"In this important volume, the authors have succeeded in deepening the current mutual embrace between psychotherapy and meditative practice. Written with clarity and featuring leading minds in both domains, this book signals the emergence of a new, theory-linked contemplative psychotherapy that crosses schools and boundaries in its pursuit of real clinical deliverables."

Zindel Segal, PhD, *distinguished professor of psychology in mood disorders, University of Toronto Scarborough*

"*Advances in Contemplative Psychotherapy* offers the most comprehensive and authoritative overview of one of the hottest cutting edges in psychotherapy today—its merger with contemplative practice. A must have for anyone in this field."

Daniel Goleman, *author of* Emotional Intelligence: Why It Can Matter More Than IQ *and co-author of* Altered Traits: Science Reveals How Meditation Transforms Mind, Brain, and Body

"While the goals of psychotherapy and contemplative practice share some important commonalities—the relief of suffering—until this volume, there was no compendium bringing these modalities together. Joe Loizzo and his colleagues have done a remarkable job in surveying this vast landscape. A must read for any clinician or provider wishing to incorporate contemplative practice into therapy."

Richard Davidson, *author of* The Emotional Life of Your Brain, *founder, Center for Healthy Minds, University of Wisconsin-Madison*

"With business leaders, healthcare providers, educators, and celebrity influencers all touting the benefits of mindfulness and other forms of contemplative practice, it is becoming increasingly difficult to sift through the data and the hype, the science and the sales pitch. This updated edition of *Advances in Contemplative Psychotherapy* provides an illuminating tour of this burgeoning field, guided by an impressive and diverse roster of researchers, clinicians, and spiritual teachers. This insightful book examines the promise and the practical challenges of applying contemplative practices to the personal, clinical, and social problems we all face today."

Doris F. Chang, PhD, *clinical psychologist and associate professor, NYU Silver School of Social Work, and co-editor of* Transformative Careers in Mental Health for Black, Indigenous, and People of Color: Strategies to Promote Healing and Social Change in Academia, Clinical Settings, and Beyond

Advances in Contemplative Psychotherapy

Advances in Contemplative Psychotherapy offers mental health professionals of all disciplines and orientations the most comprehensive and rigorous introduction to the art of integrating contemplative psychology, ethics, and practices, including mindfulness, compassion, and embodiment techniques. It brings together clinicians, scholars, and thought leaders of unprecedented caliber, featuring some of the most eminent pioneers in the rapidly growing field of contemplative psychotherapy.

The new edition offers an expanded array of effective contemplative interventions, contemplative psychotherapies, and contemplative approaches to clinical practice. New chapters discuss how contemplative work can effect positive psychosocial change at the personal, interpersonal, and collective levels to address racial, gender, and other forms of systemic oppression. The new edition also explores the cross-cultural nuances in the integration of Buddhist psychology and healing practices by Western researchers and clinicians and includes the voices of leading Tibetan doctors.

Advances in Contemplative Psychotherapy offers a profound and synoptic overview of one of psychotherapy's most intriguing and promising fields.

Joseph Loizzo, MD, PhD, is a contemplative psychotherapist, Buddhist scholar, and author with over four decades' experience integrating Indo-Tibetan mind science and healing arts into modern neuropsychology, psychotherapy, and clinical research. He is the founder and academic director of the Nalanda Institute for Contemplative Science, the developer of its Contemplative Psychotherapy Program, an assistant professor of psychiatry at Weill Cornell Medical College, and a clinician in private practice in Manhattan.

Fiona Brandon, MPS, MA, MFT, is a psychotherapist, contemplative educator, group facilitator, and the director of the Nalanda Institute's Compassion-Based Resilience Training and Embodied Contemplative Psychotherapy programs. For more than 15 years she has integrated Buddhist psychology, depth psychology, and meditation into her clinical work with adults and couples in her private practice in San Francisco.

Emily J. Wolf, PhD, MSEd, is the founder and director of Contemplative Psychology PC, where she provides psychotherapy, clinical supervision, and training for mental health providers. She has conducted groundbreaking research on the integration of contemplative methods of Indian yoga and meditation into Western psychodynamic therapy, recovery, and health education and is a former director and co-developer of the Nalanda Institute's Contemplative Psychotherapy program. She is also an adjunct clinical instructor of psychology at Weill Cornell Medical College.

Miles Neale, PsyD, is a Buddhist psychotherapist in private practice, founder of the Contemplative Studies Program, and clinical instructor of psychology at Weill Cornell Medical College. He has more than 20 years of experience integrating Tibetan Buddhism and psychology, is the author of *Return with Elixir* (2023) and *Gradual Awakening* (2018) and leads Buddhist pilgrimages throughout Asia.

The Healing Mentor, *Bhaishajyaguru* (Robert Beer, Used with Permission)

Advances in Contemplative Psychotherapy

Accelerating Personal and Social Transformation

SECOND EDITION

Edited by
Joseph Loizzo,
Fiona Brandon,
Emily J. Wolf,
and Miles Neale

Routledge
Taylor & Francis Group

NEW YORK AND LONDON

Designed cover image: © Getty Images

Second edition published 2023

by Routledge
605 Third Avenue, New York, NY 10158

and by Routledge
4 Park Square, Milton Park, Abingdon, Oxon, OX14 4RN

Routledge is an imprint of the Taylor & Francis Group, an informa business

© 2023 selection and editorial matter, Joseph Loizzo, Fiona Brandon, Emily J. Wolf and Miles Neale; individual chapters, the contributors

First edition published by Routledge 2017

Library of Congress Cataloging-in-Publication Data
Names: Loizzo, Joseph John, 1955- editor. | Brandon, Fiona, editor. | Wolf, Emily J., editor. | Neale, Miles, editor.
Title: Advances in contemplative psychotherapy : accelerating personal and social transformation / Joseph Loizzo, Fiona Brandon, Emily J. Wolf, Miles Neale.
Description: Second edition. | New York, NY : Routledge, 2023. | Revised edition of: Advances in contemplative *psychotherapy* / edited by Joseph Loizzo, Miles Neale, and Emily J. Wolf. 2017. | Includes bibliographical references and index. | Identifiers: LCCN 2022056626 (print) | LCCN 2022056627 (ebook) | ISBN 9781032153087 (hbk) | ISBN 9781032153063 (pbk) | ISBN 9781003243588 (ebk)
Subjects: LCSH: Psychotherapy. | Mindfulness (Psychology) | Empathy.
Classification: LCC RC480.5 .A32 2023 (print) | LCC RC480.5 (ebook) | DDC 616.89/14--dc23/eng/20221209
LC record available at https://lccn.loc.gov/2022056626
LC ebook record available at https://lccn.loc.gov/2022056627

ISBN: 978-1-032-15308-7 (hbk)
ISBN: 978-1-032-15306-3 (pbk)
ISBN: 978-1-003-24358-8 (ebk)

DOI: 10.4324/9781003243588

Typeset in Goudy
by Deanta Global Publishing Services, Chennai, India

We dedicate this volume to the living example
Of His Holiness the XIVth Dalai Lama of Tibet,
Who has done more than anyone to stimulate open dialogue
Between modern physical science and ancient contemplative
science,
Who has helped birth the promising field of contemplative
neuroscience,
And who inspires us all as a vibrant embodiment
Of the radical open-mindedness and unconditional compassion
We need every day as psychotherapists, caregivers, teachers, and
healers.
In the spirit of a great seventh-century Nalanda Master,
We offer one of His Holiness's favorite aspirational verses
To the heroic human spirit of altruism:

> May I be the doctor
> And the medicine
> And also the nurse,
> Until all beings are healed!
> (Shantideva, *Guide to the Altruist's Way of Life*)

Contents

Contributors

Moustafa Abdelrahman, MBA, RP, is a psychotherapist and a meditation teacher. He has extensive experience working with LGBTQ+ individuals and allies. He teaches The Foundation of Applied Mindfulness Meditation certificate program at the University of Toronto and The Compassion-Based Resilience Training Teacher Training program at the Nalanda Institute for Contemplative Science.

Tara Brach, PhD, is a clinical psychologist, influential insight meditation teacher, author, and founder of the Insight Meditation Community of Washington, DC.

Christine Braehler, PsyD, PhD, is a clinical psychologist who specializes in self-compassion, a mindful self-compassion teacher trainer, and international coordinator of the Center for Mindful Self-Compassion.

Nida Chenagstang, PhD, is the co-founder of Pure Land Farms, and founder and medical director of the Sowa Rigpa Institute: School of Traditional Tibetan Medicine.

Seiso Paul Cooper, PhD, LP, is an ordained priest and transmitted teacher in the Soto Zen lineage of Dainin Katagiri; member of the American Zen Teacher's Association; Founder: Two Rivers Zen Community. He maintains a private psychotherapy practice in Montpelier, Vermont.

Diana Fosha, PhD, is a clinical psychologist, author, the developer of AEDP—a healing-based, transformation-oriented model of psychotherapy—and director of the AEDP Institute. She is on the faculty of the Department of Psychiatry and Psychology of both New York University and St Luke's/Roosevelt Medical Centers in New York City.

Paul Fulton, PhD, is a clinical psychologist, author, meditation consultant, and co-founder of the Institute for Meditation and Psychotherapy.

Christopher Germer, PhD, is an author and clinical psychologist in private practice specializing in mindfulness-based and compassion-oriented psychotherapy. With Kristin Neff, PhD, he developed the eight-week Mindful Self-Compassion Program.

Rick Hanson, PhD, senior fellow at the University of California Berkley Greater Good Science Center, is a neuropsychologist and bestselling author who has devoted four decades to integrating meditation, brain research, and clinical psychology.

Pilar Jennings, PhD, is a psychoanalyst, author, and faculty in the Psychiatry and Religion Program at Union Theological Seminary of Columbia University and the Columbia Center for the Study of Science and Religion. She has dedicated thirty years to studying and integrating Tibetan Buddhism with psychoanalytic psychotherapy.

Kamilah Majied, PhD, is a mental health clinician, educator, researcher, and internationally engaged consultant on building inclusivity and equity using meditative practices. She is a professor at California State University, Monterey Bay, and the founder and CEO of Majied Contemplative Consulting, which uses meditative practices in Diversity, Equity, and Inclusion leadership development.

Lama Rod Owens is a Buddhist minister, author, activist, yoga instructor, and authorized Lama in the Kagyu School of Tibetan Buddhism.

Sheryl Petty, EdD, (Ngakma Shé-tsal Tsültrim Wangmo) is an organizational development and systems change consultant. She is ordained as a ngakma and teaches in the Nyingma lineage of Tibetan Vajrayana Buddhism and has been a Lucumi/Yoruba priest since 1997. Her work for nearly thirty years supports the healing and healthy functioning of organizations globally to embody Deep Equity.

Lobsang Rapgay is a research psychologist at University of California, Los Angeles (UCLA) and director of the Clinical Training Program for Mental Health Professionals at the Mindfulness Awareness Research Center, UCLA. He has a doctorate in clinical psychology and is the author of four books, including *Tibetan Medicine: A Holistic Approach to Better Health.*

Sharon Salzberg is a first-generation American Buddhist teacher and acclaimed author, co-founder of the Insight Meditation Society, and world-renowned expert on mindfulness with over forty years of teaching experience.

Daniel J. Siegel, MD, professor of psychiatry at UCLA and director of the Mindsight Institute, is a pediatric psychiatrist, education consultant, and world-renowned pioneer in the field of interpersonal neurobiology. He is author of many books and editor of the Norton Series in Interpersonal Neurobiology.

Robert Thurman, PhD, America's preeminent Buddhist scholar-translator, is president of Tibet House, US, and holds the first endowed chair in Indo-Tibetan Buddhism in the West, the Je Tsongkapa Chair at Columbia University.

Jan Willis, PhD, is professor of Religion Emerita at Wesleyan University and has a PhD in Indic and Buddhist Studies from Columbia University. She is the author of several books on Buddhism, has studied with Tibetan Buddhists for five decades, and has taught courses in Buddhism for over forty-five years.

Foreword to the Second Edition

For much of my life I have worked with caregivers in the most challenging of clinical settings—end-of-life care—as well as with activists on the front lines of pressing struggles in social justice and social action. In the course of this work, I have witnessed firsthand the insidious impact of empathic distress in caregivers and activists.

As a practitioner and teacher of Zen, I have been fortunate over the years to be able to deepen my reliance on Buddhist teachings on compassion. Not only has my practice of wise and skilled care sustained me, but I soon learned that my students and colleagues facing similar challenges found it equally helpful in sustaining their life and work. My work with clinicians and others prompted me to develop a heuristic map of compassion, based on social psychology and neuroscience, and the development of a process called G.R.A.C.E. that is a way to cultivate compassion in the process of interacting with others. This work has expanded into the many compassionate outreach programs we have developed at Upaya Zen Center, including Being with Dying, our training program for palliative care clinicians, and our popular annual Neuroscience and Zen Brain conference.

Since my work in the 1970s with pioneering psychiatrist Stan Groff, and my ongoing work with the contemplative neuroscience community of the Mind Life Institute, I have been deeply involved in the field building around contemplative neuroscience. Seeing the growing body of meditation research showing its beneficial effects on the brain, along with the mounting evidence of its practical efficacy in healthcare and psychotherapy, has been inspiring for us all. Yet the latest work done by colleagues like Richard Davidson and Tania Singer showing the beneficial effects of compassion training on the brain's processing of human suffering I find even more promising and potentially impactful for world health and well-being. Compassion training clearly has the power to protect caregivers from burnout, and to make them even more effective in helping others face the many difficult challenges of life in our age. This is why I was happy to learn of the publication of *Advances in Contemplative Psychotherapy: Accelerating Healing and Transformation*.

In parallel with the laboratory research on compassion done by my friends at Mind Life, and very much in synchrony with the practical applications of mindful compassion we teach at Upaya is the Certificate Program in Contemplative Psychotherapy (CPCP) developed by Joe Loizzo and his colleagues at Nalanda Institute for Contemplative Science. Nalanda Institute's three-year CPCP trains practitioners in mindfulness-based psychotherapy first, and then moves on to training them in the wisdom and arts of compassion and embodied compassion shared by both the Zen and Tibetan Buddhist traditions. I was very pleased to hear that Joe and his co-editors Miles Neale, Emily Wolf, and Fiona Brandon are compiling this second edition of the book, including many of my close colleagues and expanding on the social face of healing and transformation.

It is my pleasure to recommend to you this new edition of the book, which offers interested therapists and caregivers an introduction to Buddhist teachings, neuroscience, psychology, and the clinical and psychosocial dimensions of integrating mindfulness, compassion, and embodiment techniques into psychotherapy. I believe that expanding the training in mindful compassion skills to psychotherapists can enhance their ability to deepen, expand, their care of their clients, spreading the healing hand of human kindness to ever-wider circles of those most in need.

Rev. Joan Jiko Halifax
Abbot, Upaya Zen Center
Santa Fe, New Mexico
www.upaya.org

Preface to the Second Edition

As caregivers today, we find ourselves in a pivotal time—a time when our personal lives, our professional lives, our clients' challenges, our institutions, and communities, even the Earth itself, are all at once at a turning point. Over the last centuries, human civilization has made enormous strides. Modern science and technology have brought undreamed of standards of health, wealth, information, and opportunity within reach for whole populations, although many the world over still go without their fair share. After millions of years living in isolated groups and societies, most humans now have some sense of themselves as part of a global community of nations, however flawed. Despite our vulnerability to pandemics like COVID-19 and the stark inequities of access to healthcare, a growing share of humanity live longer, more comfortable, more connected lives than any of our forebears. Every day we learn more about the workings of the human genome and brain, even though the depths of the mind still elude modern science.

Yet increasingly, in an age of ever-escalating change, all the outer progress we have made sets a stark backdrop that exposes the root cause underlying the alarming rise of stress-related illness, addiction, trauma, racial and gender-based violence, extreme economic inequity, religious persecution, and environmental toxicity today. This root cause is *us*—more precisely, our self-protective stress instincts—and the real limits they put on our inner capacity to heal, thrive, communicate, and collaborate, no matter how favorable the outer conditions of our lives have become. This one hard constant has been addressed since the dawn of civilization, by great sages like Buddha, Confucius, Empedocles, Ezekiel, Jesus, Socrates, and Zoroaster. More recently, the founders of modern psychotherapy, Freud, Jung, Ferenczi, Reich, and others, took up this timeless challenge, exposing that root cause as a vestige of our evolutionary past.

Framing this hard problem in the mythic language of the Sicilian Greek thinker Empedocles, Freud (1930/1962) proposed in his *Civilization and Its Discontents* that "the evolution of civilization ... must present the struggle between Eros and Thanatos, between the instinct of life and the instinct of destruction, as it works itself out in the human species" (p.69). Now that the modern Western quest to master nature and the world has become increasingly destructive, putting much of the Earth and its life at risk, each day reminds us of the inner work which the dominant culture of the modern West has too long deferred. While many of us are just waking up to its destructive side, the fact is that modern Western culture has been destructive all along, causing escalating harm inextricably linked with the progress it achieved. This harm is evident not just in today's environmental crisis, but in the cultural systems of white supremacy, extreme capitalism, and insidious patriarchy that have left a wake of violence, oppression, and exploitation evident in the brutal legacies of slavery, genocide, colonialism, globalization, and climate change. While the West has made some real strides in counteracting this legacy of harm, including powerful movements of resistance and liberation that have advanced equal rights for Black and Indigenous people, People of Color, Asian Americans and Pacific Islanders, women, and LGBTQ+ individuals further than ever before, the specter of racial, gender, and other forms of systemic oppression in Western societies is still painfully real.

This shadow face of modern Western culture largely accounts for the fact that, while the science and technology for equitably shared global health, wealth, and well-being is ready at hand, the social will to fulfill that promise is sorely lacking. I trace this tragic lack to two main forces: one evolutionary, and one cultural. The evolutionary force at work is the biological drive for survival—the death-grip of prejudice, negativity bias, stress-reactivity, and reflex trauma that locks down our life-giving human genius for well-being, creativity, empathy, love, compassion, and altruism. The cultural force is the rising predominance of a colonizing capitalist culture based on patriarchy and white supremacy that feeds on, rationalizes, and institutionalizes the worst fears, de-humanizing biases, and destructive instincts of all those it touches—a culture of scarcity that has denied our inner potential for positive human social development and inclusive community in favor of a self-defeating and exclusive drive to accumulate wealth, privilege, and power in the hands of a few.

A child of the Enlightenment, Freud saw modern science and psychotherapy as the only hope for understanding and ending our individual and collective self-enclosure and the suffering it causes. Yet Jung believed we could not wait for these relatively young disciplines to help us know and heal ourselves fully and deeply. A child of the Romantic Age, he urged that we integrate modern physical science with the timeless inner arts and sciences of our world's contemplative traditions. In support of that vision, he advocated for a fundamental shift in psychotherapy and modern culture away from its egocentric, materialist values towards a post-modern culture of collective consciousness and timeless spiritual values.

Of course, the future of psychotherapy and its impact on the world is no longer in the hands of Freud's direct heirs. It is time for each of us as conscious individuals and concerned professionals, as caretakers of the future of humanity and our Earth, to take a stand and take action to help our families, our clients, our societies, and our world change as quickly and radically as they can. It is with this clear and present urgency in mind that my fellow editors and I have rallied our colleagues together to offer *Advances in Contemplative Psychotherapy*.

Advocating for a global renaissance in psychotherapy, this book offers a vision for the future of our field based on the recognition that Freud and Jung were both largely right. Declaring a new day for the great inner work of humanity, it highlights a confluence of traditions that holds great promise for our future at a pivotal time. What is that confluence? It is the watershed formed by the joining of two great streams of human knowhow, arisen in neighboring civilizations only to flow in opposite ways. I mean the Greek stream of evolutionary psychology and physical science, belatedly come of age in the West; and the Indian stream of evolutionary psychology and contemplative self-healing, precocious yet remarkably preserved in the meditative and yogic traditions of the East.

However contrary to our provincial sense that East and West will never meet, the reunion of these neighboring streams was bound to come with globalization. In fact, the modern father of world history, Arnold Toynbee predicted that their confluence would be the most impactful and promising event of our age. I believe I speak for the contributors to this volume when I say that finding ourselves in the thick of this historic watershed was, and is, the most potent force in our lives. When friends and colleagues feel overwhelmed by the global challenges we face today, I often share with them a thousand-year-old prelude to Toynbee's prediction, which offers a radically optimistic vision of our future. The Tibetan teaching of the *Wheel of Time* (*Kalachakra*) predicts that contemplative scientists (*vidyadharas*) will emerge from obscurity onto the world stage as East and West collide early in our present millennium, to help usher in a new global age of mindful science education, egalitarian democracy, sustainable happiness, and universal compassion.

Of course, the recent paradigm shifts that have upgraded all prior estimates of our capacity for social attunement and mindful brain integration help galvanize such hopeful visions, making them far less removed from scientific reality and human possibility than ever before. As I proposed in *Sustainable Happiness* (Routledge, 2012), the East–West confluence many great minds foresaw does seem to be evident here and now, fueling the rapid emergence and mainstreaming of long inconceivable fields like contemplative neuroscience, contemplative psychotherapy, and contemplative social justice. The discovery that our genomes are malleable, and our brains plastic, has merged together with evidence that contemplative practice promotes plasticity, social engagement, brain integration, and epigenetic change. Downstream from this new amalgam, the confluence of new science and ancient practice is giving rise to an expanding array of ever-more effective contemplative interventions, contemplative psychotherapies, and contemplative approaches to psychosocial change. So while the global challenges we face now seem unprecedented in scale and scope, the root of them all is older than our species itself. And given the global melding of modern physical science with timeless contemplative science, the empowering culture, and practical solutions we need are ready at hand. Although there is no time to waste to apply that salve to what ails us, each day I must remind myself to take in the mounting evidence that we live in times of such hopeful change.

Like all great transformations, this one began as an improbable dream, conceived simultaneously by many like-minded individuals. Raised in the heyday of psychoanalysis by an existential psychiatrist and a Catholic world history teacher, I conceived the dream that was the seed of this volume while struggling through the books on my dad's office shelves, from Freud's *Civilization and Its Discontents* and Jung's *Modern Man in Search of a Soul* to Thomas Merton's *Contemplation in a World of Action*. The world I saw reflected in that office was divided: with modern science, medicine, and psychiatry on the side of Freud's skepticism; and our ancient traditions of contemplation and ethical action on the side of Merton's mysticism. While Jung had tried to bring these two sides of our nature and culture—outer and inner, material and spiritual—back together again, the gulf proved too wide, and too deep. The fault-line seemed to threaten our integrity and humanity and led me to dream of a psychology—and a life—in which science, healing, contemplation, and action were all woven together in a seamless whole.

That dream only began to feel like it might become a reality when I met my first teacher of Buddhism, Robert Thurman, at Amherst College, in 1973. Although I knew then, as now, that Buddhism alone was no more the answer than the Catholicism I was schooled in, it did have a vital ingredient I sensed could help bridge our modern divide: a rigorous, scientific approach to self-knowledge, contemplation, and ethics. From then on, my way would be a middle way between modern medicine, neuroscience, and psychiatry on the one hand, and the Buddhist contemplative science of self-healing and ethics of social healing on the other. When I went with Bob to India in 1979, he introduced me to His Holiness the Dalai Lama and to many of the most senior teachers in the Tibetan refugee community, Yongdzin Ling Rimpoche, Tsanshab Serkhong Rimpoche, Tara Tulku, Demo Locho Rimpoche, and Ngawang Gelek Rimpoche. They would introduce me firsthand to the living legacy of Indian Buddhism, which their Tibetan ancestors brought from the world's first university at Nalanda in North India, and faithfully preserved through the centuries. These exceptionally clear and caring beings would be my inspiration through the long years of medical education and psychiatry training, along with my psychotherapy mentors, Rolf Arvidson, Leston Havens, Myron Sharaff, and Robert Rosenthal, and my research mentors, Herbert Benson, Jon Kabat-Zinn, Bruce McEwan, and Mary Charlson.

Along the way I met follow travelers, including Dan Brown, Chris Germer, Paul Fulton, and Mark Epstein at Harvard, and Dan Goleman, Vesna Wallace, Richie Davidson, and Thubten Jinpa at regular meetings with His Holiness and interested scientists, clinicians, and scholars starting in 1986. Still, the two sides of my path—Western and Buddhist—only began to merge into one ten years later, in 1996. That was the year I began a PhD program in Buddhist psychology at Columbia and was urged at the same time by my new psychiatry colleagues there to start a Center for Meditation and Healing (CMH) at Columbia Presbyterian Hospital. This was when and where the *mandala* of Nalanda Institute for Contemplative Science began to manifest itself in my life, as part of today's global renaissance of the legacy of Nalanda University and its world class contemplative science tradition. The Columbia CMH, officially founded in 1998 with my colleague Ina Becker, was the first mind/body medical center in a major academic department of psychiatry, and the first anywhere to integrate Tibetan compassion practice, role-modeling imagery, and advanced breath-control skills together with basic mindfulness and Hatha Yoga. It was there that I met a circle of very dedicated students who would help me found Nalanda Institute, including Miles Neale and Emily Wolf, who served as psychology interns, research assistants, and interventionists in studies applying Nalanda Institute's Compassion-Based Resilience Training (CBRT) to mixed groups of medical and psychiatric clients, and to groups of women recovering from breast cancer.

In 2003, at the invitation of my colleague Mary Charlson, then Chief of Medicine at Weill Cornell Medical College, I moved the CMH and its programs to the Center for Integrative Medicine at New York Hospital. At the same time, I realized that, to expand our work integrating contemplative science and practice into psychotherapy and public health education, the best vehicle would be a free-standing non-profit that could grow beyond the constraints imposed by today's corporate hospitals and universities. In 2005, I founded the Nalanda Institute for Contemplative Science, and began working with the inspired collaboration of my wife Geri Loizzo and a circle of gifted students turned board members, including Elazar Aslan, Peggy Neu, Elizabeth Rovere, David and Deborah Sonnenberg, Vance Lavelle, Tom Damrauer, and his partner Diane Bertolo, to develop and roll out the full *mandala* of Nalanda Institute and its programs.

The Nalanda Institute Contemplative Psychotherapy Program (CPP) was developed in 2011 with the help of Miles Neale and Emily Wolf. Its mission is to teach psychotherapists and caregivers from all backgrounds the foundations of contemplative science, psychology, ethics, and practice, and to support them to integrate these traditional insights and methods with the latest developments in neuroscience, clinical practice, and social justice. The CPP is a three-year program that begins with a year of training in mindfulness-based psychotherapy, goes on to a second-year training in compassion-based psychotherapy, and culminates in a final year of embodiment-based psychotherapy, all informed by the comprehensive Nalanda tradition faithfully preserved in Tibet. Over the years, we have gathered a growing, international community of faculty, students, and graduates. This volume features many of our distinguished faculty, and very closely reflects the comprehensive curriculum of the CPP. By offering this book, my fellow editors and I hope to open the *mandala* of this rare curriculum, faculty, and community to the growing network of like-minded caregivers the world over who may find them edifying and helpful.

Among Freud's contributions, perhaps the greatest was to develop a whole new discipline of health education, meant to offer a middle way between modern science and the timeless healing wisdom and arts of Greek and Renaissance humanism. Over the years, institutes of psychoanalysis and psychotherapy have trained a vast global network of professionals dedicated to helping themselves and others disarm self-protective defenses and empower their innate social capacities for empathy, compassion, love, and altruism. Given our exploding knowledge of how stress and attention shape the brain, and mounting evidence that contemplative practices can quickly turn stress-reactivity into social engagement and prosocial embodiment, the time has come for a new generation of therapies that meld the new science with humanity's most potent methods of change. The discipline of psychotherapy offers a ready-made network for the faithful distribution of this blend of new science with timeless art. Along with related disciplines in healthcare, counseling, coaching, education, and community-based social action, psychotherapy offers an existing network of people that already share the requisite aims, skills, and values, at a turning point in history when there is no time to reinvent the wheel. It is our hope as editors, as a faculty, and as a community of lifelong learning and practice, that this book and the rigorous, multidisciplinary training it represents will not only inform and inspire interested colleagues but help raise awareness of ways we can each leverage our life's work, to accelerate the transformation all humanity needs, personally, socially, culturally, and globally, right now.

On behalf of my fellow editors and the whole Nalanda Institute community, I would like to express our deep gratitude to all the inspiring individuals we have felt so privileged to work with as fellow faculty and students over these years. More specifically, I want to acknowledge our past and present partners and CPP program directors in the US, Canada, Europe, and Latin America, including Mar Aige, Fiona Brandon, Javier Garcia Campayo, Ann Campbell, Rahshaana Green, Diego Hangartner, Pilar Hurtado, Begona Martinez, Marco Mascarin, and Helen Hyunjung Park. I am equally grateful to our core faculty, Dr Nida Chenagstang, Pilar Jennings, Sharon Salzberg, and Robert Thurman; and to all of our incredible visiting faculty, including Tara Brach, Sieso Paul Cooper, Richie Davidson, Mark Epstein, Diana Fosha, Paul Fulton, Chris Germer, Roshi Joan Halifax, Rick Hanson, Sue Johnson, Rev. angel Kyodo williams, Ethan Nichtern, Lama Rod Owens, Stephen Porges, Lobsang Rapgay, Zindel Segal, Dan Siegel, Jasmine Syedullah, David Vago, and Jan Willis, many of whom have contributed chapters to this volume based on their teaching at the Nalanda Institute CPP.

Of course, this book would not have come to fruition were it not for the patience, enthusiasm, and special gifts of a whole circle of enlightened altruists. This circle includes the managing editor of the second edition Fiona Brandon, our Nalanda Fellow in humanitarian aid, Maria Thorin, our congenial editor at Routledge Anna Moore, our dynamic library science and graphic arts duo, Tom Damrauer and Diane Bertolo of Lotus and Pixel, and the extremely kind and gifted artist Robert Beer.

Last but not least, I am forever indebted for all that is good and true in my life to my soul mate, partner in all things, and Nalanda Institute Director of

Programming and Community Engagement, Gerardine Hearne Loizzo—you are my memory, love, "I carry your heart with me (I carry it in my heart)." And of course I am infinitely thankful for inspiration in this and all I do to the miraculous presence of our two great loves and joys, our remarkable sons Maitreya Dante and Ananda Rowan.

I dedicate any insight or inspiration this book may spark to the great aim that all beings throughout space and time awaken their own inner genius for profound wisdom, unconditional compassion, and embodied altruism. For any errors that may remain in what follows, I take full responsibility. May the Buddhist patron of inner science, healing speech, and empathic art, the eternal youth of Sheer Brilliance, *Manjushri*, protect me, and all who seek transformation! May all beings be well; may all minds be free; may all hearts share joy; may all earth live in peace!

Joseph Loizzo, Executive Editor
Founder and Academic Director, Nalanda Institute for Contemplative Science
Assistant Professor, Weill Cornell Medical College Department of Psychiatry
Adjunct Professor, Columbia University Center for Buddhist Studies
Manhattan, New York
June 4, 2022

Introduction

Contemplative Psychotherapy: The Art and Science of Individual and Collective Well-Being

Joseph Loizzo

Contemplative Psychotherapy: Beyond Simple Mindfulness

Now that mindfulness has earned widespread acceptance as a catalyst in psychotherapy (Germer et al., 2013), even being hailed as the next revolution in public health (Baer, 2003), it is time not just to take stock of how and why this watershed has come, but to move beyond current limits in today's mainstream approaches to mindfulness, and to expand our horizons to what lies ahead. What are the limits in today's mainstream mindfulness approaches? While the popular mindfulness movement emphasizes acceptance over change, individual over communal thriving, and attention over emotion and embodiment, traditional contemplative science and practice are far more complex and inclusive. In this book, we consult traditional scholar-practitioners to look beyond the limits to current approaches, and also expand today's narrow focus on mindfulness to include the second and third waves of contemplative science and practice—based on compassion and embodiment practices which take mindfulness-based interventions to the next level. This collection of essays, from a wide range of leading voices, provides a rigorous overview of this promising watershed in psychotherapy, including not just a retrospective review of a fast-growing field, but also a prospective survey of emerging developments and anticipated breakthroughs. We hope it will serve both as an introduction to the full scope and promise of this confluence for clinicians and researchers who are new to it, and also as a comprehensive update on the state of the field for those already familiar with or steeped in some aspect of it.

The title of this book, *Advances in Contemplative Psychotherapy*, reflects this broad aim and purpose. As mindfulness-based therapies come to rely on mindful self-compassion (Germer, 2009), as compassion techniques give rise to compassion-based therapies (Gilbert & Choden, 2014), and as embodied techniques like imagery, movement, and breath-work show promise in trauma care (van der Kolk, 2014), it seems clear that the field has already outgrown the term "mindfulness," and needs a more general framework. "Contemplation" offers one such framework, since it encompasses all forms of meditation and yoga, including recitation practices like mantra and heart-prayer, healing visualization, intensive breathing, and graceful movement (Loizzo, 2009). This may explain why, in an effort to name the neighboring new field emerging at the interface of meditation research with neuroscience, Richard Davidson coined the term "contemplative neuroscience" (Davidson & Begley, 2012). Applying the term "contemplative" to the family of psychotherapies involving mindfulness and related techniques introduces a retrospective background that highlights our progress to date, and sheds light on some larger shifts still underway in modern culture.

Science, Plasticity, and Mindfulness: The Rebirth of Contemplative Science

The very idea of "contemplative" psychotherapy may invoke some cognitive dissonance. "Contemplation" and "contemplative"—terms derived from the Latin *contemplatio*—have historically been used to describe a discipline of individual and group reflection considered central to introspective learning, especially the meditative and ethical learning practiced by lay and professional people in traditional Western religious communities. Psychotherapy, on the other hand, has evolved as a healing discipline of introspective learning based mainly on a dyadic method of reflection, informed by scientific views of human nature, and practiced in confidential relationships by mental health professionals and their clients in modern clinical settings.

In his *Civilization and Its Discontents*, Freud made the broadest possible case for a new science and art of psychotherapy: as a modern answer to the age-old dilemma described by the pre-Socratic thinker Empedocles (Freud, 1930/1962). Caught between the self-protective instinct for survival and the self-transcendent instinct for generativity, we human beings must learn to override stress and to embody love and compassion instead, in order to gradually adapt to the increasingly social conditions of civilized life. The main thrust of Freud's argument was to contrast the views and methods of psychotherapy with those of religion—Eastern and Western—and to offer his new science and art as a modern, secular, and pragmatic alternative to the age-old experiences of boundless communion and love cultivated through meditation and yoga. Although his critique of such experiences and methods as oppressively idealistic and life-negating were challenged by some analysts—notably Jung, Ferenczi, Reich, Binswanger, and Kohut—nonetheless given the reductive science of the day, Freud's view prevailed, decisively shaping the consensus and practice of mainstream psychotherapy.

A related and even more contested theme in Freud's work was his insistence that the main cause of psychological suffering is unconscious conflict within the individual psyche, as opposed to the impact of external traumas caused by poor caregiving or oppressive social forces like war, structural discrimination, and poverty. Although later schools of analysis—object relations theory, attachment theory, self-psychology, and intersubjective psychoanalysis—effectively challenged Freud's position, his medical model of psychopathology as located in the individual, and his individual-centered dyadic framework of treatment still inform most psychotherapies. This not only limits the capacity of mainstream psychotherapy to effectively address the massive human suffering caused by harmful social systems like racism, patriarchy, colonialism, and hypercapitalism, but it also stands in the way of a deeper understanding and fuller integration of contemplative approaches to healing, since these rely as much or more on healing groups, families, communities, institutions, and society at large as on working dyadically with individuals.

Over the last half-century, many disparate lines of research in biology, neuroscience, physiology, and psychology have been converging towards a more optimistic consensus on human plasticity, relational capacity, and social potential, a consensus which is transforming the landscape in which we live and practice. At the same time, groundbreaking research in stress and trauma, affective neuroscience, social psychology, and behavioral economics have been revolutionizing our understanding of the social and cultural dimensions of human suffering and healing, emphasizing the indispensable role of social safety, emotional connectedness, and group belonging in promoting individual and collective health, well-being, and creativity. Together these converging breakthroughs have led to an emerging consensus on human nature and life that supports a much more complete and robust dialogue between current neuropsychology and humanity's timeless contemplative traditions, touching not just on meditation but also on the other two core disciplines of contemplative learning and healing—wisdom and ethics.

In biology, evolutionists have resolved the age-old debate—are we naturally aggressive or social?—with a new view of our genome as "malleable" or "educable" (Dobzhansky, 1982). More recently, the young field of epigenetics has begun to show how gene regulation drives development and day-to-day adaptation (Carey, 2013). This broad vision of genomic fluidity naturally dovetails with the new paradigm in neuroscience—use-dependent plasticity—yielding a view of our brain as more dynamic, functional, constructive, and ever-evolving than we previously thought. The new science of plasticity has led pioneers like Eric Kandel and Norman Doidge to propose a more optimistic, transformational paradigm for twenty-first century psychotherapy (Kandel, 1999; Doidge, 2016).

Aligned with this new direction, breakthroughs in our understanding of the prefrontal cortex, limbic system, and brainstem have revealed the human brain to be much more geared to social cognition, social emotional development, and social autonomic regulation than was believed in Freud's day (Siegel, 2007). These breakthroughs have prompted a new generation of relational and embodied approaches to psychotherapy, like those articulated by Daniel Siegel, Louis Cozolino, Stephen Porges, and Bessel van der Kolk, (Siegel, 2010a; Cozolino, 2006; Porges, 2011; van der Kolk, 2014). Finally, two related lines of advancement—through affective neuroscience, positive psychology, and trauma therapy—have further challenged prior low estimates of humanity's potential for embodied social healing like Freud's, by revealing our robust capacity for prosocial emotions, the far-reaching benefits of motivations like love, compassion, and altruism, and the profound benefits of positive imagery, breath-work, movement, and transformational mind/body states like flow (Amihi & Koshevnikov, 2014; Brown, 2009; Lutz et al., 2008; Singer & Klimecki, 2013).

These converging lines of influence have come together to foster a sea change in mainstream science's approach to human practices long dismissed as unscientific. The shift began when the first research studies of meditation, notably transcendental meditation (TM), inspired the groundbreaking clinical paradigms of the 1970s and 1980s: Herb Benson's relaxation response and Jon Kabat-Zinn's mindfulness-based stress reduction (MBSR) (Beary & Benson, 1974; Kabat-Zinn, 1982). As these clinical paradigms were found effective in heart disease and chronic pain, they sparked the development of the first mindfulness-based interventions for mental health—dialectical behavior therapy (DBT) and mindfulness-based cognitive therapy (MBCT) (Linnehan et al., 1991; Teasdale et al., 1995).

These promising clinical studies in turn opened the door for the first phase of serious lab research on the neurophysiology of meditation and yoga. This phase came of age in a series of major breakthroughs starting very recently, in 2004 and 2005. Two teams, one led by Richard Davidson at the University of

Wisconsin, and another by Sarah Lazar at Harvard, were responsible for moving their field from its long marginal status to center stage in the new neuroscience. Lutz and Davidson's 2004 study showing that Tibetan monks can self-generate high frequency gamma synchrony at will, and Lazar's 2005 study that mindfulness meditators show increased thickness in the prefrontal and insular cortex, both directly linked meditation with neuroplasticity and neurogenesis (Lazar et al., 2005; Lutz et al., 2004). This put meditation at the heart of the new neuroscience, as one of the most effective and reproducible paradigms of neural plasticity, and the only model for the conscious self-regulation of plasticity. It is this multi-disciplinary confluence of advances that led Davidson to describe the newly central field of meditation research as contemplative neuroscience.

Fueled by the growing evidence base for the benefits of contemplative practice, the last two decades have seen a groundswell of interest in applying popular mindfulness and related practices like self-compassion in almost every sphere of contemporary life—from healthcare to business, education to wellness. One of the most important applications from a public health standpoint has been in the growing movement to bring contemplative wisdom, ethics, and practice to the epidemic stress and trauma caused by systemic racism (williams et al., 2016; Willis, 2008). As the COVID-19 pandemic highlighted the severity of chronic racial health disparities in the US and the murders of Ahmaud Arbery, Breonna Taylor, and George Floyd drew unprecedented attention to violent police interactions with Black, Indigenous, and other People of Color (BIPOC), the American Medical Association officially declared racism a public health threat and proposed a plan to counter it (American Medical Association, 2021). All this prompted new interest in the convergence of critical race theory, social psychology, and sociology into liberation psychology (Prilleltensky, 2003), and raised awareness of embodied contemplative approaches to dyadic psychotherapy like Resmaa Menakem's somatic abolitionism (Menakem, 2017) as well as therapeutic frameworks for healing racialized trauma that integrate individual with community-based strategies (French et al., 2020; Chavez-Dueñas et al., 2019).

Psychotherapy and Contemplative Healing: Two Forms of One Human Art

In the long view, the convergence of breakthroughs in neuroscience, positive psychology, meditation research, and mindfulness interventions over the last two decades has been both timely and effective. It was robust enough to clear the way for a broader integration of psychotherapy with contemplative healing, more along the lines envisioned by proponents of contemplative traditions, like Jung (Moacanin, 1986). While the growing confluence of such long-divergent fields still strikes many as unlikely or novel, there is no denying the deep resemblance in methods and mechanisms of action underlying these human practices. At the same time, the confluence has been further deepened by the growing awareness of the critical role played by broader social factors like systemic racial, gender, and economic stress, and trauma on individual suffering. And this awareness has coincided with shifts in science suggesting that positive social emotional factors, both at the dyadic level of individual work and at the group level of family and community work, are far more crucial to deepening and accelerating healing than mainstream approaches to mental health have assumed. This shift towards greater appreciation of the role of culture and community as key variables in illness and healing has further fueled the confluence of contemporary psychotherapy with timeless contemplative traditions, since contemplative approaches to healing, as exemplified by Jung, rely as much or more on healing culture and community than on conventional psychotherapy dyads.

In this book, we have the opportunity to review the family resemblances and differences between psychotherapy and contemplative healing in detail; in chapters that present the psychology behind three forms of Buddhist contemplative practice; chapters that explore their emphasis on social healing; chapters that explore their neuroscience; and chapters that flesh out their applications in psychotherapy. But first, it may help to touch on a few resemblances that have fueled the convergence of Buddhist psychology with modern psychotherapy, as well as to highlight some of the key contrasts that make these two cultural practices so distinctive.

In introducing *Sustainable Happiness*, I explained the growing confluence of Buddhist psychology and meditation with modern psychotherapy by pointing out three family resemblances in aim and method shared by the two traditions (Loizzo, 2012). 1) Both traditions base their theory and practice on the premise that every mental activity is causally effective and has determinate consequences that shape ongoing development. 2) They both view the mind as embedded in an evolutionary continuity of ever-adapting forms of life, conceiving development as an interactive, intergenerational process informed by both nature and nurture. And 3) they both base their attempts to relieve mental suffering on a practice of re-education, which combines reflection, insight, and behavior change in an enriched social learning matrix of conscious re-parenting.

At the same time, I also explained the distinctions between Buddhist and modern psychology that are often missed or minimized by modern proponents of integration, pointing out three basic differences in aim and method that distinguish the two traditions. 1) The two differ in their institutional base and disciplinary landscape: Buddhist psychology is based in monastic education in the context of Indian spirituality and contemplative science; psychotherapy in secular healthcare in the field of modern psychology and neuroscience. 2) They differ in their theory of evolution: Buddhism assumes a Lamarkian model of evolution, as driven by learned habits of mind and action transmitted across generations by social imprinting and modeling; psychotherapy is informed by a Darwinian view of evolution, as driven by random mutation and natural selection, transmitted by genetic inheritance. 3) And they differ in their healing methodology: Buddhist pedagogy involves a multimodal strategy combining individual mentoring, peer learning, group classes, and healing community, relying on a progressive path of mind-brain altering individual and group contemplation; psychotherapy involves a more targeted strategy relying on intensive individual re-parenting bonds, and milder, more limited relaxation states, sometimes combined with cognitive-behavioral learning for individuals and/or groups.

On the one hand, it is no accident that these two traditions are now engaged in an increasingly deep and far-ranging dialogue. On the other, there is still ample reason for us to be careful to respect the distinctions between them, so that we can weigh apparent similarities and differences in light of the broader cultural contexts in which they evolved. Of course, avoiding misunderstanding or misappropriating contemplative traditions like Buddhism, and respecting their distinct cultural context and roots does not require us to adopt an extreme cultural relativism. Like modern psychotherapy, Buddhist psychology claims to see and treat mental suffering in ways that are universally applicable to humans across history and culture. And, like psychotherapy, it has in fact been found helpful in several civilizations, over centuries since its inception. So, rather than thinking of Buddhist practice and psychotherapy as apples and oranges, I prefer to see them as different varieties of one and the same species of human practice. This seems not altogether contrary to Freud's view, judging by his own efforts to find historical roots for the modern practice he called psychotherapy in the ancient Greek traditions of Socratic and pre-Socratic pedagogy.

Contemplative Psychotherapy: Reconciling Science and the Human Spirit

The fact that Freud felt a need to go back to the Greeks to find the roots of psychotherapy is not surprising given the genesis story of modern science— that it emerged in the fifteenth century as a renaissance of previously lost

Greek science. What should be surprising is that he had to bypass twenty centuries to find another case of healing, re-parenting dialogue to cite as a precedent for his re-discovery. Obviously, it is not the case that humanity altogether stopped this universal practice for twenty centuries. Having grown up a young Jewish man in Catholic Vienna, Freud was well aware of two such practices embedded in the religious traditions of the Judeo-Christian West: the rabbinate and the confessional. So, his return to the Greeks suggests a move to avoid any association with these forms of spiritual counseling. In contrast, his erstwhile successor Carl Jung, the son of a Protestant minister, did not shy away from the ambiguity between the role of psychotherapist and spiritual counselor or guide. So Freud's rejection of these precedents, along with their analogues in the Hindu and Buddhist mentoring bonds explored by Rolland and Jung, may be most simply explained as an expression of his intention to align psychotherapy decisively with the side of modern science in the European Enlightenment rift between science and religion. To his credit, Freud correctly read the landscape of modern European culture and made a tactical decision that allowed psychotherapy to become a mainstream institution in an era in which scientific modernity obliged us to leave contemplative healing, pedagogy, and ethical community behind, as artifacts of humanity's religious past. Now that the modern rift between science and contemplation is increasingly being bridged, we are in a position to bring contemplative practice and its emphasis on group learning and healing community back into dialogue with neuropsychology and the practice of psychotherapy.

Viewed through the narrow lens of Enlightenment thought and science, a dialogue between the reflective practice of individual and group contemplation and the clinical practice of dyadic psychotherapy may still seem dissonant, even forced. Viewed through the wide-angle lens of anthropology, however, it appears as eminently reasonable and perfectly natural. Throughout history and around the globe, human cultures have associated spirituality, science, and healing with contemplative states, mentoring bonds, and inclusive community. The Greeks were no exception to this rule: Empedocles taught science, contemplation, and democratic ethics (O'Brian, 2009); Socrates was inspired by the Delphic Oracle (McPherran, 1999). The Rabbinic yeshivas, Christian monasteries, and Islamic madrasas of the medieval West were the cradles of Renaissance science, spirituality, and medicine (Pederson, 2009). And indigenous cultures around the world developed and preserved powerful orally transmitted knowledge-and-practice systems that wove science, philosophy, spirituality, ethics, and healing into complex integral traditions that work to promote individual and communal well-being. In fact, in the centuries since Descartes divided matter from mind, and science from reflection, the scientific culture of the West has been one of the very few glaring exceptions to the rule. So the recent trend I described towards bridging that modern divide and reuniting contemplation and contemplative community with science and healing is not really new, but a return to the commonsense view shared by most of humanity for most of history.

Five Disciplines, Three Methods, Two Traditions: The Architecture of this Volume

In the interest of advancing a dialogue that is reinvigorating psychotherapy, we have chosen in this book to approach the new landscape from the standpoint of the five disciplines we see as main stakeholders in the emerging terrain. The first of these is contemplative psychology, by which we mean the way traditional contemplative views of mind interface with and inform current advances in understanding of the human psyche, illness, and health (Loizzo, 2012). The second is contemplative ethics, by which we mean the way traditional contemplative views of healing community interface with the current thinking and practice of cultural competence, social justice, and community-based social change. The third is contemplative science, by which we mean the traditional scholarship and techniques of meditative self-healing that have contributed key practices to contemplative psychotherapy (Wallace, 2007). The fourth is contemplative neuroscience, by which we mean the convergence between breakthroughs in our basic understanding of the brain and research into the effects and mechanisms of mediation and yoga (Davidson & Begley, 2012). Finally, the fifth is contemplative psychotherapy, by which we mean the integration and application of all four other disciplines to advances in the clinical practice of dyadic and community-based psychotherapy (Germer et al., 2013). To integrate these points of view, each part of the book includes contributions by leading voices in contemplative psychology, pioneers in contemplative approaches to social justice, eminent scholars and master teachers of Buddhist practice, neuropsychologists and neuropsychiatrists working in the field, and psychotherapists working to integrate new theories and methods into clinical practice.

While our vision of a contemplative psychotherapy integrates many techniques, and opens the door to interdisciplinary perspectives that can enrich theory and practice, some may ask, "Why limit the approaches surveyed in this book to a single contemplative tradition?" On the most superficial level, we can answer this question by pointing to the avid incorporation of Buddhist techniques like mindfulness and compassion into contemplative therapies, or to the growing body of evidence that has accumulated in recent decades to support the efficacy of these therapies. On a deeper level, as I have suggested, there are of course reasons behind the natural affinity between Buddhism and psychotherapy.

Perhaps the best way to explain this phenomenon and our book is in terms of the history of modern science and psychotherapy we have just briefly sketched. In the rift—some might say the *war*—between modern science and human religious traditions, Buddhism plays a pivotal role as a middle way or intermediate case. Given its reliance on reason and evidence and its rejection of scriptural revelation and religious authority, Buddhism is more sympathetic to the methods of modern science than most religious traditions (Wallace, 2007). And given its view of life as evolved and developed by natural causal laws rather than divine creation or intervention, it is more sympathetic to the theories of modern science than most contemplative traditions (Ricard & Thuan, 2004). Finally, given its primary focus on healing and its psychological interest in understanding and transforming the mind, its aims and methods are more sympathetic to psychology and psychotherapy than most religious traditions (Loizzo, 2012).

Despite this natural affinity between psychotherapy and Buddhism, it is not our view that Buddhist theories or methods are somehow uniquely suited or helpful to clinicians or clients of psychotherapy. Rather, we feel that Buddhism helps to break down preconceived walls between science and contemplation, and hence serves to catalyze dialogue and cross-fertilization between these long estranged human disciplines. So we offer Buddhist approaches to contemplative psychotherapy as a paradigm of how other approaches and methods from non-Buddhist traditions could be integrated into new contemplative therapies, rather than as a monolithic doctrine. Our hope is that the dialogue between Buddhist psychology and psychotherapy surveyed here will stand as a touchstone that can help support a full arc of reflective approaches to psychological healing, spanning the range of human contemplative traditions and the whole spectrum of modern therapies.

Practically, our task is also made simpler by narrowing our focus to Buddhist approaches, because many of the groundbreaking findings of contemplative neuroscience, and some the most promising forms of contemplative psychotherapy, have involved insights and practices from that tradition (Varela et al., 1992; Teasdale et al., 1995). And of course, our work is also easier thanks to the growing community of clinicians and researchers who have reflected deeply and practiced extensively at the confluence of Buddhism and psychotherapy (Molino, 1999; Germer et al., 2013). This growing community provided us with a rich array of contributors who—each in her own way—has been pioneering the integration of various schools and methods of Buddhist psychology into contemporary psychotherapy and the contemporary work of fostering healing psychosocial change.

When it comes to the range of Buddhist-informed approaches to contemplative psychotherapy explored here, we have also been fortunate to be able to draw on the full spectrum of schools and methods that have recently come into dialogue within the melting pot of American Buddhism. As the most widely exported form of Indic contemplative science, Buddhism has traveled over the centuries through most of Asia. This tide of influence has taken place in three great waves during three diverse periods of Eurasian history and civilization.

In the first wave, during the five centuries after Shakyamuni Buddha's life, it spread from its cradle in Northeast India towards the west, south, and east, to Kashmir, Afghanistan, Sri Lanka, Burma, and Thailand. This first wave, which gave us the psychology of insight and mindfulness meditation (*vipassana*), is represented by the Theravada schools of Pali Buddhism, the first schools encountered by the West during the era of British colonial rule (Epstein, 1995).

The second wave dates to the first five centuries of the common era and developed with the universal kingdoms of North and South India, ruled by the Kushana, Shatavahana, and Gupta dynasties; it spread with Buddhist monks via the Silk Road caravans to Central and East Asia, and from there to China, Vietnam, Indonesia, Korea, and Japan. This wave gave us the psychology of wisdom and compassion, along with analytic insight and compassion meditation; it is represented by the Mahayana schools of Zen and Pure Land Buddhism, the second series of schools encountered by the West in the post-war era of interchange with Japan, Korea, and Vietnam (Rubin, 1996).

The third wave dates to the latter half of the first millennium of the common era, based on the rise of the world's first universities, the great monastic universities of Nalanda, Dhanyakataka, Vikramashila, and Odantipuri, which became international beacons of Indian Buddhist contemplative science and civilization, attracting scholars from Kashmir, Nepal, Tibet, Burma, Thailand, China, Japan, Korea, Indonesia, and Vietnam. This wave gave us the psychology of embodied cognition and embodied mind-brain integration, along with role-modeling imagery, affirmative recitation, and advanced breath-energy control; it is represented by the Vajrayana Buddhism of Tibet, Ladakh, Nepal, Bhutan, and Mongolia, the schools encountered by the West through the Tibetan refugee community that fled to India in 1959 (Loizzo, 2012).

Given world history, these three waves of Buddhist thought and practice, along with their counterparts in the Hindu Yoga tradition, have only recently come together again in the global melting pot of Western Buddhism. So we are fortunate in this volume to have contributors whose integration was influenced by each of the major waves, seen in the synthetic Nalanda tradition as "three vehicles" of Buddhist contemplative science and practice (Thurman, 1996).

In light of traditional scholarship, each part of the book is devoted to one of these vehicles. Part One, Mindfulness and Personal Healing, is mainly devoted to the integration of early Buddhist psychology, non-violent ethics, and mindfulness meditation with classical analytic and cognitive therapy. Part Two, Compassion and Social Healing, is mainly devoted to the integration of Mahayana Buddhist psychology, relational ethics, and compassion meditation with relational and interpersonal psychotherapy. And Part Three, Embodiment and Natural Healing, is mainly devoted to the integration of Vajrayana Buddhist psychology, liberative ethics, and embodied meditation with embodied transformational therapies.

Integrating the Triune Brain: The Science of Psychotherapy and Meditation

Of course, the alignment of mindfulness, compassion, and embodiment practices with distinctive psychologies and psychotherapy applications does not depend simply on this historical background, nor on the scholarly distinctions between different "vehicles" of Buddhist thought and practice. As the chapters on the neuroscience and clinical application of each practice show, there are ample scientific reasons behind the alignment of distinct contemplative methods with particular forms of neuropsychological healing and change. The evidence that mindfulness works largely by empowering the prefrontal cortex to enhance self-awareness and neocortical integration is consistent with current thinking about insight-oriented and cognitive psychotherapy (Siegel, 2010a). Recent evidence that compassion meditation works by empowering the limbic cortex to enhance self-regulation of social-emotional stress-reactivity and to foster the integration of prosocial emotions, empathic resonance, and proactive responses is consistent with current thinking about object-relational, interpersonal, and couples therapy (Gilbert & Choden, 2014). And preliminary findings that role-modeling imagery, affirmative recitation, arousing breath-control, and gentle movement work by transcending traumatic defenses and integrating the hypothalamic-brainstem social engagement system are consistent with current thinking about embodied approaches like Jungian analysis, Gestalt therapy, Somatic Experiencing (SE), Sensorimotor Psychotherapy (SP), and Accelerated Experiential Dynamic Psychotherapy (AEDP) (Porges, 2011).

The fact that we find synergies between such an array of contemplative practices and psychotherapies may seem improbable, but it is quite consistent with what early studies concluded about the general effects and mechanisms of meditation and psychotherapy. In a prior review, I summarized the findings of the first few decades of research on the neuroscience of these two distinct human practices (Loizzo, 2000). Meditation and psychotherapy appear to have their effects by the same common pathway: a sustained strategic amalgam of two complementary mechanisms. Both practices reduce stress using relaxation techniques to lower sympathetic arousal and boost vagal tone; and both also simultaneously enhance learning using techniques that heighten attention and promote neural plasticity (Porges, 2011; Siegel, 2007). In this way, the two work to create an optimal internal environment that disarms stress-reactive resistances and fosters the enrichment of learning. By optimizing the brain's full capacity for social learning, these practices expand the mind's openness to shared introspection and corrective dialogue; and by cultivating that shift in a stable, supportive, and equitable social learning environment, they sustain that openness through repeated practice over time. As a result, they facilitate a gradual dismantling of dissociative barriers to integration, and cultivate the growth of higher self-awareness, self-regulation, and self-transcendence though the development of integrative structures and processes in the brain (Delmonte, 1995; Siegel, 2012).

If meditation and psychotherapy in fact share a common neural mechanism and psychosocial intent, why do both cultural practices employ such a broad range of methods? The science behind the first premise—that all methods of meditation and psychotherapy work by deepening relaxation and heightening attention—helps explain the main finding of psychotherapy research, that effectiveness depends far more on psychosocial process than therapeutic technique (Norcross, 2011). The mix of safety and stimulation makes good anthropological sense, in that it recreates the secure playful bond of early childhood, the evolutionary matrix for human social learning and brain development. Yet there remain two major reasons why, within a common process of calm presence and attentiveness, these twin cultural practices of corrective re-parenting would involve a multiplicity of methods.

The first reason has to do with the complexity of the human mind-brain, a complexity mapped in various ways by all schools of contemplative psychology and psychotherapy. Most schools of psychotherapy have been influenced to some degree by Freud's tripartite model of the mind. Contemporary neuropsychology has linked Freud's map to neural structure and function, as in MacLean's triune brain schema or current models like those of Karl Pribram, Stephen Porges, and Louis Cozolino (Pribram, 2013; Porges, 2011; Cozolino, 2006). If the common pathway for meditation and psychotherapy is a process of disarming stress-reactive defenses and learning mind-brain integration, it makes sense given the complexity of mind and brain that that process takes different forms as it reaches deeper levels of structure and function. While the normal waking mind and neocortical processing may be readily accessed by free association and mindfulness, we would expect the dreamlike sensory-emotional mind and limbic processing to be more responsive to empathic attunement and compassion techniques; while deep visceral affect states and core brain processing would likely respond better to embodied therapeutic and contemplative methods that rely on imagery, prosody, movement, and breathing.

Developmental Gradualism and Therapeutic Technique

While this kind of multi-modal approach to mind is not common to most schools of psychotherapy or contemplation, it is an emerging paradigm in models of mind-brain therapeutics, such as current work on trauma. It has been the default model in the Nalanda tradition, which adopted a developmental gradualism of contemplative healing and learning as early as the second century of the common era. Hence the three-part structure of this volume not only dovetails with modern psychodynamic and brain-based cognitive behavioral approaches to psychotherapy, but also with the later

Table o.1 Interdisciplinary, Intertraditional Framework (by Joseph Loizzo)

Disciplines	Part One	Part Two	Part Three
Psychology	Personal Self-Healing	Social Transformation	Embodied Integration
Buddhist Tradition	Individual/*Theravada*	Universal/*Mahayana*	Process/*Vajrayana*
Contemplative Practice	Mindfulness	Compassion	Embodiment
Neuroscience	Neocortex	Limbic System	Brainstem
Psychotherapy	Dynamic/Behavioral	Interpersonal/Relational	Transformational

Buddhist tradition of contemplation, which mirrors cumulative Hindu traditions like the Kashmiri Shaivite (Muller-Ortega, 1997).

More compelling still is the way that Vajrayana Buddhism and Tantric Hinduism mapped deepening levels of meditation in a gradual progression onto deeper levels of the subtle body model of the central nervous system, also known to us as the "chakra" model of Hatha Yoga (White, 1996). This traditional neuropsychology followed a broadly tripartite scheme, with simpler withdrawal practices like mindfulness mapped onto the "coarse, external layer" or "sensory sheath" of mind-central nervous system, deeper focused practices like positive imagery and narrative mapped onto the "subtle, internal layer" or "thought-energy sheath," and deep affective breathing, and movement practices mapped onto the "subtlest, intimate layer" or "bliss-awareness sheath."

More to the point, we also have ample clinical reasons to foster a multiplicity of methods of psychotherapy and contemplation. This has to do not with any intrinsic superiority or neural specificity of one technique over another, but with the varied therapeutic needs of individuals who have diverse learning styles or are facing various challenges at different levels of healing and development. Traditionally, the broad-spectrum methodology behind this book was both developmentally gradual, and pedagogically "instantaneous." In other words, it was meant both to support a gradual path of contemplative healing—progressing from verbal to emotional to embodied learning—as well as to allow for accommodating individuals with specific inclinations and needs, following the Buddha's well known therapeutic art of tailoring teachings as so many medicines to the diverse ills of his students.

In a gradualist psychology like Nalanda's, it was understood that students could enter the healing and learning process using whatever techniques were most helpful or suited to them, then eventually fill in gaps in development with techniques tailored to the less pressing but vital aspects of development. Of course, there is a singular process or "taste" of healing and teaching at any point along the gradual path: progressive freedom from suffering based on the empathic attunement between a teacher's healing wisdom and the student's afflicted way of being, all taking place in the context of an equitable healing community—a healing village. So the cumulative Nalanda pedagogy which informs this volume involved an artful and mindful integration which balanced the basic need for a common healing process with the pedagogic value of a broad multi-modal array of therapeutic techniques.

The Genome and Living Legacy of this Book

While we have adapted Nalanda gradualism as one strand of the DNA of this book, partly to offer a template for the Western strand of our emerging field, our primary aim is to survey the past, present, and future of this convergence in the most synoptic and inclusive way.

In Part One, Mindfulness and Personal Healing, we survey its recent past, the already fruitful cross-fertilization of the psychology of insight and the practice of mindfulness with modern psychodynamic, cognitive, and liberative psychotherapies. Contemplative psychotherapist, educator, and equity consultant Kamilah Majied explains the vital importance for clinicians of all backgrounds to continually expose and transcend unconscious colonialist biases and surveys the rich legacy of BIPOC ("global majority") and LGBTQ+ pioneers in decolonizing, liberative approaches to psychotherapy. Contemplative psychotherapist Miles Neale explains the psychology of metacognitive awareness, where the two streams of Buddhist and Western psychology converge. Baptist-Buddhist religion scholar and civil rights activist Jan Willis explores the resonance between the Buddha's teachings on social healing and change and the civil rights movement led by Dr Martin Luther King. Renowned Buddhist teacher Sharon Salzberg then presents the psychology of mindfulness from the standpoint of the Theravada tradition of insight meditation in which she was trained. Integrative neuropsychologist Rick Hanson next explores the neuroscience of mindful-self-healing and self-change in light of the revolution of neural plasticity. Next, two eminent integrative clinicians—Zen psychoanalyst Sieso Paul Cooper and Theravada psychotherapist Paul Fulton—introduce us to their masterful integration of mindfulness practice with contemporary psychoanalysis and mainstream psychotherapy. And finally, contemplative psychotherapist, mindfulness teacher and LGBTQ+ activist Moustafa Abdelrahman shares his wisdom on tailoring mindfulness-based psychotherapy to the needs of LGBTQ+ individuals and groups.

In Part Two, Compassion and Social Healing, we are introduced to the wave of the present, the comparative social psychology of compassion, by the Tibetan doctor and research psychologist Lobsang Rapgay, who shares his unique synthesis of the Tibetan practice of cultivating compassion with the relational analysis of Melanie Klein. Acclaimed author and thought-leader Lama Rod Owens shares his take on applying the Tibetan Buddhist arts of compassion training to the challenges of healing—especially for BIPOC individuals—in a society dominated by the violence of systemic racism. Eminent

Buddhologist Professor Robert Thurman then presents the social psychology and universal compassion practice of Mahayana Buddhism from the standpoint of the Nalanda tradition preserved in Tibet. Next, leading neuropsychiatrist Daniel Siegel unpacks the interpersonal neurobiology of empathic attunement and social mind-brain development, setting the stage for the seminal convergence underway between relational psychotherapy and reflective practices of mindful awareness and compassion. Finally, three pioneering integrative clinicians—Tara Brach, Chris Germer, and Christine Braehler—unpack the powerful practice of self-compassion, which weaves the contemplative strands of mindfulness, loving-kindness, and self-parenting together with object relational psychotherapy and acceptance-based cognitive therapy. Contemplative psychotherapist Fiona Brandon presents Nalanda Institute's Compassion-Based Resilience Training (CBRT) and shares her experience and insights applying it to the challenges of building healthy intimacy through individual and couples work.

Last but not least, in Part Three, Embodiment and Natural Healing, we are introduced to the wave of the future, the embodied psychology of imagery, affirmation, posture, and breathing, by the remarkable Dr Nida Chenagtsang, one of few Tibetan doctors today who is sharing the living lineage of Tibet's integrative mind/body medicine and contemplative psychiatry in the West. Contemplative psychologist Emily Wolf shares her groundbreaking research on the medical and psychological impact of embodied contemplative techniques. Deep Equity consultant-activist, and Tibetan Tantric teacher, Sheryl Petty shares her experience drawing on embodied contemplative practices from the Tibetan and Yoruba traditions to build stamina and skill in fostering embodied psychosocial change. Distinguished author and psychoanalyst Pilar Jennings presents the comparative psychology of archetypal imagery and transformative passion based on her elegant synthesis of Tibetan Buddhism with the analytic methods of Jung, Kohut, and Stolorow. I then share my integration of the embodied neuropsychology of Vajrayana Buddhism and Tantric Hinduism with the neuroscience of archetypal imagery, embodied cognition, autonomic breath regulation, and peak performance states. Finally, groundbreaking clinician Diana Fosha and I unpack the transformational power of imagery, deep somatic affect states, deep breathing, and movement for the embodied healing of trauma and the deepest levels of mind/brain integration in our respective chapters on Accelerated Experiential Dynamic Psychotherapy (AEDP) and Embodied Transformational Therapy (ETT).

All the contributors to this volume have served as faculty for the Nalanda Institute Contemplative Psychotherapy Program (CPP). Our CPP is an unprecedented program that integrates the traditional contemplative science, ethics, and healing arts of mindfulness, compassion, and embodiment practice with contemporary neuroscience and psychotherapy, in a three-year intensive experiential learning format. Since its inception in 2013, our dedicated past and present CPP directors including Emily Wolf and Fiona Brandon, and core faculty including Pilar Jennings and myself, have led ten robust years of the program, working closely with meditation masters Sharon Salzberg, Robert Thurman and Dr Nida Chenagstang, and a rich visiting faculty including many, like Roshi Joan Hallifax, Mark Epstein, Rev. angel Kyodo williams, Jasmine Syedullah, and Richard Davidson, who despite their invaluable contribution to the program could not contribute a chapter given constraints of time and space.

This experiment has afforded us a broad overview of the state of the art, and a strong personal sense of the hunger felt by a growing community of clinicians for rigorous, multi-disciplinary training in the field. After graduating ten successive classes of the program, now thanks to online learning formats reaching students around the world in English, Spanish, and Portuguese, we have seen and felt the indispensable value of this work. In a real sense, this volume represents our wish to share this profoundly enriching experience with the growing audience of professionals everywhere looking for the deep healing wisdom and method which contemplative science and practice offer. It is with the deepest gratitude that we share some of the fruits of wisdom and healing art we have tasted on the collective journey recorded in this volume.

PART ONE
Mindfulness and Personal Healing

The Historical Buddha, *Shakyamuni* (Robert Beer, Used with Permission)

Contemplative Practices for Assessing and Eliminating Racism in Psychotherapy

Towards Dynamic Inclusive Excellence

Kamilah Majied

Fundamentally, and certainly when done well, psychotherapy *is* a contemplative practice. The dualism with which we often talk about psychotherapy and contemplative practice is illusory. If we define psychotherapy as an interactive process wherein learned, skilled healers engage dialogically with individuals seeking guidance towards emotional and behavioral wellness, then we must acknowledge that psychotherapeutic practices have existed globally for millennia in varied cultural and spiritual contexts. Centering the Western model when we talk about psychotherapy is part of how the legacy of colonialism limits our understanding of psychological pain and how humans heal from it.

This chapter discusses how racism, white supremacy, and other residuals of Western European colonialism create a reservoir of unexamined unconscious material for people of all ethnicities. The mental health professions and practices are often contaminated by the issue of that reservoir and require regular irrigation so that healers themselves do not become conduits for continued racial trauma. In my work assisting clinicians with examining their unconscious material related to racism, I have found that contemplative engagement with the work of decolonial psychoanalysts such as Frantz Fanon and contemporary decolonial clinicians such as Drs Michael Yellow Bird, Beverly Daniel Tatum, Lillian Comas-Díaz, and Jennifer Eberhardt helps guide practitioners towards excising racism from their understanding of and actions within the realm of psychotherapy.

Guided reflective engagement with anti-racist content creates space for people to manage the feelings that come up when exploring racism in their personal

DOI: 10.4324/9781003243588-2

and professional lives and lineages. The meditative practices I use in these sessions help create inner spaciousness for the therapists as well as a relational container between us that allows for the transmutation of their anxiety, grief, shame, and anger around racism so that those feelings can become fodder for personal and professional growth. Decolonial psychoanalyst Frantz Fanon describes how, whether we are aware of it or not, we have absorbed racialized messages about inferiority and superiority: "The Negro enslaved by his inferiority; the white man enslaved by his superiority alike behave in accordance with a neurotic orientation" (Fanon, 1952/1967, p. 60).

Fanon also discusses internalized racism as it sometimes manifests as identification with the oppressor. This explains how it is possible for Black, Latinx, Indigenous, and Asian people to hold racist beliefs. Hence it is important for people of every ethnicity to engage in reflective processes to examine their unconscious racism.

Contemplating Language

Often the first part of this process is reflection on language. I encourage clinicians to strive towards what I call *dynamic inclusive excellence* rather than cultural competence, because while cultural competence can connote a static state of achieved, enduring capacity to engage cross-culturally, the term dynamic inclusive excellence acknowledges the reality that we must consistently tend to the quality of our awareness of, and engagement with, diversity and oppression as ever-changing factors in order to be inclusive in each moment. This also involves awareness of our unconscious bias as it has been shaped by racism. Dynamic inclusive excellence means reiteratively waking up to and transforming one's intrapersonal and interpersonal awareness of racism to transcend the limitations it places on one's capacity to discern and engage with reality.

In her groundbreaking research-based text *Biased*, Eberhardt (2019) talks about the eye-tracking studies she did with elementary school teachers wherein the teachers' eye movements were tracked to see how they reacted when given a prompt such as "look for the troublemakers" amongst a group of elementary school students. She found that teachers of every ethnicity including Black teachers consistently looked at the Black children when given this prompt. In a parallel study, she used eye tracking devices on Oakland police officers and found that the officers consistently looked to Black and Brown persons when asked to look for who might be violent or engaged in criminal activity. These data give us insight into the ubiquitous presence of unconscious racism.

Eberhardt discusses the need for adding friction: slowing down and pausing to prevent our unconscious bias from impacting how we speak or behave. One of the ways we can add that friction is by pausing to consider how we might best describe people and places; to contemplate our language before we speak and to try on more accurate, less biased ways of speaking. For example, we can use the word "ethnicity" instead of "race" since we know that the first act of racism was to divide humanity into false categories called "races." We can also speak about geographic locations from a non-colonialist perspective by using the term "West Asia" as opposed to "Middle East" so as not to describe places in the world based on their geographic relationship to Europe.

I invite the use of a term coined by Dr Barbara Love, "People of the Global Majority" (PGM), as a reflective practice of right speech that enables us to cease using the language of enslavers and colonizers who labeled humans by color and evaluated people's worth based on their proximity to whiteness. Using the term PGM rather than the term people of color (POC) eliminates the color misnomer and in fact is more accurate since we know that skin color varies widely in every ethnicity. In practice, saying "people of the global majority" is also a way of shifting our awareness to notice that African, Latinx, Indigenous, and Asian people are not "minorities" when viewing humanity from a global perspective. Using the phrase "global minority" when referring to white people can also be helpful to add friction by interrupting our unconscious notions of white dominance.

Adjusting language can help contradict unconscious notions of white supremacy and serve as a literal reminder that the majority of the global population is not white. Such language practices can shift our cognitive distortions as they impact every area of our lives, especially the helping professions and the realm of psychotherapy.

Developing Critical Consciousness

Dr Lillian Comas-Díaz highlights contemplative practices such as engagement with art as a means to cultivate critical consciousness:

> Critical consciousness means developing an awareness of why this is happening, who benefits, against whom this is being done, and what is the effect on society of this micro-aggression, racism. One effect is the preservation of the status quo. We talk about using what is called liberation psychotherapy approaches, which is basically to help the person develop a sense of awareness, a clinical awareness, of his or her circumstances and how they contribute to their trauma, in this case, racial trauma. Once that awareness is there, they

become more liberated in terms of, well, maybe there are some things that I can do about this to cope with this situation.

(Emerson, 2019, para. 36)

She states that "in a therapeutic approach with a liberatory decolonial perspective, the provider helps the client to connect with that resilience, and that can be through art, that could be through community involvement, and that could be through social justice action" (Emerson, 2019, para. 37).

In my own research with LGBTQ global majority participants domestically and internationally, I have found that the single greatest protective factor against internalized racism having dire consequences on mental health and behavioral health is the development of this critical consciousness and engagement with social justice action (Majied, 2010, 2013, 2015; Majied & Moss-Knight, 2012). Additionally, development of critical consciousness amongst global minority folks is a resource for their own psychological hardiness (Majied, in press).

The Importance of Learning from Global Majority Thought Leaders about Psychotherapy

Consider how strange it would be to be considered an expert on cancer, but to only have read the scholarship of global minority (aka white) cancer researchers on global minority cancer patients. One could not be said to know much about cancer at all with that limited reference point. Likewise, because most clinicians are trained in models that reflect white supremacy with a dearth of study and engagement with global majority researchers' and clinicians' scholarship, their understanding of human psychology itself is compromised. Psychotherapeutic professional capacity is circumscribed by the lack of understanding of what pioneering psychoanalyst Frantz Fanon calls "colonial psychopathology." He states that "A racist in a culture with racism is therefore normal" (1964/1969, p. 40). What this means is that if we are striving to not be racist, we are in a ceaseless battle with cultural messages that indoctrinate us with racism. Hence, whether a therapist's unconscious material related to racism emerges from a family or communal lineage that ignored racism, advocated strongly against racism, or was steeped in racist values and actions, if that material has never been explored, then its impact on the intrapersonal and interpersonal life of the therapist is an area that needs attention.

To the extent that clinical training programs encourage cultural competence, they often do so from the perspective that clinicians should learn about racism and other forms of oppression to understand the experience of clients targeted by those oppressions. However, clinicians of all ethnicities need to understand their own experiences (or perceived lack thereof) with racism and the nature of their unconscious bias in order to have deeper self-awareness, including awareness of their countertransference. Janet Helms's (1992) model of white identity development elucidates how white identity presents. Her model also clarifies how a healthy self-concept and relational clarity can develop for global minority people.

Beverly Daniel Tatum's work highlights the pervasive racialization people in the United States experience in the school system and the intrapsychic and interpersonal consequences of said racialization. Global majority people are minoritized in education such that regardless of the field of study – art, science, history, technology, etc. – the contributions of Black, Latinx, Indigenous, and Asian people receive less attention than the contributions of the global minority. It is not our fault that most of us have been educated and professionally trained in paradigms that privilege global minority scholars while giving only anecdotal attention to the work of global majority scholars. However, it is our responsibility to do something about it.

Therapists can learn from the writings of global majority clinicians now to deepen their understanding of themselves and of the scope of human pain and human healing. From founders of oppression psychology such as Fanon to contemporary decolonizing clinical scientists such as Yellow Bird, therapists can learn about how their own personal psychology operates vis-à-vis various types of oppression. This is deeply valuable whether one comes from privilege, has been targeted by social oppression, or both.

Dr Yellow Bird writes about how Native American practices for healing psychological and emotional wellness have been maligned for centuries as primitive and savage. Having their healing practices outlawed, even after forced removals and genocide, has created inter-generational trauma across countless Native communities. In addition to the devastating effect on the wellbeing of Native people, it also cut the colonizers off from these paths towards wellness. Because of the tenacious commitment of Native tribes to hold onto and pass down their traditions even when facing imprisonment or death for doing so, we now know about the value of nature-based and embodied practices such as drumming, chanting, and sun, earth, and water practices. Yellow Bird describes engaging with these practices as re-indigenizing wellness.

In defining neurodecolonization, he states:

> The first part of the term in "neuro" – refers to neurons which are specialized cells in the nervous system – brain and spinal cord – that send and receive electric signals throughout the body. "Decolonization" refers to activities that weaken the effects of colonialism, facilitate resistance, and create opportunities to promote traditional practices in present-day settings.
>
> Neurodecolonization involves combining mindfulness approaches with traditional and contemporary secular and sacred contemplative practices to replace negative patterns of thought, emotion, and behavior with healthy, productive ones.
>
> Drawing on recent scientific research, neurodecolonization builds on the idea that healthy, constructive thoughts, emotions and behaviours can change our brains (and our lives) for the better. Many Indigenous contemplative practices incorporate the same principles and processes as mindfulness approaches, and are important components of physical, emotional, behavioural, and spiritual well-being. ...
>
> Along with building new empowered neural networks, neurodecolonization activities are aimed at deactivating old, ineffective brain networks that support destructive thoughts, emotions, memories and behaviours, particularly, past and contemporary oppressions associated with colonialism. For example, past colonialism that might have created negativity, sadness and anger – and activated our brain's networks of feelings of helplessness – might be our memories of our parents or grandparents' horrific treatment in residential schools or dealing with contemporary, hate, and discrimination.
>
> (*Yellow Bird, n.d., para. 1–3, 5*)

Yellow Bird's scholarship invites everyone to recover from the limitations placed on healing by colonialism and racism.

White supremacy is also evident in the way global majority immigrants are seen – or not seen – and treated in the United States and globally. Comas-Díaz's scholarship on the psychology of racism as it manifests towards Latinx persons invites us to consider our relationship to racism in immigration policy and practice. She also points out that a medical approach to trauma that does not include a sociopolitical and geopolitical perspective is limited.

Although this chapter references only a few authors, there are canons of scholarship from Black, Latinx, Indigenous, and Asian researchers, scholars, and psychotherapists that can and should be engaged to practice psychotherapy more ethically and inclusively (see Appendix A). When therapists do not do the work of exploring their unconscious bias, they unintentionally enact that bias with clients. Lack of engagement with global majority thought leadership can also cause therapists to rely on clients to educate them about racism.

When psychotherapists work with a contemplative inclusivity consultant, it helps them grow and protects their clients by preventing exploitative relationships, wherein global majority clients or colleagues are expected to do the heavy emotional and intellectual labor of explaining racism to people ensconced in white privilege. This labor is often extracted from global majority people with no compensation, thus continuing the exploitative colonialist pattern of devaluing and taking for granted the work of global majority people. Engagement with anti-racist scholarship and research guided by clinical supervisors or clinical consultants who specialize in decolonial approaches can help assure continued dynamic inclusive excellence and engagement with clients in a manner that is liberatory, and expansive for all involved.

We cannot honestly or ethically consider ourselves well-educated or well-trained in any field of endeavor, including psychotherapy, if the borders of our education and training are defined by white supremacy. Contemplative engagement with the scholarship of global majority healers and scholars broadens and deepens our self-awareness and our capacity to heal ourselves as we support the healing of all people and the environment that sustains us.

Appendix A

Suggested Reading: Scholarship from Black, Latinx, Indigenous and Asian Researchers, Scholars, and Psychotherapists

Clarke, K., & Yellow Bird, M. (2021). *Decolonizing pathways to integrative healing in social work*. Routledge.

Comas-Díaz, L. (1981). Effects of cognitive and behavioural group treatment in the depressive symptomatology of Puerto Rican women. *Journal of Consulting and Clinical Psychology, 49*, 627-632.

Comas-Díaz, L. (1987). Feminist therapy with Hispanic/Latina women: Myth or reality? *Women and Therapy, 6*(4), 39-61.

Comas-Díaz, L. (Ed.). (1994). *Women of color: Integrating ethnic and gender identities in psychotherapy*. Guilford Press.

Comas-Díaz, L. (2012). *Multicultural care: A clinician's guide to cultural competence*. American Psychological Association.

Comas-Díaz, L., & Greene, B. (Eds.). (1988). *Clinical guidelines in cross cultural mental health*. Wiley.

Comas-Díaz, L. & Greene, B. (2013). *Psychological health of women of color: intersections, challenges, and opportunities*. Praeger.

Comas-Díaz, L., Hall, G. N., & Neville, H. A. (2019). Racial trauma: Theory, research, and healing: Introduction to the special issue. *American Psychologist, 74*(1), 1–5.

Comas-Díaz, L., Lykes, B., & Alarcon, R. (1998). Ethnic conflict and the psychology of liberation in Guatemala, Peru and Puerto Rico. *American Psychologist, 53*, 778-792.

De Leon, A. (2020, April 8). *The long history of US racism against Asian Americans, from 'yellow peril' to 'model minority' to the 'Chinese virus'*. The Conversation. https://theconversation.com/the-long-history-of-us-racism-against-asian-americans-from-yellow-peril-to-model-minority-to-the-chinese-virus-135793

Eberhardt, J. (n.d.). *Academic Publications*. https://web.stanford.edu/~eberhard/publications.html

Eberhardt, J. (2019). *Biased: Uncovering the hidden prejudice that shapes what we see, think, and do*. Viking.

Fanon, F. (1963). *The wretched of the earth* (C. Farrington, Trans.). Grove Press. (Original work published 1961)

Fanon, F. (1965). *A dying colonialism* (H. Chevalier, Trans.). Grove Press. (Original work published 1959)

Fanon, F. (1967). *Black skin, white masks* (C. L. Markmann, Trans.). Grove Press. (Original work published 1952)

Fanon, F. (1969). *Toward the African revolution* (H. Chevalier, Trans.). Grove Press. (Original work published 1964)

Gray, M., Coates, J., & Yellow Bird, M. (Eds.). (2008). *Indigenous social work around the world: Towards culturally relevant education and practice*. Ashgate Publishing.

Gray, M., Coates, J., Yellow Bird, M., & Hetherington, T. (Eds.). (2013). *Decolonizing social work*. Ashgate Publishing.

Liu, F., Ye, Z., Chui, H., Chong, & E. S. K. (2022). Effect of perceived public stigma on internalized homophobia, anticipated stigma, shame, and guilt: Outness as a moderator. *Asian Journal of Social Psychology*. https://doi.org/10.1111/ajsp.12552

Majied, K. (2003). *The impact of racism and homophobia on depression*. ProQuest Dissertations Publishing.

Majied, K. (2010). The Impact of Sexual Orientation and Gender Expression Bias on African American Students. *The Journal of Negro Education, 79*(2), 151–165.

Majied, K. & Moss-Knight, T. (2012). Social Work Research Considerations with Sexual Minorities in the African Diaspora. *Journal of Social Work Values and Ethics, 9*(2), 56–67.

Majied, K. (2013). Sexuality and Contemporary Issues in Black Parenting. *Journal of Human Behavior in the Social Environment, 23*(2), 267-277. https://doi.org/10.1080/10911359.2013.747405

Majied, K. (2015). Racism and Homophobia in Cuba: A Historical and Contemporary Overview. *Journal of Human Behavior in the Social Environment, 25*(1), 26-34. https://doi.org/10.1080/10911359.2014.953428

Majied, K. (2020). On Being Lailah's Daughter: Blessons from Umieversity on Actualizing Enlightenment. In *Black & Buddhist: what Buddhism can teach us about race, resilience, transformation & freedom* (Yetunde & C. A. Giles, Eds.; First edition.). Shambhala Publications, Inc.

Majied, K. (In Press). *Joyfully Just: Liberating Meditaton Practices*. Sounds True.

Murphy-Shigematsu, S. (2018). *From Mindfulness to Heartfulness* ([edition unavailable]). Berrett-Koehler Publishers. Retrieved from https://www.perlego.com/book/580571/from-mindfulness-to-heartfulness-pdf (Original work published 2018)

Rayburn, C. & Comas-Díaz, L. (Eds.). (2008). *WomanSoul: The inner life of women's spirituality*. Praeger.

Shu, Y., Hu, Q., Xu, F., & Bian, L. (2022). Gender stereotypes are racialized: A cross-cultural investigation of gender stereotypes about intellectual talents. *Developmental psychology, 58*(7), 1345–1359. https://doi.org/10.1037/dev0001356

Tatum, B. D. (1992). Talking about race, learning about racism: The application of racial identity development theory in the classroom. *Harvard Educational Review. 62*(1), 1–25. https://doi.org/10.17763/haer.62.1.146k5v980r703023

Tatum, B. D. (1994). Teaching White students about racism: The search for White allies and the restoration of hope. *The Teachers College Record, 95*(4), 462-476.

Tatum, B. D. (1997). *"Why are all the Black kids sitting together in the cafeteria?":* *A psychologist explains the development of racial identity.* Basic Books.

Tatum, B. D. (2000). *Assimilation blues: Black families in White communities, who succeeds and why.* Basic Books.

Tatum, B. D. (2000). The complexity of identity: "Who am I?". (M. Adams, W. J. Blumenfeld, H. W. Hackman, X. Zuniga, & M. L. Peters, Eds.). *Readings for diversity and social justice: An anthology on racism, sexism, anti-semitism, heterosexism, classism and ableism* (pp. 9-14). Routledge.

Tatum, B. D. (2004). Family life and school experience: Factors in the racial identity development of Black youth in White communities. *Journal of Social Issues, 60*(1), 117-135.

Tatum, B. D. (2007). *Can we talk about race?: And other conversations in an era of school resegregation.* Beacon Press.

Tatum, B. D. (2017, Summer/Fall). "Why are all the Black kids *still* sitting together in the cafeteria?" and other conversations about race in the 21st century. *Liberal Education,* Summer/Fall 2017, 46-55.

Voigt, R., Camp, N. P., Prabhakaran, V., Hamilton, W. L., Hetey, R. C., Griffiths, C. M., Jurgens, D., Jurafsky, D., & Eberhardt, J. L. (2017). Language from police body camera footage shows racial disparities in officer respect. *Proceedings of the National Academy of Sciences, 114,* 6521-6526.

Yellow Bird, M. (2013). Neurodecolonization: Applying mindfulness research to decolonizing social work. (M. Gray, J. Coates, M. Yellow Bird, & T. Hetherington, Eds.). *Decolonizing Social Work.* Ashgate Publishing.

Yellow Bird, M., Gehl, M., Hatton-Bowers, H., Hicks, L. M., & Reno-Smith, D. (2020). *Defunding mindfulness: While we sit on our cushions, systemic racism runs rampant.* Zero to Three. https://www.zerotothree.org/resource/perspectives-defunding-mindfulness-while-we-sit-on-our-cushions-systemic-racism-runs-rampant/

Yip, T., Haskin, M., Fowle, J., Xie, M., Cheon, Y. M., Ip, P. S., & Akhter, S. (2022). Development against the backdrop of the model minority myth: Strengths and vulnerabilities among Asian American adolescents and young adults. In L. J. Crockett, G. Carlo, and J. E. Schulenberg (Eds.), *APA handbook of adolescent and young adult development* (pp. 359-374). The American Psychological Association.

Waziyatawin & Yellow Bird, M. (Eds.). (2012). *For Indigenous minds only: A decolonization handbook.* School of American Research/SAR Press.

2

Buddhist Origins of Mindfulness Meditation

Miles Neale

Mindfulness and *mindfulness meditation* have become household words. This is due to an explosion of scientific research over the last four decades, sparked by interest in the health benefits and clinical applications of mindfulness. While the efficacy of mindfulness-based interventions across a number of health indices has been well documented, the traditional Buddhist psychology underpinning the practice of mindfulness has been largely neglected. This chapter outlines the Buddhist origins of mindfulness meditation, its role in self-healing and liberation, and the psychological mechanisms of change that contribute to its clinical benefits.

Mindfulness Defined

The word 'mindfulness' refers to a psychological trait or quality of consciousness, while 'mindful' refers to a psychological state or process of being aware. Mindfulness as a type of meditation originated in Buddhist India around 500 BCE. The term is a translation of the Pali word *sati* and the Sanskrit word *smrti*, which means 'to remember.' In this and following chapters, original Buddhist terms are cited—without diacriticals—in Sanskrit, unless otherwise indicated. Mindfulness involves a voluntary, sustained, present-centered attention, which resists automatic habits of thought, emotion, and action, facilitating discernment and transformative insight. Popular and scientific definitions of mindfulness neglect its traditional aim of insight, focusing instead on simple mindfulness understood as: "clear and single-minded awareness of what actually happens to us and in us at the successive moments of perception" (Thera, 1972, p. 5); "the awareness that emerges through paying attention on purpose, in the present moment,

DOI: 10.4324/9781003243588-3

and non-judgmentally to the unfolding of experience moment to moment" (Kabat-Zinn, 2003, p. 5); and "awareness of present experience with acceptance" (Germer et al., 2013, p. 7).

Mindfulness training can be voluntarily applied—to breath, sensations, emotions, thoughts, and images. When distracted by tangential thoughts or stimuli, meditators practice re-collecting their attention and returning to the chosen focus. According to tradition, present-centered awareness trained repeatedly over time through mindfulness practice produces several distinct mental qualities: relaxation, concentration, balanced sensitivity, mental clarity, and pliancy. In addition, mindfulness affords two key skills—*recognition* and *choice*. These skills are not well documented but are traditionally seen as the active ingredients in self-healing and liberation, allowing one to leverage consciousness and override default habit-patterns. This provides an opportunity for more constructive choices about how one relates to external or internal stimuli in the moment. As the Buddha described in his theory of *karma*, with every intentionally driven thought, word, and action in the present, our minds shape our experience in the future.

Buddhist Origins and Contemplative Science

While Buddhism is clearly a world religion, it is also a practical philosophy, an ethical way of life, and one of humanity's first coherent psychologies. For this reason, some researchers now refer to a subset of Buddhist thought and practice as a contemplative science, because the Buddha based his teaching on a causal theory of mind and well-being (Wallace, 2011). On awakening to reality, Shakyamuni framed his initial teaching by applying a medical model to the human condition. His Four Noble Truths framework identifies the symptoms, etiology, prognosis, and treatment for the alleviation of human suffering. While foundational to Buddhist psychology and all future developments within Buddhist culture, the Four Truths are not a set of dogmas, but an invitation to actively engage one's experience, as the Buddha did, so that the nature of suffering is understood, its origin abandoned, its cessation realized, and the path to liberation cultivated. The Four Truths can be summarized as follows:

1 All life is prone to various forms of distress and suffering, one's conditioned reactions to which leave the mind and body poisoned by stress instincts and traumatic habits.

2 Suffering is self-perpetuated through an unconscious chain of 12 causally linked neuropsychological processes known as dependent origination (*pratityasamutpada*), comprising four stages:
   i.   Reification and misperception of self and reality, that elicits ...
   ii. ... afflictive reactions such as fear-based clinging and defensive hostility, which compel a narrow range of ...
   iii. ... maladaptive and compulsive actions that eventually hardwire themselves into one's neurobiology, causing an ...
   iv. ... adaptation to a compulsive life that conditions future moments of perception, affect, and behavior.
3 Because suffering is self-created in this causal cycle of stress (not random, innate, or predetermined), people have the ability to consciously intervene, break the links, and fully extinguish future causes of suffering. This cessation of suffering is known as liberation or *nirvana* and is considered the peak personal achievement of a human being.
4 There is a comprehensive method or path for achieving self-healing, sustainable well-being, and eventual liberation. It involves the holistic transformation of eight domains of living—known in the Buddhist canon as the Eightfold Path:
   i.   Realistic view.
   ii.   Wholesome intention.
   iii. Harmonious lifestyle.
   iv.   Truthful speech.
   v.   Ethical action.
   vi.   Joyous effort.
   vii. Sustained mindfulness.
   viii. Precise concentration.

These eight domains can be further subdivided into three categories of training, sometimes referred to as three higher educations (*adhishiksha*), each designed to counteract the major components of the conditioned stress cycle outlined in the Second Truth:

1 Wisdom training applies a realistic worldview of reality and wholesome intentions to clarify and counteract distorted or erroneous misperceptions—particularly the self-reifying habit (*atmagraha*) at the root of all mental afflictions.
2 Meditation training involves joyous effort, accurate mindfulness, and precise concentration that stabilize and refine awareness as well as counteracting afflictive emotional reactions.

3 Ethical training involves harmonious lifestyle, truthful speech, and ethical action, paving the way for a more wholesome engagement with self, others, and the world, counteracting compulsive behaviors and ensuring constructive development.

Wisdom, meditation, and ethical training each work synergistically (rather than linearly) to support one another. A harmonious lifestyle reduces fluctuations of mind and facilitates deepening insight, while insight into the nature of reality fosters tranquility and enables a responsible, caring engagement with life. Like the three-pronged cycle of self-imposed stress (misperception, afflictive reaction, and compulsive action), the three-pronged cycle of self-correction and freedom (accurate perception, balanced emotion, and harmonious lifestyle) eventually rewires one's neurobiology and coalesces positive states into wholesome traits, generating a new optimal mode of being.

So, meditation is only a third of the Buddhist approach to healing. It needs to be combined with wisdom and harmonious lifestyle to achieve the deeper transformation Buddhist contemplative science asserts is possible for all. Elsewhere (Neale, 2011, 2012), I have coined the term 'McMindfulness' for the recent trend in the Western mainstream, overemphasizing mindfulness meditation to the exclusion of the other disciplines, diluting the potency of the Buddha's psychology. My critique is based on two observations. First, extracted from the curricula of wisdom and ethics, mindfulness has been reduced to a mere stress-reduction technique. Second, diluted mindfulness is being mass-marketed as a panacea, often by those who lack knowledge of traditional Buddhist science and methodology. This dilution in the service of greater distribution risks throwing the baby out with the bathwater. While there is little doubt about the many benefits of secular or clinically applied mindfulness (Davis & Hayes, 2011), the active ingredients for liberation employed within the tradition are in danger of being jettisoned. The contemplative science of Buddhism offers humanity one of the deepest, most universal systems of personal healing and social transformation in history. It would be shortsighted and naive to reduce this comprehensive path of liberation to merely a method for relaxation or symptom reduction.

Four Foundations of Mindfulness

The Four Noble Truth framework of Buddhist science is complemented by a practical framework called the Four Foundations of Mindfulness. The aim of this meditative pedagogy is to systematically strengthen one's attention by applying it to four discrete domains of experience in order to refine the mind's natural capacities for insight (wisdom) and behavior change (ethics). The four foundations or foci of mindfulness taught within this pedagogy are: 1) the body, 2) sensations, 3) mind, and 4) realities. The specific way these foundations are taught differs widely in different traditions. What follows is one adaptation for clinicians developed by Joseph Loizzo and taught in the Nalanda Institute Contemplative Psychotherapy Program (CPP).

The First Foundation: Body

In the first foundation of breath and body, one begins meditative training by restricting the focus of attention to the smallest input or stimulus, similar to narrowing the focus of the aperture on a telephoto lens to magnify something small or remote. This is applied to the coarsest layer or scope of experience, such as the effect of posture, movement, the changing elements within the body, or simply the breath as it is experienced at the nostrils, chest, or abdomen while it flows in and out. Focusing attention narrowly and repeatedly while consciously self-redirecting one's awareness develops concentration and eventually elicits a sense of relaxation and fundamental safety, which some have equated with the so-called "safe base" of secure attachment (Epstein, 2001; Siegel, 2020).

The Second Foundation: Sensation

As concentration develops, one proceeds to the second foundation of physical sensations, opening the attentional lens to allow more input, while containing it to the field of sensation arising in the body at the present moment. Awareness of physical sensations involves an attunement to one's sensory feeling tone, specifically noting if the experience is pleasant, unpleasant, or neutral. By coupling an attitude of inquisitiveness, patience, and acceptance with this mindful observing of whatever is encountered, one learns to override habitual reactive tendencies of clinging to the pleasant, avoiding the unpleasant, and becoming disinterested in the neutral. Whereas the first foundation helps to cultivate focused calm, the second cultivates balanced sensitivity, which the tradition describes as equanimity, since one is able to remain present to the full range of internal sensations without impulsive reactions. Equanimity does not attempt to flatten experience or foster a numb detachment. On the contrary, in mindfulness of sensations one fully attends to the raw experiences of pain, pleasure, and the midrange between, but deconditions the reactive response to each state. Mindfulness actually allows for an even deeper, more intimate experience of feeling tone unobstructed by conditioned reactions.

The Third Foundation: Mind

The third foundation attunes one to the nature of mind itself, opening the lens of awareness to include awareness itself, while maintaining unbiased objectivity. Here one observes mental states as they emerge, for example noticing whether one is overstimulated or focused, afflicted or free. One learns to observe the states and qualities of awareness without being compelled by them on the one hand or needing to suppress them on the other. In the same way that one learns to override habitual reactions of clinging and avoiding physical sensations in the second foundation, in the third foundation one learns to decondition automatic reactions by applying antidotes that counterbalance the so-called five hindrances to mental pliancy:

1 Restlessness, excitation.
2 Mental dullness, lethargy.
3 Sensory fixation, greed.
4 Sensory repulsion, hostility.
5 Doubt.

As one strategically counteracts these hindrances, awareness is freed and harnessed towards deepening investigation and insight. Since this observing of mental states includes the prior foundations of body and sensation, it avoids the pitfalls of disembodied abstraction and numbing detachment. So, mindfulness of mind protects one from the escapism or disassociation characteristic of spiritual bypassing, by engaging mind/body events fully, clearly, and courageously without reactive tendencies (Welwood, 2000).

Through this mindfulness of mind, one learns to identify less with states of mind and more with the so-called nature of mind itself, traditionally described as naturally clear and cognizant (Lati Rinpoche, 1981). Mind in the West is commonly equated with thoughts themselves, but in Buddhist contemplative science it is that spacious awareness in which thoughts arise, capable of reflecting on itself (meta-cognitive awareness) and recognizing the true nature of things (meta-cognitive insight). In this practice, mind is metaphorically likened to a sky that includes all weather patterns, or a polished mirror reflecting all that comes before it. Training to rest without reactions in the so-called natural state of clarity or unobscured awareness (*vidhya*, in Tibetan, *rigpa*) is considered an advanced practice in the great perfection (*mahasandhi*, in Tibetan, *dzogchen*) and great seal (*mahamudra*) traditions, which aim at insight into the interdependent nature of phenomena. When the mind is made pliable by overcoming the five hindrances, then one cultivates seven important mental faculties known as awakening factors (*bodhyanga*):

1 Mindfulness, unwavering awareness.
2 Analytic investigation.
3 Energy, determined effort.
4 Joy, sustained well-being.
5 Concentration, sustained focal attention.
6 Tranquility, deep relaxation.
7 Equanimity, non-reactivity.

These seven factors facilitate discernment leading to insight of the three primary characteristics that define the nature of all phenomena: impermanence, insubstantiality, and dissatisfactoriness. In other words, self-healing and sustainable well-being are direct outcomes of perceptual clarity, and lead to an intuitive understanding of how subjects and objects exist beyond appearances. As one deepens insight to the profound level of transcendent wisdom, one naturally adjusts one's view, speech, and actions towards self and others to live in accordance with the principles of interdependence and universal compassion.

The Fourth Foundation: Realities

In the final foundation, mindfulness of realities (*dharmas*), two procedures are combined. The first is a process of memorizing and internalizing an extensive list of psychological phenomena, elements, or realities, and the second is observing these realities as they naturally arise in meditation. This internalization and analytic investigation then carry over into one's daily activities, as an ability to discern between wholesome and unwholesome mental factors, and to consciously direct *karmic* responses. So, based on these four foundations, mindfulness works to decondition mental hindrances, cultivate positive factors of awakening, and to generate experiential insight into the facts of life that facilitate optimal development towards liberation from self-imposed suffering.

The final frontier beyond the fourth application of mindfulness includes the domains of body, sensations, and mind, but opens the lens of awareness to embrace all experience arising in the present moment. One is free to adopt any physical posture (lie, sit, stand, walk) and attend to breath, body, sensations, emotions, thoughts, external stimuli, and all mental qualities, combining focused calm, balanced sensitivity, and discerning insight. This invokes the practice of natural wakefulness in daily life, sometimes referred to as choiceless awareness or even non-meditation. Here mindfulness is not cultivated for its own sake, but to continually yoke intuitive discernment with harmonious activity in the service of conscious evolution.

Clinical Applications and Mechanism of Change

As awareness is trained, it is more accessible for self-redirection and conscious self-healing. Over the past 40 years research in mindfulness-based interventions (MBIs) have demonstrated reductions in a wide variety of clinical issues and syndromes including chronic pain, anxiety, obsessive compulsive disorder, depression, self-injurious behavior, and addictions. Additionally, immune function, concentration, empathy, and general quality of life have been enhanced. One review (Baer, 2003) of the clinical research on mindfulness identified five major mechanisms underlying positive change: relaxation, acceptance, affect tolerance, behavior change, and meta-cognitive awareness/insight. A more recent wave of neuroscientific research correlates these psychological effects with specific brain changes (Lutz et al., 2007). Taken together, a compelling body of research exists that demystifies meditation and illuminates the mechanisms behind its clinical efficacy.

Relaxation

All meditative traditions share some techniques of concentration, applying sustained focal awareness to objects from breath and sound to image and prayer. When a client trains in mindfulness of breath, or any similar concentrative technique, s/he will usually experience decreased arousal and a sense of calm and relaxation. This is because single-pointed attention temporarily restricts external stimuli, inhibiting internal reactivity that would ordinarily overwhelm or lead to distraction. Focused attention and diaphragmatic breathing help elicit the body's natural relaxation response through activating the parasympathetic nervous system. The link between stress and medical conditions is universally accepted. Cardiac patients have been found to reduce their mortality by 41 percent during the first two years of meditation training, along with a 46 percent reduction in recurrence rates of coronary artery disease (Linden et al., 1996). Eighty percent of hypertensive patients have lowered blood pressure and decreased medications, while 16 percent were able to discontinue use of all medications for at least three years (Dusek et al., 2008). Most patients with medical and psychological syndromes would benefit from developing the capacity to relax. It serves as an optimal state of mind for learning and insight in therapy, and along with physical exercise has been correlated to increased neural plasticity (Siegel, 2020).

Acceptance

Buddhist mindfulness practice distinguishes itself from purely concentrative techniques by expanding its scope beyond an exclusive focus on a single object. Mindfulness training emphasizes an attitude of impartial acceptance along with attention control. This attitude pays dividends when one begins to encounter upsetting sensations, emotions, and thoughts. In a sort of unilateral disarmament, one contracts with oneself to suspend aggressive, punitive, or adverse reactions towards unpleasant experiences in the service of experimental inquiry and learning.

The Buddha referred to this skill of disengaging from reactivity as "removing the second arrow." Some measure of pain and stress is unavoidable in the life cycle (the first arrow), yet our reactivity towards "life as it is" creates a layer of self-imposed suffering that only compounds ordinary challenges. Since these reactions are self-imposed, they can be consciously abandoned by learning to accept things as they are, especially unavoidable moments of pain, loss, sadness, grief. To demonstrate this shift, 72 percent of chronic pain patients undergoing mindfulness training reported moderate to great improvement in quality of life up to three years post-intervention with 96 percent treatment compliance (Kabat-Zinn et al., 1987). Even while pain lingers, the suffering caused by reaction and resistance to it is diminished, altering the net experience. In a culture that has made great strides in medicine, science, and technology, many have an unspoken assumption that we should be able to eliminate all forms of suffering. Some MBIs such as dialectical behavior therapy (DBT) (Linehan, 1993) draw on contemplative science and advocate a healthy balance between striving to change what we can control while accepting conditions and circumstances that we cannot.

Affect Tolerance

As mindfulness training proceeds through the foundations, one increases exposure to more subtle stimuli (sensations, emotions, and thoughts) and consequently elicits subtler levels of conditioned reactivity. While the novice might experience this as a set-up for greater distress, it is precisely through voluntary, systematic exposure within a safe setting of self-attunement that one learns to decondition reactivity. This is similar to exposure training or systematic desensitization in cognitive behavioral therapy (CBT). When the associative links between external stimuli, internal sensation, and conditioned reaction are sufficiently slowed by introspective awareness, meditators gain access to normally unconscious micro-processes where they can decondition ingrained reactions, find more effective responses, and install new neural pathways.

In addition to relaxation and acceptance, affect tolerance is another key mechanism of change underpinning the efficacy of mindfulness. With each successive reaction to affective experience—clinging to pleasure, avoiding pain, or shutting down to vulnerability—our ability to endure those sensations and the emotions they stir atrophies. We may temporarily escape the unpleasant feeling, impulsively act out pleasure, or space out and shut down in neutrality, but we are rendering ourselves less resilient over the long term to face life's emotional vicissitudes. The fact that mindfulness increases affect tolerance and emotional sensitivity is supported by many studies, such as one that showed significant reduction in anxiety and panic maintained over three years as a result of an MBI (Miller et al., 1995). In these programs clients first elicit relaxation using the first foundation of breath, then open the scope of mindfulness to accept painful sensations, distressing emotions, and disturbing thoughts, and finally learn through exposure to endure them from an internal place of safety, impartiality, and insight. This greater tolerance allows those sensations, emotions, and thoughts to be borne with greater calm, acceptance, balance, and discernment, supporting a more realistic and effective way of relating to difficult experiences.

Behavior Change

Mindfulness meditation makes use of subtle gaps between associative links in the cycle of stress-reactivity, described at length below. These are links in a chain of conditioned responses leading from misperception to adverse emotions, stress emotions to maladaptive reactions. Whether the reactions are impulses for drug and alcohol abuse (Marlatt & Gordon, 1985), binge-eating behavior (Kristeller & Hallett, 1999), obsessive-compulsive disorder (Fairfax, 2008), or parasuicidal behavior (Linehan et al., 1991), the literature shows that mindfulness leads to successful behavior change by slowing down mind/body process to the point where linked responses can be uncoupled and changed.

For contemplative science, psychoeducation is an indispensable element of therapy, because an individual's agency and proactive choices set in motion new solutions to old problems. People require skills of relaxation and affect tolerance but can also greatly benefit from learning healthier behaviors that help them revise their personal histories, reactive impulses, and false convictions about themselves and the world. While meditative training exposes clients directly to adverse emotions to increase affect tolerance, it also leverages consciousness in the gap prior to reactions so that healthier responses can be pursued, resulting in the confidence, communicative skill, and interpersonal effectiveness people need.

Meta-Cognitive Awareness and Insight

Traditional CBT helps clients identify unrealistic thought patterns and substitute new ones that are more accurate. Mindfulness of mind fosters a radical shift in our perceiving stance vis-à-vis thoughts in general. In 2000, a group of researchers combined CBT with mindfulness, developing mindfulness-based cognitive therapy (MBCT) (Teasdale et al., 2000; Segal et al., 2013). MBCT made a nuanced adjustment to psychotherapy drawn from ancient contemplative science. Rather than simply identifying and substituting negative thoughts, clients learn to shift their whole frame of reference regarding the process of thinking itself. The shift involves relating to thoughts as mental fabrications, arising like clouds in the space of momentary awareness, rather than as "real" reflections of reality we must attend to or act on. Once the ephemeral nature of thought is exposed, then we experience more flexibility in how we choose to relate to thoughts. This flexibility creates a life-changing capacity of discernment and decisiveness. During mindfulness training, skill in meta-cognitive awareness (i.e., awareness of awareness) helps to establish an impartial open stance to all thoughts, rather than a partial, narrow stance that rejects thoughts taken to be intrinsically bad and inserts thoughts taken to be intrinsically good.

This general shift frees one's inner resources from a mental battle within oneself and provides a sense of spaciousness and restful alertness. It is as if one is able to sit on the banks of a river and watch the stream go by, rather than be in the stream fighting its currents. MBCT researchers found that meta-cognitive awareness facilitates meta-cognitive insight, as does mindfulness of mind in the third foundation. MBCT harnesses this spacious internal stance by asking clients to acknowledge thinking as it occurs, without over-involvement or over-identification with the content. At the culmination of training, a breakthrough can be made in which clients realize that none of the thoughts arising reflects the thinker of the thought: "I have thoughts, but none of them are me," a classic refrain of meditators who reach this milestone. MBCT was found to lead to a 50 percent reduction in relapse among the most afflicted population—clients with three or more prior episodes of major depression (Teasdale et al., 2000). Once skills have been established, clients are empowered to meet depressive symptoms at their onset and prevent a full relapse.

Meta-cognitive insight facilitates dis-identification from traumatic narratives that had once consumed and defined the individual experiencing them. But even when a person is no longer depressed, their mind's habit of reifying thoughts might continue to compel them to identify with some negative self-image or narrative, limiting access to their innate potential. Mindfulness of mind provides a unique training in subtle letting go, guided by perceptual discernment that is maintained through the lifespan, so that one does not substitute one self-constraining narrative trap for another, but keeps the mind open, receptive, and flexible. Further, this science affirms that intuitive discernment and insight into the true nature of things evokes fearlessness because the delusions, fabrications, and worst-case fears projected onto reality have been exposed, clearing the space of sheer interdependence and possibility.

Karma Theory: Reinterpreting the Indic Science of Causality

The whole enterprise of liberation from self-imposed suffering depends upon one of the most essential yet misunderstood insights of Buddhist contemplative science: the theory that *karma* or intentional action is the primary force shaping human development. Any understanding of mindfulness meditation without the context of *karma* theory is only partial. With the exception of Loizzo (2014a, 2014b, 2015), a thorough exploration of the scientific foundation of *karma* theory has not been attempted in the West, largely because Western beliefs about *karma* identify it exclusively with its metaphysical corollary of reincarnation or rebirth of mind across multiple lifetimes. Among Buddhist scholars, Batchelor (1998) seems to strike a balanced approach between literal traditional views of *karma*, and the modern secular dismissal of it. He argues that the core theory of karma—that intentional acts drive development—maintains the primacy of mind in the causal relationship between ethics and human flourishing. Yet he remains agnostic about the traditional cultural beliefs that *karma* refers to the mind's reincarnation from life to life. In traditional Buddhist cultures, as in the popular imagination of the West, *karma* is also taken to mean an impersonal, cosmic law of reward or retribution that explains how our past actions create either negative or positive consequences. For example, if we get a promotion, we consider it "good *karma*," a result of positive past acts, but if we are in a car accident it's "bad *karma*," the result of negative past acts.

My colleagues at the Nalanda Institute and I propose a more scientifically critical interpretation of *karma* theory, as accounting for how we *perceive* what happens to us, based on what we have done in the past (Loizzo, 2014, 2015). This slight shift of emphasis removes *karma* from the realm of speculative metaphysics and places it back into the domain of human psychology. Interpretation and perception are key. It is possible that a job promotion could be perceived as threatening and stressful just as it might be validating and exciting, or that surviving a car crash could be perceived as life-affirming, provoking a sense of incredible gratitude, as much as it could be traumatizing. Thus, *karma* theory entails a science that accounts for the variation by which individuals perceive and experience the same events differently based on their development, as well as how they can actively shift future perceptions based on present learning and behavior change. Modern stress research (Cohen et al., 1986) has drawn a similar conclusion that stress has less to do with the actual event and more to do with the subjective appraisal of one's capacity to meet the challenge.

Dependent Origination: Self-Construction Across Time

Several Buddhist doctrines elucidate the principles of *karma* theory, but the most crucial, known as dependent origination (*pratityasamutpada*) closely resembles the mind–body causality of perception revealed in current models of stress and trauma (Cohen et al., 1986; van der Kolk, 2002). Dependent origination, the second Noble Truth, teaches that all phenomena and experiences are neither determined by God, nor self-emergent from their own nature, nor random. Instead, they *originate in dependence* on psychological causes and conditions (*hetu-pratyaya*) that produce predictable developmental effects (*phala-vipaka*). This is particularly relevant to human perceptions and narratives concerning experiences of pain, pleasure, and indifference, and to broader notions of suffering (*dukkha*) and its cessation (*nirvana*).

Within this causal cycle, no single moment of human experience exists in isolation; each is accounted for by a cyclic loop of causality that resembles a chain reaction. The mental reflex of unconscious reification (*avidya*) calcifies *karmic* imprints and unconscious impulses (*samskaras*) from the past. When these are activated within the so-called continuum of consciousness (*citta-santana*), they distort our self-image and sense perceptions in the present, triggering afflictive reactions and compulsive actions that recreate future experiences of stress and trauma. This causal loop operates simultaneously at many levels: within a single moment of experience; over a single lifetime; and over the course of multiple lives. As a result, we are not completely free to experience things fully in the moment because our current perceptions are filtered by latent associations from our past. Nor are we able to act fully freely due to the force of habituated involuntary reactions that continually shape future perceptions. The whole cycle is thus conceived of as an unconscious revolving door of self-perpetuated misery that the Buddha called *samsara*, the mind–body systems contaminated and compelled by stress instincts and traumatic associations. It is from this causal chain-reaction of *samsara* that we must awaken.

In this teaching, the Buddha described the psychobiological micro-processes involved in the self-construction of experience, based on the model of a causal cycle with 12 links. The model depicts a process-oriented circular causality, in which no single link is a self-contained, independent phenomenon. Each link conditions the next step in a chain reaction that operates at many periodic levels at once: in the loop of a momentary post-traumatic stress reaction; in the arc of an individual's lifelong stress-reactive development; and in the multi-life span of intergenerational transmission of stress and trauma. At each level, the cycle involves four phases of action–reaction: 1) the imprinting of past actions; 2) the reactive formation of present perceptions; 3) the present activity of stress emotions and compulsive actions; and 4) the reactive fruition of present actions in future adaptations. While this process creates the false impression of an autonomous, independent, and reified self, our habitual sense of agency and continuity across time is not in fact so anchored but based on misperceiving a constantly changing flux of action and reaction revealed by mindful reflection and culminating in the insight of selflessness.

Examining the nuances of this causal cycle, the Buddha outlined the 12 links and their causal influence as follows:

1 Misperception (*Avidya*)—The universal instinct to reify phenomena (self, other, things) and experiences (interactions) making them appear more real, fixed, or substantial than they are.Misperception primes and conditions instinctual impulses and traumatic imprints.

2 Unconscious Instincts (*Samskara*)—Implicit memories, motivational impulses, associations, and schemas based on collective human experiences from evolution and childhood that remain latent in the psyche and color future interpretations.Instinctual impulses (from the past) condition consciousness (in the present).

3 Biased Consciousness (*Vijnana*)—Consciousness, also known as awareness, has the qualities of vivid clarity (appearance) and knowing (recognition), and arises on the basis of contact between the six kinds of objects and six faculties—the five sense objects plus ideas, and five senses plus mind.Consciousness conditions our self-construct (mind/body system).

4 Self-Construct (*Nama-rupa*)—The collected mind/body systems (*skandhas*) of matter, sensations, cognitions, instincts, and consciousness are reified collectively and misperceived as a permanent, unitary, and independent entity labeled *I*, *self*, or *person*.Self-construct conditions the six senses.

5 Distorted Perceptions (*Sadayatana*)—The six faculties (or doors of perception)—eyes, ears, tongue, nose, skin, and mind—are primed to receive input and convert it into information skewed by negativity bias and filtered by traumatic associations.The six perceptual faculties condition sense impressions.

6 Immediate Contact (*Sparsha*)—The instant a visual, auditory, gustatory, olfactory, tactile, or cognitive sense object meets its respective faculty and consciousness, triggering a moment of embodied sensory experience. Contact conditions hedonic sensation.

7 Hedonic Sensation (*Vedana*)—Sensations are pleasant, neutral, or unpleasant. The quality of every sensate experience is co-emergent with a subjective appraisal or narrative that is the consequence, or ripening result, of past impressions and processes (*karma-vipaka*).Hedonic sensation conditions afflicted reactions.

8 Afflictive Reaction (*Trishna*)—Immediate, impulsive, and afflictive reactions to sensations are classified in one of three ways: clinging to what is pleasant, avoiding what is unpleasant, or disengaging from neutral sensations in order to seek more pleasant ones. This is the weakest link in the

chain, and the gap or window of opportunity for change.Afflicted reaction conditions compulsive action.

9 Compulsive Action (*Upadana*)—The three types of afflicted reactions condition four compulsive habits to: 1) pursue sense-pleasure, 2) maintain erroneous worldviews, 3) resort to maladaptive behaviors, and 4) identify with an independent sense of self.Compulsive action conditions the process of becoming (a self).

10 Compulsive Existence (*Bhavana*)—Deterministic compulsions culminate in a reified, pervasive, and traumatized sense of personal existence, experienced as fundamentally separate, inadequate, and unsafe.Self-existence conditions the repetition of future adverse experiences.

11 Mindless Recreation (*Jati*)—The continual reinforcement of traumatic self-identification ensures that future developmental actions will also likely culminate in distorted and tainted experiences.Mindless recapitulation conditions traumatic illness, aging, and death.

12 Traumatic Aging and Death (*Jara-marana*)—A life conditioned by traumatic repetition and compulsion renders the natural processes of aging, illness, and death even more terrifying and intolerable, which comes full circle to reinforce self-reifying habits and misperceptions in future lives. Unconscious living, aging, and dying further condition misperception in future lives.

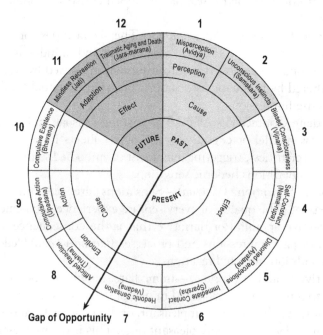

Figure 2.1 Dependent Origination (Duane Stapp, Used with Permission)

Mind the Gap: Cultivating the Garden with Recognition and Choice

Buddhist *karma* theory skillfully clears a middle way between the extremes of fatalistic determinism and moralistic free will. A small gap or window of opportunity for change exists in the present if we can locate it with mindful discernment and leverage new choices that consciously turn the wheel of causality in the healing direction. For this reason, the path of positive self-change leading to freedom and awakening (*bodhi*) is not considered a quick fix or miraculous event, but a slow, gradual process of altering causes and conditions within a psychoneuro-environmental matrix.

Because the whole process of dependent origination involves a 12-link chain-reaction, breaking just one of the links interrupts and may even help reverse the entire cycle. As mentioned, the weakest link occurs just after *Hedonic Sensation* (link 7), in the process of *Afflictive Reaction* (link 8). While there is little we can do about sense contact and the ensuing sensory appraisal of experience, we do have the capacity to consciously choose how to *respond to our experience* in the moment, creating the cause for a new future result. The traditional metaphor of a gardener planting seeds for harvest is appropriate. Most often, the untrained mind abides in a state of constant reactivity, haphazardly replanting the same weeds over and over, seeding its own future jungle. Mindfulness allows us to take advantage of the gap at this vulnerable juncture. Guided by wisdom and ethical action we can cultivate the fertile ground of opportunity by planting new seeds that bear fruit in healthy development, eventually yielding the abundant harvest of liberation.

For example, when a person is rejected by a love interest, she may perceive herself as inadequate (misperception), feel core shame (adverse emotion), and resort to isolation or substance use (reactive action) as a knee-jerk coping mechanism to numb painful affect. Our impulsive reactions, originally designed to keep us safe or secure basic needs, actually end up reinforcing a self-fulfilling prophesy of worst-case fears. While by withdrawing into isolation, a shamed individual may avoid further insult, over the long run she risks closing the door to the validation and care she so desperately needs. This reactive approach may not just deprive the individual of love but set her up for inevitable future moments of rejection, confirming a false self-image of being inadequate and unlovable. So intentional actions are so important because they seed future development of the self and mind/body process.

Complementing mindfulness with wisdom helps to deepen and refine one's faculty for insight into normally obscured characteristics of reality. Traditionally known as the "three marks of existence" (trilaksana), perceiving these qualities clearly helps us respond rather than react to the world and ourselves in more skillful ways. Phenomena and experiences are said to be qualified as: 1) impermanent (anitya) and always changing; 2) lacking any inherent, independent nature or identity (anatma); and 3) prone to pervasive preventable suffering (duhkha). Wisdom permits a more accurate way of perceiving reality beyond our myopic projections, thus enabling us to relate to the fluid and potentially constructive nature of experience with greater responsibility, fearlessness, creativity, and mastery.

While we train to slow the causal cycle of mental production down enough to gain insight (vipasyana, in Pali, vipassana) into these three characteristics, we simultaneously exercise ethical choices that, based on the developmental process of karma, create a more favorable future experience because they are more in line with the fluid, wholistic nature of reality. Because everything is empty (of fixed self)—i.e., is thoroughly relative and interdependent—perceptions, experience, and actions are naturally malleable. So, nothing could be more important than responsible, benevolent interactions that favorably change the matrix of processes and relationships in which we live. Hence the great Nalanda Master Nagarjuna affirmed "emptiness is the womb of compassion" (shunyata-karuna-garbham). While Buddhist traditions assume a set of ethical guidelines strikingly similar to those of Western religions, the Buddha contextualized ethics within the naturalistic science of active development (karma-vipaka). The ten positive actions recommended in Buddhist practice and their respective outcomes are:

1 Nonviolence leads to peace of mind.
2 Generosity leads to a sense of abundance.
3 Sexual sublimation leads to lasting satisfaction.
4 Honesty engenders trust.
5 Tactful speech engenders respect.
6 Caring speech engenders leadership.
7 Meaningful speech engenders authority.
8 Philanthropic intent results in contentment.
9 Benevolent intent results in confidence.
10 Realistic view results in clarity.

Thus, contemplative practitioners assume the role of the architect of their own evolution and development, having full confidence that by following such virtuous modes of action they may fulfill their highest aspirations for well-being, liberation, and awakening.

Western Corollaries of Karma Theory: Accounting for Responsibility and Agency

Modern corollaries in evolutionary neurobiology, attachment research, trauma therapy, positive psychology, and psycholinguistics support this scientific reading of *karma* theory. As a modern scientifically minded culture, we accept the premise of continuity over time as presented in evolutionary theories of gene inheritance and expression. Due to Cartesian dualism of mind and body, however, we have come to view mind as disembodied, and reduce it to a mere function of the brain. So, mind is given little credence as a causal factor determining our experience. Yet, recent interdisciplinary research into meditation, neuroplasticity, and epigenetics has forged a revolutionary shift in this perspective. There is a growing body of research examining the influence of mind on neural and biological processes over time. This research has helped to fuel a resurgence of popular interest in consciousness, meditation, and spirituality after several centuries of one-sided faith in scientism and its reductive materialism.

During epigenetic activation, as observed in the Dutch Hongerwinter ("Hunger winter") research, latent genetic traits such as obesity were "switched on" as a result of a mother's psychological reaction to famine, then transmitted across several generations (Ahmed, 2010). A similar phenomenon is noted in attachment research and trauma therapy where distorted psychological schemas regarding the self (as worthless) and the world (as unsafe) are solidified under traumatic conditions and passed on via transgenerational inheritance of narrative, along with insecurely attached coping strategies of clinging or avoidance (Siegel, 2010b). Such state-specific experiences happen with such automaticity and frequency that they become ingrained personality traits or self-habits, likely to continue unconsciously throughout a lifespan or even through mimicry across a parent–child bond. We often can trace back the etiology of traumas, narratives, and attachment styles to those of primary caregivers, and see them as part of a multi-life cycle of dependent origination transmitted down through the generations.

Fortunately, because of the plasticity of the human mind and nervous system, the inverse cycle of liberative, conscious development is equally possible. Current research is beginning to reveal the epigenetic activation of favorable traits such as stress resilience (Dudley et al., 2011) and the intergenerational inheritance of benevolent parental influences (Lieberman et al., 2005). One study found epigenetic alterations in as few as eight hours of mindfulness practice, where subjects showed altered levels of gene-regulation and reduced levels of pro-inflammatory cytokines, correlated with greater immune responsiveness to infection and tumorigenesis (Kaliman et al., 2014).

In sum, the ways in which we human beings think, speak, and act in relation to immediate circumstances appears to have specific enduring consequences on perceptions and subjective experience in successive moments as well as subtle impacts on other individuals' development now and into the future. The thrust of *karma* theory alerts us to the incredible primacy of mind, specifically the power of intentional actions in determining our future existence. This can inspire both a deep sense of responsibility for our actions as well as a sense of empowered agency for our evolution. Cultivating a greater appreciation for ethical and evolutionary agency need not require blind faith in either religious dogmas or in materialism. As the Buddha reminded his students, it is up to each of us to critically evaluate how mind influences behavior and experience over time, and to develop a coherent narrative that accounts for this process, knowing that all explanations are merely conventional descriptions of reality. When *karma* theory is understood as just one possible explanation for psychological causation and permitted to inform mindfulness meditation practice, it allows the meditator to guide the microscope of stabilized attention, evoking insight and behavior change of habitually unconscious micro-cycles of self-defeating reaction that perpetuate distress. By intentionally intervening to disrupt our cycles, we can steer the future developmental course of consciousness.

The Path Ahead

Mindfulness offers an inroad into the subtle sequence of causal events in mind, brain, and body, permitting skillful actions governed by insight that produce more accurate perceptions and reinforce more positive experience. When mindfulness meditation is understood in context, coupled with wisdom and ethics, its purpose and potential to radically transform experience becomes apparent. Far more than a simple technique for stress-reduction and symptom relief, mindfulness facilitates the cessation of unconscious habituation and its resulting experience of distress, while permitting the conscious reconstruction of an optimal life, up to and including one free of self-imposed suffering. Understanding this, I contend that mindfulness has never been about "being in the moment" for the moment's sake, as popular culture's dilution of it promotes. Far more powerfully, it has always been about being in the moment to skillfully direct the course of one's evolution towards optimal health, happiness, and liberation.

The Buddha and his successors offered a sophisticated theory of mind and a comprehensive path to self-healing and liberation that could benefit many, especially when approached as positive psychology and mental training, rather than speculative metaphysics or religious ritual. The recent attention paid to mindfulness meditation has opened the door for a more critical analysis of the psychology and pedagogy from which the practice arose. We are making the most of the opportunity through the cross-cultural and interdisciplinary dialogue inspired by the Dalai Lama and his Western counterparts, such as the researchers of the Mind and Life Institute. As a result, contemplative science initiatives respecting and integrating traditional Buddhist science and culture have emerged over the last decade affiliated with leading universities nationwide, and with them the promise of novel programming, hybrid interventions, and cutting-edge research.

3
The Buddha, MLK, and the Ethics of Healing Community

Jan Willis

Buddha and Dr Martin Luther King, Jr: Compassionate Social Justice Activists

When I think about embodying activism with fierce compassion, I think of the Buddha and I think of Martin Luther King, Jr. There is a lot to compare in their teachings and approach to transforming society. Many African Americans of my generation who later inclined toward Buddhism had already heard similar teachings in the words of Martin Luther King, Jr. Striving to move the United States closer to being a more just society, King and others had built the nonviolent civil rights movement around the principles of love, forgiveness, and interdependence. Hearing these same principles and practices extolled in Buddhist teachings was like coming home.

In the *Dhammapada*, an anthology of basic Buddhist teachings, there is a number of teachings that are echoed in the speeches of Dr King. For example, *Dhammapada* 5 says, "Hatred is never appeased by hatred. Hatred is only appeased by love. This is an eternal law, this is Dhamma." Dr King said it this way, "Darkness cannot drive out darkness, only light can do that. Hate cannot drive out hate, only love can do that."[1] *Dhammapada* 183 simply says, "Do no harm, practice virtue, discipline the mind. This is the teaching of the Buddhas." And from a Buddhist point of view the Buddha's teachings are meant for the welfare and benefit of all beings. Martin Luther King, Jr said it this way, "Life's most persistent and urgent question is, what are you doing for others?"[2]

The Buddha's Revolutionary Activism

People say Buddhism and activism can't come together. What? Then you don't know what the Buddha taught, and you certainly don't know what the

DOI: 10.4324/9781003243588-4

Buddha did. In the sixth century BC during the time of Aryan civilization in India, the Buddha allowed for his followers to come from all the four main castes. And that was a big no-no. At that time, in India, you didn't mix castes, you didn't share the same food. But if you wanted to be part of the Buddha's sangha, and if you had good reasons to meditate with him in the forest to become a *vanaprastha* (a forest dwelling hermit), then everyone was together.

Not only did the Buddha's sangha mix people from different castes, but he also allowed women to come into the sangha. Now that was really not accepted. Women in a place with men? That just can't happen in Aryan society. The Buddha was royal, and thought to be from the Kshatriya caste, so he was getting advice from everybody about how terrible his decisions were. "How are you going to teach those people together and how are you going to teach men and women together?" But the Buddha never seemed to have a problem with it.

In doing that, the Buddha showed a transformative vision of society. That was real activism for the benefit and the welfare of all beings. The Buddha did this revolutionary thing that was transformative for society. After the Buddha's life, one of the largest societal impacts was that people stopped killing animals and started making clay figurines to offer as sacrifices. The Buddha and Mahavira, his Jain contemporary, were both against killing, and it changed society. Because of the Buddha's teachings, and because of his own life example, many African American children of the civil rights movement have been finding their way to Buddhism. When we learned the details of the Buddha's life, he became even more of an inspiration. Here was a man who, actually, in practice, rejected the systemic oppression of his country's people by denouncing the caste, or *varna*, system of the Aryans (originally founded on color discrimination) and allowed all castes and women to enter his community of practitioners. Both actions were extremely radical—even revolutionary—for his time.

Martin Luther King, Jr's Transformative Vision of a Beloved Community

Martin Luther King, Jr also had a transformative vision of society. He believed the United States could become a Beloved Community. He was not the first one to use the idea of a Beloved Community, but his vision included abolitionism and intersectionality where beings were recognized as beings and were valued. On The King Center website it says,

The Beloved Community was not a lofty utopian goal to be confused with the rapturous image of the Peaceable Kingdom, in which lions and lambs co-exist in idyllic harmony. Rather, the Beloved Community was for him [Dr. King] a realistic, achievable goal that could be attained by a critical mass of people committed to and trained in the philosophy and methods of nonviolence.

(The King Center, n.d.)

Dr King often said nonviolence can't just be a habit that you have on certain occasions or a kneejerk reaction. Nonviolence must become an attitude. It takes discipline. It takes real training, which echoes Dhammapada 183, "Do no harm, practice virtue, discipline the mind."

The King Center further describes the Beloved Community as,

a global vision in which all people can share in the wealth of the earth. In the Beloved Community, poverty, hunger, and homelessness will not be tolerated because international standards of human decency will not allow it. Racism and all forms of discrimination, bigotry and prejudice will be replaced by an all-inclusive spirit of sisterhood and brotherhood. In the Beloved Community, international disputes will be resolved by peaceful conflict-resolution and reconciliation of adversaries, instead of military power. Love and trust will triumph over fear and hatred. Peace and justice will prevail over war and military conflict.

(The King Center, n.d.)

King had a vision of the Beloved Community, where there would be justice. Where there would be no prisons. Where people would be protected. Where people would be unafraid. Where people would be free to bring whatever talents they had. It's like Dharma rain, or Dharma cloud, in Buddhism. The rain falls on everybody equally, so does talent, but not opportunity. When I see young Black kids, talented kids who have a spark, I so want them to be able to get the opportunities to have those talents develop. In the Beloved Community, people would bring their talents, and their talents would be useful to the rest of the community, and they would be valued.

Interdependence and the Inescapable Network of Mutuality

The vision of the Beloved Community calls for fierce compassion and revolutionary transformation. It calls for us to join together in a society wherein, recognizing our interdependence, we belong and share compassionately with one another. Recognizing that "God is Love" (a New Testament Christian notion), that "we exist in dependence on one another" (a Buddhist notion), and that nonviolence and nonharm (ahimsa) and love (agape) must be our sole methods of dealing with one another. King envisioned a society in which we could be our best selves by seeking the benefit of others, knowing that when we seek to lift others up, we ourselves are raised up.

Dr King often spoke about interconnectedness, and often tied it into social justice issues. For example, he wrote,

> In a real sense, all life is interrelated. All men are caught in an inescapable network of mutuality, tied in a single garment of destiny. Whatever affects one directly affects all indirectly. I can never be what I ought to be until you are what you ought to be, and you can never be what you ought to be until I am what I ought to be. This is the interrelated structure of reality.[3]

In King's sermon "On Being a Good Neighbor" he notes that,

> the ultimate measure of a man is not where he stands in moments of comfort and convenience, but where he stands at times of challenge and controversy. The true neighbor will risk his position, his prestige, and even his life for the welfare of others.

Compare this to what the great Buddhist poet Shantideva (2006) wrote, "All the joy the world contains has come from wishing happiness for others, while all the misery the world contains has come from wishing happiness for oneself alone."

We do not exist independently. We need only breathe to know this. This is the real—not virtual—internet. We are inextricably bound together. And therefore, unless we find a way to live together, we shall—all of us—perish together. And since this is the case, since this is our reality, we must have compassion for one another. Another way of saying this is, "If you suffer, I suffer, and if you are happy, I am happy." And this is just exactly what the Buddhist Bodhisattva—and the true Christian—knows and feels. Though it is not an easy practice, this practice of love, it is the practice that gives our lives true meaning. In this interconnected world, there is no one who is not, and no thing that is not, our neighbor. With this deep recognition of our very being, we need to go forth and act in the world.

The Three Evils of Society and the Three Root Poisons of Samsara

Dr King named three evils of society: racism, poverty, and militarism. These echo the three so-called enemies at the hub of the wheel of Samsara: ignorance, greed, and hatred. Why do you suppose racism is in line with ignorance? What is the root of ignorance that keeps us in Samsara? It is the over-exaggerated investment we each make in our respective "I"'s. The conceit of "I" prevents us from seeing others—any others!—as equal to us. So, some human beings actually harbor the thought that some lives matter less than others. And so, we witness again—almost unimaginably in this 21st-century so-called "post-racial" society—the placards that must state the obvious: "Black Lives Matter." I am reminded that 50 years ago the placards read poignantly, "I am somebody." Why is this so hard for us to see and accept, and even cherish?

It seems to me that only if we harbor the deep-seated, erroneous conceit that "I am better than others" can we harbor the view that black lives—or any lives—don't matter. This conceit is our downfall. It makes us undervalue a person who is right in front of us. We think less of them. Ignorance makes a split between people. It makes a division between people. The conceit of "I" over-exaggerates the goodness of a friend, categorizes someone as a stranger because they never did anything to build our ego, and generates hatred toward perceived enemies. To use Dr King's terms, ignorance generates our militarism and poverty, a poverty that comes from greed and consumerism. Simply put, this conceit makes us view things and people as being separate from us instead of recognizing our absolute interdependence.

An Artist's Vision of Beloved Community

The artist, Natasha Marin, created a show using only sound. She banded together with a group of her friends, and they collected sound from Black people all over the United States. She describes this undertaking in the introduction to the anthology she curated, *Black Imagination: Black Voices on Black Futures*.

> We planned an exhibition that would de-center whiteness and provide space for healing and validation. We agreed to collect sound from Black folks of all kinds and craving nuance over stereotype, we sought out Black children, Black youth, LGBTQ+ Black folks, unsheltered Black folks, incarcerated Black folks, neuro-divergent Black folks, as well as differently-abled Black folks. Using field recorders, we spent months collecting responses to three prompts: What is your origin story; how do you heal yourself; and imagine and then describe a world where you are loved, safe, and valued?
>
> (Marin, 2020, p. 11)

To imagine such a space, you would be imagining something like the Beloved Community.

Here's just one response in the book from a woman in Seattle. She says,

> When I wake up, there is someone there who loves me. When I leave my home, the people living on my street, know my name, know my parents' names, and claim me as their own, drop by with soup when I'm sick, and small gifts during holidays, and I do the same for them. We break bread together. We laugh and dance and work and build together. Wherever I go, I'm known, and I know others. We greet each other with smiles and hugs. Our expressions are always genuine. We don't hide resentments between clenched teeth or anger in clenched fists. We say the words that need saying. We speak and listen and forgive and understand. We are peaceful in our hearts and our actions, and our peace is never built on the sacrifice of another's peace. We live in balance, never taking more than we need, never needing so much we can't sustain ourselves. Each of us is honored and valued and respected as equal members of a collective, irrespective of age, ability, ethnicity, gender, or any other political descriptor. We bring all of who we are.
>
> *(p. 31–32)*

Wouldn't that be great? A people-loving community.

Justice is Indivisible in the Beginning, in the Middle, and in the End

The concept of "The Beloved Community" may seem to us today to be too grandiose, too idealistic and, in the end, impossible. I disagree. It is certainly not a new proposition. If we look at the grand sweep of history, we see that no nation or people seem to have yet actually achieved it. Why? Because, where there are wars with "winners" and "losers," bitterness lingers. As King said over and over, hatred only gives rise to more hatred, and therefore only love can bring an end to hate. Only reconciliation, rather than selfish one-sided victory, can bring lasting peace and justice. Again, the King Center records,

> In his 1963 sermon, *Loving Your Enemies*, published in his book, *Strength to Love*, Dr. King addressed the role of unconditional love in struggling for the Beloved Community. "With every ounce of our energy we must continue to rid this nation of the incubus of segregation. But we shall not in the process relinquish our privilege and our obligation to love. While abhorring segregation, we shall love the segregationist. This is the only way to create the beloved community."
>
> *(The King Center, n.d.)*

One expression of agape love in King's Beloved Community is justice, not for any one oppressed group, but for all people. As Dr King said in 1963 in his Letter from Birmingham Jail, "Injustice anywhere is a threat to justice everywhere."[4]

He felt that justice could not be parceled out to individuals or groups but was the birthright of every human being in the Beloved Community. "I have fought too long and hard against segregated public accommodations to end up segregating my moral concerns," he said. "Justice is indivisible."[5] In the *Mahavagga*, the Buddha exhorted his first 60 ordained sangha members—while they were still practicing their own meditations—saying,

> Go forth, O Bhikkhus, for the welfare of the many, for the happiness of the many, for the good, well-being, and happiness of gods and men. Preach the sublime Dhamma, excellent in the beginning, excellent in the middle, excellent in the end. Proclaim the Holy Life, altogether perfect and pure.

One of the reasons King was killed was because of the anti-Vietnam War speech he delivered on April 4, 1967, at the Riverside Church. This got King into so much trouble with our national government. It might have been dangerous when you were shaking hands with Malcolm X. It might have been dangerous that so many people followed King, but when he said we should not be going overseas to kill people, his allies said, "Martin, you've really gone too far. Now, you are diluting the movement." King said, "If you don't know why I care about the people in Vietnam like I care about the people in this country, then you've misunderstood what it is I'm about." I love that. "You misunderstood what I'm about." We are interrelated.

Fierce Compassion and the Civil Rights Campaign: A Personal Account of Nonviolent Resistance

Birmingham used to be known as the Pittsburgh of the South because there was so much iron ore and coal there. One of these mining camps for coal, Docena, had closed when I was born. But my father, his father, and my uncle had jobs at the steel plant some miles away. We lived in that closed mining camp, where the White and Black families were separated by a single street. My folks, the Willises, kept their jobs. My father and grandfather were big civic-minded folk. They got the roads put in. There used to be only dirt roads. Until I later took a bus to Cornell University, that took a day and a night, I lived in this mining camp with my parents, grandparents, and my uncle. We children were very loved by all of them. My uncle had nine kids, so there were always people to play with.

Later when I got scholarships to college, the Klan came and set up a cross at the edge of the alleyway in front of our house and lit it afire. The Klan area chief lived in Docena. The Klan came to our house because there was a story in the Black newspaper, four pages folded over, that said, "Jan, the daughter of Mr Oram and Dorothy Willis, has won scholarships to Northern schools." In a couple of days, the Klan came out in 10 or 12 cars. This was part of our life. We knew that when you heard honking going through the camp, that the Klan was targeting somebody. It was a no-no for a Black kid to be celebrated, and it was a no-no to be so smart. It was never good to be conspicuous.

The Klan and their families came and set up a cross in front of our house in the alleyway. My mother had a .22 pistol in her hand. She told my sister and I to try to get under the bed. My father was working the graveyard shift at the steel plant, so he wasn't there. We were scared to death, and against my mother's will, I kept looking out the window. What I saw were these families, robed Klan people, and I was struck by the fact that their robes were colored: red robes and purple robes, not white. I was terrified, and yet I saw that their children were with them. I had this incredible urge to run out to them and say, "Wait, you're making a mistake. In this house, we're a family too. You're a family and we are a family too. There must be some mistake here." But there was no mistake.

The civil rights campaign came to Birmingham when I was 15. It was a year and a half before I went off to college. Part of King's strategy was to put the children in the front of the line for the last five days of the marches. That's why it was called the Children's March. King brought the civil rights campaign to Birmingham because he and his allies called it "the most segregated city in the South." We had a police commissioner in Birmingham named Bull Connor. It's said that Bull Connor lost one of his eyes in a fight he had with a Black man. This Black man had put his eye out. That was the story. Bull Connor hated Black people viscerally. So, King came with his retinue, and he was arrested on the second day. And we children were told to march. The marches went on for about five weeks, in April and May of 1963.

We children got downtown to the marches on school buses. The school buses would come by right after school had started. The doors would open, and the bus driver would say, "Going downtown," and we would all pile in from high school. When those buses took us to downtown Birmingham, they all stopped in front of the 16th Street Baptist Church, and we filed into the church. We took a nonviolent pledge every day and we signed it with our parents' names on it. The pledge had six pledges and then was expanded to ten over the weeks. The pledges included: "We hereby pledge to walk and talk in the manner of love, for God is love;" "Pray daily to be used by God in order that all men might be free;" and "Observe with both friend and foe the ordinary rules of courtesy. Seek to perform regular service for others and for the world. Refrain from the violence of fist, tongue or heart. Strive to be in good spiritual and bodily health. Follow the directions and the movement of all the captains about the demonstration."

And we would sign our name, sign our parents' names, and give our address. All those young people who practiced sitting-in at the counters, who practiced having ketchup poured over their heads, who practiced having taunts shouted loud in their ears, that was all nonviolence training.

My folks didn't know how often I went, but I went every day I could. Sometimes we marched with our parents. Most of the week, when my mother was home and my father was at work, we got rides with the school bus drivers, and we went downtown, and we marched. Bull Connor or the Birmingham Fire Department were there to hose us or order the police department to set dogs on us.

The last five days marked the specific Children's March. An ally of King's said, "Martin, you're going too far here. Put children in the front, that's going to be bad." Martin Luther King, Jr said, "We must arouse the conscience of the country." King knew what would happen. He knew the children would be attacked but it was strategy. Not enough people knew that children throughout the South were under attack. This was true. *Brown v. Board of Education* happened in 1954. The famous case of Emmett Till in 1955, and then, case after case, after case, after case of children being attacked and nobody doing anything. I used to wonder, "Don't they have parents? Can't somebody help?" This was the world I grew up in. Children were under attack.

We would dress in our Sunday best and my mother would have us keep the windows rolled up in daddy's old car. I said, "Mama how come we have to always have these windows up? We are dying in here! It's too hot." She would say, "Stop squirming." Then she would say, "Because mean White men want to harm you." This is a typical thing we heard all the time. If you were in a car, and you're Black, and a group of Whites pull up next to you at the stop sign, if those windows were rolled down, people threw things. They threw hot lye, or they threw acid. There was an all-out assault against children. During slavery, what was the worst thing you could do? Teach a Black person to read and write. There was an all-out assault on children, in particular in the South.

Now, we all knew this, and we were exhilarated to be able to do something about it. It was like, why didn't the rest of the country know this? This was King's way of getting the rest of the country to know about the assault on children. And it worked. The Children's March was in the beginning of May 1963. On August 28, 1963, there was the March on Washington. Then 12 days later, those White segregationists, racists—who had been seething since the May

12th declaration by the city council of Birmingham that some of the restrictions against Black people would be lifted—bombed the 16th Street Baptist Church because it had been the staging ground for sending marchers and kids every day. It was intentional that they bombed the 16th Street Baptist Church while there was Sunday school, while there were children in the building.

You Do Not Have to Like Them, But You Have to Love Them

My training with Dr King taught me about nonviolent resistance. He showed that being peaceful does not mean being a doormat. It means you do not want to kill somebody; you want them to live. You take a vow to love and liberate *all* beings. You can't say, except this one and this one and this one. That is what King meant when he said, "You don't have to like them, but you have to love them because we are all children of God." In 1970, I was talking with His Holiness the 14th Dalai Lama about college protest and fighting policemen—we called the police "pigs" then—and he said directly to me,

> If you say "pigs" in your mind, then you've got to let them get you. Instead, you can think, "I have chosen to be with these people who are protesting. Then you do what you must to stop the violence, with love."

And there are many ways to do this: vote, use your voice, be brave, and become an activist. Help people. Give rides if people are going to vote in person. If you can write, write about it. It's that simple. Do what you can. Being peaceful and compassionate does not mean being passive.

During the civil rights movement, it was mostly Black people out there marching. I'm proud of the Black Lives Matter movement as I think it is much more inclusive. You see mixed groups out there marching now. There are Whites and Blacks and Latinx and the LGBTQ+ community and everybody else out there. That's good. That to me is an improvement. All those folk make up a beloved community.

Let Love Fuel the Struggle

People often ask me, "How can we use our anger in the fight for social justice?" Well, I think you can't. You might use it for inspiration, but then if you try to use it in the struggle, you'll burn out. The second or third day, you won't be able to go anymore. Anger just wipes you out. Your energy will run out in no time. Have you ever really been angry? It's miserable. If I stayed in, I wanted to go out. If I tried to sleep, I woke up. If I woke up, I wanted to sleep.

You're crazed. You're physically just shaken. After a while I realized, "Well, this is getting me nowhere." Like King said, "I have decided to stick with love because hate is too great a burden to bear."[6]

I gave a talk once in Oakland, California, in a warehouse next to a gas station. People from the street came in, "What's going on here? Who's that?" I was talking then about nonviolence and love. This young man from the back said, "Look, I'm from El Salvador and the soldiers, they killed all of my people and they hurt the village. If I couldn't run on anger, I wouldn't have anything to run on." I thought, "Now, what can I say to this lived experience of this person?" Before I could answer, a young Chinese woman stood up. She said, "Better to run on love." I thought, "Whoa! Okay! Yes. What she said." Ultimately, my advice to him was that rather than running on hatred for the militia, let your love for your people guide you. Love is a much better fuel than hatred because hatred runs out quickly, and it burns you up. Let love fuel the struggle. Now I know you have probably heard that, but it is true. Because if you go out with anger, your fuel will soon consume you and nothing will change. But if you can act out of love—for Breonna Taylor and George Floyd, and out of love for people who are suffering—then that will be the fuel for your struggle. Then you can get creative.

I learned a lot about dealing with anger from the Tibetan lamas I met when I was able to travel to India (on a fully paid scholarship) for my junior year of college. I was part of that late 1960s phenomenon of Western students traveling to the mysterious East, part of the infamous 60s counterculture. The Tibetans took me in instantly, and I saw in them a welcoming family of compassionate and skilled people who, as I viewed myself, were refugees. I soon learned that the Tibetans possessed the type of knowledge and wisdom I longed for—knowledge of methods for dealing with frustrations, disappointments, and anger, and of developing genuine compassion. Indeed, their very beings reflected this. They had suffered untold hardships, had even been forced to flee their country. We shared, it seemed to me, the experience of a profound historical trauma. Yet they coped quite well, seeming to possess a sort of spiritual armor that I felt lacking in myself.

Confidence and Buddhist Tantra: Healing Personal and Collective Trauma

I was very fortunate to have been a close student of Lama Thubten Yeshe. We met in Nepal in the fall of 1969. Lama Yeshe kindly accepted me as his student, and I was honored that he chose to call me his "daughter." When I look back on the 15 years that Lama Yeshe was my teacher, I see confidence as his main teaching—not only to me but to countless others who over the years came to him for guidance. Once, when Lama Yeshe was visiting California, I took him to hear a lecture given by Angela Davis. She spoke one afternoon in the quarry on the University of California, Santa Cruz, campus. Lama Yeshe was visibly excited to see and to listen to Davis speak. Several times during her talk, with clenched fist, he said aloud, "This is how one ought to be: strong and confident like this lady!"

Once Lama Yeshe looked at me piercingly and then remarked, "Living with pride and humility in equal proportion is very difficult!" In that moment, it seemed to me, he had put his finger on one of the deepest issues confronting all African Americans: the great difficulty of having gone through the experience of 250 years of slavery, during which one's very humanness was challenged and degraded at every turn, and yet through it all, to have maintained a strong sense of humanness and the desire to stand tall, with dignity and love of self, to count oneself a human being equal with all others.

It is the trauma of slavery that haunts African Americans in the deepest recesses of their souls. This is the chief issue for us. It needs to be dealt with, head-on— not denied, not forgotten, not suppressed. Indeed, its suppression and denial only hurt us more deeply, causing us to accept a limited, disparaging, and even repugnant view of ourselves. We cannot move forward until we have grappled in a serious way with all the negative effects of this trauma. Tantric Buddhism offers us some tools to help accomplish this task, since it shows us both how to get at those deep inner wounds and how to heal them. Lama Yeshe (2014) explains in his *Introduction to Tantra: The Transformation of Desire*:

> According to Buddhist tantra, we remain trapped within a circle of dissatisfaction because our view of reality is narrow and suffocating. We hold onto a very limited and limiting view of who we are and what we can become, with the result that our self-image remains oppressively low and negative, and we feel quite inadequate and hopeless. As long as our opinion of ourselves is so miserable, our life will remain meaningless ... One of the essential practices at all levels of tantra is to dissolve our ordinary conceptions of ourselves and then, from the empty space into which these concepts have disappeared, arise in the glorious light body of a deity: a manifestation of the essential clarity of our deepest being. The more we train to see ourselves as such a meditational deity, the less bound we feel by life's ordinary disappointments and frustrations. This divine self-visualization empowers us to take control of our life and create for ourselves a pure environment in which our deepest nature can be expressed ... It is a simple truth that if we identify ourselves as being fundamentally pure, strong, and capable we will actually develop these qualities, but if we continue to think of ourselves as dull and foolish, that is what we will become.
>
> *(p. 29–30)*

Lama Yeshe continues,

> The health of body and mind is primarily a question of our self-image. Those
> people who think badly of themselves, for whatever reasons, become and then
> remain miserable, while those who can recognize and draw on their inner
> resources can overcome even the most difficult situations. Deity-yoga is one of
> the most profound ways of lifting our self-image, and that is why tantra is such
> a quick and powerful method for achieving the fulfillment of our tremendous
> potential.
>
> *(p. 34)*

Equalizing Self and Others: Liberation Through Cultivating *Bodhichitta*

For many years, as a Buddhist scholar and practitioner, I have been attempting
to plumb the great depths of one of the most profound and beautiful Buddhist
texts of all time, the *Bodhicharyavatara*, sometimes translated as *The Way
of the Bodhisattva*. This is the eighth-century Buddhist scholar Shantideva's
most sonorous exploration of true compassion, or *bodhichitta*.

The text offers many exercises to help us to maintain and grow compassion
once it has—almost miraculously—appeared. Among the many practices suggested by Shantideva, two are foremost. One can be summarized as "exchanging self with others," the other as "equalizing self and others."

The first exercise—"exchanging self with others"—has received the most
attention. It seems so clearly to be a prime catalyst of compassion. If we can
imagine ourselves as another, if we can put ourselves in their shoes, then we
can at least develop empathy with another's plight and in this way develop a
wish that they do not suffer. But while this may seem to be compassion, it's
often more akin to pity, offered from a position of superiority.

I think it is the second exercise—"equalizing self and others"—that is more
germane to our situation today. Yet it is so very difficult to practice. For this
second practice calls upon us to try to actualize our equality with others: neither our superiority nor our inferiority but our equality with them. Only this
flash of insight is capable of truly liberating us.

This is the liberating view held by Dr King and Gandhi, by the Buddha and
Nelson Mandela, by Bishop Tutu and His Holiness the Dalai Lama. It is
the view that we are all, ultimately, exactly the same. Not better, not worse.
Human beings reckoned as human beings only. What a marvel. If this is right,
and it is something we can contemplate, then the current "racial tensions" we

are experiencing (which are not "tensions" so much as calls for the reco⸜ tion of basic equality) can become a signal of hope.

So, how do we demonstrate that we have understood the Buddha's and Dr King's teachings? By being compassionate, by loving our neighbors, by loving our enemies. Indeed, by working "for the weal of humankind, for the welfare of the many, for the happiness of the many, for the good, well-being, and happiness of gods and men." The important thing is our doing. Compassion is our wisdom in action. Therefore, with courage, and together, may we begin to act.

Notes

1   These words were spoken by Dr Martin Luther King, Jr in a sermon called "Loving Your Enemies," delivered at the Dexter Avenue Baptist Church in Montgomery, Alabama, December 25, 1957.
2   Dr Martin Luther King, Jr said this to an audience in Montgomery, Alabama in 1957.
3   This quote is from Dr Martin Luther King, Jr's final Christmas sermon in 1967 to his Christian congregation at Ebenezer Baptist Church in Atlanta.
4   *The Letter from Birmingham Jail* is an open letter Martin Luther King, Jr penned on April 16, 1963.
5   This quote comes from Dr Martin Luther King, Jr's speech at Grosse Pointe High School, March 14, 1968.
6   Dr Martin Luther King, Jr delivered this quote during an address at the 1963 Great March on Detroit.

The Four Foundations of Mindfulness
Practicing Presence and Resilience

Sharon Salzberg

What is Mindfulness: Myth Versus Reality

Over the years, I've worked with caregivers of all sorts: teachers, trauma workers, doctors, and therapists. Through it all, I've found that mindfulness is an invaluable practice for helping them to increase their capacity for maintaining present awareness and resilience through their emotionally demanding work. In my experience teaching mindfulness to caregivers, many basic questions predictably come up—not just about how it can help and protect them, but about what mindfulness even is and how it is practiced.

For caregivers and many other students of mine, one of the most basic questions around mindfulness has to do with the various meanings of the word. Many of the ways mindfulness is described—such as being with your experience without judging it or being in the present moment without reacting—seem to imply a kind of passivity or complacency, just being with everything without judgment. The fact is mindfulness doesn't really mean that. Real mindfulness involves a very dynamic, vibrant, and creative relationship to whatever may be happening within or around us. It involves a mode of being in which we are not bound to old habits, like tunneled ways of seeing or rigid ways of responding. Unfortunately, the word mindfulness as we commonly use it today does not necessarily imply such dynamic involvement.

A corollary problem is the meaning of other common terms in the practice of mindfulness like craving, wanting, or desire. When Westerners learn that the Buddha recommended that we move toward a state of letting go of desire as a driving force toward a state of desirelessness, we often hear it as something awful. It's important to be able to distinguish the precise sense of such

DOI: 10.4324/9781003243588-5

terms, including nuances that often are not present in English words like "mindfulness" or "desire." The original terms used in Sanskrit, Pali, and other Buddhist languages often have a range of distinct connotations that may be spread across a range of different technical terms, while those meanings may all be lumped together in one English word that we use to translate all the different senses. For instance, having bold and intense aspiration and gathering all your energy behind it, in the traditional context doesn't mean craving. Knowing the difference between things doesn't mean judgment.

Mindful Judgment and the Urge for Real Happiness

Recently, when I was teaching, I began talking about the way we can distinguish pleasant feelings, unpleasant feelings, and neutral feelings. Somebody raised his hand and said, "I don't think that's mindfulness, because if you're discerning, you're judging." I answered, "No, we actually make a particular point of distinguishing between discernment and judgment. That judgment, the immediate reflex reaction of holding on or pushing away, is different from knowing something hurts or feels great."

Reactive judgment is a kind of mindless, preconceived judgment, which is really more like pre-judgment or prejudice than discerning or mindful judgment. We can tell the difference between an amazing narrative thread that is onward-leading, opening doors of possibility and bringing us together with others in a less fearful way, versus the oldest, most damaging story we have been telling ourselves about being unable to do anything well. The first is something we need to cultivate, the latter something we need to let go of. We're constantly practicing discernment as part of the philosophy and psychology of mindfulness, and that doesn't mean craving or judgment. Simply wanting to be happy is not craving.

One common complaint I've heard, especially about my last two books, *Real Happiness* (Salzberg, 2010) and *Real Happiness at Work* (Salzberg, 2013), is that wanting to be happy is somehow wrong, like craving; that it necessarily involves being selfish, self-preoccupied, or self-centered. Traditionally, the natural wish we all have to be happy isn't mere craving. In fact, the Buddha said all beings want to be happy. It's rightful, it's appropriate. The problem isn't wanting to be happy; the problem is the ignorance or delusion that makes it impossible for us to be truly happy. In fact, our urge toward happiness can be like the homing instinct for freedom. We can cut through many obstacles by saying, "I want to be happy. I deserve to be happy. All beings deserve to be happy." We just have to figure out how.

The Truth of Suffering: Craving as Tunnel Vision

But what does craving mean in this context? It's got different elements: clinging, grasping, holding on. Craving also has an element of fixation: we're obsessed with an experience, an object, with people, or with something we hope will bring us a completion we feel we don't already have. When we get lost in the state of craving, we might overlook what it will cost us to get that thing, what we're losing in the process of getting it, or how we're mistreating others to get whatever it might be.

I often teach at Tibet House in New York City, which doubles as an art gallery. One day, I was sitting on the stage giving a meditation on greed or craving and I could see a Tibetan wall hanging off in the corner as I spoke. The process I was experiencing in my own mind at the time was a typical case of craving, so I decided to share it with the audience. "That is such a beautiful *thangka*," I remarked. "I can't see the price tag, but wow—it is so amazing, I love it; I think I have to own it." From there I thought, "Okay, I'm going to buy it." But as I remembered I was living in a teensy sublet apartment, and that I wasn't allowed to hang anything on the walls, it didn't occur to me to stop my thought process. My next step was to think, "I need a new apartment." And as long as the thought of a new apartment was on the table, I considered, "Why don't I get a bigger apartment? With more space, the *thangka* could have its own room with special lighting." But then I realized that if I was going to get a new apartment in New York City, I would have to be able to afford the rent. In order to make more money, I'd have to travel more, teach more. Finally, I realized with a bittersweet pang, "Okay, I'll never be in New York, never see my *thangka*, never have time to be in my apartment, but at least I'll own it."

When we're caught in the grip of craving, we get trapped in the fantasy that this object may finally be the thing that's going to make our really painful feeling of lack disappear. When we're so lost in craving, we don't even know what we want. We're counting on someone else, or society's message, to tell us what is going to make us happy. We forget the truth that everything changes, every ordinary, fleeting pleasure passes. It's as if we are saying, "Don't change, stay exactly the same—be static." This is not going to happen, and all our resentment and protestations are not going to work, so we suffer intensely. Craving is thus the engine of ignorance that makes life an inescapable cycle of suffering that keeps us constantly going astray from the path to real happiness. When we get quiet enough to observe our minds closely, we can see this cycle driving us deeper into the downward spiral of dissatisfaction and suffering.

This is what the Buddha meant by teaching that a misguided life of mindless craving and frustration is *samsara*. This is his first Noble Truth: our minds and lives get poisoned by ignorance, craving, and resentment. When we stop and pay mindful attention to what's going on constantly in our minds and lives, even for just a moment, we see right away that they have become living, breathing hotbeds of dissatisfaction.

Non-Reactive Mindfulness: Stop Holding On, Spacing Out, Pushing Away

The usual way of describing experience is our tendency to cling, to hold on, to want to keep or own what's pleasant, while wanting to push away, discard, and separate ourselves from what's unpleasant. When we experience something as simply neutral—neither very pleasant nor unpleasant—our motivational system typically just goes to sleep. That's where numbness or shutdown comes in as a common reaction to mere neutrality. In our collective life and society, where we're not trained to appreciate subtlety, we tend to count on intensity to feel alive. When things get more neutral, we want to hype it up just to have more stimulation, to feel a connection, and are not generally able to abide the subtlety. So, the fact is we have a wide range of conditioned reactions to pleasantness, unpleasantness, neutrality. Even though those three—holding onto to pleasure, pushing away pain, and numbing out in neutrality—are the reactions most commonly spoken about in the tradition, we know from experience working with people that the human mind is a complex world of conditioned reactions.

The shorthand for this complexity is that we learn to observe and say to ourselves, "I'm holding on to the pleasant," or "I'm pushing away the negative," or "I'm spacing out or numbing out with the neutral." According to this tradition, the Buddha taught that this is the moment when we have the chance to observe and respond in a fundamentally different way. We may feel the pleasure of something fully, but we don't have to add that extra conditioned reaction of clinging. We may feel the pain of something fully, but we don't have to add the conditioned reaction of shame, isolation, anger, dread, and so on—the reactions we tend to associate with pain. The question becomes: how can we actually wake up and connect and feel alive in the more neutral realm? We need to stop picking and choosing and start learning to experience and respond wisely to whatever comes.

The extensive definition of mindfulness I was taught (again, there are many definitions of mindfulness) is that it is a quality of awareness in which we are not reacting with grasping, aversion, or delusion. We feel the pleasure, we feel the pain, we experience the neutrality, but we are practicing mindfulness of them rather than being lost in one of these habitual reactions. If we accept this traditional definition, a number of things follow. One, of course, is a better experience of our day because we're more connected, we're clearer. We're not fighting our experience.

We discover so many levels when we're looking at our experience truly mindfully. When we can let go of the big agendas about what we're going to find, the distortions of what we do find, or our preconceived need for things to be a certain way, that's real mindfulness, because we're paying attention without holding on, pushing away, or numbing out. Practicing this quality of mind creates the kind of internal environment in which we can see so much more than we could before. It's as if we're fertilizing soil for insight and wisdom to grow—and that's the ultimate reason why we practice mindfulness.

Mindful Insight: A Space for Metacognition

Mindfulness, too, is a relational quality. You may be resting your attention on the feeling of the breath and maybe this great wave of anger comes up. As a result, you find yourself not trying to get back to the breath but paying full attention to the anger. Interestingly, one way to avoid getting lost in the anger is to practice mindfulness *while* paying attention to it. Start with some questions: What does it feel like in my body? What are the sensations? What's the mood? Take a look at the anger, not just why it is there and what I am going to do about it, but what is the nature of this feeling. What do we see when we practice such open reflection or insight meditation? More likely than not, we will see moments of sadness, perhaps moments of fear, moments of guilt, moments of grief. Very likely, we see moments of helplessness which the anger is working to pick us up from. We see that the state of anger that gripped us in fact is a compound. With this broader and deeper awareness of our anger and its constituent causes, if we choose to take action, it will be based on a broader, clearer sense of what we're feeling, not just on the surface level of the experience.

According to the way I was taught, mindfulness is a compound process. That's something I like to say now to my students. Mindfulness is classically described as clear comprehension. It means that we're not just "present" (a buzzword that's often associated with the practice), but being present in a non-reactive way, a way that empowers us to see more deeply and more clearly into things. That process of seeing or insight is what actually prompts our evolution on the path. From the point of view of mindfulness, it doesn't matter what we're looking at, but it does matter how we're looking at it. I'm sure every single one of us would love to spend time at a meditation retreat and be able to say to a friend who asked how it was, "Well, first it was peaceful, then it was beautiful, then blissful, then it moved right into ecstasy, and I entered this state I can't even describe." Rather than, "First my knee hurt, then my back hurt, then I got tired and fretful, then I got restless, and then I got sleepy." From the point of view of mindfulness, these two flavors of experience are potentially the same. The question is not just *what* happened, but *how were you with* what happened? How aware were you of what happened?

If we practice mindfulness, whatever comes up is potentially useful and profound. With mindfulness, all our experience offers many possibilities for change, for transformation. We can relate to pleasure differently, we can relate to pain differently, and we can relate to neutrality differently. In this way, mindfulness practice can open up a whole new world of possibilities for us.

Methodology: Practicing the Four Foundations

There are many ways of presenting the methodology of meditation. The classic way in my tradition is presented in a Pali text called the *Satipatthana Sutta*, which lays out the main teaching within the Buddhist Canon concerning mindfulness as a meditation method (Gunaratana, 2011). My colleague Joseph Goldstein wrote a fantastic book called *Mindfulness*, explicating what he called the Four Foundations of Mindfulness based on this teaching (Goldstein, 2016). There's a lovely passage at the outset of the text that begins, "This is the direct path for the purification of beings, for the overcoming of sorrow and lamentation, for the disappearance of pain and distress, for the attainment of the right method, and for the realization of unbinding." That method involves the four foundations of mindfulness. These foundations begin with mindfulness of the body, which is described thus: "There is the case where a monk ..." or as I prefer to say, a meditator,

> remains focused on the body in and of itself—ardent, alert, and mindful—putting aside greed and distress with reference to the world. He remains focused on feelings ... mind ... mental qualities in and of themselves—ardent, alert, & mindful—putting aside greed and distress with reference to the world.
> (Gunaratana)

Practically speaking, there are so many different ways one can approach this instruction. One of the great boons of our era is that people aren't necessarily locked in their little sectarian silo, thinking, "My way is the best way, the only way." That kind of sectarianism does exist, of course, and it doesn't even take two traditions for that to happen—it just takes two people. But nowadays, we know of so many different ways of being aware of the body, of feelings, of mind, and of mental qualities—that is, of all four foundations at once; and we also know of many ways of focusing on each one separately.

The First Foundation: Mindfulness of the Breathing Body

So, we begin with mindfulness of the body. At a very basic level, mindfulness of the body is largely about posture—being mindful of when we are bending, stretching, standing, or sitting—this involves a kind of overarching sense of what your body is doing at any given moment. Classically, mindfulness of the body also focuses specifically on the breath. Finally, sometimes it involves awareness of the different qualities in your experience of your body. The text says, "The body is made of earth, water, fire, and air." What this means is that we actually experience the body's solids, liquids, heat, and gases, in their various manifestations. The fire element, for instance, refers to our experience of temperature. Sometimes we experience our body as cold, sometimes we experience its heat. This reflection on the elemental qualities of the body is one whole aspect of mindfulness meditation on the body.

Another involves a practice Jon Kabat-Zinn (2013) popularized: the body-scan. This is a practice you might learn in your first retreat, where you move your attention throughout every part of your body gradually and systematically, just feeling the presence and sensation of each part. This is simply meant to train a nonreactive, nonjudgmental experience of being in a living body, in which we practice not clinging, not condemning, and not spacing out, as we move our attention through our whole body.

Another aspect of mindfulness of the body involves walking meditation. It is said that the Buddha taught we can meditate in any one of four postures: sitting, standing, walking, or lying down. They're all equally valid platforms for practicing body mindfulness. Traditionally, all four postures are integrated into a whole system of practice. It's not like one is remedial and one advanced. If you have trouble being mindful while you sit, you may have an easier time lying down. The difference is simply one of energy and doesn't affect the integrity of the process. We tend to have the most energy while walking, the least while lying down, and a moderate amount while sitting or standing.

So, by adjusting our posture we can modulate our energy. I read a story in a traditional commentary on mindfulness about a monk who fell asleep every single time he sat down to meditate. According to the story, his entire practice became walking meditation—for sixty years. This story helped me realize the good news that there's a practice for everybody!

Recently, I've spent more and more time working with people who are very close to a traumatic experience. My work with these people tends to be a lot like the work of that monk. I find they can get more easily grounded by making simple physical contact with the world. I often ask them simply to feel the weight of a cup in their hand, its heaviness. The work can be very concrete and very physical, making a grounding connection with their bodies in the present moment. Given that grounding, our work together can more easily move from the concrete level to something far more refined, like feeling the fine sensations within your body, even letting the seeming solidity of your body dissolve. It all depends on what your experience is and how you can most easily work with it. Your body will go to work with you, your breath will go to work with you. So, this kind of mindfulness practice is a tremendous tool for integration.

The Second Foundation: Mindfulness of Feeling Tone

When we combine body mindfulness with the second foundation, mindfulness of feeling tone, it opens the door to deep understanding. Given this combined practice, we can ask ourselves,

> Where is the gravest suffering when I am feeling physical pain? Is it in my knee, or is it in my mind? Is it in my experience in the present moment, or is it in my projection—what do I anticipate it will feel like next week, the week after next, and the week after that?

These are all powerful arenas of investigation, especially when we integrate them with the reflective aspect of mindfulness, "How am I responding to the pleasant feeling in my body?" Here again, mindfulness opens up a concrete arena for that exploration. "How am I responding to the unpleasant feeling in my body? If my feeling is neutral, how often am I paying attention?" These two foundations, mindfulness of the body and of feeling tone, go together very powerfully when we really look at our day and investigate what is bringing us to greater confinement, tunnel vision, and isolation, versus what is actually freeing us, even in the face of adversity, when things are difficult or unpleasant.

A story I like to use to describe how mindfulness works came from a *New York Times* article I read a number of years ago, when mindfulness programs in schools were very unusual. The story involved a pilot program in Oakland that took place in a fourth-grade classroom, and featured two quotations I especially liked. One quote came from one of the researchers, who said, "All day long, we tell kids to pay attention, but we never teach them how." Another came when they asked one of the kids—who must have been eight or nine years old—what mindfulness is. He answered, "Mindfulness means not hitting someone in the mouth." I found that a great definition, because it implies that mindfulness helps us know there's a problem when we're starting to feel angry, not after we've said or done something regrettable, like hitting someone in the mouth. Here, too, awareness of the body is a tremendous tool, perhaps not for everybody but for most of us. When you learn to tune in to your experience, you feel a sensation in your body as it's just beginning. In this way, mindfulness offers a great feedback system, well before there's any higher cognitive understanding. With mindfulness of the body and feeling tone, you can sense implicitly what's under the radar—such as "I'm getting really angry now!" Once you feel it, you know it, and can respond accordingly.

Another aspect of mindfulness implied by that schoolboy's statement suggests the benefit of having a balanced relationship to painful experiences like anger. If every time you get angry, you get caught up in it and wind up being overwhelmed and reactive, you may end up hitting a lot of people in the mouth, literally or metaphorically. On the other hand, if you fear anger and try to suppress or deny it, you run the risk of getting wound up tighter and tighter until you simply explode. What we want ideally is something in the middle. We're better off when we can keep our balance, without getting caught up by our experience and without pushing it away. Given this balance, we can recognize our experience quickly and be with it skillfully. The balanced awareness gives us a space, and in that space we have greater choice. Within that space, there is time to reconsider: "Well, I hit someone in the mouth last week and it didn't work out that well." That kind of mindful experience is very far from an automatic reflex reaction. There are many ways in which people try to describe this balance, space, or gap, but I like this one—mindfulness means not hitting someone in the mouth.

Mindful Balance: Don't Just Be with Pain

Some people mistake the middle way of mindfulness for a kind of bypassing or suppression of emotion, but that's not the real intent or effect of the practice. Yes, there's a fine line between feeling the feeling clearly and long enough for it to register without holding on too long that we begin to indulge it, and I can't say exactly where that line is. I think it's a very complicated issue, and certainly this kind of monitoring process can be utilized to bypass feeling—many people do use it that way. But perhaps that isn't always wrong either. I think it's all a question of balance. The idea isn't to suffer for the sake of suffering, but to be able to be with pain as well as pleasure in a different way. That different way has certain components to it, including some positive energy, as well as a degree of self-compassion or self-respect (Salzberg, 2002). This practice is not about repressing emotions or hating what you're feeling. It's about seeking a different kind of balance, realizing, "I'm overwhelmed, I'm getting close to being overwhelmed. I need to pull back. I need to do something else."

In 1984, we invited one of my teachers, Sayadaw Upandita from Burma, to the Insight Meditation Society (IMS) in Barre, Massachusetts, to teach a three-month retreat. We were all going to sit under his guidance. None of us had ever met him before but we all had heard that he was a really great teacher. In fact, he was a great teacher, but he also turned out to be fierce, intense, and incredibly demanding.

One day, we were in the hall doing a question-and-answer session and somebody asked him, "How long should I be with pain"—physical pain in that case—"before I move my attention to something that's easier to be with? Listening to sounds, something lighter, something like that?" Given Upandita's personality, I thought he was going to say, "You should be with the pain until you keel over." But to my astonishment, he said, "Don't be with it for very long. Be with the pain, then move your attention to something that's easier to be with." Then he explained, "It's not wrong just to be with the pain, but you're likely to get exhausted, so why not build in balance along the way."

That was an interesting reflection for me because at that time I had a warrior spirit in practice, as many do. I thought, "I'm just going to hang in there. I'm going to break through this suffering no matter what." I approached my pain the same way when I was in psychotherapy. And once again, there's a healthy balance. We don't want to be afraid of the pain, whatever kind it is; we don't want to take the easy path of avoiding it or denying it. But we also need to face it within some sort of healing context. We need to keep restoring ourselves along the way, regenerating ourselves so there's renewal, resilience. In order to do that, we need to be with our pain—physical, emotional, or spiritual—in a different way.

The Third Foundation: Mindfulness of Mind

The next two foundations are mindfulness of the mind and mindfulness of mental objects. The precise distinction and intersection between these two have confused people for centuries. These two foundations are described in a lot of different ways in different teaching traditions and contexts. In Buddhist psychology, and certainly in classical versions of it, there are six kinds of consciousness. These refer to the different types of consciousness that arise when there is contact between one of the six sense doors—seeing, hearing, smelling, tasting, touching, or mentally intuiting the world—and its respective kind of object. For instance, visual consciousness arises when the eye encounters a visual object, auditory consciousness when the ear encounters an auditory object, olfactory consciousness when the nose encounters an olfactory object, and so forth.

The term "consciousness" and "mind" are often used synonymously. They both refer to a quality of knowing awareness, so mind in general is considered to be any kind of perceptual capacity. Part of the practice of this particular foundation is to know when we have an experience of seeing, to know when there's hearing, to know when there's smell, to know when there's taste, to know when there's touch, and to know when there's something arising through the mind—that is, the sixth sense of bare reflection on prior moments of sense experience. So, the first level of mindfulness of mind means simply being able to identify which of the six kinds of consciousness is predominant at any one time.

The Fourth Foundation: Mindfulness of Mental Factors

Although there are many factors that surround or co-arise with any given type of consciousness, they are in fact considered to be mental objects *of* the mind, rather than the mind itself. In other words, the factors we add to simple consciousness—such as thinking, emotion, memory, and so on—belong to the fourth foundation of mindfulness, the foundation of mental objects. One of my teachers, Munindra, always used to say, "The mind itself is pure." What this means is that mind, or consciousness, is simply knowing awareness, even though arising along with any and every consciousness there are various mental factors, some of which arise quite a lot. When we move to this fourth foundation, we learn to recognize what these factors are, and to discern whether they are positive, negative, or neutral. Neutral factors like attention are simply part of the basic workings of perception. Others are negative functions, including emotional or motivational factors like greed, hatred, and delusion. Some of them are positive, such as love, compassion, joy, equanimity, and insight or wisdom. One subtle aspect of the fourth foundation of mindfulness is that it's always co-arising with consciousness. It's like a filter in many ways, and consequently it is very important to notice. We can hear a sound with hatred or disappointment on one day, while on another day, after a good night's sleep, we might hear the very same sound with amusement or love. None of that variability is fixed, none of it is irrevocably or intrinsically tied to the sound, but as we hear the sound, along with a feeling tone of pleasure, pain, or neutrality, there arises some combination of these mental functions or ways of relating to that primary experience.

As you can imagine, actually recognizing the filters that color our conscious experience is a very useful part of our mindful awareness. Among the most relevant filters for practitioners to notice are the five mental functions known as the five hindrances, which are not only very common but are also talked about very often. I'm always happy to hear about them because they make me reflect, "If the Buddha described those hindrances, then it's not just me!" The first two common hindrances are grasping and aversion; the latter of which, in the Theravada system refers to both anger and/or fear. Next comes sleepiness or sluggishness, which is sometimes called sloth and torpor, and often described as a lack of the brand of courage that gives us energy when we're feeling sort of inert. Number four is restlessness or distraction, which could also be thought of as agitation or worry. The fifth hindrance is doubt. These mental factors are called hindrances not because they're intrinsically bad, but because they tend to be seductive and derail practice. If we get lost in them, we tend to veer off from the reality of things. We can easily get lost in greed or clinging, get intoxicated so we don't stop and reflect, "You know, maybe that wall hanging won't make me perfectly, finally, forever happy." So, we can easily get carried away with the seductive influence of greed or clinging, and taken very far from the reality of change. Likewise, when we get angry, we naturally become lost in hostility and aversion to what has angered us, so we can get carried away very far from reality.

The Mind Itself Is Pure, Our Afflictions Are Visitors

As I said, these five mental factors are not intrinsically bad. They may be hindrances or not depending on how we relate to them. They come up in meditation because they come up often in life, and the purpose of seeing them certainly isn't to condemn or belittle oneself but to learn a different relationship with them. Fundamental acceptance of ourselves and our basic goodness is a vital ingredient of Buddhist teaching. This is clearly conveyed in one of Buddha's teachings that I find perhaps the most helpful and beautiful: "The mind is naturally radiant and pure; the mind is shining. It's because of visiting forces that we suffer." The hindrances are just such visiting forces, and the traditional approach to these factors typifies the amazing optimism of the Buddhist tradition and mindfulness practice.

There are several layers of profundity to the Buddha's pronouncement about our luminous minds being visited by afflictions. First of all, it affirms that those forces, however familiar, are just visitors, including the greed, the jealousy, the hatred, the fear. They may visit a lot, perhaps visit nearly incessantly, but they're still just visitors. They're born out of conditions coming together in a certain way. They're not inherent to our being. Conditions shift, and with those shifts these forces or factors come and go. Another element of that statement I find very profound is that Buddha did not say, "Since we are visited by negative forces, we're negative people, we're bad." He said, "It's because of visiting forces that we suffer." Thanks to this image, I can imagine myself sitting happily at home minding my own business and hearing a knock at the door. When I open the door there may be greed, sloth, anger, whatever. I may even fling open the door and say, "Welcome home, it's all yours," forgetting I actually live here. More often, I'm so ashamed and so upset by the arrival of that visitor that I desperately slam the door and try to pretend I never heard the knock, only to find that the visitor has come in through the window, or down through the chimney.

I often think of the skill of meditation practice in terms of what happens when we're at that door, when we open it up and there's an unwelcome visitor. Not all visitors are unwelcome, there's a whole range of mental factors, but let's say it's one of the hindrances, or maybe a couple arriving together. What do we do? Can we remember who actually lives here? Can we have a kind of centeredness? Presence? Can we recognize what's happening right now, that this is what's visiting, without freaking out, "Oh my God, I'm so bad," or just caving in, "Take me, I'm yours"? Mindfulness involves a kind of balanced awareness that isn't frightened by what's come up; it's not trying to push it away, and it's not just giving in either. In this sense, mindfulness must have elements of compassion, a kind of tenderness (Salzberg, 2002). This may be especially true if your tendency is to be frightened by negative habits of mind, to feel they shouldn't be there and to blame yourself. In that case, we need a kind of balancing exercise to invite them in.

Open-Mindfulness: Greeting Visitors from Inner Space

Once I was practicing at IMS with my teacher Munindra, who was visiting from India. I was very upset about something or other, some anger that was arising in my mind, and I said, "I've been meditating for five years, I shouldn't be here anymore." He said, "This is how you should be with your anger: imagine a spaceship just landed on the lawn and some Martians come out and approach you and say, 'What is anger?' That's how to be with anger." I often ask myself, "What do I feel in my body right now? Where is the compound that is my anger?" We may hang a single label on it but let's take a deeper look. Typically, moments of anger come all mixed up with moments of sadness, moments of fear, moments of guilt, moments of grief, moments of helplessness. And within that moment-to-moment process there's the reality of change—always, inevitably. So, we use the vehicle of anger to see more deeply into the nature of life on lots of different levels. In this sense, mindfulness practice serves as a platform for insight meditation, and it's this insight that forms the real path to healing and freedom.

When practicing mindfulness, we need to train ourselves to approach our experience—positive, negative, or neutral—with the kind of open-minded inquiry Munindra recommended. That can then become a feedback system for making choices, for taking action during the day, at work, with my kids, whatever. We don't just notice but observe, and ask, "What's the nature of it? What's that rich texture of all these other feelings? And what are the deeper truths about life?" Since, classically, mindfulness is designed to lead to insight, to understanding, then even a conventionally undesirable experience, like anger, can be a vehicle for very profound insights about life, insights like the truth of change, or conditionality, or contingency, or transparency. Of course, if somebody stopped me on the street and said, "Would you rather see something deeply about the truth of change through looking at bliss or at anger?" I would say, "Bliss." But since no one stops us and asks us—we don't get a menu—we can use anything as a vehicle for deeper understanding into the nature of things. And so that's really what mindfulness of the mind and mental objects is all about. It's paying attention to whatever is arising predominately in one's experience, paying attention to awareness itself.

The Fourth Foundation as an Arena for Mindful Insight and Change

This fourth foundation of mindfulness is admittedly a little tricky. It's like an arena or field of learning and change. Some traditions take most of what I just said about mental factors—thoughts, emotions, memories, fantasies—and put them in that arena. Other traditions consider all those factors as part of the third foundation, mindfulness of mind, and consider the fourth almost like sets of insights or principles for reflection. According to the latter approach, in the fourth foundation we're observing processes like the arising of suffering or observing elements like the causes of suffering. In that process of mindful inquiry, insight, or reflection, we can see it all happen: the clinging, the holding on, the resentment, the being hostile in some way to how things are. And we hopefully can also see some kind of letting go, which is the relief. We can see all those patterns and configurations in the fourth foundation, guided by some great lists of relevant factors, lists like the four noble truths, the seven factors of enlightenment, or the five spiritual faculties.

Whichever approach we choose, this fourth foundation shows that the psychology of mindfulness is not filled with negative factors. Within the seven factors of enlightenment, for instance, we find an array of truly positive, healing factors. Three of them are considered arousing positive qualities, energy, investigation, and a factor usually translated as rapture or raptness, meaning an intense interest in something. There are also three quieting qualities: calm, concentration, equanimity. And then there's mindfulness in the middle, which brings all the others into balance. One of the classical themes in the description of that last foundation is, "You can be mindful of the presence or absence of equanimity." As I hear it, that theme expresses a kind of radical acceptance. It gives me the option to be mindful of my complete absence of equanimity right now, rather than accelerating it, escalating it, compounding it, and judging or hating myself for the absence of equanimity.

This is just one example of how this foundation of practice allows us to appreciate how many different ways the factors of mind can come together. I also think seeing mind and mental factors combining in all kinds of patterns helps us appreciate the causality of the mind in a somewhat different way than the third foundation.

Despite the conventional wisdom that we're afraid of the unknown, I've found through observing my own mind that fear is much more likely to visit when I think I do know what's happening and expect that it's going to be really bad. It's the stories I tell myself that most terrify me, until I remind myself, "Actually you don't know." Then there's some space to observe, and from there, real relief. It's like watching something over the course of time: as you observe the changes, you can say, "Oh, look at that! It turns out it's just a story not reality."

In terms of practice, the way of doing this I'm most familiar with is to begin by simply sitting. Next, you pay attention to something neutral, like the breath, taking that as a home base. Then you include feeling tone, then tactile consciousness, which we call physical sensation. When your consciousness of physical sensation becomes really prominent, you then switch your attention to the fourth foundation. I usually offer the option of placing a mental label on whatever seems to emerge with predominance, whether an emotion comes up strongly, or a thought pattern comes up strongly. The fourth focus or arena of practice is to be with and investigate that predominant object. When this works, your meditation may come to resemble looking at an anger movie or looking at a joy movie. We apply words or labels as expressions of curiosity or interest. As an illustration, you could imagine you're in a movie theater and there's the screen and you're just going to watch those scenes go by, just like subtitles in a movie. Or you could imagine you're watching the sky, a see the beauty of the sky and the clouds. There are many, many ways to do this fourth form of mindfulness practice.

All of this is in the realm of mindfulness. And again, from a particular system or tradition, there are so many different ways of categorizing meditative styles and practices. One of those ways is to consider that all these practices are geared to help us see the reality of things more clearly, just as they are. And that's how I see the whole range of mindfulness practices—not just simply as minding the present, but as insight meditation—with the help of which freedom comes from becoming aligned with reality.

5
Positive Neuroplasticity
The Neuroscience of Mindfulness

Rick Hanson

In this chapter I share some ideas about the intersection of three circles: neuroscience, clinical psychology, and Buddhist contemplative practice, which I informally call "applied neuro*dharma*." (In Sanskrit, *dharma* means both reality and an accurate description of it.) Let's begin with a review of some relevant neuroscience.

The Science of Experience-Dependent Neuroplasticity

The function of the nervous system is to process information, and the brain is constantly changing—both functionally and structurally—due to the information coursing through it. Most of the immaterial information represented by material neural substrates is forever unconscious, but the fraction of this information that composes conscious experience is particularly influential in shaping the brain. This is what researchers call experience-dependent neuroplasticity. The idea that changes in the nervous system underlie learning and memory dates back, in the Western world, at least to Hippocrates. But beginning in the 1940s, accelerating in the past couple decades, our scientific understanding of the breadth, depth, and underlying mechanics of neuroplasticity has grown tremendously. For example, you may have encountered the saying based on the work of the psychologist Donald Hebb in the 1940s: "neurons that fire together, wire together" (Hebb, 1949/2002).

It turns out that neurons fire and wire preferentially and maximally with regard to whatever is in the field of focused attention. In a sense, awareness is like a stage. Right now, in this moment, you are conscious of many things, both in the foreground and in the periphery of the field of awareness. What's front and center in awareness is more likely to become neural structure, because as the nervous system evolved over 600 million years, what our

DOI: 10.4324/9781003243588-6

ancestors paid attention to was usually most relevant to survival, and therefore most important to learn from. And when I use the term "learning" or a related word like "memory," this includes the emotional, somatic, attitudinal, motivational, social, and sometimes even spiritual residues of our experiences. Traumatization is a kind of learning, as is healing, the acquisition of psychological resources such as mindfulness and compassion, personal growth, and spiritual awakening.

Consequently, one's own path of development is a process of changing one's own brain. Similarly, therapists, educators, meditation teachers, executive coaches, and parents are helping others to change their brains as well. Whether you are encouraging beneficial brain change in yourself or in others, the fact that learning is heightened for what's in the field of focused attention has profound implications. As William James, the grandfather of American psychology, wrote over a century ago, "The education of attention would be the education *par excellence*" (James, 1890/1950). Because attention is like a combination spotlight and vacuum cleaner, it illuminates what it finds on the stage of awareness and sucks it into our brain. Improving regulation of that spotlight/vacuum cleaner is the foundation of harnessing the ongoing structure-building processes in the nervous system. This highlights the importance of helping our clients (the term I will use here) to get more control over attention, so they can place that spotlight where it's useful and keep it there, or pull it away from what's harmful, such as anxious rumination, grinding resentments, obsessions, compulsions, or addictions. In essence, mental health—brain health—means being able to pull the spotlight of attention away from what hurts and hold it onto something that helps.

The Powerful Potential of Mindfulness for Healing and Change

The problem is that most people don't have much control over that spotlight. Since learning—in some sense a process of internalization—is turbocharged for what's in the field of focused attention, mindfulness training (or related contemplative training) is vital for improving therapeutic outcomes. Of course, implementing this understanding requires the modesty not to skip over the foundational steps. This reminds me of an experience I had learning the clarinet in sixth grade. I got bored with the scales, and I wanted to skip over the fundamentals to the cool stuff, in which I'd be playing songs like a rock-and-roller. Predictably, after a few weeks I got frustrated because I didn't have the foundational skills to do what I wanted to do, so I lost interest, and unfortunately that was the last experience I had with learning a musical instrument.

Explaining to clients how mindfulness training will help them take charge of the structure-building processes in their brain—in effect, taking charge of the person they are becoming—a little more resilient, a little less anxious, a little more loving each day—is really quite motivating. It's not airy-fairy: the changes are *physical*. More generally, it is also highly motivating to clients, as well as to ourselves as therapists, to appreciate that therapy changes the brain. Although it may be common sense that psychological growth must involve neural change, it can be really helpful to have MRI findings or other hard evidence showing that skillful mental activity, repeated over time, leads to lasting beneficial changes in neural structure or function. The physician Jerome Frank, in his book *Persuasion and Healing*, argues that the effectiveness of psychotherapy depends critically on motivation (Frank & Frank, 1993). Joseph Goldstein says something similar about contemplative practice: "Everything rests on the tip of motivation" (Goldstein, 2016). How do we help our clients be motivated to change? For many, it is truly inspiring to know that their efforts in psychotherapy are actually producing lasting physical changes in the tissues of their own body.

Self-Healing and Transformation in Buddhism

Far afield from modern neuroscience, ancient contemplative traditions like Buddhism offer many time-tested ways of boosting people's motivation for change. Sharon Salzberg alludes to this in the previous chapter. One such way involves the powerful therapeutic optimism or fundamental trust in our potential shown by the Buddha and his teaching. The path of contemplative practice in the Buddhist frame of reference starts with acknowledging the universality of suffering, while promising that our suffering can end in complete liberation. The basis of this promise is the Buddha's personal experience that we all are naturally capable of radical transformation, because of what he calls the stainless purity of mind. In other words, we start out naturally fundamentally free of the suffering that afflicts us, so the path of liberation involves not so much a fierce uphill struggle to force something new "over there" into being, but a progressive and intrinsically rewarding process of revealing what was already present "in here." The Buddha called this process, and the factors that support it, the Noble Eightfold Path. We start with suffering but end up with the "highest happiness which is peace." Along the way, we need a path made up of intermediate steps, including the gradual removal of the obscurations of our always already true nature.

Perhaps that's what the Buddha meant when he said, "Rejoice in your goodness" (Easwaran, 2007). Appreciate your own good heart, your own good intentions, the sacredness of your own aspirations and daily efforts, and the development of your own good qualities and the fruits of your virtuous efforts. You deserve that gladness, and it's motivating for practice down the long road, which isn't always easy. Spiritual practice, life practice, psychological practice, career practice, parenting practice—any kind of practice can be a long hard road. To motivate ourselves down that road, it's very helpful to periodically feel glad about what's good in yourself, and there's a lot that is good in all of us. I think one of the great taboos these days is the recognition that you actually really are a good person. A taboo against claiming that knowing for yourself, and especially against expressing that knowing to others. This knowing is something like: "I'm not a perfect person, except perhaps in some ultimate sense of having perfect potential. I'm not a perfect person in the conventional sense—but I am a basically decent, *good* person." How can we help our clients claim an authentic confidence about their own goodness? More importantly, how can we help them claim that confidence if we don't have any authentic feeling of claiming it ourselves?

Therapeutic Optimism on the Path of Psychotherapy

If it's appropriate to wish for the end of suffering, it's also appropriate to wish for less suffering. If through psychotherapeutic means we can help people clear out some of their hindrances of greed or hatred or doubt or remorse or restlessness, or help them exercise right speech in their relationships so they cause less harm to themselves and others, perhaps we can see those simple improvements as intermediate steps on the more ambitious path that leads all the way to exceptional happiness. Likewise, if we help people clear out, bit by bit, the legacy of their own childhood trauma, so that they can access more capacity to enjoy an undisturbed mind, perhaps this healing process in psychotherapy can also be part of a contemplative path to greater peace and well-being.

There are obviously pitfalls on either approach to self-healing and transformation, whether by psychotherapy or by contemplation. For instance, one could get overly obsessed with short-term self-improvement and fail to recognize that perfecting the contents of mind is like polishing Jell-O, an impossible task. On the other hand, approached from the spiritual side, some may be prone to what John Welwood called "spiritual bypassing," using spiritual insights or practices to skip over the hard work of cleaning out their own psychological basements (Welwood, 2000). Yet while there are pitfalls on either side, if we take care to avoid them, I think the psychotherapeutic and contemplative approaches to well-being can each be very effective, perhaps even more so when practiced together.

Of course, there's a lot of misfortune and suffering in the world, but one thing we can be sure of is that if there is to be mental change for the better there must also be neural change for the better. Even if we don't yet have the technology that could document what those neural improvements are, we have thousands of anecdotal examples and many studies that show that, given the right healing causes and conditions, even those who have been hit hardest by life can make dramatic recoveries. If people can make dramatic recoveries in terms of their mental functioning, their mood, outlook, sobriety, impulse control, whatever, it must therefore mean that their brains are changing as well. That's a very important point to appreciate, and an easy way to talk about therapeutic change with clients, colleagues, or the media. If the mind is changing the brain must be changing as well.

Brain Vulnerability, Prevention, and Mindfulness

The brain consists of roughly three pounds of tofu-like tissue inside the coconut shell of the skull. It may not look like much but is arguably the most complex physical object currently known. It has roughly 1.1 trillion cells, about 10 percent of which—100 billion or so—are neurons. Neurons on average make about 5000 connections with other neurons, giving us a network with several hundred trillion nodes called synapses, each so tiny that roughly 5000 of them would fit in the width of a single human hair. The realm of the brain is the realm of the very small, the very fast, and the very complex. Neurons are firing away typically five to 50 times a second. Even though it's just 2 to 3 percent of body weight, the brain consumes roughly 20 to 25 percent of the oxygen and glucose circulating in our blood.

With regards to the plasticity of the brain, it is particularly vulnerable to changing for the worse through negative experiences. There are some vicious cycle dynamics we are increasingly aware of, one of which involves cortisol, a stress hormone that is also released when we feel irritated with a partner or worried about money, or when we recall an upsetting experience. Released from the adrenal glands on the kidneys, cortisol enters the brain, where it has a one–two punch. It sensitizes the amygdala—in some ways the alarm bell of the brain—and weakens the hippocampus, which (among other functions) helps us put things in context while also calming down the amygdala and signaling the hypothalamus to quit calling for more stress hormones. These very physical processes create a feedback loop in which negative experiences yesterday make us more vulnerable to them today, which then sensitizes us even more to the negative tomorrow. Unfortunately, there's no comparable process of sensitization to positive experiences. We need to bring repeated sustained mindful attention to beneficial experiences (which usually feel good because they are good for us) in order to help the brain become increasingly efficient at internalizing them.

We have a brain that's vulnerable to change for the worse. So, we have to take care to stop the causes of stress, as well as to protect our minds and brains from the powerful effects of chronic stress and trauma. An ounce of prevention is worth a pound of cure. The good news is that in addition to the mental evidence for the possibility of healing and recovery from trauma, there is a growing body of neural evidence for the possibility of preventing our natural vulnerability to stress and trauma. For example, the activation of the amygdala can be downregulated by simply noting your own experience through mindfulness practice. Literally just naming anger, rage, or trauma increases processing in the prefrontal cortex, the executive system of the brain, and downregulates activation of the amygdala. That's good in the short term.

Over the long term you can actually also get neuro-structural change in the amygdala itself through contemplative practice (Hölzel et al., 2010). For example, you can get an increase in receptors in the amygdala for oxytocin, the social bonding and connecting hormone. So, people become more and more able to use social experiences of feeling nurtured and included and seen. Even when the hippocampus has shrunk in size due to chronic overexposure to cortisol, you can still get neurogenesis there, the birth of baby neurons, through healthy exercise of your body and stimulation of your mind (Spalding et al., 2013).

Some people, such as Alan Schore, have advanced the view that very vulnerable young children who've had horrifying traumatic experiences can be permanently damaged by them (Schore, 2012). This may turn out to be true—though in general I prefer to bet on the human spirit, on the possibilities of neuroplasticity. The stress diathesis model basically says that healthy human development is based on the three variables. The first of these are life challenges, demands on us like stresses, traumas, and injuries. The second variable is our genetic or constitutional vulnerability, physical and psychological. The third factor is resources. The greater our vulnerabilities, the more we need to be careful to dial down challenges and increase resources wherever possible. Similarly, the greater the challenges, the more we need to protect vulnerabilities and increase resources. We tend to have less influence over our challenges, though we may be able do some things to regulate the environment and the demands we're grappling with. We can do a little bit about our vulnerabilities, especially over time. But where we usually have the most opportunity is increasing resources of various kinds. To me, this possibility is really, really hopeful and helpful. If people do the best that they can in the next minute, which is the most important minute of our life, minute after minute, the *experience* of living can certainly improve—even if bodily or environmental conditions are stubbornly slow to change.

Overcoming Therapeutic Pessimism through Mindful Cultivation

I think Freud was grossly mistaken when he called psychotherapy an "impossible profession" (Freud, 1937/1964, p. 248). I find the efficacy evidence for psychotherapy is extraordinary. If Pfizer or Merck could patent psychotherapy in terms of its benefits for physical health outcomes, let alone mental health outcomes, we'd be seeing ads for it every night on television. Of course, the challenges are huge, and often it's hard to deliver resources to people in the direst need. But we can do a lot to help. From an evolutionary standpoint, certain experiences have a very high restorative value. Everyday beneficial experiences—relaxing while exhaling, taking in the friendly smile of another person, recognizing some good quality in oneself—have the power to bring us out of the "red zone" of stress and trauma back into the "green zone" of well-being, which is our resting state, our home base.

One aspect of the restorative power of internalizing beneficial experiences, taking them into yourself to build durable psychological resources, is that they often help you to register that in this moment you are basically all right. How does this work? Consider the fact that most of the inputs into the brain originate from inside the body, since our ancestors—going all the way back to jellyfish, worms, crabs, jawless fish, turtles, and mammals from rodents to primates—had to know what was going on inside their bodies. Of course, there are times when things inside our bodies are not all right. We may be in extreme pain, on the edge of death, when something terrible has happened. But most of the time, the vast majority of signals coming up from the viscera into the hypothalamus, which monitors your interior and is a key control center for craving (subtle to gross), are like the reassuring calls of a night watchman: "All is well, in this moment there is actually enough air, you've had enough food, you're not extremely thirsty, not in agonizing pain, things are actually all right, right now."

The opportunity, especially for those hit hard by life, is to recognize that at least in this moment they're actually all right in a fundamental sense. It may not be a great moment, a perfect moment, but it is basically all right. We may wish we had more food, more money, more love, but it's vital to realize what is *also* true: that we're basically all right, right now. Each of us has an incredible opportunity to register again and again and again, thousands and thousands of times, one or five or ten seconds at a time, "I'm all right, right now." The fact is, we need to consciously choose and practice recognizing this, since most of us, especially those who have been traumatized, live with a background trickle of anxiety. Through natural selection, evolution has bred us to be ever vigilant. To truly register that we're basically, fundamentally all right here and now, we have to push against the well-intended lie that Mother Nature is continually whispering, like the evil minister Wormtongue in *The Lord of the Rings*, "Be afraid; watch out; be very afraid."

Besides recognizing that you are basically all right when you actually are, another usually accessible source of authentic well-being involves feeling cared about by other beings, in some way, shape, or form. Any time you have a chance to feel included, seen, appreciated, liked, or loved, that is a beautiful opportunity to experience a sense of well-being in the moment—and to internalize that experience to develop an increasingly unconditional sense of confidence and worth hardwired into your own nervous system. As our primate, hominid, and early human ancestors lived and evolved in small bands, for instance on the Serengeti plains, exile was effectively a death sentence. If you were separated from your band, you were likely to die. Consequently, today, surrounded by all our fancy technology, the experience of social support is still primally vital to the sense of basic safety.

So, repeatedly having and taking in these two simple and down-to-earth experiences—of feeling all right, right now, and feeling cared about in one way or another—has become an important part of my day as well as my contemplative practice. Sometimes, there's so much fear as well as mistrust of others that doing this practice is a kind of "cultural disobedience" akin to civil disobedience. For instance, when I used to pass through airports with signs and loudspeaker announcements that "the threat level is orange, the threat level is orange," I would remind myself that the actual odds of a bad event on my flight that day were like a swimming pool of green paint with one drop of yellow. And I kept registering in my own body, "No, I'm green, I'm green, I'm green." Likewise, with others, it doesn't have to be a perfect interaction or perfect relationship, but in some fundamental sense we can register feeling included, seen, appreciated, even loved.

Natural Constraints on Neuroplasticity

Of course, there are constraints on neuroplasticity. For example, I could not will myself to lose a language. Or, someone who's suffered a stroke that mildly affects certain parts of their brain might be able to recover a fair amount of function, but there can also be irrevocable damage that can't be undone by even the most persistent practice. I also think there are limits in terms of core things like temperament. And, of course, there may also be constitutional limits on certain capacities or talents. We can't suddenly make ourselves mathematical geniuses, for example. Closer to home, there may also be constraints in terms of the negative habits that grip us each day. How quickly or easily can we help ourselves be less gripped by hatred, heartache, or delusion, or less affected by a parent's critical voice in our head, or by childhood losses or traumas we've had? The evidence is that people can change dramatically, but it's rarely quick or easy.

The fact is, we have a brain that did not evolve to be enlightened. It's been shaped by the harsh survival needs of our ancestors to suffer and crave and suffer some more. Animals that fought or fled or froze in reaction to real or potential pain ... that chased or gorged on or tried to mate with whatever was pleasurable ... that clung to relationships, with loyalty to their own band and fear and disgust toward other bands ... that moved quickly past what was neutral, looking for something better—well, these animals were more likely to pass on their genes. One useful way to think about practice, when it comes to underlying biological, neurological, or psychological causes of suffering and how to end them, is to appreciate how much power those ancient causes have. When we practice, we are dealing with 600 million years of evolution in the nervous system, on top of another 3 billion years of evolution of life. This said, we did not evolve to play chess or ping pong, or to make symphonies or skyscrapers, and yet we can do these things and more. With practice, we really can extinguish the fires of craving over time. And through repeated insight and practice, we can even deconstruct the conventional sense of "I" that hooks us into taking the largely impersonal processes of life so very personally. We can help ourselves learn from beneficial experiences, gradually coming home to the green zone, in which there is less and less need to presume a unified, stable, and independent "I" (Hanson, 2009, 2013).

The Neurobiology of Mind and Meditation

The Buddha was one of the pioneers in describing the mental causes of suffering and happiness. Nowadays, we can complement his hard-won wisdom with an evolutionary neurospsychology that sheds new light on the underlying causes of suffering and happiness. Of course, the Buddha and many of his peers and heirs became awakened without having an MRI. In this chapter, I have been exploring our experiences, and consciousness altogether, inside what is called the "natural frame" of science. In this framework, phenomena are considered to have causes within the material universe—including wildly exotic causes such as mass bending space to produce gravity, quantum entanglement, and dark energy—even if we do not yet understand them fully. This framework does not argue against potential causes that lie outside it but does ask whether it is necessary to posit such causes for a full account of a phenomenon.

Within the natural frame, scientists and scholars explore how what we see, what we hear, what we think, our hopes, our joys, our sorrows could be the result of causes within the material universe. From this perspective, there are still great mysteries, such as the two-way causal link between mind and brain. There might be causes of consciousness that are supernatural or transcendental, by definition outside of the natural frame, but science does not engage these causes, and looks instead at the human body, embedded in nature and culture, both now and over the course of deep time. Science investigates how the mind—which I define as the information represented by the nervous system—could be a natural process that is grounded in life.

Correlations between mental activity and physical processes within the brain are increasingly well established. Yet there still remains what is called the "hard problem" in consciousness studies: an explanatory gap between the meat and the mind that profound scholars and teachers like Francesco Varela and Tenzin Palmo have written about (Varela et al., 1992; Palmo, 2002). As Palmo has said, "We're thinking all the time, but we still don't actually know what a single thought actually is." As we explore, inside the natural frame, the processes of mind and how to shape them for our own sake and that of other beings, it is important also to respect the mystery and majesty of mind. Immaterial information (mind) represented by a material substrate (brain, embedded in a nervous system embedded in a body embedded in life) is an example of what philosophers call "dual-aspect monism," the notion that there can be two categorically distinct features of a single system. Looking at things in this way allows causality to flow in both directions, from mind to brain and brain to mind. Information has a logic of its own, its own causal streaming. It enlists underlying material processes to represent it, but its own logic is driving the underlying flow of neural activity, which then can leave lasting traces in neural structure. This way of understanding the mind respects its dignity, while also locating mind as a natural process arising dependently upon its material substrates.

If we're being deliberately mindful, whether it's in contemplative practice, attending to our partner, or learning long division, we're stimulating certain kinds of brain activity. If we observe the brain of someone paying attention in an MRI, we might see heightened activation in the cingulate cortex, especially the anterior part of it that supports top-down processing. MRI imagery—humorously described as the new science of "blobology"—may make it look as if the rest of the brain has gone dark, sort of like the orange glow of a little campfire late at night in a lonely wood, but the whole brain is still busy. It's just that the anterior cingulate cortex, in this case, is about 2–3 percent more metabolically active: a difference that makes a difference. This is just one illustration of how mental activity, in this case paying attention deliberately, entails underlying neural activity, which shows up as greater activation in a part of the brain that performs that particular function. Then we go to the next step: repeated patterns of mental activity entail repeated patterns of neural activity, and repeated patterns of neural activity build neural structure. Here we have the essence of experience-dependent neural plasticity; our thoughts, our feelings, and how we respond to them are continually sculpting our brain.

The brain is the organ that learns, and any form of learning—from personal growth and cultivation of loving-kindness to non-ordinary states of absorption—all that learning involves alterations in brain structure or function. For example, comparing the brains of long-time meditators to those of non-meditators, as in the well-known study by Sarah Lazar and her colleagues (2005), found that the meditators' brains had measurably thicker cortices in two key regions. Number one is the insula, on the inside of the temporal lobes, which is very involved in interoception. The second is the prefrontal cortex behind the forehead, involved in the control of attention, emotion, and action. These findings make sense given that meditators are constantly regulating their breath and body awareness, as well as their attention, emotions, and responses. They work the "muscles" in the parts of the brain involved with these functions' regions until they get bigger, metaphorically speaking, as a result. Now, we naturally lose several thousand brain cells a day. That's a lot but since we have 1.1 trillion to start with, we only lose several percent by the time we are elderly. In the cortex, this process is called normal cortical thinning and it is related to normal cognitive decline due to aging—not dementia but forgetting names and where you left your car keys. Lazar and her colleagues found that the non-meditators did in fact develop a thinner insular and prefrontal cortex as they aged, but older meditators did *not* have such thinning: they preserved these portions of their brains, apparently through regular meditative practice. They used it so they did not lose it—which has obvious implications for everyone, including an aging population.

The Neurobiology of Wholesome Experience: Installing States and Traits

Whether looked at from the vantage of modern or traditional mind science, what is fundamental to healing is the cycle of states and traits, activation and installation. States are momentary, temporary conditions, like a moment of loving-kindness, anger, or determination. Traits are more enduring tendencies of heart and mind that can incline us toward better or worse. This brings us to the question: how do we develop wholesome traits? Traits come from states. On average, roughly a third of our personal qualities are innate, grounded in our biology, in our DNA. The other two-thirds of our traits are acquired, not innate. They start out as states, experiences of one kind or another, and then through repetition they become gradually installed in enduring neural structure as a trait. This process offers us the welcome possibility of a virtuous circle of positive traits. Activated, positive states can become installed as enduring positive traits, then these installed positive traits can foster positive states in turn, which then become another opportunity to reinstall and reinforce the trait.

How do we cultivate this virtuous circle? The opportunity here is one of self-directed neuroplasticity, in which we can use the mind to change the brain to change the mind for the better. In order to do this, we have to get on our own side, to be a friend to ourselves. Otherwise there will be no traction, no motivation to activate wholesome mental states, and no motivation to install those activated mental states as enduring neural traits. It's helpful to appreciate in Buddhism or in other traditions various rationales for being a friend to ourselves, as an act of benevolence. Most people treat others better than they treat themselves, but the Golden Rule is a two-way street: we should do unto ourselves as we do unto others. If it's a moral value for us to be benevolent toward all beings, that includes the one being who wears our own name tag. In general, we have the highest duty to use power well over those that we most influence, and the one being we influence most is our future self, a minute from now, a year from now, perhaps a lifetime from now. As Pema Chödrön says, "The root of Buddhism is compassion, and the root of compassion is self-compassion, compassion for oneself" (Chödrön, 2000).

There are so many implications to this process of growing inner strengths. It makes me think of a famous story you've likely heard in some form. A Native American woman was asked toward the end of her life, "Grandmother, how did you become so happy, so strong, and so wise? Everybody listens to you; everybody wants to be your friend. How did you do it?" She paused, reflected, and replied, "I think it was because when I was young, I realized that in my heart were two wolves, one of love and one of hate. I also realized that everything depended upon which one I fed each day." Who among us does not have some kind of wolf of hate broadly defined, a capacity for hostility, for envy, for resentment, for aggression, even violence? Modern evolutionary studies indicate that the wolf of love and wolf of hate coevolved in our ancestors, in hominid and early human groups that bred mainly inside the band. Groups that were better at cooperating internally could outcompete other groups. Bands that were more aggressive than other bands at claiming resources in hard times were also more able to pass on their genes. Of course, evolution gives us inclinations and options, and it is up to us to respond to these wisely today. Which wolf will we feed?

The Buddhist View of Cultivation and Resilience

A frequent metaphor in early Buddhism is the Vedic image of the sacrificial fire. So perhaps a Buddhist way to ask this question is, "Which fire are we fueling?" For instance, the Buddha described greed, hatred, and delusion as fuels for the fire of suffering and harm. By contrast, generosity, love, and wisdom are fuels for the fire of happiness and welfare. Whether as therapists, parents, meditation teachers, or business consultants, much of our efforts in life are devoted to cultivating strengths, broadly defined. Inner strengths include things like character virtues. In the Buddhist context, these include qualities like the seven factors of enlightenment: mindfulness, investigation, energy, bliss, tranquility, concentration, and equanimity. Another list involves positive emotional factors called immeasurable states or divine abodes (brahmavihara): loving-kindness, compassion, altruistic joy, and equanimity. As positive psychology has increasingly shown, many of these states of mind promote lasting happiness (Lopez et al., 2014).

Unfortunately, most positive experiences are wasted on the brain. This is the fundamental weakness of psychotherapy, character education for kids, mindfulness training, recovery work, or dealing with trauma. As teachers, therapists, coaches, people in the humanities broadly, we may be quite good at activating positive states. But historically we've assumed that these states would just stick to the brain. As it turns out, the real problem is less around activating positive states than it is around installing them in the brain as neural traits, so we don't waste them. We've hit the bottleneck in our brains; now we need to open that bottleneck up. That's where the practice of taking in the good comes in. With a little bit of mindful attention, five, ten, 20 seconds at a time, we can heighten the conversion of positive, useful, activated mental states into lasting, useful, positive neural traits.

H-E-A-L: The Four Stages of Wholesome Learning

I've described the practice of taking in the good, wholesome learning, as a two-stage process: we start by activating a useful state, then we install it in the brain. But if we really want to ensure that we install the positive state, there are at least two other things we can do to help the process along. I summarize the four-step process of taking in the good with the acronym HEAL. H reminds us that first of all we need to *have* positive experiences. E reminds us that we are more likely to register and install them if we *enrich* that experience. A reminds us that we need to *absorb* the experience. L reminds us that we can more fully install the experience if we *link* it to other experiences which are significant to us.

Having positive experiences is simple enough, but how do we enrich them? There are five major factors that are known to heighten or enrich learning. First, duration is fundamental, the longer the better. Second, intensity counts, the more intense the experience the more readily we remember it. Third, multimodality, which means the more you feel it in the body, the more it's enacted, the more it's sensate, the more it's emotional, the more neurons are going to be firing together and wiring together. Fourth is novelty. The more we see things afresh rather than just presuming, "I know what this is," the more likely we are to install it. Fifth and last comes personal relevance. We remember what's salient, what matters to us. Why would it help me to have this particular positive experience?

As for the third step, we need to *absorb* the experience. Research shows that we can sensitize or prime underlying memory systems through the top-down intention to remember. We've probably all had the experience of getting the phone number of some cool person we meet in a bar, but we can't write it down: we just say it again and again and again. Or we may have a really meaningful moment, maybe at meditation or the birth of a child or a particularly beautiful sunset, and we tell ourselves to remember this one.

Finally, we can help install the state we're experiencing by linking it to other states. One way to do this is to hold an awareness of both positive and negative material at the same time. That's since neurons fire together, they wire together, the neural substrates of the positive material start associating with, and linking with and wiring together with, the neural substrates of the negative material. When the negative material goes back down the memory hole to be reconsolidated in a very dynamic process, it takes some of those positive associations with it. Then, repeatedly, with repeated linking of positive to negative, eventually the negative can be soothed, eased, minimized, and even gradually replaced. Many people do this naturally or intuitively. Increasingly therapists are learning to do this. Focusing is an example of using this technique in therapy, and others include forms of trauma treatment like eye movement desensitization and reprocessing (EMDR) or somatic experiencing, addressed in Diana Fosha's chapter later in this volume.

If you think about the first three steps, it may help to use the metaphor of fire—much as the Buddha did long ago. In the first step, Have, we light the fire. In the second, Enrich, we add fuel to the fire to keep it burning, burning ever more brightly. In the third step, Absorb, we warm ourselves by the fire. We let the warmth, the heat of the fire, sink into us. We let what's useful and wholesome about this experience really come in.

To put the HEAL practice in context, there are three fundamental ways to engage the mind. The first way is to just be with what is, feel the feelings, experience the experience, witness it, hopefully hold in it in a vast space of awareness, possibly even direct some friendliness or compassion towards what's there. Hopefully we can also disidentify from it, maybe even investigate it. We sense down to what's younger, more vulnerable, or more central to us. But we're not trying to change it. We're simply being with it. The second way to engage the mind is to prevent, reduce, or end what is negative. (Throughout this chapter, I mean "good" and "bad," "positive" and "negative," in pragmatic not moral terms as that which, respectively, promotes the happiness and welfare of oneself and others, or promotes the suffering and harm.) We release greed, hatred, and delusion, relax tension in our body, let go of thoughts that are not helpful for us or other people, control or abandon desires that are harmful for ourselves and others. The third way to engage the mind is to create, preserve, or grow the positive. We open to wise view, we cultivate good intentions, we develop mindfulness, grit, gratitude, and compassion. We can be mindful in all three forms of practice. Using the metaphor of a garden, we can witness it, pull weeds, or grow flowers. While all of these are vital, the first one—being with the mind—is most fundamental since you can't always release the negative or grow the positive. Still, it is not the only mode of practice, and I think that many people overvalue it.

How do we understand cultivation in a Buddhist frame of reference? We're taught the root of all suffering is craving—but what is the root of craving? In terms of evolutionary neuropsychology, craving is a drive state that arises dependently upon an invasive internal sense of deficit or disturbance. Through repeatedly internalizing wholesome experiences of core needs being met, we can gradually replace the roots of craving with a growing sense of fullness and balance hardwired into the nervous system. Over time, cultivation undoes craving. Having and taking in experiences of core needs met— experiences of safety, satisfaction, and connection—builds up the neural substrates of a green zone brain, with a mind increasingly colored by peace, contentment, and love. Do this practice of wholesome cultivation again and again and again, 10,000 times, ten seconds at a time. Again and again and again and again and again, growing the internal sense of core needs met no matter if the world or other people are flashing red.

Doing this will deepen the keel in the sailboat of your mind/brain, and you will be able to manage inevitable challenges in life more resiliently and gracefully and joyfully. As the eight "worldly winds" blow—praise and blame, gain and loss, fame and ill-repute, pleasure and pain—it will be much harder to knock you over. And if you get banged hard, you will recover more quickly. Then you can afford to dream bigger dreams, and head on out into the deep blue sea. As Mary Oliver (2004, p. 94) asks, "Tell me, what is it you plan to do/ with your one wild and precious life?"

6
Mindfulness Practice as Advanced Training for the Clinician

Paul R. Fulton

Just a few decades ago, discussing meditation and psychotherapy together was frowned upon, as meditation was regarded as religious, new age, or spiritual, with little to do with the science of psychotherapy. Of course, this is no longer true. Meditation has become a legitimate object of clinical interest. A key element in the clinical integration of these practices is the clinician's own meditation practice and understanding why it may be crucial to the therapeutic process and outcomes. Over the course of this chapter, I share both personal and professional experiences that inform my understanding of the value of the clinician's own meditation practice as a form of advanced clinical training.

Many years ago, I spoke with a woman who was a psychologist and a meditator and asked her if she was interested in getting psychoanalytic training. At the time, psychoanalytic training was the gold standard for advanced training. She said that she could best serve her patients by being "as enlightened as possible." She had expressed a thought I had never dared to say out loud. While there are problems with the notion of "trying to be as enlightened as possible", her stance felt like an invitation to begin exploring this idea.

There are many ways to understand how meditation and psychotherapy interact. For instance, one might consider psychotherapy as preparation for meditation. A dear friend wanted to practice meditation but felt fundamentally too crazy to sit with herself until she had done a number of years of therapy. For others (myself included) the benefits of psychoanalytic therapy were elusive until retreat practice started to deepen meditation. I had harbored a low level of simple fear I had not yet fully recognized. Once the meditation practice took hold, I began to see the fear more clearly, and came to feel less possessed by it. In this respect, meditation was preparation for psychotherapy.

DOI: 10.4324/9781003243588-7

Meditation, and the perspectives it cultivates, can inform psychotherapy covertly and overtly. At the 'covert' or implicit end is the psychotherapist's own meditation practice, which may remain invisible to the patient. It may contribute no particular markers to the therapist's technique. More overt are mindfulness-based strategies, using the techniques or insights that come out of the meditative traditions, whether or not identified as such. Yet more explicit are mindfulness-based approaches, such as dialectical behavior therapy (DBT; Linehan, 1993b), mindfulness-based stress reduction (MBSR; Kabat-Zinn, 2013), compassion-based stress reduction (CBRT; Loizzo et al., 2009), and mindfulness-based cognitive therapy (MBCT; Segal et al., 2013), that explicitly utilize and teach various meditative practices. Lastly, explicit use of meditation practices by the patient may be suggested as an adjunct to ongoing treatment, or as a 'next step' for the patient who has received the benefits of therapy and wishes to continue along a path of self-development.

Regardless of the particular discipline or theoretical approach, the practice of mindfulness cultivates qualities of mind that arguably influence any type of treatment, irrespective of theoretical orientation. Lambert & Barley (2001) provide a meta-analysis of treatment variables and effects to discern what effects therapeutic change. Their findings suggest that patient variables (i.e., motivation, resourcefulness, intelligence, and support system), account for approximately 40 percent of the outcome variance. Placebo or expectation effects account for an additional 12–15 percent. Surprisingly, the therapeutic model and technique of the clinician also accounted for merely 12–15 percent of variance. Most relevant to our discussion here is the final set of variables, the implicit "common factors" that seem to be present in any effective treatment relationship. These account for the remaining 30 percent or so of outcome variance in successful treatment. I would argue that mindfulness is an essential practice for the cultivation of factors that facilitate effective psychotherapy, independent of the particular theoretical orientation of the clinician. What are these common factors, and how might mindfulness help their development?

Empathy

Empathy is the single best-researched common factor in psychotherapy outcome literature. It is beyond dispute that empathy is positively associated with successful outcomes. Though we know its central importance, how many practitioners took courses in cultivating empathy, especially as it is applied across lines of difference such as gender, race, religion, education, and more?

The concept of empathy is easy to teach, becoming empathic is not. And the fact is that clinicians differ in their capacity for empathy. How does mindfulness grow our capacity for this personal quality essential to a positive treatment outcome?

There are a number of ways in which meditation cultivates empathy and compassion. In meditation, we learn to be attentive to our own experience, which will inevitably include the experience of suffering. With the long term committed practice of meditation, we begin to discover that our suffering, which always seemed to be a sort of personal affront, is in fact baked into the experience of being alive. In this sense, it is shared with all other humans, and becomes a basis on which we discover our affinity with others – it is not just *my* suffering, rather we all are subject to the same natural laws of suffering. Just as I suffer, so do others, and we share the wish for this to be overcome. This is a basis for empathy and compassion.

In addition to the intrinsic unpleasantness of pain is the accompanying sense of estrangement we often feel around it: "I alone am suffering this." It is astonishing how frequently clients feel ashamed because they look around and see a world of others who do not appear to be suffering their particular affliction. Therefore, not only are they in pain but they are also suffering a sense of alienation of being excluded from participation in the human experience. This kind of alienation is also pervasive in groups that are marginalized by dominant society, whether based on race, gender, class, ability, or some other difference. By contrast, as our understanding of our own suffering grows with sustained meditation practice, we actually begin to see it as universal, a basis of our shared inheritance as humans. Indeed, the first Noble Truth, the axiom around which all of these teachings turn – is that no one is immune. When we begin to see our own suffering and engage our own experience fully, it becomes the actual basis on which we begin to feel our affinity with others. Compassion and empathy naturally emerge from this understanding. In other words, the sense of a separate self starts to attenuate, and in its place comes an appreciation of a deep, shared humanity.

If empathy is the factor most associated with a positive treatment outcome, then the importance of learning to cultivate this quality in ourselves is paramount. With this capacity we become attuned to the experience of accurate empathy, as well as its failures. To see the power of both empathic connection and its breaches is to be drawn to investigate more deeply; we cannot address what we cannot accurately perceive. A quote from Rumi says: "Every forest branch moves differently in the breeze, but as they sway, they connect at the roots."

Present-Centered Attention

As clinicians, we give undivided attention to our clients to the best of our ability. We know from our experience that the quality of our attention varies from one client to the next, from one day to the next. Ordinary attention, which may be far better attention than our clients generally receive elsewhere in their lives, creates an environment where they feel listened to. But very often we are not completely present either. We have learned all these techniques to mask our inattention by asking the well-timed question whose purpose is probably nothing more than to say, "I'm here. I'm awake."

But we also know the experience of paying extraordinary attention or being paid attention to. If you have ever been in distress and have reached out to just the right person who could listen (maybe it was your therapist), you know there can be that moment when attention is alive, when it cannot be faked, when you are on the edge of your seat. It is compelling, electric, and full of possibility. Sometimes this happens because someone is actually speaking from the living edge of their own experience, without any defense, as opposed to blandly reporting the day's events. We also know the flip-side moments, when you can't keep your attention on what the patient is saying to save your life.

I imagine these two extremes at the far ends of a bell curve, representing the natural distribution of our attentiveness. We still have days when we are somewhat sluggish or inattentive. Most of the time we are within "normal limits," and present enough. I would argue that our meditation practice moves the entire bell curve, so we are learning to sit still and pay deep attention for more of the time. We have learned to pay closer attention simply because we have practiced it in meditation. We know from empirical studies, as well as in the laboratory of our own experience, that attention is improved with meditation practice.

This shift in attention became most clear to me upon return from a meditation retreat, when I noticed that every session seemed to be going outstandingly well. It did not take much to figure out this was not because every patient was primed to do really good work. Rather, I was effortlessly and simply present because all the background noise in my own head had settled, if only temporarily. Doing therapy under such circumstances is just delicious.

Attention can be trained, and it is essential that we learn to pay attention. Ordinary treatment progress can be made with ordinary attentiveness, but when we are really awake and alert to the other one before us, they know it.

We know it when we are being listened to in the same way. I have a friend who is a *vipassana* teacher in Los Angeles who trained in mental health at Massachusetts Mental Health Center. As a student she was invited to attend a senior seminar. At the time, these were all run by what I like to call "the silverbacks" – the senior psychoanalysts in the department, almost always male, who would gesticulate with their pipes and make pronouncements. In one seminar, a very senior instructor whom she held in high regard admitted it was hard for him to pay attention to his patients, and his mind wandered to the point that sometimes he couldn't even hear what they were saying. As a student of Zen, she was appalled. Although she was a trainee and knew little about clinical practice, she knew how to sit with clients and how to listen. And she wondered how anything useful could occur when someone was so distracted or lost in his own thoughts. This point is pretty evident: mindfulness is direct training of attention.

Affect Tolerance and Holding Space

Marsha Linehan (1993) speaks about affect tolerance in DBT as a quality to be cultivated by all patients. But the term was originated by Elizabeth Zetzel (Zetzel & Meissner, 1974), a psychoanalyst who talked about this as a kind of ego function or ego strength. Its meaning is self-evident learning to hold painful affect without retreat, without folding, without resorting to primitive defenses. If we cannot tolerate our own pain, we cannot tolerate the discomfort that comes from sitting with our clients. We may not even realize the degree to which we wind up turning away from other's experience out of our own discomfort – this can be especially true when working with clients who have a significantly different life experience based on gender, race, sexuality, ableism, and socio-economic standing. This discomfort can masquerade as a premature effort to seek a cure, to figure out what is supposed to be done, because sitting with something intolerable feels intolerable.

If we cannot bear our clients' pain (and perhaps our own moments of helplessness), they will recognize this consciously or unconsciously, and will seek to protect us. They're going to stop sharing anything they feel we can't manage, or possibly leave treatment. So, we have now put a ceiling on what can be said, tolerated, or accomplished in psychotherapy.

On the other hand, if our clients intuit that we are able to hold whatever they offer, it provides a vast freedom typically not available elsewhere in their lives. When we're doing intensive practice in meditation, we're making space for *everything* that arises. If you sit long enough, you're going to see the whole complex show. We make space for it and allow it to be because it is there and it is true, whether or not it is to our liking. We are learning to set aside all of the habitual avenues of escape and avoidance and allowing the experience to be. In this process, we can see so much of our inner reactivity, but we just allow it, soften around it, and make space, minute after minute, hour after hour.

In this process, we also become a larger container capable of holding whatever happens. Indeed, often the real benefit is only seen when it really hits the fan, when the rug has been pulled out from under us, as when there's some intolerable loss, like a death or a life-threatening diagnosis. Then we suffer, but we also realize we are not going to drop out of the bottom of the universe; this experience, too, can be met. When we practice this holding for ourselves, we become a larger container for being able to listen to what our clients have to share.

While I am not a trauma therapist, a number of years ago I saw a woman in therapy who endured a tremendous trauma. When she began treatment, she was very clear with me that she was seeking help for something related to the application of mindfulness to stress. She wasn't interested in any emotional archaeology. One day her affect was quite different. She spoke haltingly and slowly in a near whisper, eyes downcast, and started to tell me about a memory of abuse she had endured as a child. Even if only half of it were true, it was by far the worst thing I had ever heard. As I'm hearing this. I thought to myself, "What am I going to do? I don't have the skills for this." I was quite frightened because I felt immediately out of my depth, and considered saying, "Have you considered seeing a professional?" I caught myself reeling back, recoiling in the moment, but since I noticed it and saw my turning away out of fear and defensiveness, I had the possibility of deciding instead to just lean into it and allow myself to be present with the full horror of what she was telling me, to just letting it be so. Finally, toward the end of the session, she ran out of story, and it was my turn to say something. I said it was more than I felt any human being should ever have to bear. I didn't know what else to say.

She left the session, and a few days later I got an email from her thanking me for listening, for not rejecting her, because in her view all of these things took her outside the domain of ordinary human experience, and it was not her expectation that I or anyone else would be able to bear this story. She came back in the next week and again thanked me for seeing her because she had felt certain she would get fired. There's no magic in this. I did feel intimidated by her level of suffering, but remembering to apply the skills learned in meditation, I could turn toward it again and make space for it. If we cannot do this, how do we expect our patients to engage with the deepest levels of their own suffering? It's imperative that we learn affect tolerance, making room for the full scope of our own suffering, because otherwise we wind up putting limits on what can be accomplished, and patients will be cheated out of what might be a once-in-a-lifetime opportunity to seek and receive real help. It's not a substitute for technique, or knowledge, but those things alone are not going to get us through these places of deep torment.

Sometimes our clients say things like, "I don't know how you can do this hour after hour." This is how. We become that larger container. I think of the expression about the salt in the cup: you can put a tablespoon of salt in a cup of water and it's going to be very salty, but if you take the same tablespoon of salt and drop it into a freshwater pond the salt is still there but the taste is no longer distinguishable. With mindfulness practice we become that larger container. The salt is all still there, but it loses its pungency, or does not spill out over the edges quite so much.

Acceptance

Meditation is itself the practice of acceptance and self-acceptance. Sitting with non-judgmental open attention is to allow whatever arises to find a temporary home in the spaciousness of awareness. While the notion of self-acceptance certainly speaks to the goals of much of psychotherapy, it is not a conclusion one reaches, finished once and for all. One cannot wave a wand and say, "I hereby forgive myself and accept myself just as I am." Our habits of self-criticism are persistent and well-practiced and overcoming them requires practice. We may be accepting in one moment and an hour later find we are ridiculing ourselves for some thought or experience. In my view, our meditation is the practice of acceptance and of self-acceptance because we are simply allowing ourselves to be present with whatever is happening, surrendering the habits of judgment, censorship, and control as much as we are able. In that process we allow a lot in, and it is often shocking, and at moments ugly to see what surfaces.

So we learn to accept, and we learn to accept by practicing. Something unacceptable arises within us – and we think to ourselves, "Can I be with this?" When something difficult arises, such as a difficult mind state, we ask ourselves, "What is already present and wishes to be known? Can I be with it? How can I be with it?" Or a variation on this, "Can I drop all agendas for this moment?" Practicing acceptance in this way includes self-acceptance because the self, in this instance, is not the self as an abstract concept, but rather the totality of our moment-to-moment experience.

As we grow in our ability to accept each moment with full attention – without regard for whether it is mean, petty, ugly, or jealous – and make space for it without clinging or pushing it away, then we can extend this quality of heart and mind to whatever our patients bring, with non-judgment, interest, and simple acceptance. This is another way to talk about affect tolerance. Clients are so often astonished that they can tell us their most shameful secrets and our greatest strength is that we are not knocked down, which is to say we are not burdened by the sense of shame that they may carry. This offers a felt sense of safety that permits a new degree of openness and honesty largely missing in ordinary relationships. That is of enormous value and, most importantly, it can be learned and expanded. Acceptance, cultivated toward our own moment-to-moment experience, extends naturally to others.

Equanimity

Equanimity seems to carry a few different, though related, meanings. One is simply the ability to remain steadfast in the presence of whatever arises, a very valuable quality of mind. A more specific meaning comes from the *Brahma Vihara*, the four "limitless or divine abodes." In this latter sense, it is a particular quality of mind that one cultivates having already practiced the three other more prosocial qualities of loving-kindness, compassion, and sympathetic joy. When practicing these for any period of time, people can become so loving, warm, and committed to reaching out and saving all sentient beings. On the basis of these three, one moves to the fourth: equanimity practice (*upekhkā*, in Pali).

The phrases traditionally used to cultivate equanimity go something like, "All my wishes for the welfare of another being cannot save them from the consequences of their own actions." Or, "All beings are the inheritors of their own *karma*, the bearers of the consequences of their decisions." One can spend much time cultivating this huge store of love and compassion, and the commitment to do whatever is possible to free another from their suffering and then, with equanimity there is this cold shower that says, "And there are limits to what you can do for them." To me, this is the essence of what makes doing clinical work a challenge, because we really want to help, but there is a point at which we can do very little. If we do not understand the limits of our ability to help, we are going to step into something by overselling our abilities and making promises to clients we can't keep. Our clients are going to wind up leaving angrier and more impoverished because of our failure to deliver.

As effective clinicians, we create the conditions that allow a person to make the decision whether to move toward growth and health, or not. We are careful in our efforts to identify the influences of projection and transference, in order to avoid recreating the sorts of obstacles they have felt in much of their life. We learn to get out of their way again and again. One way we may get in their way is through arrogance regarding our own skill. An essential remedy here involves equanimity as recognition of the limits of our own ability. At times, this may clash with the business of being the expert and being able to model our expectation of treatment efficacy. The line from T.S. Eliot expresses this understanding of equanimity: "Teach us to care and not to care. Teach us to sit still."

This is the heart of our dilemma: we have to care *and* we have to maintain equanimity and balance. We have to allow for the limits of our ability to save anybody from themselves if they are not prepared for help, and that can be extremely challenging to the earnest and hardworking therapist. When you see someone making a bad decision, what do you say and how do you relate to it? What do you imagine are the limits of your own ability and impact? When I was a trainee, I remember once thinking I had to cancel my vacation because I had a very fragile client I was very worried about. Of course, my supervisors were all over me about that, as they should be. The idea that I alone am going to stand between her and some self-inflicted harm offered nothing of benefit to her.

I think of equanimity as this sober balancing – a recognition of the limitations of our ability to save another person and how essential it is to be able to hold that, because I think humility is the truth of the matter. We offer the best of what we have and recognize that it may well not be enough for the particular circumstances. Clinicians may fall short when we are not fully cognizant of how our social location may impact our ability to fully empathize with our clients, as well as being unaware of biases we may have around gender, race, sexuality, religion, economic standing, and ableism.

Learning to See

Meditation hones our capacity for accurate perception. As this capacity is strengthened, we apply it to the observation of ourselves, our minds, and our lives. With practice, we become more acute observers of our own minds. With this clarity of seeing comes insight; we come to see what we're up to, our habits, and reactivities. It may not be that they've gone away, but we see them with greater clarity.

When I worked at a state hospital, there was a nurse who was friendly but also very needy and "sticky," and I found that I did not much care for her. One day, when I had just returned from retreat, I was walking down the hall and she called to me from the nursing station. I felt a wave of aversion and the impulse to turn away. But because I felt it and it arose as an experience in awareness, I could see it. Now, instead of acting it out by racing past, I had a choice. In that moment I simply turned toward her, and we had a fine and delightful conversation. My initial aversive impulse could be set aside long enough to treat this as an utterly unique encounter, worthy of full attention. Through mindfulness, we are learning to put our energy into the experience of observing and seeing clearly rather than automatically reacting to something in a habitual way.

Of interest to the clinician is that the more adept we are at seeing our own minds, the better we become at seeing the minds of others. The more we know how we get hooked and entangled, the more we are able to see how our clients are similarly ensnared in unskillful ways, and the traps they are laying for themselves. Needless to say, this is a tremendous (and generally unheralded) benefit of mindfulness training for the clinician.

I recently saw a man who had been in psychoanalytic therapy, and he described being annoyed and wanting to quit because he wanted his analyst to tell him what she thought of him, but she wouldn't. He came to see me for a one-time consultation. He had some interest in Buddhist psychology, but he said to me at the end "You know, I'm too old for that." Without thinking, I replied, "That's just an idea." It startled him because he had already closed the door on the idea that he had anything to learn from it. But I could see his fixed view of himself was just a concept. He's not too old for anything, he is still breathing, so what more does he need?

Early in our training, we learn how to formulate our patients' plights. Conversely, in the fullness of the attention to our patients and the ability to see their minds, the natural and correct formulation arises almost spontaneously. When we speak from that place of attunement, patients know we are not repeating some theoretical formulation derived from our training. Those formulations and responses come out of being completely marinated in the fullness of the moment and seeing clearly. Our ability to see others comes from our ability to see ourselves and simultaneously, of course, to quiet our voice a bit so we can make space for another.

Reframing the Nature of Suffering

As psychotherapy has found its home in medical science, our training is rooted in learning to diagnose. We are taught to see people's distress as symptoms, and piece them together into a formulation. This becomes the frame of reference for our work. However, unlike somatic medicine which can often draw on lab tests, x-rays, and visible signs of illness, nearly all of our diagnostic categories come from reports of subjective suffering, consensus statements, expert panels, prevalence reports, and other less direct forms of evidence. Tethered less clearly to visible markers, the diagnostic categories in mental health change over time because they are basically social constructs. When people come to us and speak about their suffering and difficulties, we generally treat such distress as a clinical matter, and all that connotes. If we keep in mind the Buddha's teachings about the ubiquity of human suffering, it really puts a different frame on it. It is enormously useful to understand that suffering is not always evidence of a disorder or a treatable condition, but rather a human condition with birth as its original cause. In this way, we are able to help reframe people's expectations to a degree and, for ourselves, to begin to distinguish those forms of suffering that might be properly considered clinical from those that are more properly considered culturally and institutionally constructed, existential or spiritual, requiring a different approach.

Someone dies and you feel grief. What do you do? Perhaps you go to a psychotherapist as though it's treatable. Yes, it is often invaluable to be able to speak to someone who is not otherwise involved in your life. But grief is not always a clinical matter unless you meet the Diagnostic and Statistical Manual of Mental Disorders (DSM) conditions for persistent complex bereavement disorder. I think our practice helps us understand that not all suffering is reducible to a treatable clinical condition, and we actually can work with suffering differently. We can relate to it differently and set aside the idea that our wellbeing depends on fixing something that may be fundamentally unfixable. I would argue that as meditating clinicians we have a leg-up here because we begin to have a different perspective on suffering and its causes. We are not so easily drawn into the myth that suffering equals disorder and therefore is treatable. There are forms of suffering, such as racism, sexism, homophobia, loss, and disappointment, that call upon a completely different approach of learning how to meet and embrace experience (painful and otherwise) with equanimity, kindness, and compassion.

Such an understanding helps us avoid the pitfall of overselling psychotherapy, to our patients and to ourselves. It is often simply more realistic.

Professional Self-Esteem and the Problem of Narcissism

In psychoanalytic training, it is understood that clinicians need to undergo a good analysis themselves. This offers some defense against the risk that one may not really recognize when they are engaged in transference (or counter-transference), and so is more likely to re-enact and recapitulate old dysfunctional patterns, relational dynamics, and unconscious biases. I would suggest that even a good psychoanalysis doesn't go nearly far enough in its ability to begin to identify the degree to which we are relating to others as a kind of projection of our own expectations, our own needs, and cultural conditioning.

Meditation goes further than psychoanalysis in this regard because it does not give us any place to hide. If we are really practicing with honesty and diligence, we begin to see the manipulations of the self that wants to possess, own, and control everything. Clear seeing of this process does not bring an end to living in a world of our projections, but with growing insight, we are less likely to buy into – and act from – the narratives generated out of our self-centered preoccupations.

One example of this involves insight gained in mindfulness practice into our incessant conscious and unconscious motivation to establish and preserve our self-esteem. If we are being attentive to the rising of self in meditation practice, we can see how much of the time we are subtly (or maybe not so subtly) trying to position ourselves for the purpose of enhancing and establishing our view of ourselves, reflected in others' eyes. This unpleasant business is bundled with the habit of comparing ourselves to others. In the Theravada Buddhist model, there are stages of awakening during which fetters or obscurations drop away at each stage. One particular fetter (*mana*, in Pali), is typically translated as conceit. This involves the persistent impulse to say, "I'm here," or "I exist." This is the urge to speak up just to put yourself in the room, or the tendency to compare yourself to others, whether favorably or unfavorably. That particular fetter does not completely vanish until full awakening. This is good news and bad news. The good news is that because most of us are going to be stuck with this in some fashion for the long haul, we don't need to get too worked up about it. And though it is workable, the bad news is that we are stuck with it.

Our meditation can be used as a means of beginning to explore how the self arises and how it shapes our relationship to so much of our experience. We can have moments where self does not arise, and moments where we see it at every turn. I think this is an extraordinarily powerful and subtle tool in terms of beginning to root out and directly apprehend those narcissistic impulses.

However, they are not easily eradicated, even for people who have had very deep experiences of awakening; under the right circumstances the self reasserts itself, but we do not need to fear it or repudiate it as fiercely because we understand the self in and of itself is empty of self. Self comes and goes, and paradoxically, is empty of an essential self-nature.

This persistent concern with our self-image and our self-esteem can be seen in our work. As clinicians, we want to be seen as effective. When you think about the clients for whom the treatment is going well and those for whom things are going really poorly, who do you typically look forward to seeing most? I saw a woman many years ago who worked as an industrial designer, and apparently, had been successful. Her parents had been highly demanding with high professional expectations for her and being a designer barely qualified in their eyes as a legitimate enterprise. She did it dutifully but, she harbored a secret. One day, with great difficulty and shame – and with an intensity more befitting a murder confession – she admitted she really wanted to be was a hairdresser. In light of the strength of her feeling, I was relieved because her secret was, to me, utterly unshameful. I said to her, "Well, then, why don't you be a hairdresser?" My comment struck her like lightning. This encouragement from a paid stranger that she could be a hairdresser, led her to feel I was the most brilliant clinician and therapist she had ever met or could hope to meet.

We love those patients because they make us feel effective and competent. The problem is that the quality of our professional self-esteem is being renegotiated pretty much on an hourly basis, and we are only as good as our last client. But we want to feel good about the work we do. In a subtle way, that can wind up infecting how we are with our clients, because we want to be – and seen as – effective. We have our own narcissistic needs, and we would like to see ourselves reflected in a positive way through their eyes.

It is not a problem that this tendency exists within us. The problem arises when it remains unseen, because only then is it likely to wind up steering us in ways we didn't intend. Through our mindfulness practice, becoming aware of those moments when we are tempted to say something for our own needs and our own purposes, allows us to make a more conscious decision. If we don't see it, we are often mindlessly compelled by these self-centered needs. When we are embedded in our own need to be an effective therapist or to be seen in a certain way, we have prematurely eclipsed the patient's freedom. When that occurs, we are not attending to them, but subtly dealing with ourselves, and neither party is the wiser for it. It takes a lot of discernment to be aware of this process, and it becomes a hindrance in therapy when we blur our own narcissistic needs with the therapeutic needs of the client.

Mindfulness can root out some of the ingenious ways we have of deceiving ourselves about what we are really up to and can be extremely painful. I suggest a little experiment. Ask yourself where your attention is when you're sitting with a patient. It is appropriate to be attentive to your own inner state, but if you are absorbed there, you will lose contact with the patient. Conversely, when not attuned to yourself, you miss some very important data. But take a few moments in a therapy session to bring your mindful attention to the fluctuation in your own self-appraisal and experience. You may think, "Oh, crap! That was stupid," or "Oh, she liked it!" and then there's a moment of pleasure. If we're attuned to it, the cycle of pleasure and displeasure happens constantly, and we begin to see what we are up to – dealing with our own wish to be effective, to put ourselves in the room to try to be smart, helpful, and avoid being stupid or exposed. The Buddhist approach offers the capacity for taking this examination to a much more profound level than is possible simply by discursive thinking alone, which is prone to the distortions of our unconscious needs and drives.

Learning to 'Not Know'

Therapy informed by our mindfulness practice facilitates overcoming our infatuation with theory. We have all sorts of fixed ideas about how things are supposed to go, and we wind up clinging to those ideas because we want certainty. Our knowledge, our training, background, and degree justifies our work, and reassures us that we have a specialized understanding that gives our patients the confidence to seek help from us. It helps us have the confidence to overcome that sense of insecurity that may arise when we're sitting with someone new. We find it aversive to sit with insecurity; our ignorance in the face of a new client feels unpleasant.

We might consider our meditation practice as learning to not know, to sit with the uncertainty of not knowing what comes next. As applied to our clinical work this sounds a bit subversive. Does 'not knowing' mean all our training comes to nothing? Are we supposed to jettison everything that we've ever been taught?

There is a quote attributed to Samuel Butler, "Life is like music, it must be composed by ear, feeling and instinct, not by rule." He goes on to say, "Nevertheless, one had better know the rules for they sometimes guide in doubtful cases …" We do not abandon our knowledge, but rather learn to hold our clinical constructs more lightly. For example, we begin to see that our diagnostic categories are not descriptions of some clinical truth. They are just heuristics meant to organize our observations, and, while that's useful at times, it can also be enormously limiting, even damaging. Having sat in meditation with the arising of thinking, noticing it is thinking, noticing how we get entangled in thinking and how it drags us into compulsive and repetitious ways of responding, we start to recognize that these are constructions, and not to be mistaken for reality. The constructs are just things we employ, and they don't merit our slavish devotion.

I had a client when I was a trainee and continued with her in my private practice for 14 years, until she moved away. It was a real privilege to work with someone that long. She might have legitimately been considered to have borderline personality disorder. During the course of our work together she entered graduate school in psychology, took a course in abnormal psych and, of course, does what everybody does, which is to diagnose herself. She came into therapy and said, "So, what's my diagnosis?" and insisted on being told. I said, "I think you're really unhappy." She continued to pester me, and I kept finding experience-near ways to answer in non-clinical terms, and still to tell the truth as I saw it. Years later, after she moved away, she came back to visit me. She recalled these exchanges and actually thanked me for not answering her question as she originally framed it. Reading the diagnostic categories and criteria she might well have known how to diagnose herself, but what I did not do was saddle her with a label that could only have been damaging. This is what we need to do with ourselves as well. We need to be very careful about our premature efforts to know out of our own need, or to manage our insecurity.

Our concepts, conclusions, and judgments do naturally arise, but we learn to hold them lightly because we realize they are just constructions, concepts, or ideas, undeserving of our devotion. It takes a lot of consistent practice to see mental constructions as mental constructions. The process of generating thoughts and ideas never stops; it is what our minds do. What we can begin to do is recognize that any time we try to arrest that process we are already wrong, because now we have a false representation of a process that by its nature is in endless change. Far from stopping that process, we are simply learning to allow it to spin, to take what is useful but not mistake it for the real thing, that is, the person sitting before us, who is fundamentally mysterious. What could be more mysterious than another person or, for that matter, your own mind?

Can we restrain ourselves from that process of needing to conclude? What does it mean to not know in therapy? It means understanding that the play of the self, or ego, constantly tries to get control of the process and appropriate everything for itself. It means being very cautious about the impulse to jump in and try to fix something prematurely rather than allowing ourselves to simply explore. It means appreciating that resistance may actually reside within us and not within our patients. For me, a take-home lesson on returning from a retreat was noticing how every session seemed to go exceptionally well. In this I realized that 'resistance' was within me, and if I drop my resistance (which is to say, my need to know, or pushing for a certain outcome), the therapeutic process happens naturally and organically. This points to the adage, "Don't just do something, sit there." The correct formulations are going to arise not out of our knowledge, but rather spontaneously out of a full recognition of the fullness of the moment. This is trust in the process, not in my personal expertise.

Holding a Vision of Happiness

As a kid I remember seeing a magazine article with a photo of Sigmund Freud. He had a grim expression, and under his photo was a caption that read, "Herr Freud, why do you always look so unhappy?" and his answer, "I am unhappy. I'm unhappy with humankind." This was because from his vantage point as a master diagnostician, he had formulated a problem that was fundamentally unresolvable. In his view, the best one could hope for was a compromise between the insatiable needs of the instinctual drives and the constraints of the social world. His best formula, his best treatment – if it can even be considered a treatment – was to become as conscious as possible about what you were up against, and hopefully replace inadequate, immature defenses with mature defenses. At best, psychoanalysis offered to turn misery into ordinary human unhappiness.

In the Buddhist model, full awakening means the eradication of the inner forces of greed, hatred, and delusion. The profound value here is that these sources of our suffering are not immutable defining instincts, and can be pulled up by the roots, never to return. In the Mahayana tradition, these instincts are granted even less currency, opening the possibility of a very different conception of what happiness looks like. It is no longer limited to the notion of simple adjustment or even extinguishing the causes of suffering, but rather a positive conception of happiness as being complete, moral, psychological, and emotional emancipation, a concept that cannot be adequately described in clinical terms.

When we get a taste of this for ourselves, we can also begin to see what is possible for our clients. Rather than imagine that their happiness is dependent on fixing an insoluble, neurotic problem, or mistaking existential suffering for something clinical, we can begin to entertain a different response to our experience, in which well-being can be known *in spite* of difficult conditions, and not because conditions have been remedied. This opens up the possibility for our clients that they do not need to become perfect or solve all the problems as a precondition for greater peace of mind and self-acceptance. A quality of profound relief can be found, even without reaching the end of their long laundry list of things they need to correct about themselves or society at large. This sort of happiness is invaluable to know for ourselves, and to hold as a possibility for our clients, so we do not put an artificial constraint on what is possible in the treatment relationship. This is only possible if we know it for ourselves, and it cannot be gained in a book. You have to do your homework, returning to your cushion day in and day out.

7
Meditation, Wisdom, and Compassion in Psychoanalytic Psychotherapy

Seiso Paul Cooper

I'd like to share my orientation, or what you might call my biases, with regard to an area of overlap between Buddhist practices and psychoanalytic psychotherapy. What I want to focus on is how the two approaches are not mutually exclusive due to their emphases on the primacy of experience. In my view there is an underlying basis, or principal, that both Buddhist and psychoanalytic practices share: they are two of the most highly subjective and experience-based disciplines. I believe that both Eihei Dōgen (1200–1253), the 13th century founder of Soto Zen Buddhism in Japan, and Wilfred Bion (1897–1979), the influential 20th century English psychoanalyst, have taken this orientation as the epitome of their respective approaches. The primacy of experience functions as a shared point of contact. In fact, it is their subjective and experience-based foundations that I believe energize these disciplines as unique, deeply penetrating, and impactful processes.

The Groundless Ground of Psychoanalysis

Bion emphasizes this experiential and subjective orientation in the opening of his book *Attention and Interpretation* published in 1970. The opening paragraph of the book reads,

> I doubt if anyone but a *practicing* psychoanalyst can understand this book, although I have done my best to make it simple. Any psychoanalyst who is practicing can grasp my meaning because he, unlike those who only read or hear *about* psychoanalysis, has the opportunity to experience for himself what I in this book can only represent by words and verbal formulations designed for a different task.

> (Bion, 1970, p. 1)

DOI: 10.4324/9781003243588-8

Note that Bion emphasizes the word *practicing*. He's setting up his argument that language is based on and designed to communicate what he calls sensuous experience, which is not in the intuited experiential realm of the psychoanalytic process, and not the subject of psychoanalysis. In fact, according to Bion, language clouds over the intuited awareness of a psychoanalytic experience, except one that intuits awareness of the elusive "O" or ultimate truth of the session. Something that before too long evolves into what Bion refers to as "K," which is his term for logical sense-based knowledge. For Bion, the fundamental ground of psychoanalysis is "O." This is a groundless ground that is constantly in motion and at once both empty and full. "O" designates the ultimate, ineffable, infinite reality. Bion uses "O" to keep the psychic space open and unsaturated with preconceived meanings. "O" evolutions are central to Bion's later views. He defines "O" as follows:

> I shall use the sign O to denote that which is the ultimate reality represented by terms such as ultimate reality, absolute truth, the godhead, the infinite, the thing-in- itself. O does not fall in the domain of knowledge or learning save incidentally; it can be "become," but it cannot be "'known."
>
> (1970, p. 26)

However, Bion doesn't refute or discard language since the ineffable experience of "O" can only be intuited experientially and becomes known through an evolution into language. That is, an ineffable intuited experience of "O" transforms from the initial experience, either suddenly or gradually, into usable language and can then be communicated in the form of an interpretation or a notation. At first, he argues "O" only approximates experience, both of the analysand and the analyst's intuition. To draw upon Bion's notion of what he calls "transformations," there's an ongoing and paradoxical consensus of the intuited—or perceived—reality of the moment. The experience is simultaneously consensual and paradoxical because the two perceptions of reality are unique, yet, at the same time the two individuals agree what, for instance, the object of perception is. To use a concrete example, let's look at two individuals who agree that an object of perception is a teacup. However, the actual perception and experience of the teacup is really multi-determined by many internal and external factors such as: past experiences, light, shadows, and vantage point, etc. Bion uses painting as an example in his discussion of transformations. He argues that each individual's experience and perception of any particular scene will be expressed differently in the resulting artistic production. Bion notes that through what he calls an invariant—the transformation between objects of perception, a field of poppies in his example— the artist's process and the final rendition of the field on the canvas will be recognizable to the viewer as a field of poppies, but if you think about how

Picasso, for example, and Van Gogh would paint the same image, you can see how differently they would come out.

Karmic Formations and the Enactment of Transference and Countertransference

This point can be developed further from a Buddhist perspective by considering the notion of karma—simply translated as action or activity—and *samskara* or karmic formations, which can be thought of as underlying, often unconscious, preconceptions and repetitive organizing principles. From this Buddhist perspective the activities, perceptions, and interactions with the environment that influence each individual's experience, result in a unique perception of reality and each individual's unique patterned way of being in the world. Over time, these influences develop into unique, consistent, habitual, and often automatic and unconsciously motivated ways of perceiving and interacting with the world both internally and in terms of interpersonal relations. Habit formations are unreal, but they have very real consequences when they are not addressed. For example, misperceiving a friendly stranger as a dangerous threat that leads to a violent encounter, such as the recent murder of Ahmaud Arbrey in Georgia, tragically and poignantly exemplifies this problem. On the other hand, from the Buddhist perspective, conscious awareness of internalized habit formations holds the potential to transform fear, hate, greed, and aggression into wisdom and compassionate actions.

In the psychoanalytic situation, the enactment of transference and countertransference dynamics, when not addressed, can be acted out with negative consequences. The repetitive quality of *samskaras* finds visual representation in the Buddhist *Bhavachakra*, the wheel of life and death. At the second link of dependent origination there is a potter at the wheel who enacts the pattern of continuously making the same pot repeatedly. It brings to mind the expression, "Ignorance is doing the same thing over and over again and expecting to get a different result."

Experience as Primary for Buddhist Practitioner and Psychoanalyst

As I see it, experience is primary for both the Zen practitioner and the psychoanalyst. Cognition is secondary. For example, two therapists will have the same experiential understanding of the patient's state of being. However, any response, such as an interpretation, will depend on what theories any individual analyst has internalized. For example, a classical Freudian might emphasize the libidinal and aggressive drives. A self-psychologist will emphasize the self-state of the patient. As an alternative, emphasizing experience opens the gate to entering an approach to psychoanalysis, by way of John Milton, who Bion quotes, "The rising world of waters, dark and deep are won from the void and formless infinite." Milton argues that opening into this formless void, this intuitive reality, requires moment-to-moment presence by the action of relinquishing sensory input. This is the rationale for Bion's recommendation to relinquish memory, desire, and understanding. Bion's mandate includes, for example, a memory, a wish for a result or some kind of understanding. In other words, previous learning needs to be set aside, including what the therapist has previously learned about the patient. Bion's approach is extremely radical in this respect, and it's also all-inclusive. For example, he writes, "The psychoanalysts should aim at achieving a state of mind so that every session he feels he has not seen the patient before. If he feels he has, he's treating the wrong patient" (Bion, 1967/2013, p. 138) This is Bion's version of being as present in the moment as possible.

Similarly, Dōgen advocates bringing the intention of *mushotoku*, or "no gain in mind" to the Zen practice of *shikantaza*, or "just sitting." In this way the practitioner sits with whatever rises and falls free from attachment or aversion. He describes this process poignantly in *Zanmai O Zanmai*, "The Samadhi that is the King of Samadhis" (1244/1997):

> Just in the moment of sitting, investigate whether the universe is vertical, and whether it is horizontal. Just in the moment of sitting, what is the sitting itself? Is it a somersault? Is it a state of vigorous activity? Is it thinking? Is it beyond thinking? Is it doing something? Is it not doing anything? Is it sitting inside of sitting? Is it sitting inside of the body-mind? Is it sitting that is free of "the inside of sitting," "the inside of the body-mind," and so on? There should be investigation of thousands and tens of thousands of points like these. Sit in the full lotus posture with the body. Sit in the full lotus posture with the mind. Sit in the full lotus posture being free of body and mind.
>
> (p. 281)

The Impact of *Zazen* on the Practicing Therapist

My interest in the primacy of experience that I have so far shared with you also extends to how practices such as *zazen*, that is, Zen meditation, a Buddhist sitting meditation, fundamentally impact the practicing therapist. Not necessarily as a technique to introduce to the patient, rather as a way for the therapist to better understand their unconscious motivations and the infinite creative possibilities that have the potential of becoming open in the psychoanalytic encounter. As a therapist, if you take on the commitment to meditate, "As if your head were on fire," to quote an old Zen proverb, it's going to influence you. It's going to have an impact on the way you are in the world—what I like to call your mode of being in the world—and influence the unconscious. Our mode of being in the world is going to influence other people, and it's not limited to psychotherapy, but that's certainly an area of focus here.

After Eihei Dōgen went on a retreat in China looking for true dharma, and returned to Japan, he wrote in his chapter *Genjōkōan*—which means manifesting or actualizing present reality—that Buddhists, being Buddhists, do not know they are being Buddhists. Now, what does that mean? Well, to me, it means that somehow our practice has affected how we are in the world. It might be something really simple. For example, how do you greet a new patient when they come to see you for the first time? They come to you, a stranger, to share—or try to share—their problems that they are anxious about. How do you greet them? To me, the idea of a mode of being in the world is very important. In other words, can we simply be who we are? For me, I often notice retrospectively that a confrontational situation with someone goes differently than how I would have handled it in the past. It works out, and two people make a compromise and walk away somewhat happy. It's like, "Wow, I handled that differently," but it's more of a retrospective thing. We're always keeping an eye on ourselves in that regard. As Dōgen writes in *Bendowa*, "Wholehearted Practice of the Way," "Because practice is just experience, the experience is endless; and because experience is practice, the practice has no beginning" (Dōgen, 1231/1994, p. 12).

The particular form of Zen Buddhist meditation that I mentioned above and emphasize is called *shikantaza* in Japanese. *Shikantaza* means just sitting, or only sitting, and that's all we do. There's no mantra, there's nothing to concentrate on. No visualization, no goal, no object of attention. We just sit. That's my practice and the practice of the Zen teachers who have directly influenced me. Most importantly, I feel that it's the most compatible practice with the highly subjective experience-based internal listening and intuitional process that is unique to psychoanalytic therapy when conducted from, what I like to describe as, a realizational perspective.[1]

When I first started practicing psychoanalysis in 1986, I maintained, in retrospect, a rather rigid boundary between psychotherapy and Buddhist practices. My orientation was primarily classical at the time. However, over time, this

early position softened over the years through the support and encouragement of my colleagues and teachers.

I now frequently find myself in a position of asking during an initial consultation whether the individual is seeking me out as a psychotherapist or
as a Buddhist teacher. Of course, I'm both, and both will be present during
sessions because I'm, of course, one person, and I've been deeply influenced
by both practices. The influence of both practices has become internalized
which deeply affects my mode of being in the world. However, the emphasis
that I take, and my responses, will shift depending on the needs and concerns
and interests of both students and patients.

The Experience of *Shikantaza*

Since I've been talking about experience, I'd like to bring you into the experience of the *shikantaza* form of meditation, which Dōgen really doesn't refer to
as meditation. In fact, in *Fukanzazengi*, "Universal Promotion of the Principles
of *Zazen*," he writes, "The *zazen* I speak of is not learning meditation. It is
simply the Dharma gate of repose and bliss" (Dōgen, 1227/2002, p. 4). (His
perspective has a history to it as it is a critique of some early misconceptions
from centuries before him.) *Zazen* is a blanket term that covers many forms
of Zen practice. For example, the *zuisokukan* method of following the breath;
susokukan, the practice of counting the breath, *kanna-zen*, or koan concentration; and *shikantaza*, just sitting, which is my preferred form in relation to my
clinical work.

Shikantaza, is a non-concentrative, goalless and objectless form of *zazen* practice that functions as an all-inclusive awareness. Preparing for meditation,
for *shikantaza*, is very important. It's a very important aspect of the practice,
just as important as the practice itself. It is the practice. Preparation is the
practice. There's no difference. This way, everything becomes practice. We
bring the mind of *zazen* to all of our activities. Make your preparations with
the same mindful and attentive awareness that you give to the *shikantaza*
session itself. This will help bring your practice into your everyday life more
effectively and increase the benefit.

Here are some keys to igniting an effective practice. Begin by making sure that
you're very comfortable. Whether you're sitting on a *zafu*, a cushion, a chair
or a bench, it's really important to be comfortable. A relaxed posture makes a
calm mind. A calm mind makes a comfortable body. If you are not comfortable, you'll become preoccupied with the discomfort, and the discomfort will

ironically become a source of attention or an object of your meditation. Even though it's an irritating object, it still becomes an object. We don't fix our attention on anything except what we might call the basic ground of being. We remain open to all experience, both internally and externally, as the present moment continuously evolves and changes.

Now that you're comfortably seated, just check that your spine is erect but not stiff. The shoulders are relaxed. The chin is tucked in a bit so the back of the neck stretches a little in response. Next, place your right hand in your lap with your palm facing up. Gently rest your left hand in your right palm so that the tips of your thumbs are gently touching, as if you are holding a very thin piece of paper with your thumb tips. This position of the hands is called the Cosmic Mudra. During practice, if you feel pressure or tension in your thumbs, or notice that you're pressing your thumbs together tightly, that means you're working too hard. You're taking a middle way here. Not too easy, not too hard. You can back off mentally, readjust your thumbs and your posture, and reset yourself. If your thumbs drift apart, you're probably drifting off on a train of thought, daydreaming, or maybe even falling asleep. Again, just simply readjust yourself.

Next, gently rock your body slightly back and forth, and from side to side, to find your own balance point, and then simply be still. This rocking also helps to ground you in the present moment. In *shikantaza* we sit with our eyes open. Notice that your eyes are open about halfway. The gaze is set at about a 45-degree angle to the floor. Open eyes help to prevent sleep and daydreaming and represent being open to all of reality. Just like *Avalokiteshvara*, the Bodhisattva of compassion, has many arms open to all beings. In *shikantaza* we let all reality flow through us without judgment or preferences and without trying to block out anything. No picking or choosing. Remember, we're just sitting. If you are new to sitting with your eyes open, you might have some difficulty at first. Your eyes might close. That's only natural and it's okay. Simply notice that you're sitting with your eyes closed. When you're ready, gently open them again and continue. No judgment, no pressure, no forcefulness. Just sitting. Keep in mind that you're centered in the middle, relaxed. Not lazy, firm. Not rigid or forced.

I'll explain here why sitting with your eyes open is important. When we sit with eyes open, we maintain a soft focus. We're not concentrating on anything which can create an alteration in perception, rather eyes open can help us experience a shift in perception where our vision becomes wider. With extended practice, we start to take in a whole universe, everything, even if we don't see it. That leaves us more widely open for taking in our clients' or our patients' experiences. I mentioned before that I like to share why I use this particular style of meditation in relation to psychotherapy, and that's why. We're not concentrating on something like, "When is he or she going to talk about that thing that they brought up last month?" That blinds us. Instead, can we be wide open to experiences like stepping into a big globe and there're no channels or pathways except for the ones that we create ourselves? Here's a haiku I wrote to illustrate this:

> Morning walk;
> no footprints in the snow—
> but those left behind.

Can we do the morning walk with our patients or our clients and let them show us the footprints?

Next, three rings of the bell is a traditional Zen Buddhist signal that we're about to start a period of meditation. When you hear the bell, allow yourself to hear it with your whole being. Feel it with your body. If your thoughts take over, as they often do, simply come back to the sound and the feel of the bell. This attention to the bell sound is called the *samadhi* of the bell. *Samadhi* means absorption. Fully soak up the sound.

As the sound fades, become aware of the deep sense of peaceful presence and sense of grounding in the moment that you feel. Now exhale through the nose completely and take a slow, full, deep inhalation, feeling the tummy, the abdomen, and the chest filling up and expanding without straining. When you reach capacity, very slowly exhale, letting all of the air out until the tummy contracts. The next inhalation will come by itself, as if the breath is breathing you. You can do this breath practice a couple of times. This will refresh you and help you develop a non-grasping attitude toward the meditation. In Zen, we call this attitude *mushotoku* or "no gain in mind." Now simply allow the breath to rise and fall at its own pace.

During the meditation, you'll sometimes notice the breath and sometimes you won't. Some folks count the breath, or concentrate on the breathing, or follow the breathing. In this practice, we simply notice the breath when we do, and we don't notice it when we don't. It's the same with sounds, with thoughts or any other sense input. At the end of the practice you can ring a bell that'll signal the end of the session. Once your sitting is over, begin to move very slowly. No rushing. Maybe you want to stretch out your legs or roll your head a little bit if you need to. You can also pause for a moment and ask, "Do things feel different now than they did before we sat?"

To me, *shikantaza* helps with how we are listening to our patients and clients. It helps keep the field open in a different way. Buddhist traditions talk about the concept of skillful means and offer lots of practices and medicines, if you will, for lots of unique individuals. Every legitimate method has its purpose and place. I'm not a critical of the different methods. I'm just pointing out that I find this particular method especially useful for the practicing psychotherapists.[2]

If you do the *shikantaza* practice, if you think you want to investigate it and give it a shot, I recommend just doing it for a few minutes so you don't have a boomerang effect of overdoing it and then not doing it again. Five or ten minutes a day is plenty until you can build it up to between 25 and 40 minutes. Remember, since there's no goal, no gain in mind, we're expressing our enlightened being, we're not looking for it. And since there's no goal, starting over again is not really starting over again, is it? Because we weren't going anywhere. As Zen teachers often say, to paraphrase a common Zen truth, if it's not right here, where is it? If it's not right now, when is it? The same with Bion, if it's not right now, it's not important. If I'm having a particular day where something's just caught ahold of my head, I'll just ring the bell right in the middle of my meditation period and start all over again and re-presence myself. So how does *shikantaza* practice help us when we are with our patients and clients? Let's look at a case study.

A Case Study

I refer to this person as Aida. Aida was a young woman, and we had been working together for quite a while. She expressed some concerns regarding her feeling very sensitive and vulnerable to "crossing boundaries." She said to me, "How can I make any impositions on you or expect any favors from you?" I said, "In terms of what?" She then hesitatingly explained that she needed to reschedule our sessions to accommodate changes in her new work schedule. The required change was related to a promotion that she had successfully competed for and had just been awarded. Her increased responsibilities as a project manager demanded increased hours and possibly unpredictable work schedule. We had covered various versions of this situation many times, and both knew the transference origins of her sensitivity, of her vulnerability, and her hesitation. We both knew why this felt to Aida like an imposition and evoked the fear of crossing boundaries. This time we simply continued to silently sit together with our concerns, with our feelings, with the situation, and with her internal fears, and her very real needs.

She soon began to describe a feeling of calmness and peace, which surprised me, but that's what happened. The session ended, and she left without further dialogue between us except for the usual, "See you tomorrow." The following day, Aida arrived 20 minutes early. She usually arrives right on time, if not a few minutes late. I asked her about it by simply saying, "Oh, you arrived early today." That's a notation. It's just noticing like when you're sitting in *shikantaza*, you're just noticing. I didn't want to make a big deal out of it. So I noted, "You arrived early today." She said that she had wanted to recapture the feeling of well-being she felt when sat together the day before. She began the session by explaining her understanding of the transference dynamics. In her experience, any shift on my part, either toward her or away from her, such as through making an interpretation, would have destroyed the intimacy of the silence that she was feeling and would have felt like an abandonment to her. Whether the interpretation was accurate or not, I would have been experienced by her as abandoning the experiential space of the silently lived moment. I would have disrupted the deep connection that she was feeling in the moment through the shared silence. If you are a self-psychologist, for example, you might interpret the disruption and generate what we would call a transmuting internalization. We create a shift in our psychic structure supposedly to the better, but in this situation, I believe that an interpretation would have functioned as a resistance on my part to the evolution of what Bion refers to as the "O" or the emotional truth of the session and to the unitive nature of the experiential moment.

We pursued this shared understanding further in the following session: Aida's self-hatred, which she experienced as her greed and aggression, with her wish for making a request that felt like a violation of our boundaries. She also felt that I would view her as greedy and aggressive for competing for the promotion and higher salary. She was afraid that I would view her negatively and then I would act out my negativity by withdrawing my attention, or even with harsh criticism. This was far from the truth because my counter-transference reaction was more like, "Oh, good, she's getting a raise. I can raise her fee. She's paying me a very low fee from a clinic."

Two different realities happening in one place. She experienced her promotion and her increase in salary as manifestations of greed and aggression and imagined that I would be judgmental of her achievement. We both understood the early object relations that perpetuated her fears as they have been spoken about many times before during our work together. These self-perceptions and imagined expectations of my reactions, we discovered, despite their harshness, actually felt safer for her than the deeper more vulnerable feelings that were emerging with my undivided attention and silent presence no matter what. Aida imagined that she would be aggressive if she had asserted these needs. As I noted, she also considered her wish to express her needs as a violation of our boundaries. She was welling over with feelings and fear that she would "flood the room and wash me away." Not unlike her early objects. I simply could not and would not handle them. She wondered if I would be strong enough, compassionate enough, and present enough to willingly sit with and hold her feelings, which she felt were an acknowledgment of her needs, her hunger, and longings. In short, when I love her unconditionally, no matter what, my capacity for acceptance to love unconditionally meant sitting still, staying right where I was, in the present moment, attending to the moment, embracing the moment in full acceptance of what the Zen teacher Shunryu Suzuki often describes as, "Being as it is." Together, could we, as the old Zen teaching story asserts, "taste the strawberries?"

At this point, she said that she felt anxious, but it was a good kind of anxiety. She said that there was something fundamentally anxious about feeling fully alive, mutually present, and feeling loved. From Bion's perspective, we might say that Aida communicated the importance and significance of true and genuine presence in the not knowing, and sitting with, and patiently waiting for, the evolution of the uniqueness of Aida's "O" or emotional truth. This is what Bion (1970), quoting the poet John Keats, called "being in uncertainties, mysteries, doubts, without irritable reaching after fact and reason" (p. 125). In contrast, though, and this is a point of difference that I think is important, Dōgen views the truth as always present. Waiting for evolution is not necessary. In this regard, I could respond only to Aida being as she is, in the present moment, or as the psychoanalyst Thomas Ogden describes it: "Without trying to ferret out what the story was really about" (2004, p. 297). The story was not about anything. The story was the story. O is O. In conclusion, we could say that Aida's experience, I hope, conveys the difference between talking about an experience, such as through an interpretation, and simply being the experience of the evolving now of the emotional truth of the session.

Some psychotherapists who I have shared Aida's case with have been surprised that I would sit in silence for a period of time with my patients. They have seen this as something unusual and wonder how long the silence lasted. I've had sessions where there was no talk at all for the entire session, which would have been 45 minutes, not with Aida, but with other patients. The question becomes, "What is sitting in silence like for you as the therapist?" The intuition comes out of a process that psychoanalysts refer to as projective identification. That's where the intuition comes from. Now, some psychoanalysts and other traditions might call it intuition or empathic attunement, or what Freud (1912/1958) describes as follows,

> The technique, however, is a very simple one. As we shall see, it rejects the use of any special expedient (even that of taking notes). It consists simply in not directing one's notice to anything in particular and in maintaining the same "evenly-suspended attention" (as I have called it) in the face of all that one hears.
>
> *(p. 111)*

The bottom line is there's an experience. What is that experience communicating? It's a very important question to ask yourself, "What is it like for me to sit with a patient in those moments?" Does it make you feel anxious, neglect or ignored? Does it make you tired or sleepy? Does it make you impatient? Does it make you feel like you have to say something? In the case of Aida there was a very deep sense of intimacy when we sat in silence together. We both seemed to be tolerating it. But what if there was a sense of intimacy and one of us was not tolerating it? As a psychoanalyst, I might make some clever interpretation that really functions as a resistance to get off the hot seat, but what happens if you just stay with that silent, intimate moment? Now, with some patients I might say, "I noticed that you got quiet," or, "Oh, where did your thoughts go off to?" With Aida I felt that we had worked long enough together and there was enough mutual trust. And it is not just the patient feeling trust in me as the analyst, but I have to feel trust in the patient too. We're both human beings, we are both vulnerable. I believe that, in this case, there was enough of that to be able to stay in the snow without the footprints.

I think it is important to ask ourselves, "Can we let the intimacy evolve?" Here is an example in the opposite direction. There's been a lot written in the psychoanalytic literature, especially in the mid-80s, about how mindfulness practice helps to increase your attention; your ability to attend to a patient's free association; and therefore increases psychoanalytic listening. What about the value of inattention? What if you're not paying attention to the patient? Do you beat yourself up over it? "I don't like this guy. Let see what time it is. Oh, another half an hour. Oh, boy." Do you beat yourself up for not being attentive? Or do you take a backward step and notice it, and turn your subjective experience into an objective experience and ask yourself the questions: "Where is this intention coming from?" "What does it tell me about the internal object world of the patient?" "Who is inattentive to him or her?" "What does he know about inattention in his or her own life?" Those are the questions we need to ask. "Was he an inattentive little rascal?" "Was mom or dad inattentive to him?" Now we're experiencing it. We're living it. Can we live and sit with it and tolerate it long enough until an awareness evolves and maybe we could say something? With these kinds of experiences, I usually won't say anything until I can connect it to their narrative. Otherwise, I might get, "Oh, what the hell are you talking about?" Bion talks about digesting the experience and feeding it back to the patient in a useful way.

When sitting with a patient, it's important to maintain an open mind, fully receptive to the awareness of what might be intuited. It is equally important to attuning to what is being communicated unconsciously beyond words through this process of projective identification, or whatever you might call it depending on your theoretical orientation. What parallels, intersections, identities are evolving into the moment? What arises spontaneously? What thoughts, feelings, memories, anticipations? Yes, they might be about you. For instance, a memory that arises in you spontaneously, what Bion would describe as an evolution, might certainly be your memory. However, I believe that we need to ask ourselves, "Why is this memory coming up now at this moment with this particular person? What does this experience, this memory, tell me about this person's inner life?"

As I mentioned before, we take a subjective experience like a particular memory, feeling, thought train, bodily experience, and turn it into Thomas Ogden's term "an object of analysis." For example, I experience a moment of impatience. I glance at the clock. I wonder when this session will be over. Sure, it's my real reaction. I need to own that, but why is it coming up now with this particular person? Let's keep in mind that from this perspective—which I describe as a realizational perspective—all of experience is fundamentally neutral without exception. I want to say that again, all experience, internal or relational, is fundamentally neutral without exception. This includes the experience of impatience that I just noted. This also includes, and this is important because quite a bit has been written regarding how Buddhist meditation can deepen attention, but attention to what? What happens is, and I say this about the meditation practice and I say this about our work as healers, our relationship to the experience will determine whether it's a negative, positive, or continues to be neutral. Dōgen and Bion were both very big on that, on the relationship, not the object. For Bion, the object would maybe be the patient or some figure from the patient's past. For Dōgen, the object would be whatever is predominant in a consciousness at a particular moment.

Concluding Comments

As I mentioned in my opening comments, both Buddhism and psychoanalysis emphasize the primacy of experience. This emphasis functions as a potent connecting thread between these two disciplines. However, it must be kept in mind that they are clearly not identical. Rather, to varying degrees, depending on the Buddhist sect and the various psychoanalytic theories, they both contain areas of identity, areas of similarity, and unrelatable differences. As a result, many unique "blends" have been developing over the past several decades.

This discussion has centered on one specific integration that draws from Wilfred Bion's psychoanalytic ideas and the Soto Zen Buddhist work of the 13th-century monk and teacher Eihei Dōgen. Given this highly subjective and experiential emphasis advocated by Bion and Dōgen, I would like to conclude this discussion with a few questions. What was your experience of reading this text? What did it evoke in you? Hopefully, you will experience openings into your own creative peregrinations. What is your experience of the individuals with whom you work? What do they evoke in you? How does your innate capacity for empathy, intuition, compassion, and wisdom evolve for you? How do these capacities change, grow, expand, and affect your mode of being in the world? I personally believe that these are ongoing questions that we need to constantly ask ourselves to keep our analytic instrument honed and sharp. Perhaps you can add your own unique questions so that, to quote Bion:

> The theoretical implications can be worked out by each psychoanalyst for himself. His interpretations should gain in force and conviction—both for himself and his patient—because they derive from the emotional experience with a unique individual and not from generalized theories imperfectly "remembered."
>
> (Bion, 1967/2013, p. 138)

Notes

1 For a detailed explication on "Realizational Perspective" see: Cooper, P. (2020). Realizational Perspectives: Bion's Psychoanalysis and Dogen's Zen, *American Journal of Psychoanalysis*, 80, pp. 37–52.
   Also: Cooper, P. (In Press). *Psychoanalysis and Zen Buddhism: A Realizational Perspective.* London: Routledge.
2 To listen to Seiso Paul guide *hikantaza* visit https://soundcloud.com/paul-cooper -290569931/basic-fact-of-sitting-12-20-2020mp3

8
Toward an LGBTQ+ Affirmative Approach to Contemplative Psychotherapy

Moustafa Abdelrahman

Differentiating General Stressors and Minority Stressors

As human beings, we have a fundamental need to connect with each other in safety; to care and be cared for. It is through social connections that we thrive. Similarly, when social connections are under threat, our instinctual stress reactivity is invoked as a way to survive. Researcher Amy Edmondson coined the phenomenon "psychological safety," an inherited safety-in-numbers notion, more commonly known today as pack mentality or herd mentality (Edmondson, 1999, 2019). The pack mentality is governed by the pecking order of societal hierarchies. From this perspective, unfortunately, the social need to connect and belong is frequently defined by heteronormative structures. Divergence from societal norms is often met with an underlying sense of fear, correction, and even hostility towards what is unfamiliar and different. Hence, it is crucial to recognize that both visibly and non-visibly identifiable minority communities take on unique and hostile everyday life stressors that intersect in complex ways with their multiplicity of identities.

The Lesbian, Gay, Bisexual, Pansexual, Transgender, Gender Queer, Queer, Intersex, Agender, Asexual, and other Queer-identifying communities, commonly abbreviated as the LGBTQ+ community, experiences a wide range of social stressors above and beyond general population stressors. LGBTQ+ individuals' experience of stress is not only caused by single isolated events but also by years and years of everyday prejudices that are pervasive across different stages of life. Some examples of these stressors arise from conscious or unconscious familial rejection; internal conflict during identity development; the tribulations of coming out; challenges in relationship development; and

DOI: 10.4324/9781003243588-9

the isolation and mistreatment of elderly members of the LGBTQ+ community in senior homes.

Despite the advancement in mental health studies, the research and literature on stress and healing are often limited to heteronormative structures and cultures, which may further hinder clinicians' understanding of the LGBTQ+ community's needs and effective therapies. The concept of minority stress (Brooks, 1981; Meyer, 1995) was originally developed as a framework to help psychologists understand sexual orientation-based stressors and may also be applicable to gender-variant stressors. The framework describes minority stress as "the relationship between minority and dominant values and resultant conflict with the social environment experienced by minority group members" (Meyer, 1995; Ross & Mirowsky, 1989; Pearlin, 1989).

Reflecting on LGBTQ+ Stressors

Based on the minority stress model, LGBTQ+ individuals face two distinct types of stressors: objective and subjective. Objective stress relates to the pressure caused by external factors or conditions in the individual's hostile environment. This includes long-term discrimination and victimization, which can manifest in various ways such as harassment, verbal abuse, non-affirmation, maltreatment, exclusion, isolation, stalking, and assault. LGBTQ+ people are susceptible to these stressful and devastating events being inflicted consciously or unconsciously by loved ones such as friends and family, as well as different segments of one's social structure, including schoolmates, teachers, employers, colleagues, mentors, heroes, religious leaders, healers, therapists, politicians, police, lawmakers, acquaintances, and even strangers.

Subjective stress, on the other hand, is frequently caused by identity concealment and internalized homonegativity brought about by the awareness or expectations of social stigma and rejection. Being in an environment plagued by objective stressors for an extended period of time can condition LGBTQ+ individuals to construct a negative and conforming judgment of themselves and other members of the LGBTQ+ community.

From childhood and throughout life, many gender and sexual minority groups are taught negative overt or covert messages about themselves that perpetuate an endless cycle of self-stigma and shame. These include the idea that being different is wrong, immoral, or unworthy, and that you should not be yourself. Otherwise, you are deemed unlovable. These messages are often internalized as homonegative self-schemas that impact mental health and can manifest in subtle and not-so-subtle ways. Some examples include denial of sexual orientation or gender identity, excessive rumination, attempts to conceal or change oneself, feelings of fear, shame or anger, low self-esteem, compulsive behavior, heterophobia, projection of stigma to other members of the LGBTQ+ community or other minority groups, harm to self or others, and developing a contingent sense of self-worth and perfectionism in other areas of life as a bid for external validation and acceptance.

The notion of stress as subjective, or an appraisal process of one's challenges and resources opens up the possibility for cultivating coping skills and resilience in the face of minority stress. This appraisal process can include cognitive reframing and flexibility, emotional regulation, positive self-regard, and cultivating a support system.

The Role of Therapeutic Alliance

It is sometimes difficult to distinguish between mental health challenges caused by minority stress versus other psychological factors. As clinicians and healers, it is pivotal to grasp that prejudice and social discrimination play a role in causing psychological distress (Meyer, 2003), which requires the development of coping strategies for LGBTQ+ clients that affirm a positive self-identity. This LGBTQ+ affirmative stance encourages therapists to become culturally competent and well-versed in the challenges experienced by the LGBTQ+ community; and to work through their own biases and comfort level to discuss and hold space for these challenges as a necessary step in establishing an affirming therapeutic relationship which Fassinger et al. (2010) describes as a "warm, supportive, and unconditionally respectful relationship." Meyer's (2003) minority stress model, Feinstein's (2020) rejection sensitivity model, Cass's (1984) identity formation model, and Testa and colleagues' (2015) gender minority stress and resilience measure, offer useful frameworks that identify LGBTQ+ specific stress processes, including but not limited to prejudice, discrimination, fear of rejection, internalized stigma, negative expectations for the future, and other ameliorative coping processes.

Toward an Affirmative Approach to Contemplative Psychotherapy

A contemplative therapeutic approach is an integration of modern psychotherapeutic modalities, informed by scientific research, with traditional contemplative practices, most notably, mindfulness and compassion-based interventions. The synergies between these Western and Eastern practices have been advanced through ongoing dialogue between scientists and Buddhist practitioners, and were further ignited by breakthroughs in neuroscience. There is growing evidence (Kabat-Zinn et al., 1992; Segal et al., 2013; Siegel, 2007; Loizzo et al., 2009) that provides insights into the benefits of contemplative therapy, including fostering a supportive client learning environment, lowering sympathetic arousal, facilitating neural integration, cultivating attention and self-awareness, and supporting introspection and corrective dialogue. Contemplative practices that support mindfulness and compassion encourage such introspection and intersubjectivity, providing helpful tools that cultivate LGBTQ+ individuals' capacity to recognize the reactivity associated with stigma stress and develop the resilience to shift into self-care.

The Wisdom of Fullness of Being

From a developmental perspective, starting at an early age, we gradually develop over time the illusion of a unitary fixed sense of self. This is described in Buddhist psychology as self-reification and a misperception of self. Within our family of origin, often, there are unspoken messages about which self-states are favored and which ones are unfavored. Children are often faced with two choices in response to those messages, either a) rebel and push away the unfavored self-states and risk losing the loving connection with caregivers, or b) use dissociation to try to split off from the unwanted self-states or unaccepted parts of self. It is common for a child to feel consciously or unconsciously pressured into expressing the parts of themselves that the family structure finds most lovable, even if this leaves the child feeling inauthentic or frustrated. Having psychic distance from the parts of one's being that are not favorably responded to by loved ones, close community, and the dominant culture does not mean that these parts go away. For example, one might be inclined to project unwanted parts into others (projective identification) and relate to the other as if this is their dominant part (e.g., homophobia). Philip M. Bromberg (1996) argues that a person's ability to live with both authenticity and self-awareness depends on the presence of an ongoing dialectic between separateness and unity of one's self-states, allowing each self to function optimally without foreclosing communication and negotiation between them.

From this perspective, integration is the process of standing in the space between all wanted and unwanted parts with non-judgmental awareness and loving-kindness instead of trying to merge or change these parts. This is the wisdom of knowing the fullness of being, rather than negating or bypassing parts of our humanness. Instead, the totality of our experience is embraced with acceptance and kindness. Accordingly, healing can begin when the therapist becomes highly attuned in a non-coercive fashion to the client's shifting states of mind which may include the parts of self that are protective and rigid, the parts that are frustrated, the parts that are longing and wanting to be felt, and the parts that are spontaneous. Gradually, both therapist and client can begin to map out and name these different parts so that the client can experience themself with enough sense of safety to withstand other people's input without it threatening to overwhelm their experience of selfhood or reactively dissociating some parts of themself.

Similarly, according to Buddhist teachings (Thurman, 2005), the main cause of suffering is our misperception that a static and absolute self (an independent essence) exists. A simple example of this is mistaking the empirical "I," "me," "mine" for our true self. This misperception leads to self-protection through clinging or avoiding (suffering). Self, in reality, is multiple, both uniquely relational and uniquely individual. From a Buddhist perspective, it is through self-investigation to locate the "absolute self" that one discovers that an unrelated or isolated self is nowhere to be found. One also discovers that all the components that make up the self are constantly changing. Buddhist psychology term these components as aggregates and they include the physical body, sensations, thoughts, emotions, and consciousness. Upon reflection, one can recognize self as a relative, open, flexible, adaptable, and ever-changing field of awareness. With this recognition, both relative and conventional absolute sense of self can become self-complementary.

Bringing into therapy this definition of self as inherently changing and relational helps challenge the cycle of stress that is fueled by static and absolute self-schemas, such as "I am unlovable" or "I am a shameful." When negative self-schemas arise, they trigger negative emotions. Negative emotions then drive reactive behavior and habits, such as fear of negative evaluation and social avoidance and distress, to which the client's external environment responds by confirming the self-schema. This does not negate the importance of addressing and eliminating objective external stressors. However, investigating the suffering that comes from the illusion that there exists an independent and invariable self offers the potential to break the cycle of stress-stigma and shame, as it relates to subjective stress. Being able to break this cycle allows the client to step back from the negative self-schemas, find support, and shift into a more resilient mindset.

From a clinical perspective, this approach could be viewed as deep affect therapy that connects clients to the core of their being from a deeply positive space. This slowly helps them to unlearn maladaptive and protective habits of stress reactivity by relaxing the dualistic fixations of self/other and gradually expanding the window of tolerance to different experiences. This includes dissolving the grip of negative core beliefs about self, such as shame, into the totality of one's true nature where there is no idealized state to reach.

Integrating Whole Self through Mindfulness

Thanks to research on neuroplasticity, we know that the brain keeps remodeling (rewiring) itself throughout life, and day-to-day experiences can have measurable effects on brain structure and function. With this empowering understanding, both client and therapist can explore mindful awareness as a training to cultivate intrapersonal attunement to help balance existing stress stigma biases. Within the safety of the therapeutic relationship, mindfulness practices can help clients shift from autopilot reactive states by developing non-judgmental open-focused attention in the present moment – a state of awareness where clients can live life as it unfolds and access a range of choices to respond in helpful adaptive ways.

An affirming approach to mindfulness is one that recognizes that the intention of the practice is not to bypass aspects of oneself or to practice with the goal of adapting to heteronormative social values and norms of "good" and "bad," as this is a recipe for more suffering. It is through accepting and welcoming deeper vulnerabilities that one can be wholly present with these experiences and, in turn, be able to access more of who we are. By bringing equanimity to our psychic reality and our inner life, nothing needs to stay concealed, including the parts that we dislike, feel foreign, are frustrating, etc. Together, the client and therapist can bring non-judgmental and kind awareness to the multiplicity and fullness of self as it comes to light. Meanwhile, gradually expanding the client's window of tolerance for oneself and others. This is the therapeutic scaffolding through which clients can shift back to cognitive, emotional, and embodied states of resilience.

Practicing mindfulness in this context is not limited to relaxation or short-term stress management techniques. Beloved Buddhist teacher, author, and nun Pema Chödron describes this process perfectly when she says, "Meditation practice is not about trying to throw ourselves away and become something better. It is about befriending who we already are" (Chödrön, 1991). This not only includes the parts of ourselves that are loving, generous, grateful, and forgiving but also the parts that are jealous, angry, shameful, and fearful. All of these parts make us perfectly human.

Compassion: An Act of Declaring Love for That Which Society Imposes Stigma

Compassion involves both the heartfelt wish that all beings be free from suffering and the readiness to act on their behalf. It arises from a deep sense of affection for others. According to a growing body of research, compassion can be trained. In one study published in *Psychological Science* (Weng et al., 2013), researchers found that not only can adults learn to be more compassionate, but teaching compassion could also result in more altruistic behaviors and lead to changes in the brain.

As a therapist, compassionately embracing what arises in session for the client as well oneself is key. For the client, being told that something that feels natural is wrong from an early age (such as sexual attraction or gender identity) can result in distrusting their own emotions and disconnecting from their own needs. This is an outcome that can limit emotional awareness, affect tolerance, and emotional regulation. The introduction of compassion-based practices in session can be beneficial as it can help clients cultivate emotional resilience in the face of past trauma and emotional dysregulation.

Self-compassion can be a powerful coping resource (Vettese et al., 2011) and an antidote to self-stigma stressors such as shame, emotional dysregulation, and relational difficulties. Through non-judgmental awareness in the present moment, LGBTQ+ individuals can begin adopting an attitude of kindness and genuine care towards themselves during the process of reappraisal and restructuring of homonegative schemas. This may include the positive regard of LGBTQ+ gender identity and sex as natural, validating all the positive aspects of oneself, and recognizing that one is not alone or isolated in the experience of suffering as it is a common experience for all humans.

Instead of editing or changing oneself, self-compassion allows one to gradually cultivate an attitude of kindness toward inner experiences, including thoughts, memories, images, beliefs, emotions, and sensations. Gently inviting all aspects of oneself to show up in practice: 1) the aspects that are admired and proudly shown to the outside world, 2) the aspects that are neutral, fairly common or even unknown and mysterious and 3) the aspects that vulnerable, challenging, disliked, suppressed, or shunned away. Self-compassion is a practice of learning to gradually be with and integrate the whole of oneself in the present moment. welcoming what arises so that all aspects of oneself may be seen, held, soothed, and loved in awareness. To quote Marian Caplan (2012),

> Learning to soften into ourselves is a skill that is often learned rather than innate. Our deep vulnerabilities are revealed and integrated through skillful and loving approaches to the trauma and psychological wounding that resides within. The interior walls that separate us from ourselves and the world are penetrated through self-love rather than smashed with the wrecking ball of forceful techniques. There are no shortcuts.

A Supportive and Loving Community

Besides our basic survival needs for food, water, and shelter, neuroscientists have marked human connection as equally fundamental for our survival. To build resilience, we need to feel accepted, loved, valued, and have personal protective structures such as family, society, and the environment (Dale et al., 2014). This need for interpersonal connection has been embedded into our psyche for millions of evolutionary years (Lieberman, 2013). This is a basic need that can only be fulfilled by an emotional bond with other people. However, given the social stressors placed on LGBTQ+ individuals, they often experience interpersonal challenges throughout their lives as a result of minority stress. Given that same-sex couples can face rejection and devaluation of their relationship from family and friends (LeBlanc et al., 2018), an LGBTQ+ person's decision to come out to others is often complicated at best. It is also common for members of the LGBTQ+ community to have conflicts with their biological family due to a lack of acceptance. To survive complex family dynamics, some LGBTQ+ individuals may find themselves needing to either conform to heteronormative demands, or be excluded from their biological family.

To complement traditional family and social ties, LGBTQ+ individuals may need to seek social connectedness and relational resilience by intentionally and purposefully cultivating a family of choice. This may include non-paternal mentors, supportive friends, and community. The wisdom of equanimity, a balanced mind toward all experiences, regardless of whether they are pleasant, unpleasant, or neutral, can help deal with relationships' complexity. Instead of ignoring or numbing the pain of stress reactivity, intimately engage with the others in the present moment and gradually cultivate an even mind towards all beings beyond likes and dislikes. Such is a recognition that we are connected, and yet, each of us has our unique path.

The foundation of a contemplative community can be particularly supportive for LGBTQ+ individuals, as it supports healthy individual and group reflection, catharsis, belonging, and purpose. Belonging to a Sangha can reduce psychosocial and social isolation through shared experiences. A Sangha brings together individuals who share similar values. Through a sense of refuge and strength in affirming personal experiences rather than neglecting and suppressing fundamental needs and desires, individuals can become a source of support for each other.

This affirming environment can facilitate LGBTQ+ people's need for a supportive community that validates personal characteristics and expressions. It is a braver space where LGBTQ+ can feel comfortable being themselves and expressing their identities and unique experiences. The Sangha offers a smaller microcosm for fostering positive and loving attachments so that individuals build the relational skills needed to establish and maintain their own chosen families and a community as a whole. Such peer acceptance and psychological association can also bolster an intrinsic motivation to explore reasons for living and allow individuals to find meaning and a sense of purpose.

Counterproductively, a non-affirming Sangha that builds community connectedness based on heterosexist assumptions deeply embedded in society can trigger stress stigma, internalized homonegativity, and/or spiritual bypass. Hence, a Sangha should be not only non-judgmental but also inclusive and affirmative. Its elected leaders should be knowledgeable and conversant in LGBTQ+ experiences and challenge traditional teachings that invalidate LGBTQ+ people. Because many LGBTQ+ individuals crave favorable and supportive role models and a functional social system, positive LGBTQ+ leadership and peer representation in Sanghas can play an important role in the lives of LGBTQ+ people.

A Profoundly Intimate Mentor Relationship

In Buddhist mentor-bonding tradition, the seven-limb mentor bonding practice is a reparative interpersonal meditative process that can be seen as following the arc of what Kohut called transmuting internalization, in four key phases: mirroring, idealization, twinship, and integration (Loizzo, 2012). As a way to repair childhood wounds experienced by the LGBTQ+ community, the use of a role model involves developing a profoundly intimate relationship with a new parental figure, someone that has the qualities one needs, someone that can represent a loving and accepting parent to help complete the original task for the mentee to become the best parent for and within her/himself/themselves. To elaborate, the following is a brief comparison of the mentor-bonding practice with Kohut's self-psychology theory.

According to Heinz Kohut's self-psychology (Baker & Baker, 1987), the development of a cohesive self occurs along three axes:

(a) Grandiosity axis (feeling valued and developing a sense of pride).
(b) Idealization axis (admiring and identifying with parentified figures).
(c) Alter ego–connectedness axis (belonging, connecting, having empathy, and navigating social roles).

Additionally, Kohut described three core needs for healthy development:

(1) Mirroring: the need to be acknowledged by others for one's qualities and accomplishments, leading to the development of one's self-concept and self-awareness.
(2) Idealization: the need to admire and identify with significant others (parents) and to experience a sense of merging with the resulting idealized self-objects. Idealization leads one to proceed through development in a more secure fashion while internalizing the ability to hold ideals and set high but realistic goals.
(3) Twinship: the need to feel included and part of a community (Banai et al., 2005).

Kohut (1971, 1977, 1984; Kohut & Wolf, 1978) describes that in optimal caregiver relationships, needs are naturally fulfilled in early development, and over time the individual can internally regulate self-esteem and ambitions instead of requiring admiration from others. When unmet needs disrupt the process of internalization, pathological narcissism may develop and result in a constant hunger and endless search for satisfaction of unmet needs.

From a psychological point of view, Tibetan role-modeling visualization practices combine the natural developmental mechanism involved in parenting, the power of human imagination, and the subtle neurochemistry of love and openness to create effective flight simulators for positive growth.

The mentor bonding practice involves the development of trust, safety, confidence, and an interactive and mutually engaged relationship between the practitioner and the mentor. Envisioning both parties' engagement, responses, and actions is key to accelerating the healing and bonding process. The mentor bonding may occur through direct contact and proximity. It can also take place at a distance, where the intimacy occurs more in the meditation/visualization practice and is augmented by support from the community (Sangha). As a result, the person can internally regulate self-esteem and ambitions instead of requiring admiration from others. The person can develop his or her own system of ideals and goals and maintain a sense of direction in life instead of needing to identify with a powerful other to fulfill self-object functions.

That said, Loizzo (2012) acknowledges that it can be challenging to find a mentor who exemplifies the qualities one hopes to develop, suggesting infusing the abstract knowledge of a mentor's qualities with one's personal encounters through a courageous, inspirational, or expansive mental process. LGBTQ+ affirming mentor qualities may include a mentor that a) represents the unique LGBTQ+ themes of identity, self-exploration, and self-expression; b) understands the complexity, contraction, and self-determination of the LGBTQ+ experiences; c) is affirming of these experiences and hold spaces for deeper experiences such as loneliness, felt difference, sensibilities, lovelessness, hopelessness, and isolation; and d) inspires and reframes how LGBTQ+ individuals can see their lives.

Celebrating Inherent Resilience

To survive another day for the LGBTQ+ community means being on the constant lookout to protect oneself. This, on its own, requires monumental strength, grit, and flexibility. Such is the reason why celebrating LGBTQ+ pride is a privilege, an act of self-kindness, and an important peaceful defiance LGBTQ+ community members must practice in every moment. It is a testament to LGBTQ+ individuals' daily achievements of survival and the entire community's strides in overcoming prejudice. Validating sexual and gender identity and embracing the unique gifts and rejoicing in them as part of a common human experience.

Research supports the adoption of a strengths-based approach to buffer against LGBTQ+ minority stress (Meyer, 2003). The LGBTQ+ community endures many adversities and holds endless stories of resilience, recognition, warmth, and generosity. Riggle et al. (2014) highlighted eight themes exploring the positive aspects of the LGBTQ+ community: 1) authenticity; 2) self-awareness, personal insight, and growth; 3) freedom to create new rules; 4).

stronger emotional connections with others; 5) freedom to explore relationships and sexuality; 6) compassion and empathy; 7) mentors, role models, and activists; and 8) belonging to an LGBTQ+ community. There is a growing body of research shifting the narrative towards building strengths within the community. For example, LGBTQ+ are capable change agents who have experiences from which they can draw from (Dominelli, 2002; Weick et al., 2009). Many are self-reflective and introspective in nature when coming to terms with a sexual minority identity and developing strategies to come out to others (Meyer, 2003). Fassinger et al. (2010) also commented that "LGBT leaders engage in effective leadership utilizing characteristics based on sexual orientation alongside relational, emotional, and motivational styles to lead people to fight for individual rights." Similarly, through mindfulness, compassion and wisdom, LGBTQ+ individuals are able to further cultivate their inherent resiliencies.

Further Notes on Affirmative Contemplative Psychotherapy for LGBTQ+ Community

The lack of evidence-based contemplative psychotherapy practices centered around the LGBTQ+ community requires genuine effort from clinicians and healers to adapt heteronormative practices for the LGBTQ+ community. The following are additional reflections when considering an LGBTQ+ affirmative approach to contemplative psychotherapy.

Affirming LGBTQ+ experiences requires the recognition that safety within the therapeutic relationship may not always be replicable in the outside world. There must be a realistic view that difficulties will lie ahead. Paradoxically, while the world might not be safe at all times, it is only in the here and now that LGBTQ+ individuals can begin to access (enough) inner safety.

While research shows that contemplative practices such as mindfulness practice can help decrease rumination (Chambers et al., 2008) and develop affect regulation in the brain (Siegel, 2009), it is important to recognize the shadow side of spiritual bypass such as excessive mental disengagement from lived reality, passive acceptance of homonegativity, and skipping identity development stages. Taking refuge in practice should support and affirm the lived realities of the LGBTQ+ community and the need for engaged adaptive resilience.

Finally, holism is not only bringing all of oneself to the present moment and in practice; it also includes all the different relational factors of how an individual experiences the world. It is, therefore, ethically important to not only view sexual and gender minority stress as issues of individual appraisal that require individuals to cope or change. Interventions at the social level are also necessary to eliminate prejudice and stigma (objective stress). As a society, we should aim for a multifaceted approach that cultivates individual resilience and also lifts societal and systemic barriers.

May we find the courage to celebrate our differences and recognize our interconnectedness.

PART TWO
Compassion and
Social Healing

Nagarjuna, Champion of Profound Wisdom (Robert Beer, Used with Permission)

9

Traditional Buddhist Perspectives on Modern Compassion Trainings and a Proposal for an Integrated Relational Emotional-Analytical Framework

Lobsang Rapgay

Introduction: Comparing and Integrating Compassion Trainings

Today there is a growing interest in compassion in the West, especially in self-compassion, as evidenced in both popular and scientific literature, and contemplative practices. From a global perspective, Eastern contemplative traditions have made immense contributions to the contemporary understanding and practice of compassion, informing psychological, philosophical, and religious studies, and inspiring new approaches to health and well-being. While current compassion interventions have been inspired by Buddhist teachings, the two are not necessarily fully aligned, and divergences between modern and traditional approaches to compassion deserve attention.

The Nalanda tradition preserved in Tibet offers an especially advanced psychological approach to the cognitive, affective, and behavioral dimensions of cultivating compassion (Arpaia & Rapgay, 2003). In this chapter, I will revisit the Nalanda perspective on the complexities, challenges, and benefits of cultivating compassion, focusing on insights and techniques which have been overlooked and are yet to be incorporated by today's mainstream compassion movement.

First, I review the Tibetan understanding of compassion and its developmental roots, comparing this to current concepts and practices such as self-compassion. Finally, I outline the different ways in which compassion is practiced, both in the psychological literature and in the Buddhist tradition, concluding with a reflection on how the two approaches can be integrated.

DOI: 10.4324/9781003243588-11

What Buddhist Compassion Is and Is Not

From a historical, cross-cultural perspective, what compassion is, and is not, is a much-debated topic. When individuals speak about compassion, it is safer to assume that they mean various things, as one's individual view of compassion is only one type within a typology of multiple views in the world. In contrast to the unilinear idea of compassion in the West as a feeling of co-suffering, compassion in the Buddhist tradition is a more complex, multifaceted moral phenomenon (Hopkins, 1980). Moreover, compassion in modern literature has routinely been seen as a derivative of other social emotions like love or reduced to prosocial behavior (Davidson & Begley, 2013), whereas the Nalanda tradition sees it as distinct from empathy, sympathy, love, kindness, and concern, as well as from prosocial gestures of kindness, generosity, care, and the concern it may motivate.

Traditionally, compassion is seen as a whole arc of perception and response which involves cognitive, affective, motivational, and behavioral aspects. The arc of compassion includes a clear cognitive recognition of pain and suffering; the equal value of all beings; a heartfelt empathic concern for those whose pain and suffering we recognize; a motivational response of deep personal responsibility to help; along with any behavioral expressions of that deep response. In this conceptualization, it is *not* necessary to feel the painful feelings of the person suffering, but it is necessary to have a heartfelt sympathetic affection towards them (Hopkins, 1980). The characteristics of compassion can be summarized as follows:

A. Cognitive: accurate recognition of pain and suffering, and the equality of self and others
B. Affective: a heartfelt empathic concern for the pain and suffering of the other out of affectionate love
C. Motivational: altruistic ("other"-directed) urge to help without seeking personal gain
D. Behavioral: a personal sense of responsibility and capacity to effectively help even at a personal cost

What makes a compassionate person? In general, someone who manifests compassion in a powerful way that integrates all these levels will stand out as one who embodies compassion. Yet, as we look closer at specific contexts in which an individual expresses compassion, we realize the complexity of assessing its degree and scope. The levels of altruism in our motivation matter, as does the size of the circle of beings towards which we feel and express compassion. For instance, how would we assess the degree of compassion in a person who is very kind, protective, and caring towards animals, but is indifferent or even cruel to their fellow humans? What about a person who often helps and is friendly to strangers, but who actually acts out of self-guilt, or is showing compassion publicly to compensate for being short tempered or harsh to their own children? How compassionate would we consider a person who shows great courage, generosity, and effort to help a certain suffering child, based on identifying that child's suffering with their own childhood traumas, but who is not equally moved to help other children with whom they do not identify?

Three Levels of Compassion: A Traditional Buddhist Framework

The Buddhist tradition offers categorizations of different levels of compassion, meant to help distinguish degrees of ethical and spiritual maturity. One threefold categorization distinguishes progressive levels of altruistic motivation based on the scope of beings towards which compassion is manifested. The three levels are common, immeasurable, and great compassion. Each of these includes many incremental levels of progressively expanding scope or more profound expression or embodiment (Erdynast & Rapgay, 2009).

Common compassion refers to the basic capacity to objectively recognize suffering, feel a deep concern for the person suffering, and manifest a genuine strong motivation to do something to relieve it. While prosocial activity is not a criterion, and one may or may not take action, common compassion requires that we feel a deep wish to help another person based on other-concern. For many of us, compassion may be restricted to people we see as close, and we may have difficulty extending it to others outside our inner circle or comfort zone. But we may also feel compassion for a limited number of people outside our circle, people we identify in some way as other, such as people from other backgrounds or political parties. This scope of capacity may include compassion both for people we see as part of our in-group and for people we see as part of an out-group.

Immeasurable compassion is the next scope of capacity, one which is recognized by both Theravada and Mahayana Buddhism. Like common compassion, this scope of capacity presupposes a deep concern for the suffering of others, coupled by a wish to free them from that suffering. But there are two added dimensions that make compassion immeasurable. The first is that we not only wish to relieve others of their suffering, but also to free them from the causes of their suffering. The second is that our empathy and concern are more fully objective, based on directly experiencing the pain of others, without the intermediary step of trying to imagine their pain by projecting our own prior suffering onto them.

The causal criteria make it necessary to really understand the other person's suffering, both why it exists and the way it manifests. This scope of compassion involves both more wisdom and the added effort to go to the root of the problem. As an example, instead of simply giving someone who's in need some time-limited financial aid, immeasurable compassion would involve the more profound and demanding work of investing time in fully understanding the difficulties the person is having, focusing on the causes of economic distress, and then trying to completely end those root causes, thus irreversibly relieving the other's suffering.

So, the empathic awareness involved in this scope of compassion operates both at the surface expression of suffering, as well as at the deeper processes causing that expression. You may be empathically aware of another's suffering based on directly what your senses tell you, such as seeking someone crying, but immeasurable compassion would also involve a willingness to go deeper and become aware of the underlying causality of suffering being expressed through that crying. This deeper awareness should generate a much deeper and more powerful level of empathic concern.

This deeper empathic awareness and concern leads us to the second feature of immeasurable compassion, that is, feeling the suffering of others through unbiased intuition, as they actually feel it, rather than through the filter of your own memories of pain projected onto them. The empathic concern that springs from this more accurate empathic experience is thus based on identifying altruistically with the pain of others, seeing it as they do, feeling it within oneself as they feel it, and then responding to it more accurately without any personal narratives or projections. This more accurate and objective empathy and concern allows for a far more powerful urge to help and a more precise and skillful expression of compassion.

The third scope of capacity for compassion, called great compassion, involves a practice more fully articulated in later, Mahayana Buddhism (Shantideva, 1987; Shamar Rinpoche, 2014). This great scope of compassion adds to common and immeasurable compassion a powerful resolve to act one's intention to help others. In this sense, great compassion is distinguished not just by the greater power of one's altruistic urge to take responsibility for relieving others' suffering, but also by an unconditional and unwavering commitment to act, to do whatever it takes to relieve to the suffering of others and its root causes. Thus, great compassion places a much greater demand on us not just to wish, or try, but to do whatever we must to succeed, a sense that we absolutely must see the other person set free, not only from their immediate expression of suffering but from its deepest root causes. Of course, it does not mean we can actually achieve that aim in practice given our own limitations, the other's limitations, or limits imposed by external conditions. It simply means that we feel that duty and will do anything in our power to follow through.

Buddhist Self-Compassion through Renunciation of Own Suffering

Self-compassion as a concept and practice has become immensely popular in the West, almost as widely accepted as mindfulness, with which it is becoming increasingly integrated. There's a growing body of research and academic literature showing that self-compassion is highly accessible and effective at improving well-being in diverse populations (Neff, 2015). His Holiness the Dalai Lama, prominent Buddhist leaders, and Western psychologists frequently promote practices of self-compassion. However, the place of self-compassion in traditional Buddhist psychology and practice is not as obvious as many now understand it to be. There are good reasons to ask whether self-compassion, as presently taught in the West, is a traditional Buddhist teaching or not. This is an overlooked issue in the Western–Buddhist dialogue which calls for further investigation. Of course, any conclusion depends on what precisely is meant by the term "self-compassion" in the West, versus "loving-kindness," "compassion," or "giving-and-taking towards oneself" within Buddhist traditions.

By now, many in the West are aware that the Theravada tradition focuses more on "loving kindness" (Skt. maitri, Pali. metta), while the Mahayana tradition has a stronger focus on "compassion" for others (karuna). We can also see that self-compassion as a theme plays a different role in the respective traditions. The Theravada tradition gives it more prominence, as we see in the practice of mindfully repeating phrases like, "May I be happy," "May I be free from suffering," "May I have joy," and "May I live in peace." Theravada Buddhism teaches that it's important to be concerned about one's welfare and also that one must have compassion for oneself before one can have compassion for others. On the other hand, the basic practice within the Mahayana tradition, repeating phrases called "The Four Immeasurables," doesn't replicate the more self-oriented opening sentence of the Theravada practice.

Instead, it immediately starts off with other-oriented aspirations: "May all beings have happiness and its causes," "May all beings be free from suffering and its causes," and so on. Mahayana teachers in the East seldom refer to self-compassion in those terms.

Because of the growing importance of self-compassion in the mainstream and the mounting evidence of its benefits, there is now a tendency among Buddhist teachers in the West towards a sort of reinterpretation of Mahayana practice to suggest that affirmations like "May all beings be happy," etc. includes oneself. As modern Buddhist teachers increasingly present the Mahayana doctrine of compassion as including a major focus on compassion for self, it's important to note that this is a new way of presenting compassion more common in the West.

Exploring the issue further we can see that the meaning given to self-compassion is quite different in the West versus the East. In the modern self-compassion literature, the notion is presented as a radical form of self-acceptance, self-esteem, or self-worth. In contrast, when Theravada Buddhists talk in terms of compassion for self what they mean is more than just having the self-worth to know we deserve happiness, but the capacity to know your own suffering and its causes, along with the knowhow it takes to realize inner happiness, without letting the outside world dictate how you react or feel inside. This critical practice, known as renunciation (Tib. *Nges 'byung*, Skt. *nihsarana*) in my view is not discussed enough in Western Buddhism (Rapgay & Bystrisky, 2009)

Contrary to widespread misconceptions, renunciation does not mean renouncing family life, material comfort, or turning away from others' suffering, but being able to let go of one's own internal suffering through learning and practice. Through renunciation we come to feel truly worthy of lasting happiness and to understand how to reduce our misperceptions and afflictions, thereby developing joy and well-being. From a traditional Buddhist standpoint, if this deeper sense is not woven into the idea or practice of self-compassion, vital steps towards self-awareness and transforming our mind/body state risk being sidelined. This vital work is foundational to all traditional Buddhists teaching and practice, even when not explicitly stated. Reading between the lines of the Theravada practice of compassion for oneself, for instance, you will find a vital first step needed before wishing oneself happiness; the practitioner must have regulated the three poisons of desire, hatred, and ignorance. This is a tall order, which clearly speaks to the fact that, to do this practice, you need to have a very high level of emotional and mental competence. That competence is the true meaning of self-compassion. The distinction between self-compassion and renunciation is not merely theoretical. When traditional Buddhists say, "May I be happy," it assumes this foundation which is not being presented in the West today (Rapgay & Bystrisky, 2009).

Renunciation is not only the basis for your own happiness but the necessary foundation for practicing compassion for others. It's about letting go of what makes you suffer and learning how to develop happiness yourself which gives a basis for helping others do the same. Trying to practice other-compassion without the foundation of knowing how to take care of ourselves really doesn't work. When taking on the suffering of others, you have to really be conversant with your own suffering and the freedom that comes of ridding yourself of it. It is necessary to first come to know quite precisely the nature of your personal suffering and its root causes, and then to be able to work towards getting rid of it. And as you do so, you develop a level of confidence, resilience, and the resultant joy gives you the inner strength to help others. This competence for renunciation, or genuine compassion for self, is what you should wish for all others.

Four Risks of How Self-Compassion Is Taught in the West

There are four main risks with how self-compassion is taught in the West today. First, modern teachers talk about developing compassion for oneself by thinking about how one is capable of showing compassion towards others, but if self-compassion practice is not firmly grounded on renouncing one's own suffering it risks bypassing the deeper foundation of transforming negative mind/body states, covering up the painful spots which we actually must investigate and heal. If we overuse methods that are simply reassuring to boost our self-esteem, we may run away from the need to fully view and deal with the causes of our suffering (Erdynast & Rapgay, 2009).

Second, a less obvious risk with self-compassion as taught today is that, from a traditional perspective, it can bypass the need for seeking compassion from others who may have greater renunciation and freedom or may just be able to help us see causes for our suffering that we are blind to. Third, relying too much on self-compassion may hinder social connection through compassion from/for others which generally proves to be the most effective path towards healing. Being able to request and receive compassion from others stands out among the top factors for mental and physical health. Reluctance to seek help to avoid interdependence with others can contribute to social isolation, and hence pose a risk for depression, anxiety, and physical illness. Finally, the fourth risk is that, in emphasizing caring for yourself, you deprive your fellow humans of the opportunity to exercise their social competence for compassion. From a traditional Buddhist perspective, this is vital because we all need our interdependence with others to have frequent opportunities to practice compassion.

Self-Protective Instincts Move Us towards Compassion

Another key difference between the way compassion is taught by Western Buddhist teachers, and within traditional Buddhism, is the issue of the origins of human compassion. Many modern Buddhist researchers and teachers put forth the idea that compassion is an innate feature of human infants, and that it is basic to our nature to be compassionate (Davidson & Begley, 2013). Traditional Buddhist teachers and texts, on the other hand, place more emphasis on the primacy of self-protective instincts, describing human nature as innately self-interested and self-cherishing (Shamar Rinpoche, 2014). Current claims for humanity's innate basic goodness draw on studies that show prosocial features from very early on in human development. While it is striking and encouraging that babies as young as three months show a preference for attending to behavior that is prosocial rather than antisocial—behavior commonly considered good rather than bad, right rather than wrong—it seems problematic to interpret these findings as direct evidence that humans have compassion or basic goodness as our primal inborn nature.

The traditional interpretation of Buddhist psychology lines up more closely with modern Western psychology, based on a nuanced understanding of the role of social cooperation in evolution. Instead of jumping to the conclusion that infants are basically altruistic rather than self-interested, Buddhist psychology identifies self-preservative instincts as the main source of infants' innate preference for prosocial behaviors like compassion. Like Western psychology, Buddhism explains how self-interest for humans dovetails with a preference for the prosocial, since the infant's survival is ensured by an interest and attachment to prosocial beings over those who may harm, reject, or deny care.

Of course, from the perspective of our potential for positive moral development, Buddhism teaches not only the basic self-interested condition of human nature, but that all humans have a higher capacity that lines up with modern claims of innate goodness. Traditional Buddhists are committed to the idea that each and every human has innate capacities for luminous brilliance and for unconditional compassion known as our Buddha Nature (Skt. *Tathagatagarbha*). These two sides of our nature—basic self-interest and the capacity for unconditional compassion—line up with the traditional claim that life can be viewed from two perspectives: from the relative standpoint of our natural baseline condition, and from the ultimate standpoint of our potential for higher development. This mixed, complex view of human nature contrasts with the current tendency among Western compassion research to overemphasize our moral goodness (Davidson & Begley, 2013). It also helps explain the sobering evidence that humans have a darker side to their nature, as shown by the alarming historical, epidemiological, and research evidence that humans are all too capable of inflicting harm, pain, and even death on innocent others, especially in social contexts like the Stanford Prison Experiment where we are encouraged to do so by perceived authorities (Zimbardo, 2008).

From a traditional Buddhist perspective, the self-preservative instinct that drives a human infant towards prosocial caregivers is a natural expression of a basic drive innate in all living things. Even the smallest forms of life, single-celled organisms like the amoeba, have a similar self-protective drive. If you disturb the water around an amoeba or put something aversive into it, the organism will move away from the potential threat. If you add a vital nutrient such a bacterial sugar to their surroundings, amoebas will instinctively be attracted towards it. From a traditional standpoint, all living beings including humans have very similar innate self-protective instincts to avoid threats and pursue what is nurturing, and this is what underlies our innate preference for things we experience as pleasant and aversion towards things we experience as unpleasant. That is the biological basis for our attraction to kindness.

In the course of normal development, through experience of relationship and an expanding mind, a child comes to realize, "I'm interdependent. I'm not alone, as I thought I was as an infant." This leads to a sense that self-preservation depends on the well-being of others, equally as on oneself. As people continue to mature, especially with help of contemplative practice, we grow to recognize how everyone and everything is impermanent and interdependent. This helps each of us realize it's not all about me, even though we started life with a deep sense of being the one at the center of everything. This shift away from self-focus is the beginning of our journey to awakening compassion. With this realization, the insight Buddhists call the wisdom of selflessness or emptiness begins to dawn on us, and we begin to realize that compassion towards others is more important—even for self-preservation—than compassion for self. So that is how the drive towards self-preservation and compassion become intertwined.

While a child is born self-centered, a healthy family environment can speed up the maturation of compassion. For instance, an infant raised by adults who are more prosocial will learn much faster to be compassionate than someone raised in a home with adults who for a host of reasons—developmental, economic, or social—may be more preoccupied with their own survival needs. The primary caregiver is enormously influential in how fast self-centeredness can gradually turn into more expansive compassion (Kohut, 1971). That's also why Buddhists use the mother–child relationship as a template for understanding compassion.

In short, our self-preservation drive is critical not only to our survival but also to the development of compassion. Our primal survival strategy as infants is to seek and receive compassion. Later, especially if mature love and care have been modeled for us in early childhood, we develop the capacity to provide care and compassion for ourselves and others. So self-protective instincts move us towards compassion because it's in our deeper self-interest. Thanks to social evolution, healthy development, and adult experiences including contemplative practice, we all have the capacity to become other-cherishing.

Comparing Modern and Traditional Compassion Trainings

Western compassion education has developed rapidly in recent years. Today, seven or more institutes based in the West offer distinct compassion training protocols, often based on an eight-week step-by-step program. I begin by exploring some of the pros and cons of these programs, and then present some of the advantages I see in traditional Buddhist compassion education, especially based on Asanga's Seven Point Training in Cause and Effect. My discussion also draws on the model of compassion development based on Kleinian psychoanalysis, which I believe can inform and help improve modern compassion education.

While some modern compassion trainings are more elaborate in their conceptualization and techniques than others, common to them all is that they're prescriptive: each week students are told exactly what to do and there are standardized ways to assess progress in the practice. Big cohorts cover one step at a time and then jointly move on to the next step in the program. The big advantage of such trainings is that they can be applied to large groups, enabling effective outreach in the world where prosocial training, even online, is much needed. A problem with this type of standardized training, however, is that it is not personalized to individual needs. Considering that individual attention often allows for deeper more personal emotional-analytical processing, a group format has its limits, especially for personality types prone to resistance and drop-out. For example, when standardized activity is prescribed to anxious clients, it can activate early memories of a dominant, demanding, punitive parental figure. Modern compassion trainings that do not actively facilitate emotional processing are limited because compassion is an affective state. Those that do facilitate group emotional processing may still be limited in their effectiveness for students who have trouble with emotional processing in a group, especially a structured skills learning group.

I believe these limitations can be addressed by integrating traditional Buddhist and Western psychological sources that more directly foster emotional-analytical processing and that this will strengthen modern compassion education. The big picture is that Buddhist psychologists and Kleinian analysts agree that unless we work through emotional and perceptual conflicts—typically rooted in childhood—in our own minds adequately, it will not be psychologically possible for us to cultivate the emotional capacity for mature love, let alone the higher capacities for universal love, great compassion, or altruistic resolve. All Buddhist traditions are full of methods for exposing and working through such deep-rooted conflicts, such as the cognitive-affective-behavioral method of working through anger offered by the seventh century Nalanda master Shantideva (Rapgay & Bystrisky, 2009).

The Benefits of Practicing Compassion within a Relational Context

For compassion to really hit home for us it has to be practiced within a relational context. The Tibetan Buddhist tradition offers a process-oriented, individualized approach to compassion training based on engaging compassion developmentally with a relational practice. While modern compassion education presents compassion as necessary for individual health and well-being, compassion practice in the Nalanda tradition is relational from day one. In fact, the relational dimension of learning compassion is built into the structure and context of contemplative learning in and through the teacher–student relationship and the peer-to-peer relationships of the learning community (sangha). Having a relationship with a teacher, as well as with other peers who are practicing in a similar fashion, is critical to the affective dimension of developing compassion. The teacher–student relationship is especially important because it offers mentoring and modeling in compassion as a reference point for all learning (Kristeller & Rapgay, 2013). A traditional teacher is there to support your individual journey, explain what and how you are doing, and why you're doing it. This mentoring and modeling is equally essential to modern compassion trainings, as is the peer-to-peer support that may happen in the group learning environment, but in modern trainings these relational factors tend to be less explicit and more time-limited.

The teacher–student relationship is considered important from a modern psychological perspective because it provides a relational context for transference dynamics, where students project feelings for early caregivers onto the teacher. Ideally, in this context as in psychotherapy, the teacher can help the student become aware of such projections, to process them, and learn to address issues that strained or limited key relationships in early development.

In Buddhism, in general, the relationship with early caregivers is seen as the most loving and compassionate of all human relations and used as a template for compassion training and practice. The prime example of this method is the Seven Step Cause-Effect practice of compassion training, which is an advanced relational practice in the Nalanda tradition (Hopkins, 1980). The method is based on a personal focus on the mother, or early caregiver, and then extends whatever love and gratitude one feels towards that figure to recognize and appreciate all beings, all life, universally as equally dear "mother-beings."

The "Seven Step Cause-Effect Practice" for Relational Compassion

Nowhere in the Nalanda tradition is the cultivation of compassion more naturally evoked and methodically cultivated than in this Seven Step Cause-Effect Practice handed down by Tibetan masters. I believe it offers the most accessible way of developing real love, which is the foundation we need to cultivate compassion. So, the template used to generate real love is motherly love, or love from any other primary caregiver. Based on the real affection and gratitude we feel for this person, practitioners learn to transform and extend this natural emotional-mental state and progressively shift from personal to universal love (love directed equally towards all beings); then from great compassion to altruistic resolve; and finally, towards awakening an enlightened altruistic spirit called *Bodhicitta* (Hopkins, 1980). The seven steps in the training are:

1. Recognizing all beings, all life, as your universal "mother"
2. Remembering the kindness of all "mother beings"

3. Gratefully wishing to return their kindness
4. Developing nurturing love for others as a way to return the kindness you've received
5. Developing great compassion that aspires to end all beings' suffering and its causes
6. Engaging an extraordinary altruistic resolve to help all beings end their own suffering and its causes
7. Cultivating Bodhicitta, the altruistic spirit that awakens all beings' enlightened altruism

This Seven Step Cause-Effect Practice is in essence a fast-track method for lay and monastic practitioners, which embodies the essence of Mahayana compassion practice in a step-by-step developmental approach. It is considered advanced because one commits to delaying one's own liberation in order to develop the fully mature compassion and altruism that can help inspire others to reach their full capacity for awakening and embodying compassion and altruism. It's also considered advanced because the basic requirements needed to engage in the practice effectively are demanding in their own right. The preliminary requirements include developing a deep appreciation for having a human body and life. This appreciation allows for a deeper recognition of the immanence of impermanence and death, as well as of the inexorability of the causal laws of development. The Training in Cause and Effect is practiced in conjunction with trainings in affect tolerance that sustain equanimity as well as the profound insights of selflessness and emptiness, which help expose and transform negative emotions, distorted perceptions, and maladaptive behaviors. Since this compassion training is developed in conjunction with the self-transcendent wisdom of emptiness, it enables a deeper type of unconditional compassion which is actually an exceptionally demanding practice.

The Seven Step Cause-Effect Practice is one of two main methods offered by the Nalanda tradition for developing unconditional compassion, and it normally is seen as laying the foundation for the most advanced practice, Exchanging Self for Others, which forms the basis of the Compassion-Based Resilience Training (CBRT) described in Chapter 15. Traditionally, Buddhists would recommend that you first practice the Seven Step Training, because it involves emotional analysis and processing that foster an insight-based affective experience of compassion which helps prepare for more advanced compassion practice. However, for individuals who already have a solid foundation in relational compassion, it is possible to start with the practice of Equalizing and Exchanging Self for Others (Shantideva, 1987).

The Resonance Between the Buddhist Psychology of Compassion and Modern Kleinian Psychoanalysis

One modern approach to relational compassion that resonates deeply with the core insights of the Steven Step Cause-Effect Practice is Melanie Klein's psychoanalytic approach to human development. Buddhists and Kleinian psychoanalysts share the recognition that genuine compassion as a very mature affective state that supports the highest level of emotional development we can aspire to. Identified by Klein as a high-level defense, compassion is seen as an act of taking a negative experience and transforming it into a positive experience, the highest level of sublimation possible (Klein, 1975). According to both Buddhist and Kleinian psychology, in order to develop authentic compassion, one must first learn to regulate hate and negativity through emotional-analytical processing. Compassion practice can only be truly fruitful if we can base it on personal experience, training ourselves in the capacity to face the deepest suffering of ourselves and others. This explains why genuine compassion practice requires us to work with and from real feelings, including both love and hate, rather than avoiding or "bypassing" intense emotions in our meditations. Learning how to face, tolerate, and work with strong emotions—such as transforming anger into acceptance, or gradually extending personal love into universal love—is indispensable if we are to be able to truly cultivate genuine compassion.

So, relational compassion education must include deeply personal emotional-analytical processing to work effectively. Ideally, one would learn to regulate negativity and hate to a large degree before engaging in compassion practice. By revisiting our primary relationships from infancy on, we can come to understand how they continue to affect us as adults through lingering childhood feelings of anger, resentment, and sadness which we unconsciously project onto others (Schienbaum et al., 2015). Depending on the level of childhood trauma involved, emotional-analytical processing can be a daunting task which requires much mental preparation, trust, and courage.

From a Kleinian perspective, the process of moving towards love and compassion requires that we work through the defensive splitting of our negative and positive experiences of childhood caregivers to restore wholeness to our primary relations (Spillius, 1988). The starting point in this process is to work through aggression and hate by developing "healthy guilt" that allows us to feel remorse for our rage at caregivers who disappointed us. Remorse allows us to anticipate the grief inherent in the harm rage and hate does to even our most positive relationships. As we grieve the actual or experienced loss of connection caused by anger and rage, we can access our deeper longing for reconnection with the other, and out of that longing develop the willingness to repair any harm and restore the connection. This process is what finally allows us to sustain the capacity for mature love (Segal, 2004). I explain these steps in more depth below when I discuss the integrated method I propose for compassion education.

Towards an Integrated Relational Compassion Training

Since the Kleinian perspective on compassion shares key features with the Buddhist approach, I want to suggest how to integrate the two into a method of compassion education that may help address some of the limits of modern compassion trainings. The proposed Integrated Relational Compassion Training is organized around the first three steps of the Buddhist Cause-Effect Practice—remembering the good-enough mother/nurturer, developing gratitude for their kindness, and repaying that kindness. The program starts with experiential self-discovery and goal setting and concludes with an evaluative element.

Behavioral experimentation and meditation are integrated at all stages of the training and used to deepen practice, insights, and results.

Behavioral experimentation in daily life is essential because it allows all the insight and hard work of emotional processing to bear fruit in real transformation. It involves people who activate the internal conflict not yet resolved with the primary caretaker. Other strategies for processing negative emotions towards primary caregivers are imagery and role-play, which can help people recognize the conflicting parts activated in the primary relationship and allow for conscious integration and working through.

Meditation is used to further confirm and deepen insights revealed intellectually or analytically throughout the training. Even when working in the context of psychotherapy, encouraging clients to develop a meditation practice can help deepen the integration of cognitive or analytical insights from therapy sessions. Once such transformative insights register deeply enough to correct prior misperceptions, they can yield a new conviction that can be a powerful source of motivation for change. In contrast, merely intellectual insight can still be subject to distortion or obstruction by ongoing stressors and deeper conflicts that have not been fully exposed or resolved. Therefore, each stage of the training requires meditative practice to deepen insight, motivation, and perceptual learning.

Stage One: Self-Discovery and Goal Setting

The first stage of the training is to experiment with cultivating compassion to determine whether compassion practice feels worthwhile for you and if so, to define your compassion training goals. In order to assess how worthwhile it may be for you to engage in serious compassion practice, you must have a clear definition of real compassion so you can recognize it when it arises in your mind, and then assess how beneficial the emotional state feels to you. Rather than deciding to practice based on what your religious tradition says, or based on some psychological model or research evidence, or even on the opinion of a trusted friend, the Buddhist template is to determine the value of compassion in your life based on your own personal experimentation. Through self-discovery you can assess whether any mental state is wholesome, growth oriented, and positive, or unwholesome, unproductive, harmful, or destructive. So, in this stage, we take some time experimenting by observing how different emotions including compassion feel and work for you in your life and arrive at your own personal assessment of which emotions help you grow mentally, emotionally, and spiritually.

The Buddhist template of self-discovery is based on the Four Scopes of Mindfulness practice, as classically taught within the Theravada tradition (Rapgay & Bystrisky, 2009). The first scope focuses on mindfulness of the breath and body; the second scope on the pleasant, unpleasant, or neutral quality of any experience; and the third focuses on the mind and its contents, such as perceptions, thoughts, and emotions. The fourth and final scope involves using the experience and insight gained from the three previous scopes to eliminate misperception and unhealthy patterns, and to cultivate wise perception and healthy habits. So, the first three scopes provide a basis for experimenting with the whole spectrum of mind/body states, processes, and behaviors; and the fourth scope is about gathering the findings about experiences, like compassion, so that you can then act on them to benefit your daily life. In the second scope in particular, the Buddha taught that we can investigate whether specific states, processes, or behaviors lead to pain and suffering, to neutral feeling tones, or to positive feelings of joy or well-being. It's essential to self-discover this vital information through direct personal experience, rather than simply relying on outside recommendations. Once you come to a conclusion, you can begin to integrate it into your life though daily practice, using the fourth scope of mindfulness. This is the basic template of behavioral experimentation and change that supports the foundational practice of renunciation which underlies healthy self-care, and it is also the template we need to use to come to a clear conviction of the tangible benefits of cultivating compassion in this integrative approach to compassion training.

Based on this preliminary step of experimentation, we move on to setting appropriate compassion training goals. Since compassion training is demanding in many ways, getting organized is key and this includes both planning and goal setting. In regard to planning, schedule your compassion practice based on what works for your particular lifestyle, life demands, and your current emotional strengths and challenges. As for goal setting, it's best to set very modest, incremental goals. The traditional way to guide your goal setting is to analyze compassion into its prerequisite—i.e., renunciation—and its three component parts. Its three component parts include the cognitive component, which is awareness of another's suffering; the affective component, which is empathic concern for another's suffering; and the motivational component, which is the wish to see the other freed from suffering and its causes.

Another factor to consider in setting goals is the scope and type of compassion you plan to cultivate. If you plan to practice common compassion, you're free to limit the scope of your practice to one or two individuals you'd like to cultivate greater compassion for, such as significant others or family members. With this scope you can better track your progress because you're encountering the people you choose more intimately and frequently, so you are more likely to make progress that way. Of course, the intimate nature of the relationship, including the proximity and frequency of your contact with them, makes this scope in some sense more challenging—it will offer you many opportunities and challenges to practice. On the other hand, if you can make progress practicing this scope, it will be much easier to move to the two larger scopes, which both involve higher capacities of compassion. If you plan to practice great compassion, for instance, its scope includes not just every single human being, no matter how close or distant your relationship to them, but also to each and every living entity on earth.

Determining the type and scope of compassion practice can be challenging because of the human impulse to choose the highest, most ambitious option first. It's vital to recall that any form of training is equally beneficial, and that you can expect added resistance and challenges if you choose to skip the first scope of common compassion. There are good reasons why the mother–child relationship is the traditional paradigm for cultivating compassion. While the tradition recommends that you try to see everyone as a beloved mother, in practice the advice is to work with your primary caretaker as the most profound way to start. This also resonates with the Kleinian perspective and modern psychology in general. If you can start with cultivating compassion for your primary caretaker, it will build a solid foundation on which you can gradually expand the scope of your compassion practice, as you see fit.

Stage Two: From Personal to Universal Love through Integrated Emotional-Analytical Processing

One of the challenges of working with a primary caretaker, such as your mother for instance, is that by its very nature such an early bond is a complex relationship charged with conflicting positive and negative emotions—love and hate. In fact, even such polar opposite emotions tend to be complex in themselves. Such primal love, for example, is often colored by other emotions like fear of retribution, which further complicate the process. Working through these complex early relationships is crucial to be able to deal with deep conflictive emotions effectively. A first step could be to list the harms you suffered in your early ties, and then to assess whether you're currently feeling confident or strong enough to work with this material towards healing. Without this kind of assessment, and without challenging yourself emotionally, it is very difficult to move towards acceptance and healing simply through intellectual insight, particularly when you've been seriously harmed by a primary caregiver.

This stage of compassion practice involves a cleansing, analytical process which moves towards internalizing the good mother, according to Klein (1975). Of course, this requires working through the unresolved hurt, resentment, and hate you feel towards "the bad mother/caregiver" who hurt you, at least enough so you can remember and internalize whatever good there was in the relationship. If it helps, you can access the full intensity and range of anger and rage towards the caregiver by acting them out imaginatively in your mind's eye, either with the help of a protective presence—a friend, mentor, or therapist—or simply by yourself. Facing and owning the power of your primal destructive emotions can actually be a very liberating and empowering experience. Once you are able to face and accept the rage and hate from early wounds enough to regain some appreciation for any good shown you, you will need to work through any mixed feelings including any healthy or unhealthy guilt and remorse for the rage directed at someone who cared for you in some way.

Unlike unhealthy guilt in which we wrongly blame ourselves for the harm done by others, healthy guilt means simply taking responsibility for having hateful thoughts and emotions towards the caregiver for harms they've caused. Healthy guilt is crucial because it allows us to emotionally integrate our experience of the good caregiver as connected to one and the same person who was bad to us, empowering us to take responsibility for having both constructive and destructive thoughts and impulses towards the whole person. By taking responsibility for your aversion, you can more readily feel remorse for the destructive side of your emotions, and this in turn allows for a sense of self-inflicted loss of connection to the whole person of the caregiver. That sense of loss generates feelings of grief and sadness, which in this case is positive because it allows us to access memories of the good caregiver and to long to repair and restore the connection. For those who have suffered abuse, accessing neutral to good memories of the caregiver can elicit the ability to disarm the aversive feelings connected with traumatic memories and reconnect with their caregiver's complex humanity.

You will need to process the heat towards the primary caregiver because, if not worked through, your past hurts will dictate and color your current relationships, both in overt and covert ways (Sheinbaum et al., 2015). The risks of not doing so are many and range from identifying with the caretaker who harmed you and harming others, to becoming avoidant, passive aggressive, pleasing, compliant, or even self-sacrificing and self-destructive. When you've done enough working through your anger and frustration with the primary caregiver, a good question to ask yourself is: what needs and desires of your inner child would you wish your caregiver had been able to fulfill? This deeper processing can offer a very strong foundation for greater self-acceptance and self-care, as well as for identifying the needs you bring to adult relationships. Through meditating on the analytical-emotional processing at this stage, you practice holding in mind both the image of the good caregiver and the bad caregiver at once. Inevitably, one of these images will predominate and when it does you practice going back and forth between the two images over and over again. Eventually, you become more able to see this individual person as having both good and bad qualities, a major developmental step in working through the roadblocks towards cultivating mature love and compassion.

This capacity for integrated emotional processing empowers us to develop a capacity for unconditional love and compassion, which in turn supports a more profound and consistent memory of the kindness of the caretaker. Gradually you can try to expand the scope of remembering the kindness of that one person to more and more beings, including other loved ones and benefactors, strangers, and challengers, and eventually to all beings. While most people will eventually be able to move through this stage, some with deeper levels of trauma may do better doing this processing in the context of psychotherapy together with the traditional Buddhist approach.

The next step, after internalizing the good caretaker and starting to long for reconnection, is to access and cultivate gratitude. The power of this step is supported by a large body of research on the importance of gratitude for mental health and well-being (Wood et al., 2010). As you overcome the hurt from the bad caregiver you can remember the good and begin to sense feelings of gratitude spontaneously emerging. Gradually you learn more deeply to recall and enjoy a sense of gratification for the love and kindness that the primary caretaker has shown to you. It's important to focus on cultivating gratitude towards the primary caretaker instead of directing it towards somebody else who you might feel gratitude towards today. The gratitude should not be derived from other positive loving relationships that compensate for feelings of past deprivation. You must instead search for your capacity to recall and appreciate the early love you received from the primary caretaker, which requires a certain degree of hard work including trusting, honoring, or at least respecting the other person as a complex, limited human being.

The previous steps helped you develop the capacity to return what you have received in full measure to others in need. This is based on a particular type of gratitude, referred to both in the Buddhist and the Kleinian tradition, which fosters the ability to repair any damage you may have caused the other and restore the positive dimension of relationship. A mature way is to first fully restore the other person to wholeness and wellness in your own imagination and then eventually repair any harm done to the relationship interpersonally. True restoration involves not simply doing a favor to compensate the other but requires a deep and genuine feeling of gratitude.

According to Klein, this process is critical because it leads to sublimation and creativity which means taking your aggressive energies and transmuting or translating them into appropriate social activities. There are different levels of sublimation and creativity including taking the energy of anger and transmuting it for example into exercise, or on a higher level, transforming anger into philosophy, art, music, writing, and so forth. The essential feature of sublimation is transforming negativity into spiritual, developmental, and prosocial practice. All of these creative processes arise, according to the psychoanalysis, because you are able to repeatedly repair and restore relationships with a significant other. Each time you repair and restore on an interpersonal level you develop more mental capacity, emotional flexibility, and fluidity to be creative beyond the individual relationship, through activities with larger social outcomes. This is the basis of moving from mature love and compassion that is personal to universal forms of love and compassion.

Stage Three: Continuous Self-Evaluation and Adaptations

You can assess the outcome of the practice at the end of the day or the end of the week, depending on what works best for you. It is vital to continuously assess what helped and the benefits you derived. It's very important to not only identify what worked more generally, but to identify very specifically what you got out of the practice, locating actual evidence of progress. Can you, for example, see a change in how you talk to your partner, child, parents, etc.? Can you notice any shift in your meditation practice Are you starting to experience greater well-being, connection, and belonging in general?

Similarly, when you identify parts of the practice that you might be having problems with, make sure to identify the specific source of the problem. It is not necessary to address the whole problem. Trying to address the whole rather than specific sources of the problem is not the best way to deal with psychological challenges. Instead, learning to identify components of the problem, and exactly which of these maintain the root cause of the problem,

Table 9.1 Integrated Relational Compassion Training Summary (by Maria Thorin)

Integrated Relational Compassion Training:
From Personal to Universal Love
through Emotional-Analytical Processing

Stage 1: Self-Discovery and Goal Setting
Key Questions

- *What causes suffering and pain in your life?*
- *Is compassion a wholesome state for you?*
- *What are your compassion goals (type and element, personal relation)?*

Stage 2: Integrated Emotion Analytical, Experimental, and Meditative Training*

1 *Learn to regulate anger, hate, and resentment through the practice of renunciation*
2 *Remember the kindness of the good enough caregiver and the kindness of all beings*
3 *Experience healthy guilt and sadness at the loss of connection to the primary caregiver*
4 *Develop the ability to transcend anger, repair, and restore the disrupted connection*
5 *Develop gratitude for the caretaker's kindness and try to extend it towards all beings*
6 *Develop the intention to return the kindness and try to extend it towards all beings*
7 *Develop the resolve and capacity to love the caretaker and extend it towards all beings*
*Mainstreamed Training Components: Behavioral Experimentation and Meditation

Stage 3: Continuous Self-Evaluation and Adaptations
Key Questions

- *Are you making progress in real life relations, feeling more connection?*
- *Do you experience greater well-being, deeper self-insights, and compassion?*
- *Does your training design need readjustment (type, element, goals, etc.)?*

---

is what gives you the mental skill to quickly address it. Based on this assessment of obstacles to growth, next consider if your training plan, goals, or scope of practice needs major or minor adjustments.

Concluding Summary

Now that mindfulness has become well known in the West, and found its way into new forms of psychotherapy, the next phase in the integration of Buddhist psychology involves the many methods of cultivating compassion which were refined and preserved in Tibet. Nowhere in the Nalanda tradition is the cultivation of compassion more methodically and meaningfully presented than in Seven Step Cause-Effect Practice handed down from Nalanda master Asanga by Tibetan masters.

This chapter has reviewed the current state of dialogue between Buddhist and Western psychology and identified some different approaches to conceptualizing and practicing compassion. The Tibetan Buddhist perspective offers insights on the nature of compassion and techniques for compassion cultivation which have thus far been overlooked and are yet to be incorporated by the modern mainstream compassion movement.

Interesting resonance and synergies have also been identified in the dialogue between Buddhist and Western psychology, particularly between the Kleinian psychoanalytical tradition and the Buddhist practice of the cause-effect method. An integrated framework is proposed based on these two traditions, with a focus on the first three steps of the Buddhist practice—remembering the good-enough nurturer, developing gratitude for their kindness, and repaying that kindness—as the most accessible way of developing mature love, which is the foundation we need to cultivate compassion. The framework outlines how people can build a regular practice of these steps, to accelerate psychotherapy and transform daily life.

10

Compassion Practice, Social Justice, and Collective Liberation

Lama Rod Owens

Compassion and Spaciousness: Antidotes to Contraction and Violence

Compassion is one of the most important practices that we can embrace. It's also one of the hardest for us to be working on because it's so easy for us to shut down and contract. It's so easy to try to protect ourselves out in the world by erecting walls and barriers, and to energetically shut off the empathic part of our bodies – particularly the heart center – or the part of our energetic bodies that deeply sense, deeply experience and feel. And we do this because there's so much happening in the world, and it is quite overwhelming.

For me and my practice, when I feel overwhelmed, that's a sign of being super distracted. This kind of overwhelm is similar to when you're sitting in meditation and you want to do open awareness practice, but you're focusing on every single thing that's arising, instead of actually cultivating an openness, an expansion that holds everything that's arising. If we can hold everything, then we're not so distracted. That holding is a way for us to practice a profound kind of agency. When I have space, then I get the choice to focus my attention within the spaciousness. And that spaciousness is also where my joy, happiness and contentment arise from. The difficulty is holding the pain, the woundedness, the suffering, the sorrow, the broken-heartedness that exists in the spaciousness.

If there is no space to hold these painful things, we end up contracting around them, and these difficult situations become the totality of what we experience. Contraction is the root of violence. Contraction means rigidity. Contraction means being stuck and being set. Contraction means there's no movement. When there's no movement and there's no space, nothing but tension arises from that. You can directly apply that analysis to systems of violence. When

DOI: 10.4324/9781003243588-12

we're shut down and contracted, when the heart center closes and there is no space, we end up saying things like, "You know what? I'm pissed, I'm tired, I'm sad, I'm overwhelmed." The issue is *I am*. When we shut down and have no space, then there is no room for us to differentiate the painful situation itself from our sense of self. I essentially begin to self-identify with my afflictions. There's no space to do anything else, so I have to become the anger, I have to become the burnout, I have to become the rage. What we're trying to cultivate instead is this expression of spaciousness so I can do more than just be. I can have experiences in space. I can have the experience of anger; I can have the experience of sorrow and it's not the totality of my experience.

Rigidity and Oversimplification: Dehumanizing Tools of Oppressive Social Systems

Patriarchy is this system that forces us into rigidity. When we try to overcome that rigidity by getting fluid, then we're punished. Part of that rigidity is the way in which the system of patriarchy labels us and tells us that these are the labels within which we're going to stay, and if we don't stay there, then we're going to get our asses kicked. These labels oversimplify us, and oversimplification is yet another act of violence. Oversimplification is the opposite of fluidity. Oversimplification is an expression of being rigid because you don't get a lot of choice in simplicity. It's either *this* or *that*, which is how systems like patriarchy function; it's either this or that. There is nothing in between, and there is certainly nothing outside. That's a hard way to live, and a hard way to be, but that's how many of us are living our lives. We're living our lives within this experience of deep rigidity which gets reinforced by fear. "I don't want to take on the responsibility of being fluid because if I do that, then I have to start negotiating the complexity." In a way, simplicity is comfortable, though it breeds violence.

Fluidity and Impermanence: Countermeasures to Harmful Social Systems

We're living through a time where a lot is happening. I call such periods of reckoning apocalyptic times. For me, the apocalypse means the unveiling of truth-telling. The apocalypse is the way in which the truth is being told and the ways in which we're struggling to be in relationship to that truth. And it's also the ways in which we're being reminded that things have always been fluid and moving and shifting. We're being reminded that we have pretended to build our houses on rock, but they've actually been built on sand, and so everything is beginning to slide. You might think, "This isn't supposed to happen," and then you have to realize, "But it's always been sand." This system that I've invested a lot of energy in has always been kind of unstable. This has always been – as we say in the Tibetan language – a situation of *jig-ten*.

In Tibetan, *jig-ten* is the word for world. A direct translation would be destructible foundation, a foundation that can be destroyed. The Tibetan word for the world is impermanence, but we have forgotten that. We've tried to convince ourselves that everything is permanent, and nothing will change, but instead the truth of phenomenal reality and the essence of reality itself is perpetual shifting, perpetual change. The nature of everything is essentially empty, without form. This is something important for us to come into relationship with because many of us have forgotten. We've forgotten the truth of perpetual change. We've let ourselves get rigid and buy into the illusion of rigidity. Now we're trying to get fluid again, but some of us don't know how to do that. We don't know who we are if it's not *this* or *that*.

What happens when this and that get completely wiped away and we're asked, "Okay, who are you now?" Without a reference point, without systems, without policing, without hierarchies, who am I? How can I prove that I'm successful if the system of capitalism completely disrupts? Who am I if I can't be a woman or a man? Who am I if I can't be White? Who am I now? In actuality, the rug is always being pulled from under us, but we've created this sophisticated system of completely ignoring that and increasingly we can't ignore it anymore.

Expressions of Love: Choosing Discomfort and Accepting Suffering

"What am I going to do?" I can feel hopeless and find myself in a lot of despair, and that's important to notice so that I can begin to do the hard work of really opening to the reality of everything that's happening. In doing so, I am entering into a co-creative process where I'm actually beginning to create the future that I most want to see, but in order to do that, I have to be really uncomfortable. Matter of fact, I want to choose to be uncomfortable instead of being victimized and terrified by discomfort. How can I do that? How do I choose discomfort? Some of you, of course, are saying, "I'm always uncomfortable. I've gone through this and this, and I've survived that." Absolutely, but I wonder if you've been able to choose the discomfort? We're going to go through it anyway. Why not choose it? Why not shift our intention – not just our attention, but also our intention – and say, "You know what? You're coming, you're here, and I want to welcome you." I'm going to be miserable, absolutely, but I can cut through a layer of suffering by welcoming the discomfort. I add a layer of suffering on top of suffering when I am resisting the basic suffering to begin with. When I choose discomfort, I'm saying, "You know what? I'm allowing you to be here. I'm accepting it." For me acceptance is an expression of love. Accepting doesn't mean condoning. It doesn't mean celebrating. It doesn't mean I'm throwing a parade for all the discomfort. It means that I am acknowledging that the discomfort is here, that it is happening. I am acknowledging and saying, "Now, let's take the step to be in a relationship to suffering and begin to transform it into something worthwhile."

At no point am I saying be a victim and just let things happen to you. I'm saying that in order to really begin the work of transformation, you have to genuinely accept the thing that you want to start transforming first. In a way, you have to put your hands on it in order to start shaping it. I can't change anything that I'm afraid of touching. I can't walk until I touch the ground. I can't make anything until I touch it. We're afraid to touch it because the thing itself can be something really intense, like racism, white supremacy, something like that. And before I can touch the thing itself, I have to first move through my broken-heartedness around that thing. Often, we can't even see the thing because we're being distracted by this aversion, this broken-heartedness, this lack of being with the deep disappointment that this thing actually exists. Many of us can't even get to the thing because we can't touch into our deep disappointment that we have to do the touching to begin with.

That's where we're stuck in the world today. We have a mountain of broken-heartedness that manifests as trauma, woundedness, hurt, violence, all kinds of stuff that we're not touching and not being in relationship to. That heartbreak doesn't just disappear. It doesn't go away. It becomes a part of the thing that we're habitually avoiding. That habitual avoidance also turns into deeper experiences of suffering, and it also turns into acts of violence against ourselves and against others.

Systemic Racism: Touching into Broken-Heartedness and Metabolizing Trauma

What I see in the world is not only a bunch of people who are pissed off, but also a tremendous number of people who are deeply hurt. Their hearts are so deeply broken that we have absolutely no methodology to really get into touching that broken-heartedness and to metabolizing it. And this is so essential – the touching into and metabolizing – because it allows us to move through the broken-heartedness to finally get to touching the thing itself. When I came into Dharma practice through the door of meditation, I was told that the only way that I could ever achieve liberation was to move into the broken-heartedness, to move into everything that I was running away from. I had to let my heart break in order to begin to touch into the reality of systematic racism. I had to move through my deep unwillingness to acknowledge that this isn't fair. It's not fair that I have to be Black in a racist country, which will arguably be racist for the rest of my life. It's not fair, so I'm not going to deal with it. It's not mine to deal with. I had to wrestle with that for a while.

For me, racism isn't a thing that I have overly studied. I don't have a degree in anything related to racism. My first level of expertise came from being Black, but that doesn't necessarily mean I had a precise critique of racism. But I think what makes my view so interesting and unique is that I've done this work of moving through the broken-heartedness, and so I've gotten really close. I've gotten to touch the actuality of racism and I see it clearly now. I can see it functioning because I'm not being distracted by my aversion to it. I'm not being distracted by my trauma. I'm not being distracted by my broken-heartedness. I'm seeing racism as it is. It's not actually personal. On the other side of my broken heart, looking at the system of racism, it seems very personal. It's about me and being impacted in silence, and about being repressed and restricted from resources. But when I get closer to it, I see, "Oh, this isn't even about me." Systematic racism wasn't created to make Rod's life horrible. It wasn't created to particularly attack me. It was created as this system that's really about domination, and I just happen to be the subject of that domination, but it wasn't about me, so I stopped taking it so personally.

When I got into *Buddhadharma*, I thought, "Oh, I'm this Buddha. I'm this enlightened person. Okay, I can roll with that. That sounds great." Then I moved deeper into study and practice, and I realized I am much more than what a system tells me I am. That's when I could say, "This isn't about me. Systemic racism is trying to create me in a way that *Buddhadharma* has taught me to start rejecting. That's not who I am anymore." That's how all the systems work: they are trying to create us, trying to define us. What happens is that we buy into it to our detriment, not for our good. Unless the system is telling you that you're brilliant and amazing, and that you're enlightened like Buddhism is telling us, then it's not telling you the truth. There's a level of release, of freedom, of liberation when you get to the point of seeing things as they are, not viewing things through the lens of our trauma. For me, I believe that's where the real change begins. That's where the real liberation starts:

touching into the thing and beginning to transform it by no longer believing in it. Having that disbelief completely alters everything in your life. But nothing, none of this is possible if we don't have the capacity to experience our woundedness, our broken-heartedness. We have to ask ourselves, at what point do we take responsibility for touching into the broken-heartedness as individuals, as well as collectives and communities?

The United States is nothing but one collective experience of trauma and broken-heartedness that has been left unattended to, unmetabolized. We're in trauma, our systems are in trauma, our institutions are in trauma, our leaders are in trauma, the air is in trauma, the water is in trauma and the land is in trauma reverberating with the initial violence of genocide. We also have traumas passed from generation to generation. We have intergenerational trauma and transhistorical trauma that exists along with all the daily traumas that we're experiencing by living and moving through a world that is hostile to many of us. The resistance that we have to engage in also creates woundedness and trauma that impacts how we are in the future. Trauma is an energy that saturates everything. And there's no collective liberation for any of us until there is a collective emphasis on metabolizing and moving through this broken-heartedness, this trauma and this woundedness.

As a country we don't have a language for this collective trauma. So how do we move forward? This is why I come back to the beginning, which is compassion. Again, compassion being the most important practice that we can utilize to open the heart, to metabolize trauma, to stay connected; but also to use compassion to hold the broken-heartedness so I can move into it, and move through it, and touch the thing that I'm trying to touch in order to begin to liberate it. I can't be afraid of the pain anymore. I have to begin to see the pain as a teacher, as a friend, as a guide, as a guru. This pain, my pain, my woundedness, my broken-heartedness is teaching me something important. It's teaching me how to stay connected to the world. To do that I have to also choose that discomfort. I have to choose to be there. I can't keep running away from everything and thinking that's going to get me free. I have to essentially choose to show up to my broken-heartedness, choose to show up to my trauma.

It's Not Right, But It's Okay – Owning the Capacity to Heal

Maybe initially I have no idea what to do beyond just showing up. Showing up is the beginning. Showing up allows me to start slowly taking responsibility for my pain. It doesn't matter if I've been a victim of so much. It doesn't matter if I've had to survive all kinds of things. I am still responsible for my healing. This is when I evoke Whitney Houston and say, "You know what? It's not right, but it's okay." It means that, yes, I don't think it's right that I have to be a victim of certain forms of violence and then still have to do my own work of healing, but it's okay because I can embrace the practices, the methodologies and free myself from these experiences. I can deeply experience and metabolize these experiences and release that energy. I have the capacity to do that so it's okay.

Aspirational Compassion and Compassion in Action: Tools for Individual and Social Transformation

I define aspirational compassion as the wish for others to be free from suffering. Compassion in action, which is the compassion that I'm more interested in, is not only I want beings to be free from suffering, I'm actually going to get involved in that freedom struggle for myself and for others. We start with aspirational compassion, "I want everyone to be free," then we move into compassion in action, or the fruition of compassion, which is, "This is the work that I'm going to engage in to become an agent of benefit for others." The first steps of our aspirational compassion work are truth-telling and empathy. First, I have to tell the truth about how I'm experiencing things and what's going on. I can't fool myself and think that I'm going to somehow authentically show up to other people's pain if I lie to myself about my own pain. So I tell the truth about what I am experiencing. I begin to tell the story and the narrative of my own deep discomfort. Then from there, I engage my empathy and turn my attention to the world around me, to others, and I say, "Oh, you know what? I think others are in some kind of discomfort that is maybe similar to mine, maybe greater, maybe lesser." That's really the most important piece of this developmental stage of compassion: I have to link my discomfort to the discomfort of others around me. I have to link my discomfort to everyone's discomfort, actually. Eventually – not at the beginning – if I really want to do this for real, I need to connect to the pain of the people that I can't stand. Go ahead and pick a person that you can't stand and say, "When I get to this person, I'm going to be enlightened. When I start considering the pain of this difficult person then I have gotten somewhere. Give me my certificate," but many of us don't go there.

So we start really small and we take our time. We connect and we say, "Okay, we're similar, right?" Then there's a kind of sympathy that we experience, and sympathy means abiding with. Not only am I touching my discomfort, I'm touching into the discomfort of others. It's helpful to sit with this experience because we can move too quickly through all of this. When I sit with my own discomfort, and when I sit with the discomfort of others, I'm allowing myself to hold space for all of the discomfort. It's like allowing the pot to simmer, to give rise to this rich beautiful stew of compassion. I have to really feel the discomfort. It's more than just touching and saying, "Oh, yes, I'm uncomfortable, they're uncomfortable. Okay, I'm done." No, I'm sitting with it. I'm allowing that discomfort in a way to break my heart. I have to understand discomfort in that way. This understanding begins to lead us into the aspiration to be free.

What does it mean for me to be free from this deep heartbreak, discomfort and trauma? What would that be like? What is my dream of freedom? Many of us have actually lost our ability to dream and envision ourselves beyond the hurt. We don't know who we are beyond the hurt because we've lost the spaciousness. Again, if we've lost the spaciousness, then I am hurt, I am wounded, I am traumatized. There's no space anymore to differentiate the hurt from our sense of self. By cultivating spaciousness, I can have the experience of hurt without it being the totality of my experience. There needs to be space for me to begin to understand that indeed this is just an experience within this vast amount of spaciousness. And within the space itself, in and around the broken-heartedness and within the trauma, I can experience liberation. I want to do that for myself. I want to experience liberation for myself. If other people are like me then I'm sure others want to experience that liberation as well. That opens the door to actual aspirational compassion, which is I want all of us to be free. Even the people that I can't stand.

You may not be ready for aspirational compassion right now. Maybe there's a group of people you can't wish compassion for at this time, and that's fine. We have to start somewhere, but we have to commit to getting there. We just can't say, "I want everyone to be free except for these folks." That's fine to start, but that's not where we're going to continue to be for the rest of our lives. Our work should always be to want everyone to be free, but that doesn't mean your actions will reflect aspirational compassion. In the world of Buddhism, there's a lot of people who walk around talking about how they want everyone to be free and they do inappropriate things that are not in line with compassion.

We have to move into compassion in action, which means I am beginning to enter into a deep discernment about what I am going to do to bring about the liberation of all beings, including myself. "What am I going to do? What am I going to get involved in? What are the practices that I'm going to deeply commit to?" The practices are important, but we also have to think critically about how to move into action:

> How am I going to start talking to people now? How am I going to start treating myself? How am I going to start setting better boundaries? How am I going to start interrupting violence around me as it happens? How am I going to take responsibility for my communities that I belong to? How am I going to repair the harm in my life with others? What am I going to do?

We're going to do something. And not only are we going to do something, we're going to do something that's likely to be really uncomfortable because compassion is helping us to choose the discomfort. People ask me all the time what their work is. I often say if it's easy, it's probably not your work. If you want to get free and it's easy, it's probably not liberation work. If it's hard, then that's a good sign that's where you need to be. If you're thinking right now, "I don't want to do that." Bingo. That's it. You found your work. Our aspiration has to be so strong that it propels us into the fruition of compassion, into compassion in action.

This is Where I'm at: Ethical Care, Clarity and Boundaries

Wisdom guides our expression of compassion. When we bring wisdom and compassion together, we create this intense momentum that drives us into enlightenment and realization; but compassion needs wisdom, and wisdom needs compassion. A more secular way to put this is that ethical care needs clarity, and clarity needs ethical care. Like two wings of a bird, wisdom and compassion fly us into enlightenment and realization. When we get compassion and wisdom together they can inspire us to develop a level of integrity that can seem self-righteous. That level of integrity means that I am getting really clear about who and what I am, and what I will and won't do. I'm getting clear about my boundaries. I'm getting clear about what's healthy for me and what isn't healthy because I care about myself, and I care about the well-being of others. Drawing the line and saying, "This is where I'm at," and holding that line is compassion in action in the moment. It could make you seem super self-righteous because we're living in a world where people are really struggling with integrity, where a lot of people don't know who and what they are. They don't have a sense of ethics, they don't have a sense of the practices of compassion and love. They're too afraid to touch into the energy of these practices for themselves. You show up with your boundaries, your compassion and your clarity, and you're going to seem self-righteous, but it's not self-righteous. Integrity is going to take us into tough places. It's going to take us into relationships with people who resent integrity and clarity. You have to take responsibility for that. This is part of the practice; this is part of the work: the choices that I make to get free will be misread by others around me. It's not right, but it's okay.

The Practice of the Seven Homecomings

The practice of the Seven Homecomings is a foundation practice this is going to help us hold, and over time move through, the broken-heartedness. This practice came directly out of the ways in which I was trying to figure out how to be in the world and have the support that I need to move through situations. The word homecoming comes out of this idea that when I find my refuge, and allow that source of refuge to hold me, it's like coming home to my favorite place where I feel really held, taken care of, seen and restored. It can be a room in your house or your house in general, or somewhere you grew up. Maybe it is outdoors, in nature? What does it feel like going to your favorite place and being in your favorite place? We don't have to go to those places to feel cared for, we can summon those places, those experiences, here with us in this moment, and in every moment that we need those experiences to be with us. It's a very personal practice and not set in stone. I think you can have as many homecomings as possible.

The Seven Homecomings, or what I call the seven sources of refuge, are based upon the three traditional sources of refuge that we find in Buddhism, beginning with the Buddha, the Dharma and the Sangha. Traditionally we take refuge in these Three Jewels. With the Seven Homecomings practice, I added four more sources of refuge: Ancestors and Lineage, The Earth, Silence and Ourselves. The seventh refuge, Ourselves, is the most important because our experiences and our bodies are the vehicle for liberation, so if we can't take refuge in ourselves, then it's going to be hard to obtain freedom. While you practice, offer yourself spaciousness. We're never about contracting and shutting down. We're always about expanding and opening. That's how we reduce violence; that's how we get free.

First Homecoming: Teachers, Guides and Mentors

Turn your attention to the First Homecoming: Teachers, Guides and Mentors. Any being, spirit, deity or saint who has been a teacher that we've gone to for advice and support or love. Invite those beings into this space and welcome them so they sit around you and form a circle of care.

Second Homecoming: Wisdom Texts

Next, turn your attention to the Second Homecoming: our Wisdom Texts. Invite the energy of any material that has been a source of clarity or wisdom for you, including scriptures, books, ideas and philosophies. This can include visual and performance arts, dance, music, poetry; anything that's helped you to experience openness, clarity, deeper love, deeper compassion. Invite the energy of this material into the circle as well.

Third Homecoming: Community

Next turn your attention to the Third Homecoming: Community. Reflecting on and calling into the space any community, group or space where you feel a sense of belonging; where the group wants you to experience happiness and freedom from suffering. This community also allows you to love it in return, and to express a deep wish for freedom and liberation back to the group. Invite those groups to come and sit with you in the space. If you don't have communities like this in your life then invite in the aspiration, so one day you'll be a part of communities where you experience love and are able to return love back.

Fourth Homecoming: Ancestors and Lineages

Next turn your mind to the Fourth Homecoming: Ancestors. This is simply opening your heart and mind to those ancestors who want to benefit you, who are trying to help you. Invite only those ancestors to sit in the sacred circle. Next turn your mind to the second part of the Fourth Homecoming: Lineages. This can be your spiritual lineages, lineages of great artists or activists or those within a certain school of thought that you've received great benefit from. Invite those beings into the circle as well.

Fifth Homecoming: Earth

Next turn your mind to the Fifth Homecoming: Earth. Acknowledge the earth under you, knowing that it is the energy of the living earth that supports your practice in this moment. You may also want to acknowledge the ancestral indigenous name of the land that you're living and practicing on, as well as the indigenous peoples of the lands.

Sixth Homecoming: Silence

Next turn your attention to the Sixth Homecoming: Silence. Invite the presence of silence into the circle so you may deeply turn within yourself.

Seventh Homecoming: Ourselves

Lastly, turn your attention to the Seventh Homecoming: Ourselves. Acknowledge your own experiences, mind and body. Allow yourself to show up and be present within the middle of the sacred circle that you have called upon.

Bringing the Circle of Care to the Experience of Broken-Heartedness

Slowly begin to imagine that your circle of care radiates the energy of care all around you. This energy of care can feel like whatever is appropriate for you. It can feel like love or compassion. It can feel like being seen, celebrated and validated. Begin to imagine that this energy slowly seeps into your body, into your skin, bones, muscles, tissues and even into your bloodstream. Begin to slowly be saturated with this deep, profound energy of care.

Maybe in this experience, you begin to identify your experience of broken-heartedness and how that manifests for you. You can begin to imagine that this broken-heartedness is being held and surrounded by this energy of care. Maybe you can even imagine your broken-heartedness dissolving into this energy of care.

Closing and Dedicating the Practice

To transition out of the practice, shift your attention back to your seat, noticing the weight of your body and your body making contact with the seat. Shift your attention back to your circle of care. Thank your circle of care for their support, for their guidance, for their love. You can ask them to remain sources of refuge and care for you from now on. Imagine that they dissolve into a white light and that white light is absorbed into your heart center. Return your attention back to the earth. Thank the earth for holding and supporting you during this practice. Thank your seat for holding you during this practice and your body for being a vehicle for this practice. Thank your breath for supporting you, and your mind for being the seed of enlightenment itself, for being awakened, actually, already. You can dedicate the merit of this practice, the energy of this practice, to the benefit of all beings. May all beings experience freedom and liberation from all suffering.

11
The Supreme Medicine of Exchanging Self-Enclosure for Altruism

Robert Thurman

In this chapter, it is my pleasure to introduce the essential teachings of Nalanda University, which integrated and transmitted the full legacy of all the Buddhist traditions throughout ancient India, including those of the Individual Vehicle or *Theravada*, the Universal Vehicle or *Mahayana*, and the Esoteric Vehicle or *Tantrayana*. That means distilling the oceanic intellectual and scriptural legacy contained within the entire gradual curriculum and all three great libraries of Nalanda, such as Ratnagiri, a legacy shared with many other great Indian Buddhist universities of the first millennium. Perhaps the greatest gift—the jewel in the crown—of this legacy is the holistic, analytic, and highly sophisticated mind/body medicine and psychology developed in India and most fully preserved in Tibet.

Although we are rightly proud of our modern medicine, with all its high-tech science and interventions, Tibetan doctors and psychologists are concerned that our worldview is too reductive, too materialistic. Many in the West now agree that our healthcare system has some real problems. Given its limitations in the realm of prevention and end-of-life care, its overuse of surgery and pharmaceuticals, and its access inequality, some think our medical system is in crisis. Increasingly, committed professionals have seen the need to complement conventional training and practice with alternatives, and many have become interested in the spiritual dimension of healing. As the evidence of brain science and clinical applications of meditation grow, I believe this will happen more and more, thanks to the effort of a few pioneers including the contributors of this volume. We are all very grateful to be able to teach caring healers from within the sacred circle or *mandala* of the Medicine Buddha, *Bhaishajyaguru*. Although psychology and psychotherapy actually fall more within the broad healing science and art of the

DOI: 10.4324/9781003243588-13

Buddha's teaching than the realm of Buddhist medicine, some of you may be doctors and nurses, and in any case the two overlap in the sophisticated neuropsychology of Tibet's Tantric Buddhism. So it is only fitting that as I set out to explain what is considered the essential nectar of Buddhist psychology, the art of exchanging self-enclosure for altruism, that I do so by first invoking and inviting you into the visionary world of healing offered by Tibetan medicine.

Envisioning the Buddha as Archetypal Healer

Traditionally, when a person aspires to become a Tibetan doctor or healer, not only does she work very hard to cultivate the altruistic spirit of universal love and compassion, but she would also imaginatively and ritually enter into the sacred circle or visionary world of the Medicine Buddha. What that healing individual does with that initiation or consecration into the world of the Buddha's healing is to cultivate a deep sense of connection. The ritual and contemplative art she enters into is meant to cultivate a sense of connection with the healing wisdom of the Medicine Buddha, and the healing presence of the Medicine Buddha; a sense that there are those who once lived or still live on this Earth who know at the deepest level what promotes health and eliminates sickness, who have the compassion to share that, and who are deeply concerned for the well-being and health of all life.

If you were to become a Tibetan doctor, psychologist, or healer, you would first learn to protect your heart and mind and to recharge your batteries, so that you can avoid the burnout that happens to many doctors, nurses, and psychologists, simply by being exposed to the immense amount of sickness and suffering in the world. The ritual consecration that placed you into the domain of the Medicine Buddha would also teach you a yoga in which you visualize the Medicine Buddha, and practice identifying yourself with him, so you can make yourself a vessel of healing wisdom and power. That doesn't mean that you must become a strictly spiritual healer. A Tibetan doctor doesn't live in a fantasy world that she can shine a light at you that makes you magically heal. Although there are some who focus on developing the psychic healing power of unconditional love and compassion, most are normal doctors who practice taking a medical history, doing pulse-diagnosis, analyzing the evidence, and prescribing lifestyle changes, meditations, acupuncture, or herbal pills. Yet they themselves sense the Medicine Buddha is with them and within them. They are protected, empowered, and focused in their energy by the exceptional healing power of the Buddha, understood as the supreme healer of the human condition, the preeminent mentor of doctors, nurses, psychologists, and all who seek to heal all the suffering of life on earth.

As a patient who is trying to heal, when you take the medicine, or do the recommended lifestyle therapy, you might also invoke the presence of the Medicine Buddha, say the *mantra* of Medicine Buddha, feel connected to that. This is meant to enhance the treatment by putting your mind into a positive state. This amounts to a consciously cultivated placebo effect. Buddhist medicine harnesses that power. So part of the reason to take an initiation or learn about the Medicine Buddha, whether as a healer or as a patient, is to engage the mind's full healing power. For the doctor or healer, that serves to intensify the potency of their bedside manner. For the patient, it serves to intensify the potency of the placebo effect in their mind. In fact, the healing power of mind is harnessed at all points in the medical system.

The Role of Mind and Heart in the Buddhist Medical Tradition

Of course, Tibetan medicine, Buddhist medicine, is not seen as in any way magical. It is seen as a science, based on an analytical understanding of the causes and conditions of illness and health. For instance, each herbal remedy is composed of as many as twenty to thirty separate herbs, grouped into three main categories: herbs that counteract a particular diagnosed disease process; herbs that mitigate side effects caused by the active ingredients of the compound; and herbs that promote the basic health and balance of underlying tissues to intensify and accelerate the healing process. In addition, the medicines are given within a complex healing regimen that usually involves prescribing a change from unhealthy behaviors to healing alternatives, psychological prescriptions to transform negative mind-states into positive ones, and even ethical prescriptions to renounce negative motivations and meaningless lifestyles in favor of positive motivations and lifestyles of greater meaning and purpose. So the doctor's recitation of the *mantra* and visualization of the healing environment are understood as subtle interpersonal and psychological factors that add to a highly rational and sophisticated multi-modal approach to healing (Dhonden, 2000).

The contemplative approach of Buddhist medicine does not only apply to conventional physical medicine and psychiatry but to all forms of care and teaching in all Buddhist civilizations, including those we would think of as spiritual counseling, psychological caretaking, and contemplative education. Compassion and its systematic cultivation play a fundamental role in all these forms of practice. This is evident in the fact that the capacity for empathy and compassion is considered a prerequisite for anyone embarking on a healing profession of any kind. Of course, basic intelligence, scientific knowledge, and practical expertise are all vital ingredients to effectiveness as a healer, but none of them is more fundamental than compassion. Just as Shakyamuni Buddha is praised not just for realizing enlightenment—including the relative, therapeutic omniscience we often attribute to our doctors—he is also praised for having the universal compassion that motivated him to become a healer and teacher for others. Without that compassion, all the knowledge in the world becomes a source of bondage, since without kindness it can lock us into an arrogant stance in which we are unwilling, even unable to help ourselves and others break free of self-enclosure and transform illness along with the pervasive suffering of fear and loss, aging and death, as well as the collective suffering of oppressive social systems.

Not only is compassion considered the basic foundation for any healing role but it is also seen as the quintessence of all healing training and practice. This is why modeling our own actions of body, speech, and mind after the Buddha—understood as *Bhiashajyaguru*, the Mentor of Healers, or *Bhaishajyaraja*, the Lord of Healers—becomes the natural place for us to enter the path of contemplative healing in the Nalanda tradition. Just as modern psychotherapists model themselves after Freud and his heirs in their training, by developing a transferential relationship with their own analyst—a living representative of the art—so Buddhist doctors, psychologists, and healers model themselves after the Medicine Buddha by means of a transferential art of meditation that aligns them with living mentors who embody Buddhahood for them (Zopa, 2001).

Exchanging Self-Enclosure for Altruism: Shantideva's Approach to Compassion

The essence of the Nalanda tradition is the extension of the Buddha's Individual Vehicle teachings of personal freedom into the mainstream of Indian civilization, based on the teachings of non-dual wisdom and universal compassion expressed in Universal Vehicle texts like the *Transcendent Wisdom Scripture* and *Medicine Buddha Scripture* (Thurman, 1996; Birnbaum, 2003). Historically, the Nalanda curriculum took shape based on the interpretations of these scriptures by a series of great masters beginning with the champions Nagarjuna (c. 150–250 CE) and Asanga (c. 350–450 CE). Although the father of the Nalanda tradition, Nagarjuna, is best known for his explanation of the profound wisdom of emptiness, he began his career as a physician, and in his capacity as a royal minister also gave shape to the healing art and science of universal compassion. His healing teachings on compassion contain the quintessence of this tradition, crystallized in his *Jewel Rosary, Ratnavali* (Hopkins, 2007). Tibetan scholars often quote one famous passage from that classic which distills that quintessence:

> Just as the grammarian teaches grammar,
> Buddhas give teachings appropriate to their disciples.
> To some, (they teach) abstaining from vice,
> To others, accomplishing virtue.
> To some, (they teach) reliance on dualism,
> (And finally to others) non-reliance on dualism:
> The profound, awe-inspiring practice of enlightenment,
> The emptiness that is the womb of compassion.

The word translated here as "emptiness," the Sanskrit *shunyata*, is Nagarjuna's term for the profound, ultimate nature of reality. It could equally be translated as "voidness," "freedom," or "openness." What is remarkable about this formula is that he calls emptiness "the womb of compassion." What he means by this is that realizing that all people and things lack their own intrinsic, independent, isolated nature or reality, realizing that they are entirely made of infinite interdependence or relativity, naturally gives rise to a sense of interconnection and compassion. The reality of emptiness itself is a kind of openness, like a sensitive and nurturing membrane that ties together all beings' sensitivities.

For a person who realizes that reality, another's suffering is as intolerable as her own. This way of seeing—called the spirit of enlightenment or *bodhicitta*—naturally leads to the development of a kind of enlightened altruism that became the focus of the Nalanda tradition. For six centuries after Nagarjuna, Nalanda masters continued to refine his wisdom and methods to cultivate that altruistic spirit and way of being. How to live in and with this radical openness and compassion—as an enlightened altruist or *bodhisattva*—became the special focus of the lineage of Asanga (c. 350–450 CE), who taught the cultivation of compassion by extending the emotional recognition, gratitude, and responsibility we feel for kin outwards towards all beings in seven steps. The two lineages of wisdom and compassion, championed by Nagarjuna and Asanga, came together in the philosophies of Chandrakirti (c. 575–675 CE) and Shantideva (c. 675–775 CE). It was their legacy that was transmitted into Tibet by the Nalanda abbot Atisha (982–1054) (Thurman, 1991). So we can appreciate the essential Nalanda teachings on wise compassion by looking at the work of Shantideva.

The Story of Shantideva and His Guide
to the Altruist's Way of Life

The story passed down to Tibetan scholars about Shantideva revolves around one of the great masterpieces of Indian literature and world spirituality, called the *Guide to the Altruist's Way of Life*, *Bodhisattvacharyavatara* (Shantideva, 1997). The story begins in a humorous way. A humble monk at Nalanda University, Shantideva was such a recluse that he had developed a reputation as the laziest and worst student of his day. This reputation earned him the name Bhusuku, which means "he who eats, sleeps, and defecates." Given his reclusive ways, his peers assumed that that was the sum of what he did. Nalanda for centuries had been India's preeminent university. People would come from all over the subcontinent, and beyond, from the farthest reaches of Asia. They would study for a number of years, and when they had finished, they would graduate and return to their home region to become a teacher, ruler, doctor, or government official.

Shantideva had been living in solitude at Nalanda for many years, so his professors insisted that it was time for him to defend his doctoral thesis. Traditionally, a thesis defense at Nalanda was a large public lecture given to the whole university community, which in his day numbered as many as 10,000 students and faculty. As the word circulated that the date for his defense had been set, the assumption was that Bhusuku would simply embarrass himself, and finally be dismissed from the community. The humble monk agreed. At the appointed date and time, he appeared on the lecture platform. Then he asked his audience, "Would you like to hear something similar to what you have heard before, or something unprecedented?" Some of the senior monks replied with a challenge, "From you, Bhusuku, we want something unheard of." "Very well, then," he agreed, "I will share with you my unprecedented work, but if anyone is curious, my references are compiled in a *Compendium of Teachings*, *Shikshasammucchaya*, which I have in my cell, hidden under the bed."

As he began his address, legend has it that he levitated slightly over the platform, about three feet in the air, because some of the audience in the back couldn't see him. Then he began to recite his *Guide* from memory. The entire audience gradually became fully absorbed in the poetic verses of his masterpiece, some who were scribes were actually transcribing his words as he uttered them. When he reached the ninth chapter, he arrived at the verse which begins the ultimate analysis of self in four keys: "Without contacting the phenomenal (self as) designated by delusion, you cannot realize its nonexistence."

Figure 11.1 *Shantideva,* Poet of Unconditional Compassion (Robert Beer, Used with Permission)

At that point, it is said, he suddenly began levitating higher into the air and floating away. But before he left he announced that he had chosen to call himself "Shanti-deva," which in Sanskrit means "God of peace." His intention was that he wanted everyone who heard his name to feel at peace.

The chapters of Shantideva's *Guide* are arranged according to the six transcendent virtues. These refer to refined and extended visions of ordinary virtues, which arise when the practice of good qualities is inspired by enlightened altruism, guided by the self-transcendent wisdom of emptiness, and motivated by universal compassion. So the first two chapters introduce the nature and benefits of the spirit of enlightened altruism. The following six explain the practice of the transcendent virtues—generosity, justice, tolerance, creativity, meditation, and wisdom—based on conceiving and realizing that spirit. And the tenth chapter explains the dedication of this work to the benefit of all living beings. Although there is no one chapter devoted exclusively to compassion, the understanding is that all these virtues involve the integrated practice of wisdom and compassion in different forms. Shantideva shares his profound method of transforming the mind by this non-dual practice in the latter part of the eighth chapter devoted to transcendent meditation. In the Nalanda tradition, there is also a system of ten transcendent virtues related to the ten stages of an enlightened altruist's development, in which the seventh virtue is the practice of compassion in action, known as empathic art or *upaya*.

The Chapter on Meditation and the Practice of Exchanging Self and Other

Within chapter eight, starting at verse 90, Shantideva introduces the art of compassion after explaining how meditation depends on solitude: "Thus having considered the excellence of solitude, by the many themes appreciating its value" (Thurman, 1996, p. 152,). The idea here is to prepare oneself for contemplative solitude by renouncing bodily pleasures and attachments, then to practice concentration, and finally to transform the mind.

He begins explaining meditation on compassion by introducing what he calls the equality of self and other: "First of all, let me strive to contemplate the equality of self and other. Since we are all equal in seeking pleasures and avoiding pains, I should guard all others as I do myself." What kind of person, with what kind of experience, does it take to realize such a radical equality? A person who sees the ultimate equality of all living beings in Buddhism is called a noble individual, following the fundamental framework of Buddhist teachings: Shakyamuni's Four Noble Truths. Although we are most familiar with that framework from the Theravada tradition, it is also fundamental to Mahayana and even Vajrayana traditions. The word translated as "noble" here is the Sanskrit term *arya*. Although historically it had referred to the social standing of the Indian nobility as opposed to the common people, the Buddha transformed it into a spiritual term. In Buddhism, the word noble distinguishes a person who has seen and feels that there is no real separation between living beings. This way of being is contrasted with that of an alienated individual who sees and feels that he has a self that is truly separate or different from others. While the noble truths apply to personal happiness and freedom in the Theravada tradition, in the Mahayana we recognize that the laws governing transforming our own suffering into happiness apply equally to all other beings. And in the Vajrayana we see that they apply to the transformation of unconscious, compulsive modes of embodied life into fully integrated, blissful ways.

Shantideva begins his discussion of compassion with this principle of radical equality since (as Nagarjuna taught) universal and natural compassion comes out of a direct, nonconceptual realization of emptiness. A person becomes a noble person when she has had the direct experience that all people and things are without a substantial, separate self, because she no longer sees or feels any real separation or difference from others. The mind of such a noble person is a "womb of compassion," because she experiences all beings universally and naturally as one field of sensitive life, all deserving the same love and compassion as herself and her loved ones.

How does nonconceptual experience of emptiness lead to compassion rather than to a trance-like absence of feeling? Direct realization of emptiness includes not just the space-like equipoise concentration, where everything seems to disappear, including oneself. It also and equally includes the return of appearances in the dream-like aftermath concentration. In other words, the realization of emptiness is more nondual than we think. It's not just about a seeming disappearance but also about a distinctive reappearance. Both aspects of this experience—the nonconceptual and the conceptual— are considered equally "noble" intuitive wisdoms. This non-duality is clear from the teaching that authentically experiencing emptiness also includes experiencing "the emptiness of emptiness." When, after emerging from the dissolution or disappearance of space-like wisdom, you experience the emptiness of what you first thought was emptiness, people and things reemerge out of emptiness, all things come out of the space or womb where it seemed there wasn't anything. An equal part of the nonconceptual realization of emptiness properly understood is when emptiness *itself* disappears, and the world is back, only less clearly solid or separated.

So what Nagarjuna and Shantideva are saying is that when you achieve that realization, one of the natural effects is an expansion and extension of compassion. Once you get out of yourself, and then come back to yourself, having lost yourself in one sense, then the way you perceive yourself is completely different because you perceive yourself as an other, in a natural equality with all beings. Therefore you begin to be a person who automatically and naturally considers the feelings of others as well as your own. As the verse says, we all come to seem and feel equal because we are all in fact equal in wanting and deserving no end of pleasure, and in our wish and right to avoid pain.

So the noble person, according to the Buddhist psychology and phenomenology of human awareness, is the person who perceives another as equal to themselves automatically. They know what the other is feeling because they feel it. When you see a certain expression on someone's face, or even when you hear them say "ouch," even an ordinarily sensitive, empathic human being will automatically think "ouch" as well. What we may not know is that there are higher degrees of that sensitivity, where you automatically feel the pain empathetically through seeing the expression or being in the presence of that person, rather than having to think, "Oh, that person said 'Ouch,' and grimaced so they must be in pain." Of course such heightened sensitivity requires facing and seeing through personal and social biases that limit our ability to feel the suffering of others with very different social location and lived experience. That intuitive capacity is what makes you "noble" in the Buddhist view.

You may be a ruler or warrior, born into the aristocracy, but still be psychologically a common, self-centered individual. But when your self-centeredness has melted down even once, when you return to yourself, you now realize, "I'm not as central to this world as I thought." This is not a merely verbal experience. You feel different, and become more of a field of awareness, in which other people's sensitivity begins to feel like your own. Of course there are degrees of that transformation; it's a gradual process. People involved in caregiving are said to realize this transformation more easily, whether as part of their embodied experience of child bearing or child rearing, or some other form of caregiving.

Field Awareness: The Emptiness That Is the Womb of Compassion

Once we open into that field awareness, simple self-satisfaction is not so easy. From the noble person's point of view, even enjoying simple sensual pleasures may be felt to involve suffering when others around us are suffering. In the Buddhist tradition, there's a saying that the pain in the world is like a grain of sand in the hand of an alienated person, but like a grain of sand in the eye of a noble person. The sensitivity is much greater for the person who is automatically and empathetically aware of what everyone around them is feeling. Shantideva makes this expanded field sensitivity the subject of another verse:

> The parts of the body such as hands are many. They are one in needing to be protected. In pleasure and pain, all living beings are just like me in only wanting to be happy. So why not regard them as all parts of one body?

This verse gives you some sense of what it might be like to be enlightened and to feel that another person is actually yourself. How complicated that must be. When you look at your own hand, you may think, "If I am the consciousness seeing the hand, then the hand must be other than me." Of course, we would still exist if for some terrible reason our hand was amputated. Without that hand, I would still be me, so in a sense, the hand is *not* me. Yet when I look at the hand, even as something separate from me, it feels like me at the same time. Now, given that thought experiment, imagine if you were looking at another person and suddenly felt that person was you, in the same way as your hand is you. Imagine your sensitivity extending out to and encompassing their sensitivity. Of course, in one sense, they *are* different. Such an enlightened, field awareness is far more complex than normal myopic awareness. It requires a tolerance of cognitive dissonance. It means being able to combine different levels of perception simultaneously. Those of you who work as psychotherapists likely experience and develop this kind of field awareness.

In the next verse, Shantideva's own mind poses an objection, "But I don't actually feel their pain." Then he answers, "The pain of others may not be inflicted on my body, but still becomes unbearable to me when I identify their pain as if it were mine." For instance, consider a person who is hypnotized. You may light a match under their feet, but in a trance they may not feel it. If you apply enough heat, their skin may burn and blister, although in some cases the injury itself may be reduced by hypnosis. The point is, even though the pains of others do not affect me directly, once I identify their pains as mine, they too become hard to bear. Such is the case for parents when their children suffer, or for lovers when their beloved suffers. Shantideva is saying that after some direct realization of emptiness, you do begin to feel the pains of others. When you identify their pains as your pains, and they become equally hard to bear, that is what compassion means. When the suffering of others is unbearable to you, because you feel that suffering with them, you have compassion. Conversely, when we lack a sense of common human identity or compassion we are at risk of inflicting harm on others, or not being helpful to others, because of our insensitivity or self-enclosure.

Spontaneous, Unconditional Compassion: Breaking the Unconscious Self-Habit

This reflection leads to Shantideva's next simple yet powerful verse, "So I must dispel the pains of others, because they are pains, just like my own." When you have pain, say you put your hand on a stove burner, you do not think, "Should I take it off? Should I be compassionate to my hand?" You just automatically take it off, because you feel pain. Likewise, if you have this field sensitivity, others' pains are unbearable to you automatically; you just don't want them to have those pains. You feel, "All these beings have bodies like mine, when they hurt I must help." Shantideva drives this home,

> When I and others both are alike in wanting happiness, what is so special about me that I strive for my happiness alone? When I and others are alike in both not wanting pain, what is so special about me that I guard myself but not others?

Then again, Shantideva's mind objects, "I do not protect them since their pains do not hurt me." This time in answer he points out that insensitivity is only a function of our myopic, alienated sense of identity, "Then why do I guard myself from future pains, since they also do not hurt me now?" When we identify with our anticipated future pain, and act to protect ourselves against it, we only do so because we imagine that we are going to have that pain. In fact, we typically tend to do that too much; we worry about the future pains that may never come. The following verse pushes the argument further, "'I will experience that [future pain]' is a mistaken notion, for the one who dies here is almost totally different from the one reborn." What Shantideva means is that whoever you are today, you will be different tomorrow. In fact, you are different in this moment from what you were just this morning. We ourselves, like the cosmos and everything in it, are totally and continuously changing. We have this exaggerated sense of continuity, which we then reify into an absolute sense of self. That is what Buddhist psychology calls our "self-habit." It is all wrapped up in creating a fantasy of unchanging, independent, intrinsically identifiable, objective and substantial self, in order to deny the obvious reality of our complete interdependence and constant change.

Of course, this does not mean that Shantideva or Nagarjuna believe that there is no continuity linking different parts of our lives or even different lifetimes in the multi-life process Buddhists describe as rebirth or reincarnation. The Buddha gave the famous analogy that one life continuum carrying over into the next is like one candle lighting another: the flame carries on as a continuum of heat, a causally based stirring of molecules, even though the newly lit candle contributes new wax and a new wick. It is said to be difficult to remember past lives (whether we consider them ours or our parents') because most of our memories from this life are stored in coarse level memories we now call "explicit." Our deeper, "implicit" level of memories reach further back into our development, or ancestral past. While many of us are forced to actively face and struggle with traumatic memories from adverse childhood experience or systemic forms of trauma, others may tend to repress memories of personal and collective trauma and compartmentalize them within our subtler, unconscious level of mind and body. Buddhist psychology is not merely a matter of dismantling repressions in the unconscious, although that may be healing and helpful. It actually aims at our becoming fully awakened, fully conscious of the personal and collective unconscious.

Just as we anticipate future pain even though we are not immediately feeling it, identifying empathetically with others' suffering is not exactly the same as feeling it. Still, it does stir compassion; and compassion does motivate compassionate action. Let us return to Shantideva's argument that real compassion is not a calculation, but a natural sensitivity and a natural response. "Although such self-concern is not rational, it happens because of the self-habit. There is no possessor of pain, so who can take control of it?" His point here is that whatever pain and suffering we face in life, our experience of it is heightened when we over-identify with that pain and suffering, adding worst-case narratives, emotions, and reactions that compound the primary experience. Something similar happens when we encounter pain and suffering in others since this naturally evokes in us our own memories of pain and suffering, including thoughts and feelings of over-identification that added to our past suffering. His reminder not to over-identify with or fixate on our pain and suffering opens the door to a healing awareness of such difficulty as a part of our common human experience that actually connects us to all other life through compassion. He concludes, "There being no owner of pain, all pains are without distinctions of self and other." In other words, because there is no owner of pain, then others' pain might just as well be mine. It must be dispelled not because of some issue regarding personal identity, or some narrative construction of life—past, present, and future—but simply because it is pain.

Unblocked Spontaneous Compassion and the Altruist's Heroic Resolve

This understanding amounts to a sort of universal imperative to alleviate all pain, to which his mind poses another objection: "Why should the unknown pain of all be abolished?" To this he replies, "This is no argument (but a simple fact): to abolish my own I must abolish all. Otherwise I must stay in pain with all other beings." This recognition of our total interdependence with all life becomes the foundation for the extraordinary rationality of the *bodhisattva's* altruistic resolve. For instance, when we recognize that a cultural system of racial oppression harms everyone involved, albeit in very different ways depending on whether it puts us in positions of privilege or targets us for oppression, then we can develop a very strong resolve to dismantle it based on a sense of deep solidarity with those oppressed by it as well as with those whose access to compassion and inclusive community is blocked by any complicity or denial of that systemic harm. This universal, enlightened self-interest is the basis of the altruist's spirit, the heroic resolve that I be the one to save all beings from suffering. But despite our natural wish to aspire to such an uplifting ideal, unless our view of reality (of our own life and the infinite lives around us) makes this a plausible and practical solution to our predicament, we are just paying lip service and actually missing the seriousness of this vow.

If we approach this compassionate spirit from the alienated perspective of an ordinary human, how could we possibly vow to save all beings? Unless we have first broken out of our shell and come to understand that who and what we really are is part of a selfless network of infinite interdependence over infinite lives, this vow makes no sense. It's ridiculous, maybe even a delusion that requires medical treatment. The point is we have to have reworked our underlying conditioned assumption of being identified myopically with just this one body, one life. We realize that what we truly are has been here evolving forever, and will carry on and on, in some way forever. The point of the vow then becomes painfully obvious: unless I do something special about it, my life and others like it will go on in this unhappy way forever. The *bodhisattva* vow offers a rational, logical way of being, when you realize your infinite entanglement or entwinement with other beings. We save for retirement, buy life insurance to protect our loved ones, but what about planning for a better psychological future for us all? If our field awareness will in some way go on beyond this one body and life, do we want to be harming, disliking, and irritating each other forever? Of course not. We want to be all loving with each other. So therefore, I must help diminish and finally eliminate all pains—my own and others—because otherwise, I will remain enmeshed with all others in suffering.

The Buddha Solution: Emptiness, Compassion, and the Infinite Web of Causality

Given this understanding, the best we can do for ourselves and each other is to each become a Buddha for the sake of all. The best solution to our human condition is for everyone to become blissfully happy, which is only possible when we become enlightened. The point is, there is no escape from the web of infinite relationship that our lives depend on. So it becomes only rational that we take even tiny baby steps to ameliorate all our relationships. In this view, the tiniest positive cause has an infinite effect, and the tiniest negative cause has an infinite effect. In *The Compendium of Teachings*, Shantideva quotes the *King of Concentration Scripture*: "Who understands causality," that is, the *karmic* causality of intentional action and development, "understands emptiness." Everything being a web of causality means that everything is empty of any non-causal element. Therefore, emptiness is relativity, and relativity is emptiness; they are fully equivalent. It is vitally important to remember that emptiness is not nothingness, but the relativity of infinite somethingness, the causal interdependence of all relative things. So, one who understands emptiness becomes minutely observant of the tiniest things. This is the ultimate meaning of being mindful. Being mindful of the tiniest things, when you know relativity and emptiness, means realizing that every little thing has infinite repercussions. This doesn't just apply to what you physically do, or what you say, it's also what you think. The most powerful *karmic* causality is what you're thinking. Hence the Tibetan saying, "If you want to know what your future is like, look at your mind in this moment."

The engine of *karmic* causality never idles, either at the mental, verbal, or physical levels. This is why Buddhist cultures have so many Nalandas, so many contemplative universities, because the society and everybody in it wants to go clean up their mind. They have become poignantly aware that even thinking is either evolutionary or devolutionary action. When your view of reality includes the fact that the tiniest little piece of selfishness and the tiniest little piece of generosity both have infinite effects, then you're very careful of what you do. And if you are careful of what you do, you quickly realize you have to take much better care of your mind, because all actions begin with acts of mind.

So Shantideva concludes, "She who attunes her mind like this, delights in eradicating others' pains, and can plunge into the fires of hell like a wild goose into a lotus lake." And he continues:

> The vast ocean of joy, when all beings are free, why am I not satisfied with that? What can I do with a solitary freedom? Accomplishing the welfare of beings, I should not be conceited or amazed with myself, but enjoying singlemindedly the welfare of others, I need not expect any rewarding fruit. Just as I protect myself from unpleasant things, however slight, I should have a protective concern and compassionate attitude for others. Through the power of familiarization, I have come to regard as myself a few drops of others' sperm and ovum, in themselves quite insubstantial. Since I learned to do that, likewise why can I not come to regard others' well-developed bodies as myself? Having understood the flaws in self-concern, and the ocean of advantages in other concern, I must abandon self-preoccupation and cultivate concern for others.

(Thurman, 1996, pp. 154–155)

This conclusion is one of Shantideva's key formulations of the art of exchanging self and other. Of course, it isn't necessary to wait until you're totally empathetic before you can begin this practice. All it requires is that instead of constantly thinking about, "What am I getting? What do I want? What do I have?" you focus on, "What does she want? What does he want? What do they have?" You simply start to think primarily about others, and then you'll naturally practice altruism. Shantideva goes on to explain:

> One who desires as soon as possible to give refuge to self and others should practice the holy secret teaching of the transposition of self and other. If I give it away, what can I enjoy? Such selfish thinking is the demons' way. If I enjoy it, what can I give? Such altruism is the way of the gods.

Finally, he follows these powerful verses with what I call Shantideva's challenge:

> All suffering in this world arises from the wish for one's own happiness. All happiness in the world arises from the wish for others' happiness. What need is there to say more. The immature work for their sake alone, Buddhas work for the sake of others, just look at the difference between them! If I don't truly exchange my happiness for others' sufferings not only will I not attain (the bliss of) Buddhahood, I will not gain even fleeting happiness.
>
> (Thurman, 1996, p. 156)

Shantideva's Heart Practice Finds its Way into Tibet

Shantideva's art was eventually transmitted into Tibet, where it forms the basis for the practice called *lojong* or mind transformation. This particular tradition came through the great Bengali prince/the abbot of the eleventh century, Atiśa, who was invited to Tibet in 1042 (Jinpa, 2005). The story goes that Atiśa had a statue of Tara, the female Buddha, who used to speak to him. After being invited to Tibet, he asked her what to do. She said,

> You should accept the invitation of the Tibetans, and go up to that cold, harsh, difficult land. It will shorten your lifespan by seventeen years, but the years you spend there will have a thousand times more impact for the Buddhist teaching than if you stay as the abbot of Nalanda.

Atiśa listened, and lived for twelve years in Tibet. Those years hugely impacted all schools of Tibetan Buddhism. The tradition coming from him is called the *Kadampa*, the tradition of personal instruction, which refers to the personal transference of teachings from mentor to disciple. In this tradition, the right teacher is one who applies the teaching appropriate to the needs of the particular student, just as the Buddha gave the teachings tailored to a particular person. Within the tradition of the *Kadampas*, there are many famous anecdotes describing the encounters between different masters and their students.

Atiśa Meets His Mentor: The Nalanda Abbot in Indonesia and Tibet

These anecdotes include the story of how Atiśa met his mentor for the practice of transforming the mind, whose name was Dharmakirti of Suvarnadvipa (the island in Indonesia he originally came from). The story is that at a certain point in his career, Atiśa was in Bodhgaya, circumambulating the great shrine around the enlightenment tree, when the statue of Tara on the wall there spoke to him. "That's nice, Atiśa," she said, "but wouldn't it be better if you practiced the teaching?" "What do you mean?" he asked the statue, "I'm circumambulating, bowing, and saying *mantras*, what else should I do?" Then Tara replied, "You may be doing all those things, but you're just going through the motions. You have no spirit of enlightenment, no compassionate mind, no *bodhisattva* vow, and no will to benefit all life." Confused, he questioned her again, "What do you mean? I took the *bodhisattva* vow." Then she replied, "No, you could not possibly have taken that vow, because there is no spirit of enlightenment left in India, the lineage has been broken." Naturally he inquired, "So is it unbroken anywhere else in the world?" And she answered, "Yes, it remains unbroken in Indonesia." So he traveled all the way to Indonesia to meet this Dharmakirti. After spending years there with his mentor, he came back to India and started spreading the authentic transmission of the spirit of altruism, inspired by the wisdom archetype Manjushri. That is the exchange of self and other lineage passed down to Dharmakirti from Jayananda, a disciple of Shantideva.

This practice is universally accepted by all schools of Tibetan Buddhism, and is considered the heart practice of the Nalanda tradition by the great master scholars of Tibet from Tsong Khapa down to the present Dalai Lama. Its essence is the spirit of heroic altruism inspired by universal love and compassion. There are two types of this spirit, the will to enlightenment and the active spirit of enlightenment. The will means that although you are not yet enlightened, you do have that deeper feeling that we are all connected in love to each other. Therefore you're inspired to make the altruist's vow: "My life purpose is to make all beings happy. To remove all the suffering of all beings, I will take it upon myself if necessary, and eventually get rid of it."

This is considered like the second birth of all beings, to create this spirit. The irony is, even if you take this vow, you don't want to become a person overly sensitized by too many mirror neurons. Our discouragement in the face of suffering, our burnout, exists only because we worry too much about controlling and fixing things. With the genuine spirit of enlightenment, however, whether we are succeeding right away or not, we are happy. We are happy simply because we feel we are doing our utmost and that at least our mind is headed in the right direction.

This practice has to do with understanding the transformative power of mind when we shift its orientation to a positive mode of field awareness, a field of concern uniting us together with all life. This reminds me of Rupert Sheldrake's theory of morphogenetic resonance (Sheldrake, 2009). Sheldrake is an Oxford biologist who talks about a sociobiological force by which the energy and information patterns of all our brains are isomorphically interconnected with each other. When one person's mind–brain patterns shift, it affects the whole field of beings around her. The power of transforming the mind through practices like Shantideva's comes from the realization that when we make even a small victory over negativity in our own minds it naturally improves the field of resonance linking us to all living beings. Our change of mind resonates out and helps others shift theirs, like a flock of wild geese who are flying together in formation and then very suddenly all turn together at once. If you practice mindfulness because you are trying to clean up your own life, then your practice has usefulness and a certain power. But if you practice mindfulness in the sense that you are doing it for everyone, knowing your transformation of mind will radiate out to impact everyone, then your intensity is so much more powerful. This is Mahayana practice, because it is for everyone.

Living for Everyone: The Higher Purpose of Infinite Competence

When you live for everyone you simply live better. As the Dalai Lama says, if you want to be happy, or if you want to be selfish, be wise-selfish, be compassionate. Being altruistic will satisfy both others and yourself, being selfish will satisfy neither others nor yourself. Our lives may not have an intrinsic purpose, but we can choose a purpose. In fact, our lives can become eminently purposeful. That purpose is to really find happiness and bliss ourselves, and to share them with every other being, no matter how close or far they are from us, or how easy or challenging we find them. Real bliss or happiness doesn't come from having some ice cream, or winning the lottery, or winning the

Olympics. It comes from understanding that reality is naturally blissful when we attune to it, because reality is infinite connectedness, the infinite creative energy that fulfills any kind of desire. When we discover that and work to share it with every other being, that is called becoming a Buddha. Then we have an evolutionary purpose, and we have an evolutionary goal. This is not something to be reified as a fixed state, but more like an infinite competence. If you have a friend or a loved one, and they break something, you naturally want to help fix it. If you are a doctor, you would like to provide this treatment, or offer that medicine. If you are here infinitely, you are capable of infinite improvement in your ability to help. You can become the ultimate doctor, who has the bedside manner par excellence, who just comes in and helps a person feel infinitely better. So I like to say, Buddha is not omnipotent, but omni-competent. Luckily there are an infinite number of potential Buddhas, because there is no limit to the potential of life, much less to the universe. We have an infinite field of omni-competence circling around waiting for us to get the message, to wake up to real understanding and to make better choices for ourselves and others. So let's wake up and get to work.

12

Interpersonal Connection, Compassion, and Well-Being

The Science and Art of Healing Relationships

Daniel J. Siegel

In this chapter I'd like to explore what the field of interpersonal neurobiology has to teach us as psychotherapists about the role of human relationships, especially compassionate relationships, in health and well-being. This field is one in which we approach human life from multiple disciplines—physics, biology, psychology, sociology, anthropology—and try to bring them all to bear on understanding things from the standpoint of consilience. Consilience refers to those ways in which all the disciplines that shed light on different aspects of our human experience, health, and well-being converge or overlap. Based on this broad foundation, we can begin to understand the importance of a key dimension of human health and well-being that is only now being fully appreciated; that is, the dimension of integration.

Integration refers to a way of being of any complex system in which the connections between parts or elements of the larger whole exist in an optimal balance with the distinctness of those parts or elements. Whether this balance involves the parts of an individual mind and body, of the individuals within a given relationship, family, or society, or of humanity as one species within the complex ecosystem of the earth, integration is a sign of health and promotes well-being. Given the vital importance of integration to health and well-being, we can better understand those human capacities that foster integration within individuals and relationships. In this context, I will focus on two in particular: mindful awareness as a capacity that fosters the integration of an individual mind, brain, and body; and compassion as a capacity that fosters the integration of individuals with any given relationship, family, or society.

DOI: 10.4324/9781003243588-14

Mind and Empathy: The Missing Ingredients in Modern Healthcare

I'd like to begin exploring integration and the capacities that foster it with a story. It's a sad story but I think it's important. When I was in medical school, back in the late 1970s, many of my professors shared an approach to patients I found concerning. After they would get their lab data, they would walk with us, the medical students, into the patient's room. They would say to the patient, "I've received the results of your testing. You have a fatal disease, and you probably have three or four months to live. I'm sorry. Goodbye." When they would leave the room, I would tug on their white coat and ask, "Don't you want to talk to the patient about how she feels?" In retrospect, I don't really know what they were attending to. One after another, my professors would say, "Why would I do that? I've tested what's going on in their bodies. I've given them the information they need. There's nothing more I can do."

If you were a young medical student, how would you take that in? We were being taught by example how to be representatives of this stance on healing, to simply say, "I'm reporting on the physical state of your body." Of course, these were very smart professors; I was at Harvard University. These doctors were giving their patients data about the physical nature of the world. Ultimately, I ended up dropping out of medical school, and thought about entering all sorts of other professions. Instead, I chose to go back, and to begin to think deeply about how to understand and describe the nature of that subjective experience we call "mind." As a physician, psychiatrist, psychotherapist, scientist, and educator, throughout my career I have been saddened and dismayed to find a firm grounding in the healthy mind absent even from our professional education and our work. After surveying over 100,000 mental health clinicians and nearly 10,000 teachers, the results are in: over 95 percent of these professionals focusing on helping others develop their minds have never been offered a working definition of what the mind is!

So, I have worked over the years with many colleagues to develop the field of interpersonal neurobiology, where we combine over a dozen branches of science to address the question of what a working definition of the mind might be and, based on that, try to understand what a healthy mind is. While we have a bunch of chemicals that make up the structure of the body with all their interesting molecular combinations, there is also something more, something equivalent to the whole being greater than the sum of its parts. That something more is the mind, which at a minimum has subjective experience, what you feel. When someone tells you you'll be dying in three to four months, you have an inner subjective core that is not the same as the molecular structure of your body. That is mind. The ability to see it involves something more than mere eyesight. In 1980, I decided to call that ability "mindsight." I understand mindsight as the ability of mind to see itself. It's insight into your own inner subjective world. And it's also empathy for the inner world of someone else. The fact is, we human beings, and perhaps all living beings, have an internal subjective experience that is the fundamental nature of what we mean when we say, "mind." In addition to mindful awareness and empathy or compassion, the third component of mindsight is something that is a consilient finding across all different disciplines; that is, that well-being, including the full capacity for seeing into one's own mind and other minds, is dependent on a singular process: the process of integration.

In this context, I'm using the word integration in a very specific way, to mean the linkage, the connection of differentiated parts of a system, the linkage of things that are unique, specialized. For example, in the system of medicine, a patient has a differentiated role in relation to a clinician, whether a psychologist, nurse, occupational therapist, or physician. Then other third parties are involved in the whole system. Or within any one individual, integration refers to the connectivity or linkage between differentiated aspects of mind, brain, and body. It turns out that what I call mindsight is the capacity to see and promote such integration, whether it's expressed as insight into oneself, honoring the complexity of our own inner life, or empathy for others, honoring their complexity and differentiation (Siegel, 2010a). Sadly, when I go to medical schools around the world, even to departments of psychology or psychiatry, most never teach their students or clinicians how to understand and heal their own inner life. Without that basic capacity, it becomes very hard for us as clinicians to understand and heal the inner lives—the mind, brain, and body—of the others we call patients or clients. That is why I felt I had to use my professors as anti-role models, as examples of how not to practice medicine. Fortunately, 25 years later, we have a growing body of evidence in neuroscience and medicine that is leading to a gradual shift in perspective, and the beginnings of a shift in practice.

The Impact of Mindsight on Health and Healing

When I was invited in 2005 to return to Harvard Medical School and speak about the neuroscience of emotion and narrative and its role in medicine, I was able to point to a number of new studies showing the power of mindful awareness and empathy in healing. For instance, I pointed to one double-blind study of students being seen with a common cold in a college infirmary during exam period. In the control group, the students were simply informed by their providers that they in fact had a cold and should recover soon (Rakel et al., 2009). In the experimental group, the provider spent 30 seconds inquiring about the student's level of stress and making an empathic comment such as "It must be really hard to be sick during exam period." The study found that the immune response in the experimental group was more robust, and that that group recovered faster.

What we can say now is that empathy is not a luxury for physicians. Empathy is a fundamental part of the system we're working in as clinicians. That system is one of human relationships. Relationships can be defined as the sharing and flow of energy and information. When we talk to each other, with the movement of air molecules, we can hear one another. We can see each other because of photons. A clinician who puts her hand on a patient's hand when they're upset is using physical contact. That's energy. Our work in psychotherapy is all about how we derive information, which is energy with meaning and symbolism, from the energy patterns of our interaction with clients. In many ways that's what our mental lives are all about. By mind I mean the subjective experience, the consciousness of meaning and symbolism, a distinctively human, psychological form of information processing. Of course, it involves the brain, and we'll come to that in a moment. But my point is that since our work concerns relationships, it involves the sharing of energy and information flow. So, this kind of care requires that we differentiate, that we have our own inner subjective experience, and then link that with the inner subjective experience of another.

P-A-R-T: Applied Mindsight for Clinicians

When I teach physicians or psychotherapists, this is where I start, by understanding healing relationships (Siegel, 2010b). Relationships that promote health are integrated relationships, honoring differences, promoting linkages. As a clinician, you don't become the patient, but you attune to their internal world. I like to unpack this process using an acronym. When people ask me, "What is the part in the healing relationship a psychotherapist needs to take?" I frame my answer using the word "P-A-R-T," which stands for these four elements. P stands for presence. We can now study the idea of a clinician or any human being present for another person. This requires a receptive state of mind that allows you to receive things without judgment. Some people like to overlap this capacity with the practice of mindful awareness. In the research center I co-founded at UCLA, we recognize mindful awareness as a way of developing presence.

Presence allows for the second aspect of PART, the A, which stands for attunement. Attunement is the focusing of our attention on the inner nature of a person. It's usually used to mean interpersonal attunement. I believe that mindful awareness is actually a form of internal attunement. Attunement emerges from presence, so you attune to your own internal nature as well as that of another person. The clinician who offered the 30-second empathic comment in the study I mention had to be present to realize that the patient was a student in final exams. Then that clinician was able to attune to the student's internal world, and that attunement allowed her to engage in the third aspect of PART, the R, which stands for resonance, resonating.

To resonate means that, as a clinician, I don't become my patient with a cold who's facing final exams, but I do feel connected and resonant enough to sense their feelings. They change me because of the resonance I'm experiencing in my attunement, and the resonance and attunement can only happen because I'm present. Resonance is like a guitar string. You don't become the lower-pitched strings if you're a high-pitched string, but you do resonate with them. This is where the phrase "The whole is greater than the sum of its parts" begins to make sense. Instead of two individuals in a clinical encounter, it becomes a "we." This understanding is everything. A "we" created from presence, attunement, and resonance creates the fourth aspect of PART.

When you're present, attuned, and resonate literally through the connected nervous systems of the two individuals involved, what is created is trust. Steven Porges has elegantly referred to this process in terms of something he calls the social engagement system, which is turned on when we can be present, attuned, and resonant (Porges, 2011). All sorts of physiological benefits emerge from this engagement, benefits that contemplative neuroscientist Richie Davidson and many others have demonstrated and described (Davidson & Begley, 2013). So, presence, attunement, resonance, and trust are the fundamental parts we play when our relationship is integrated and healing.

The Interpersonal Neurobiology of Mind and Integration

Since I promised to say something about the neuroscience of integration, you might ask, "What does the body and brain have to do with this?" The nervous system of the body begins as ectoderm in the conceptus. Once the sperm and egg fuse together, the work of neural development is not far behind. One cell becomes two, two become four, then eight and 16, then 32, 64, 128, until finally some tissue differentiation has to occur, the embryo's mass of cells is so big, some are now on the outside and some are on the inside. That's the first differentiation of embryonic tissues. At this point, the cells from the outer skin layer, the ectoderm, invaginate inwardly to become the neural tube. The nervous system begins with skin cells. The ectoderm is the interface of the outer world with the inner world. The nervous system, though it's embedded deep inside the body, stays aligned with this original commitment. It remains central to the interface between the inner and the outer worlds. In this sense, the brain is not so much up in the head but linking our whole inside with the outside world. I often refer to the central nervous system that gradually develops in the womb as an embodied brain. The term reminds us that the central nervous system is so much more than what's in the head. Thinking of it as just in the head is almost meaningless since its biology is all about interfacing the entirety of the body with the entirety of the natural and social surround. We humans are amazingly social creatures, and the next big phase of neurobiological development is embedded in a social world.

Simply put, integration happens interpersonally. Although it took us 20 years to flesh out, when you think about it, this is incredibly obvious. Interpersonal integration—relationships in which connection links two unique and distinct human beings—stimulates the activity and growth of fibers in the brain that are integrated. I draw your attention to three key examples: the prefrontal cortex, the corpus callosum, and the hippocampus. When I present this to new audiences, I ask them to use their hand as a very simple model of the brain. If you put your thumb in the middle of your palm and wind your remaining four fingers over the top of your thumb, you have a very rough brain "handout." Your spinal cord is represented by your wrist. Your brainstem, roughly 300 million years old, is represented by your palm. Your thumb curled over the palm of your hand represents your limbic area. And the other four fingers curled over the thumb represent your neocortex. This simple model overall represents a super complex system. With 100 billion neurons up in the head, and an average of 10,000 connections to each other, that nets out to trillions of connections. The number of on–off firing patterns in this brain has been calculated to be 10 to the millionth power, a number larger than the number of atoms in the known universe. What you have, even just up in your head, has more potential firing power than anything we know about.

The way this complex system coordinates and balances itself is very simple: differentiate and link. We can see this simple principle at work in the three areas I mentioned as examples. The corpus callosum, like the underbelly of your four top fingers, is a bridge of fibers linking the left cortex to the right. The hippocampus buried deep within the limbic area, like the underbelly of your thumb, links widely separated implicit and explicit memory systems together. The prefrontal cortex, roughly analogous to your pinky with its fingertip and fingernail, connects with and links all three systems together, while also linking all three outwards to the social world.

To return to early development, the formula I offered was, "interpersonal integration cultivates neural integration" (Siegel, 2007). Recent decades of neuroscience have found masses of evidence supporting that formula, and not a single piece of research to disprove it. Of course, you can never say in science, "We've proven it," but that's the conclusion that now stands. Interpersonal integration catalyzes or cultivates neural integration. What that means is that these integrative regions develop fully and well when children are raised in secure bonds, where they enjoy presence, attunement, resonance, and trust with caregivers. And as these regions develop, they support the higher personal and social faculties of mindsight, such as mindful awareness and empathy. Conversely, when children experience an insecure attachment with caregivers or disorganized environments in which they are subjected to trauma or abuse, their integrative regions fail to develop fully and well, and so do their higher personal and social capacities.

Why is this link between interpersonal integration and neural integration so important? Because we know that every form of regulation we've been able to look at, regulating attention, regulating emotion or affect, regulating mood, regulating thought, regulating physiology, regulating relationships, and behavior—in other words every aspect of self-regulation we explore depends on integration in the brain. This fact brings us back to the question, why did a 30-second empathic comment improve the immune system and help subjects recover a day sooner? The answer lies in understanding the power of integration.

Interpersonal Integration and the Nature of the Mind

We don't live in isolation. We live in connection with each other. Of course, we live in separate bodies. That's a differentiated experience we all have as an "I." I live in this body. This is me, right here. Dan is here in this body. He's got a name. He's going to live, hopefully, about 100 years. But what we're learning from current research is that our bodies develop in intimate linkage with the bodies of others, through development. Consider the Adverse Childhood Experience Scale Study done at Kaiser Permanente in California (Felitti et al., 1998). Sadly, relationship experiences that are stressful early in life lead to serious medical problems later on. Why? Because energy and information flow that happens relationally in the social world directly affects the molecular structure of the body. We've defined relationships as the sharing of energy and information flow. We defined the body as this collection of molecules in a system full of differentiated parts. The nervous system is very important, because when it's integrated, the whole body does well. What is that nervous system really all about? It's the embodied mechanism of energy and information flow. Relationships are the sharing of energy and information. The nervous system is the mechanism of that flow within the network called yourself. It's the node of the network. Now we're ready to ask the next, almost never-asked question: "What is the mind?"

First of all, in thinking about this vital and subtle question, I ask you please to think with care. Most, in fact, nearly all of what is said in current science about the mind comes down to one, deceptively simple article of faith: "Mind is what the brain does." According to the conventional wisdom, "mind" is nothing but brain activity. Of course, that's part of the story. But if you limit your understanding of mind to that commonplace, you won't have a clue as to how the mind relates to medicine and psychotherapy. In 1992, I was asked to convene a think tank of 40 scientists to discuss the connection between the mind and the brain. They couldn't come to any consensus, because there was no definition of mind besides brain activity, which didn't make the anthropologist in the room happy. She would say, "That's not true. It's not just brain activity. Mind is central to what I study, to human culture." At our Center for Culture, Brain, and Development at UCLA, we study how culture shapes synaptic formation in the brain. We don't believe the mind is just brain activity. Brain activity is an important part of it, but not all.

If relationships are the sharing of energy and information flow, and the brain is the embodied mechanism of that flow, then of course its electrochemical energy transformations sometimes contain symbolic meaning: information. If energy and information are embodied in the nervous system, and outwardly in a social system of shared relationships, what would the mind be? Since it's clearly embedded within a vast web of complexity, in order to understand the mind, we must apply the mathematical science of complex systems. What that science tells us is that the mind as a living system is open to the flow of information from all around it; that it is capable of operating chaotically, embracing and transforming chaos, not just order and organization; and that it's nonlinear, in that it constantly adapts and changes in unpredictable and creative ways. These properties of mind mean that it meets the mathematical criteria of a complex system. All complex systems have what are called emergent properties. Emergent properties are those that arise from the interaction of the elements of the system, although they are not found within the separate elements considered in isolation. They are properties that come out of the complex system's interaction.

Mind as an Embodied Self-Organizing Flow

One emergent property scientists of complexity have described is the property of self-organization. My proposal to the think tank I called in 1992 was that the mind is an emergent, self-organizing property of human life. In other words, it is an embodied, relational process that regulates the flow of energy and information (Siegel, 2012, 2017). If mind is a self-organizing process, where is it located? It is located within you and between you and other people, and also between you and the whole planet. One small sample of the evidence supporting the view of mind as a self-organizing embodied process comes from the groundbreaking study done by Nobel Prize winner Elizabeth Blackburn, psychologist Elissa Epel, and two of my interns (Entringer et al., 2013). That study showed that presence—the experience of embodied, mindful awareness in the present moment—leads to improvement in telomerase levels that repair and maintain the ends of your chromosomes. When you apply your mind to presence, the initial P of our PART acronym, it actually raises the enzyme level to repair and maintain the ends of your chromosomes to keep you healthy.

Another set of studies supporting this view relates to something called *eudaimonia*, the Greek term for well-being (Ryff, 2014). One aspect of *eudaimonia* is said to be the aspect of compassion; a second aspect involves connection with other people; a third aspect is having a sense of meaning or purpose; and a fourth aspect is equanimity, achieving some degree of emotional balance. Equanimity, meaning, connection, and compassion are all said to contribute to lasting well-being, called *eudaimonia*. Studies of *eudaimonia*, cultivated through practices like mindfulness, show that it may be associated with epigenetic changes in the non-DNA molecules that help our cells produce chemical messengers called cytokines that prevent inflammatory diseases, including some kinds of cancer and some kinds of diabetes (Fredrickson et al., 2013). What you do with your mind actually changes the methyl groups and histones, the non-DNA molecules, that sit on top of the DNA altering its physical shape in ways that shift gene transcription and expression towards well-being. One common denominator we notice about the aspects of mind that promote well-being is that they all seem to involve a sense of connection to something larger than the bodily self.

Compassion involves *feeling with* another person, wanting to help them. Connection involves an awareness of being linked with and belonging to social relationships and a larger community. Equanimity involves being able to regulate your own internal state so that you can maintain compassion and a sense of connection. A sense of higher meaning or purpose also involves an awareness of how we can contribute to others and the larger whole. All these positive, healing capacities of mind therefore relate to integration.

In modern culture we have made a serious mistake that is embedded in the way parents raise children, the ways teachers teach kids in school, the way the media are portraying everything. That mistake is congruent with the mistake we make by reducing the mind to nothing but brain: we have equated "self" with the body. The point is that the self is not isolated within the brain and body, nor simply a node within the self-organizing process of mind, brain, body, and society. The self is a node in that process along with all the interconnections within the person and between persons. We do have a differentiated experience of self. Yes, there is a Me, but there is also a We. We don't want to give up on taking care of the body. We all need to be attuned to our bodies. But we also have a larger socially interconnected identity as a We.

When you see integration take hold in the mind, when you see mind emerging as a self-organizing process, you see how self-organization involves differentiated linking, linking internally to our parts, externally to others and our world. Otherwise the system tends towards extreme modes of self-destruction or self-protection; that is, towards chaos or towards rigidity. This perspective on the healthy mind as a process of integration also sheds light on mental illness. When we integrate, when we can differentiate and link, we get individual and social harmony. We get flexibility. We're adaptive. We're coherent. We're energized. So the integrated mind can be stable even in the face of the hardest realities of life, including aging and facing death. Integration is the fundamental basis of health. Integration made visible is kindness and compassion.

Integration, Empathy, and Compassion: Receptive vs Reactive States

How does interpersonal neurobiology help us understand and develop compassion? We're all familiar with the term kindness, but "compassion" requires some definition. In my view, compassion is more than just helping people who are suffering, but also entails actually helping people flourish. Viewed in this way, compassion merges into what we know as kindness, as well as related terms like care, love, altruism, and empathy. What do these terms have in common? Interpersonal neurobiology helps explore these related capacities, by reminding us that our brains and bodies have two binary basic states. One is the state of being reactive, the state we slip into when we hear "no." That state of reactivity is very different from the receptive state we slip into when we hear "yes." So I begin by suggesting that every one of the capacities I mentioned—care, love, altruism, empathy, kindness, compassion, connection— all have to do with the receptive state of our minds, brains, and bodies.

We all know that the reactive state of stress has a historical, survival value. When we feel threatened, our minds, brains, and bodies fall into this reactive state, which is expressed in one or more of the forms described by four Fs. We fight back, we flee, we tighten up our muscles and freeze waiting to see how to respond to threat, or we faint, which is also called feigning death. Such reactive states are interesting in many ways because the whole field of positive psychology has shed new light on a contrast that is controversial for professionals and the lay public—the contrast between positive emotions and negative emotions. What this means basically is that if you have negative emotions like anger, fear, sadness, anxiety, despair, all these states come about as a response to threat. The "no" reactive state actually is the gateway to what some call destructive emotions. If they persist for long periods of time, they undermine health.

Of course, as psychotherapy teaches us, all emotions are fair and natural; we all feel them and when we do, they should be expressed and explored. But these negative states are based on threat and so they affect our whole system adversely. Overexposure to them eventually becomes unhealthy. These negative states, these reactive "no" states, are in fact pathways to non-thriving, non-flourishing. In contrast, receptive states have the dramatically distinct quality of opening us up and out, are pathways to positive emotions like love, joy, elation, awe, and gratitude. What positive psychology has taught us in recent decades is that all these positive emotional states, when you can attain and maintain them, actually foster well-being. In what follows, we'll take compassion as a prime example of all these positive states.

To begin with, what does the word "compassion" mean? This word comes from Latin, and is a compound of two words. Literally "com" means with, and "passion" feeling. So we can think of it simply as "feeling with" another person. A common interpretation of this is expressed in the phrase, "I feel your pain, and I'm able to hold that pain inside of me enough to think about how I'm going to skillfully take an action to reduce your suffering." But we can also widen the definition of compassion beyond this standard sense, to include what people usually associate with love or kindness. In that broader sense, compassion is not just about sharing and reducing suffering, but also about promoting flourishing. Of course, these different senses are all aspects of one positive social emotional process. This process involves being open to another person's feelings, which is usually called empathy; then based on that it involves responding or taking action in some way to reduce suffering, which is usually called compassion; and it may expand to include the wish to share happiness by responding or taking action in some way to help foster flourishing, which is usually called love or kindness. We could even include another emotion here that is usually called empathic joy, a state of openness that shares and rejoices in the well-being of others.

What do these all shades of compassion have in common? What do reactive states and receptive states tell us about creating a compassionate inner life for inner transformation, interpersonal thriving, even a compassionate care for our planet Earth? In terms of the interpersonal neurobiology of mind, compassionate action, kind action, and empathic action are all integrative acts. Since integration is enhanced in a state of receptivity, and reduced in states of reactivity, all positive emotional states are also integrative states. What this means in terms of the brain is that they tend to enhance the activity of integrative regions like the prefrontal cortex, corpus callosum, cingulate cortex, and hippocampus. This activation is essential for us to access and maintain our full capacities for mindful presence, empathic attunement, emotional resonance, and basic trust or confidence. In contrast, when we are in distressed emotional states, reactive regions in our brain like the amygdala and hypothalamus tend to be more activated, leading to the shutdown or "hijacking" of our brain's social engagement system. This kind of reactivity is naturally increased by trauma, whether in childhood abuse, insecure attachment, or trauma in later life. So negative emotions not only impair internal healing and social adaptation, but also basic well-being.

Mirror Neurons, Positive Affect, and Vagal Tone

Three current research areas in neuroscience lend support to this broad picture. Recent work on the mirror neuron social empathy system by my colleague Louis Cozolino and others has helped us understand the way our social brains try to understand others' emotional states: by reading their facial expressions and body language, and then mapping the information we gather onto our own archive of embodied emotional memories (Cozolino, 2006). This groundbreaking work has been further clarified by current compassion research by Tania Singer and others, which distinguishes two modes of the empathy system (Singer & Klimecki, 2014). One is a reactive mode in which the negative emotions we detect in others trigger negative emotional memories and states in ourselves. The other is a receptive mode in which we connect with the suffering of others while preserving a sense of differentiation that allows us to feel safe and respond with positive states like compassion that enhance well-being.

The second research area that sheds light on the integrative role of positive emotions is the field of affective neuroscience led by pioneers like Barbara Fredrickson (Fredrickson et al., 2013) and Richard Davidson (Davidson & Begley, 2013). In study after study over recent years, we have found that positive emotions like compassion have an expansive, social self-organizing function that brings the mind, brain, and body into healthy receptivity and prosocial engagement with others and the world. Negative emotions like fear and anger not surprisingly increase reactive, self-enclosing states of mind, brain, and body that promote anxiety, traumatic reactivity, depression, and isolation.

A final field of study that has given powerful support to this model of compassion as an integrative process is the research on the autonomic nervous system done by Steve Porges (Porges, 2011). Steve's work shows how negative emotions trigger the primitive sympathetic fight–flight and parasympathetic freeze–faint systems that disable the brain's social engagement systems at all levels—cortical, limbic, and brainstem—while positive emotions like love and care help promote and stabilize the mammalian neurobiology of those systems, based on the smart vagal nerve and the peptides oxytocin and vasopressin. So, compassion and related emotional states are vital to promote the integration and self-organization of mind, brain, and body on which healing relationships like parenting, teaching, and psychotherapy depend.

Mindful Awareness, Compassion, and Contemplative Practices

We are all in great need of a new way of being—in ourselves, in our schools, and in our society. Our modern culture has evolved in recent times to create a troubled world with individuals suffering from alienation, schools failing to inspire and to connect with students. We live in a contemporary society overly focused on self and material things, often devoid of a moral compass to help clarify how we can move forward in our global community to create a more meaningful, sustainable, and compassionate way of living. Part of our journey towards rediscovering such a compass has involved linking the universal principles across scientific disciplines to clarify the true nature of mind and well-being. Another part has led us to explore the mechanisms of strengthening our mental skills through methods of attentional training, especially those developed and preserved with ancient traditions of meditative practice. One of these traditions belongs to what is sometimes considered a "religion" but at other times is seen as a form of practical "mind science," the contemplative tradition of Buddhism. One facet of Buddhist meditation is the cultivation of a quality of attention that enhances the ability to be aware of present-moment experience and free oneself from the burden of often self-created anxiety, despair, and isolation.

In many ways, learning to train the mind to become more mindful has been demonstrated in a range of scientific studies to enhance immune function, improve cardiovascular health, increase telomerase, balance emotions, decrease fear and anxiety, increase empathy, and even strengthen self-compassion. Being mindfully aware, attending to the richness of here-and-now experiences, creates scientifically recognized enhancements in our physiology, our mental functions, and in our interpersonal relationships. Being fully present in our awareness opens our lives to new possibilities of well-being. In addition, what is called "interpersonal attunement," focusing attention on the internal world of another, harnesses neural circuitry that enables two people to "feel felt" by one another, promoting longevity and resilience. Mindfulness may in fact be a form of "internal attunement" in which an observing self-function approaches a more directly experiencing self with curiosity, openness, acceptance, and love. This internal attunement may lead the brain to grow in ways that promote balanced self-regulation via the process of neural integration, which enables flexibility and self-understanding, empathy, and compassion.

Almost all cultures have practices that help people develop awareness of the moment which we know enables attunement toward self and others. Each of the major religions of the world utilizes some method to enable individuals to focus their attention and feel connected to their inner and outer worlds, from meditation to prayer, yoga to tai'chi. Among these cultures, the Buddhist traditions of Asia have received growing attention from researchers and clinicians in recent years, in part because they approach our human needs for reflection and attunement as a science and healing art of individual and communal well-being. "The Buddha" was a man who sought a new way of living free from the self-created suffering that drove him to explore his inner world. The realization of a way to view suffering as inherent in the human condition and to outline the path to alleviate that suffering is the "awakening" that came with his journey. "Buddha" means the awakened one, and this awakening, this shedding light on a universal human condition, is the essence of Buddhist philosophy and practice.

The key to these practices is that the way we learn to focus our attention can prime new neural patterns of activation and ultimately stimulate the growth of new synaptic connections in the brain itself. This is how we use the focus of attention with awareness—a function of the mind—to change the structure of the brain. Such tools of training attention may be especially helpful in bringing mindfulness and attunement to high performance social roles and intimate relationships. In many ways, these are "mindsight skills" that enable us to see our own and others' minds with more clarity and depth, and then to transform this energy and information flow in our bodies and in our relationships toward a process called integration—the linkage of differentiated parts of a system. Modern science can be interpreted to suggest that physiological, interpersonal, and psychological health emerge from such integration, experienced as harmony and flexibility. Ancient contemplative practices may reveal a rigorous form of mental training that ultimately can be seen to promote such integrative states in body, mind, and relationships.

In fact, within this ancient tradition, as in our own current science, the conscious mastery of differentiated elements brought about by rigorous methods of mind training is viewed as catalyzing a deep form of integration across many layers of mental life. This synergy helps make explicit the potential of applying this new science together with traditional practices to psychotherapy. The result of this kind of exploration is a productive confluence of both traditional and a contemporary science of mind that offers glimpses into the promise of an ongoing dialogue between these two very distinct disciplines of discovery.

Given the challenges we face throughout our global community in cultivating well-being in this troubled and alienated world, it is vital to our future well-being, and even our very existence, that we preserve and explore all human strategies to strengthen self-regulation and promote the internal and interpersonal integration needed to help us build our natural capacities for mindful awareness and interpersonal attunement. Integration can ultimately shift the pathway of cultural evolution in a positive direction—and a strengthened capacity for mindful awareness may be the essential starting place to cultivate such an intentional shift, helping our increasingly interconnected and rapidly changing world to survive and even thrive as we move into this new digital era. Science brings knowledge and technology but not necessarily wisdom. If we take our human family's accomplishments in exploring the nature of our mental lives, it is natural to then seek a weaving of the important contributions of all the sciences with the deep understanding of our subjective mental lives in the wisdom traditions of contemplation. Such moral living does not arise from a vacuum but can be cultivated with integrative practices. Integration is the source of well-being and health that provides a secular ethic around which we can focus our efforts to bring the world to a scientifically grounded place of positive growth. Integration made visible is kindness and compassion. Whether we come to such integrative practices as individuals seeking lasting happiness through caring relationships in the world, or as professionals seeking to heal, teach, or lead, these insights and methods can inspire us all, and offer vitally relevant strategies to all walks of humanity, and to the future of the world, this fragile and precious Earth, the home we all share.

13
Compassion in Psychotherapy

Christine Braehler and Christopher Germer

When I (Christine Braehler) first met Kate,[1] she was in her late thirties and working as a pastor in Germany. She had attempted suicide during a major depressive episode and was admitted to a psychiatric hospital. When her depression began to subside, Kate was referred to a psychosomatic hospital for intensive inpatient psychotherapy where I worked. During our intake assessment, Kate reported that she was still struggling with low energy, lack of pleasure in ordinary activities, intense guilt, and shame. She worried about failing at her job, judged herself harshly, ruminated, and felt generally hopeless. Kate was avoidant and did not like the idea of engaging in psychotherapy, clinging to a biological explanation of her suffering.

How could the resources of mindfulness and compassion inform Kate's healing? And how might the skills of mindfulness and compassion help a clinician care for Kate? Thanks to the growing neuroscientific evidence supporting mindfulness training and practice (Hölzel et al., 2011), mindfulness is now being integrated, both theoretically and practically, into clinical practice (Germer et al., 2013). However, a key aspect of mindfulness that is often overlooked is the attitude of kindness and compassion. These heart qualities are especially necessary when a person is in the grip of shame or despair and needs *acceptance*—acceptance of one's experience and one's self, just as they are. Recently, a program of Mindful Self-Compassion (MSC) has been developed to train the skill of *self*-compassion in non-clinical groups (Neff & Germer, 2013) and compassion has been integrated into a cognitive behavior therapy called Compassion-Focused Therapy (CFT) (Gilbert, 2009). At the same time, we are witnessing the emergence of a new field of research—the science of compassion (Singer & Bolz, 2013). This chapter explores how compassion and self-compassion are integral to the psychotherapeutic journey for both therapists and clients, and how ancient Buddhist teachings and contemporary scientific findings are lending support to the anecdotal evidence of clinical experience.

DOI: 10.4324/9781003243588-15

Compassionate Commitment:
The Essence of Therapeutic Intention

How did you react when you read Kate's story? Some readers may have felt Kate's despair with a sense of hopelessness and defeat. Others may have felt warm wishes arising for Kate. Still others may have tried to understand the origin of Kate's suffering by linking her past experiences to present events. All these responses are part of compassion: empathic resonance, goodwill, and perspective-taking. Taken together, this complex response would enable us to hold Kate and her suffering long enough to understand what she is avoiding and, hopefully, to help her transform it. The following quote by a Theravada Buddhist teacher, Nyanaponika Thera, illustrates these three components of compassion,

> The compassion of the wise man does not render him a victim of suffering. His thoughts, words and deeds are full of pity. But his heart does not waver; unchanged it remains, serene and calm. How else should he be able to help? May such compassion arise in our hearts! Compassion that is sublime nobility of heart and intellect which knows, understands and is ready to help. Compassion that is strength and gives strength: this is highest compassion.
>
> (Thera, 1994)

Psychotherapists and other helping professionals are faced with others' suffering on a daily basis and have taken a professional vow to care for others and alleviate others' suffering to the best of their abilities. It could be argued that helping professionals aspire to the "highest compassion" Thera describes. Professional codes of conduct typically contain an implicit ethos, often summarized as vowing not to harm. Knowing what to avoid is necessary, but not sufficient to know how to help. Following significant failures in both management and care leading to the loss of life, some healthcare systems, such as the UK's National Health Service, have recently included "compassion" as an essential and necessary value to aspire to (Mid Staffordshire NHS Foundation Trust Public Inquiry, 2013). In Buddhist psychology and medicine, practitioners take a vow to remind them to manifest compassion toward themselves and others to alleviate suffering: the Bodhisattva vow. "Bodhisattva" refers to a committed or enlightened altruist who works to embody universal compassion and act as a role model for all who wish to help. Reminding ourselves of this motivation is meant to activate our natural capacity for open-heartedness and empathic insight, referred to as bodhicitta, the altruistic spirit of enlightenment. Even though we may be imperfect as human beings and professionals, limited in our capacity to alleviate suffering, we may benefit from reorienting our hearts again and again toward the qualities of wisdom and compassion we aspire to develop and manifest.

Compassionate Strength: The Antidote to Caregiver Fatigue

The daily reality of professional caregiving is often far removed from Bodhisattva qualities. It is very common for dedicated psychotherapists to suffer from burnout or "compassion fatigue" (Figley, 1995), and to lose their capacity to be compassionate. Symptoms of burnout—helplessness, feeling overwhelmed, physical exhaustion, restlessness, insomnia, nightmares, irritability, cynicism, withdrawal, anhedonia, numbing, and loss of empathy—appear to many as a result of being *too* compassionate. Advice commonly given to professional helpers includes seeing fewer patients, taking more time off, or developing a nurturing hobby. While tending to the needs of heart, mind, and body outside of work is vital, such self-care strategies do not sufficiently protect the helper when exposed to clients' suffering. Other advice may include not getting too emotionally involved with clients, to become more detached. What makes implementing this advice difficult for psychotherapists is that they need to connect with, rather than disconnect from, their clients in order to build a working alliance and do therapeutic work.

Luckily, discoveries first made in 2009 have provided us with a new definition of compassion (Singer & Klimecki, 2014). Neuroscientific studies of empathy have discovered that opening to the pain of others triggers pain and distress in the observer, eventually leading to burnout and disengagement (Singer & Klimecki, 2014). Studies with both meditation-naïve participants and experienced meditators have demonstrated that our default, reflex reaction to the suffering of others is sympathetic pain, which many identify as "empathy" (Singer & Klimecki, 2014). In some ways, this aversive state can be viewed as a universal side-effect of an open-hearted person who wants to help, not as a sign of weakness. If we remain in this state, however, we run the risk of becoming "a victim of suffering," to use Thera's words. "Compassion fatigue" may be more appropriately referred to as "empathy fatigue" or better still "sympathy fatigue." (Note: the use of "empathy" for mindless mirroring of others' pain is not consistent with the classical definition of the term in poetics and phenomenology, from which it entered psychoanalysis and psychotherapy. In most psychotherapeutic discourse, "empathy" is understood as an accurate, reflective perception of another's state of mind, not as a mindless reaction— "sympathy" is a more historically and linguistically accurate term for this subliminal reactivity and resulting "social contagion.")

What would allow the therapist to connect emotionally with the patient and give compassion without the negative effects of the exposure to suffering? Recent studies have shown that compassion is primarily experienced as a positive energizing state, which protects us against burnout. On a neural level, compassion meditation and the positive emotional states that correspond to it reflect activation of the ventral striatum—associated with positive affect—and of the prefrontal "theory of mind" network associated with cognitive perspective-taking (Singer & Klimecki, 2014). If we attempt to translate these neuroscientific findings into Buddhist concepts, we may parallel positive affect with loving kindness or goodwill (Pali: *metta*), and cognitive perspective-taking with a wise deep knowing and understanding (Pali: *sampajanna*). The phrase by Theravada Buddhist Thera "The nobility of the heart and nobility of intellect, which knows, understands and is ready to help," beautifully illustrates the emotional and cognitive manifestations of compassion (Thera, 1994). Compassion arises when goodwill and insight meet suffering and remain loving. Another inherent quality of compassion, which helps goodwill to stay loving, is equanimity (Pali: *uppekha*). Equanimity refers to unbiased impartiality and non-attachment. By not preferring one outcome or object of compassion over another, compassion becomes stable, relaxed, and universal, much as sunlight shines on everything and everyone without discriminating: "his heart does not waver; unchanged it remains, serene and calm" (Thera). Equanimity provides the spacious awareness in which goodwill and wise understanding can transform into compassion when any kind of suffering is met, personal or collective.

The challenging task of the psychotherapist, then, is to turn toward the pain of the other instead of avoiding; to remain present with suffering instead of dissociating or getting entangled; to take the perspective of the other instead of solely one's own; to sensitively tune in to the needs of the other, instead of presuming what the other may need; to try to alleviate as much of the suffering as one can instead of imposing or withholding help. At times, psychotherapists may unwittingly identify with the client's suffering, which can lead to feeling overwhelmed, to trying to rescue or fix, or to becoming dismissive—even contemptuous—and disengaged. Similarly, psychotherapists may become attached to improving the client's well-being, which may be tied to their own self-esteem as a therapist. Frustration and disengagement may occur when no improvement occurs.

Self-compassion exercises (Germer & Neff, 2016) adapted from the Tibetan art of giving-and-taking (Tib.: *tong-len*) offer a remedy in those moments of feeling overwhelmed by a client's suffering. They can help soothe our own sympathetic pain by breathing compassion in for ourselves and reconnect with the patient by breathing compassion out for the other, creating a balanced flow of care between therapist and client. Research suggests that such meditations can help protect from burnout, even with a relatively brief period of practice. Practicing loving-kindness over a three-week period (average five total hours) significantly helps meditation-naïve women switch from a habitual distressing response of sympathetic pain to the energizing and sustainable state of compassion when exposed to the distress calls of children (Klimecki et al., 2013).

When I first met Kate, I sensed her ambivalence—wanting help, yet showing strong resistance to it. Equanimity helped me make space for her resistance rather than trying to convince her that psychotherapy would help. Understanding the shame surrounding depression and treatment helped me to validate her resistance authentically. Goodwill for both of us helped me to stay with her and to inwardly commit to helping her in whatever way I and my team could.

Re-Parenting through Self-Compassion

An implicit goal of most psychotherapies, including mindfulness- and compassion-based therapy, is *self*-acceptance. Self-compassion provides us with the tools we need to gradually embrace challenging emotions and parts of ourselves, helping us move toward greater self-acceptance. The term refers to a relatively new psychological construct derived from ancient Buddhist contemplative psychology, defined by Kristin Neff (Neff, 2003). Self-compassion has three main components: (1) mindfulness, (2) common humanity, and (3) self-kindness. When applied to a moment of suffering such as the pain we feel when we have failed at something important to us, we can apply mindfulness by simply acknowledging the suffering of disappointment rather than avoiding or becoming fused with the emotion. Rather than isolating ourselves from others or from our own experience out of shame, we remind ourselves that every human being experiences suffering at some point in their lives, so that we feel connected in the midst of our pain. Rather than beating ourselves up when we feel down, we hold ourselves in a loving embrace until we recover our strength. In other words, self-compassion describes loving, connected presence in the midst of our own suffering.

Self-compassion appears to be a core mechanism of change in different forms of psychotherapy. One team discovered that therapy outcome was largely predicted by the increase in self-compassion in clients across two different types of therapy, neither of which explicitly trained clients in it (Schanche et al., 2011). Following short-term psychodynamic treatment, decreases in anxiety, shame, and guilt, and increases in the willingness to experience sadness, anger, and closeness were associated with higher self-compassion. In the same study, increases in self-compassion predicted fewer psychiatric symptoms and interpersonal problems. How did clients develop self-compassion over the course of therapy?

We could hypothesize that the transmission and internalization of self-compassion takes place to a significant degree within the therapeutic space. Firstly, how a therapist relates to herself affects the degree to which she can embody and model self-compassion authentically. One study found that self-critical therapists achieve worse outcomes compared with less self-critical colleagues, since they eventually treat clients in a less caring, more critical manner (Henry et al., 1990). Receiving compassion in an attuned way may serve as a corrective emotional experience that helps clients feel truly felt-for, accepted, and supported. To help transfer this corrective experience into daily life and beyond the therapy, interventions can be used to train the client in self-compassion, both within and between sessions. Explicit self-compassion interventions aim to activate the innate compassionate self within the client, which will guide and support her in the long term.

Modern psychology describes the process of internalizing representations of secure, caring, and reliable self and other as a limited re-parenting, which may correct early attachment experiences and help clients move toward attachment security (Travis et al., 2001). Buddhist traditions promote models of lineage and transmission. Qualified teachers transmit their wisdom to their students from one generation to the next through embodiment, direct instructions, and ongoing guidance on the way, with the goal of the student manifesting qualities of wisdom and compassion within himself or herself.

In compassion-based psychotherapy we combine both models. The psychotherapist acts as a supportive guide and companion to help uncover the client's innate potential for compassion, also referred to as "Buddha-nature," while navigating the intricacies of his or her attachment system. The psychophysiological basis for compassion lies within our innate caregiving and care-receiving system, which calms, soothes, and regenerates the body when activated by threat or competition, and also opens the mind outwards to include a broader and more inclusive social perspective (Depue & Morrone-Strupinsky, 2005). The psychotherapist shares in the client's common humanity, by inwardly offering her services humbly as a fellow human rather than a detached professional; and by acknowledging her own limits in an authentic way. Compassion-based psychotherapy aims to activate inner resources of mindfulness, love, joy, and self-compassion to alleviate the client's suffering in a safe and individualized way.

Resisting Compassion: Overcoming Fears of Emotion and Connection

Tibetan Buddhism suggests we practice universal compassion by loving all beings as if they were our aging mother. Theravada Buddhist practices of loving-kindness begin by extending kind wishes toward ourselves before moving on to loved ones. Most clients are likely to encounter difficulties when trying to follow these instructions. Granting yourself the same attention, kindness, and understanding you would readily grant a loved one is a goal many clients would like to achieve through therapy. Such difficulties are often rooted in early experiences of care, and likewise may make it difficult to extend compassion even to one's own mother. Our attachment system is shaped by our experience of how our caregivers responded to us when we were infants or children in distress. If in times of distress, we experienced neglect or some form of emotional or physical abuse, we likely will have formed ingrained emotional memories linking the experience of needing and/or receiving care with negative emotions of shame, anger, loneliness, fear, or vulnerability. Our ability to feel affiliative emotions such as love, joy, compassion, longing, and grief toward our primary caregivers, and subsequently toward ourselves or significant others can be compromised.

Our sense of self is also shaped by the degree to which we experience belonging to and appreciation by the communities and wider culture that we have grown up in and live in. When a person has identities that are marginalized or oppressed by mainstream culture, those experiences are also internalized and make it difficult to interact with potential oppressors, whether they be individuals or groups. Empowering the individual through fierce self-compassion involves firstly validating the harm experienced and experiencing validation and coaching them to by transform healthy anger and outrage into clarity and wise action against harmful cultural biases and oppressive institutional structures and the courage to find safety and support in a community of peers (Braehler, 2020). The process of developing fierce self-compassion is particularly relevant for clients with complex posttraumatic stress disorder (PTSD) (Braehler, in press; Braehler & Neff, 2020).

Psychotherapy is one place where the client can be gradually desensitized to the receiving of compassion including the genuine validation of whatever abuse, neglect, or oppression they have encountered. This kindness and understanding might be the first step in establishing a more secure relational template in the client over time. Yet many clients experience receiving compassion from another as aversive. Why would clients be rejecting the very quality they need to alleviate their suffering? Paul Gilbert and his colleagues shed light on this by exposing common meta-cognitive beliefs in such cases: "I worry that people are only kind and compassionate if they want something from me," "I will become dependent on it," "I do not deserve it," "It will make me weak/lazy/selfish," "I will be overwhelmed by distress," "I will let myself off the hook" (Gilbert et al., 2011). Such resistance to receiving and to giving compassion has been associated with greater anxiety and depression in the general population and in clinical cohorts (Gilbert et al., 2012, 2014c). In both depressed and non-depressed cohorts, fear of receiving compassion from others was strongly correlated with fear of receiving compassion from oneself. A combined fear of compassion factor predicted 53 percent of variance in depressive symptoms and correlated strongly with self-criticism, which is a known predictor of depression (Gilbert et al., 2014a). Fear of compassion has been associated with greater attachment insecurity in clinically depressed individuals (Gilbert et al., 2014c, 2014a). Higher fear of compassion and lower self-compassion in eating disorder patients at the start of treatment was associated with greater pathology and worse treatment outcome after twelve weeks, suggesting that therapy must first address such resistances (Kelly et al., 2013). Although research refers to "fears of compassion," it really taps into people's fears about what *reactions* they have to compassion. More in-depth research shows that fear of sadness, in particular, is associated with depression, and that fear and avoidance of sadness and anger correlate with fears of happiness and compassion (Gilbert et al., 2014b). These findings suggest that the expression of difficult emotions appears threatening if we cannot build on representations of others lovingly validating and holding our emotions.

My client, Kate, exhibited such fears. Her mother left her family for "periods of respite" when Kate was a one-year-old. When Kate needed medical treatment at the age of four, she remembered feeling guilty for burdening her mother. As a child, she was afraid of her irritable and violent father, since he would regularly beat up her brothers. Since neither mother nor father offered a safe haven, she learned to suppress all emotions and to become "self-reliant." Kate's unmarried aunt and other female relatives had suffered from severe and debilitating depression. They were seen as useless and lazy, and as a burden and disgrace for the family, which highly valued hard work. As an adult, Kate was afraid that she would burden others and ruin their day if she were to share her distress, or in any way ask for help. Suffering from depression and needing a psychiatric admission was associated with intense shame, since she felt it threatened to render her "useless," "a burden," and "a disgrace." She believed receiving compassion would make her weak, and that she would be overcome by an all-encompassing depression that would never lift.

Our first goal during therapy was to develop a joint understanding of the causes and conditions that had led Kate to these difficulties. I invited her to recognize that she had not chosen her genes or the circumstances of her birth, and that it was understandable that she had developed strategies like suppressing emotions, avoiding help, and working hard, as ways to stay safe and connected to the family on which her survival depended. She could gradually begin to see that even her depressive episodes were simply the unintended consequences of her conditioned safety strategies and a possible genetic predisposition. The motto, "It is not your fault, but you can take responsibility," introduced by Paul Gilbert, summarizes this de-shaming stance, which cuts through unjustified self-blame and opens clients to the possibility of change.

Rescuing the Observer: The Antidote to Shame and Self-Hatred

Typically viewed as strong and caring in her role as pastor, Kate understandably felt great shame about having depression and being admitted to a psychiatric hospital. She worried about losing her capacity to contribute to society if she lost her job and became a "useless depressive," like some female relatives. In the years leading up to this episode, Kate and her husband had been trying to conceive. The shame of potentially not contributing either by motherhood or by professional service threatened her sense of self, so that suicide had seemed like a viable option. Now, she reacted with anger toward herself, the depression, and the mental health system.

A therapist who focuses their treatment approach on compassion considers the following question: "What does the person really need in order to be with this difficult experience in a way that would support her well-being in the long-term?" Since I could feel Kate's helplessness, I sensed that she needed me to receive her concerns with genuine kindness, as well as to validate her fears. By describing treatment options and the typical course of recovery, I hoped to instill hope and trust. Most importantly, I hoped to reduce her sense of shame, which seemed most toxic to her at this point, as it led her to turn away from these seemingly unbearable and unresolvable difficulties.

When we feel shame, we experience ourselves as appearing unattractive in the minds of others (Gilbert & Andrews, 1998). Sometimes we have a clear sense of what others may reject us for, such as our race, ethnicity, religion, sexual preference, physical appearance, or personality traits that fall outside of what is deemed socially desirable. Often, shame manifests cognitively as a negative core belief, such as "I am useless" or "I am selfish." Its evolutionary function is to alert us to disapproval from others in the group so we can adjust our behavior to conform to the group's desired norms and thus remain a member of the group. As humans, we depend on membership in a group for our physical and psychological survival. We implicitly monitor whether we exist as positively in the minds of others and adjust our behavior accordingly (Buss, 2000). Sometimes, we have no clear indication of what others object to but a vague sense that "Something is fundamentally wrong with me." Such core shame is intensely threatening, as we have little or no indication of what we can do to feel loved and appreciated again. Shame isolates and excludes us from any benevolent company, including our own. A meta-analysis showed a large effect size linking shame and depression (Kim et al., 2011).

When we feel shame, typically we become completely identified with our experience, so that we come to lose our mindful awareness. If we were shamed by caregivers in early life, or because our identities are marginalized by the dominant culture, shame itself can be experienced as traumatic (Matos et al., 2013) and a central part of our sense of self (Pinto-Gouveia & Matos, 2011). Shame schemas have been linked to paranoid anxiety and to depression (Matos et al., 2013). Depending on how shame-prone we are, we may need a kind person on the outside to rescue our inner observer, in order to become disidentified with our shame. One antidote to shame is to reconnect to our common humanity, or at least to a collective of people who share our identities, to overcome our sense of separation and inferiority.

Typically unhelpful questions which revolve through the mind are: "What is wrong with me?" "What do others think about me?" "How do they perceive what I have done?" "What can I do for others to like me more?" In the attempt to prevent social exclusion, our mind is preoccupied with inferring and anticipating the social evaluation of our self. Depending on the sense of self constructed by our default mode network—the autopilot in our brain that generates offline self-images and narratives—we may come up with more or less favorable answers. In fact, brain areas associated with the default mode are involved in error processing and behavioral inhibition, suggesting a negative bias toward thinking about what went wrong rather than what went well. Depression has been associated with getting stuck in default mode activity of negative self-referential rumination. Whereas non-clinical populations can shift more easily out of default mode activity when asked to focus on a task, people with recurrent depression stay caught in depressogenic rumination even during a task (Marchetti et al., 2012). Default-mode self-referential processing in major depression has been shown to involve higher levels of maladaptive depressive rumination and lower levels of adaptive reflective rumination compared to healthy controls (Hamilton et al., 2011).

The Neurobiology of Self-Compassion

While mindfulness training helps people gain distance from such depressogenic default activity (Kuyken et al., 2008), self-compassion helps to rescue the observer more directly by instilling a sense of existing positively in the mind of another. It capitalizes on the social and relational nature of our brain. Default-mode activity is highly social, and we are typically engaged in a self-to-self or self-to-imaginary other conversation. Rather than focusing on negative aspects of ourselves, we can develop a kind and encouraging inner dialogue, which acknowledges both negative and positive aspects of ourselves. Experimental studies have repeatedly shown that the induction of a self-compassionate inner dialogue versus self-critical inner dialogue was associated with increased motivation to work after failing an exam, increased positive affect and reduced depression, anxiety, and shame (Leary et al., 2007; Breines & Chen, 2012; Ehret et al., 2015). The only neurological study to date to test this paradigm found self-criticism correlated with increased activity in lateral prefrontal cortical regions and in the dorsal anterior cingulate, whereas self-reassurance correlated with left temporal and insula structures (Longe et al., 2010).

Self-Compassion in Psychotherapy

The goal of compassion-based psychotherapy is to help the client find a safe access point to self-compassion. On a physiological level, we seek to activate our mammalian caregiving/care-receiving system, which is thought to release oxytocin and endorphins via the part of the vagus nerve that facilitates flexible approach behavior and social engagement as a way to soothe, comfort, and care (Porges, 2007). In mammals, the parasympathetic vagal system and its neuropeptides oxytocin and vasopressin have evolved to down-regulate the sympathetic threat system, which releases adrenalin and cortisol and is typically overactive during states of shame, self-hatred, and depression (Depue & Morrone-Strupinsky, 2005). On a basic physiological level, the system can be activated through offering oneself physical warmth, soothing or supportive touch, a genuine smile, and soothing vocalizations (Porges, 2007). Therapists can explore with their clients which point of access (warmth, touch, smile, tone of voice/vocalizations), from which direction (self-to-self, self-to-other, other-to-self), in which form (real, imagined memory, imagined fantasy), and with which degree of mindedness (inanimate object, nature, animal/pet, human being, or supernatural being) allows him or her to access the felt sense of care most easily and without activating the threat system. Once vagal activity has led our organism to feel safe to approach, the social engagement system is activated, allowing higher cortical processing to take place.

On a more existential level, therapists can help their clients to access compassion, for example, by connecting with core values like justice or peace. Therapists can also explore significant relationships to look for safe and uncomplicated experiences of giving and receiving kindness, such as with pets or children, to install a felt sense of compassion. Other ways of cultivating compassion are by sharing one's struggles in group therapy or with people who share one's identities, or by reflecting on common humanity. People who have been marginalized by the dominant culture may not find "common humanity" a useful concept, and it may trigger painful memories, but realizing that one's experience is shared with at least one other person, even if it is a person in public life or a movement, can be enormously healing.

Early in her hospital stay, Kate received a letter from a colleague and friend which was deeply compassionate and de-shaming, reminding her that her difficulties were not her fault. Over time, Kate was able to take in the meaning of the words and experienced great relief from the heavy burden of shame she had been carrying. When asked to view herself through the eyes of her friend, she was gradually able to internalize a more benevolent view of herself. For Kate, the wish to return to her pastoral work to help others was a great motivation. It also helped to access memories of caring for others, which she could use as a safe access point to feeling compassion for others.

As she felt safer within herself and with me and the group, Kate expressed more despair, shame, and fears of failure and rejection as well as anger toward the depression. I validated her experiences and gave her space to share without wanting her to change, trusting that she would be able to take the next step in due time. To counteract her typical pattern of hiding her emotions and vulnerabilities, she shared some of her difficulties in our group therapy as well and was positively surprised that she received compassion and care without burdening anyone. The common humanity and care received from others helped Kate to turn toward her own emotions rather than away from them.

However, she still felt vulnerable and in need of help. The resurfacing of painful emotions based on older relational wounds is a normal part of the healing process and referred to as "backdraft" (Germer, 2009). A reassuring metaphor that can be offered to help to tolerate the temporary arising of difficult and long-suppressed emotions is that of the pain we feel when we enter a warm room with ice-cold hands: since the warmth is just what we need, we can tolerate this pain as it is temporary and necessary to save our hands.

Resource-Building through the Four Heart Qualities

Mindful awareness remains open and spacious when it is suffused by the four heart qualities, also referred to as the four immeasurable contemplations (Pali: *apamada*, or *brahmaviharas*). These are the boundless social emotions of love (Pali: *metta*), compassion (Pali: *karuna*), joy (Pali: *mudita*), and equanimity (Pali: *upekkha*). *Love*, known to us as loving-kindness, refers to the goodwill we extend to all sentient beings as we recognize everyone's inherent goodness and wish to be happy. *Joy*, commonly called sympathetic joy, arises when we extend this goodwill to what is beautiful in the world and in all beings, rejoicing together. When the goodwill of loving kindness meets suffering, *compassion* arises as the wish for all beings to be free from suffering, and a natural willingness to help. *Equanimity* is the quality of unbiased impartiality and non-attachment, which helps to balance love, joy, and compassion. The resulting "even-mindedness" provides an unwavering stability of mind and heart. Joy is also helpful to maintain emotional balance in the presence of suffering.

When we begin cultivating compassion for ourselves and others, we may not only fear that difficult emotions could surface, such as grief or despair or anger, but we may also fear the arising of positive emotions like happiness and joy. Some depressed patients experience pleasure as a taboo, and they worry that something bad will happen when they feel happy. Such fears may have developed due to a lack of attuned mirroring of joy by caregivers, or by caregivers reacting to happiness and joy with envy or punishment. In fact, fear of happiness predicted increased depression, anxiety, and stress in a sample of 53 moderately to severely depressed individuals (Gilbert et al., 2014c). Increased suppression of the outer signs of both positive and negative emotions and the active dampening of positive affect have also been linked to depressive symptoms (Beblo et al., 2012).

One goal of compassion-based therapy is to gradually desensitize the client to the sense of threat that has been linked to positive affiliative emotions and blocks positive emotions. Psychoeducation and behavioral experiments can help clients test whether their meta-cognitive beliefs about compassion and happiness hold true or not. Increased mindfulness of pleasant events and practice of loving-kindness meditation have been shown to lead to an increase in positive emotions and social connectedness, and these practices reduce the downward spiral of negative affect in depression, anxiety, and schizophrenia (Garland et al., 2010). The upward spiraling effect of experiencing positive emotions and improved social relationships is thought to be mediated by a change in vagal tone (Kok et al., 2013). A common pitfall in the compassion-based treatment of individuals with complex PTSD, including due to systemic abuse and oppression, is to bypass the processing of anger and outrage out of a misconception that compassion needs to empathize and forgive all. Such "idiot compassion" or "submissive compassion" lacks the wisdom to discern what supports the long-term well-being of the individual. In such cases, therapists need to develop fierce compassion and wisdom to be able to be steadfast in accompanying and coaching the client through the process of feeling and validating righteous anger, outrage and eventually and in their own time moving into a sense of inner distance from the perpetrators, which some might describe as form of forgiveness.

Kate had learned to suppress any outer signs of emotion, including joy, depriving her of the natural reinforcement of joy that comes of sharing it. As we began to explore the function of her anger and defiance, she discovered that it was driven by an unmet need to express the simple joy of being alive, which she associated with the image of a carefree, lively, and happy little girl sitting on a swing. Having learned that she no longer needed to suppress her joy in order to stay connected to her parents as an adult, she quickly embraced her innate capacity for enthusiasm, joy, and gratitude as a natural antidote to shame and the resulting depression. By purposefully paying increased attention to joyful and pleasant experiences in the present and reliving memories in the past, gradually she was able to broaden her awareness to include more joyful experiences and to strengthen her capacity to share joy and her natural sense of humor with others (Garland et al., 2010).

Re-Integrating All Parts with Compassion

In Tibetan Buddhism the peacock is considered to have the power to transform the venom of snakes into the cobalt blue color in its plumage, and into the wisdom eyes on its tail feathers. This myth symbolizes the transformational power of compassion, which can turn the mind poisons of anger, greed, and ignorance into nectar, and which ultimately creates something as beautiful as peacock feathers. In compassion-based psychotherapy, all aversive or shameful emotions and parts of us are considered to serve a function, such as to alert us to an unmet need, which, when met, can lead to a greater sense of wholeness, and relieve us of the burden of resisting disliked parts of ourselves. When we bring these shadow feelings and parts of us into the light, and meet them with goodwill, anger can be transformed into clarity and assertiveness, sadness into grief, shame into the shared human vulnerability that connects us, and loneliness into longing for love.

The safety of the therapeutic relationship can help the client to develop greater trust and safety within her own resources. Safety and trust serve as a foundation for the development of compassion and wisdom. Kate felt supported by the therapeutic team and her group, such that she was able to practice imagery of being in a safe place on a regular basis outside of therapy. Rather than avoiding hopelessness, anger, and sadness by surrounding herself with others, she was able to actively comfort and soothe herself when painful emotions arose on her own. Over time, we expanded these imagery practices to invite an ideal compassionate other (Gilbert, 2010), who would manifest the qualities of deep understanding, strength, calm, joy, and unconditional love toward her. A wise old woman appeared in the exercise, which she gradually came to recognize as her older wiser self. She was able to receive comforting and supportive words and gestures from this wise and compassionate part of herself, which helped her to validate her anger and to hold the emerging grief in a tender way. The power of self-compassion through imagery helped her regain trust in life and confidence in her own abilities to master challenging moments. She had fully accepted even the most shamed and shunned part of herself, which were her angry, sad, and hopeless parts and which together made up her depression.

A study by Tania Singer provides support for how compassion practices can help increase our resilience, by generating feelings of positive affect, reward, motivation, and affiliation in the face of acute distress (Engen & Singer, 2015). Compassion appears to up-regulate rather than down-regulate positive responses to distress. These findings explain how we can have the experience of simultaneously being the holder and the held, when we give ourselves the compassion we need, just like a parent.

Several months after being discharged from psychosomatic hospital and day hospital, Kate wrote to me to share her reflections on how her relationship to her *experiences* and to herself as the *experiencer* had changed:

> Even if I still sometimes feel sad or down since the inpatient treatment, I do no longer feel as despairing and hopeless as I did on the worst days during my deepest and darkest depression. When I do, I try to allow my emotions simply to be there, without judging them or pushing them away. I try to meet the feelings of fear and defeat with feelings of hope and ease, without pushing away the difficult feelings. I try to meet myself with understanding and love and to hold myself in a supportive and comforting embrace by contacting the whole and wise parts of my soul. I remind myself that my life is held and supported by God ... and I trust that God cradles my heart in his.[2]

The compassionate self-part can then be activated through ongoing tailored practices, in order to send compassion to the part of oneself which is in distress. Over time, as we listen to these distressed parts of ourselves, we develop a deep and refined understanding of what they need and how they are best able to receive it. Our compassionate self may reassure an anxious part of ourselves through words, gestures, or imagery. Over time, we may also be able to develop understanding of the personal, intergenerational, and collective historical context in which these parts emerged. We may be able to honor their good intentions to protect us, and to assure them that they are no longer needed to keep us safe or connected to caregivers and our group.

Preliminary Conclusions: Compassion in Psychotherapy

Research has increasingly focused on identifying trans-diagnostic mechanisms of change in psychotherapy. Experiential avoidance, rumination, and self-criticism have been shown to maintain a range of clinical disorders. Mindfulness offers an effective way of turning toward experience and disengaging from ruminative self-critical thinking (van der Velden et al., 2015). The recent integration of mindfulness into psychotherapy offers a significant conceptual breakthrough in cognitive behavior therapy (Hayes et al., 2011), and has shown considerable success in treating a wide variety of clinical conditions (Khoury et al., 2013). Acceptance is the emotional or attitudinal component of mindfulness (Bishop et al., 2004); and acceptance of *oneself* as a suffering individual is self-compassion (Germer, 2009). Self-compassion is increasingly understood as an underlying mechanism of action in mindfulness-based treatment, and in psychotherapy (Schanche et al., 2011). It is also a robust predictor of emotional well-being (Zessin et al., 2015).

Both mindfulness and compassion trainings have been found to improve emotion regulation on a neural level (Desbordes et al., 2012). Compassion and loving-kindness, in particular, appear to improve affect regulation by increasing positive affect (Engen & Singer, 2015) and by improving understanding of others (Mascaro et al., 2013. Compassionate imagery has also been shown to lead to a reduction in cortisol and increase in heart rate variability, even in a group with secure attachment and low self-criticism (Rockliff et al., 2008), suggesting that compassion training improves self-regulation by strengthening the vagal tone that promotes our abilities to safely connect, care for, and connect with others.

Because self-compassion is predicated on connecting with difficult emotions without self-judgment, it appears to lead to healthier psychological functioning. Self-compassion has been linked to greater psychological well-being

(Neff et al., 2007), and to reduced anxiety, depression, and stress (MacBeth & Gumley, 2012). The affective and cognitive components of self-compassion (kindness, balanced awareness, common humanity) are critical capacities for regulating distressing emotions. Fostering the capacity for self-compassion in patients strengthens their emotional regulation, helping them respond in a wise and kind way to difficult emotions rather than trying to fix them or make them go away. Self-compassion also improves a person's ability to cope with stressful events and it can provide the self-confidence needed to stand up to injustice.

Recent research on clinical applications of self-compassion is supporting these clinical insights. Self-compassion is associated with reduced harsh self-criticism (Gilbert & Procter, 2006) and with reduced experiential avoidance and rumination in depression (Krieger et al., 2013). Self-compassion has been found to be a protective factor in major depression (Diedrich et al., 2014), in PTSD (Dahm et al., 2015) in eating disorders and body image disturbances (Braun et al., 2016; Kelly & Tasca, 2016), and in psychological adjustment following chronic physical illness (Pinto-Gouveia et al., 2014) and divorce (Sbarra et al., 2012). Self-compassion has also been shown to enhance cognitive reappraisal as an emotional regulation strategy in major depression (Diedrich et al., 2016). Another study provided evidence that increasing attachment security led to an improvement in state self-compassion, pointing to the potential of compassion-based interventions to strengthen the attachment system (Pepping et al., 2015). Research also suggests that self-compassion can buffer the deleterious impact of social stigma (Wong et al., 2019). Self-compassion was specifically found to dampen the impact of internalized racism on anxiety, depression, and stress (Emery, 2020).

Several pilot studies of CFT in group-therapy settings support the effectiveness of applying compassion with patients suffering from eating disorders (Gale et al., 2014), PTSD (Beaumont et al., 2012), personality disorders (Lucre & Corten, 2013), psychosis (Laithwaite et al., 2009) and mixed chronic conditions (Gilbert & Procter, 2006). A first randomized controlled trial by Christine Braehler demonstrated the feasibility of conducting group-based CFT with clients with chronic psychotic disorders, showing increases in compassion associated with reduced shame, depression, and a greater sense of social inclusion (Braehler et al., 2013; Braehler et al., 2013).

Compassion is at the heart of the psychotherapeutic process. Self-compassion offers an emotional resource for psychotherapists to care for ourselves, prevent burnout, and become more resilient and effective. Compassion is a state of loving-connected presence with suffering, which has been found to energize us so we can actively help. It also helps us to stay with the suffering of our clients as well as our own in an effortless way. Whereas mindfulness dismantles the separate self into moment-to-moment experience, self-compassion melds the separate self through love in the heat of suffering. Self-compassion is the loving hand our clients learn to extend to themselves when caught up in the midst of shame and despair.

Notes

1   Kate was treated by Christine Braehler in German. Both are German natives.
2   Kate (name changed) kindly agreed for her story and citation to be published in book chapters to help other professionals learn about what helped her. The original citation in German was translated into English by Christine Braehler.

14
The RAIN of Self-Compassion
A Simple Practice for Clients and Clinicians

Tara Brach

In *The Song of the Bird*, Anthony de Mello (1984), a well-known Jesuit priest, writer, and sage, described a key moment of his waking up—a moment of what I call *radical acceptance*. He said that he had spent decades being depressed, anxious, and selfish—despairing about how to change. The worst part, he said, was that even his friends had told him that he needed to become less self-absorbed. Then, one day his world stopped when a friend said, "Don't change. Please don't change. I love you just the way you are." *Don't change. I love you just as you are.* Father de Mello said the words were pure grace; they flooded through him. He said that, paradoxically, it was only when he got permission *not* to change—to be as he was—that he was able to transform in a profound way.

To me, this story describes one of the deep principles of healing and transformation: it's only when we stop the war—stop the accusations toward ourselves about how bad and wrong we are—that we are actually free to flower and become all that we can be. Father de Mello was fortunate that he had a friend to help him. Many of us have friends who are mirrors in a positive way but, ultimately, to really move forward on our path we need to be able to regard ourselves with deep love and acceptance to open the door to change. To cultivate this ability in myself and my clients, I have developed a practice that I teach using the acronym RAIN. I find the R-A-I-N practice to be a powerful way to deepen self-compassion. It is a simple practice that has been really helpful to many of those I work with (Brach, 2004).

The Trance of Unworthiness and Our Negativity Bias

Before I explore the RAIN of self-compassion, some context may be needed. I have written and spoken about the suffering of self-aversion and the need for

DOI: 10.4324/9781003243588-16

self-compassion perhaps more than any other single theme and I come back to it again and again because self-aversion is such a pervasive form of suffering. It also happens to be one I am personally familiar with—while the frequency has decreased, the self-critic continues to appear in my mind. When I recognize it, I acknowledge what's happening, "Oh, I'm back at war with myself again," followed by, "Ok, this is the time to offer some kindness inwardly." In my own life and work, I have found, over and over, that self-compassion is essential for healing. Perhaps that's because I've noticed self-aversion at work even when other emotions seem to be predominant. While it might feel like I'm stuck in anger, fear, or blame, deep down there's a sense that *something's wrong with me*.

If we look closely at our minds when we're distressed, whatever the difficult emotion is, we find not just that emotion—not just the fear or the jealousy— but something deeper. That something deeper is an underlying belief—*I'm bad for having this feeling. This feeling reflects badly on me.* There's an unconscious leap from *I feel bad* to *I am bad*. In the Buddhist tradition, this is described as *second arrowing*. The first arrow is the feeling of fear (or whatever emotion is arising); the second arrow is the experience of being bad for having the feeling. Rather than bringing healing energy to the fear, we all too often lock into what I call the *trance of unworthiness* and condemn ourselves and the feeling as bad or wrong. When I talk about that trance, I'm talking about a narrow, distorted state of mind that impacts all our feelings, thoughts, and behaviors.

I once received an email from a woman who wrote,

> Dear Tara, my twelve-year-old niece is quick to worry and often gets wound up with anxiety. After one such experience, she and I left to run some errands and she started apologizing in the car and told me how bad she feels about herself for having panic attacks.

This woman understood that her niece's self-judgment was the second arrow and how that is what perpetuates the trance of unworthiness. I suggested that she teach her niece to recognize the second arrow and, when it arises, to instead bring a gentle attention to the inflow/outflow of her breath. I also talked about the phrase *real but not true*—that while her niece's judgments felt real, their content was not truth. She could learn not to believe these stories. I heard back that, after sharing this with her niece, she got this response: "The second arrow of self-judgment can be really difficult … but then there is the third arrow—when you realize that what you're worried about isn't even true!" These stories resonate because we all have experiences of personal deficiency and badness, and because the conviction we have of being bad is usually the most stubborn of our beliefs. In my experience, such beliefs are typically the hardest for us to wake up from.

Of course, we are all familiar with what seems like the converse, when someone says, "You may feel less than, but I usually go around feeling special and better than other people." We humans tend to be emotionally bulimic. We either feel like we're the worst or we feel superior and self-important. We go back and forth between extremes. Underneath the sense of specialness there is, invariably, a hollow feeling—some feeling of separateness. Despite the bravado, our sense of superiority is predictably fragile and, deep down underneath it, there is a suppressed vulnerability.

So despite different surface appearances, the trance of unworthiness—of feeling deficient and unlovable—is one of the most common and pervasive forms of trance we fall into. What we're often not aware of is how many moments of our lives are distorted by an undercurrent of *not enough* or *should be more* or *something's wrong with me*. In the grip of this undercurrent, we have a sense that there's a problem and we see that problem as ourselves. In fact, like fish unaware of being in water, most of us are so familiar with that sense of insufficiency that we don't realize that we're living and breathing in a toxic cocktail of *not being okay*.

Many people wonder, and many clients and students ask me, "Why is this insecurity about self so pervasive?" And of course, I've asked myself the same question: "Why do so many of us, deep down, feel we're not okay?" We can certainly see this insecurity as a mirror of the larger culture we live in. There is so much striving, competition, bias, and fear that, for most of us, rather than living with an assumption of belonging, we are convinced that we have to meet certain unrealistic standards in order to be acceptable or lovable. Such standards are implicit in the messages regularly conveyed to us by our culture beginning in early childhood. Our culture, and all too often our families, tell us that we have to think, feel, behave, and look a certain way in order to be accepted or to get the approval we need to develop in a healthy way. We learn to conform as a way of gaining a positive response from others, which may work in the short run but, ultimately, undermines real confidence. Of course, the standards in any society are set by the dominant culture. So, if we don't belong to the dominant culture or if we don't want to live in the dominant way, or if we simply can't meet those standards, there are even more hurdles. For instance, if we are a person of color rather than white, we receive ongoing messages that, due to our race, we are "less than," and a likely target of hostility and violence. If we don't fit into the dominant culture in terms of religion—right now, for instance, by being Muslim—we get the message that we're perceived as dangerous, and not welcome in many places. Each additional hurdle to acceptance and belonging deepens the trance of insecurity and unworthiness (Powell, 2015).

The trance of unworthiness is sustained and amplified by our ingrained negativity bias—a deeply conditioned tendency to remember and dwell on the things we feel are wrong. This negativity bias is a part of an instinctive survival mechanism and there is a growing body of research that shows how our minds and brains are preset to recall and focus on what is or could be wrong (Hanson, 2013). Through most of our evolution, we were likely, at some point, to have predators, like the lion, stalking us. Given that, it was highly adaptive to remain vigilant that something might go wrong at any moment. In modern life, while some of us continue to be threatened by physical violation, many others are stalked by our own psychological fears rather than any sort of clear and present danger to our lives. Nonetheless, this survival bias persists and disposes us to fixate on whatever might be problematic. And usually, that means our own weaknesses and mistakes. Though we tell ourselves that this is rational to ensure that we don't repeat our mistake or that we improve ourselves, the hyper-vigilance just makes us more anxious and prone to make other mistakes. In short, this bias locks us in—it draws us into the trance.

I have a memory from when I was six or seven years old that highlights how our mind narrows when we fear mistakes. My parents had taken me to a restaurant and the waiter chatted to me, saying something like, "Well you look like a smart young lady. I have a question for you. What color was George Washington's white horse?" My brow furrowed and I really started trying to figure the riddle out. In my mind, I turned over everything I remembered from any of the stories I'd ever heard about George as I tried to remember if I'd seen pictures of the first president on his horse. I finally made my best guess that the horse was black. When the waiter exposed my mistake, I was flooded with embarrassment and shame. True story. That was one lived experience in which insecurity led to error and set in motion more embarrassment, more fear of failure, more vigilance. It's as if the mind and brain make a contract with themselves, saying, "Let's remember this, so we don't ever do it again!" And here I am, many decades later, still remembering.

Of course, I'm not unique. We can all look back and find memories like this that jump out to us. A physician I know described a humiliating experience during his training. As a young, newly graduated MD doing his residency in obstetrics, he would become deeply embarrassed while performing pelvic exams on his female patients. To further his embarrassment, he had unconsciously formed a habit of whistling softly while performing them. During one such exam on a middle-aged patient, the woman suddenly burst out laughing, further embarrassing him. He looked up from his work and sheepishly said, "Oh, I'm sorry. Was I tickling you?" She had tears running down her cheeks from laughing so hard. "No, doctor, but the song you were whistling was 'I wish I were an Oscar Mayer Wiener'!"

While this is a funny story, the reality is that when we are insecure about ourselves, we are not operating in full awareness. We're in a trance—our attention is narrowed, and we're driven by the beliefs and feelings that something's wrong with us. And then we add the second arrow (and third and fourth) that we should not have these beliefs and feelings or be driven by them. This proliferation of arrowing keeps fueling the trance of unworthiness.

Three Core Dynamics that Perpetuate the Trance of Unworthiness

When we encounter the trance of unworthiness, what we most need is to catch ourselves and open our eyes so that we can consider what is really happening. For instance, when you're defensive with a colleague or too harsh in parenting, or when you find you're drinking too much or you are insensitive to your partner's needs, you might very well turn on yourself and accuse yourself of being a bad person. The only way to wake up out of such a trance is to shine the light of awareness on it. In my experience, there are three key dynamics that arise in moments like this, when we're at war with ourselves. The first is that *we're taking it personally*. The belief is: *What's going on is my fault. I'm bad.*

Self-blame overlooks all the past causes and conditions that we had no control over that may have contributed to the problem. Causes and conditions might include intergenerational trauma—the epigenetic traces that pass down memories of violence—as well as the influence of our family and culture that shape our development in this lifetime.

Recent research shows that if someone grows up in a situation with a lot of violence, it literally changes their biochemistry so that they get locked into stress mode—where there's a feeling of impending danger and a potential for violent reactivity. Beyond overt trauma, there are many degrees of severed belonging that we all experience when we don't receive the kind of nurturing we need. What happens when we look at our early years and ask,

"Did my parents really listen, and understand, and get who I was? Was I given the kind of mirroring that helped me trust myself and trust my core goodness? Did I feel a sense of trust that I belong and am acceptable, lovable, and worthwhile?

If we were able to view this wisely, we might realize, *I get it that I was often judged and criticized, and I've internalized this as self-aversion, which leads to defensive or aggressive behaviors that protect me from feeling worse about myself.* Then when those unwanted behaviors arise, we wouldn't take it so personally as "my fault." Remembering the chain of conditioning, we wouldn't add the second arrow of, "I'm a bad person for being so judgmental."

Recognizing the multitude of causes for our behavior doesn't mean we are not responsible for our actions, it just means we are not condemning ourselves as *bad* and directing aversive blame at ourselves. This is a vitally important distinction. I frequently encounter people who admit that they're afraid of easing up on themselves. "If I don't blame myself," we often think, "I won't be taking responsibility." We are not able to respond with wisdom and compassion if we are struck by that second arrow of self-blame. The fact of the matter is that releasing aversive self-blame is the necessary precursor to taking authentic responsibility and being more intelligent and creative with our solutions.

Typically, we do take it personally, and in a similar way we are hooked into judging others. Our nervous system picks up other people's insecurities, and we react to them just as we do to our own feelings of inadequacy—with judgments and aversion that are trying to change or make up for what we don't like (Siegel, 2015). Then we add on more self-blame for those judgments and behaviors towards others. In other words, the first dynamic in the trance of unworthiness is to forget the causes and conditions and target ourselves and others with aversive blame.

The second thing that happens when we're in the trance of unworthiness is that, because our attention is narrowed and tightened, *we lose touch with key dimensions of our authentic being* and with the actual vulnerability that is current in us—our feelings of hurt, woundedness, sorrow, or fear. This makes it much more likely that we'll aggressively turn against ourselves, since we're not actually registering the simple truth, *Oh, I am suffering. This is hard. This hurts.* We are cut off from both the rawness of our vulnerability, and the natural compassion that arises when we touch that rawness. If we can't touch the vulnerability, we can't feel compassion. In addition, the negative fixation of trance creates blinders that keep us from being aware of our goodness. We forget how much we long to be honest and to see what is true. We forget how much we really want to love, and not to hold back our love. We forget the light of awareness that shines through us, the goodness of our being. We have lost touch with the wholeness of our being, with our heart awareness. This is the crux of the second characteristic of trance—forgetting the truth of who we are.

The third dynamic when we are caught in the trance of unworthiness is that *we are propelled into reactive behavior in a misguided attempt to cope and feel better.* We react automatically with an unconscious defense or adaptation designed to lessen the sting of our shame, guilt, or fear. These reactive behaviors sustain the trance because they create psychological and behavioral tendencies that only reinforce the entire experience of distress and trauma. Trance begets behaviors that draw us more deeply into trance, in a seemingly endless cycle.

The three dynamics operant during the trance of unworthiness lock us into an identification as a deficient person. Consider instances when you're feeling insecure or bad about yourself. How do you habitually cope? What are the behaviors that get triggered? One habit some of us fall into is sustaining an inner dialogue that seeks to self-justify and convince ourselves that we are okay. The flip side of this inner dialogue may be to blame other people for how we are feeling or reacting badly. We may then start working to compensate for our negativity or try too hard to please others in order to prove that we're worthwhile in spite of it. Add to that our attempts to self-soothe with many addictive behaviors like overeating, immoderate drinking or drug use, and gambling. Whatever reactive habits we fall into to try to feel better about ourselves, we end up solidifying the identity of the *not-okay-self,* and actually intensifying the hurt rather than relieving it. Finally, we often add insult to injury by blaming ourselves not just for feeling bad, but for our defensive efforts to cope—*I'm bad for the ways I'm trying to feel better.* In other words, we feel ashamed of our trance and then shame ourselves for our trance behaviors. So, these three parts of the trance of unworthiness—taking it personally, not seeing our vulnerability and goodness, and then reacting out of shame—consolidate an identity as a *not-okay-person.*

RAIN: Dissolving the Trance with Self-Compassion

Awakening out of our deep sense of unworthiness begins when we start to see that we're living in a trance and recognize how this is keeping us from living and loving fully. This motivates us to find a path of healing and homecoming.

To bring a quality of healing presence to the suffering of unworthiness, I use a practice based on the acronym RAIN:

- Recognize what is going on.
- Allow the experience to be there, just as it is.
- Investigate with interest and care.
- Nourish with self-compassion.

First, we *recognize* that we're in a trance. We might notice that we're judging ourselves—that's the big one. Usually, there's that voice of the inner critic going on. We also might notice that we're justifying ourselves. We are rehearsing what we're going to say to somebody else. We might know that we're over-eating or over-drinking. We might notice that we're speeding up or worrying.

There may be many different aspects of our trance but, in recognizing them, we prepare for the second step—to *allow* what is happening to be just as it is. We can stop and say, "Okay, in some way I'm not feeling good about myself." Recognize it and allow it. We can let the unpleasant feeling be there, which gives us a pause—a chance to deepen our attention in a healing way.

The "I" in RAIN refers to the next step in the practice, which is to *investigate* what is happening. It's important to investigate our feelings and state of mind with curiosity and gentleness. We begin by asking: *What's really going on inside me right now? What am I believing? What feeling is most asking for attention?* We investigate further by discovering what the felt sense of our experience is like and where we are feeling it. We might ask: *How does this vulnerable place want me to be with it?* or, *What does this part of me most need?* In this way, we sense into what might most comfort or heal—be it love, compassion, understanding, or forgiveness.

The final step in the practice, the "N" of RAIN, is to *nourish* ourselves with compassion. Perhaps we offer words to ourselves like: "It's okay, sweetheart" or "I'm sorry," or "I love you." Thich Nhat Hanh uses the beautiful and powerful phrase, "Darling, I care about this suffering" (Thich Nhat Hanh, 2014). Or it might be that you sense the love of God or the Divine flowing through you, bathing the parts of you that feel most vulnerable. Some may visualize themselves as a mature parent attuning to and caring for the part of themselves that feels like a terrified child, gently placing a hand on their heart as a way of communicating care. Whatever it is, we sense the possibility of calling on love (from our own awake heart, or from a source perceived as beyond) and offering it inward. That's how we *nourish* with self-compassion.

Just like with a real rain, where fresh life flourishes in the aftermath, the moments after practicing RAIN are an essential part of our healing and awakening. After applying the practice, we simply rest and notice, *Okay, what's it like right now?* What we often discover is that the moment when we began the practice of RAIN, we were in the trance of unworthiness and identified with a small self that felt separate and deficient. In contrast, after applying the practice of RAIN—after we've recognized and allowed our feelings of vulnerability and investigated and nourished them with compassion—we open to a sense of who we are beyond the trance. At that point, we can rest in that beingness—savoring our natural spaciousness, wakefulness, and tenderness.

The RAIN of Self-Compassion: The Minister's Story

Here is an example of how the RAIN of self-compassion works. I was working with a minister who had reached an impasse in his marriage which left his wife really dissatisfied. She wanted him to be more intimate, more vulnerable, more real with his feelings, and not so spiritually detached. She wanted him to feel more connected, to look in her eyes and say, "I love you," and let her know, "I feel scared." The more she asked for this, the more he felt blocked, pressured, and even offended. As we began working together, he started to get in touch with those moments in which he felt this way. Soon, we began to discover that, in those moments when there were opportunities to connect, he felt a real sense of deficiency and was visited by a harsh inner critic who said, "You're a hypocrite." In other words, this voice was saying to him, "You're preaching love, but you don't embody it. You can comfort and guide as a spiritual adviser and you're fine with people as long as you're in the role of the minister, but as soon as you're the one hurting you can't be close. You know all your life you've never been close to anybody." Naturally, this self-criticism was accompanied by a great deal of shame.

His practice with RAIN was to recognize when those thoughts and feelings would arise and pause, allowing them to be there. We did this together as he recollected a recent, very shame-filled incident of not being able to engage authentically with his wife. I asked him, "What does that shame feel like, and where is it in your body?" He replied, "It feels like a sinking hollow ache, and I can feel it in my heart and in my belly." And he continued, "Then I'm gripped by the belief that I'm an impostor, I'm defective, and people will find out." Though he was clearly a sincere and caring man, he was terrified that his wife would find out how he really felt and dismiss him as defective. When I asked him, "What does that hollow shame place most need?" he responded with conviction, "It needs forgiveness, it needs love, it needs somebody … a presence that sees my goodness."

As mentioned earlier, when we nourish, we want in some way to bring love and compassion to our place of suffering. At this point, in my own practice of RAIN, I often put my hands on my heart because I have found—as have many others—that touch really makes a difference. Current research seems to be supporting the healing potential of touch (Field, 2014). There's a whole neural nexus in the area we touch when we put our hands on our heart, and this simple gesture helps bring the warmth of human contact to these nerves, possibly activating the parasympathetic nervous system—which calms and soothes the "fight–flight" response of the sympathetic nervous system. Nourishing often happens through some combination of touch, words and messages, imagery, and energy.

For my client, the minister, nourishing involved the sense of calling on God's love, as well as on his own love, placing his hands on his heart, and sending all that love to his wounded places. He described trying to let that love pour into his chest, and into his belly. He shared with me that it helped him to say, "It's okay, you can surrender into love. It's okay, surrender."

In the moments after offering these compassionate words and gestures to himself, when he paused to observe the effects of the RAIN practice, he reported feeling a sense of spaciousness and that he felt one with a vast field of vibrating, loving awareness. Naturally, this was not a one-time experience, as our conditioning is deeply wired, and it takes many rounds of RAIN to uproot the old patterning. For this minister, the old feelings and beliefs kept coming back. But after many rounds of bringing his hands to his heart, calling on God's love and his own love, and pouring it inwards to heal his hurt, he began to connect more regularly to an enlarged sense of his own being. And importantly, this enabled a growing sense of trust in his own inherent goodness. Months after we began working with RAIN, he shared with me that, for the first time in twenty-six years, he and his wife were feeling each other's hearts. I believe this profound shift and opening came from his repeated practice of self-compassion.

For this minister, the trance was actually a kind of inner stoniness around his heart, where he played his role but was armored against fear of exposure. By practicing RAIN, he gradually dissolved that stoniness, and in its place was a space of loving openness that gradually transformed his relationship with everyone in his life.

My Own Experience of the Nourishing RAIN of Self-Compassion

The most challenging experiences for most of us are when self-doubt and shame solidify at our core. It's not only a *belief* of personal badness, but it's visceral. So often when we try to offer compassion towards ourselves, there is a sense that there's really no one home to offer it. It's almost like we're too regressed, too tight, or too small to offer ourselves real compassion. So I want to reiterate that, in the RAIN of self-compassion—in recognizing, allowing, investigating, and then nourishing—it's vital to draw that sense of loving presence from whatever source we can—whatever is closest and most accessible. It doesn't have to be Buddhist, Muslim, Hindu, Christian, or Jewish—just personal and authentic (Brach, 2016). Ultimately, that love is our very nature but, because our hearts are constricted and contracted and alienated, we often don't feel that it's present or available. By reaching out and touching some expression of love, we reconnect with the loving that flows through our own being.

The RAIN of self-compassion is a practice like any other. We have to do it repeatedly because our conditioning to regard ourselves as a deficient self is so strong. Even if we can only go through the motions, I have found this practice to be extremely healing and effective. As we've heard, *neurons that fire together wire together.* We need to de-condition our sense of unworthiness and badness, over and over, by *recognizing, allowing, investigating,* and *nourishing with compassion.* Each time we do RAIN and then pause, the true flourishing and flowering happens. In the rest after RAIN, we can inquire, *Who am I, when meeting this moment with an allowing and caring presence?* It is in these moments that we begin to realize and trust the depth and beauty of what we are.

© Tara Brach

15
Compassion-Based Resilience Training (CBRT)

A Contemplative Therapeutic Intervention for Self-Regulation and Cultivating Loving Intimate Relationships

Fiona Brandon

Demystifying and addressing the roots of relationship stress is a fundamental aspect of my psychotherapeutic work with clients. At our core we are all relational beings, and learning to be in a wise, supportive, and compassionate relationship with ourself and others is the backbone of building a psychologically resilient and meaningful life. One of the tools I use with my clients to inspire and support an architecture of psychological well-being, resilience, and relational health is Compassion-Based Resilience Training (CBRT). The training was developed by psychiatrist Dr Joseph Loizzo to reduce stress and build resilience by combining the wisdom of traditional contemplative practices from India and Tibet—including mindfulness, compassion, imagery, and breath-work—with contemporary discoveries from stress research, neuroscience, and positive psychology. Using a health-educational group format, the CBRT program is taught by certified teachers to lay and professional groups who are curious about an integral healthcare approach to relieving personal and social stress while increasing mental, physical, and emotional resilience and well-being.

CBRT's modular therapeutic curriculum educates participants about the root causes and pervasive impact of personal and social stress and trauma on our mind, heart, body, and nervous system. The curriculum then offers a range of antidotes to stress-related suffering and its root causes using contemplative practices that reduce stress, enhance resilience, and accelerate personal and relational well-being. The first four modules of the training cover four basic practices of mindfulness to address personal healing. Participants learn to be

DOI: 10.4324/9781003243588-17

thoughtful observers and caregivers for themselves. In the final four modules, participants learn ways to use the wisdom and compassion garnered from the personal healing modules and apply them to all their social relationships with close loved ones, acquaintances, and challenging others.

For the purposes of this chapter, I will focus on the ways I use CBRT's therapeutic framework as an adjunctive support for individual clients and couples who struggle to cultivate loving and supportive long-term intimate relationships. As a psychotherapist, I find the CBRT approach a vital tool to help clients become conscious of, get curious about, and shift out of, stress-reactive or traumatic states of mind and into more equanimous and compassionate mindsets that support them to engage in, and nourish adult intimate relationships. The mindfulness, compassion, and breath-work practices that CBRT offers are the medicines that directly counter the reactivity of stress and trauma, along with the distorted perceptions of self and others informed by them. The practices encourage clients to go beyond an intellectual understanding of their personal and relational blocks to an embodied curative experience of progressive change that brings about an optimal mindset for love, intimacy, and care.

I have found that CBRT compliments my psychotherapeutic work by facilitating a client's *direct experience* of unburdening themselves from adaptive problematic relational strategies that hinder a fuller experience of intimacy. This direct experience can also give clients conscious access to positive mental, emotional, and visceral ways of being that have been kept out of awareness by chronic stress and trauma. So even though CBRT's contemplative insights and methods are taught discursively to clients—to be practiced inside and outside of classes or sessions—the CBRT approach includes an appreciation for the normally unconscious, pre-verbal layers of the psyche, and is designed to access our capacity for implicit and embodied learning to facilitate personal and relational healing.

To begin, I describe how CBRT presents the common roots of relationship stress; along with the personal and interpersonal costs of attachment stress and overidentification with a negative sense of self. I then offer an overview of CBRT's eight modules, their respective companion practices, and how these practices reduce personal and relationship stress. Finally, I give examples of how to apply the CBRT framework in clinical practice to improve self-regulation, self-care, and the capacity for intimate relationships; and how the contemplative therapeutic process utilizes mindfulness and compassion practices to build a bridge between conscious relational experiences and unconscious traumatic beliefs, fears, projections, and embodied stress-reactions that clients need to work through.

The Common Root of Relationship Stress

The CBRT framework gets right to the heart of clarifying the common root of relationship stress and our blocks to love: it is the negative sense of self that we develop in early childhood, and carry with us into our adult relationships. It is this traumatic sense of self that distorts our perception of ourself and others creating resistance and blocks to intimacy and the experience of belonging. Naming this common root of relationship stress gives clients an anchor from which to contextualize and grapple with how early childhood relationship wounding has affected their ability to maintain healthy intimate adult relationships. Acknowledging and investigating their negative sense of self, along with the associated stress-reactive relational patterns, gives them the opportunity to take responsibility for their part in dysfunctional intrapsychic and interpersonal dynamics while holding others accountable for their role in relationship stress.

How does the negative sense of self get constellated in our psyches? And how does it generate personal stress that foments interpersonal difficulties later in adulthood? To explain the development of the negative sense of self the CBRT framework draws on the neuropsychology of attachment and developmental trauma (Baradon, 2009; Loizzo, 2021; Schore, 2010; Treisman, 2016); affect theory (Kernberg, 1990, 2006); the dynamics of shame (Erskine et al., 1994; Wheeler, 1997); relational and intersubjective psychoanalysis (Nemirovsky, 2021); and contemplative psychology (Loizzo, 2012, 2017; Strong, 2021; Van Gordon et al., 2022). As a starting point, this modality builds on the foundational insight of developmental psychology: in early childhood, we are entirely dependent on our caregivers for safety and well-being. We instinctually orient ourselves to critically needed others for comfort, protection, guidance, and love. Brain research shows that healthy brain development relies not only on our genetic information, but also on the dynamics experienced with an attuned and attentive caregiver with whom safety and connection are readily accessed (Brotherson, 2005; Siegel, 2020). Without these relational factors, the brain can have difficulty regulating basic physiological functions, including respiration, metabolism, immune responses, and heart rate, not to mention healthy psychological development.

For healthy brain and nervous system development in infants and young children we need to "borrow" our caregiver's nervous system to calm and co-regulate us (Brotherson, 2005; Porter et al., 2022; Porges & Furman, 2011). Not only do we learn from our caregiver's nervous system how to self-regulate, we also develop executive functioning (working memory, mental flexibility, and self-control) (Schroeder & Kelley, 2010) along with our understanding of interpersonal dynamics. Developmental psychology and attachment research (Banai et al., 2005; Stern, 1985; Trevarthen & Aitken, 2001) show that we learn about ourself and the world through the dynamic exchange of mental, emotional, and visceral messages between ourself and primary caregivers. At its best this multi-dimensional interpersonal exchange produces an intrapsychic experience of safety and resilience that helps us cultivate affective self-regulation, nourish intimacy with others, manage life's stressors with the capacity to recover, and experience happiness. At its worst it can produce a sense of alienation from self and others, low self-esteem or self-attack, and mistrust (sometimes even terror) of intimate connection. All this to say that the mental, emotional, and physiological states of our primary caregivers powerfully impact how we experience and perceive ourselves and the world. Another way to understand this is that the development of our sense of self, and our sense of intimate connection, is embedded in this crucial relational process that begins in infancy (Siegel & Bryson, 2011; Stern, 1985).

The Effects of Attachment Stress

CBRT draws on attachment theory (Ainsworth, 1978; Duschinsky, 2020) to explain that during our initial emotional development with primary caregivers we all experience varying degrees of rupture and attunement. Even if a child does not experience traumas such as exploitation, abuse, war, or natural disaster, they will inevitably suffer some attachment stress. This idea is informed by the work of John Bowlby, Mary Ainsworth, Mary Main, and subsequent attachment researchers who have shown that our attachment system is biological as well as psychological. Ainsworth laid out the three initial primary infant attachment styles: secure, ambivalent, avoidant, while the disorganized style was later added from Main's research. The central premise of attachment theory is that having a responsive and stable caregiver early in life provides a child with the confidence to go out and explore the world, while a child who is not securely attached tends to be insecure and have difficulty venturing out into life. Attachment research also shows how a child's early bonding experiences greatly affect personality development and the formation of adult relationships (Karen, 1994).

The study of early ruptures of safety and connection in infants and young children shows that attachment stress can vary in intensity depending on whether a caregiver is out of sight for a few minutes, to a caregiver being chronically stressed and unable to care for their child's physical and emotional needs.

This upset in attunement—a loss of connection with our caregiver—can lead us to feel that we are under threat. If this experience of threat remains insufficiently cared for by needed others, our nervous system becomes dysregulated and prompts survival-based reactivity (Mikulincer et al., 2003): as infants and toddlers we do not yet have the mental capacity to understand that our caregiver will return and the connection will be restored.

It is normal for babies to experience threat states, such as separation panic, when they are missing their primary caregivers. The degree to which a caregiver is able to repair these ruptures, and reestablish needed attunement, will inform the development of our adult attachment styles based on how well we recover from the distress or learn that we must self-manage chronic and unresolved stress. If we do not receive the necessary support the stress will be carried both physiologically and psychologically into adulthood; and leave us with feelings of abandonment, helplessness, and lack of control. As adults we may then carry the self-perceptions: "I am alone," "I am powerless," and "I can't rely on others" into our adult relationships, informing how we navigate our intimate relationships (Dobson et al., 2022).

The Repercussions of Overidentifying with Attachment Stress

CBRT points out that when the overwhelm from attachment rupture is coupled with our instinctual negativity bias,[1] an overidentification with the negative experience of feeling small, disempowered, and out of control, will likely develop. For example, if our parents are predominantly emotionally unavailable and dismissive, as a child we will have unmet emotional needs. If we overidentify with this attachment stress, we may adopt an avoidant attachment style to manage the hurt and disappointment associated with connection and vulnerability. It is this repeated process of overidentification with our attachment stress and trauma that is the common basis for our negative/wounded/sensitive sense of self. We learn to organize our sense of self around this experience of abandonment, separateness, dysregulation, and shame, and then mistake it for the core of who we are (Loizzo, 2021).

As we mature into adulthood, we are not aware of the influence our negative sense of self has on our personal well-being and our ability to relate to others. Depending on the type of early attachment stress we experienced, we may react in a number of ways to adult intimacy. If we had caregivers who were emotionally distant and did not respond to our cues of upset, we may feel the world is a place where others cannot be relied upon and as adults fear emotional intimacy (a dismissing adult attachment style). If we received inconsistent love and care from caregivers we may be nervous and insecure about relationships as adults. We may cling to relationships to the detriment of our own well-being and live in constant fear of abandonment and rejection (a preoccupied adult attachment style). If our caregivers fluctuated between expressing care and being frightening/terrifying, this can result in a state of mind that bounces back and forth between alarm and disorientation. This early attachment stress ties the experience of intimacy to some degree of terror making it difficult as adults to maintain intimate connections and have any consolidated mechanism for self-soothing (a disorganized attachment strategy) (Hazan & Shaver, 1987). For those of us who also experience varying degrees of stress and trauma from discrimination against our race, gender, sexual preference, ability, religion, body size, socio-economic standing—to name a few—our identification with the negative sense of self can be further intensified if we consciously or unconsciously take on the dominant culture's devaluing perspective.

The majority of individuals and couples that I work with are unaware of the stress and dysregulation that their negative sense of self creates in regards to their perception of themselves and how in turn this affects their intimate relationships. They are innocent to the ways in which we bring a frightened, shame-based, and chronically stressed part of ourselves into our relationships. And they are unaware how, more often than not, we unconsciously react from this part of ourself in response to an exchange or experience with our intimate partner. Unless more mature ways of relating are modeled to us over the course of our emotional development, and more developed defenses are consolidated to navigate relational difficulties, our negative sense of self—like a child—will continue to consciously or unconsciously seek security, love, and emotional regulation from external sources. There is little understanding that love and security can also be sourced and regulated internally.

Because of this unidirectional expectation and focus, our wounded sense of self places unrealistic expectations on our relationships, including the expectation that our partners will *always* be able to care for us when we are feeling upset and/or discomfort in the relationship. Our negative sense of self does not take into account that our partner may also be feeling vulnerable and upset, and therefore lack the resources to soothe us. Our younger sensitive sense of self does not see that our partner also has attachment wounding (J. Loizzo, personal communication). Instead, our negative sense of self holds a fantasy that our partners will fulfill the developmental needs that were not met by our primary caregivers.

The Cost of Putting Others in Charge of Our State of Mind

In this way our wounded sense of self asks our partners to be a parent/caregiver instead of accepting them as an adult who equally suffers and wishes for happiness and love. It is as if our wounded sense of self is saying to our partner,

> I do not see that it is possible to create my own happiness, so you need to create it for me. You need to make me feel loved. I cannot do this for myself. I cannot validate myself, you need to give me validation so that I feel a sense of self-worth.
>
> (J. Loizzo, personal communication)

If we unconsciously ask our adult partner to be in charge of our sense of security and self-worth, then we are abdicating our responsibility to care for and regulate ourself. This externalization of a sense of well-being puts others in charge of our state of mind. We effectively outsource our locus of control and position our partner's state of mind to have an outsized impact on our ability to feel safe, loved, grounded, and regulated. As adults, if we turn over control of our state of mind to another, then in a sense we are falling into a regressed parent–child dynamic with our partner. It is appropriate for a child to look to their caregiver for help regulating. As an adult we need to relate to a peer not a parent. It is up to us to tend to, and regulate, the stress reactive mindset born out of our negative sense of self.

To consciously unlearn the tendency of overidentifying with a negative sense of self and its unconscious survival-based reactive relational habits, CBRT offers mindfulness-based and compassion-based practices that directly address how to reduce personal stress and become a good-enough observer, self-regulator, and caregiver to ourself, followed by ways to extend the knowledge gained from caring for ourself to heal interpersonal stress.

The following is an overview of the nine contemplative practices offered in CBRT.

Personal Healing and The Four Noble Truths—Modules I–IV

Before we can uproot and heal our main block to intimacy—our overidentification with our negative sense of self—we must first begin by healing the stress-reactive habits that get constellated when we meet difficulty in our own mind and body in the here and now. We need to learn methods for self-awareness and equanimity to regulate our nervous system which affords us the capacity to act skillfully and connect deeply in intimate relationships. To do this, the initial four modules of CBRT offer a step-by-step therapeutic intervention modeled on *Shakyamuni* Buddha's "four noble truths" framework.[2] The four mindfulness practices build on one another so we learn progressively (J. Loizzo, personal communication):

1. In module I, how to face and accept our personal suffering (the first noble truth) and unwind our stress conditioning in the here and now with the practice of Body Mindfulness;
2. In module II, how to be less reactive to the causes of our suffering (the second noble truth) and tolerate difficulty in the moment without succumbing to misdirected survival reactivity with the practice of Mindful Sensitivity;
3. In module III, how to recognize our ability to expose, divest, and unlearn stress as a way of being (the third noble truth) with the practice of Mindful Awareness;
4. In module IV, how to follow a life-long path of pruning what is harmful from our life and growing what is helpful (fourth noble truth) with the practice of Mindful Insight.

The four mindfulness practices illuminate at mental, emotional, and visceral levels how to witness our stress-infused mind in the present moment, how to calm and balance this dysregulated body/mindset, and how to re-engage with the contents of our mind with equanimity and the insight we need to shift away from a stressed body/mindset to a more healthful perspective. In tandem with the introduction of mindfulness-based contemplative practices, the first four modules refer to discoveries in the fields of stress-research, neuroscience, epigenetics and positive psychology that give scientific backing to what contemplative traditions have known for centuries: that our minds have the boundless potential to unlearn stress reactive habits, and with consistent practice, tap into deep reserves of resilience, compassion, and well-being (Amihai & Koshevnikov, 2014; Kaliman et al., 2014; Loizzo, 2014, 2016).

Social Healing, Shantideva and Lo-Jong—Module V–VIII

The second four modules in CBRT take the basic framework of the first four modules and extend it to our interpersonal relationships. CBRT moves us beyond tending to our own stress in the present moment and supports us to understand how to continue to take care of ourselves in light of the fact that we are all members in social systems where we are exposed to other people's stress and trauma. Without understanding the basic factors of social stress, and tools to face and heal social stress, we will struggle to navigate our relationships and interactions with others.

The social healing modules are structured using compassion practices that reflect Shantideva's "four steps of social self-transformation,"[3] as distilled in the Tibetan compassion-training called *Lo-Jong*.[4] CBRT uses Shantideva's steps for social healing as a method to build upon and amplify the social implications of *Shakyamuni* Buddha's "four noble truths." Extending the logic of the first four modules, the second four modules teach us (Loizzo, 2021):

1. In module V, how to face and bear with social stress/social bias with the practice of Equal Empathy. Here we extend our knowledge from module I in regards to the suffering we experience in our own mind and body, and learn to face the suffering in our relationships. Facing social stress and bias is the social aspect of the first noble truth of suffering;

2. In module VI, how to understand the ways in which our interactions with other people trigger our social survival reflexes and insecurities; and how to reparent our negative sense of self with the practices of Mindful Self-Compassion and RAIN. Our ability to tolerate difficulty in the moment without succumbing to misdirected survival reactivity learned in module II is extended to our social-emotional life by acknowledging there are evolutionary and historical roots to why we become stressed when we encounter difficulty, pain, or discomfort in our social relationships;

3. In module VII, how to tap into our unlimited capacity to develop and cultivate positive social-emotional intelligence with the practice of Wise Give and Take. We learn to bring mature social emotions into our interactions with others. Accessing this ability to tap into prosocial emotions is built upon our ability to unlearn stress as a way of being from module III;

4. In module VIII, how to use our interaction with others to become socially healing change agents who are resilient to emotional stress using the visualization practice of Emulating Mentors. This capacity is built upon learning what to prune from our lives and what to grow from module IV so that we can use wise compassion to help transform our families, communities, and institutions.

Alongside the introduction of compassion-based contemplative practices, the second four modules point to decades of scientific research and evidence from affective neuroscience, positive psychology, and compassion training which demonstrates the critical role of compassion and care for health, happiness, and the ability to thrive socially (Gilbert, 2017; Seppälä et al., 2017). The CBRT student manual (Loizzo, 2021) explains,

> Among the most problematic myths ... is the widespread belief that being caring, emphatic and kind somehow makes us weak and vulnerable. Compassion has been largely conceptualized as a misguided aversive emotion entirely disconnected from human reason and cognition ... These myths persist despite the fact that empathy and compassion are usually the most effective skills for understanding and dealing with human adversity, and also come not just in gentle forms of kindness and tenderness, but also in fierce forms like tough love and fierce compassion ... What is emerging is a broad new consensus that compassion is not a cultural sentiment or luxury, but a basic social capacity and vital necessity if we are to survive ... Cooperative traits based on social emotions are not weaknesses, as science once taught us, but the right evolutionary tool for the job of civilized life ... The capacity for compassion is a mammalian feature built into the human heart and brain; and this capacity is by no means limited to kin, tribe, or mutual benefit. Compassion is a common human instinct and natural potential that can be endlessly cultivated and extended, fostering healthier individuals and groups, with more efficient, integrated and creative brains.
>
> (p. 136–137)

Compassion is like any other muscle, it is use-dependent, and the more we use it, the more we reduce the costs of negative emotions on our brain, mind, and heart. The CBRT manual further explains, "Compassion gives us the power to face distress—our own and others—without getting triggered into unconscious reactivity. It also deepens and expands our emotional resilience, social connectedness, joy and skill" (Loizzo, 2021, p. 86). The last four CBRT modules offer us a compassion-based framework that advances a prosocial way of being at intersubjective and interpersonal levels.

Misperceptions That Trigger Relationship Stress

The CBRT framework maintains that when the part of us that holds our attachment wounding—our negative sense of self— has not had the benefit of learning self-regulating skills (mindfulness-based practices from modules I–IV), and interpersonal resilience (self-compassion practices from modules V–VIII), it is difficult to break the narrative of fear, worry, anger, shame, and blame that our negative sense of self expresses when in relationship distress. Our wounded sense of self gets caught in a state of mind that misperceives any stress in intimate relationships as an overwhelming threat that triggers childhood attachment stress. The present moment attachment stress brings to the fore reactive coping strategies that were developed in childhood, and imposes them on the present moment. We were doing the best that we could when we came up with these protective strategies in childhood, but they rarely are up to the job of addressing adult relationship conflict as they are sourced from a time when we did not have the ability to hold the complexities of relationships or a larger picture beyond self-defense. With our wounded sense of self in the driver seat, we are blind to the fact that we are bringing in a pandora's box of suffering, disappointment, and trauma from childhood into our adult relationships.

Applying CBRT Mindfulness-Based Practices in Clinical Practice

How can the CBRT therapeutic framework be applied to working with clients who suffer from persistent stress in their intimate relationships? How does cultivating a more balanced, open, and discerning state of mind increase the likelihood of a sustained intimate relationship? The first practice, Body Mindfulness, teaches us to bring a non-judgmental unbiased awareness to the present moment experience of our breathing body so we can calm and ground ourself. With a more focused and calm mind/body state we are better able to observe and tend to our present state of mind instead of impulsively acting out from unconscious fears, frustrations, and survival reactivity. The second practice, Mindful Sensitivity, helps us investigate and take responsibility for our unconscious stress reactive habits by bringing attention to how we meet pleasant, unpleasant, and neutral experiences in the here and now. The practice helps us develop a conscious nonreactive presence and an unbiased awareness to our lived moment-to-moment experience which further reduces knee-jerk reactivity. The third self-healing practice, Mindfulness Awareness, tunes us into the natural clarity of mind. Here we have the opportunity to consciously soften our overidentification with a stressed state of mind and begin identifying with immersive and expansive mental and somatic states that help us access our full capacity to heal, learn, and hold complexity. This builds to the fourth practice, Mindful Insight, where we actively use our clarifying awareness to see the links between our conscious reactive habits and the unconscious material that anchors them; along with the ability to discern that which supports a balanced and spacious state of mind, and letting go of whatever thoughts, emotions, and perceptions that might cloud our moment-to-moment experience.

These initial CBRT practices directly address at an experiential level how to become aware of, investigate, and shift into a more conscious, spacious, flexible, and mature state of mind. The practices encourage an internal sense of well-being regardless of what is happening externally, and shift us out of unconscious knee-jerk stress-reactivity and into direct awareness of our mental, emotional, and visceral experiences and needs in the present moment. With a conscious understanding of how to care for ourself and self-regulate, we can chip away at the negative sense of self's propensity to look solely to our partner for comfort and reassurance, and begin to offer ourself these internal conditions. Learning to turn inward to become a good-enough observer and caregiver to ourself cultivates our own capacity for self-awareness, self-understanding, and self-care. We continue to shift away from our wounded sense of self's dependency on others to self-regulate, and the regressive belief that others are better qualified to care for us. Conversely, these practices can help those of us who may need to shift away from reactively shutting down as a way to self-regulate, and let go of reactively projecting onto our partner the early belief that others are unreliable. In both of these scenarios our negative sense of self falls into a habitual reactive pattern of self-regulation depending on the closeness or distance of our partner. The mindfulness-based practices help us stop leaning into unconscious reactive ways of soothing our self, and instead encourage a proactive cultivation of equanimity as a basis from which to engage in our relationships. These practices teach us how to balance our need for connection and belonging with the skill of self-regulation and self-care.

This is not to say that we do not reach out to our partners for support and care, rather we learn to discern what is realistic to ask of others versus what we need to tend to ourselves. Our early attachment wounding cannot be healed by our partner, and neither can our negative sense of self. If over time we continue to ask our partner to be our caregiver/parent/personal regulator, this invariably creates an enormous strain on the relationship; the relationship becomes about *getting* something rather that mutually creating something (personal conversation with J. Loizzo). Our partner is reduced to an object that should gratify us, make us safe, make us happy. If they go outside of the boundaries of how we perceive our needs should be met, they are wronging us, and our negative sense of self reactively retaliates at the injustice of not being cared for (Holmes, 2014; Karen, 1998). This is not to discount the healing impact of attunement offered in adult romantic relationships, but it is important to name the burden of placing too much heightened need for emotional corrective experience on our adult relationships.

The first three scopes of mindfulness are preliminaries that build on each other to afford direct contact with an open, grounded, and flexible state of mind that uses the contemplative therapeutic process of Mindful Insight to prune unrealistic relationship needs; grow taking responsibility for our part in problematic interpersonal dynamics; and recognize that our partner is another sentient being who also has trauma and wounding. The practices can illuminate that when our defenses are engaged, we unconsciously project our need to change onto our partner. They become the one who needs to change. They are the problem, not me! And if *they* could change, then everything would be better.[5] The four scopes of mindfulness can give clients the felt visceral experience of shifting out of this projected child-like/distorted mindset, along with the benefits of being responsible for their state of mind (such as pausing before acting mindlessly or experiencing the agency inherent in mindful skillful action). In this way, the practice of Mindful Insight is the workspace where clients can build a bridge between conscious automatic reactivity and dysregulation, and the unconscious beliefs, fears, projections, and embodied reactions clients need to work through so they are not held back from deeper experiences of connection and intimacy.

Investigating Our Part in Relationship Stress: Mindful Insight in Clinical Practice

If we want intimacy and connection, we need to ask ourselves,

> What is it about my mental state that keeps me from being able to love and connect? What keeps me from being in a more positive and realistic state of mind? What keeps me from being able to bring into my awareness the distress of my partner as well as their ability to love, share, and connect?[6]

Mindful Insight, the culmination of the four scopes of mindfulness practices, is a powerful practice I use with clients in session to answer some of the above questions. Though CBRT is not a cure-all, and clients do not necessarily experience immediate relief, here is one example of a way to bring Mindful Insight into session.

A long-term client of mine, who has experience with mindfulness meditation, had been struggling with why she easily becomes overwhelmed and shuts down when her wife expresses difficult feelings such as frustration, sadness, and fear. Intellectually, my client understood that it was hard to tolerate her wife's emotions; as a child she learned from her family of origin that any edgy emotions such as anger, disappointment, or resentment were not to be expressed. When I invited my client to practice Mindful Insight with me in session, she used the practice to ask herself why she becomes overwhelmed and shuts down in the face of her wife's edgy emotions. My client reported experiencing, at a visceral level, how emotional distancing was a way to maintain safety. She became aware that her reactive impulse to shut down comes from a problematic belief that her wife's emotions make her unsafe. My client was able to see the reactive pattern her negative sense of self employs, and subsequently, was better able to tolerate her wife's feelings and stay engaged during emotionally charged conversations because she could be mindful of what was happening internally for her. She could tend to her internal experience with a grounded, focused, and calm state of mind that maintained her sense of safety while her wife was expressing difficult feelings, such as anguish, unhappiness, and exasperation. By practicing Mindful Insight, she gained perspective on her negative sense of self's habit of turning away from feelings. She could then take responsibility for this reactive state of mind and choose to lean into, value, and be present for emotional moments with her wife. By working in session with the practice, I could help my client process the specifics of her meditative experience in the context of the psychodynamic and somatic work we had been doing together for a number of years.

The CBRT framework is clear that taking responsibility for our part in a relational dynamic does not imply that those who cause harm should not be held accountable. Taking responsibility for how we participate in dysfunctional dynamics is rather a way to own our agency to care for and protect ourselves from suffering instead of being overrun by mental, emotional, and visceral reactivity that deny us our resourcefulness and ability to respond with discernment.

The relative health of any relationship begins with the capacity for the individuals in the relationship to address their own unconscious material. The more we can use the self-healing mindfulness-based practices to make conscious, investigate, bear with, and shift the specifics of our wounded sense of self's unconscious reactive habits; while immersing in our mind's natural clarity, spaciousness, and healing capacities, the better chance we have to connect and experience intimacy in our relationships; or know when to leave a relationship with the confidence that we will be able to find another partner. In this way CBRT nurtures the bridge between conscious and unconscious experience, helping us learn ways to acknowledge, stay with, and feel into subtler psychological realms that are active in how we relate to ourself and others.

Clinical Applications of Compassion-Based Practices to Cultivate Healthy Intimacy

Encouraging clients to work with the compassion-based practices, during and outside of session, can lead to a deeper experience of intimacy with their partner. If we think of intimacy in the moment as the capacity to share emotionally charged experiences (Johnson, 2008, Johnson & Brubacher, 2016) then we need to learn how to share heated emotions without getting overwhelmed and/or going into survival strategies inherent to our specific attachment style. We cannot share affect in a responsible and connective way if we are hyper-vigilant, shut down, or in a heightened state of self-defense. The compassion-based modules offer practices that short circuit our reactive relational reflexes and prime a prosocial state of mind so that we can be vulnerable with our partner and successfully build intimacy (J. Loizzo, personal communication).

Module V digs into the practice of Equal Empathy, the purpose of which is to look at the costs and remedies for biased behavior towards loved ones, strangers, and those who challenge us. When our wounded sense of self is in charge of how we relate in our intimate relationships we might worry, cling to, push away, and overidentify with our partner; we are relating to them from the standpoint of a child. For those of us working through an anxious-ambivalent attachment style, if our wounded sense of self perceives that our partner is moving too far away—either physically or emotionally—it is experienced as a great threat. We may react by holding on tighter, which in turn can feel suffocating to our partner who then takes more distance. This dynamic facilitates the very experience which our wounded sense of self feared. For those with an avoidant attachment style, or a history of early mal-attunement involving over-stimulation (Stern, 1985), they may react to relationship stress by ignoring their partner and actively take more distance. Whether we reactively hold on tighter, or loosen our grip, our fears of rejection restrict our ability to love and trigger relationship stress (J. Loizzo, personal communication). I encourage clients to work with Equal Empathy as a way to unhook from relational biases and postures of exaggerated self-defense, while building compassion. The practice helps clients tolerate relationship stress without getting triggered into their own stress-reactivity.

Mindful Self-Compassion and RAIN, the two practices introduced in module VI, help to address reactive defenses, and correct early childhood distorted perceptions by nourishing an intrapsychic relationship between our negative sense of self with a mature internal caregiver. The CBRT manual (Loizzo, 2021) explains,

> In effect, the practice of Self-Compassion identifies, and connects us to, the traumatized child and cornered animal within us, and equips us with the self-knowledge and inner strength to heal. This inner transformation has two components—emotional nurturance and cognitive-perceptual correction. The care that we need to give to ourselves is both nurturing care that soothes stress emotions and care which helps correct our misunderstandings, or false beliefs, from the trauma of early childhood. Beliefs that we are bad, helpless, powerless, or all alone. So it is not only about softening the inner critic with a

warm inner voice, but also about correcting the false criticisms that we have made of ourselves unconsciously since early childhood.

(p.118–119)

The practices cultivate an internal caregiver who brings compassion, cognitive-perceptual discernment, and a realistic lens to our negative sense of self. They help us to re-parent our wounded sense of self so whatever care or attunement was lacking in our original attachment with primary caregivers can be constituted in the here and now intrapsychically. Over time, as this intrapsychic relationship grows, the most sensitive parts of our psyche have a safe space to go for care, soothing, security, connection, love, empathy, guidance, mentoring, and coaching from the wisest parts of our psyche. With practice we learn to be with, analyze, and amend the hurts and worst-case beliefs that undergird our negative sense of self while in the care of our internal wise counselor.

In this intrapsychic holding environment of deep care and love, we can look at our part in dysfunctional relationship dynamics using wise perception without shaming or being overly critical towards ourself. We learn to disarm our wounded sense of self when we are in the midst of conflict and find more mature ways to engage with our partner. By moderating our edgiest feelings, we can step back from reactively blaming our partner when in a conflict, and increasingly grow more curious about the conflict's complexity. We can recognize our part in the dynamic while acknowledging what our partner brings to the conflict. If we can cultivate compassion towards our most difficult and awkward parts of our psyche, then we can also eventually extend this compassion and care to the parts of our partner that are wounded and reactive.

I encourage clients to work with these practices to develop a more compassionate sense of self and to steer away from focusing (sometimes obsessively) on their partner's struggles/limitations. Self-compassion practices can also guide clients to better understand what they have control over, including changing their attitude, perceptions, and behaviors rather than fixating on the ways their partner needs to change. This is not to say that we do not hold our partners accountable for their actions and state of mind, especially if we find ourselves in an abusive relationship. Rather we are diligently stepping outside of our negative sense of self's point of view and getting our good-enough caregiver in the driving seat (Winnicott, 1958). If we are in an emotionally neglectful or abusive relationship, self-compassion practices can help us move towards a greater understanding of the parts of ourself that may find it difficult to leave an unhealthy relationship, and give us the courage to eventually do so.

Addressing the Shame–Blame Reflex with Compassion Practices

Shame stirs a tremendous amount of stress, chaos, and hurt in relationships. And therefore needs a lot of tending to so as not to persistently disrupt the connection with our partner. Shame, which takes root in our childhood experience of attachment distress, arises when there is an attempt to expose and share a vulnerable state (e.g., love, the desire for affection, the desire for closeness) that is ignored, rejected, or not received in some way by our partner. This can lead to a crippling combination of disappointment, dejection, and despair. The experience of not being met in our excitement and/ or vulnerability can be excruciating due to our deep need to feel seen and connected to. These fraught experiences of not being received by our partner can trigger and confirm our negative sense of self's belief that we are fundamentally unlovable and unsafe in the world. This activation is particularly true for those of us who have a history of shame-inducing relational dynamics. CBRT offers that the cure for shame is the experience of wise self-acceptance/self-love over time. Mindful Self-Compassion and RAIN are critical practices for cultivating a state of mind infused with self-acceptance/ self-love so we can de-fuse/dissipate our reactive shame reflex. Over time, if we can care for our shame in a safe intrapsychic holding environment, we will be less overwhelmed by shame-based reactivity and have a better chance of sharing our hurts and suffering with our partner while feeling connected to them.

On the other side of the shame reflex is blame. Blame is one of the most common default reactive defenses our wounded sense of self employs to manage shame with an intimate partner. Often when loved ones express unhappiness in the relationship, shame gets stirred and defensive efforts to attack the partner with blame ensue. A blaming state of mind can include going into dualistic thinking: "my partner is wrong/bad and I am right/good;" "I need them to see how bad/wrong they are and how right/good I am." In the heated exchange that ensues, we forget that our partner also suffers from a negative sense of self who is feeling vulnerable, small, and powerless. But it is hard to see this when they look like a fire-breathing dragon or a frozen iceberg. Our negative sense of self experiences the overwhelming intensity of our partner's emotional expression, but does not see that their negative sense of self has taken over and is trying to protect itself. We are equally blinded to the fact they see us as scary in our powerful reactive survival responses and we each blame the other for "making me feel X." Whatever "X" is, did not pop out of thin air due to our partner's actions. The difficult emotions that surface for each person have in fact existed since childhood, and the conflict is the medium through which each person is getting back in touch with their respective historical painful attachment stress (J. Loizzo, personal communication). In this way we are choosing to read the situation through the lens of our negative sense of self and not our mature adult self that recognizes the complex emotional history on both sides.

Defusing Shame–Blame Exercise

To help clients out of the shame-blame dynamic: shame leads to blame, which promotes the other's shame—which ultimately keeps both contributors belaboring childhood attachment wounding and validating stress reactive responses—I guide clients through what I call, Defusing Shame–Blame Exercise. The exercise builds on Mindful Insight and RAIN, and can be an additional tool to counter the shame-blame reflex. Here is an example of the exercise you can do with your clients:

> Take a moment to think of an experience where you were blaming someone else for something. Maybe this person made you sad because they forgot your birthday or mad because you felt they were being self-centered.
>
> What feeling(s) arise? What sensations do you notice in your body? Are you trying to push something away? Getting caught up in the story more? Or maybe feeling numb?
>
> Now drop the narrative of blame and investigate how the feeling(s) is operating inside yourself. What is your experience of the emotion? Does your body react in some way? Are there thoughts about yourself that appear? Is there an image related to the feeling that appears? Or maybe some beliefs about yourself come into focus?
>
> What is the quality of your relationship to the emotion? Does the emotion change, become a compound of different emotions? Are you experiencing any shifts in your body or mind?
>
> Whatever you notice, see if you can bring care and compassion to the elements of your experience.

The point of the exercise is to help clients make conscious, witness, and better understand, their wounded sense of self's shame-blame reflex while cultivating the ability to turn towards their woundedness with compassion, and tease out their own part in perpetuating the dysfunctional dynamic.

How Equal Empathy and Self-Compassion Practices Benefit Our Relationships

Over time, as we practice self-compassion and build a strong intrapsychic bond between our sensitive sense of self and our mature caregiver, we are able in heated moments to put our wise self in the driver seat and soothe our wounded sense of self. When our more mature part is in charge during relationship stress we can: recognize that both parties are feeling distress; we see that the shame-blame dynamic keeps us in our wounded self's perspective; we stop blaming our partner and own our feelings; we remember that our ability to love is based on an internal state and not on external circumstances; and we are able to acknowledge the suffering of our partner, along with our own, and make room for all of it.[7] In this way we hold a fuller, more complex, and more realistic understanding of ourself, our partner, and the relationship.

Here is an example dialogue that illustrates a couple using mindfulness and compassion techniques to express relationship frustrations without going into reactivity:

> Partner A: "I noticed my throat got tight and I started to feel some frustration when you interrupted me at the dinner table with our friends last night. I appreciate how enthusiastic you are about sharing your perspective and I also want to be able to share mine. Is there a way we can work on this together so we can both share our ideas with friends?"
>
> Partner B: "Thank you for sharing this. I do not have the same memory of the situation. I may be misremembering and this makes me feel vulnerable. Can what I remember be respected by you? Can you tell me what you recall and give me a moment to remember what I recall? Can we help each other think through this together?"[8]

The practices of Equal Empathy, Mindful Self-Compassion, and RAIN help us take care of, and be responsible for, our triggers in intimate relationships. With practice, they support a wise and compassionate internal caregiver to be in charge of our state of mind when we face relationship stress. I offer these practices to clients who struggle to see their part in dysfunctional relationship dynamics, as well as to those who struggle with a strong inner critic that can be relentless when relationships do not work out or hit a rough patch. These practices help us: regulate our social stress-reactivity; feel safe enough to listen to our partner; and give us a better chance of responding skillfully to relationship stress.

Though our negative sense of self and a stressed state of mind are the prime drivers for relationship stress, it is important to name that negative systemic projections can also get introduced into our relationships and cause distress. There are many ways biases rooted in systems of oppression show up in relationships, so I will share just a couple of examples to illustrate the point. If we are in a mixed-race couple, there can be an unspoken power imbalance which erodes needed safety and trust in the relationship. This creates a need for the couple to talk more openly about racial inequality and how this might present itself in the relationship. In session it can be important to investigate who is closer to the dominant culture due to race or ethnicity, and if that partner is aware of their privilege. It is equally important to explore if the other partner can trust that their experience of being part of an oppressed group is sufficiently understood by their partner. If we are in an LGBTQ+ couple there may be the need to look at gender and power dynamics. How might heteronormative gender roles and patriarchal values be operating in their relationship and creating stress?[9] These questions should also be introduced when working with heterosexual couples.

How Wise Give and Take and Emulating Mentors Reduce Relationship Stress

The final two practices, Wise Give and Take and Emulating Mentors covered in modules VII and VIII respectively, amplify our ability to stay simultaneously connected to ourself and our partner when there is relationship stress. The practice of Wise Give and Take teaches us to give love and care to ourself, and then to extend this ability to those around us. By taking on our own suffering with compassion we establish a refuge of self-care from which we can bring awareness to the suffering of our partner and offer them care. Wise Give and Take marries self-compassion with skillful attention to our partner. It potentially helps us observe if our negative sense of self is triggered, and care for ourself if it is, all while analyzing the state of mind of our partner. Using clear awareness, we look to understand the degree to which our partner's state of mind is triggered, then we can assert ourself skillfully. The CBRT manual (Loizzo, 2021) explains,

> We must bear in mind that this shift in mindset is ... not about being "nice" to everyone or exposing ourselves to harm or abuse from others driven by destructive emotions like cruelty and hate. It simply means taking responsibility for bringing awareness and care to our interactions with others, including those driven by destructive forces, so that we are fully prepared to deal as wisely as possible with the challenges they pose with full self-efficacy and social power ... By practicing taking on as much responsibility as we can for our own wounded sense of self and giving as much help and care as possible to our loved

one, then rather than having unrealistic expectations of others generated from the perspective of our inner child, we learn to gradually grow into a position of being able to care for ourselves and turn to our own capacities to improve our social lives. This way, we focus on what we actually have control over and therefore feel more empowered.

(p. 146)

Broadly speaking, this practice can be an antidote for those of us who suffer from ambivalent/preoccupied attachment patterns; it teaches us to consider our hurts, needs, and care alongside our partner's without fearing the loss of connection. This practice also helps those of us who may be more dismissive/avoidant in our relationships to stay in connection with our partner and not fall into the belief that our loved one's needs are too burdensome, overwhelming, and intrusive.

The final practice, taught in module VIII, is Emulating Mentors. During this practice we visualize a mentor who has the qualities of emotional well-being that we wish to grow for ourself. The powerful process of visualizing a healing mentor awakens and connects us back into the experience of emotional development within a relational field. This time, instead of our social-emotional learning being deeply impacted by the emotional limitations of our primary caregivers, we can experience mental, emotional, and visceral social-emotional learning with an altruistic mentor who ignites a profoundly positive intrapersonal attachment experience.

Emulating Mentors involves us in developing a sense of self, and a sense of intimate connection, by way of a dynamic exchange with a mature and loving guide. Our mentor fully accepts us, is delighted to care for us, and shares their confidence that we have the ability to embody the altruistic qualities we admire in our mentor. There is no rupture in attunement in this relationship. Rather we learn to identify with the experience of an unconditional loving bond that invites us to nourish intimacy and be a resource for others.

Over time, our overidentification with our negative sense of self decreases in acuity, and we see ourself as a loving being who has the resilience and skills to care for ourself and others in the face of stress. This practice is particularly helpful for those of us who suffer from low self-esteem and chronic self-doubt especially as these relate to relationship and intimacy issues. The CBRT manual (Loizzo, 2021) explains,

> The practice of emulating mentors of unwavering kindness, compassion and altruism empowers us to re-envision ourselves and the world in a more optimistic way that supports our developing a more resilient and compassionate way of living. Like a flight simulator, this practice primes our minds and nervous

system to rehearse and master more proactive and compassionate ways of seeing ourselves and others, supporting our ability to embody greater resilience and care. Through this practice we can speed the natural process of positive human development, allowing us to flourish together in mutual happiness and well-being.

(p. 165)

This practice helps us to improve our self-confidence and self-image by correcting limiting self-perceptions, and allows us to see ourself through an empowered, loving, and optimistic lens.

Evolution of Consciousness in Intimate Relationships

As we work with individuals and couples to develop more intimacy using the practices offered in CBRT, there can be an evolution of consciousness along these lines:

1) The problem isn't me, it's my partner;
2) The problem isn't me or my partner but our relationship;
3) The problem isn't the relationship but the traumas we get stuck in;
4) The problem is my partner's childhood trauma;
5) The problem is my childhood trauma and my partner's;
6) The problem is how we learned to survive our childhood trauma;
7) The problem is we can't access compassion in trauma mode;
8) The problem is we need our partner's cues of safe connection;
9) The problem is we need to give ourselves and our partners those cues.[10]

This evolution in perspective can manifest with the support of CBRT as a therapeutic intervention. The framework and practices offered in CBRT are highly effective in accelerating the shift from a stress-based state of mind to a balanced, prosocial state of mind (Bankard, 2015; Gilbert, 2017; Klimecki et al., 2013; Lee, 2005; Loizzo et al., 2010; Weng et al., 2013). Clients learn to take responsibility for self-regulation at mental, emotional, and visceral levels; their part in dysfunctional relationship dynamics; cultivating a compassionate sense of self; and attuning to their partner with the wisdom of mindfulness and the loving care of discerning compassion. By offering clients the contemplative practices showcased in CBRT, in tandem with a trusting therapeutic relationship, clients can move beyond an intellectual understanding of self-healing and intimacy to an embodied experience of love and belonging.

Notes

1 Paul Rozin and Edward Royzman coined the term negativity bias and defined it as "The principle, which we call negativity bias, is that in most situations, negative events are more salient, potent, dominant in combinations, and generally efficacious than positive events."

2 The Buddha's four noble truths are the essence of Buddhist psychology and explain the human condition: 1) the truth of suffering; 2) the origin of the truth of suffering; 3) the truth of cessation; 4) the truth of the path.

3 Shantideva was an eighth-century CE Buddhist monk and philosopher who expanded on the four noble truths to address social healing through the practice of exchanging self for others. His book, *A Guide to the Bodhisattva's Way of Life* offers a roadmap to the Bodhisattva's altruistic way of living.

4 *Lo-Jong* is a Tibetan Buddhist mind training practice derived from the teachings of Atisha, Shantideva, and Nargarjuna. The pithy teachings, in the form of slogans, can be memorized and easily incorporated into one's daily life.

5 For more sources to explore the complexity of projection in couples check out Young-Eisendrath, P. (2019). *Love between Equals: Relationship as a Spiritual Path,* and Spillius, E. B. (Ed.). (1988). *Melanie Klein Today: Developments in Theory and Practice (Volume 1: Mainly Theory).*

6 These questions come from a discussion with Dr Joseph Loizzo.

7 This list of benefits comes out of discussions with Dr Joseph Loizzo. It is important to note that these capacities may require the slow and patient therapeutic processes reinforced by the working alliance of the clinical dyad, particularly for patients addressing complex trauma or developmental thwarting.

8 Partner B's response was crafted in conversation with Dr Pilar Jennings.

9 These examples were discussed in conversation with Dr Pilar Jennings.

10 This evolution in relationship consciousness was shared in a lecture given by Dr Joseph Loizzo.

PART THREE
Embodiment and Natural Healing

The Healing Mother, Noble *Tara* (Robert Beer, Used with Permission)

16
Tantra, Imagery, and Integral Dynamic Therapy

Emily J. Wolf

The Indo-Tibetan Tantras offer a comprehensive set of power tools for optimal well-being, oriented toward realizing one's highest prosocial potential. Tantric practices utilize our innate capacity for imagination, work with the subtle energetic networks in the body, and draw on fundamental relational processes to realize our full capacity for conscious transformation of our selves and lives. In this chapter, I contextualize these traditions historically, describe their philosophy and psychology, and illustrate their profound healing methods by presenting the role-modeling imagery of the seven-limbed mentor-bonding practice through the lens of self-psychology and psychotherapy.

Tantra comes from the Sanskrit word for "loom," and refers to the warp threads that fabrics are woven onto. It is best understood as a metaphor for the process of enlightened cultural transmission (Loizzo, 2018). In this, Tantra refers to the cultural art of consciously shifting the course of human development by means of a mentoring bond (loom), which allows us to culturally replicate (weave) an enlightened way of integrating the information-matter (pattern-fabric) of a human mind and nervous system (tapestry). The Tibetan Tantras emerged in India as the third wave of Buddhist contemplative science, stemming from teachings attributed to the historical Buddha. According to tradition, Shakyamuni gave over 84,000 teachings, providing a variety of methods to accommodate individuals' divergent needs, motivations, and capacities (Yeshe, 2014). Since its formative years, this tradition has been integrated in a number of cultures across Asia and is currently being assimilated in Western cultures.

Historically, Buddhist contemplative science took shape in three major vehicles connected with various teachings and cultural influences: the Individual Vehicle (*Theravada/Hinayana*), the Universal Vehicle (*Mahayana*), and the Process or Diamond Vehicle (*Mantrayana, Vajrayana*; Loizzo 2000; Wallace

DOI: 10.4324/9781003243588-19

& Shapiro, 2006). Tibetan scholars assert that both the exoteric Mahayana and the esoteric Vajrayana were secretly taught by Shakyamuni to some of his disciples, and that seeds of those teachings took root and blossomed when Indian civilization was ripe for them (Thurman, 1996; Dalai Lama, 2009; Loizzo, 2018). The central aspects of Tantric practice were clearly taught in Shakyamuni's day, as we can see from the literature of the Upanishads. Yet they were passed down from teacher to student in secrecy and were not published until much later, based on cultural and historical trends in India and Asia (Thurman, 1996; Loizzo, 2018).

While the core principles of Buddhist psychology are similar across all its forms, each vehicle of practice developed distinct approaches to implementing that basic science (Thurman, 1996). The first wave of the Buddha's teachings, the Way of the Elders or Individual Vehicle, represents the classical monastic approach to personal self-healing and self-liberation. The second wave known as the Universal or Great Vehicle emerged during the first centuries of the common era, and represents a lay-oriented approach emphasizing love, compassion, and altruism, and a prosocial ethos geared toward social transformation. The third wave of teachings emerging from about 500 CE is referred to as the Diamond or Process Vehicle, and also falls under the larger umbrella of the Universal Vehicle. This last wave represents the esoteric tradition of Buddhism preserved in Central Asian cultures, which remained largely unknown to the West until the Tibetan Diaspora of 1959. Tibetan Buddhism integrates all three vehicles into one, since it is maintained by monks who live according to Theravada tradition, who teach the exoteric Universal Vehicle, and who practice the esoteric Diamond Vehicle. As part of that three-in-one approach, Tibetan monks and lay teachers emphasize the complementarity of the exoteric teachings of Transcendent Virtue (the *Paramitas* of generosity, justice, tolerance, creativity, meditation, and wisdom) with the esoteric arts of embodying blissful openness as an expedient way of cultivating those virtues (Cozort, 2005; Thurman, 1996; Loizzo, 2012).

The Process Vehicle: Tantric Buddhism

The Vajrayana is characterized by an insistence on realizing and enjoying the ultimately blissful nature of reality, here and now. The ideal of the *Mahasiddha*, the Great Adept or Master conceived as a living Buddha in human form, also emerges in this tradition (Thurman, 1996), as well as the social inclusion of marginalized groups, women, and people of lower socioeconomic class. Vitally important to this tradition is the idea that Tantric practice rests on the foundation of Theravada and Mahayana wisdom and ethics, specifically the prerequisites of true renunciation, universal compassion, and non-dualistic wisdom.

Renunciation can take many forms, but in essence it involves realistic assessment and subsequent abandonment of the causes of suffering. Often misunderstood as extreme asceticism or austerity, renunciation more accurately involves a moderating practice based on the determination to be free of unconscious cycles of stress and trauma that perpetuate suffering. The Buddha's initial teaching of the Four Noble Truths provides a medical framework from which to diagnose our suffering and discover its origins in the unhealthy workings of our own minds. Vital here is the active letting go of the core causes of suffering: misapprehension, attachment, and aversion. In renouncing these sources, we can taste the natural liberation or freedom from the poison we feel enslaved by. For some, behavioral restraint is key, for others more important is deep analysis, and for still others, strengthening self-love and compassion—all of which depend on help from others. These helping reliances are referred to as the three refuges: the Buddha, the Awakened Mentor that has overcome suffering and can show us the way; the Dharma, or Teaching of principles and practices we can draw on and experiment with in our own lives; and the Sangha, the Community of enlightened friends providing support.

Compassion practices involve a reorientation away from self-involvement and toward care for others. The Buddhist tradition refers to great compassion as *bodhicitta*, the altruistic resolve to reach awakening to benefit others. Compassion practices are geared toward cultivating this aspiration, rooted in the self-healing renunciation and self-compassion of Theravada practice. While others are still suffering in the world, one cannot truly be free and happy, as we are infinitely intertwined. From this perspective, the Theravada awakening of the individual Ascetic (*Arhat*) is incomplete and misses the truth of our deep interconnectivity. While we cannot be fully free and happy when those around us are suffering, we can taste the freedom and joy that naturally arises when we help others. Of course, compassion has to be skillful, rooted in our own self-awareness so as to avoid co-dependency, and based on a clear analysis of what is truly helpful. This concept of empathic art (*upaya*) involves drawing on the most skillful means to help each individual, whether that takes the form of mirroring and listening or of analyzing and challenging, of being permissive or being fierce.

The teachings on selflessness and emptiness are unique to Buddhist philosophy and psychology. In the Buddhist perspective, insight into selflessness facilitates the path to health, lasting happiness, and liberation (Wallace, 2005). Teachings on emptiness extend beyond the individual self and describe how all phenomena lack inherent existence. Emptiness can be defined as "the absence of an inherent identity or self; the lack of an intrinsic nature that exists in and of itself. Physical phenomena, the mind, and the self all are empty, all are dependently related events" (Wallace & Wilhelm, 1993, p. 182). This insight points to the absence of any fixed, permanent, unchanging, or non-relational aspect of self or things that exists independent of everything else. Key to understanding emptiness and selflessness is the insight that the self *does* exist as a vital social construction, referring to a relative, insubstantial confluence of aggregates (*skandhas*) and elements (*dharma*) in constant flux and change (Thurman, 1996). These insights reveal the sheer relativity, interdependence, and interconnectivity of what we experience as our self and world. Of course, misconceptions of emptiness abound, the most insidious being that it entails a negation of real persons and things, i.e., nihilism. The key point here is that emptiness does not negate existence, it negates the reified view of existence as an inherent or intrinsic reality. Upon analysis, one cannot find an essence or self that exists in a singular, permanent, and independent way. Emptiness therefore reveals how all subjective selves and objective phenomena are in fact only possible based on this pervasive reality of relativity.

Transformational Practice Based on These Preliminaries

In Tantric practice, the practitioner renounces his or her ordinary perception and experience of self through imaginatively dissolving them in the wisdom of emptiness. Then moved by the spirit of compassion, she re-envisions herself in the form of a heroic archetype or deity (*devata*), revises her inner and outer dialogue in the form of enlightened speech (*mantra*), and engages in enlightening activities or embodied gestures (*mudra*). These aspects of Tantric meditation are symbolic manifestations of the blissful wisdom of emptiness, expressing ecstatic compassion and altruism (Dalai Lama et al., 1987). These practices create an enlightened frame of reference from which the practitioner can deconstruct his or her compulsive misapprehensions of self and world and reconstruct them in the mirror of enlightened realization (Loizzo, 2012, 2018).

Tantric practice harnesses the insight of emptiness, in that seeing the emptiness of all things opens the space for visualization practice. The visualization process trains the ability to see one's ordinary perception of self and world as a projection of mind, helping one become experientially familiar with emptiness by dissolving that unconscious projection into the "womb" of emptiness, and rebirthing a new, transparent self and world. This process facilitates a softening of the mind's habitual processes of reification, undermining the habit pattern of inherent existence that makes self and world seem solid and fixed (Dalai Lama et al., 1987). Furthermore, that greater mental flexibility not only frees one *from* reifying habitual perception but also frees one *to* identify with and internalize a new sense of self and life, envisioned in the image of an idealized mentor-archetype. This combined practice of perceptual deconstruction and reconstruction further facilitates the realization of one's capacity to gradually reshape oneself in the image of the ideal mentor-archetype.

Visualization: The Art of Self-Transformation

The psychological understanding of emptiness and the power of visualization practices are supported by current neuropsychological theory and research. The quantum theory of consciousness developed by Llinás (2001) describes how the brain works as a dynamic system similar to a virtual reality simulator, rather than as a static mirror of reality. Llinás's research in brain wave patterns during dreaming and waking states reveals how a forty-cycle-per-second bioelectrical rhythm generated by the thalamus and basal ganglia creates coherence and connection between various functional brain processes. This wave involves an interaction of internally generated images and mental events evoked from the previous wave of perception along with novel external input in order to create a coherent simulation of reality. This model of perception as a synthesis of sense-input with memory, fantasy, and association suggests that the world we experience is not as objective as it seems but is in large part a virtual reality projected by the mind and brain, as predicted by the Buddhist understanding of emptiness. This mentally generated inner world would seem to be what psychoanalysts and shamans have recognized as the subconscious dream-world of unresolved past fears, wishes, needs, hopes, and traumas. The only difference between this waking simulation and the dream state is the incorporation of a few bits of corrective external data to update the waking simulation. So, whether we are waking or dreaming, the basic process of perception is one of an active imaginative construction of reality. This constructivist psychology provides the basis for self-conscious visualization practice, designed to serve as a natural method for enhancing healing and internal development by activating the best associations and qualities within us, rather than what we habitually project through self-protective worst-case scenarios (Loizzo, 2012).

Recent research further demonstrates the power of internally generated imagery, suggesting that the brain registers internal imagery and external stimuli with the same neural activity. Studies of mental imagery and brain activation have shown the overlap in brain activation during visual imagery and direct perception (Kosslyn et al., 1998; Mellet et al., 1998). Kosslyn et al. (2000) demonstrated through brain imaging that a vivid mental visualization of a color (i.e., purple), can override the sense data and perception of color in the actual visual field (i.e., gray). These studies reveal that from the brain's perspective there is little difference when the object is internally generated or externally located, supporting the power of visualization practices. The science of vivid imagery helps us understand how to create a positive vision of life that prepares us to act in ways that match our true values and helps us realize our highest aims for ourselves and our world. Such a method of reliably changing our perceptual software and responsive engagement could dramatically expand our horizons of healthy change.

Four Levels of Tantra

There are four classes of Buddhist Tantra that involve practitioners' increasing intimacy and identification with divine archetypes. These are Action (Kriya), Performance (Carya), Integral (Yoga), and Unexcelled or Optimal Integral (Anuttarayoga) Tantra. The four levels are designed to meet the particular needs, capacities, and skills of diverse practitioners and are characterized by increasing intensity of blissful energy and increasing intimacy (Cozort, 2005). In Action Tantra, the mentor-archetype is encountered with a sense of awe and refuge, and the practitioner engages in ritual actions of cleansing, fasting, and sustained concentration on the mentor-deity and mantra. Performance Tantra involves admiring the mentor-deity and receiving guidance; it is marked by greater proximity and engagement with one's ideal. Integral Tantra emphasizes the internal practices of mind, envisioning communion with the mentor-deity as a catalyst for transformation, and envisioning arising as the mentor-deity oneself. Finally, Optimal Integral Tantra involves advanced methods of simultaneous internal and external transformation, based on meditating on the nature of mind (clear light), and the subtle body (virtual body) of energies (prana), drops (bindu), channels (nadi), and hubs (chakra). This fourth level emphasizes male–female archetypes in intimate union, inner and outer offerings, transformative worlds (mandala), affirmative statements (mantras), and expressive gestures (mudras) (Loizzo, 2018).

Each of these levels of Tantra meets the needs of diverse practitioners to help them sublimate their passions to develop greater emotional maturity and psychosexual intimacy. The Optimal Integral Tantras are further classified as Father and Mother, based on the particular approach they take to sublimation. Mother Tantras such as *Chakrasamvara* "specialize in sublimating instinctive delusion into the objective intuition of emptiness," while Father Tantras such as *Guhyasamaja* "specialize in sublimating addictive desire or compulsive anger in to pure bliss-void intuition" (Loizzo, 2018, p. 362). Each type of Unexcelled Tantra provides a path to work with a unique personality type or disposition, in order to reach spiritual awakening.

Creation and Perfection Stages

Optimal Integral Tantra distinguishes two stages of practice: creation and perfection. These two stages can be practiced sequentially or simultaneously depending on the particular Tantra's scripted practice (*sadhana*). Visualization during the creation stage focuses on developing single-pointed vision of and identification with the mentor-archetype, as well as internalizing a heroic life narrative. In the perfection stage, the practitioner works with the subtle energies in the body to actualize the gradual transformation of the mind and nervous system into the enlightened mind and body of a Buddha. These stages transform perception, instincts, energies, and capacities into optimal psychosocial and psychospiritual functioning. Teachings on the two stages take place within a confidential collaboration between a spiritual mentor and practitioner, guided by specific guidelines to ensure effective transmission of practice, based on the specific developmental level and capacity of the practitioner. For example, private instruction on perfection stage practices will be given to the most adept students, while creation stage practices are appropriate for group instruction (Loizzo, 2012, 2018).

The Optimal Integral Creation Stage

Similar to a flight simulator, the creation stage of Optimal Integral Tantra empowers the practitioner to re-envision his/her self and world in light of a heroic ideal vision of life. This occurs through an imaginative conversion, transforming the human body–mind from its natural, compulsive state into a triumphant, cultivated form fully adapted to a life of spiritual self-mastery and cultural creativity (Loizzo, 2018). Visualization in the creation stage is a powerful means of regulating affect through the symbolically charged content of its imagery. Similar to a schema in cognitive science (Corsini & Wedding, 2000), the transformative impact of Tantric visualization is based on its implicit, depth-psychological meaning, which encodes healing insight and emotion within the imagery. Furthermore, each image is a symbolic representation of a philosophical insight, which the practitioner actively recognizes and reflects on. There is an interpretative quality as one moves through the symbolically potent visualization, along with a narrative storyline enacting a heroic life plan of creativity and prosocial action.

Overlap of Creation Stage with Western Psychotherapies

Athletes and coaches, as well as integrative medical therapists, have increasingly turned to visualization and imagery (Rossman, 2000; Banyan & Klein, 2001). Use of imagery cognitively encodes new information, but more importantly accesses emotional responses and rehearses new action-patterns. Narrative Therapy (White & Epston, 1990) works along similar lines, recreating and reconstructing optimal stories about oneself that serve to support living more value-based lives. Similar to the relationship between the spiritual mentor and practitioner, the role of the therapist in Narrative Therapy involves co-creating the narrative and emphasizing the implicit message that the client already has the capacity to reach their aims.

Jung (1934/1981) pioneered the concept of archetypes in his psychoanalytic theory and practice, based on his observation of the power of universal symbols in the human psyche. For Jung, universal archetypes are narrative patterns from which individuals can organize personal experience, as natural manifestations of the collective unconscious, accessed in order to resolve developmental complexes. They also personify ideals that the individual can access to realize her deepest potential through active imagination.

Affirmations are used in a number of behavioral therapies including Beck's cognitive behavior therapy (CBT), rational emotive behavior therapy, reality therapy, and self-instructional training (Ellis, 1962; Glasser, 1965; Beck, 1976; Meichenbaum, 1977). Affirmations in CBT replace habitual negative thought patterns that have developed and been reinforced over time with repetitive positive statements that become ingrained in one's inner narrative and speech. In creation stage Tantric practice, the power of affirmation is strengthened by the relationship between practitioner and mentor. Rather than convincing oneself that the affirmation is completely self-generated, one imagines communication coming from an external idealized person and eventually becoming an internalized resonance.

The Optimal Integral Perfection Stage

In the perfection stage, the practitioner accesses and manipulates the most primal layers of the mind and nervous system. Perfection stage practices are based on an extensive map of the subtle body that represents a qualitative, interoceptive analogue to modern maps of the central nervous system. This map explains the flow of energy and drops through channels and hubs in ways that bear some resemblance to our model of neural impulse and synaptic transmission (Lutz et al., 2007). According to this system, embedded in the subtle nervous system are core instinctive patterns of life, including attachment, aversion, and delusion, as well as love, acceptance, and wisdom. The practitioner's capacity to influence and control the subtle energies and drops in this stage consciously regulates instinctual drives and transforms the nervous system on the most basic structural and functional levels. By mastering the male and female energies of the polar side channels of the subtle nervous system and infusing them into the central channel, "the practitioner gains full access to the deepest sources of blissful energy and chemistry" (Loizzo, 2018, p. 366). Levels of sexual arousal may also be utilized in perfection stage to enhance access to euphoric states, which reinforce learning and empower the practitioner to shape the direction and culmination of his or her transformation and development. The perfection stage involves a mind/body science and art of harnessing the sexual response to seed psychospiritual healing, maturation, and communion with the world at large. In this, it represents a rare cultural system of know-how to facilitate the cultivation of Eros in the service of helping humanity adapt more quickly and fully to the unnatural condition of civilization (Loizzo, 2018).

Overlap of Perfection Stage with Western Psychotherapies

Somatic therapies have their roots in early psychoanalytic thinking and the search of analysts like Reich to glean important information about the unconscious from the body. More recently, therapists have developed somatic approaches that explicitly attend to internal physical experience as a means to heal psychological trauma and emotional disorders (Caplan et al., 2013). These approaches emphasize the importance of working with the body and identifying ways in which repressed traumatic affect coalesces in the physical body and our embodied nervous system. By working from the bottom up, somatic practitioners use visceral experience to enact somatic experiments meant to engender emotional discovery, tolerance for deep affect, embodied insight, and awareness (Baum et al., 2011).

Recent research on the vagal nerve such as Porges's (2011) Polyvagal Theory align with somatic therapies and help us understand the psychosomatic impact of Tantric practices. This model proposes that the autonomic nervous system underwent a sea change from reptiles to mammals in order to support increasing demands for maintaining social safety, regulating social emotions, and mobilizing behavioral responses for social engagement. Key here is the new, myelinated vagal nerve or "smart vagus" designed for rapid mobilization and bonding. The smart vagus travels from the brainstem to face, throat, heart, and lungs, inhibits fight–flight (sympathetic) reactivity, stimulates safe arousal, social emotions like compassion, social mobilization in the face of danger, as well as communication and creative collaboration when safe. There is also a complex interaction between the smart vagus, the heart–face connection, and middle-ear muscles, which uses social cues of facial expression and vocal tone to assess the safety of the social environment. Central to this system is the way vagal tone inhibits sympathetic reactivity and supports social emotions and social engagement. Porges links poor vagal tone to clinical syndromes such as autism, borderline personality, social phobia, and posttraumatic stress disorder (Porges).

Embodied practices like those of the Tantras are key to developing vagal tone. Practices like chanting and mantra recitation simulate human vocal tones and prosody, indirectly stimulating vagal tone. Deep breath work such as abdominal breathing, alternate nostril breathing, extended exhalation, and breath retentions, as well as visualization of mentors with calm, warm facial expressions and embracing postures, stimulate vagal tone. A recent study measuring neurohemodynamic correlates and visceral resonance of chanting demonstrated significant deactivation in limbic brain regions (Kalyani et al., 2011). These findings are consistent with the findings of vagal nerve stimulation in epilepsy and depression, lending empirical evidence to the theory that mantra recitation can increase vagal tone.

Positive psychology and positive affective therapies (Peterson, 2006) further align with the perfection stage model and vagal theory in terms of harnessing the healing power of prosocial emotional states. These modalities do not deny suffering, but rather embrace and cultivate the positive that is already present but under-utilized. One study examining the relationship between deep positive affect and cardiac vagal tone showed a significant increase in vagal tone after a sixteen-week positive psychology group intervention (Lü et al., 2013). The new mammalian circuitry elicited by perfection stage practice allows us to stay calm and socially engaged while accessing core transformative affect states that facilitate learning, healing, and transformation. The effectiveness of somatically oriented practice such as embodied imagery, recitation, posture, and breath-work, as well as mental states of health and connection, appears to be due to higher neural integration of the autonomic nervous system.

Defining the Uniqueness of Buddhist Tantra

According to Tsongkapa, founder of the Gelug lineage of Tibetan Buddhism, the power and efficacy of tantric practices does not lie in the harnessing of subtle body energy or ritual objects/experience, but rather in three core processes (Dalai Lama et al., 1987). These unique characteristics include (a) simultaneous training in non-dual wisdom and compassion, (b) use of mentor devotion and role models, and (c) working with a fruitional (or resultant) approach.

In the exoteric Universal Vehicle, training in wisdom and compassion are developed individually, which facilitates a slow maturation. In contrast, the Vajrayana involves simultaneous training by conjoining symbolic images of altruism with consistent insight into the emptiness of that imagery (Thurman, 1996). This entails first envisioning a new self and world as altruistic archetypes on the basis of emptiness, then giving the mind/body system a coherent neuropsychological pathway from the old reactive self to a new one of proactive engagement. The symbolic imagery of the mandala allows one to let go of the familiar self and reconstruct a new self within an optimal learning environment. The touchstone of the visualization practice is the constant insight that it is inseparable from emptiness, as well as an art of routinely dissolving and recreating the self and the world within each practice. This facilitates a profound experiential insight and creates checks and balances that protect the practitioner from grandiose or depressive extremes.

Furthermore, Vajrayana practice cultivates multiple levels of internal capacity simultaneously that speed transformation relative to the sequential structure of exoteric practice. When the symbolic tools of visualization and affirmation are applied to the nervous system and conjoined with advanced breath control, they can induce profound altered states by accessing deeper levels of consciousness and neural function (Loizzo, 2012). Mastering these states gives the practitioner access to normally unconscious processes as well as state-specific faculties for influencing them, allowing the practitioner to expose and reform learned and instinctive habits of mind on their own level and providing the experiential basis for rapid maturation. These levels include: the (a) cognitive/perceptual layer accessed through the de-reifying insight of emptiness, converting conditioned traumatic perceptions into direct healing intuitions; (b) the positive affective level of universal compassion, converting reactive habits of clinging and aversion into deeper positive emotions; (c) the ethical behavioral level converts reactive action patterns into a more mature lifestyle and aspirations; (d) the creation stage level transforms ingrained reified self-images and the pride of ordinariness into an ideal self-image with awakened dignity, accompanied by affirming inner dialogue, and prosocial gestures; (e) the perfection stage level involves an alchemical conversion of reactive neural energy and chemistry into the positive neural energy and chemistry of blissful openness.

Social learning from role models is core to our evolution and development as mammals. The bonds of kin provide current cultural know-how to navigate an ever-changing environment. While parent and child remain in a long pattern of dependency, the mammalian advantage over reptiles is that current learning can be imparted to enhance adaptation quickly. The narratives that have been internalized through primary relationships with parents set the stage for one's current worldview and relationships, some healthy, others maladaptive. Understanding that this internal landscape is co-created in the child–parent relationship serves as the basis of seeking a "better" role model when one commits to consciously growing oneself.

The tradition of mentor bonding involves developing a profoundly intimate relationship with a new parental figure, someone with the qualities to help one complete the process of healthy development. From the Tibetan standpoint, this could occur through proximity with a mentor or more at a distance, where the intimacy takes place virtually within the visualization practice augmented by support from a like-minded community. Key to the relationship is the interpersonal contract to embark on the path together, in which the practitioner commits to maintaining the practice, and the mentor to skillfully guiding the practitioner along the path.

The Process Vehicle of the Tantras takes a resultant path, bringing the future result of full awakening into present practice, rather than the gradual approach of the Universal Vehicle that focuses on creating the causes of future maturity, concentration, and wisdom. In essence, the Tantric practitioner starts at the goal, acts-as-if, and "learns to think, speak, and act now as if he or she were already a fully enlightened Buddha" (Yeshe, 2014, p. 3), thereby simulating and habituating to the final attainment of full awakening. This fruitional approach involves "trying on" the mentor's enlightened experience, speech, altruistic actions, and view of herself as a living Buddha within a Buddha's perfected natural, social, and cultural sphere of action. Creative imagery, poetic formulas, and performative gestures provide a working linguistic construction and imaginative simulation of enlightened perception that serves as an alternate system of reference by which the individual can critique his or her compulsive misperception of self and world. By choosing to enhance a positive view of self and other, one essentially begins to build and connect the neural structures that support the optimal experience, thereby making it more viable to elicit that positive experience again. This creates a mind–brain–body feedback loop, simulating and reinforcing new integration.

This fruitional path further involves a profound worldview that informs working with others, in line with some forms of psychodynamic thought and practice (i.e., Orange et al., 1997; McWilliams, 2004). The basic assumption is one of openness and plasticity. In working with others therapeutically, it is essential to address the relative suffering presented by the client, but equally important to maintain the fruitional view; that the client has an enlightened nature, and that his/her challenges are temporary obstacles that can be overcome. By relating to this underlying truth, the therapist maintains hope and flexibility, and overtly and covertly evokes the openness for the client to manifest rapid transformation.

Therapeutic Integration of Mentor Bonding: The Essence of Tantra

All preliminary practice of Tantra involves what is called the seven-limbed practice of mentor bonding. This is core to the Tantras, whether the lower-level practices or more intricate integral and optimal integral performance scripts (sadhanas). In fact, this fundamental art structures the more elaborate practice of all sadhanas, and in many ways is the quintessence of the Tantras. As a preliminary practice, it is accessible to everyone, and does not require traditional initiation. As such, Loizzo has integrated and implemented the mentor bonding in clinical settings and populations with significant positive outcomes (Loizzo et al., 2009, 2010). He has also developed an in-depth explanation of the psychological mechanisms by which it effects change, connecting it to the work of Heinz Kohut. I first briefly highlight some of Kohut's key theories and concepts underlying self-psychology and the relational approach to therapy. The developmental needs and therapeutic goal of Kohut's transmuting internalization serves as the base from which to understand the depth of the mentor bonding practice.

Kohut (1971) described three core needs for healthy development: mirroring, idealization, and twinship. Mirroring involves being acknowledged for one's qualities and accomplishments, often subtle non-verbal approval and validation of emotions and experience, leading to the development of one's self-concept and self-awareness. Idealization involves a need to admire and identify with parentified figures with whom children are associated. This provides a sense of inclusion in the caregiver's positive qualities and allows children to internalize the capacity to develop ideals, set realistic aspirations, and move through development with a secure sense of self and attachment. The third relevant process is twinship, a fundamental need to feel included and part of a community (Kohut, 1984).

Kohut called the internalization of these self-regulatory factors "transmuting internalization," and applied this same concept to the process whereby patients internalize a healthy sense of grandiosity, idealization, and connectedness through the therapeutic relationship. The seven-limbed mentor practice entails a reparative interpersonal process in which these core elements take place in a contemplative bond, guided by visualization. Loizzo (2012) builds on Kohut's theory to explain how mentor bonding can facilitate psychosexual healing and integration, delineating four phases of the internalizing process: idealization, identification, internalization, and integration.

The Tantric Art of Mentor Bonding

The seven-limbed art of mentor bonding is based on a real relationship with an admired person, one's teacher, mentor, or any role model one considers further along the path of development. For some, identifying a mentor is a simple proposition, for others it can be more challenging. When proposing identifying a mentor, we suggest considering a range of options. Traditionally, the mentor is a spiritual guide and friend that one has forged a connection with, either through direct experiences or indirect connection, including past and present historical figures that one feels an affinity with, e.g., Mohammed, the Virgin Mary, Gandhi, Mother Theresa, Moses, Jesus, Socrates, Shakyamuni. Most important is a genuine sense of safety, admiration, hope, inspiration, even affection for a person who embodies qualities one wishes to develop. Of course, mentors we have direct experience of often elicit complex emotions. The intention here is to connect with the mentor's primary positive regard, so that one can work through complex emotions, and eventually accept the common humanity of oneself and the mentor. As in idealizing transference, the aim here is not to deny one's experience, but to intentionally harness the intersubjective power of the positive mentor bond as a crucible for insight, healing, and transformation (McWilliams, 2004). This opportunity rests on a foundation of mutual trust, safety and understanding, based on a reciprocal agreement to work through challenges as they arise.

I The Idealization Phase: Action Tantra

First Limb: Admiration

The first phase of the mentor-bonding practice begins with three elements of idealization: admiring, offering, and disclosing. In admiring the mentor as an ideal model, we consciously identify qualities we admire by seeing them in another person. Developmentally we need to idealize, admire, be in awe, feel safe and worthy of love by someone more capable than we feel. The ideal is someone from whom we seek refuge, validation, and positive reinforcement of healthy self-esteem. This entry point harnesses the creative and positive use of what ego psychologists refer to as regression in the service of ego (Knafo, 2002). In mentor bonding, as in therapy, the close tie allows for lowering defenses, while a relaxed-state consciousness primes the mind for new learning and insight. Key here is to evoke the qualities one seeks to emulate from the mentor, so they are not abstractions, but based on personal experience. One does this by blending real life encounters with the idealized image of a mentor as hero archetype. If one chooses an archetypal or historical mentor like Mohammed or Martin Luther King, the idea is to infuse an abstract knowledge of his qualities with personal experience of inspiring individuals that helps enliven the transference. This conscious transference initiates a positive limbic resonance between practitioner and mentor, in which both freely enjoy and appreciate the connection forged between them.

Second Limb: Offering

The next limb involves offering, an act of giving freely. As the mentor shares his or her personal qualities for both to enjoy, the practitioner actively deepens the bond and welcomes the connection through sharing experiences, potentials, and resources. This is traditionally rehearsed in the real or imagined ritual of offering things for mutual enjoyment: water to drink and wash, flowers to please the eyes, light to find one's way, perfume to breathe in, food to eat, and music to enjoy, as well as offering an ideal vision of the world. This builds confidence and a kind of entitlement that overrides self-protective guardedness and insecurity and deepens the sense of reciprocity in the relationship. Most importantly, one envisions such acts of generosity having a positive effect on the mentor, seeing the mentor smiling, enjoying, and feeling gratitude. The resonance of this exchange is key—opening to the experience of deriving pleasure from making others happy.

Third Limb: Disclosure

On the basis of this safe bond and resonant circuitry, the next step is to disclose one's limits, fears, and doubts to the mentor. Personal struggles, conflicts, maladaptive behaviors are shared, to help dismantle shame-based fear or anger that blocks the flow of mutual closeness and interchange. Disclosure reduces the sense of isolation, and helps transform toxic emotions of shame, fear, and hate into prosocial emotions like empathy and humility through the active acceptance of the mentor. While this limb is usually translated as confession, disclosure may be a more appropriate term because it speaks to the interactive nature of this kind of openness. One envisions the mentor taking in the disclosure, accepting the limitations expressed from an enlightened perspective, seeing that the practitioner can move past the difficulty and realize his/her full healing potential. The mentor maintains the simultaneous view of the practitioner's relative suffering and ultimate freedom.

II The Identification Phase: Performance Tantra

Fourth Limb: Rejoicing

The limb of rejoicing evokes a developmental shift from idealizing to identification through the engagement of gratitude and vicarious enjoyment. In this phase, the mentor is a mirror of our own potential, and the power of this fourth limb lies in opening to the reality that an open, plastic nature exists within us, as reflected by the mentor. Rejoicing involves a vicarious enjoyment of the mentor's qualities and accomplishments but implies that we too can be free from personal challenges and traumas and fully connect with our inner potential. Often those personal qualities can be overlooked in the spirit of avoiding pride or indulging self-criticism. This limb encourages the practitioner to develop a sense of enlightened dignity or pride in his/her personal "good." Having disclosed personal challenges in the prior limb, the practitioner balances this by sharing and rejoicing in personal strengths and potentials.

By enjoying qualities that could be ours, we distance ourselves from identification with our old traumatic narratives. This involves conscious supplementation of parental models, worldviews, and ways of acting with those we deem more effective. One begins to let go of the shame-based comparison or jealousy fueled by chronic trauma and opens to the sense that "I too can develop these qualities." This empowers the practitioner to relate to the mentor as both an idealized other and a potential equal; both parties ultimately share the same nature.

III The Internalization Phase: Integral Tantra

Fifth Limb: Requesting Guidance

Requesting guidance includes a number of steps that foster internalization. In requesting guidance, one is not asking the mentor to magically transmit positive qualities, but rather for support and guidance to find those qualities within oneself. The process of asking for help comes from an empowered sense of agency, that we too can develop these qualities with some help, as well as a confidence that the mentor has already taken the necessary steps, so has the experience to help us on the way. This marks a distinct shift in the power differential away from the childlike awe and idealization as well as the identification phase in that the mentor here is even closer to a peer, one who has developed her own mind and potential, is a bit further along the path, and can show the way.

In this internalization phase, the mentor's presence is relocated from external to internal as an inner presence. Here, one visually rehearses taking in the mentor's help, downloading the support without one's own selfhood being replaced or obscured. It is a mixing of subjectivities, and a discovery of one's open potentiality. This internalization traditionally takes the form of a visual and linguistic affirmation transmitted from mentor to practitioner, which are essentially potent seeds of meaning that ripen over time. Over time, the mentor's thoughts, speech, and actions find their way spontaneously into one's daily life, and this inner presence can be drawn upon in between sessions. This resembles the internalization of a therapist's voice, a symbolic presence and sense of connection that can be experienced independent of the therapist being actively engaged in one's daily life.

IV The Integration Phase: Optimal Integral Tantra

Sixth Limb: Requesting Constancy

Requesting constancy deepens the internalization by envisioning the essence of the mentor's qualities merging with one's own. Here one imagines the mentor's mind stream coalescing into a drop of light, which enters through one's crown, travels past the throat, and finally reaches the heart, where it merges inseparably with one's own. The merging here is a deeper level of mixing subjectivities, not an overriding of the practitioner's subjectivity, but a kind of twinship, a congenial sharing of mental qualities, affirmative language, and embodied altruistic spirit. The request for continued guidance comes with the understanding that the path is long and that one may need access to the mentor's support at any time. Again, the mixing of minds is not a replacement or graft, but rather a discovery and harnessing of what is already there.

Seventh Limb: Dedication

The dedication limb focuses on the empowered commitment to oneself and the work that lies at the end of the path. It is a conscious redirecting of one's energy towards fully embodying the mentor's qualities in one's daily life, relationships, and mind/body processes. This also draws on the power of twinship, a deeper and wider sense of solidarity with the community, and a personal commitment to the social development of a fully conscious species and awakened planet.

Flipping the Practice: Psychotherapist as Mentor

Given this background, one can see how the seven-limbed offering could be an excellent training ground for a therapist's sensibility and maturation. Not only is the mentor internalized through the practice, but the relational healing that occurs within that practice provides a corrective experience we can draw on and relay in our work with others.

The first limb of idealization evokes the responsibility of the therapist to hold the relational capacity of being idealized. In order to take on that responsibility, one has to develop confidence in one's role in the therapeutic process, continue to work on one's own conflicts and interpersonal concerns that would block taking on the idealized relational role. Therapists may feel some reluctance and resistance around accepting this role by diminishing or denying clients' transference due to their own unexamined neuroses, shame, or fear, or conversely may exaggerate and reify the transference to serve narcissistic validation. So it is incumbent on therapists to face their particular nuances and reactions to taking on the idealized role. This limb further speaks to harnessing and developing the positive attributes of the mentor. Current psychodynamic approaches to optimal therapeutic attunement suggest giving one's "best self" to the therapeutic relationship, attending to and learning from one's subjective responses to patients, and skillfully using the subjective response in a way that patients can hear, take in, and learn from (McWilliams, 2004). So we bring our best genuine selves to the therapeutic encounter for the benefit of healing, and this requires the personal development of the optimal aspects of one's relational capacity.

The second limb of accepting generosity involves an overall appreciation for the extremely sensitive material that clients are sharing, or offering, in therapy. Therapeutic content and relational processes can be the most intimate material that one can entrust with another and being able to take in clients' content as though it were a precious offering impacts the therapeutic landscape. This is a practice of openness for the therapist, keeping perspective on what is truly happening when clients are exposing their inner worlds.

The relational dynamic of accepting disclosure in the third limb shifts the field from purely focusing on the immediate concern or pathology to including the view of a patient's ultimate potential. As a therapist, one can see both the client's challenges and the freedom from those challenges simultaneously, avoiding getting stuck having the difficulty obscure the full landscape of the client. By relating to the healthy nature of open potential in our clients, we are also able to help clients find this internal capacity within themselves. We relate and attend to what is already covertly there in order to help clients discover it for themselves. This limb also speaks to the key element of love as a healing process in psychodynamic therapy. McWilliams (2004) highlights the therapeutic power, and actual necessity for therapeutic healing, of coming to genuinely love the full subjectivity of one's patient. It is the relationship between the therapist and client that heals, and this rests on the bond of mature and reciprocal empathy developed over time.

The fourth limb of shared rejoicing can extend beyond the positive circuitry of appreciating the positive qualities between client and therapist, to include a connection to the positive qualities of all people psychologically present in the room. As clients share about problematic relationships, this inclusion involves a radical practice of discerning and acknowledging the full spectrum of humanity even in the most difficult or harmful dynamics. Rather than reducing those difficult others to "all good" or "all bad," we develop empathy by seeing the underlying sources of their harmful behavior (delusion, anger, or unhealthy attachment), and maintain the openness of possibility that this person has done some things right. This is not to deny, justify, or minimize the negative impact, harms, and traumas caused by others as these require validation, processing, and exposure. However, maintaining the connection to the full spectrum of all human beings allows for greater power and flexibility in our clients' and our own relational landscape.

The fifth limb of sharing guidance and inspiration from the therapist's perspective draws on one's skillful present attunement to clients' evolving and developmentally maturing needs over time, and not getting stuck in old perceptions or analyses of the client. The imagery here involves the mentor distilling the unique inspiration and guidance in the symbolic form of sending light to the practitioner's heart, a symbolic merging of minds or subjectivities. From the therapist or mentor's perspective, this involves both wisdom and compassion. The therapist has enough wisdom and insight into the truth of emptiness that s/he has the freedom to let go and merge with another's subjectivity as well as enough ego strength to maintain a relative sense of self and differentiation. This commitment also involves the profound compassion and resolution to enter another's subjectivity, go to the depths of hell with each client (Orange et al., 1997), and to be the beacon of light to find the way out.

The final two limbs of continued presence and commitment to altruism from the therapist's perspective invokes the determination to continue on the path toward the deep relational healing with each client. This can broaden the scope of the intersubjective dynamic in that the therapist not only commits to the relational work regardless of duration, but also reaffirms the dedication to one's own development and inner work as a means to help ripen the awakened nature in all our clients and all people we encounter.

17

Skill, Stamina (Noticing Avoidance), and Embodied Connectedness

Realizing Our Vows to Be of Service

Sheryl Petty

I am an organizational equity and systems change consultant and strategist. Much of my work attends to organizational transformation and healing (at *individual, interpersonal, institutional,* and *community/societal/field* levels). I have been in the fields of equity, education, systems change and organizational development for nearly 30 years. I am also a black woman, a *ngakma* (one form of Tantric Buddhist ordination), and teacher in Tibetan Vajrayana Buddhism (Nyingma tradition), which I've practiced for nearly 25 years. I have also been a priest in an African-based tradition (Yoruba/Lucumi), for 25 years as well. These strands inform how I think about systems change, the embodiment of my vows as a professional and spiritual practitioner, healing, and what it means to "be of service."

This chapter is focused on:

- *The meaning of "depth" in our practice as aspiring (or current) healers and contemplative practitioners;*
- *Attending to both the universal & the particular (and how one of these often gets lost);*
- *The nature of "being of service" related to healing, race, gender, and other dimensions of difference;*
- *Will, skill, stamina, and pitfalls in maintaining presence with the above (especially related to white dominant habits); and*
- *Embodied connectedness (to ourselves, one another, the earth, and to all beings).*

DOI: 10.4324/9781003243588-20

Intended Audience and Purpose

I have written this chapter mainly for those for whom reconnection with the particular (i.e., race, gender, and other dimensions of difference) is new, unusual, unfamiliar, challenging, scary, undesirable, and/or potentially seen as not relevant to spiritual or therapeutic practice. That is, for those I assume to be this volume's main audience(s) – therapeutic practitioners who operate from a largely white dominant cultural mindset (whether or not they are white and/or male). Hence, the audience I mean to address could also include those who operate with such a mindset either by assimilation or by choice, despite being part of, having been raised in, and/or living in predominantly multiracial, multigendered communities. Of course, there may be other practitioners who read this volume as well – e.g., equity-minded and BIPOC (Black, Indigenous, and People of Color) practitioners for whom connection with the particular and with difference is not at all new.

(Note: "White dominant" should not be confused with *white culture*, in general. *"Dominant culture"* or *"dominant identities"* refer to groups who hold widespread positional power in an organization or society. In the US, some of the most prevalent dominant identities are white, male, heterosexual, able-bodied, cis-gender, native English-speaking, among others. There's nothing "wrong" with male or white or heterosexual, or any other dominant identity. The issue is a *value-hierarchy* and denigration of those who do not conform to dominant approaches in ways of being, doing, thinking, seeing, understanding, analyzing, communicating, etc. There is current and generational harm toward non-dominant groups as well as our collective well-being and ability to recognize, honor, and benefit from variety in human manifestation and expression.)

Thank you and bear with me and the density here. Some common issues in the fields of *equity capacity building* and *healing* that this chapter attempts to address, relate to **audiences** who have different *starting* places, and therefore different *support* needs and desires in a chapter like this. Namely:

1) Some people operating with a *dominant culture* mindset (white and other) may be <u>new to equity, *but very receptive*</u>. Hence, the issues here may include: A) steepness of learning curve, B) accessing appropriate resources & training, and C) sufficient practice;

2) Some people operating with a *dominant culture* mindset may be <u>new to equity *and defensive/not receptive*</u> in relation to it. Hence, some issues here may be: A) determining whether or not one has interest in learning

and growth, and if so, B) softening the borders of what we think we know and fostering receptivity, and then C) addressing the issues from #1;

3) Some people operating with a *dominant culture* mindset (white and other) may be <u>very equity-minded and (potentially) equity-skilled</u>. Hence, the tasks here include being of humble, compassionate, and rigorous support, and a resource to others, especially those in #1 and #2;

4) Some *BIPOC (and other non-dominant) people* may be <u>new and/or defensive</u> in relation to equity (despite deep lived experience), if/when we have assimilated effectively (*unconsciously* or by *choice*) to dominant culture. Hence, the issues here are similar to #1 and #2, <u>*but*</u> with the added dimensions of reflecting on the – (often highly skillful and at times, detrimental/unhelpful) – coping strategies we may have developed to live and survive as BIPOC (or other non-dominant) people in many dominant culture communities around the world.

5) Many *BIPOC (and other non-dominant) people* are <u>very equity-minded and may also be very equity-skilled</u>. Hence, the tasks here potentially include being of humble, compassionate, and rigorous support and a resource to others, especially those in #4, and possibly in #1 and #2 as desired/moved to do so; and in partnership with those in #3.

A note on "intentions" and the four levels of equity (i.e., *individual, interpersonal, institutional,* and *community/societal/systemic*): *individual* growth and good "intentions" related to equity <u>*are necessary but not sufficient*</u> in our endeavors in the focus of this chapter. We are trying to address <u>*systemic*</u> problems and the implications for contemplative and therapeutic practice – which include <u>*and*</u> go beyond *individual* and *interpersonal* dimensions – to support the emergence of a healthier world <u>*for all*</u>.

Hence, for these different audiences, sometimes my tone might be direct, subtle, controversial, provocative, nurturing, fierce, calm, etc. – or anything in between, to try *to shake us out of* potential *complacency*, into kinder (which may not necessarily mean "softer"), more present, *feeling/affected/impacted* human beings, who are not insulated from one another's suffering and pain. We may then become more capable of discerning or manifesting in each moment *right/appropriate/beneficial action*, which can emerge spontaneously for the liberation of all.

(A few additional thoughts: without presence, we can be dangerous when we are *disconnected* from each other. This "connectedness" [as will be discussed later in the chapter] is *specific/particular*, not just *universal/general*. We are *particular* human beings, in *particular* bodies, and those *particularities* matter in terms of *communication* with one another. The same reason we would learn another language in order to speak and be understood by those from other cultures, *is the same reason we would attend to areas such as race, class, gender and other dimensions of difference*: because they impact how we experience the world, and hence require *translation* of the dharma or psychotherapeutic approaches to *meet and honorably attend* to our particularity – as individuals, as families, as communities, as societies.

(I am going on and on about this because my experience over the last nearly 30 professional years is that what I am speaking of *was largely ignored* [or addressed only cursorily with "diversity" and "inclusion" efforts], until about two years ago when race suddenly became visible to more and more dominant-culture people, as a domain requiring societal attention. There are still significant efforts fighting or continuing to avoid such a focus – some school districts, philanthropists, spiritual teachers, and others. This "fighting" or "avoiding" takes the form of believing that such "focus" is "divisive" or a "distraction" or a "distortion." This is an important part of what we have to address to be of greater aid, support, assistance, partnership, presence, kindness, honor, and love with and for one another. These are at the heart of both Deep Equity and Tantric practice in my work, life, practice, teaching, and experience.)

Depths of Practice

The framing for this revised edition of *Advances in Contemplative Psychotherapy* – "*fleshing out the social context and ethical dimension of contemplative practice and … the intersection of this work with the impact of systemic racial and gender oppression on personal, interpersonal and collective health and well-being …*" – is very helpful and (in my training and practice), not "new" to Buddhism nor to contemplative practice at depth. Such framing is also core to the professional, sacred, and secular training of Deep Equity[1] and social justice[2] practitioners.

The deep meaning of "compassion" requires or *compels* us to be <u>*fully*</u> engaged in the world and profoundly <u>*in touch with*</u> the suffering of beings. "Engagement" may mean different things or look different ways – (as my mother once said to me, "We don't all have to engage in social justice in the same way"). Prayer from a cave in the woods can be just as profound and dangerous as complex social engagement in highly political circumstances, and vice versa.

The question becomes, <u>*what does our practice require of us DEPENDING on what type of engagement we are called to have in the world*</u> (in any given moment)? i.e., _different conditions require different tools and capacities to be effective, successful, and beneficial_. At different moments in our lives, we may also be called to different "practice" or "service" in the world, which, in turn, will require different skills of us, different capacities to manifest to meet, partner with, and best serve the needs and beings of the moment. This is the "skillful means" of Tantra, a view and method we find ourselves at certain stages of our Bodhisattva vows. Equity and social justice – at depth – is this. It is _infinitely creative, dauntless, unwaveringly rooted in compassion, dogged_, and _loving_. It is innovative to meet the needs of the moment, whatever they may require of us; come what may. Buddhist Tantra, in particular, is one system that is well suited to support individuals and collective bodies/systems in _metabolizing_ the toxic residue of social ills, such as racial, gender and other forms of oppression.

Deep Equity and social justice[3] is also precise. (It also, at depth, displays all the Enlightened/Wisdom Families of Tantric Buddhism – _pacifying, enriching, magnetizing, wrathful_, which are descriptions of the ways that compassion can manifest.) It is _specific_ in its engagement with phenomena so that its prescriptions/methodologies/activities can be equally precise. White dominant habits[4] (which any of us may display), have had the tendency in this hemisphere[5] to _erase_ or _minimize_ the "_particular_" in favor of the "_universal_." The _universal_ can seem easier/simpler/less complicated, generalizable. The _particular_, on the other hand, may seem messier, more complicated, less neat, non-conformist. We have heard terms such as "wild" used to describe both female-identified people as well as Black, Indigenous and people of color. While there is nothing _per se_ problematic about the term "wild," how it has been used is less than desirable to honor the varied ways that human expression can manifest. Both Equity _at depth_ as well as Tantra allow and celebrate the varied ways human manifestation may occur, because they are both grounded in profound wisdom and compassion. In fact, by some definitions, Equity at Depth _is_ Compassion, and Tantra is called the "path of Skillful Means," another phrase for infinitely creative Compassion.

Attending to the "Particular"(As Well as the Universal)

There is a _running_ away from the particular in white dominant habits; a "melting pot" mentality which _erases_ the specificity of human experience. Many of us may do this – from time to time and/or because of how, when, and where we were raised or trained by our families, professionally, and our communities of practice. As we emerge from either oblivion or from conflicted states of being, seeing our shared humanity can be liberating, a boon, and a revelation that we had heretofore not seen or been in touch with. (This emergence is similar to the stages of grief [beginning with *denial* and *anger*], and the IDI continuum, which may be useful, though it does <u>not</u> include the full focus of Deep Equity and Social Justice [DE&SJ]. DE&SJ includes attention to differential power, cumulative impact, and societal conditions, among other areas.)

To deepen our practice from this state, from *this revelation* of the (non-intellectual) *experience* of our common humanity, *requires us to <u>stay in the (sometimes very intense)</u> **heat of the moment***; the "warp and weft of life,"[6] which is *relentless* in its manifestations. It is not *"neat"* or (always) *"pretty;"* (but it is always "good," in the Bodhicitta/Buddhist sense of deep compassion way of saying this word; as in *Samantabhadra*, the primordial Buddha, meaning "All Good"). From the Vajrayana Buddhist Dzogchen view, the current moment is perfect; though we may not be able to realize/perceive it. In our states of confusion about the perfection of reality, we create all kinds of chaos and mayhem. Our practice aims to *stabilize* our ability to be *with* the present moment, so that we do not run from our innate freedom and our ability to be of service to each other. This is part of the depth of practice. In *both* Deep Equity *as well as* contemplative practice, we find our *capacity* and *repertoire of action* **EXPANDS** to be able to <u>encompass</u> the totality and limitlessness of creation, of manifest reality.

Enter again, equity – or *Deep Equity* in my use of the term. What are we talking about here, as spiritual practitioners, clinicians, therapists, and healers? *Our collective commitment to promote the well-being of individuals, groups, and the planet* – both the <u>universal</u> and the <u>particular</u>. The particular in this case, means <u>with radical attentiveness to our identities</u> (racial, gender, sexual orientation, and others) – <u>not</u> with gripping, fanatic attachment, but with <u>presence</u> and <u>honor</u> for the <u>particularity</u> of our lives and their precious, unique, magnificent manifestations. This is at the heart of many of our vows – *to honor phenomenal reality*. Such "honoring" and "attention" allows us to *discern* in the moment, appropriate behavior, and action. We are <u>not insulated</u> from life, people, and situations. We commit to being *present* to whatever is arising at any moment.

The Multifaceted Nature of *"Being of Service:"* Healing, Race, and Other Dimensions of Difference

What does this mean and have to do with psychotherapy or contemplative practice? It means that <u>we expand our repertoire of being able to be of service to EVERY DIFFERENT KIND of human being</u>; that we can actually be of service to *the many*, and not only the few. And we can do this <u>without</u> erasing the *specificity* and nuances of race, gender, or any other dimension of human difference. Just as different spiritual teachers are more effective with particular students – (sometimes *not* based on identifiable characteristics) – we become <u>open</u> to being aware that race, gender identity, and other dimensions of difference *may impact how we perceive* and *can (or cannot) communicate with <u>specific</u> people*.

Though we may *specialize* in certain capacities or faculties or skills (i.e., everyone doesn't have to be a carpenter, or know how to work with children and families, etc.) – we know that we *can*, if we choose to and apply ourselves diligently – expand our repertoire and skills to be of more effective support for wider and wider ranges of beings, including multiracial and multigendered communities. This is no small matter and is more complex than "diversity" or "inclusion" or even learning another language; Deep Equity includes and goes beyond these. These dimensions of human difference become <u>important</u> for us to attend to because of our commitment to be of service. Our commitment <u>requires</u> us to attend to the particular as well as the universal. (This is an aspect of Discriminating Awareness.[7] We are not all the same, *and* we are not all different.

We do not shy away from life; which means, *we do not shy away from people, in our <u>specificity; and <u>particularity</u>* (not just in the "universal"). We can develop the capacity to *see* and *meet* and *stay fully present* with the <u>*particular*</u> *dimensions of our lives* (and those who come to us for support). "*Staying present*" in this way, is core to many aspects of Deep Equity and to contemplative practice, at depth.

Will, Skill, and Stamina in Contemplative Practice and Equity

What I often see in white dominant contemplative (and other) communities and organizations is either:

- Inability to stay **present** when engaging equity; to want to run from or alleviate the "discomfort" as soon as possible – This is a "stamina" issue, so we need to <u>deepen</u> our practice to <u>remain</u> with intensity, until it subsides or transmutes; and/or
- Lack of **skill** – with regard to either *awareness, knowledge*, and (beyond *intellectual/brain*) *understanding*, and capacity to *effectively engage* race (and other dimensions of difference) with kindness and rigor when they arise and present themselves.

A corollary to these *skill* and *stamina* domains is lack of "*will*" and/or "excuse-making." These forms of **avoidance** are contrary to our Bodhisattva and Tantric vows, which compel us to be present and attentive "*as refined as the grains of flour …*"[8] These *avoidance* tactics take the form of something like: "those things don't matter," or "that's a distortion of the teachings." At depth, our commitment to be of service also requires *willingness* and practice to maintain awareness of our *own* condition and conditioning – both *before/as a prerequisite* to being of support to others, and *during* our attempts to be of support. This is "putting our own mask on first" before seeking to help/support others.

"Will" promotes openness and receptivity to growth and learning. "Stamina" promotes endurance and bravery when/if things get intense. "Skill" is *capacity* in actually engaging in the work itself. With "will" and "stamina" only, without "skill," there is a limited capacity to actually *do* anything, make a difference, and be of service.

"Staying present" in terms of Deep Equity requires us to build the STAMINA and SKILL to be able to stay present with race, gender identity, sexual orientation, class, and other dimensions of difference *which are impacting* the individuals and/or groups who may come to us for support. These dimensions of difference are not solely "individual" or "interpersonal" "*issues.*" Viewing them in these ways can confuse and obscure our perception of them influencing our collective life – i.e., the organizations, systems, and structures within which (most of us) exist in the world (such as neighborhoods and parks, educational systems, healthcare systems, the job market, housing, systems for receiving food, and other areas) – which are all radically impacted by race, skin color, class, language, accent, and other dimensions of difference, globally. The degree to which we pay attention to what is *specifically* happening in these areas when individuals or groups come to us for support, is *precisely* the degree to which we will or will not be able to be of assistance *in the particularity* of the life circumstances of those who come to us for support and guidance.

Said another way, if we are ignoring or avoiding these areas (i.e., race, class, gender, etc.) we will be limited in our capacity to be of aid, because individuals and groups are *always* experiencing *both* the universal *as well as* the particular/specific at the same time. They are non-dual, and the depth of our practice (equity and/or contemplative) requires us to attend to the particular.

"Stamina" also relates to our contemplative practice and not being *overwhelmed* by phenomena or whatever is manifesting. "Skill" is about developing the actual *knowledge, understanding, awareness, & capacity* to 1) *notice,*

2) *effectively engage/meet* (i.e., with what I like to call, "rigor + kindness"), 3) *address*, and (if appropriate), *transform* conditions as they arise.

"Noticing" is about *paying attention to what is arising, as it is.* To "notice"/recognize that I am Black, female-bodied, and human is *to have enough awareness and skill* to know that it may likely be less effective to engage me as generic or white or Asian, or male-or-other-gender-bodied, or as a four-legged animal. That is *skillful.* To *not* notice (or rather, to not pay attention), would be highly unskillful. "Ignoring" race or other identities can *limit our actual efficacy,* as well as our *enjoyment☺* of the particular and myriad, wonderful manifestations of reality. Spiritual bypassing of race and other dimensions of difference, taking refuge in "melting pot" or assimilationist approaches to contemplative practice and therapy will be less effective with BIPOC and other non-dominant communities who are navigating both dominant and non-dominant cultures. (See for instance *"Spiritual Bypassing in the Contemporary Mindfulness Movement,"* by Carla Sherell and Judith Simmer-Brown, in *Social Justice, Inner Work & Contemplative Practice: Lessons & Directions for Multiple Fields,* 2017, p.74–93.)

The way we ensure that addressing and engaging the particular, does <u>not</u> become exoticizing or remain "surface," is to *actually* put in the *time and effort* to <u>learn</u> about marginalized/non-dominant communities and history (i.e., women, gender-expansive people, BIPOC, etc.) so that we appropriately share the responsibilities of living in this world together. We deepen and broaden our understanding of our collective life, how we have arrived at our current state of affairs collectively (at least from a physical/material perspective), and therefore deepen our capacity to make this (apparent) world better. Just like a plumber or electrician would do – *we continue to learn about our craft, because the history of its evolution <u>matters</u> for doing good work today and even more beneficial work tomorrow.*

To not pay attention to race and other dimensions of difference in our practice (whatever our professions in the world), is an abdication of our *responsibility* as practitioners, craftspeople, and fellow human travelers who aspire to embody Bodhisattva vows. Tantra is where we significantly <u>*expand our repertoire of capacities to be of service*</u>. We become more <u>*capable*</u>; we build greater *stamina, endurance,* and *determination.* We become *dogged & unwavering/unflinching* in our commitment to be of service toward the liberation of everyone and everything, everywhere.[9]

We are living in a time when (in many parts of the world) a "case" no longer has to be made for a focus on equity and race (in particular), with the rise of widely available, video-taped murders of Black, Brown, and Gender-Expansive people in the United States. For the first time in my lifetime, wide swaths of people are (finally, many for *their* first time) making the connection between *individual* (or *interpersonal*) "issues" of "discrimination," and historical, systemic, widespread racism and oppression that impacts the ability of *specific*, very large groups of people to even have a hope of access (or consistent access) to healthy food, decent housing, quality education, beautiful, safe neighborhoods, and so on. We are seeing the beginnings of a greater consideration of *our* COLLECTIVE responsibility for our *collective* well-being, (especially in countries and environments where there are the financial and resource means to attend effectively to the "many" and not just the "few").

So, we have to ask now (as many have been for the last two years): *What does a moment like this require of us – to deepen our embodiment of our commitment to be of true & authentic service? (And where and when are we shying away from that? And what is the impact, one way or the other – when we <u>are</u> in embodiment, and when we are <u>not</u>?)*

Skill in Intensity

We've been talking about how one of the **functions** of practice then becomes building our **stamina** for *staying fully present* to the <u>intensity</u> of the moment, **whatever it may hold.** This is no small matter and may be part of the reason folks shy away from the work of attending directly to race and other dimensions of difference: it can become VERY intense (some/much of the time because of many centuries of denial and repression, and lack of adequate capacity *en masse* to fully attend to it). We may collectively be called to build such stamina *en masse* in this historical period for the benefit of future generations. This lack of stamina often shows up *physiologically*, *emotionally*, and/or *mentally/cognitively*. Contemplative practitioners may recognize these as the domains of *body*, *speech*, and *mind*.

All of life is not "calm" and this is not the goal of practice (though that may very well be the *internal* state, no matter the *conditions* or *behavior* we may be manifesting *externally*). Sometimes things are intense (for us individually, in our families, in our communities, societally, and/or globally) – and require various methods to support the most beneficial progress and the liberation of all. Sometimes those moments (especially in intensity) require a sharp instrument to cut through (like childbirth). Some Tantric (and other) Enlightened Beings have ritual knives and other "intense" instruments to fulfill their work and duties in support of the *maturing* and full realization of beings. Wielding such instruments or *tools of intensity* well, requires an *unwavering* heart of compassion, lest we become dangerous. *This warrants repeating* and significant meditation.

We (sometimes) have to build up the capacity to be able to handle a more powerful or intense "electric current" – in our bodies, in our relationships, and in the world. **This increased capacity for more fully engaging the complexity, intensity, and multifaceted nature of life – (including skillfully addressing the *individual, interpersonal, institutional,* and *systemic/structural* forms of racism, sexism, and other manifestations of social oppression) – is part of what Buddhist Tantric and Deep Equity practice can yield.** (Sometimes it's also fun to ride a rollercoaster, or surf, or paddle in white water rapids ...) Sometimes the degree of confusion, (either *our own* or that of "others" around us), causing harm and damage to those near and far, wreaking havoc on the planet – *requires an* **intense tool & method to disrupt & get our/their attention.** This is (part of) the methods of Buddhist Tantra and other wisdom traditions.

When one trains to deepen equity practice to <u>notice</u> and *reduce/release* racist, sexist, and other conscious and unconscious inequity tendencies, one domain of skill-building is **healthy engagement with conflict.** There are corollaries and entire teachings on this in Vajrayana Buddhism; some teachings (and wisdom beings) specialize in these capacities. It is actually a set of capacities/muscle group(s) in one's psycho-physical-subtle-energetic sphere/field that can be cultivated <u>*so that one can become more stable and compassionately centered, under any conditions*</u>. One also comes to realize in Vajrayana as well as in Deep Equity, that "compassion" can manifest itself in ANY manner of ways – *gentle, intense, vivid, soft, loud, hard, wild, peaceful, seductive,* or **any** *unpremeditated manner* needed to serve the Enlightened needs of the moment ...

In this/these ways, we have the possibility of *actually* **becoming** kind & loving, and experiencing the fruit of our contemplative practice, teachings, and our healing aspirations. Then, we can be greater agents of well-being and positive change, for the collective good – that emerges spontaneously for the benefit of others.

Some Pitfalls to Depth, Service, Will, Skill, & Stamina: *White Dominant Habits*

Many have written in recent years on such attentiveness to the "particular" as it relates to race, gender, social systems, and contemplative practice.[10] As we've noted above, we still need to be attentive to the danger of equity spiritual bypassing and avoidance as they relate specifically to race and other dimensions of difference. A fuller elucidation of some of these pitfalls can be found in the pervasive literature now present in equity communities of practice around white dominant culture or *white dominant habits*. As many know, these habits are sometimes conscious, sometimes unconscious, and not always used by white or other dominant culture people and institutions. (The reader is encouraged to familiarize themselves with these habits, with skilled coaching and/or facilitation support alone and in groups – to notice how such habits may be manifesting in one's own life and practice, to practice releasing these patterns, and building new, more compassionate, skillful muscle …)

Harm, Un-Numbing, & Healing: Disconnection & Reconnecting with Ourselves & Each Other

For those (of any race, gender, or other manifestation) for whom focus on the *particular* (race, gender identity, etc.) in the ways we are talking about, is new, unfamiliar, scary or undesirable – this often marks a state of <u>disconnection</u> – with ourselves, with each other, and with the planet. There are many practices (across multiple wisdom traditions, tantric and other) that support us to *reconnect* and "unknot" contortions inside of our mental, emotional, physiological, relational systems. Receiving intensive training *and* deeply practicing these approaches can support us to become better practitioners, better therapists, better loved ones, better social systems change agents, better neighbors, and community members – who care for and attend to one another.

Without this level of <u>reconnection</u> (as I often tell my organizational clients), we are <u>numb</u> to our own pain and to the pain of others – like when our foot or hand is numb. With this numbness, it is <u>very</u> difficult to know *when we have hurt ourselves* or *when we are hurting others*. In such a state, we do not feel our own pain, let alone anyone else's, and all the intellectualizing in the world cannot solve that. Hence, we have to be un-numb, *sensitized/sensitive/present/aware* enough to notice. And we have to be *WILLING to NOTICE*. Here again enters "will," because sometimes we *ignore* our own <u>and</u> others' pain (even when it is quite obvious) – and this is how it becomes possible to harm ourselves, others, and the planet. We lose awareness of connection and our fundamental interconnectedness (in some Buddhist systems this is referred to as "*tendrel*").

(I led a day-long workshop on the relationship between deep equity and contemplative practice for a multiracial group of about 50 people in early 2020,

and a Black woman said at the beginning of the day that she had no familiar-
ity or relationship to "inner work," contemplative practice, or being "sensitive" to her internal state. After the group engaged in practice and exercises
with the breath, natural elements, subtle body, etc. – she said something to
the effect of, "Now I get it. It's *re-sensitizing*" to these things that have gone
dormant ...)

Avoidance is a form of *disconnection* and (as has been noted) can take the
form of "excuse-making." Even when we *see* what's happening, we may create
"explanations" for what we are seeing that enables us to avoid actually dealing
with it. We all know this and have likely done it (in some forms), whether in
our personal relationships, in work, or in relation to social systems and race.

In our societal and interpersonal dynamics (for simplicity's sake), we might
say there is the experience of those on the *"receiving"* end of harm, and the
experience of those on the "perpetuating" end. **For those causing harm**, this
can be thought of as a state of *disconnection* from self and (so-called) "others." From the "self," this can be at the *subtle body* level (as it's understood
in Tantric Buddhism), it can be on the level of mind/brain, it can be on the
more gross, physical body level, and/or in our relationships with "others."

For those experiencing harm, whether or not we go into a state of "suffering" with the experience of oppression, abuse or harm, is a matter of choice,
skill, and may be a matter of timing (i.e., our capacity in the moment). This
is *very important*. Whether or not we take "experiences" as "suffering" (from
a Buddhist perspective), has to do with our degree of *presence, awareness*, and
non-grasping onto our experiences. When we are experiencing what appears
to be estrangement from our Natural Condition (from a Buddhist perspective), we suffer. When we are connected to and aware of it, we are Free – *no
matter the external conditions*. This is one of the most important parts of this
chapter.

Now, we need to be careful <u>not</u> to make social oppression the problem of
individuals and *his/her/their own* healing. In a collective life full of love and
caring, *we all have the responsibility to be of service to the liberation of everyone and everything, everywhere*. This is the life of (spiritual) practitioners and
healers at certain depths of our practice. We've noted that "healing" is **not
(solely) an individual matter**. It is about the **collective** as much as it is about
the so-called "individual" because 1) we are <u>connected</u>, and because 2) we can
create social conditions (families, institutions, societies) that decrease harm
and support the well-being of all. (Whether or not, when and to what degree
we *feel* connected is another matter; and is another of the main subjects of

this chapter – because the greater our *felt-sense* of connectivity, the greater our capacity to make wise, compassionate, and skillful choices based on that clearer awareness…)

Upping Our Game …

We now know that this *reconnection* (with self, "other" and the world) becomes a core *function* of practice and any healing methodology. When we are connected, we feel deeply, we are **attuned & aware**, *and therefore have the CAPACITY to ACT in ways that serve our "individual" & "collective" liberation*. Processes, habits, and approaches that disconnect us from our Natural Condition and each other, will not serve us as practitioners, healers, or those who would be healed. *What makes us MORE SENSITIVE to the MOMENT, and to EACH OTHER will*. We may shy away from this, with the perspective that it "is too much; or 'too overwhelming' …" This is precisely why we would practice: *as we are called to deeper service, we may need to "up our game"* (i.e., our capacities) to be of effective and proper service to what is arising before us. This "upping our game" is a **deepening of skill & stamina**. (If we are not called to this, perhaps our current capacities, methodologies, and approaches are sufficient … and perhaps they are not? …)

For BIPOC and other non-dominant culture people who are reading this – we are called to "up our game" to 1) use and/or find contemplative practices that support us to *not grip* onto experience in a way that causes us or others to suffer, and 2) deepen our skill and stamina to be more effective change agents with individuals, organizations, and systems who may be resistant, oblivious, and/or unskilled in relation to matters of race, gender, or social justice, and 3) to find adequate resources, supports, and communities of practice for us to heal where there has been damage to our physical, emotional, subtle, and/or mental bodies. #2 relates to both A) a sensitivity to readiness/current state of those we are engaging with, and B) ensuring that our heart of tenderness and compassion (with *rigor*) is pervasive and unwavering in the face of intensity, abuse (sometimes generational), gaslighting, and massive harm.

For all of us: *What is our heart of Bodhicitta in the charnel ground*[11] *(in this case, families, communities, institutions, and societies that continue to cause harm, even when they become aware of it)? Where is our unwavering commitment to develop the skill, will, discipline, stamina, and undauntable fearlessness in the face of ANYTHING?*

- For dominant culture people: *How do we maintain* presence *with specificity/particularity of experience without "taking refuge" in the "universal" (i.e., "melting pot/assimilationist/we are all one human family")?*
  - It's not that the universal is not present; it's that it is not *all* that's present;
  - As practitioners and healers, *we commit to not ignoring the specific* and *to deepening our capacity to effectively and skillfully* engage *it,* in this case, as it relates to race, gender and other dimensions of difference.
- For non-dominant people: *How do we not become contorted by the experiences of oppression and frequent harm? How do we maintain our heart of Bodhicitta/loving-kindness* with *a wild fierce compassion* as it becomes necessary *to break old patterns and catalyze ourselves, people, and situations into more liberated states?*

Do we have (and are we *using*) the resources we need to *do* and *become* what the above requires, for the benefit of all? And if not, *what are we gonna do about it?* (And *when* are we gonna do it?).

So What, Now What? Reflection & Application

Now that we have come to the crux of the matter, **some reflection questions** as practitioners (therapists, contemplative practitioners, would-be or current social change agents, or other identities we may find ourselves within at the moment☺):

1) To what degree am I *fully present* with MY OWN identities (*even knowing they are transient and don't last* from a Buddhist perspective) – in my attempts to be of service to and with others? (Note: some may take presence with our identities as not part of Buddhist practice. We have been talking about the need to pay attention to the particular *especially* in Tantric practice, because the very *texture* of life and reality is experienced as *sacred*. Our "attentiveness" is part of how we honor it. The point is not to *attach* to it.)
   a. To what degree do I shy away from such presence?
   b. How aware am I when this is happening?
   c. What do I do when I become aware?
2) To what degree am I *fully present* with the identities of THOSE WHO COME TO ME for service and support?

a. To what degree do I shy away from or reject such presence and noticing?

b. How aware am I when this is happening?

c. What do I do when I become aware?

3) How **SKILLED** and **KNOWLEDGEABLE** am I about race, class, gender identity, and other dimensions of difference in their historical & current *individual*, *interpersonal*, *institutional*, and *systemic/societal* manifestations?

a. What have I done/am I doing to *deepen my awareness, knowledge,* and *skill* at **all of these four levels?**[12]

b. How much does such focus on the *specific/particular* matter in my current work? How much do I think it makes a difference (or not) in my efficacy with those who come (or might come) to me for support?

4) What are my goals in the **_depth_** of my practice (professional, personal, contemplative, psychotherapeutic, other)?

a. What do I actually hope is different for people and their capacities and actions in life after engaging with me? What do I hope the effect(s) is/are of engaging with me?

5) To what degree do I have **stamina** for the *intensity* of engagement that may be necessary with this level of *specificity* (related to race and other [apparent/ephemeral] identities)?

a. What will be required to deepen the efficacy of my practice and presence in the world?

b. How am I deepening this stamina and capacity for intensity?

c. What supports or resources do I need, and how and when will I bring them to bear?

If we seek to ...

- Be *healers in support of individuals*, we will be motivated to learn and refine modalities & approaches that support those we would seek to benefit;
- Be *healers in support of the collective*, we will be motivated to learn and refine modalities and approaches that support those organizations and groups who desire our services and partnership.

Each of these – *individual* and *collective healing* – have their own *sacred* and *secular* sciences, approaches, methodologies, histories, practitioner groupings, "certification" rituals and bodies, etc. Transformation at individual, interpersonal, institutional, and systemic/societal levels requires considerable learning and practice. Collective healing of "ills" like racism, colorism, and sexism (among all the other isms), includes the field of *equity-embedded organizational development* (which is different than "equity" as an add-on ...).

Closing & Applying Practice ...

As we end, we return briefly to the issue of "stamina" and what we do when we notice _discomfort_, irritation, annoyance, cringing, fear, loathing, and potentially gymnastic approaches to rationalizing distance from seeing race, one another's pain, systemic harm, and the _specific_ suffering we see around us, in our communities and families (not only "across the world"). We can reflect on _what is tenderness_[13] in our practice? To what degree are we willing to be _touched_ and _moved_ into skillful, compassionate action? "Moved" not in a syrupy, overwhelmed, distorted, pity-motivated way – but _moved_ in a way that is _powerful, centered, grounded, anchored in our innate goodness & brilliance, fierce and fearless, undauntable, skillful, clear & kind_? Without preferences or aversions for particular groups of people AND without _ignoring the particularities_ of those groups of people (history, societal impacts, cultures, languages, race, genders, etc.)? Can we be _that_ <u>discerning</u> and <u>precise</u> in our action and engagement with phenomena and the world – _at all times_?

Can we be this for and with each other because this is what the world needs right now – for us to be _fully_ present with one another and of service? And finally, <u>_are we willing to put in the work and the time_</u> that it will take for us to <u>_actually_</u> build the STAMINA and SKILL to _live into_, FULL embodiment of this call that both Deep Equity and Tantra (as two of the countless/limitless doors to the _same thing_) – require of us, as radical acts of _love_ and _kindness_?

Capacity may not magically emerge and manifest because we _want_ it to and because we have "good intentions." For many things, we have to actually <u>_apply_</u> ourselves – i.e., learn the language(s), study the material, practice the sadhana(s)/methods, shadow our mentor(s), get the substantial equity training, and practice in real-time with discomfort and uncertainty, etc.

This is life; this is (part of) Tantra; this is Equity (at depth); this is what is required for (deeper) embodiment of our vows and commitment to be of service to the liberation of everyone and everything, everywhere.

Notes

1   Sometimes used interchangeably; hence, singular here. _"Deep Equity"_ is a term and approach coined in my practice some years ago to distinguish more nascent approaches to "DEI" (diversity, equity, and inclusion) work, from approaches with a depth of rigor and compassion that could lead to more lasting, beneficial changes at individual, interpersonal, institutional, and community/field/societal levels. See these publications as examples: _Seeing, Reckoning & Acting: A Practice_

Toward Deep Equity (S. Petty, 2016), and *Systems Change & Deep Equity: Pathways Toward Sustainable Impact, Beyond "Eureka!" Unawareness & Unwitting Harm* (S. Petty & M. Leach, 2020).

2   See for example the *Deep Equity Practitioners Network (DEPn)*, 2021.

3   Deliberately singular here, as these are interchangeable in my use in this chapter. For an elucidation of these terms and their relationship to contemplative practice, please see S. Petty, *Waking Up to All of Ourselves: Inner Work, Social Justice & Systems Change,* in *Social Justice, Inner Work & Contemplative Practice: Lessons & Directions for Multiple Fields,* Initiative for Contemplation, Education & Action (ICEA), July 2017, p. 1–14.

4   Not be confused with *white culture,* in general.

5   Often referred to as the "West."

6   A phrase I have heard one of my Buddhist teachers, Ngak'chang Rinpoche, use in referring to Tantra.

7   A description of the wisdom quality of the *magnetizing* Buddha Family.

8   As the father of Tantric Buddhism, Guru Rinpoche/Padmasambhava has said …

9   For the liberation of "everyone and everything, everywhere" is a phrase used by one of my Buddhist teachers, Ngak'chang Rinpoche.

10   E.g., *Radical Dharma: Talking Race, Love & Liberation* (by Rev. angel Kyodo williams, Lama Rod Owens, and Jasmine Syedullah); *The Way of Tenderness: Awakening through Race, Sexuality & Gender* (by Zenju Earthlyn Manuel); the Arrow Journal; therapist, author, healer Resmaa Menakem; and *Waking Up to All of Ourselves: Inner Work, Social Justice & Systems Change* (p. 1–14); among others.

11   In Tantric Buddhism, a *"charnel ground"* is traditionally a place of intense practice where corpses are left to rot and be consumed by vultures and other animals who inhabit the place. In this case, I am using the term to refer to the intensity of the widespread experience of systemic racism and other forms of oppression, in places where danger, abuse and harm are nearly constant (not just for individuals, but for entire groups, generationally).

12   Some potential equity training programs readers might be familiar with or choose to participate in include: White Awake; the Racial Equity Institute; Crossroads Anti-racism; Race Forward; and Wayfinding Partners; among other providers. (*Note* that not all include a contemplative approach.)

13   In the way Zenju Earthlyn Manuel uses this term in *The Way of Tenderness: Awakening through Race, Sexuality & Gender.*

18

The Essence of Tantric Medicine

Embodied Healing in the Yuthog Nyingthig Tradition

Nida Chenagtsang

Buddha, Tantra, Mantra: Awakening Through Mind-Energy-Body Protection

What is the most important word in Buddhism? It's "Buddha." The root of the word means "to wake up," and describes the essence of Buddhism—it's a wakeup call. As we wake up from confusion, we become free. That is the one goal, waking up, because it's the ultimate freedom. The problem is, we are imprisoned in confusion and can't experience freedom. We are not free with our thoughts, we are not free with our emotions, we are not free with our past, we are not free with our future, we are not even free with our present. Instead, our minds are totally conditioned and lost. The confusion that keeps us trapped in our own nightmares may be the common root cause of all forms of suffering, but the way confusion proliferates and manifests—its branches and leaves—are endlessly varied. During the Buddha's six years of diving into the human mind, he saw all its nooks and crannies, every aspect of its suffering, reactions, and activities. After he woke up, he said, "We humans suffer from 84,000 mental afflictions" (kleshas). Luckily, through his life, he offered 84,000 teachings or specific solutions for those 84,000 problems. So every type of poison has its medicine.

The Buddha taught different teachings for different people struggling with different afflictions and different mentalities. There is no single way to think about Buddhism—it can be approached as a religion, a science, a philosophy, a psychology, a way of life—and all these approaches are fine, as long as they work for people. As long as our approach works to tame and transform our minds, to help us work skillfully with our thoughts, emotions, sensations, and reactions, then that's good. In the end we all have to wake up. Among the

DOI: 10.4324/9781003243588-21

many different kinds of methods for awakening Buddha offered, one of the most powerful is the profound transformational psychology called Tantra.

Tantra: The Science of Protecting and Expanding Mind/Body Health and Freedom

Tantra is a Sanskrit word, translated as Gyu in Tibetan, which means a continuation or lineage of embodied wisdom and learning. This is very important because today people think they can just read a book on Tantra to become a Tantric practitioner, then become a Tantric master in a year or two. Tantra is a very systematic method for transmitting embodied learning, and must be studied and practiced in the proper way, otherwise it's easy to get it wrong, and that is more serious than commonly believed. To make matters worse, there is widespread confusion about Tantra, including how it relates to yoga and mantra, as well as the serious misunderstanding that it's all about sex.

Tantra is the name of an extended family of practices, which includes many family members. One branch of the family is called Mantra, one is called Yoga, one is called Yantra, and there are many other practices under the Tantric family umbrella. But all of these are related and not separated from the larger methodology called Tantra. That methodology is focused on guarding and expanding positive energy, the light of love, joy, and compassion, to be shared with everyone. The importance of understanding this focus on transmitting and spreading the embodied energy of love and compassion is that enlightenment in the Buddhist tradition is not seen as a strictly individual accomplishment, but rather as an interpersonal and psychosocial process through which successive generations and whole communities reach enlightenment together.

Another distinctive aspect of Tantra is that it combines practices that help cultivate and protect the health and well-being of the body, practices that cultivate and protect the health and well-being of the mind, and practices that cultivate and protect the health and well-being of our embodied life energy. How does Tantra protect the body? It includes practices that are similar to physiotherapy, involving the body-work of stretching ligaments and tendons, strengthening and toning muscles, massaging fascia, etc. It also includes other guidance for physical health, hygiene, and well-being including how to maintain a healthy diet and lifestyle.

Under the umbrella of Tantra we also find many practices focused on psychological health, hygiene, and well-being. These practices are often called

Mantra. Mantra means guarding and cultivating the mind. In that sense, anyone who is studying or practicing some form of psychology is engaged in Mantra—caring for the mind. This would include what in the West is called psychiatry, psychology, and psychotherapy. There are Mantra practices meant to protect the mind from anxiety, depression, panic, addiction, and trauma. If we want genuine well-being, we need to care not only for the body but also for the mind. This includes the ultimate practice of protecting the mind from itself—that is from the proliferation and reification of misperceptions and mistaken constructs, and from unhealthy emotions and reactive habits, a protection that can only come from wisdom based on healing insights into impermanence, selflessness, and emptiness.

Finally, according to Tantra, the link between body and mind is energy, including the energy of the breath as well as the energy of the nervous system and body. So Tantra includes a wide range of practices for training life energy, including methods of controlling the breath and harnessing it to manage the energy of the nervous system and body. These are known as Yantra Yoga. Finally, the "Yoga" in Yoga Tantra refers to the way both Tantra and Mantra must work holistically to care for the whole human mind/body process in an integral way, offering an embodied approach to unifying mind, body, and energy around optimal health and well-being.

Tantra: The Inclusive Path for Everyone

The history of Tantra in India includes both Buddhist and Hindu Tantric traditions. Within Hindu Tantra, the most highly developed forms are found in the Kashmiri Shaivite tradition. The Buddhist Tantric tradition is the legacy of the world's first university at Nalanda, whose masters transmitted Tantra into Tibet, along with the Mahayana practice of compassion, and the profound philosophy of emptiness taught in the Middle Way (Madhyamika) and Mind-Only (Yogacara) schools (Wedemeyer, 2007).

Within the Nalanda Tantric tradition preserved in Tibet, there are several systems for categorizing different levels of Tantra. According to the tradition of the two newer schools of Tibetan Buddhism, there are four levels of Tantra: Action (Kriya), Integral (Yoga), Performance (Carya), and Highest Yoga Tantra (Anuttarayogatantra). The first three are considered lower, more introductory levels, while the Highest Yoga is considered the highest, most challenging, and most effective. You can think of these as forming a pyramid, with the three lower levels forming the base, and the fourth being the apex.

Action Tantra focuses on cultivating healthy external behavior, such as excellent hygiene, pure diet, careful, and devoted action. Integral Tantra focuses mainly on internal cultivation of the intuitive wisdom of emptiness and the profound, embodied bliss and joy that comes of accessing deeper levels of meditative concentration and absorption. Performance Tantra focuses on a combination of external behavior and internal mindset, adding to healthy lifestyle the cultivation of healthy inner states and qualities of mind, such as devotion, bliss, and joy. Finally, Highest Yoga Tantra focuses on cultivating profound intuitive wisdom, orgasmic bliss energy, and fully compassionate action touching equally on internal and external domains and pervading all levels of the body-mind.

The first three levels of Tantra empower practitioners to transform unhealthy habits of action, expression, perception, and motivation into qualities like healthy hygiene and lifestyle, devotion, wisdom, and compassion. But only the fourth, highest level of Tantra, can empower practitioners to fully awaken and transform all aspects and levels of mind, body, and energy, both internally and externally, allowing the complete realization and embodiment of full awakening. This is based in part on its methods of accessing and transforming the subtlest levels of mind, energy, and body by means of its art and science of working with the extremely subtle clear light mind and the blissful nervous system of the subtle body (Cozort, 2005). Since these levels of Tantra are all part of one family of practice, another way I think of them is as sisters, with the three introductory levels being little sisters, and the fourth, the big sister. What makes the big sister big is that she is open to everyone, and has practical solutions for all problems. The big sister doesn't discriminate about who we are, where we come from, our what our challenges are. Whether our challenge is caring for our body, our mind, our energy, or all three, the big sister of Highest Yoga Tantra is ready with powerful practices that can help us.

Once we recognize the main categories of Buddhist Tantra, we can begin to understand why this method of embodied contemplative healing is so inclusive. Tantra shares the main focus of ordinary Mahayana teaching (or Sutra)—cultivating and embodying non-dual wisdom and compassion—yet is more open, flexible, and friendly to lay practice in everyday life in the world while Sutric practice tends to be more geared to monastic life. For instance, while both Sutra and Tantra address the whole scope of human existence— birth and development, adult life, death and dying—Tantra offers many more explanations and practices geared to understanding and engaging with these different phases. These include practices related to sleep, dreams, death and dying, and sexuality that are easy to integrate into our normal, busy lay life.

Another inclusive aspect of Tantra is that it focuses on our embodied existence and energies as much as on the mind, and that it speaks to those embodied and energetic levels of our being through accessible arts. These go from medicine and psychiatry to aesthetic practices like visual and performing arts, and include a whole range of embodied mind/body practices like visualization, recitation, meditative gestures, breath exercises, posture yoga, and self-massage (Chenagtsang, 2020).

Another dimension of Tantra's inclusiveness is its openness to every human being, from all races, genders, and classes. This spirit of inclusion is clear from the way Tantra disregards and inverts the order of race and color, gender, and class built into the caste system and many societies. In Tantric art, the images of awakened beings come in all colors; and in the Kalachakra system of Highest Yoga Tantra, each of its awakened couples portrays the union of partners of different racial classes (varna), with the explicit message that diversity enhances creativity and society. When it comes to gender, there are as many images of awakened female beings as there are male counterparts, and the female images portray the same range of qualities—wisdom, compassion, meditative power, gentleness, ferocity, etc.—as the male images. In addition, the couple images do not just portray the union of male and female genders but also the different aspects of one human individual. This reflects the mixed male and female aspects of every human mind and body, as well as the third "mixed" or "intersex" gender which some scholars have aligned broadly with LGBTQ+ individuals and others more specifically with people who identify as bisexual, transgender, or non-binary. Conventional gender roles are also challenged in Tantra since people who identify as female commonly meditate on their bodies as male and as both in union, people who identify as male see themselves as female and both, and people who identify as neither male nor female see themselves in all three forms. Finally, the order of classes in the caste system is also inverted. Each of the four levels of Tantra is associated with one of the four social classes—Brahmin priests, warrior rulers, merchants, and workers—but the lowest Action Tantra is linked with the highest priest class, and the Highest Yoga Tantra with the worker class, the general public (Wallace, 2001).

The inclusiveness of Tantra is clear when it comes to the big sister, Highest Yoga Tantra, because a big sister doesn't care whether you're black or white, what gender you are, what your social status is, whether you're rich or poor. She cares for you because you are human, and honors you because she sees your human body as an Indivisible or Diamond Body (Vajra-Kaya). Since you have an Indivisible Body, you can practice the Indivisible Vehicle (Vajrayana), the most powerful vehicle of transformation. Given its power, the big sister first has to make sure that you will trust in yourself and believe in yourself deeply enough to engage in the practice.

Beyond pointing out that we have an Indivisible, Diamond Body within our coarse physical body, the Highest Yoga Tantra builds our trust and confidence in ourselves by trying to wake us up to the truth that the ultimate nature and essence of our body, energy, and mind is great bliss. Beyond any mere faith, beyond all philosophy, psychology, and ritual practice, great bliss is great because it transcends dualistic constructs like subject and object, mind and body, yours and mine. It is great because it provides the natural ground for our human capacity for profound and complete transformation. In fact, our innate capacity for great bliss is not only the basis of transformation but also the path that leads to transformation, as well as its final fruit. This profound teaching—that we are made of great bliss—is the ultimate method the big sister uses to build our trust and confidence in our capacity to completely transform ourselves and our lives. In this level of Tantric practice, we focus on accessing this essential reality, and this deep transformational path takes priority over other aims, such as ritual purity and good conduct, or communing with Tantric Buddha-Deities—the many archetypal images used in Tantra to help us envision a Buddha's full awakening. All these outward forms can easily distract us, so we have to go beyond even Buddha-Deity yoga to unite with our essential nature, the basic reality of primal blissful intuitive wisdom.

Finally, the Tantric tradition is inclusive because its many methods make it so flexible and open; it does not impose restrictions in the way the Sutric tradition does. We don't need to live a monastic lifestyle. Whoever you are, you can practice just as you are. Tantra is the kind of school that's open to everyone; anybody can access and receive the teachings so anybody can practice.

Troublemakers and Transformation: The Optimism of the Tantras

Where Sutra practice is most suitable for monks and nuns, Tantra is most suitable for lay people. One difference between monastics and lay people is that we lay people have more problems to deal with. In the monastery, you meditate, sleep, and never worry about paying the rent or having food, everything is free. What you do is train your mind, you meditate, and eventually you can help the lay people around you. But while the Sutra path can be very effective, it requires a lot of renunciation. We have to renounce not just material comforts, alcohol, and drugs, but even the attachments of love. As lay people, we don't want to develop addictions or have emotional dramas or traumas, but we are still human and want to experience life. We know that love is dangerous, but still we want to experience it, and in the course of living and loving, we create problems for ourselves and others. We have a different orientation from monastics, and that's why we lay people can think of ourselves as "the troublemakers" when we choose to live this life fully. Tantra is the path for us troublemakers, because it the path of transformation. Yes, we create problems but when problems arise, we don't crash and burn. We learn to use the negative things that happen and to transform them into positive things.

Tantra offers us good news. Everything can be transformed, so everything is possible. Once we can tap into the fundamental blissful nature of our bodies and minds, we can transform anything that afflicts us. With access to that primal power through the many methods of Tantra, we can use the mind to heal the mind, or we can use our energy to heal the mind, or we use the body to heal the mind. Likewise when the body is in trouble, given the many tools that help access our primal power, we can use the body to heal itself, or we can use energy to heal the body, or we can use a mind to heal the body. In the Tantric view—even though we may all be afflicted with different traumas—we may all have some version of post-traumatic stress disorder (PTSD) and we also have the methods to turn it into an opportunity for growth and transformation. With Tantra we can access what I call post-traumatic stress power—PTSP! This radical optimism, along with all the methods to back it up, may be the most important difference between Sutra and Tantra. Tantra empowers us to access deep strengths we didn't know we had to do something better with our lives. When we look at our lives, especially when we look around us at our society, we see so many problems. We have political problems, economic problems, health crises, relationship problems, family problems—everything is kind of a mess. Tantra and its optimism, based on its powerful transformational practices, can empower us to do something better with our personal lives and our society.

Highest Yoga Tantra: The Smart, Speedy Path

We're all aware of the trend in modern society for everyone to be constantly busy running towards happiness. And now we're becoming aware that all that running isn't actually leading towards happiness. That's when we turn towards a more spiritual life and practice, which normally tells us to slow down. Unfortunately, given the pace of everyday life in our society, if we really slow down, we often cause ourselves other problems. According to

Tantra, practitioners don't necessarily need to slow down; we can keep pace with our busy lives yet still stay on a spiritual path, provided we practice in a really smart way. The big sister, Highest Yoga Tantra says, "If you're going to engage in spiritual practice in the midst of your fast paced life, fine—just be smart about it." Do you drive a smart car? Do you have a smartphone? Do you have smart TV? Why not get a smart spiritual practice?

Through the smart path of Tantra, we can make quick progress while still avoiding accidents, because Tantra offers methods that allow us to protect our mind, energy, and body from the negativity that causes harm. In a sense, Sutra is like allopathic medicine—it directly targets and counteracts our afflictions. Tantra offers a homeopathic path—it allows us to work with the strong forces of our body, energy, and mind that might cause harm and instead harness and channel their power into accelerated healing and development. Sutra says we're going too fast, slow down; Tantra says, yes, we're going too fast, so we need to work smarter. So, if like me, you choose to follow a spiritual path in the world, you may need to learn Tantra's smart meditation techniques to speed your path. Of course, when we say quick, we're not talking about overnight results. The path of Tantra still takes diligent practice and sustained commitment, but compared with Sutra, which is said to work only gradually over many eons, the Tantric path promises that we can reach full, embodied awakening in the course of this one present lifetime.

The Medical Science of Tantra: Caring for Our Human Mind

Tantra is known as the path of deep emotional transformation. Yet actually, we humans naturally know how to transform our emotions. Even small children are able to learn to access their power to transform their emotions. We humans are blessed with a nature that is innately self-healing. We notice how our body heals itself; and know our immune system protects our body from infection and illnesses. Our minds and energies also tend to be naturally self-healing. We have a kind of mental and emotional immune system that operates on its own. This profound insight is built into Tantra, which is like an ancient wisdom or secret doctrine of self-healing. Of course, it's still true of our nature even if we've never heard of Tantra. That's why healing doesn't have to be allopathic, like an intervention that fixes things mechanically. Some healing needs to happen organically, homeopathically. Even if we may need to give it a little push to get it started or lend support to sustain it, the deepest healing more or less works by itself. I think psychotherapy is like that. We push a little to help get the healing started, we lend support to help sustain it, but in the end the mind naturally heals itself (Loizzo, 2012).

Within Tantric medical science, we make a distinction between helping people heal their mind with mind—as in conventional psychotherapy—and helping people heal the mind with their body or with their breath energy. The strictly mind approach, like talk therapy, we call Mantra; the embodied or energetic approach we call Tantra. In one embodied approach, we work with the body to balance our neural energy, and that more balanced energy naturally helps the mind to become more balanced. So when it's too complicated to use the mind to heal the mind, Tantra lets us take a step back, and try to shift and balance the energy, using breath practices like pranayama, to indirectly heal the mind. This practice is based on something very simple, very organic—inhalation and exhalation—a basic sign of life. The living body has bioenergy and this bioenergy—operating in the nervous system and other mind/body systems—sustains consciousness and so supports insight. So in Tantric medicine and psychiatry, we use breath control to access the mind-energy body (also known as the subtle body or Diamond Body), and then work with that subtle energy body to heal the mind. Of course Tantric medicine recognizes many different kinds of energies that run various systems in the living body—such as the cardiovascular system, respiratory system, digestive system, and nervous system—but the most essential energy is the life supporting energy of the breath (Loizzo et al., 2009). Without breath, we have no bioenergy.

In addition to using breath energy to heal the mind, Tantra also offers many other embodied practices that allow us to use the body to indirectly heal the mind. These Tantric practices offer a third approach to healing the mind. They include systems of posture yoga and self-massage, which work like physical exercise or physical therapy to promote health and well-being, mental as well as physical. Since a sedentary lifestyle predisposes us to anxiety and depression, we have to get our body moving through aerobic exercise, yoga, biking, hiking, whatever. Of the three approaches, whichever method makes most sense for any given individual at any particular time is best.

Our Inner Alchemy Can Turn Poison into Medicine

Anger, desire, and confusion. These three states of mind are what we call the three mental poisons. They are seen in Buddhist psychology as the roots of both mental and physical illness. Tracing mental and physical ills to three poisons is very interesting, because science today tells us that a large part of our physical and mental health problems is related to chronic stress and trauma. Why are we so prone to stress? When we look at the psychology of stress, that's where we find the three poisons at work. Desire can be a good emotion, when it leads to healthy attachment or love, but it's such a powerful energy that when we don't know how to control it, it can lead to the psychologically stressful states of anxiety, panic, clinging, lust, and craving. Likewise, anger can be healthy when it steps in to protect us from physical or psychological harm, but it's also so powerful that, uncontrolled, it can lead to stressful states of frustration, resentment, rage, hatred, and even self-hatred. What about confusion? Confusion or misperception is actually at the root of both desirous and angry emotions, so in a sense it is the root of all forms of stress. When we overestimate the extent and constancy of the pleasure we expect from people and things we desire, it leads to stressful mind states like anxiety, panic, or craving. And when we overestimate how threatened we are by a person or thing that evokes anger, it routinely leads to stressful mind states like resentment, hatred, and rage. Modern science has shown in great detail the negative impact of chronic exposure to the fight-or-flight, faint-or-freeze response to stress, and these toxic reactions clearly relate to the emotional poisons of unhealthy anger and desire (McEwen & Lasley, 2002). At the same time current science has also shown that underlying the stress response is confusion—distorted worst-case perception that overestimates how threatening challenges are and underestimates our capacity to meet them.

The fact that these three toxic forces lie at the root of the majority of our mental and physical disorders is basic to Tantric medicine, which considers them the primary cause of all disease, with the secondary cause being diet and lifestyle (Rapgay, 2005). It is also basic to the transformational method of Tantric healing, which provides us with the methods and practices we need to harness and channel the power of emotional states like anger, desire, and confusion. So the fundamental framework of Tantric healing is not just homeopathic but also alchemical. It starts with the basic nature of our potentially toxic emotional states, applies practices that offer a path of working to transform those states, and finally yields the fruit of a new capacity to turn these common poisons into medicine—the healing forces of assertiveness, love, and wisdom.

Tantric Yogas as Homeopathic Medicines

In the Sutric forms of Buddhist psychology, we see powerful emotions like anger and desire negatively as poisons—as the root of our problems. And it's true that when we're unable to recognize and control our emotions, they can end up becoming very destructive. But in Tantra, we don't consider anger, desire, or even confusion as negative emotions. Yes, we may call them poisons, but we know that poison can be both good and bad. As we know from modern chemistry, all chemicals can be poisons, but dangerous chemicals can also make the best medicines. Whether they are poisons or medicines depends on how they are used. This is precisely the view of Tantra. Tantra adopted the ancient chemical tradition of alchemy that India shared with the West, based on the insight that everything is transformable (White, 1996). In Tantra, however, the system of alchemy is internalized. Tantra teaches an inner alchemy, based on transformations that take place within the human mind, energy, and subtle body.

As in chemistry, trying to work with poisons can cause harm, unless we know precisely what we're doing and have the necessary skill. For that we need not just a few books or workshops but a whole education. That is how Tantra works—by providing a rigorous education and training in how to transform the three poisons into medicine. That is why we find systems that categorize Tantric practices according to which of the three poisons they help us transform. In the early classification system of the Nyingma tradition, for instance, the three types of Tantric Yoga—Maha-Yoga, Anu-Yoga, and Ati-Yoga—are prescribed to help us transform anger, desire, and confusion. That is why Maha-Yoga practices have us meditate on ourselves as wild, wrathful, mainly male deities—to own and transform anger, while Anu-Yoga practices have us meditate on ourselves as sensuous, passionate, mainly female deities to own and transform desire. And it is why Ati-Yoga practices focus on accessing the primal blissful awareness that is our essential nature directly, without binary constructions like fierce or loving, male or female, self or other, angry or desirous—to own and transform confusion. Within the new classification system, the three categories—Father Tantra, Mother Tantra, and Non-Dual Tantra—are prescribed in a similar way (Wedemeyer, 2007).

Freeing Yourself from Past, Future, and Present

In Highest Yoga Tantra we find two main paths of meditation: Creation Stage meditation (Skt. Utpatti-krama; Tib. bsKyed-rim) and Completion Stage meditation (Skt. Nispanna-krama; Tib. rDzogs-rim). So the path has two stages: first, we fix our past; and then we fix our future. What happens after both stages of the path are complete? We are free from all the conditionings of the past—from the karma of our multi-life evolution and of this life's development—and we are also free from the future we would have had based on that conditioning. It means we are free from now on to write our own future, since without dealing with the past we cannot really be open to the future, because we are bound by the imprints of so many memories, dramas, and traumas. Once our mind is fully open, we are free to see the past, future, and present simultaneously without conditioning. We are not only free from our conditioned perception of the past and future but even free from the present, from any conditioned sense of the here and now.

In this sense, Tantra opens the door to a kind of psychological time travel. We are free to travel back into our past, to purify our perception and rewrite it; free to travel into the future, to the moment of our death, to purify our perception and write a new destiny. When we can purify the conditionings of stress and trauma, remove the poisons from our minds, we can live life fearlessly, not stressed about what has happened or what will happen. And this leaves us feeling freedom here and now. We can see how the here and now includes the past and includes the future. That's how we can begin to rewrite the whole picture of our human life. With the Creation Stage we rewrite the story of who we are, where we came from, and where we're going—we travel back to free the past. And with the Completion Stage, we transform the embodied way of being that shapes our individual destiny—we travel ahead to free the future. So altogether, it's complete—we see our lives around all 360 degrees and I'm free from all my dramas and traumas, and free from the poisons that afflict me. This completeness is the fruit of Tantra. So now let's look at how it all works.

Preliminaries: Stable Roots, Strong Tree

As I've said, if we want to learn or practice Tantra, it is vital that we remember to strengthen our roots, otherwise our practice will be unstable and ungrounded, and will not bear fruit. The preliminaries required for a stable Tantric practice are grouped into three broad categories—common, uncommon, and routine. The broader context for understanding these preliminaries is that the Nalanda tradition of Buddhist psychology preserved in Tibet sees the contemplative path as a unified journey with progressive stages of healing and healthy development. Since Tantra is considered the most advanced practice, which yields the final result or fruit of the path, in order to be truly stable and fruitful, it must be grounded on the more basic paths of Sutra, which nurture the causes or roots of awakening. Sutra includes two fundamental forms of practice—the practice of renunciation called the Individual Vehicle

(Theravada) and the practice of compassion called the Universal Vehicle (Mahayana). Without being deeply rooted in renunciation and compassion, the Indivisible, Diamond Vehicle (Vajrayana) of Tantra cannot bear fruit. So in the Nalanda tradition, we practice respecting the unity of Sutra and Tantra, that is, we practice the three vehicles as one gradual path (Yarnall, 2013). This is absolutely vital.

Practicing the common, uncommon, and routine preliminaries together is one way the three vehicles act as one gradual path. The common preliminaries are reflections from the basic paths of Sutra derived from the Four Noble Truths—the basic framework of all Buddhist Psychology and healing—and promote the first main prerequisite for successful practice of Highest Yoga Tantra—renunciation. The uncommon preliminaries are specifically Tantric and promote the second and third main prerequisites for successful practice of Highest Yoga Tantra—the capacity for compassion, and the profound wisdom of selflessness and emptiness. The routine preliminaries take the reflections on renunciation, compassion, and wisdom explored in the common and uncommon preliminaries, and shift them from aspirational states to foundational traits we actively engage in all the activities of our daily lives. What follows is a more detailed description of the three categories of preliminaries.

The Common Preliminaries

The common preliminaries involve four successive reflections on the nature of life based on the foundation of the Four Noble Truths. They are meant to promote a deep motive of renouncing our poisons and the whole way of life driven by them. The first reflection is on appreciating the preciousness and full potential of life, especially this human life which allows us to learn, grow, and transform our fundamental way of being. Secondly, we need to reflect on the challenging reality that, however precious this life is, it is not permanent but transient and impermanent. Whatever happens, we need to practice facing and accepting the fact that we ourselves and everyone and everything else are constantly changing and transforming, that change is the very process and fabric of life, and that eventually we all die, and all things pass. Thirdly, while everything is always changing, that change is not causeless or random, but moves according to laws of causation that govern the way all change occurs.

In Buddhist science, causality does not just govern the physical dimension of nature, but also the biological, psychological, and social dimensions of life.

So this third reflection focuses on the causal laws by which our own intentional actions or karmas shape our ways of thinking, speaking, acting, and living. Specifically, the laws of karma mean that our intentional actions are either directing the change in our lives towards bondage and suffering or towards freedom and happiness. Seeing the way our own minds direct the course of our lives, through the causality of intentional action, leads to the fourth reflection. Even if we can improve our lives by cultivating healthy habits, we cannot find freedom from unconscious life (samsara) and hence real, lasting happiness, unless and until our minds can transform the poisons of confusion, anger, and desire into medicine. From a Buddhist perspective, the human condition driven by the three poisons is actually considered an insidious chronic disease we can treat, even when it offers a wide array of experiences of fleeting happiness. This reflection leads us to the urge towards the real, lasting freedom and happiness called Nirvana, the third Noble Truth, and moves us to engage in the Fourth Truth, the path of self-healing. These reflections are meant to promote renunciation, the first main prerequisite for a successful Highest Yoga Tantra practice.

The Uncommon Preliminaries

The uncommon preliminaries include a series of seven specifically Tantric preliminaries that work to prime the mind, energy, and body to be able to successfully engage and sustain the challenging practice of Highest Yoga Tantra. These seven practices are meant to promote the second main prerequisite for successful practice of Highest Yoga Tantra—the positive emotional capacity for compassion. At the same time some of these practices, especially the seventh, also promote the third main prerequisite for Highest Yoga Tantra—the profound wisdom of selflessness and emptiness. All seven of these uncommon practices are specifically Tantric in two ways: they involve an embodied dimension such as verbal recitation, embodied movement, or gestures; and they involve embodied learning through repetition of the practice, most commonly up to 100,000 times.

The first of the uncommon preliminaries is taking Tantric refuge, which adds an embodied dimension to the common practice of taking refuge in Buddha, Dharma, and Sangha, namely: adding a fourth refuge in the Guru or living Mentor who embodies all three other refuges. The practice involves committing to becoming a Tantric Mentor who embodies all refuge by emulating one's own Mentor. The second is cultivating the spirit of awakening (bodhicitta), which harnesses the energy of great compassion—unconditional compassion for all beings—to generate the altruistic resolve to embody awakening in order to inspire everyone to seek their own individual and collective awakening. The third uncommon preliminary is an embodied practice of humility, conscientiousness, and devotion—prostrating oneself before the community of Buddhas, Bodhisattvas, Tantric Mentors, and Deities as an act of releasing pride, acknowledging one's limits and faults, and requesting the aid and blessings of the awakened community.

The fourth uncommon preliminary is an embodied practice of generosity, devotion, and dedication—ritually recreating the whole universe including the microcosm of one's body in order to offer it repeatedly to the whole community of the awakened. The fifth uncommon preliminary is an embodied practice of commitment and engagement—ritually circumambulating a sacred reliquary (stupa) symbolizing Shakyamuni Buddha's fully embodied awakening. This practice cultivates the positive energy needed to travel the path of awakening through Highest Yoga Tantra. The sixth uncommon preliminary is an embodied practice of acknowledging and transforming negative habits rooted in the three poisons—reciting the 100-syllable confessional mantra in the visualized presence of the whole awakened community. The seventh and last uncommon preliminary is an embodied practice of the wisdom of selflessness and emptiness—the ritual of repeatedly cutting (Tib. chod) the root of confusion, the self-protective instinct to see our bodies and ourselves as separate, fixed, and central, by rehearsing in words and images the ritual sacrifice and transformation of our gross physical body into an elixir of awakening we offer to nurture and heal all beings.

These uncommon preliminaries all work together to strengthen the two capacities that will protect us from the most serious risk of Tantra, namely— misusing the power of its practices to inflate our ego, pride, entitlement, desire, or anger rather than to dismantle and transform them into embodied awakening. Those two vital capacities are the great compassion which seeks to free all beings, and the profound wisdom of selflessness and emptiness that matures and guides that compassion.

The Routine Preliminaries

The last category of preliminaries for Highest Yoga Tantra, the routine preliminaries, includes a range of embodied practices of continuous altruistic engagement with all the individuals and communities we meet in the course of our day-to-day lives. These eight practices include: supporting spiritual teachers and communities; offering material aid to those who need it; providing free healthcare and medicine for those who can't afford them; offering free spiritual teaching; saving human and animal lives; restoring spiritual institutions and spaces; improving public facilities like roads; teaching widely; and hosting spiritual gatherings. These "routine" practices take the common reflections on the importance of mental and spiritual development and the uncommon practices for cultivating renunciation, compassion and wisdom beyond theory and good intentions to the level of daily activities. These simple forms of daily practice help practitioners evolve from mere aspirational compassion to a fully, actively engaged compassion, supporting the gradual development of an altruistic way of being that is not just psychological but also energetic and fully embodied. This kind of development is the foundation we need to avoid the risks of Tantric practice being co-opted by our poisons and to build the solid grounding for a stable, successful, and fully embodied practice of transformation.

Although these preliminary practices are absolutely necessary for a grounded, fruitful Tantric practice, they are not sufficient. Full protection from the very real risks of misusing the powerful methodology of the Tantras requires all practitioners, however well-meaning, well-educated, or well-prepared, to form an intimate relationship with another human being who is qualified to serve as their Mentor or guide on the path. In fact, the capacities the preliminaries help develop are vital precisely because they give practitioners the stable personal qualities it takes to form and maintain a mentoring bond with an expert practitioner, a Diamond Master who has successfully travelled the Highest Yoga Tantra path. Although the Buddha taught that we must all become our own masters, both Sutra and Tantra depend on our having the wisdom of proper refuge—to know that we need to rely on more experienced teachers and guides until we are ready to step into that role for ourselves and others. So at the beginning of the Tantric path, our self-reliance involves humbly understanding that we need to train in the preliminaries to be truly ready for practice, and wisely choosing a mentor who has the knowledge, experience, and integrity to help insure that we use the power of Tantric practice skillfully and effectively.

Initiation: Empowered Seed, Ripening Fruit

Initiation, often translated as empowerment, is a very interesting concept. Traditionally, it goes back to the Buddha's early life as a prince. In ancient India, when a prince or princess came of age and the King and Queen were ready to step down, the prince or princess would undergo a ritual of empowerment or consecration which pronounced them the new King or Queen. So the ritual of initiation that empowers us to practice the Tantra is modeled on this royal consecration, except it doesn't matter what our ordinary social status is—what our race, class, gender, or lineage. According to the Tantra, every single one of us should be empowered as if we have the throne for ourselves. So the empowerment is really like an enthronement process in that it's designed to give you self-confidence and self-trust. Developing that trust is what we call "ripening the seed;" it means really recognizing that this is your life, it is entirely, in your hands. Remember, like a fruit, it takes time for us to fully ripen. It's vital that we know ourselves, know our own nature, and that we let ourselves experience life deeply, so we have the time it takes to become mature like a ripened fruit.

In this sense, since the actual ripening or development takes time, the empowerment really offers a wake-up call that helps us recognize that we are the kind of fruit that can and will ripen, that is—we have the potential for full awakening. As part of that wake-up call, empowerment helps us understand the process—the path of practice—by which our potential will gradually come to fruition in full liberation. It also gives us a preview of the teachings, the instructions on how to practice, that will empower us to undertake and complete the process of development that results in our fully embodied awakening. So the empowerment reveals to us that our life is really like a beautiful seed, planted in fertile soil, and it shows us how that seed will be nurtured by sunlight, clean water, fresh air, and rich soil, and how it will naturally grow, unfold, and ripen. It tells us that we are like teenagers, ripe for full development; that there's nothing wrong with us, nothing missing; that now is our time to manifest who we really are.

Of course, some people think that just being empowered will be enough to ripen our potential, as if they don't need to do much to support that ripening. In that case, we gradually lose our initial awakening, motivation, and power. In order to maintain it, to keep it fresh, we must commit to doing a little bit of practice every day. That is how you protect your empowerment and nurture the ripening of your potential over time. Remember at bottom we are talking about a fundamental transformation of our way of being and living through an inner alchemy of our poisonous habits of mind, energy, and body into the blissful wisdom energy and awareness.

In the Highest Yoga Tantra, empowerment includes five distinct parts: the Vase empowerment; the Secret empowerment; the Wisdom empowerment; the Word empowerment; and the Total empowerment. Traditionally, each empowerment is connected with a specific chakra within the subtle body. The

Vase empowerment is connected with the crown chakra; the Secret empowerment is connected with the throat chakra; the Wisdom empowerment is connected with the heart chakra; the Word empowerment is connected with the navel chakra; and the Total empowerment is connected with the base or root chakra. Each chakra also holds a specific seed syllable that represents the subtle mind, energy, and drops that work within the subtle body.

So the five empowerments together point out the five basic elements tainted by the five poisons (confusion, desire, anger, pride, and envy), which our practice must purify and transform into our full awakening. At the same time, they also give us basic instruction in, and permission to, practice the methods that will help us transform our poisoned mind, energy, and body into medicine. Specifically: the Vase empowerment permits us to practice visualizing ourselves as Buddha-Deities and our world as their Mandala; the Secret empowerment permits us to practice mantra recitation, which transforms our thought and energy into a Mentor's thought and energy; the Wisdom empowerment permits us to practice sublimating sexual energy into a Mentor's pure joy and bliss; the Word empowerment permits us to practice the Great Seal, which transforms our awareness into a Mentor's ultimate non-dual wisdom of emptiness; and the Total empowerment permits us to integrate our whole being into a Diamond Mentor's.

According to the alchemical framework of the Highest Yoga Tantra, the depth psychology of the fundamental shift we are empowered to practice is spelled out in terms of the transformation of the five poisons into five intuitive wisdoms. At the crown, confusion is transformed into the Wisdom of the Dharma Realm. At the throat, desire is transformed into the Discriminating Wisdom. At the heart, anger is transformed into the Mirror-like Wisdom. At the navel, pride is transformed into the Wisdom of Equality. And at the base, envy is transformed into the Accomplishing Wisdom (Thurman, 2010).

So this is what empowerment means. It's kind of ritual in which we are really enthroned in our own potential for transformation. At the same time, it also helps you access and open your subtle body channels and chakras, so that you can really see and feel for the first time—through guided meditation—that it is possible for you to transform your inner poisons into the nectars of the five wisdoms. So it's not just a ritual, but a real teaching based on the guided meditations that give you a felt sense of the meaning and power of the Tantric path. That's the psychological transformation—the inner alchemy—you're empowered to practice. Of course, the first time you experience this empowerment, you should receive it from a qualified Mentor. Afterwards, based on maintaining daily commitments to practice, you eventually become able to empower yourself with the help of an imaginary Mentor. This is called self-empowerment—it's as if your Mentor showed you how to open the door to your potential, then once you've learned how to open it, you go through it every day until you truly realize your inner Buddha-nature, your inner Mentor (Berzin, 2010).

Creation Stage Meditation

In the Creation Stage—the first stage of Highest Yoga Tantra—we practice re-envisioning ourselves and our environment, starting with revising our self-image in the image of an awakened Buddha-Deity. In a sense, the practice is like modifying your perception and revising your story through the processes of rebirthing or regenerating yourself as a strong, empowered, protected, high performance figure. The template for your self-creation depends on which Tantric deity you've been empowered to practice. Each form has a precise impact, helping us transform specific poisons into wisdoms. The actual meditation works similarly to the Sutric practice combining concentrative meditation with analytic insight, although the method of the creation stage uses visualizations and mantra recitation instead.

Creation Stage practice is specifically done to clean up and heal our past. So we usually begin by imagining everything inside and outside us restored to a primordial void or emptiness. It's as if you've traveled back in time, to the beginning of your personal life, the beginning of human existence, the dawn of the planet, or the origin of the universe. There we imagine emerging out of the void a lotus, symbolizing the origin of matter or the mother's womb. Then at the center of the lotus we envision a solar disc and a lunar disc, symbolizing sun and moon, or the egg and the sperm, coming together. Then out of the discs there emerges a syllable or hand implement, symbolizing our consciousness, which finally transforms into the Deity that is our Buddha-self. So it's as if through the Creation Stage we imagine ourselves to be a creator God or the universe itself, and then retrace the causal process of our evolution and development until finally we are reborn as completely awakened Buddhas, such as the lapis blue Medicine Buddha.

What is the psychology of the Creation Stage? It's as if our whole sense of ourselves and our lives, everything we've learned until now, is like a bad case of PTSD. The really beautiful thing in the creation stage is that, by going back in time, and separating our minds from everything we've learned along the way, we can start over to recreate our sense of ourselves and our whole life and world in a totally mindful, caring, and positive way. We started out stuck in our dramas and traumas, but we end up manifesting as a Buddha, free from the past and fully open to the present and future. Everything is good here and now, and we can access our full energy, our full wisdom, our full power, and our full compassion.

Why are there so many Buddhas and Deities? They all represent the many aspects of our human nature. We humans emerge from nature, like the forest. We talk about biodiversity—just look at the Amazon, filled with so many different kinds of trees, flowers, lifeforms, all harmonizing together to make a beautiful rainforest. This is exactly how we should create our human minds and societies—celebrating our complexity and harmonizing our diversity. So the really beautiful thing about the Creation Stage, where we find so many different Buddha-Deities, is that it represents the rich diversity of our human nature and potential. If you look at ancient Greek mythology, it's very similar. If we embrace the diversity of life, we can always find our own version of Buddha, representing our particular potential for fully embodied awakening. If we are involved in the healing field, we have the Medicine Buddha. If we are interested in feminine energy, we have the Goddess Tara. If we're interested in leadership, we have Vajrapani. If we're interested in maximal flexibility, we can visualize ourselves as different Buddha-Deities. In the end, the Creation Stage is really a rich and complex self-psychology, where we can learn, practice, and manifest for ourselves and others the full range of our rich and complex human potential.

Guru, Deity, Dakini: Three Creation Stage Yogas to Free The Mind

In the Yuthog Nyingthig tradition, formulated by the great Tibetan Tantric scholar-healer Yuthog Yonten Gonpo (1126–1202), we practice the Creation Stage through three yogas: the Yoga of the Mentor (Guru); the Yoga of the Meditation Deity (Devata); and the Yoga of the Wisdom Goddess (Dakini) (Chenagtsang, 2016). Mentor Yoga connects you with the inspirational energy of your empowerment, and focuses on the Mentor as an external support or mirror of your transformation. Through the Yoga of the Meditational Deity, you transform yourself into the form of a chosen Buddha image (Yeshe, 2014). Through the Yoga of the Wisdom Goddess, you connect with the blissful energy and awareness that allows you to transform your poisons into wisdoms (Gray, 2007). This particular progression reflects the fact that most Tantric practitioners in the past have been male, and may tend to pick a male

Meditation Deity. That, plus the traditional link between ultimate wisdom and femininity, explains why the yoga of transforming bliss energy into wisdom is linked with a female form. Of course, female practitioners may tend to choose a feminine Meditation Deity, in which case connecting with blissful energy and awareness may involve using a male Wisdom Deity (Daka) (Shaw, 2022). So the progression from Mentor to Deity to God or Goddess doesn't actually depend on the gender of the figures we meditate on, or on whether those figures are fierce, peaceful, or joyful. It simply reflects our progression from the more basic phase of Creation Stage practice to more advanced stages.

One key function of the Creation Stage is to build our power to maintain our inner peace of mind without being controlled by external factors. In this practice, we try to free ourselves from conditioned reactions to our environment, like what is going on with our family, our work, our community, or our society at large. It's not that we're trying to ignore these factors or avoid the need to cope with or change them. Of course we need to cope and change them, but we will have much more energy and capacity to do that if we are not overwhelmed or controlled by external events. Changing external conditions takes time—we need to be patient. That's why it's best to change ourselves first, to prepare our own minds, so that we're ready for the outer change we are working towards. When we can visualize, we transform our perception of ourselves and the world so that we can stay unconditionally calm, present, and mindful. This way everything stays clear for us, we have a clear direction. Otherwise, there are so many ways in which we are conditioned by external events, like the news; so if we can't protect our minds, we get confused. That's why we need the Creation Stage to help us wake up, calm down, and get ready to make change.

Five Types of Guru Yoga

As a reminder, we practice three types of yogas in the Creation Stage. The first is Guru Yoga. So what is Guru Yoga in a simple way? What is a Guru and what isn't? Guru Yoga is a practice for getting an extra boost of energy to help you speed up the alchemy of deep transformation in smarter and faster ways. Traditionally, this practice involves five types of Gurus:

1. The Outer Guru—the human teacher and guide, who can act as a doctor, a provocateur, a road, a bridge, a vehicle, and a driver.
2. The Lineage Gurus—the ancestral lineage of mentors who have transmitted embodied wisdom from the Medicine Buddha down to our own Outer Guru, like an unbroken streaming wireless internet.

3. The Black Guru that never gets angry—the texts that empower us to learn, contemplate, and meditate on Highest Yoga Tantra.
4. The Guru of All Things—life as the teacher that every day offers perfect instruction, from positive experiences that make for good life to negative experiences that carry good lessons.
5. The Inner Guru of Awareness—the optimal function of our human brain, experienced as pure orgasmic bliss and open, luminous, non-dual, and all-pervasive awareness.

This teaching of five types of Guru is vital because normally we tend to get fixated on one person. The word "Guru" in the Indian tradition literally means "elder" or "heavy," but in Buddhism, it really refers to the light of guidance, the light that opens our eyes. Of course, the Outer Guru is our spiritual master, guiding us, helping us, supporting us, and teaching us so many things. But in reality, one person is only one small part of our whole learning process. The outer human teacher is part of a larger living system like a tree within a forest. Like any one tree, the teacher is there because of a lineage—a continuum of prior teachers that stretches back many lifetimes to the tree of the Buddha's own awakening. And like any tree, in order for the Outer Guru to be non-harmful and truly helpful, we need to know how to rely on that person—in what way, at what time, for what purpose—otherwise like a tree the Guru can be poison and not medicine. I love the way Yuthog also teaches us to rely on books as Black Gurus, since unlike human teachers our texts don't have feelings or personal quirks we have to be concerned with. The fact that they teach us impartially and impersonally can empower us to grapple with them more freely and deeply.

As for the Guru of All Things, I always believe our best Guru is our own life. We learn about theories, about philosophy, about science, we can learn so many things but it can easily remain theoretical. Life is different—it can be tough, it can be ugly, it can be beautiful, but as we experience it, life can be a very powerful learning process. The Guru of life allows us to have a wider understanding; and it's also the Guru who is always with us, 24 hours a day, seven days a week, 365 days a year—it covers everything, like a rainbow, and it is always teaching.

Last but not least, there's the Inner Guru. I compared the Outer Guru who empowers us to the one who opens the door for us. Once someone outside us opens that door, we know we can open our own inner door. That's our Inner Guru. Some people talk about the true self, our physical individuality, but from a Buddhist point of view, that self is constantly changing. But deeper inside us there is this profound self that is our universal self—our blissful, non-dual wisdom awareness. Once you see that as your own nature, you are seeing your Inner Guru, your Buddha-nature, your Inner Goddess, your Inner God. That is the natural basis for our capacity for conscious transformation and awakening, the real god-like wisdom and creativity symbolized by all Tantric Deities. Say I have a very precious glass from my grandmother, but suddenly I get distracted and it's broken. I could blame you because you distracted me, or I could see it as a Guru, teaching me that everything is always changing. The breaking glass has become my Guru, and because my Inner Guru listens and sees the light, I realize one more moment of freedom.

Recreating Oneself as a Buddha-Deity

The most interesting aspect of the Creation Stage is that it empowers and guides us to recreate ourselves and our lives. Specifically, in the creation stage we recreate ourselves in the form of our own Chosen Deity (Skt. Ishtam-Devata; Tib. Yid-dam). Literally this means a divine archetype or ideal self-image we prefer, choose, and hold close, like our own inmost core or secret lover. Why visualize ourselves in the form of a Buddha-Deity? This profound practice serves as way to counteract and expand our own limiting image, concept, or story of ourselves. When I visualize myself as a Buddha-Deity, I have this feeling that I'm free from this body and my habitual mindset. I feel I'm somebody more than myself—I can do more, I can feel more, I can always be better, and I can always be useful. Physically, I'm here as usual, but energetically and mentally I experience an expansion. This expansion is one of the enhancements referred to by the essential meaning of the word of Tantra. And the expansion is not just helpful for ourselves as individuals.

Once we can see ourselves and practice manifesting as a Buddha, it can help us to change our whole world, and this is the main reason to see ourselves as a Buddha, a Deity, as pure love and light, and so on. This expansion of our potential to manifest love and light empowers us to recognize and actively engage the full potential of our whole living environment. It does not stop with seeing only ourselves as Buddhas or Deities—in the Creation Stage we practice seeing every other living being in the same way. This is a powerful practice of equanimity—we're equal to everyone and need to share whatever we have, since the root of our existence is interdependence. Without understanding this, we never can be 100 percent happy, right? If we're happy but our partner isn't happy, our kids are not happy, our friends or neighbors are not happy, then our happiness is a kind of transient, small happiness. So if we want to be more able to share our happiness by helping others, we can begin by expanding our limited sense of our own capability. That's Buddha-Deity Yoga (Yarnall, 2013).

Of course, imagining we are Buddhas or Deities doesn't make us Buddhas or Gods. So one could say in Deity Yoga we're just pretending or faking. In a sense, that's true, but if you look deeper, there are very tangible benefits that come from changing our outlook and mindset. For one thing, simply replacing our habitual, limiting self-image and self-concept with a more expansive, empowering image and concept of ourselves can help us see possibilities and access capacities we otherwise assumed were not there. When children do imaginative play, seeing themselves as the queen or king, they are transported into that other dimension, free from the limiting ideas and stories of the adults around them. And those early experiences of play can have a powerful impact on their development. Likewise when we practice the Creation Stage and choose to identify with any Buddha or Deity we feel drawn to, it can transport our hearts and minds to another plane of our own adult development. One of our biggest problems as humans is the way we get stuck with ourselves, we can't get away from ourselves. Since we all have too many problems, too much stress, too much drama, and too many traumas, we find ourselves trapped in our own past, and in our own stress-conditioned present lives. Carrying this burden as "I," "me," "mine," is not only limiting and exhausting, but blocks our capacity to keep developing in new ways that expand our ability to cope with our own problems, others' problems, and the collective problems we share. This is often the predicament people face when they want to kill themselves—they've become their problems and can only imagine freedom by eliminating the self they feel stuck in. So the practice of Buddha-Deity Yoga allows us to take a more expansive, creative break from ourselves. If we don't just try it once but meditate on that expanded sense of self every day, even for just for five to ten minutes, we would not only be able take a fresh look at ourselves and our lives, but gradually see and pursue possibilities we couldn't see before.

Finally, when it comes to the many Buddha images and Deity images to choose from, the diversity is meant to help us access and cultivate specific human qualities. For instance, the form of the Bodhisattva Avalokiteshvara is meant to help expand our capacity for embodied love and compassion. Each of his four arms symbolizes one of the four immeasurable emotions—love, compassion, joy, and equanimity. From the standpoint of Buddhist psychology, these four qualities are the foundation of health and well-being, benefiting both the individual and all those around them, not only all humans but animals and the planet as well.

While Avalokiteshvara specifically focuses on the embodiment of love and compassion, this focus is also the basis for all the different spiritual manifestations in the Tantras. Without cultivating and embodying love and compassion, the Tantras, especially the Highest Yoga Tantras, can be dangerous and leave people prone to misusing it (Yeshe, 2014). This is why any form of Mahayana Buddhism, Sutra, or Tantra, focuses on developing a positive motivation—the spirit of awakening compassion and altruism, in Sanskrit, Bodhichitta. Once we have that as a foundation, we may be drawn to Buddha-Deity images that manifest compassion in many different forms. Some forms are peaceful, expressing the gentle face of love and compassion, like the Medicine Buddha or the female Buddha Tara. But sometimes we also need to access the deeper sources of love and compassion—the capacity to transform desire into love and compassion. That second form of Buddha-Deity image is considered blissful or joyful—it often shows the male and female faces of awakening embracing as a couple. These are also called images of male-female union or communion (Gray, 2007). The third main type of Buddha-Deity images are fierce or wrathful, symbolizing the transformation of anger into tough love or fierce compassion. Although anger can be a destructive emotion, essentially it's an energy whose impact depends on how we embody it, how we use it. An example of this kind of wrathful Buddha-Deity is the fierce flame red male Buddha Hayagriva.

Of course, the peaceful Buddha-Deity images tend to be easier to relate to for my Judeo-Christian friends, despite their multiple forms and unusual features, like many arms or faces. But when we get to the joyful Buddha-Deities in union and the fierce Buddha-Deities, they can strike people as very provocative, especially given their erotic and aggressive symbolism. Hayagriva for instance has many faces, a crown of skulls, and an extra horse's head, so people may find him disturbing. But this initial reaction reflects a lack of understanding the deeper meaning, symbolism, and intent of such images, which causes confusion. The point is to help us face and own the often unconscious sexual and aggressive forces within our nature, so that we can bring the clear focus, wisdom, and compassion needed to transform and harness them as forces for good. Have you ever taken a good look at your face in the mirror when you're really angry? Have you ever taken a selfie when you're enraged? Have you asked your friends or partner how scary you are when you're mad? We often just gloss over how our powerful moods or passions strike others, and imagine ourselves as always kind and cool. But in fact, we have powerful often volcanic energies inside us—anger, desire, drama, and trauma. So whatever it is, with Buddha-Deity meditation, we can bring the clear awareness we need to let the energy come up mindfully, then express it while balancing and redirecting it. In that way, practicing Buddha-Deity Yoga is like practicing acting in the theatre—you're not being mindlessly driven by your passions, you're consciously evoking them in order to artfully transform and perform them. This is what makes this practice far more effective at transforming and harnessing our primal passions than ordinary Sutric practices combining calming meditation and analytic insight. Generally, when we engage in Sutric practice, we try to calm our minds, so we can reflect on anger, desire, or confusion, though we are not actually feeling those disturbing moods. But creation stage practice gives us a method for meditating on confusion, anger, and desire when those forces are actually arising. So not only are we more able to transform them because we are working with them in real time, but also we can harness the intensity of the forces to add energy, clarity, and focus to our practice. That's why Creation Stage practice offers a smart, quick, and dynamic method for building skill in transforming and harnessing our emotions.

Completion Stage Meditation

Once we have developed a stable practice of Buddha-Deity Yoga in the Creation Stage, we're ready for the deeply embodied transformational practice of the Completion Stage (Skt. Nispanna-krama; Tib. rDzogs-rim). In this stage of Highest Yoga Tantra practice, we get in touch with the essential nature of our body, speech, and mind by working with the Indivisible Diamond Body—the subtle anatomy of channels, chakras, energies, and drops—to deepen and speed our transformation (Loizzo, 2016). This stage of practice combines imagery and mantra recitation with physical Tantric yogas that transform the subtle body in ways that help us quickly access and embody all the wisdom and potential that lie dormant within us. Unlike the gradual approach of Sutric meditation and insight, the Tantric methods of the Completion Stage can help us access these potentials quickly, through empowered, enhanced meditations that work directly with the body, senses, energies, and primal emotions.

There are two main reasons we call this the Completion Stage. First, the work of transformation we began in the Creation Stage in this stage is completed. Having transformed our mind and perception through Creation Stage practice, we now begin transforming our energy and body so that our transformation is complete. The second, deeper reason why we call this the Completion Stage, is that in this stage we fully realize that we are already perfectly complete—we have everything we need already inside us. One hundred percent of the happiness we are seeking is already within us, the only problem is we don't see it and can't experience it. That's why we feel something is missing and go searching everywhere outside us for what we already have. This wholeness is emphasized in Completion Stage teachings: the whole universe is contained in our individual human bodies, as we see in the phrases, "As above, so below," and "As without, so within." These phrases teach that the expansive deity imagery of the Creation Stage actually refers to processes that take place within the body; and that the macrocosm of the outer world—our social and natural environments—is actually contained within the microcosm of the human individual.

Of course, the human body according to the Completion Stage, is not the gross anatomy of the physical body, or the image of the physical body we hold in mind, but the subtle anatomy of the Indivisible Diamond Body, Diamond Speech, and Diamond Mind. This subtle body refers to the three main channels that travel from the crown to the base of the spine along with the chakras and many branch channels that spread out from the central channel at the crown, throat, heart, navel, and base. The subtle speech refers to the five main energies that travel through the channels and chakras and support speech and thought. The subtle mind refers to the drops that originate within the central channel and are carried by energies through the side and branch channels. Of course, various Hindu and Buddhist Tantras have slightly different models of the subtle body, some with six, seven, or more chakras some with three or four chakras, each with its own specific reasons. Most often the Tibetan tradition points to five main chakras, aligned with the five elements, and also the five main energies, although there are notable exceptions like the yoga of dying where we focus on head, throat, and heart. The right side channel is red and associated with the sun; the left is white and associated with the moon; the central channel is dark blue and associated with the eclipse or black hole (Loizzo, 2014b). Within the Kalachakra system, each of the chakras is associated with a galaxy. So within our subtle bodies we have sun, moon, black hole, the galaxies, and the five elements—a microcosm of the natural universe that is our outer environment (Wallace, 2001).

Why travel into outer space when you can find the whole universe in your inner space? We imagine the universe is nearly infinite, with its billions of trillions of stars, yet each and every human nervous system is just as infinite, with nearly a billion trillion neural connections. Then think of the even larger infinity of possible ideas and things a single human brain can invent based on that neural circuitry, and multiply that by how each individual human brain is also a microcosm reflecting the inner worlds of the eight billion other human brains on this planet. According to the Tantras, our internal universe and external universe are not just equally vast and complex, but mirror and include each other. Reflecting the reality of our infinite complexity as individuals is one of the ways the Tantras point to our divine completeness and creativity.

Finally it's important to know how the subtle body also maps out the path of Tantric practice. I've already mentioned in discussing empowerment how the five chakras map the alchemical process of Tantric practice—transforming five main poisons located in each of the five chakras into five wisdoms. The Kalachakra Tantra, also aligned with the Yuthog tradition, does this somewhat differently from most other Highest Yoga Tantras. It first links the drops at the four higher chakras with the four basic states of mind—waking at the crown, dreaming at the throat, sleeping at the heart, and orgasm at the navel. It then describes the alchemy of Tantric practice as the work of transforming those four drops from their basic condition tainted by the poisons to their purified condition as four embodiments of our fully awakened Buddha-nature (Wallace, 2001).

The model of four states of consciousness is vital to how Yuthok's Tantric medical system views the basic human condition as well as the yogas of the Completion Stage (Chenagtsang, 2018). Normally, every day we cycle through the three or four of the states of consciousness—in the daytime we are in the waking state; at night we cycle through dreams and deep sleep; and some of our days we also experience the fourth state of orgasm. Although Tantra teaches that we can discover the blissful, luminous, nectar-like Clear Light of our primal Buddha-nature through all of these states, most of us experience them normally as afflicted with various kinds of stress and trauma. We tend to get more stuck in an unpleasant way of cycling through the routine states—waking, dream, and sleep—under two adverse circumstances: when we don't experience deep sleep or orgasm often; and when we don't bring full awareness to the deep sleep or orgasmic experience we have.

The waking state is wonderful when we're able to calm the tendency to stress through practices like mindfulness or calming meditation, although most people don't make full use of this state and are troubled in it. Deep sleep and orgasm are different in being non-dual states, where there is no concept of self and others, where—in a beautiful and profound way—we are free from everything. But while the healing power of deep sleep and orgasm are amazing, the problem is we don't get enough of them. Light sleepers who stay stuck in stress and trauma often don't fall into deep sleep. Even those of us who get deep sleep normally experience it as a sort of blackout in which we lose full awareness. Likewise with orgasm, most of us don't enjoy that beneficial state every day or often enough, and even when we do, we often tend to move through it too quickly or with less than full awareness. We wonder why we're not happy, when not even making proper use of deep sleep and orgasm which are not only the best medicines for us but also totally free (Varela, 2002).

Here is where the Tantric yogas of the Completion Stage come in. Tantra is life—it doesn't just work with the waking state, it works with all four states of consciousness using specific yogic practices. Highest Yoga Tantra offers two embodied practices for the waking state—the daytime yogas of the Inner Heat and Illusory Body. It offers embodied practices for the dream and sleep states—the nighttime yogas of Lucid Dreaming and the Clear Light. And since sex and love are part of our embodied lives, it also offers three embodied practices for the orgasmic state—the yogas with a live Intimate Partner (Karmamudra), an Imaginary Partner (Jnanamuda), and the Yoga of the Great Seal (Mahamudra), in which we commune with the whole universe as a partner. These practices have been seriously misunderstood and misused, leading to the confusion that Tantra is all about sex. In fact, they are simply part of its systematic practices touching on all aspects of our embodied lives. That even includes two practices for the altered states of death and dying— the yogas of the post-death Transition (Skt. Antarabhava; Tib. Bardo) and the Transference to a positive afterlife (Skt. Amashaya; Tib. Phowa).

The Daytime Yogas: Inner Heat and Illusory Body

In the daytime, Completion Stage practice is based on the Yoga of Inner Heat (Skt. Chandali; Tib. Tummo). This is based on an intensive breath-control practice similar, though not identical to, Indian Kundalini Yoga. Based on exercises that allow us to control deep abdominal breathing, we develop the capacity to access and transform the energies that flow within our subtle body. The practice combines breath exercises with visualizations of the subtle body and with physical exercises. It involves a comprehensive training, but even with minimal training you can have some experience and understand how it works. The practice is also called Inner Fire, because it works to activate the subtle body's solar energy, which allows us to experience more clarity in the waking state as well as more bliss and joy in our daily life (Yeshe, 2015).

Next we come to the second daytime yoga, the Yoga of the Illusory Body. I find this yoga very interesting, because it offers a powerful practice for training the mind, a Tantric form of psychotherapy. We call it Illusory Body yoga because you practice seeing yourself as a reflection, like your dreamlike better half. It's as if you're recognizing yourself in a mirror—in this case in the mirror of your Buddha-Deity image, the image of your full potential—and you practice using that dreamlike image of the realized you as a way of accessing and consulting your Inner Guru, as your own inner therapist. Without feeling shame, without judging, repressing, or rejecting anything, you practice sharing all your deepest emotions and self-talk with this guide in you. You share everything without withholding—all the good, and all the bad, from the best to the worst. It may feel very strange at first, but the more you engage in this inner dialogue, the more you start to identify with this wiser, freer, more joyful version of you. Thanks to your inner therapist or guide, you gradually start to access and own the wisdom and compassion you need to hold your powerful emotions and their energies, to not be swayed or controlled by them, and to transform them into forms of blissful awareness and wisdom energy. Eventually, no matter whether you hear, think, or feel something good or bad, you're able to stay in the flow of blissful awareness and wisdom energy. It's like developing a very strong psychological immune system.

Nighttime Yoga: Dream Yoga and Clear Light Yoga

Normally, we are controlled by our dreams. In Dream Yoga, we do the opposite, we train ourselves in lucid dreaming, so we can practice controlling our own dream life. To practice Dream Yoga, first we have to learn how to stay lucid through the transitions of our nighttime lives. If you remember, when I talked about the normal sleep cycle, I said that, for most of us, falling asleep is like falling into a black hole. So when we sleep and dream, we essentially lose consciousness and have a long nighttime blackout. When we wake up, we typically remember very little, if anything. So if we want to train in lucid dreaming, we first need to practice falling asleep while maintaining some degree of mindfulness. When we practice staying mindful as we drift into sleep, our experience is not one of falling into a black hole or blacking out. Entering sleep mindfully, we feel as if we are dissolving into the light. And we can practice maintaining awareness through that light. That is the Yoga of Clear Light. So if a dream arises as we rest in that Clear Light, we have the presence of mind to choose to enter the dream dimension lucidly. When we become able to do that, we are able to play with our dreams, to direct it freely in ways that deepen and speed our transformation (Mullin, 2005). For instance, if we begin dreaming with a self-image and self-concept afflicted by our emotional poisons and the energies of stress and trauma, we can have the presence of mind to shift our sense of ourselves towards the healing image and blissful energy of our Illusory Body.

Normally, when we practice the two nighttime yogas, we start by first focusing on Dream Yoga. In order to dream lucidly, we have to practice entering sleep lucidly first, but since dreams are the lightest part of our sleep cycle, they are closer to the waking state yogas of Inner Heat and Illusory Body than deep sleep is. So it is usually easier in the beginning to practice lucid dreaming than lucid deep sleep, the subtler of the two nighttime yogas.

When we begin the Yoga of Clear Light, we do so in much the same way as we begin Dream Yoga—by approaching sleep in a state of embodied mindfulness based on the daytime yogas of Inner Heat and Illusory Body. We then practice easing into sleep mindfully by imagining the dissolution of our Illusory Body into the Clear Light of sleep, a transition like the natural experience of dissolution during death or orgasm. Over time, we practice immersing our minds more and more fully in non-dual blissful awareness, and resting there as long as possible. This helps us see the luminous blissful clear light in all our states of consciousness and empowers us to transform the poisons that afflict those states into wisdom nectars. For instance, if we choose to transition out of the Clear Light of sleep into dream, we then shift our practice into Dream Yoga, shaping our dream body into the form of our Illusory Body to help guide our dream life. When we're done lucid dreaming, we once again gradually dissolve our dreaming Illusory Body into the Clear Light of sleep. And we do this repeatedly until we can fully enter into the Clear Light. This gives us all the benefits of deep sleep or orgasmic experience, enhanced by the fact that we are maintaining full awareness of those beneficial states, really absorbing their medicine.

Union Yoga: Traditional Tantric Sex Therapy

As I said, Tantra is all about our embodied human life. And of course, love and sex are a vital part of human life, especially for laypeople. This dimension of Tantric practice includes three yogas to help us transform all aspects of human sexuality from our normal experience in which it is poisoned by confusion and desire, to the healthy condition in which it becomes medicine. First, we look at two yogas that work with sexuality in its basic condition—as a primal force of love and desire—one yoga that involves embodied work with an Intimate Partner, and one that involves meditative work with an Imaginary Partner. These are the Tantric yogas that have been misunderstood and misused in the West to misrepresent Tantra as all about desire and better sex. This is really unfortunate, since Tantra actually offers a much needed traditional practice for working with the blocks and dysfunctions of ordinary sexuality, something like an enlightened form of sex education and sex therapy (Chenagstang, 2018).

We all see the conventional love stories that begin with couples bonded by intense desire that gradually turns into the couple stuck in chronic frustration and fighting. This is when people go to couples therapy or sometimes modern sex therapy. But these Tantric yogas offer a deeper understanding and methodology for transforming ordinary sexuality not just with the mind, but also with the body, and with breath energy. These Tantric practices allow us to work with sexuality not just at the level of the ordinary waking mind and gross physical body, but also at the subtler, deeper level of orgasmic consciousness including the channels, energies, and drops of the subtle body. This empowers us to free sex and love from the poisons of desire, confusion, and anger, and transform them into the non-dual blissful awareness of the Clear Light. The embodied form of this practice involves a true Intimate Partner Yoga, in which both partners are practicing the same yogas, though in slightly different ways based on their gender identification, whether heteronormative or LGBTQ+.

Fortunately, there is also a form of sexual yoga for people practicing not as part of a couple but as an individual. This form of the practice relies on simulating physical intimacy with a meditative, Imaginary Partner. The way we work with the body and energy in this Imaginary Partner practice is similar to the way we work in physical intimacy. Essentially, we use our own sexual energy to simulate the experience, as in a sexual dream. This practice extends the Creation Stage yoga of visualizing ourselves as a joyful Buddha-Deity with our male and female parts in union. In the Completion Stage, we deepen and enhance that visualization practice with the yogas of Inner Heat, Illusory Body, and Clear Light. This practice is especially helpful for individuals who are single or celibate, including monastics, although it can also be helpful for people in couples who want to prepare for or supplement their Intimate Partner Yoga.

The third Tantric yoga for working with human sexuality is the Yoga of the Great Seal (Mahamudra). Of course, it does not work with sexuality in the ordinary sense, like the yogas with an Intimate Partner or Imaginary Partner. Instead it works with what you might call sensuality—our capacity to feel a sense of blissful sensual connection with a wide range of different kinds of experience. Some of us seek bliss through the enjoyment of food, some through enjoying clothing, some through enjoying nature, some through enjoying art or music. We are all searching for something that brings joy to our lives, something that helps us feel a real sense of transcending our ordinary condition of suffering. From the Buddhist standpoint, the suffering we long to transcend is the primal sense of alienation or separateness that makes us feel lonely or disconnected from life, so that no joy ever feels truly satisfying, truly enough (Dalai Lama & Berzin, 1997).

This mindset of separation, this isolating sense of extreme individualism, is what leads us to get fixated on "I," "me," "mine," and poisons love and sexuality with confusion. This poison of confusion also locks us in a prison of false pride and loneliness, a prison in which we long for the connection with others, with life, with nature, and the whole universe, which is the real source of all our joy and bliss. In Completion Stage Yoga, we practice to break out of our self-made prison of separateness, and immerse ourselves in the blissful awareness of our deep interconnection with all beings and things. This is the Yoga of the Great Seal. This yoga empowers us to taste the bliss of our deep interconnection with everything by learning to sense how we ourselves, all beings, and all things are empty of any truly separate or unrelated nature. The yoga works by accessing the non-dual bliss awareness that naturally arises in deep sleep and orgasm to practice seeing all beings and things as characterized by the "Great Seal" of that emptiness. This practice helps transform the poison of confusion that disconnects us into the medicine of blissful connection, just as the practice of the two partner yogas helps transform the poison of desire into the medicine of joyful communion.

Death and Dying: The Yogas of Transition and Transference

While modern culture treats death as the opposite or enemy of life, the Tantras see death as an essential part of the fabric of life. Since Tantra works to help us engage our whole life, death is simply one of the key parts of life we need to deal with. Would you prefer to die in a traumatic way, or to die peacefully? This is not just a question for ourselves but also for our family and friends. If we die in a traumatic way, they are traumatized with us; if we are able to die peacefully, they can be at peace too. According to the Tantras, death is life's final journey. So if we want our journey in life to be joyful and peaceful, we need to take that final journey in a mindful and beautiful way. This is why the Completion Stage offers two yogas for death and dying: the Yoga of Transition—called Bardo in Tibetan—and the Yoga of Transference—called Phowa (Thurman, 2010).

Bar-do literally means something in-between. While the most common meaning of bardo, given the Buddhist view of existence as a multi-life continuum, is the state between one death and the next birth. In the Tantras, Bardo refers generally to any transition between one state of being and another. That is why traditionally we define not one bardo but six. The Bardo of Birth is the transition of pregnancy, from conception to delivery; the Bardo of Dreaming is the transition in the sleep cycle from deep sleep to waking; the Bardo of Meditation is the transition from the ordinary waking state to the altered state of meditation; the Bardo of Death is the transition from the moment of death to the moment of the next conception; the Bardo of Reality is the transition of the spiritual path, from delusion to awakening; and the Bardo of Existence is life seen as one great transition from birth to death.

Many people approach the Bardo teachings as something mysterious or magical. But the Tantras use Bardo Yoga to prepare us to understand the deepest nature of life as a continuous process of constant impermanence, constant transformation. By viewing all the different parts of the life-cycle as transitions, the Tantras are trying to prepare us to face death not as other than life but as simply another form of the same basic process that all life is made of—continuous transformation.

The essence of the practice is to train our minds to be able to see that process clearly for what it is, so that we can embrace it and stay connected to it through all life's transitions with the full clarity of our deep, non-dual bliss awareness, in other words, with the luminous wisdom of the Clear Light. If you think of your consciousness as a kind of light, this light is making its journey through different spaces, from one dimension to another. Wherever this light goes, the space may be different, but the light is always the same. That's the journey we call the bardo—a journey of maintaining continuous lucid awareness through all life's great transitions. That also includes the final transition after death, when the mind that can stay consistently clear can move through whatever might arise without being triggered into confusion and the related poisons of desire, anger, envy, pride, or greed. And since death not only involves the person dying but all those connected to that individual, the Bardo Yoga is not only meant as a practice for those imminently facing death but also for those who wish to support that person by staying clear and connected to their loved one's transition.

The second Tantric yoga around dying is the Yoga of Transference. For those who have the training, the transference yoga allows a more directed approach to guiding the end of life transition by consciously choosing a destination for the post-death journey. The practice actually involves a forceful ejection or projection of consciousness towards a chosen destination—such as a Pure Land (Buddhist heaven), or a voluntary reincarnation as part of a Bodhisattva mission to help specific beings by assuming a specific future form. You can think of this as a faster, more directed way to engage death that avoids the inevitable uncertainty of the end of life transition, a kind of escape hatch, but of course it's only one option and not for everyone (Mullin, 2005).

There is one more best-case scenario in the Tantric practice of death and dying, based on the training for death offered by the yogas of dissolution within both the Creation Stage and Completion Stage of Highest Yoga Tantra. That is the possibility for practitioners to use the death process as a path to fully embodied awakening. According to the Tantras, there are two Completion Stage practices using especially deep altered states to realize the final Clear Light which is the subtle lucid body-mind of awakening. These two states are the natural release of orgasmic bliss fully accessed by the yogas of sexuality and the natural release of dying accessed by the yoga of the Clear Light of death. In this practice at the end of life, we bring full awareness to the dissolution of our subtle mind, energy, and drops at the moment of death. Then we follow the dissolution of our lunar and solar energy and enter into a dark space where eventually we experience the final Clear Light called the Mother Clear Light. This is the innate Clear Light of our subtlest mind and energy body—our true nature, who we really are. When we know that as our origin, our self, we return to our true mother, our true origin, reuniting the smaller Child Clear Light of our individual sense of separate experience with the great mother of infinitely connected experience that makes death a path to full awakening and spiritual liberation (Thurman, 2010). For Christians, Muslims, Jews, and Hindus, that mother clear light is the God that is our origin and our source. For Buddhists, it is the Nirvana that Buddha awakened to, experienced as the complete embodied joy and contentment we have when being embraced by our loving mother.

The Final Stage: The Great Perfection

If we are lucky enough to receive an empowerment in Highest Yoga Tantra, and faithfully practice both the Creation Stage and the Completion Stage, we may have the even greater fortune of realizing the Mother Clear Light before death, through practicing one or more of the yogas of transforming ordinary sexuality (Chenagtsang, 2018). This is one of the ways in which the embodied path of the Tantras may be even smarter and quicker for lay practitioners than for celibate monastics.

If we follow the Tantric path this far, we find ourselves entering the final stage of Tantric practice—the Great Perfection Stage (Skt. Ashadharna-Nispanna, Tib. Dzog-chen)—which focuses much like Sutric meditation on cultivating the profound wisdom of emptiness. The difference between Sutric and Tantric emptiness meditation is not so much in the wisdom as in the method. Unlike Sutra, which bases emptiness practice on concentrative meditation and the calming energy of renunciation and compassion, Tantric emptiness practice relies on accessing the subtle mind, energy, and drops that support non-dual blissful states of awareness.

In a sense, Sutra and Tantra offer two distinct methods of therapeutic psychology. Sutric psychology focuses on counteracting the problem—understanding and eliminating stress and trauma. While Tantric psychology focuses on the solution—understanding and embodying happiness, peace, joy, and bliss. When it comes to wisdom, both these psychologies teach that facing and embracing reality is the most critical factor in healing and transformation. And both traditions point to that wisdom using the insight of emptiness—that all phenomena are empty or devoid of any permanent, essential, independent self, nature, or identity. Emptiness is presented not as a mere philosophical theory or concept but as the basic reality of things just as they are. This insight fits with the more scientific view—shared by modern physics and Highest Yoga Tantra—that the ultimate nature of everything is not solid matter but extremely subtle energy and space. In both Sutric and Tantric views, emptiness is not seen as an absolute nothingness or total void, but rather as inseparable from the infinite variety and relativity of mental and physical forms. This is conveyed somewhat differently in Sutra and Tantric views, with Sutra emphasizing the inseparability of emptiness, relativity, and compassion; and Tantra emphasizing the inseparability of emptiness—understood as Clear Light—with the diversity of lived experience and the embodied energy of bliss. While these two therapeutic psychologies may seem at odds, in reality they are quite complementary. Sutra cultivates the wisdom of emptiness to realize freedom from suffering; and Tantra cultivates it to realize the freedom to embody happiness.

How do we meditate on emptiness in the Great Perfection Stage? Once we have an initial experience of the Mother Clear Light at the end of the Completion Stage, we arise from that deep realization in the form of our self-created, blissful Illusory Body. From here, the practice of the Great Perfection Stage involves working to further refine and integrate these two faces of wisdom into one fully embodied awakening. In Sutric meditation on emptiness, we first achieve two separate but complementary insights into emptiness: the ultimate, spacious insight that all beings and things are free from self-identity;

and the relative, illusory insight in which the apparent diversity of all beings and things appears like an illusion. The advanced practice in this case involves slowly realizing that the two insights are not separate at all but two sides of the same hand—the non-duality of form and emptiness, relative and ultimate reality. In Tantric meditation on emptiness, the two complementary wisdoms are the ultimate realization of the Mother Clear Light and the relative realization of the Illusory Body and its whole diversity of embodied experience. You can think of the great perfection stage as the advanced Tantric practice of gradually refining and integrating these complementary embodied wisdoms until they can be fully realized as two inseparable faces of one living, breathing embodiment of non-dual, blissful awakening.

Conclusion: Embodied Healing in the Tantric Medical Tradition

The Tibetan medical tradition handed down from Yuthog Yonten Gonpo offers the world's oldest system of integrative healthcare complete with a very unique and effective methodology of embodied psychological healing. The wide ranging, multi-dimensional methods of Tantric healing allow us to work with the mind not just directly through teaching and meditation, but also indirectly through shifting energy with breathing and adjusting the body through self-massage and movement. Also, the Tantra's radically optimistic alchemical approach, based on its unique way of working with the subtle body of channels, energies, and drops, offers a very powerful system of deeply embodied psychological healing and transformation. In the current environment of growing interest in trauma and embodied approaches to healing, this rare and powerful tradition has a lot to offer psychotherapists and other health providers working with the many conditions caused by stress and trauma.

In a larger public health sense, the radical optimism and embodied practicality of the Tantras can offer therapy clients and the general public empowering perspectives and accessible methods for facing the many challenges of everyday life. This is especially true in areas where modern psychotherapy offers only limited perspectives and methods, such as transforming trauma or sexual dysfunction and facing and working with death and dying. Finally, its focus on transforming the universal poisons of confusion, desire, anger, greed, and pride into the healing wisdoms and energies of love, compassion, joy, and equanimity offers a positive embodied approach to psychological health and well-being far more radical and practical than the West's recent approaches to positive psychology.

19
Imagery and Trauma
The Psyche's Push for Healing

Pilar Jennings

In the small but robust and rapidly growing world of spiritually oriented therapists, some of us came to discover a Western understanding of psyche through spiritual practice, and some the reverse. I found myself in the former camp, with a budding interest in clinical work that grew out of an early exposure to Buddhist meditation. By the time I hit adolescence, I had learned that working with the mind in a thorough, but deeply compassionate, non-coercive way had clear psychological benefits. As I moved into adulthood, with all the psychic tumult that comes with efforts at individuation, I began to appreciate and grow curious about the ways in which certain methods within the Tibetan Buddhist tradition seemed to offer me needed ways to stay the course of psychological development. Understanding and separating from my family of origin seemed to be a process that my spiritual practice was effectively addressing, in ways that were different but just as relevant as my work in psychotherapy. Healing images were evoked that simulated the feelings I still longed for, of safe belonging, maternal holding, and paternal pride in my being.

When several years later I began my psychoanalytic training, I was reminded of my appreciation for images of parental care when encountering the work of D.W. Winnicott, the British psychoanalyst. Winnicott wrote with remarkable insight into the terror so many of us face as we seek somehow to remain connected to the people who brought us into this world, while blazing some psychic new trail away from them, a trail with no clear roadmap (Winnicott, 1975). With his characteristic humor and warmth, Winnicott encouraged parents not to expect a thank you note from their children when they traverse this journey successfully, but instead to survive the many ways they may come to feel psychically killed off as their children traversed the choppy waters of individuation (Winnicott, 1965; Ulanov, personal communication). These waters never fully ebb, he rightly suggested. The hero's journey away from

DOI: 10.4324/9781003243588-22

our origins, even origins that have been treacherous or fraught with danger, unleashes in the psyche a primordial longing for safe merger that is typically defended against through the mosaic of jarring behaviors parents of teenagers throughout the globe have come to know well.

Tantra and Individuation

In the Tibetan tradition of Vajrayana Buddhism, also known as Tantra, I had been learning and practicing a form of meditation that seemed to touch on the primordial longing for love and connection free from all the shadow content that comes with human closeness. Like many of my American-born spiritual friends, I was aware of the profound psychological impact of these meditations. Together, we utilized the mindful concentration we'd been learning to hold our attention on the imagined presence of certain images— green shimmering Tara Mother Buddha, indigo Blue Medicine Buddha, fiery red Wisdom Mother Vajrayogini—that we were encouraged to commune with imaginatively and, over time, to internalize as manifestations of our own deepest level of awakened mind, our Buddha-nature.

The practice of Tantra, one quickly finds, is powerfully relational. Unlike the increasingly secularized practice of mindfulness meditation, in which one can feel that the ability to cultivate heightened non-reactive awareness comes solely from one's own efforts, in the Tantric tradition, practitioners learn to rely on external images that are considered to be both powerfully healing *and* empty of any external reality. For many, this conundrum of supreme reliability and absolute emptiness can take some time to work out. These symbols are meant to represent manifestations of our own healing nature, our own mind infused with insight, receptivity, love, and compassion, which require another simply to jump-start an untapped internal resource. In the concept of *trikaya*, usually translated as triple body, these images are referred to as *sambhogakaya*, or enjoyment bodies. Having grown out of *dharmakaya*, or the truth of emptiness that is all-pervasive, they can be utilized to evoke a felt sense of other, both healing and caring, that is always available to be relied upon, even as we seek to understand that such images merely reflect our own deepest nature, our own internal resource of well-being. *Nirmanakaya* are thought to be the incarnate beings, teachers, and helpers, who manifest to bring forth these resources we all harbor (see Gross, 1998, pp. 171–186).

For the many developmental challenges faced in the terrain of human intimacy, the process of evoking and communing with such images can offer another method for using one's imagination and archetypal imprints for healing. The psychoanalytic method has similarly had a deep and abiding appreciation for the importance of symbolizing. Freud mused endlessly on the ways in which we symbolize psychic life via dreams and learn to sublimate desires not readily met through art, poetry, and the myriad ways we represent unmet needs symbolically. Jung suggested that our efforts at symbolization were critical for mental health, affording us ways to access layers of meaning and longing that he believed we inherited from the evolution of human consciousness (Jung, 1983). Clinicians such as Melanie Klein and Hanna Segal suggested that through a developmental capacity for symbolization, we are able to relate to external reality, most notably our primary caretakers, while protecting ourselves and others from misperceptions of objective truth.

In other words, when children learn to distinguish their symbolic representations of experience from experience writ large, they can play with it, reflect upon it, and mentalize, or think about it. Such a child might find herself comparing a grumpy parent who is short-tempered after a difficult day at work to Cruella de Vil. And while such a comparison, if expressed directly to the parent, might cause some embarrassment, it will save the child from losing touch with a parent's fuller, more multiple, and external psychic reality. Such a child might begin to see in herself the capacity to feel and act like Cruella on given days, and Santa Claus on others. These images, or archetypes, offer us ways to symbolize highly charged affective experience, to integrate our own and others' dynamic multiplicity. In so doing, we are better able to be spared the suffering that comes with overly restrictive images of self, other, and self–other interaction.

In all schools of psychoanalytic thought, there is a deep appreciation for the ways in which restrictive notions of self and other resulting from trauma, or a prolonged experience of mis-attunement within one's family of origin or culture, create complicated and multifaceted forms of pain and suffering. The psychoanalytic method seeks to use the relationship between therapist and client as a way of better understanding how the individual has come to experience herself, and to anticipate her treatment of others. In Jungian depth psychology, now mirrored in the work of Internal Family Systems, there is also a fundamental reverence for the client's ability to access healing resources within her own mind (see Schwartz, 1995). Thus, the therapist is encouraged to work as more of a translator, or receptive psychic radar, for the client's unconscious, where such resources live (Ulanov, 2004). With this work comes a deep and abiding respect for the client's images, dreams, and fantasies. It is a way to honor the healing imagination that exists in us all.

As the traditions of Buddhism and psychoanalysis began to mix in my own clinical journey, I came to utilize those healing images from Buddhist cosmology that resonated so viscerally for me, while learning to connect with the healing images arising from my clients' psyches, often informed by their own religious traditions. What I hope to explore in this chapter are the ways in which my relationship to the healing imagery found in Vajrayana Buddhism has allowed me to more fully enter into and utilize the healing imagery of my clients. Like all clinicians who respect their client's capacity for healing, I have made efforts first simply to notice these imaginative interactions free from interpretation, then to more directly utilize them for healing. In the following clinical example, I explore how my own meditative practice seemed to intersect with my clients' use of healing imagery.

Margarite: A Case Vignette

My first session with Margarite took place on a blazing hot day in July. From the window of my office, I could see the heat rising in waves from the asphalt street. My *mantra* throughout the day was directed at my air conditioner: please freeze me like an ice cube for the benefit of all beings. This emphasis on climate is relevant only because when I opened the door to greet Margarite that afternoon, I was struck by a Latina woman clad in elegant purple batik from head to toe and wearing a thick woolen hat. My mind flashed to a supervision session years back when we had discussed a severely depressed patient who wore winter hats in the summer. My typically jovial and steadfastly non-pathologizing supervisor had looked distressed: "Winter hats in the summer," he'd said, shaking his head, "that's *bad.*"

I shook Margarite's hand and invited her in. Before long she began to describe in great detail the many ways she had felt alternately hurt, disappointed, and altogether misunderstood by her previous therapists. "Totally incompetent," she said, shaking her head in disbelief, reminding me of my supervisor's note of alarm. I stood forewarned, watching her adjust her hat when it occasionally slipped too far back, revealing a high regal forehead with rivulets of sweat pouring downward and landing in small pools on her pretty shirt.

Despite her previous disappointments in therapy, Margarite quickly began to share with me the sense of profound aloneness and abject despair that had been haunting her throughout her life. It was a despair so jagged and unrelenting that it left her willing to try therapy "one last time." She looked up, her almond-shaped black eyes searing into me. She described her mother as an extremely hard-working and keenly intelligent woman who had put herself through college and completed a master's program in history after she moved to New York City from her native Dominican Republic. Her father had been a librarian, also from the Dominican Republic, and had died from pancreatic cancer when she was fifteen years old, leaving her and her mother to care for themselves and Margarite's three younger siblings.

Her mother had become a high school history teacher in a well-respected school and continued working full time, and continued growing increasingly, though quietly enraged. It seemed to my client as if her mother had wished Margarite had died instead of her father. When I asked, she confirmed that she'd noticed her mother's rage before her father died, a noxious presence of categorical disapproval she often felt. But it became more obvious and over-powering to her in those last years before she left to attend an Ivy League college where she studied biology, "It was as if she hated me, and I couldn't figure out why. I was a good kid."

Margarite eventually had become a professor of biology at an elite college and a well-known researcher. As we continued our work, she spoke to me of losing faith in her ability to ever be a genuinely happy person. She had limited contact with her family of origin—her siblings and mother had all dispersed to different corners of the globe—and she was in a relatively new romantic relationship with a man whom she experienced as benign but self-centered, and unable to challenge her in any significant way. A previous ten-year marriage had ended in divorce. Margarite spoke honestly of the ways she felt herself treating her former and current partners as her mother had treated her, "With an oozing though somehow contained contempt. Something impossible to talk about or see clearly, yet totally pervasive, like an *odorless gas*."

While I appreciated Margarite's laser insight and psychological curiosity, I found it difficult, even treacherous, to help her reflect on the ways in which the aggression she'd gotten the brunt of was getting mobilized and enacted with her partners. She quickly followed any such association with a litany of the ways her partners had deserved her wrath. They couldn't keep their focus on her, they couldn't offer support when she most needed it, they were self-ish, unable to acknowledge the ways in which they hurt her, unwittingly or not. "Total *fucking* idiots," she said, shaking her head in a dismay so thick and condemning it sometimes made me laugh with discomfort. Sometimes we laughed together in what felt like a joint appreciation for her blunt honesty, even if it had an edgy protective function that caused her and her partners a good deal of suffering.

What I felt in my initial work with Margarite was her need for copious amounts of unrushed, attuned, non-judgmental listening. My early efforts at interpretation were met either with confusion or affront, and so I opted for a long period of time to offer a more supportive therapy, a place where she could be heard without interruption, and begin to more fully feel into the complexity of her losses. Slowly, we mapped out the various parts of herself she had noticed in her professional and personal life, and the ways in which these parts needed care and attention. We talked through her understanding of her family's history, the way her parents were parented, the culturally supported tendency toward inflexible expectations, the value of hard work, and the scorn unleashed when any hint of vulnerability or overwhelm was revealed. Margarite was aware that these values had helped her accomplish a great deal, but she was growing more curious about the emotional toll such grueling expectations had taken.

It seemed to her that before her father died, the edginess of these expectations was somehow made more palatable by his presence; that it felt normal to be so hard-working in an immigrant family. It seemed that her father somehow offered a softness that served as a buttress for the overwhelm she sometimes felt. He had been the real love source in the family. A hard-working, but kind and decent man. After her father died, Margarite felt that the meaning drained out of life, that her work felt driven by a sense of obligation and fear of failure, rather than any sense of real inspiration. Her father had been the rock in the family, her North Star.

Enter Primordial Woman: Dream Imagery and Transformation

Almost a year into our sessions, Margarite began to share with me a compelling image that came from her dreams, of an ethereal yet fiery woman whose power seemed to pervade all reality. She had long black hair, was sometimes small like a doll, and other times massive like a redwood tree. She stayed in the background of her dreams but always communicated to Margarite by her very presence that she was there, watching, helping, unafraid. Together we used my version of Jung's active imagination to work with this archetypal image. I encouraged my client to speak to her, ask her what her role was in her life. The woman told Margarite that she could take her rage, it wouldn't hurt her. She had the strength, and she understood Margarite's need for safe expression. Margarite envisioned her unexpressed rage—toward her mother, toward her father for leaving her, toward herself for feeling so undone by his death—as a blaze that burned her up; in our guided visualizations she handed the woman her fire, which the woman gladly received.

I noticed after these sessions a palpable relief in Margarite, that there was finally somewhere to put feelings that had formerly seemed to have no place except within her own mind. She'd been burning up without someone to help hold these feelings. Together we sat in moments of rare quietude, as if we'd together survived some unexpected rescue after a drawn-out catastrophe. "I feel better," she said. I nodded, feeling better too. The ambiance in the room had shifted, becoming somehow quieter, less riled.

Unbeknownst to Margarite, at the end of our first year of treatment, my father died suddenly. It was a loss I could not have anticipated or imagined. Like Margarite, I too had experienced my father as a North Star, a person who had offered me throughout my life a sense of direction, even in the midst of great family tumult. A person of character whose work ethic was only surpassed by his capacity for decency and kindness. In addition to the shock of his death, which I had witnessed, was a most unexpected rage in its wake, a rage that seemed to have a lethal impact. Before I finally fell asleep for rare periods of rest in the months following his death, I fantasized about who I would kill and how: his absentee surgeon who had failed to show up; my family members who seemed unwilling to suffer any real feelings of loss; myself for having failed to adequately protect him.

As a long-term Buddhist, such ferocious feelings were not easily managed. I worried about their influence, the way they riled my mind, leaving me feeling extraordinarily wrathful. During this time my appreciation for the conversation between Buddhism and psychoanalysis deepened, as my own mentors—people conversant in both traditions—encouraged me to allow for this wrath without judgment. One cherished colleague said she was a "big fan" of my new-found aggression. It offered zest to my personality. When I expressed fear that it would eat me alive, she looked at me tenderly and asked what I could do with it. How to use it for good? My gratitude for the question was immense, as I realized yet again that there was no inherent problem with aggression—it too was empty—but in need of skillful expression.

In the weeks to come I found myself flashing on the image of Manjushri, the Buddha of compassionate wisdom, a big gleaming sword in hand that was meant to symbolize his capacity to cut through delusion. I thought of the sweet and mild-mannered chaplain who had accompanied the surgeons to tell me that my father was in distress while recovering from what was supposed to be a minor medical procedure. When I met with him again two days after my father had died, consumed with a jagged rage toward the hospital for making it impossible for me to be with my father at the end, and toward his surgeon for abandoning him on the day of his death, he wisely reminded me that "anger can be an indication of something important."

When I returned to work two weeks later, I met with Margarite on my first day back. While I tended toward revealing little about my personal life, with clients who needed to know my whereabouts for their sense of safety, I was honest and direct. For this reason, Margarite had some insight into how I'd spent my summer vacation. She walked in, a big and generous smile spreading across her face. "How's your father?" she asked. I waited for her to sit down and told her that I was very sorry to tell her that he had died. She grimaced, looking stricken. She shook her head, still grimacing. "I'm so sorry," she said. "God!"

I felt tears forming, which I fought. But when one tear slipped out, she softened, even as I braced myself for the anger my vulnerability might incite in her for having to feel concerned about me. I asked her what it was like for her to see me cry. She took a breath. "I see a woman devastated by the loss of her father." Even as I took in her response with palpable feelings of gratitude and tenderness, I worried that my tears would be too much for her, indicating some limited capacity to tolerate her pain, or my own. Interestingly, she seemed unconcerned about this, and more concerned about my capacity to get pissed. "What the fuck, Pilar?" she asked. "I hope you sue those bastards."

My mind flashed on Vajrayogini, a feminine Buddhist wisdom deity known for her "semi-wrathful" properties. For many years, this powerful symbol had been a central part of my spiritual practice. In Buddhist artwork, she is depicted as deep red in color, with long black hair, drinking blood from a human skull and wearing a garland of fifty freshly severed heads. I'd found these images to be quite compelling, the way she seemed joyfully to revel in her aggression, which from a Buddhist perspective spoke to her capacity to relinquish or "kill off" all non-truths. She is understood to be blissful and, in her dynamic bliss, to realize the truth of emptiness, that everything is relational in nature, and therefore lacking any fixed, unchanging, or independent being or essence.

While I could not have fairly described myself as blissful during that time, I nevertheless had come to feel that the presence of wrath, or aggression, could be a means through which deeper truths were encountered. I thought of the mild-mannered Southern chaplain, the way he'd seemed to understand the need for my upwelling of anger to shake up a hospital system disinclined to face the truth of mortality, as if patients would never die on their premises, and their surviving family members would never feel the devastation of sudden loss. As if they were so powerful that this basic fact of life—that we are impermanent—was not applicable in their self-made cocoon.

In the days just following my father's death, I had been turning for support to the more peaceful images—of shimmering Green Tara Buddha—known for her capacity to offer swift compassionate action. This gentle but nimble healing presence was a primary source of care for me in those first days of radical loss. But in the weeks and months to follow, volcanic spurts of a furious rage would surge through my mind, with a violence that took me far from Tara Buddha. Swirling among these fiery feelings were distressing images of my sweet-natured father putting his trust in a hospital system that did not care for him properly, of a culture of hubris I encountered in the administration when I went to address the circumstances of his death. I experienced a quality of wrathful upset that was quite foreign to me. In these moments, the image of Vajrayogini holding her ascetic's *khatvanga* staff, stepping on two squirming gods who lay powerless beneath her, gave me a way to work with and envision my own experience of wrath that could be used for something generative, a way to cut through the delusion of an outmoded healthcare system.

The Hidden Tender Heart

In the sessions with Margarite that continued through this challenging time in my life, I noticed an interesting and unexpected shift. It seemed to me that as I felt increasing aggression, she felt less burdened by rage, and more connected to a sense of her own tenderness, a capacity for love that I had seen in her from the start of our work. She had moments of real mirth when recalling a tepid effort from her partner to listen to her with more sensitivity, "He honestly looked constipated, like he was trying to push out understanding another person." The image made us both guffaw. She seemed to recognize in herself an ability to be patient and empathic, qualities she associated with her father, which had remained camouflaged by a distorted self-image created in response to her own feelings of misdirected rage.

But when a few weeks later she was denied a large research grant for which she was clearly the front-runner in her field, a grant she had poured herself into over the course of two years, to a white male colleague with half her resumé, the tenderness she had allowed for seemed to evaporate into an oceanic depression. "I feel like the universe is against me," she said. I shook my head and blurted out, "Fuck the universe!" She looked up and laughed. I was not prone to such outbursts but felt in that moment that the impact of the injustice should not deflate her sense of worth. That this was the real injustice, the way those victimized are often left feeling disempowered and valueless for being so. I went on to say that while I was sorry for swearing, I meant to express that her rage was rightly directed at the fractures in our world that allowed for misogynistic and racist behavior. She had done nothing to deserve this. I would take a stand against *karma*-theory as it was popularly understood, which would somehow hold her accountable for such setbacks. She laughed again, knowing that I was a practicing Buddhist, and having read about *karma*, or the laws of cause and effect.

I continued,

> The cause for this suffering, as I understand it, is unconscious bias and racism. The effect is your sense of having been ripped off. But that loss, I think, is putting you in touch with other losses in which you were made to feel responsible. Not the least of which was the loss of your father.

Margarite quickly wiped away a tear, having explained to me early on that she was not interested in crying her eyes out in therapy like every white woman on Manhattan's Upper West Side she'd ever known. But I felt her taking in my response, sensing into it that she did not deserve to take on the rage that rightly should be directed toward those structures that would thwart the achievements of formidable women of color.

We sat together in a few rare moments of silence. Margarite was a terrifically verbal and expressive person, who spoke freely and openly with me, something I had come to enjoy and appreciate in our work. But in this session, I felt in her a powerful need to let the rage that had been triggered in the wake of a major professional loss work its way through her psyche, opening up corners of her mind and heart dearly in need of attuned care. As I reflected on this session, I felt that my recent increased capacity to feel aggression without judgment had made it easier for Margarite to be relieved of her own. I was more available to join her in such feelings and, in this way, allow them to come up more fully and move out with greater ease and authenticity.

During this time, Margarite shared with me that she had awoken the morning before our session feeling immobilized with a deadening depression. A stack of papers to read and grade, two lectures to complete, and another grant proposal to research all remained untended to. She spoke of feeling a strong pull toward death, a sense of being in the wrong world. I nodded, knowing such feelings, but also sensing that Margarite was re-experiencing a state in which acute pain was actively denied by those who had caused it. I understood her depression to be symptomatic of feeling pain that is unrecognized by others, rendering a sense of unreality engulfed in hopelessness. But then, surprisingly, she went on to tell me about her image of a powerful female presence, an ageless woman, dark but almost without skin, and eyes that seemed to hold her, that had appeared and said: "I'll help you do one thing today, whatever you most need to do. I *will* help you." Margarite felt her reaching out to take her hand, something that made her feel both youthful and capable. She looked like Margarite's notion of the "original woman." In response to her presence and offer, Margarite got out of bed and worked for one hour on a new grant proposal. It was an hour that gave her a needed sense of survival, of psychic restoration.

We stared at one another, jointly feeling the relief and amazement that Margarite had connected with this healing presence, allowing herself to feel helped in the midst of such a powerfully disappointing and triggering time in her life. I pointed this out to her, affirming that a part of her had been available to facilitate this feeling of being supported in the right way, a trusting part that could envision that another being might be desirous and capable of helping her. She listened, nodding in agreement, and said in a tone I hadn't heard before, "I think that's right. It usually feels too dangerous even to imagine that someone could help. As if I'd disappear into the abandonment. As if asking and getting nothing back could kill me."

Healing through Imagery and Deep Affect

Aware that I felt a powerful identification with Margarite, I made efforts to consciously note that our circumstances, and our psychic resources, were not the same. I too knew the feeling of needing help that was not forthcoming and feeling undone by loss. But the specificity of Margarite's experience and ensuing feelings were not the same as mine. As such, she needed to make use of the imagery that *her* psyche put forth, not mine (see Ulanov & Ulanov, 1999). In this way, I worked to cull meaning from the nuances of her healing female presence. We talked about her associations to a teacher in her early childhood, an elderly neighbor who seemed to have a knowing way about her, a grandmother Margarite had loved dearly who died when she was a teenager. We talked about this small community of women who knit together an image that was available to her when it seemed that no one or nothing else was. A collective body of women who could offer a strength and sensitivity of awareness that felt specifically feminine in nature, a capacity to take in the experience and reality of another.

Interestingly, throughout this time, I found myself less able to access the healing presence of Vajrayogini, the semi-wrathful yet simultaneously blissful Buddha who had been such a central part of my own spiritual practice. I felt my own capacity to call forth the resources I had come to utilize and rely upon receding into the background of my psyche as the tumult of changing circumstances continued to reorganize my life. But I knew and trusted that what she symbolized—that nothing is without the elemental capacity for meaningful change—was available to me when I could make use of this awareness. Her stance of joyful confidence, that she could stomp out delusion, was a needed resource, a way for my mind to weather seemingly unending inner tumult. A way to stand on and stomp out delusional notions of reality. One such delusion, I had come to appreciate in a new way, was that the devastation of loss could be put to rest once and for all. With Margarite, I came to understand that major losses reorganize the psyche just as they change the circumstances of one's life, creating new spaces for profound feelings of devastation, rage, and ideally a quality of sacred gratitude when one's suffering is responded to with needed sensitivity and care. Room must be made in all our methods of healing for the full and powerful range of affect that accompanies us as we are changed by life and death.

Throughout my work with Margarite, and many other clients who have taught me needed lessons of human experience, I have developed a deepening respect for the many ways in which the healing methods found in Tibetan Buddhism can be used for recovery from psychological trauma. As a relational psychoanalyst, and a practicing Buddhist, I am continually reminded of how these contrasting healing traditions are powerfully enriched when they actively converse, and most importantly how suffering can be reduced when clinicians make efforts to let their own spiritual healing endeavors infiltrate their clinical work.

With Margarite, I rediscovered the remarkable ways in which the psyche pushes for wellness, especially when it is in communion with others, both incarnate and imagined, available to bear witness without judgment, and to help in the specific ways most needed. This is how we come to feel a sense of inherent value, and how I believe Margarite's feeling of value was slowly restored. It wasn't enough for her to know that I would be reliably present and emotionally attuned during our sessions. I could not be the sole facilitator of change she needed. Nor was it enough for her to have other people in her life who were available to her, though such people of course were vital resources as she made efforts to heal from past and current loss. What I believe she needed and came to rely upon with greater ease and trust, was a deepened relationship to her own caring and emotionally responsive capacity, as it was modeled by her image of the "original woman." She needed those psychic structures in her own mind that could hold more of her experience with empathy, understanding, and a willingness to respond with a sense of fellow feeling. In Buddhism, this is known as our Buddha-nature, that part of the mind that is entirely free from judgment, with the spaciousness necessary to open to all reality at all times. In psychoanalytic theory, this is sometimes referred to as needed self-structure, or an internalized good object, that offers the care and kindness that we need to be able to show ourselves, particularly when in the midst of radical change.

It is possible that the psychoanalytic tradition has relied too heavily on the therapist as the primary agent for change. Modern psychotherapeutic methods could be greatly enhanced by the Buddhist trust in the psyche's push for healing, a trust reinforced by the work of Carl Jung, and others. And Buddhist notions of healing could be enhanced by the psychoanalytic appreciation for the power of an attuned other to jump-start these needed resources. It seems that we are able to have a fuller experience of our own psychological reality when it is known by another. Both traditions, I have come to find, want to hold up the healing impact of imagery that we so easily miss in a culture that prizes discursive thought and linear thinking. When engaged skillfully and whole-heartedly, our psyche's images have the power to help us navigate even the most unexpected trauma and loss. They are those critically needed resources for our ongoing psychological and spiritual development that can offer what is most needed and least expected.

Embodied Practice, the Smart Vagus, and Mind–Brain–Body–World Integration

Joseph Loizzo

The Third Wave of Contemplative Science and Psychotherapy

As the neuropsychological mechanisms and benefits of mindfulness become clearer each day (Tang et al., 2015), and research has begun to elucidate the neuroscience of compassion (Engen & Singer, 2015), it is time to turn our attention to the least understood forms of contemplative practice: the embodied methods of imagery, recitation, breath control, and mindful movement. In this chapter, I hope to offer an accessible introduction to this most complex and least studied frontier in contemplative neuroscience and psychotherapy.

Before we can focus on these practices, we must address some misconceptions and challenges that have blocked understanding and study of them thus far. The misconceptions we face come from several sources—modern and traditional, Eastern and Western, religious and scientific—all of which overlap. The challenges come from the legacy of mind/body dualism, and the inherent difficulty of studying the normally unconscious processes and exceptional mind/body states tapped and harnessed by these practices.

Facing Misconceptions and Challenges

One broad preconception of meditative practice is that it is exclusively of the mind. Neither open monitoring methods like mindfulness nor focused attention methods like concentration do much to challenge this bias, despite their focus on body awareness, vivid imagery, and recitation. Through studying compassion, we have realized that contemplative practice can deeply engage the heart, literally and figuratively (Desbordes et al., 2012). Yet while we often

DOI: 10.4324/9781003243588-23

lump meditation with yoga, we still tend to think of them in binary terms, relegating yoga to the body and meditation to the mind. This tacit bias may explain why the whole domain of embodied contemplative practice has all but fallen through the cracks.

Unfortunately, the binary lens through which researchers see contemplative practice is far from limited to science or to modernity. Although ill-suited to a clear view of embodied practices, it has also been applied by scholar-practitioners of most traditions. Whether they focus on vivid imagery, recitation, movement, or deep breathing, embodied practices meant to access unconscious somatic processes and deep affect states have often been regarded with suspicion by their ambient culture (Wedemeyer, 2007). This is as true of the subtle mind/body practices known as Tantra in India and Tibet, as it is of the practices of alchemy and mysticism in the West, Sufism in the Middle East, and Taoism and Shingon Buddhism in East Asia (White, 1996).

In India, the Hindu Yoga and Vajrayana Buddhist traditions co-evolved systems of embodied practice using related forms of archetypal imagery, mantra recitation, advanced breath control, and core body yoga (Cozort, 2005). Together these practices serve to access normally unconscious deep affect states, then harness them to cultivate exceptional mind/body traits like ecstatic openness and spontaneous altruism (Varela, 2002). Unlike most practices of meditation, these methods cultivate high arousal flow states rather than low arousal calm states, and map their actions and effects onto an embodied, interoceptive model of mind and nervous system called the subtle body, also known as the "chakra system" from Hatha Yoga (Loizzo, 2016).

Such practices have historically been misunderstood in part because they offer techniques that activate and inspire practitioners outside the bounds of religious scripture, ritual, and authority (Sanderson, 1985). In effect, they offer an internalizing model and direct route to innate sources of personal inspiration and social empowerment that most societies restrict to contemplative elites and control through institutionalized religion (Thurman, 2010). But beyond the embodied, activating nature of these practices, their least understood, most controversial aspect is that they apply their methods to access and sublimate the most primal, deeply embodied drive energies and chemistry of sexual desire, consummation, and self-protective fear of death (Loizzo, 2012). The depth-psychological orientation of these practices, combined with their spiritual individualism, led them to be viewed in India and the West not just as anomalous but as suspect (Yates, 1991; Muller-Ortega, 1997).

These perennial misconceptions are further compounded by the critique of religious symbolism and contemplative practice in the West since the Reformation and Enlightenment (Ferngren, 2002). Subsequent science and psychology in the West approached embodied practices with both kinds of skepticism, dismissing imagery and recitation as religious, and dismissing flow states of bliss and openness as primitive and regressive (Freud, 1930/1962). This "hermeneutic of suspicion" was woven into the fabric of psychotherapy, leading not only to a wholesale critique of religion but also to marginalizing therapeutic approaches—like Jung's and Reich's—which made use of imagery, sublimation, breath control, and embodied peak states. Until recently, this suspicion was extended to all therapies that involve embodied techniques beyond relaxation.

Compounding these misconceptions, our understanding of embodied contemplative practice also faces special challenges that spring from its distinctive nature. First, our received outlook on life is filtered through a polarizing mind/body dualism that has been part of the framework of modern culture since the Enlightenment (Thomson, 2008). By adapting interpretive tools from humanism and romanticism to give an embodied account of mind, Freud tried to heal the split between modern psychology and neuroscience (Sulloway, 1992). While he set the stage for current efforts to bridge the divide, the perspectives and languages of mind and body are only just beginning to come together (Cozolino, 2006). So current research on the embodied methods of the Tantras faces the special burden of forging a new scientific consensus on mind/brain interaction adequate to study and explain them. In what follows I will touch on several lines of research and thinking that seem to be converging towards such a consensus.

The second special challenge facing the study of embodied practices is methodological: both the states of consciousness and the neurobiological processes involved in these practices are extraordinary, poorly understood, and little studied (Amihai & Kozhevnikov, 2014). Vivid mental imagery, although most accessible, is unfamiliar to most, and its complex cortical processing is just beginning to be understood (Kosslyn et al., 2006). Inspiring recitation, while more familiar, is less well studied, and its mixed cortical-subcortical processing less well known (Lazar et al., 2000). This is even more true of the bottom-up experience and neuroscience of movement, which involves the poorly understood network of embodied cognition based in the cerebellum, brainstem, and neocortex (Broussard, 2013). Finally, forced abdominal breath control and the non-dualistic flow states it supports are the least commonly experienced, while its subcortical-brainstem processing remains unclear, given the paucity of studies that touch on it (Kozhevnikov et al., 2013). Since these practices are so unfamiliar, the challenge of understanding them is multiplied by the difficulty of studying them.

Recent Neuroscience and Embodied Methods

Recent developments in neuroscience and psychotherapy have begun to converge in several ways that show the fundamental role of bodily posture, movement, and somatic experience in mind–brain processes, mental suffering, and psychological healing. First came the discovery of embodied cognition, that specific postures, movements, gestures, and facial expressions promote specific modes of neural processing, neurochemistry, and mood states (Ekman, 2007). This breakthrough helped reveal a missing link that explains how postural alignment and somatic therapies impact mind and brain.

More recently, the science of embodied cognition was reinforced by an explosion in our understanding of the cerebellum. This expanded our narrow view of the cerebellum's role—coordinating fine physical movements—to recognition of its holistic role in coordinating the planning and execution of all the complex cognitive, intentional, imaginal, and emotional actions supported by the neocortex (Broussard, 2013). While early research sought to analyze mind–brain function into modular systems, it makes more evolutionary sense that mind, heart, gut, and body live and work in a holistic gestalt or interlinked network of integrated systems and elements (Siegel, 2007).

Perhaps the most promising breakthrough in this field is also the most recent. A refined understanding of the autonomic nervous system as it evolved in mammals is taking center stage in current models of meditation and psychotherapy. The explanatory power of this new science revolves around the study of a new myelinated branch of the vagus nerve called the "smart vagus," with its nucleus in the ventral vagal complex of the medullary brainstem opposite the older, dorsal vagal nucleus (Porges, 2011). This smart vagus co-evolved with the trigeminal, facial, auditory, and glossopharyngeal nerves, and the mammalian neuropeptides oxytocin and vasopressin, to support enlarged capacities for social-emotional communication, sustained social engagement, and prosocial autonomic mind/body regulation.

This new autonomic science dovetails with current research on stress, affect, meditation, and psychotherapy, because smart vagal activity is vital to sustaining prosocial modes of mind–brain processing and embodiment. In the context of perceived threat, smart vagal dominance shifts to sympathetic and/or primitive vagal dominance, hijacking the social brain and engaging fight–flight–freeze–faint reactivity and embodiment. By enhancing breath awareness and breath control, meditation and yoga both activate the smart vagus, stabilizing its dominance and fostering embodied social engagement (Shannahoff-Khalsa, 1991, 2007, 2008). By combining more intensive methods of breath control with prosocial imagery, recitation, and gentle movement, embodied practice further activates the smart vagus via interneurons it shares with the four other mammalian cranial nerves, deepening its dominance over primitive autonomic reactivity and modulating the release of mammalian neuropeptides.

In this neurobiology, embodied practice internalizes the holding environment of psychotherapy, replicating the sociobiology of kin-recognition, secure attachment, limbic resonance, mammalian caregiving, and early development (Porges, 2011). So, these practices overlap with those of Jungian and Reichian analysis, bioenergetics, deep affect therapies, and somatic experiencing, harnessing the power of archetypal imagery, deep abdominal breathing, disarming posture and movement, and transformational affects to reach into the normally unconscious mind–brain, deepening insight and accelerating transformation (Loizzo, 2000, 2009, 2012). This may be why these techniques seem to show real promise in treating the implicit learning and aversive conditioning of trauma (van der Kolk, 2014).

Taken together, the breakthroughs of embodied cognition, cerebellar integration, and vagal social engagement provide basic science that can help us study and understand the previously obscure workings of embodied contemplative practice, and embodied psychotherapy. They also help us understand the claims of Indian Tantric traditions that such practice offers the quickest possible path to radical healing, self-transformation, and mind/body integration.

The Quick Path: Traditional and Modern Perspectives on Embodied Practice

Traditionally, this mode of practice is thought to be quickest by virtue of three distinctive aspects of methodology. First, it is practiced within an embodied social modeling bond—between mentor and student, master and apprentice—explicitly meant to replicate and revise the formative process of early development (Loizzo, 2012). Second, it involves a multi-modal system of contemplation that affects multiple levels of the mind–brain simultaneously, as in development (Wedemeyer, 2007). Third, its contemplative re-parenting works to access and transform the very deepest and subtlest layers of the mind and central nervous system, where innate instincts interface with implicit learning and traumatic conditioning (Thurman, 2010). In short, the traditional rationale for embodied contemplative practice anticipates both the emerging neuroscience of mind–brain–body interaction, and the clinical logic of embodied psychotherapies.

This recent confluence helps us appreciate modern and traditional claims that an embodied approach to contemplation and psychotherapy promise not just to complement familiar approaches but to outperform them. The complementarity of embodied approaches is obvious from the growing recognition of major differences in learning styles (Gardner, 2006). Of course, visual, auditory, emotional, intuitive, and somatic learners may respond more deeply to methods of contemplation and psychotherapy that harness their learning style. Less obvious is the emerging consensus that repressed imprints of traumatic events split off into sensory, emotional, or somatic processing networks may be more directly accessed and integrated into waking consciousness by embodied methods than by talk therapy (van der Kolk, 2014). Finally, the idea that deep healing and character change may happen more quickly and fully by embodied social modeling than by analytic insight or empathy alone is plausible given that the imprints of early images, preverbal affect, conditioned response patterns, and raw sensory impressions are largely preserved in subcortical structures of implicit memory more readily accessed by these practices.

Understanding the Indic Tradition of Embodied Contemplative Practice

Given the confluence of groundbreaking science, time-tested practices, and clinical promise, the time is right for us to understand and integrate embodied techniques. In what follows, I will offer one perspective on the neural substrates, mechanisms, and effects of these practices, based on my work comparing the contemplative science of the Indian Tantras with the latest social neuroscience of embodied learning and mind–brain–body integration (Loizzo, 2014b, 2016). On the Indic side, I draw on the Buddhist Tantric tradition developed at Nalanda University in dialogue with the Hindu Shaivite Tantras of Kashmir (Muller-Ortega, 1997; Gray, 2007; Thurman, 2010). From the sixth to the eleventh century CE, this syncretic tradition was refined by Nalanda masters into a complete system of embodied neuropsychology called the "optimal integral process" (*anuttara yoga tantra*). Preserved in the

Vajrayana Buddhism of Tibet, the most modern, transparent, and synthetic form of that system—known as the *Wheel of Time Process* (*Kalachakra-tantra*)—put embodied neuropsychology at the heart of Nalanda's classical tradition of multidisciplinary sciences (Arnold, 2009).

In order to sequence the DNA of this system to cross-reference it with brain science, and cross-fertilize it with psychotherapy, we must understand its vital matrix. Unlike most ancient traditions of contemplation, including most Buddhist traditions, this one shares with Hatha yoga an embodied psychology that maps consciousness and its meditative integration onto a model of the central nervous system called the "subtle body" (*suksma-sharira*) (Loizzo, 2014b). While some proponents of the subtle body view it as somehow transcendent to the physical body, this tradition sees it as intimately related to the gross mind/body process. This is especially clear in the *Wheel of Time* system, where its structure and function are described in terms that anticipate modern views of the central nervous system (CNS).

According to this system, the channels, hubs, energies, and drops that make up the subtle body are aligned along the neuraxis, and made of subtle, molecular matter that interacts with four levels of consciousness on the one hand and with the gross physiology of the body on the other (Wallace, 2001). That the subtle body is functionally analogous to the CNS is clear from the fact that its structure and function are said to support mental processes and changes in state of consciousness, as well as the gross physiological functions of cardiorespiration, sensorimotor activity, vocalization, metabolism, and excretion-reproduction (Loizzo, 2014b). At the same time, given its subtle, functional nature, it is also distinguished from the gross anatomy of the brain and spinal cord. This distinction is clear from the fact that its molecular structure and function are said to be altered and even sculpted through top-down causation by mental activity, including the transformational practice of meditation.

The Neurophenomenology of the Subtle Body

If the subtle body is functionally analogous to the CNS, why is it mapped along the entire length of the neuraxis—from the forebrain to the pelvis—instead of onto the gross anatomy of the brain? I have cross-referenced the subtle body with the modern brain map and argued that the discrepancy between them stems from a divergence of methodology and application. The subtle body maps neural structure and function based on expert introspection rather than gross anatomy, and is intended to serve as an

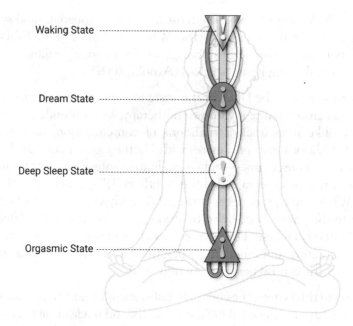

Figure 20.1 Subtle Body Map of States of Consciousness (Lotus and Pixel, Used with Permission)

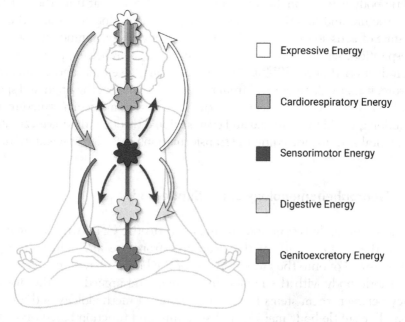

Figure 20.2 Subtle Body Map of Five Main Neural Energy Circuits (Lotus and Pixel, Used with Permission)

interoceptive neurofeedback aid for contemplative practice rather than an aid in mechanical CNS study and intervention (Loizzo, 2016). In the language of Francisco Varela, the subtle body is a guide for neurophenomenology; it maps those points in the human body where the processes of the CNS can be most readily *sensed and modulated* by means of afferent feedback loops (Varela et al., 1992).

I align the six main hubs mapped along the subtle body—at the forehead, crown, throat, heart, navel, and pelvis—with the prefrontal cortex, sensorimotor cortex, limbic system, midbrain, pons, and medulla. While we may intuitively locate our executive and sensorimotor agency in the forehead and crown, in line with our organs of sight, smell, and hearing, we most readily feel our emotions in the throat, where we voice them; our mental state in the heart, where we sense our autonomic tone; our level of arousal in the gut, where we sense our wake–sleep energy balance; and our life-force in the pelvis, where we sense our vital rhythms (Loizzo, 2016).

Beyond being an interoceptive map of the CNS, the subtle body is also viewed as a multi-life embryonic network that links the mind/body process back to its early development and remote evolution, as well as ahead to the eventual maturation of its natural potential for mind–brain–body integration

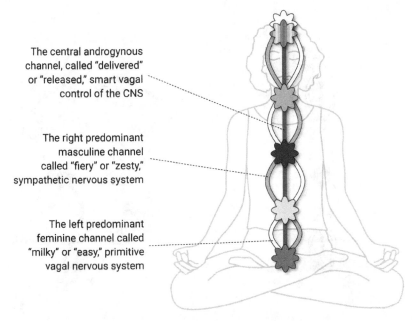

The central androgynous channel, called "delivered" or "released," smart vagal control of the CNS

The right predominant masculine channel called "fiery" or "zesty," sympathetic nervous system

The left predominant feminine channel called "milky" or "easy," primitive vagal nervous system

Figure 20.3 Subtle Body Map of the Autonomic Nervous System (Lotus and Pixel, Used with Permission)

(Lati Rinpoche & Hopkins, 1985). According to the *Wheel of Time*, the subtle body branches out from one central channel that began as a neural tube from the union of egg and sperm and developed as the embryo recapitulated the ten stages of evolution—from fish to human—during the nine months of pregnancy (Wallace, 2001). In its default mode, the subtle body's core network of bliss chemistry and primal awareness within the central channel is blocked by the reflex activity of two side channels that support the stress chemistry and emotions of fight-or-flight aggression on the one hand and freeze–faint aversion on the other. When this stress reactivity and its blocks are dissolved by embodied practice, the core bliss network and primal awareness of the central channel can be fully accessed and harnessed into a wholly integrated mode of mind–brain–body social engagement.

The reason embodied practice systems are embedded within a reparenting practice of social modeling is to help de-condition reactive character habits and cultivate prosocial ways of being (Berzin, 2010. Within the Nalanda tradition, this ambitious practice of social self-transformation is mapped onto the subtle body as a heroic journey of mind–brain–body integration, divided into three main phases (Loizzo, 2014b).

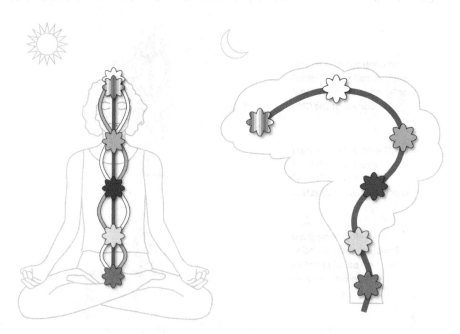

Figure 20.4 Six Subtle Body Hubs and Their Corresponding Brain Mapping (Lotus and Pixel, Used with Permission)

The first phase is devoted to cognitive, affective, and behavioral preliminaries to embodied practice. This includes the low arousal methods of mindfulness, compassion, and insight meditation, although practiced here in the context of envisioning an archetypal ideal self and bonding with a congenial mentor. The second phase called the creation stage is devoted to the cognitive, affective, and behavioral restructuring of thought and perception through role-modeling imagery and affirmations that help de-condition reactive self-world constructs and simulate the experience of embodying an ideal prosocial way of being. The third phase called the perfection stage is devoted to dismantling emotional, intuitive, and somatic reactions and instincts, and to fully tapping and integrating the blissful chemistry and open embodiment of natural flow states and optimal social performance, as modeled by one's chosen ideal and mentor (Lamrimpa, 1999).

In the *Wheel of Time* system, progress along this path is tracked as a heroic journey towards embodied integration, measured as progress in accessing, transforming, and integrating the CNS mapped by the subtle body.

Specifically, the path is divided into six key stages of progress: the first continuous with preliminary practices; the second with the art of creative imagination; and the third through sixth with the embodied process of perfectly realized mind–brain–body integration (Wallace, 2001). In what follows I will align these stages with contemplative access to and integration of the subtle body, as well as with relevant findings from current meditation research that help clarify their neural bases, mechanisms, and effects.

Stage One—Withdrawal: Mindfulness, Compassion, and the Third Eye

At the first stage called withdrawal, mindfulness helps expose and renounce stress-reactive behavior, compassion helps modulate stress-reactive emotions, and insight helps free the mind from worst-case thought and outlook. All three preliminary practices are said to work by withdrawing coarse energy and awareness from sensory and mental distractions and then channeling them into the first "command" neural hub at the forebrain, aligned with the intellectual faculty called the third eye (Lamrimpa, 1999).

In terms of current meditation research, a growing body of evidence supports the traditional claim that these preliminary practices work on the forebrain to calm and awaken self-awareness, emotional intelligence, and presence of mind. Mindfulness has been found to increase prefrontal activity and cortical

Table 20.1 Subtle Body Hubs, with Wind Energies, Neural Drops, and Mind/Body Functions, Cross-Mapped with Brain Level and Neurochemistry (by Joseph Loizzo)

Hub	Network	Wind/Drop	Functions	Structure	Chemistry
Command	6 Elements Caudal Links	Vital/Male Waking	Cognition Conscience	Prefrontal Cortex	Glutamine Norepinephrine
Great Bliss	32 Elements Ventral Links	Vital-Sensory/Male Orgasmic	Sensation Motor Control	Sensorimotor Neocortex	GABA Dopamine
Pure Enjoyment	16 Elements Rostral Links	Expressive/Male Dream	Imagination Emotion	Limbic Cortex	Serotonin Dopamine
Primal Truth	8 Elements Caudal Links	Pervasive/Male/Female Sleep	Reward Activation	Subcortical Midbrain	Dopamine Opioids
Emanation	64 Elements Rostral Links	Digestive/Female Waking	Metabolism Vital Rhythms	Pontine Brainstem	Serotonin Acetylcholine
Sacral Genital	32 Elements Internal Links	GU/Female Sleep-Orgasm	Reproduction Elimination	Medulla Oblongata	Oxytocin Vasopressin

thickness, enhance metacognition and interoceptive awareness, promote emotional regulation, and lower fear-reactivity, reducing right amygdalar size and activation (Lazar et al., 2005; Hölzel et al., 2010). Compassion practice works to enhance prefrontal executive activity, increase "top-down" regulation of limbic cingulate cortex, and increase amygdalar empathic activity, while promoting prosocial emotion and reward reinforcement in the limbic system and midbrain (Leiberg et al., 2011; Desbordes et al., 2012; Klimecki et al., 2013; Weng et al., 2013). Finally, mindful insight has been found to enhance medial prefrontal activity, reduce self-referential default processing, and promote moment-to-moment presence and self-awareness (Brewer et al., 2011; Vago & Silbersweig, 2012).

Stage Two—Reflection: Creative Imagination and the Crown Complex

At the second stage called reflection, attention focused on vivid images of an ideal role-model hold up a mirror in which to envision having such a model self, thinking and acting heroically to make a better world (Yeshe, 2014). Role-modeling imagery and affirmations are said to work by withdrawing coarse sensorimotor energy and awareness from the distraction of external sense objects and bodily actions and by channeling them into the second "thousandfold" neural hub at the crown, aligned with the power to create self-world images, narratives, and actions (Wallace, 2001). This practice not only offers a corrective to reactive childhood images, memories, narratives, and habit-patterns, but also frees up the creative power to vividly imagine and rehearse proactive self-world visions modeled on chosen ideals, which guide future perception, performance, and development.

In terms of current research, mental imagery and internal narratives play a powerful role not only in processing visual and auditory perception but in interpreting all sensation, and in the planning and execution of all motor action. It turns out that the brain treats such internally generated content as indistinguishable from sensory and interoceptive data (Kosslyn et al., 2006). The majority of what we perceive of ourselves and the world at any time is virtual rather than actual. This is exemplified by default mode network (DMN) that keeps the brain idling in between tasks. The DMN runs virtual self-world loops made of both internal narrative generated in the middle prefrontal cortex, angular gyrus, and temporal cortex, and of virtual self-world images generated in the posterior cingulate cortex, inferoparietal cortex, and precuneus (Brewer & Garrison, 2014). While meditation reigns in this self-referential autopilot, consciously generated imagery and narrative specifically exposes and replaces it with a lucid vision of personal experience, drawing less on memory scenarios stored in the hippocampus and parahimpocampus. The result is not just replacing one loop with another, but deconstructing a limiting childhood rerun with a transparent template that guides an empowering reconstruction of self and world, allowing the kind of virtual rehearsal athletes use to prepare for new performance highs (Brown, 2009; Dahl et al., 2015). The transparency of this reconstruction reflects the fact that it not only involves vivid imagery but also metacognitive self-awareness and insight (Kozhevnikov et al., 2009). This explains why such imagery heightens rather than blocks visual discrimination and processing, and also explains how it can preserve the increased interoception and perceptual accuracy resulting from mindfulness alone (Fox et al., 2012; Farb et al., 2013). In addition, the content of the imagery—the attentive faces and heroic body-language of the archetypal figures envisioned, along with their radically affirmative voices and messages—helps stimulate mirror neuron facial recognition and auditory nerve feedbacks to the smart vagus via the empathy system, activating limbic, and brainstem systems of prosocial engagement (Leiberg et al., 2011).

Stage Three—Breath Control: Calming Reactive Emotional Energy

The third stage called breath control involves deepening role-modeling imagery by reciting affirming phrases while practicing breath-slowing, forced breathing, breath-locking, and breath-holding to balance polar energies and gather them into the central channel (Yeshe, 2015). The combination of recitation and breath control is said to work by displacing binary fantasies and emotions, while centering the reactive energies driving them, until those energies can be infused into the central channel at the third "pure enjoyment" hub at the throat and/or the fifth "emanation" hub at the navel (Mullin, 2005). This practice not only helps de-condition reactive internal dialogue, distorted memories, and traumatic emotions, but also helps dissolve stress-reactive energies and chemistry, allowing access to deeper, more centered mind/body flow states, and eventually tapping into the core neural network of bliss chemistry and open embodiment.

In terms of meditation research, the best analogues for this stage are the Hindu practice of Kundalini Yoga and the Vajrayana Buddhist practice of Tummo (Benson et al., 1990; Lazar et al., 2000). Both practices combine activation of frontal, temporal, and parietal cortex supporting auditory-visual processing with the activation of limbic and subcortical areas supporting memory (hippocampus, putamen), autonomic arousal (anterior cingulate, hypothalamus), and internal reward (striatum and midbrain). The picture that emerges is that these practices induce a high level of arousal that is not only unusual for meditation, but exceptional in that it involves a balanced mix of sympathetic and parasympathetic activation—as in flow states and natural highs—suggesting not only the modulation of primitive autonomic reflexes by the "smart vagus," but also a simultaneous stimulation of the internal reward system (Benson et al., 1990; Kozhevnikov et al., 2013). The two subtle body locations at which energies are said to enter the central channel reflect anatomical regions where the stimulation of afferent feedbacks from the smart vagal and glossopharygeal nerves (throat hub), and of involuntary vagal afferents from the abdomen (navel hub) takes place. So conjoining recitation with deep abdominal breath control simultaneously activates both voluntary and involuntary branches of the vagal system, promoting conscious self-regulation and integration of the two—one branch active above the diaphragm and the other below—presumably by prompting the growth of interneurons between their respective nuclei in the medulla (Porges, 2011; Loizzo, 2014b).

Stage Four—Holding: Accessing the Core Network of Bliss Awareness

The fourth stage called holding involves deepening access to the core bliss network by breath-slowing, forced breathing, breath-locking, breath-sound awareness, and breath-holding, to the point where immersion in flow states and ecstatic highs is complete, and can be sustained more or less at will (Yeshe, 2015). This stage is said to work by fusing the energy and chemistry of the side channels so fully into the central channel that it stimulates the maximal flow of bliss energy and chemistry up and down that channel, dissolving stress-reactive blocks along the way (Mullin, 2005). Eventually the whole nervous system's energy and chemistry coalesces into an unwavering field of blissful openness centered in the "primal truth" neural hub at the heart (Thurman, 2010). This practice not only helps de-condition reactive mind states and primal affects, but also helps reform the innate stress-reactive instincts underlying them, allowing access to the most centered and profound mind/body flow states, and eventually fostering conscious self-regulation and integration of the core neural network of bliss chemistry and open embodiment (Wedemeyer, 2007).

In terms of meditation research, a handful of studies done on advanced practitioners of the Buddhist and Hindu Tantras offer evidence for the cultivation of core states of ecstatic arousal and unconditional mind/body flow (Benson et al., 1982; Heller et al., 1987). Through prolonging breath-holding, often conjoined with sexual imagery, Kegel-like pelvic movements, and the awareness of primal breath sounds, these advanced practices push the simultaneous activation of the new and old vagal systems to the extreme, triggering an exceptional state of paradoxical activation that shares features with orgasm, hibernation, and estivation. The archaic mechanism elicited by these practices, known as the diving reflex, triggers a unique suite of mammalian adaptations to the sustained hypoxia caused by long underwater immersions (Heller et al., 1987). These paradoxical adaptations—joining hibernation-like depths of musculoskeletal immobilization with orgasmic/REM-like heights of cardiac and cortical activation—reflect a limiting case of co-activation of the smart vagal system of heart–brain social engagement with the old vagal system's self-protective freeze–faint response (Benson et al., 1990). Chemically, this state appears to mix the smart vagal neuropeptides, oxytocin and vasopressin, with the sympathetic mood-elevating transmitters, dopamine and serotonin, spiking the mix with the pain-protective old vagal transmitter acetylcholine and endogenous opioids (Loizzo, 2012).

Porges calls these "fearless immobilization" or "immobilized love" states, because their strategic blending of old and new vagal systems appears to form the biological substrate of mammalian social capacities like romantic pair-bonding, sexual-emotional intimacy, and parental caregiving (Porges, 2011). The subtle body location of this stage at the heart not only reflects the fact that the heart is highly activated by this practice but also that its location just above the diaphragm is where the distribution of the two branches of the vagal system bifurcate. Within the subtle body map, this bifurcation is represented by the fact that the polar side channels are said to constrict the central channel three times more tightly at the heart hub than any other, and by the claim that the polarity of the side channels switches below the heart (Loizzo, 2016).

Stage Five—Sublimation: Harnessing Bliss Energy and Chemistry for Life

Once the core neural network of bliss energy and chemistry has been fully accessed, the fifth stage called sublimation moves to harness them into a new, fully integrated way of being. As the reactive habits and molecular patterns that supported the old self and life have been melted down into the primal reservoir of bliss energy and chemistry, the old self has effectively died. This practice involves reconstructing a transparent new self and life out of the primal bliss energy and ecstatic openness accessed in the fourth stage (Thurman, 2010). This new self assumes the form and character of the ideal archetypal self envisioned in stages two and three, only now it can be infused with the vital energy, chemistry, and ecstatic openness of pure flow tapped in stage four. This infusion makes the virtual ideal self actual, transmuting it into a subtle, bioenergetic form known as an open embodiment.

By repeatedly melting this open embodiment down into the primal reservoir of unconditional bliss—rehearsing the near-death dissolution of self through the arts of breath control, breath-sound awareness, and bliss-holding—this lucid self is progressively purged of residual stress energies, moods, and instincts (Wedemeyer, 2007; Thurman, 2010). So it becomes an open embodiment of pure, sublimated life energy, a fully integrated way of being, open to the flow of caring social engagement and unconditional love (Loizzo, 2012). Sublimation is linked to harnessing and guiding the energies and chemistry that emerge from the primal sources in the central channel, initially from the heart hub, and then from the neural hubs at the throat and navel. In the *Wheel of Time* system, this process of building a fully open prosocial way of being is seen as an energetic and chemical transmutation, in which masculine and feminine drops of blissful openness are gradually accumulated up and down the central channel until they fill and transform the whole neuraxis from the "secret" genital hub to the crown hub and back again (Lamrimpa, 1999; Wallace, 2001).

In terms of research, one window onto this stage can be found in studies of non-dual awareness practice. Traditionally called "the great perfection" or "great seal," these methods are popularized forms of the advanced stages of optimal integral process, collectively called "the great perfection stage." Recent studies show that these methods—aimed at melting stress energy and chemistry into open bliss-awareness, then reshaping pure energy and mind into more connective ways of being—have important impacts on brain function and structure. One study showed that non-dual awareness enhances connectivity between internally and externally oriented cortical systems, and others that non-dual awareness practice increases the grey matter density in the brainstem region of the nucleus of the smart vagus (Vestergaard-Poulsen et al., 2009; Josipovic, 2014; Josipovic 2011, et al.). A final study lent support to the idea that non-dual bliss-awareness states allow practitioners to channel their energy into a more effective "open" mode of higher cortical processing, by finding that cognitive performance is enhanced in these subjects, while the high frequency beta EEG waves thought to indicate stress are simultaneously reduced (Amihai & Kozhevnikov, 2014).

Stage Six—Integration: Fully Embodying Flow and Openness

The sixth and final stage of integration completes the work of extending bliss energy and chemistry through all levels and functions of embodied mind, bringing them all within the sphere of optimal connectivity and prosocial performance by mastering the union of continuous flow and open embodiment (Lamrimpa, 1999). This stage continues to cycle between the orgasmic near-death dissolution of self and world through global melting and blissful holding, and the dream-like rebirth of new self and life through harnessing bliss energy and chemistry to non-dual awareness and compassion. Based on an increasingly refined oscillation between these poles, it gradually unifies all forms of being and acting—coarse and subtle, internal and external, personal and social, local and global—into a newly integrated self-world sphere of optimal connectivity and prosocial performance. The fruit of this all-embracing rehearsal is the final embodiment of masterful integration, based on filling the whole central channel with male–female bliss-energy drops that support non-dual awareness and continuous flow across all four levels of the mind–brain–body process. This complete integration at all levels maps onto the subtle body as the filling of the central channel with bliss drops from the genital hub up to the crown, and from the crown down to the genital hub (Wallace, 2001).

In terms of meditation research, some compelling findings on the neural substrates and mechanisms of this culminating stage have emerged from several key studies of the most advanced Tantric practices. The idea that this final stage involves the conscious self-regulation of all cortical processing gains support from a study that found non-dual awareness practice increases the gray matter of the anterior cerebellum, which coordinates the planning and execution of complex cognitive and social-emotional activities, as well as bodily movements (Vestergaard-Poulsen et al., 2009). In addition, the claim that this stage allows for integration of different levels and states of consciousness within a broad spectrum awareness is supported by a study of a Hindu Tantric practice, which found that the EEG profile of the experimental group practicing sleep yoga had a distinctive hybrid which combined a theta-alpha wave pattern characteristic of the calm attentive waking state with the delta wave pattern characteristic of dreamless sleep (Mason et al., 1997). This brings us to a third claim of optimal integral science, that tapping core bliss states and channeling them into non-dual awareness of others is the most effective way to cultivate unconditional care and love. This claim has found support through a recent study of Tibetan compassion techniques. In this study, the brains of experts engaged in a non-dual caring awareness practice called non-referential compassion were found to be far more attentive and responsive to all sounds in general, and distress sounds in particular, than the brains of normal controls and novice practitioners (Lutz et al., 2008). Together, these studies offer preliminary evidence for the promising claims made for this culminating stage of practice: that it supports the integration of all mind–brain–body activities; that it promotes the integration of all four levels and states of consciousness—waking, dreaming, sleeping, and orgasmic; and that it fosters the development of a fully integrated and responsive capacity for unconditional social emotions of love and compassion.

Conclusion: The Alchemy of Embodied Methods and Therapies

I hope this overview has helped clarify both the obstacles to understanding embodied contemplative practice, and its potential to accelerate mind/body learning and psychotherapy. While embodied methods of meditation, yoga, and psychotherapy have long fallen outside the scope of mainstream psychotherapies, recent breakthroughs in neuroscience have finally brought their study and integration within reach. Although these high arousal mind/body methods differ from common practices like mindfulness and compassion, they assume those calming practices as preliminary steps on the way to deeper healing and change. Embodied methods are not incompatible with more familiar techniques but offer power tools to deepen and speed progress along one and the same path of contemplative life.

Addressing the misconceptions and challenges that have blocked integration of embodied techniques, we explored three distinctive aspects of their methodology. First, while all meditative techniques, like all psychotherapies, work best when set within close positive mentoring bonds, that setting is generally implicit in low arousal practice, but explicit in embodied practice. Second, whereas all forms of cognitive and affective experience are generally welcome in all meditative learning, embodied practices intentionally use multi-modal tools like archetypal imagery, heroic narrative, and transformational affect to work with normally unconscious mind–brain–body processes. Finally, though all meditation techniques, like all psychotherapies, are tacitly understood to work through a biological basis, embodied methods explicitly map progress in

Table 20.2 Six Stages of Optimal Integral Process Mapped onto Subtle Body, Mind-State, Brain Structure, and Research Findings (by Joseph Loizzo)

Practice	Substrate	Effect	Mind-State	Structure	Findings
Withdrawal Mindfulness	Command Hub Coarse Nervous System	Calm Energy Lateral Balance	Mindfulness Mood Balance	Prefrontal Cortex	Self-Regulation Neurogenesis
Reflective Focus	Bliss Hub Subtle Nervous System	Energy Focus Subtle Balance	Awareness Compassion	Sensorimotor Neocortex	Self-Aware More Empathy
Breath-Work Recitation	Pure Joy Hub Core Channel	Energy Control Core Access	Absorption Bliss	Limbic Cortex	More Proactive Reinforcement
Retention Breath-Locks	Truth Hub Extremely Subtle Nervous System	Fused Energy Bliss Drops	Immersion Great Bliss	Subcortical Midbrain	Autonomic Nervous System Balance Bliss-Reward
Sublimation Sex Energy	Emanation Extremely Subtle Heart Drop	Stilled Energy Bliss Flow	Equipoise Orgasmic Bliss	Pontine Brainstem	Mixed Arousal Smart Vagus
Integrative Awareness	Genital Hub Entire Central Nervous System	Integral Energy Constant Flow	Integration Altruistic Bliss	Medulla Oblongata	Epigenetics Neurogenesis

learning, healing, and change onto an interoceptive model of neural structure, function, and transformation.

One way to see the distinctive methodology of embodied contemplative
practice is that it actively tries to access and shape the depths of the unconscious mind–brain, while more familiar forms of meditation and psychotherapy prefer to influence those depths indirectly and gradually. Both modern
depth psychology and ancient Tantric science agree that the deepest, subtlest layers of the mind–brain–body drive processing at higher, coarser
levels, and hold the imprints of reactive stress and trauma that condition
mental suffering. So whether we use low arousal methods that work from
the top down, or high arousal methods that work bottom up, unlocking and
shaping the oldest, earliest layers of mind and brain is the final common
pathway of mind/body healing and transformation. Both the challenges
and the potential of embodied contemplation and psychotherapy stem from
the fact that their methods more quickly and actively address that final
common pathway of change.

While the challenges of studying and applying this path of practice are
real, new findings in neuroscience and meditation research help establish
its promise and affirm that the time to seriously study it has come. In fact,
embodied approaches to healing and change are no strangers to modern
psychology. Kohut's view that narcissistic defenses are best disarmed by the
client's "transmuting internalization" of the therapist as a model loving self
bears some resemblance to the *Wheel of Time*'s first stage—bonding with
ideal mentors. Jung's use of archetypal imagery and alchemical sublimation
to guide the deconstruction of a neurotic self and the reconstruction of
a more integrated way of being bears a resemblance to the second, third,
and fourth stages—reflective imagery, emotional energy work, and holding flow states. And Reich's bioenergetic approach of dismantling embodied
character armor, accessing the flow of blissful life energy, and channeling it
into a fuller embodiment of love resembles the fifth and sixth stages—sublimating bliss energy and chemistry, and integrating them into a fully open
embodiment.

Not only should the therapeutic logic of embodied approaches be familiar to
us from the history of psychoanalysis, but they can also be seen reemerging in
contemporary methods like intersubjective therapy, narrative therapy, accelerated emotional dynamic therapy, and somatic experiencing. Integrating
embodied contemplative methods into approaches like these holds out the
promise of a new generation of contemplative therapies tailored to the diversity of learning styles and equal to the deeper challenges of early neglect,

abuse, or trauma. Finally, developing a sound understanding and accessible methods of teaching these powerful practices also promises to address a broad, overarching need we all feel acutely; that is, the need for forms of contemplative practice equal to the demands of the high-performance roles, disembodied digital connectivity, and complex cultural challenges of contemporary life.

21

How to Be a Transformational Therapist

AEDP Harnesses Innate Healing Affects to Rewire Experience and Accelerate Transformation

Diana Fosha

Science, Phenomenology, and the Transformational Process

Unburdening. Rebirth. Enlightenment. Making whole. Transcendence. Love. Illumination. Alchemy. Letting go. Be it by ordinary mortals, poets, phenomenologists, mystics, sages, contemplative scientists, or transformationally oriented clinicians, these are all words used to describe the transformational process. In the essay "The Hidden Self," William James, reflecting on who "will be in the best possible position" to study such phenomena, concluded that their study would be best served by investigators—like James himself—who "pay attention to facts of the sort dear to mystics, while reflecting upon them in academic-scientific ways" (James, 1890). As a clinician interested both in promoting and studying transformational experiences, like James, I have sought to be the kind of investigator who does "pay attention to facts of the sort dear to mystics," facts that routinely emerge in transformational therapy, "while reflecting upon them in *neuroscientific and phenomenological ways.*"

Accelerated Experiential Dynamic Therapy (AEDP) is a healing-oriented mind/body treatment that puts positive neuroplasticity into systematic action (Fosha, 2000b; Russell, 2015; Yeung & Fosha, 2015). Its therapeutic practice routinely accesses innate healing affects and yields transformational phenomena. The assumption that informs this volume—that transformation happens, and that our practices, be they therapeutic, contemplative, or a blend of both, can accelerate naturally occurring processes to do so—is in full resonance

DOI: 10.4324/9781003243588-24

with AEDP. The assumption that healing and transformation are natural embodied processes that are there for the entraining is at its very core. How does AEDP—as an example of an embodied contemplative approach to psychotherapy—accelerate transformation, and how does it make the entraining of naturally occurring transformational processes systematic, rather than serendipitous? That is the question this chapter aims to address.

I address how AEDP works under three headings. First, I explain aspects of AEDP that are key to its transformational effects. Second, I focus on the phenomenology of the transformational process that guides AEDP. Third, I show AEDP in therapeutic action, using a transcript of a videotaped therapy session. I conclude with brief reflections on rewiring and on what it takes to be a transformational therapist.

How Does AEDP Promote Rewiring and Accelerate Transformation?

AEDP's change-based metapsychology and transformational methodology reflect an organic integration of many sources: the science of neuroplasticity, affective neuroscience, attachment theory and research on developmental dyads, interpersonal neurobiology, emotion theory, memory reconsolidation, transformational studies; contemplative practices, other experiential and somatic treatments, and two decades of AEDP practice by a growing number of practitioners worldwide. In developing AEDP, I have elaborated a phenomenology of the transformational process (Fosha, 2009a, 2009c), revealing an arc that organically links suffering with flourishing, trauma with transcendence, stuckness with flow (Fosha, 2005, 2013b). Key to AEDP's systematic access to transformational phenomena is the moment-to-moment guidance of its clinical practice by this phenomenology.

Four factors promote rewiring and allow AEDP to be a transformational therapy: 1) a healing metapsychology, i.e., a theory of therapy rooted in naturally occurring change mechanisms, as expressed in the construct of *transformance* (Fosha, 2005, 2008); 2) an embodied, reparative therapeutic stance aimed at "undoing the patient's aloneness in the face of overwhelming emotional experience" (Fosha, 2000b); 3) an experiential methodology for accessing and processing the somatic states and deep affects associated with trauma and emotional suffering to help transform them into resilience and well-being; 4) a methodology called *metatherapeutic processing*, through which systematic work with transformational experiences organically leads to further rounds of transformation and upward spirals of energy and vitality that culminate in highly integrative new self-states.

AEDP's transformational practices blossom because they are rooted in a positive, embodied, and intersubjectively engaged therapeutic relationship that seeks to replicate "the sociobiology of kin-recognition, secure attachment, limbic resonance, mammalian caregiving, and early development," described by Joe Loizzo in the previous chapter. Eschewing neutrality, the stance of the AEDP therapist is characterized by active emotional engagement, embodied dyadic mindfulness (Fosha, 2013b), a strong "being with" (Pando-Mars, 2016), and affirmative advocacy on behalf of clients and their deep knowing (Fosha, 2013a). What follows is an elaboration of four factors that explain how AEDP's clinical methodology can achieve rewiring and transformation.

Healing from the Get-Go: The Construct of "Transformance"

Unlike traditional models of therapy that are psychopathology-based, AEDP roots itself in *transformance* (Fosha, 2008). The manifestation of neuroplasticity in therapeutic action, transformance names the innate, wired-in motivational drive toward healing and self-repair present in all of us (Yeung & Fosha, 2015). This drive, which comes to the fore in conditions of safety, is marked, moment-to-moment, by positive affective/somatic markers.[1] Also known as the *vitality affects* (Stern, 1985), these positive affective/somatic markers cue the therapist that the therapeutic process is on the right track. Therapists can thus become *transformance detectives*, moment-to-moment tracking fluctuations in the client's experience, being on the lookout for and privileging the manifestations of this natural healing process (Fosha, 2009b).

The Positively Engaged Therapeutic Stance: A Departure from Neutrality

Grounded firmly in an understanding of the bidirectional relationship between the neurobiology of attachment and intersubjectivity (Bowlby, 1988; Lyons-Ruth, 2006; Porges, 2009), AEDP offers a brain-based, relationally rooted, and affectively affirming therapeutic stance. The AEDP therapist strives to engage the client from the get-go, so that, together, they can co-create a safe dyadic environment in which challenging emotional experiences—both negative and positive—can be accessed, worked through, and processed to completion.

The stance of AEDP is intentionally positive (Lipton & Fosha, 2011). In a clear departure from neutrality, the AEDP therapist takes a page from security-engendering mothers. The aim is to maximize time spent in positive attuned interactions, and to metabolize as rapidly as possible the negative affects associated with misattunements and disruptions, so as to quickly restore coordination with positive affect (Tronick, 1998) and avoid chronic stress states (Schore, 2001). Positive relational tone characterizes the positive vitalizing experiences of intersubjective delight that are the stuff of secure attachment, resilience, optimal brain growth, and mental health (Fredrickson, 2009; Schore, 2009; Trevarthen, 2009).

Emotion Processing to Completion and the Shift from Negative to Positive

Because evolution has wired emotion and other affective processes of transformation into our brains, bodies, and nervous systems, when an individual is properly supported, full experiential processing of each emotion has a positive conclusion: the release of the resilience and adaptive tendencies that are wired into the emotions (Darwin, 1872/1965; Frijda, 1986; Damasio, 2003). Trauma and insufficient support for dyadic affect-regulation interfere with that process. The methodology of AEDP has client and therapist emotionally engaged, tracking momentary shifts in affective experience, energy, somatic contact, and connection. Within the field of safety co-constructed by the dyad, the focus of the work is on helping the client access, process, and work through previously overwhelming emotional experiences, through a variety of experiential emotion-processing techniques (Fosha, 2000b, 2003), until there is a shift from a negative to a positive affective valence. The emergence of positive affect signals the release of resilience and other adaptive action tendencies which are the hallmark of successfully processed adaptive emotions (Russell & Fosha, 2008).

Processing Transformational Experiences: Metatherapeutic Processing

Metatherapeutic processing, or *metaprocessing*, is AEDP's contribution to a systematic methodology for working with transformational experiences and the healing affects associated with them (Fosha, 2000a, 2009a, 2013b). In AEDP, transformation is not *only* a desired goal or process to be entrained; it is also an *experience* to be harnessed. We have discovered that processing the *experience* of transformation is itself transformational, giving rise to yet another round of healing affects, and so on. Progressive rounds of metatherapeutic processing lead to a *nonlinear, nonfinite transformational spiral*, an ever emergent upward movement (Fredrickson, 2009) which fuels the system with more and more energy and vitality (Fosha, 2009a, 2009c).

What is often an endpoint in other treatment modalities is the starting point of a new round of exploration in AEDP: we process transformational experiences and positive affects as assiduously as traumatizing experiences and negative affects. When metaprocessing, in response to each experience of change for the better, be it big or small, the therapist explores the emergent positive experience and asks, "What's that like?" Then, with each new experience that arises in response to that inquiry, the therapist follows that up by asking, "And what's *that* like?" The recursive process—in which each round's reflection on an experience of change yields a new experience, which then in turn becomes the focus of the next round of experiential exploration and reflection—calls to mind Iyengar's saying, "Transformation is sustained change, and it is achieved through practice" (Iyengar, 2005, p. 224). The practice of metatherapeutic processing involves experientially investigating what is healing *about* healing, in the context of a healing relationship. Extensively written about (Fosha, 2009c; Russell, 2015), metaprocessing has also been the subject of empirical interest and investigation (Iwakabe & Conceicao, 2016).

Phenomenology: On Transformational Work in Therapy

This section is devoted to naming the mainstays of transformational practice. AEDP's four-state phenomenology of the transformational process differentiates between (a) defense-dominated states in which transformational work cannot happen and (b) states where there is embodied somatic access to deep affective change-processes. Its transformational phenomenology goes beyond the elaboration of naturally adaptive affective change processes to elaborate the realm of transformational phenomena, the innate affects of healing that emerge systematically as a result of metatherapeutic processing techniques. In addition to describing the phenomenology of the transformational process, I also discuss the transformational arc that seamlessly links suffering with flourishing, and the *gaze-up* phenomenon, a bio-somatic-affective marker of transformational processing.

Moment-to-Moment Guidance of AEDP by Transformational Phenomenology

The moment-to-moment guidance of clinical practice by the phenomenology of four states of the transformational process is foundational to AEDP's systematic transformational work. It allows therapists to orient themselves within the transformational process, with phenomenology operating both as a map and as a compass.[2] The flow chart in Figure 21.1 identifies the phenomena that characterize each of the four states.

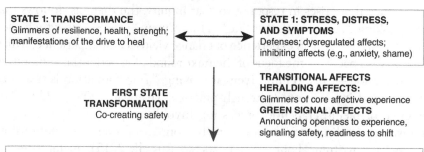

THE PHENOMENOLOGY OF
THE TRANSFORMATIONAL PROCESS
The Four States and Three State Transformations

STATE 1: TRANSFORMANCE
Glimmers of resilience, health, strength; manifestations of the drive to heal

STATE 1: STRESS, DISTRESS, AND SYMPTOMS
Defenses; dysregulated affects; inhibiting affects (e.g., anxiety, shame)

FIRST STATE TRANSFORMATION
Co-creating safety

TRANSITIONAL AFFECTS
HERALDING AFFECTS:
Glimmers of core affective experience
GREEN SIGNAL AFFECTS
Announcing openness to experience, signaling safety, readiness to shift

STATE 2: THE PROCESSING OF EMOTIONAL EXPERIENCE
Categorical emotions; attachment experiences; coordinated relational experiences; receptive affective experiences; somatic "drop-down" states; intersubjective experiences of pleasure; authentic self states; embodied ego states and their associated emotions; core needs; attachment strivings

SECOND STATE TRANSFORMATION
The emergence of resilience

ADAPTIVE ACTION TENDENCIES POST-BREAKTHROUGH AFFECTS:
Relief, hope, feeling stronger, lighter, etc.

STATE 3: THE METAPROCESSING OF TRANSFORMATIONAL EXPERIENCE
THE TRANSFORMATIONAL AFFECTS
The mastery affects (e.g., pride, joy); emotional pain associated with mourning-the-self; the tremulous affects associated with the experience of quantum change; the healing affects (e.g., gratitude, feeling moved) associated with the affirmation of the self; the realization affects (e.g., the "yes!" and "wow!" affects; the "click" of recognition) associated with new understanding

THIRD STATE TRANSFORMATION
The co-engendering of secure attachment and the positive valuation of the self

Energy, vitality, openness, aliveness

STATE 4: CORE STATE AND THE TRUTH SENSE
Openness; compassion and self-compassion; wisdom, generosity, kindness; clarity; calm, flow, ease; the sense of things feeling "right"; capacity to construct a coherent and cohesive autobiographical narrative

Figure 21.1 The Phenomenology of the Transformational Process (by Diana Fosha)

The chart begins with how our clients arrive, with suffering and demoralization, along with transformance and hope, side by side with the trauma. *State 1* is one of stuckness, stress, and distress, resulting from both the success (hyper-regulation) and failure (dysregulation) of defenses and the inhibiting affects, i.e., anxiety, shame, etc., that power them. Side by side with the sequelae of trauma and defensive functioning, we also see transformance phenomena. The former, the realm of psychopathology, are marked by negative somatic affect markers, while the latter, the realm of transformance, are marked by positive somatic affect markers. The goal of State 1 work is to co-construct safety, privilege transformance phenomena, and minimize the impact of defenses and inhibiting affects. This helps clients "drop down" into embodied, somatically based affect states, where they can be in contact with emotions that previously were too overwhelming to be dealt with alone. With aloneness undone and active dyadic affect regulation, what could not be processed previously can begin to be processed in the here-and-now.

State 2 is where emotional processing takes place. It involves accessing, regulating, and working through to completion some of the client's deep somatically based, core affective experiences. Core affective experiences include but are not limited to *categorical emotions* of sadness, anger, fear, joy, and disgust; *coordinated relational experiences; ego states and their associated emotions; attachment strivings; somatic "drop-down" states*; and *authentic self states*. State 2 experiential work begins with processing the negative affects associated with trauma and emotional suffering, then gradually works them through until resilience and the adaptive action tendencies of the emotions are released. When a whole wave of emotional processing is completed, it is as if an alchemical change has taken place. The pain of suffering has been transformed into a positive experience. We see the release of *breakthrough affects*, i.e., experiences of relief, release, and hope; and we also see the *adaptive action tendencies* wired into each emotion come online. The resilience and motivation to act on behalf of the self, which had been split off along with the core affects, can now come to the fore.

State 3, where the metatherapeutic processing of transformational experience takes place, is characterized by the emergence of the affects of innate healing, deep somatically based *transformational affects* that are invariably positive[3] and associated with transformational experience. AEDP is unique in articulating in detail the phenomenology of the positive, adaptive, high arousal affects of transformation, along with the upward spiral of further transformations that comes from metaprocessing them (Fosha, 2009c). Five *metatherapeutic processes*, each with their respective *transformational affects*, have been identified to date: 1) the process of *mastery*, evokes the *mastery affects*, the "I did it!" feelings of joy, pride, and confidence that emerge when fear and shame are undone; 2) the process of *mourning-the-self*, accompanied by the transformational affect of *emotional pain*, involves painful but liberating grief and empathy for one's self, and one's losses; 3) the process of *traversing the crisis of healing change* evokes the *tremulous affects*, fear/excitement, startle/surprise, curiosity/interest, even positive vulnerability, maintained with the support of the therapeutic relationship; 4) the process of *the affirming recognition of the self and its transformation* evokes the *healing affects*, gratitude and tenderness toward the other, as well as feeling moved, touched, or emotional within oneself;[4] 5) and finally, the process of *taking in the new understanding*, evokes the *realization affects*, the "yes!" and "wow!" of wonder, awe, amazement, associated with the grasping of the magnitude of transformational changes taking place.

Metaprocessing oscillates between experience and reflection, between right brain and left brain, between insula and anterior cingulate, between the limbic system and prefrontal cortex. The steady oscillation between experience and reflection while metaprocessing the high arousal transformational affects of State 3 leads to recursive cycles of transformation, and culminates in State 4, where we see the cultivation of "exceptional mind/body traits like … spontaneous altruism" (Loizzo, Chapter 13).

State 4. Core state is one of calm and neural integration and is characterized by the natural emergence of the same qualities of mind—well-being, compassion, self-compassion, wisdom, generosity, flow, clarity, joy—that mindfulness and contemplative practices seek to bring forth (Fosha & Yeung, 2006). Guided by the *truth sense* (Fosha, 2005), this parasympathetically mediated low arousal state is where the fruits of the transformational process are reaped and folded into self. Core truths about the self emerge: "this is me" revelations are a common feature of core state. In State 4, the embodied new meanings, new truth, and new sense of self that emerged through the healing process become integrated into a larger self (Fosha, 2009a). A new, coherent autobiographical narrative, a correlate of resilience and secure attachment (Main, 1999), naturally comes forth as well.

The Transformational Arc Seamlessly Links Suffering with Flourishing: The Gaze-Up Phenomenon

AEDP's fundamentally experiential metatherapeutic process is able to not only transform trauma but also set in motion a non-finite spiraling process of change which brings vitality and energy into the self. By working with both the high arousal transformational affects of State 3 and the low arousal calm of State 4, affectively processing emotional suffering becomes a "direct route to innate sources of personal inspiration and social empowerment," (Loizzo, Chapter 13). The transformational arc seamlessly and organically links biology and spirituality (Fosha, 2005, 2009c, 2013b). It entrains the innate healing forces within the individual. Through its alchemy, the negative affects associated with trauma and emotional suffering, i.e., emotions that require energy expenditure, are transformed into the affects of resilience and flourishing, i.e., the energy-rich emotions, the sources of growth and expanded affiliative unitive states (Craig, 2005; Fosha, 2013b).

A specific biomarker of transformational processing is the *gaze-up* (head straight, eyes gazing straight up, neither to the right nor to the left) phenomenon. Over the years, I have found this type of gaze to accompany the healing affects and herald the emergence of resilience (Fosha, 2000a). Austin (2014) and Bays (2011), both of them physicians, Zen practitioners, and Zen teachers, have also observed the *gaze-up* phenomenon and written of its importance.

AEDP in Action: The Case of the Woman Warrior

The case of the Woman Warrior is a single session of AEDP in which we see the movement of the transformational process from State 1 to State 4. The client, whom I will call Rosalind, is a twenty-five-year-old married teacher, the mother of a young daughter. Two years earlier, Rosalind's marriage suffered a crisis occasioned by her husband's sexual addiction. That crisis led to her husband's committing to recovery work, and the two of them getting into couples therapy. The consultation reported here occurred eight months after the beginning of couples treatment. It involved both a couples consultation (conducted by a colleague) and individual therapy consultations (conducted by me) for each of the members of the couple. We join the session as Rosalind, having regained compassion for her husband, Neil, is speaking of her renewed motivation to support him and save the marriage, a motivation that was resparked in the context of the couples session that preceded the individual session with me reported below.

Getting Started: State 1

Ct: A huge part of me is still wanting to fight for him and fight for us, ... (*head nod*)
Th: That is so beautiful to witness ... What about Neil's pain touches you?

Ct: Just knowing how his family is with him ... and just seeing that poor little boy who's never had anybody really fight for him ... I can't imagine what he must feel ... the loneliness I hope he can believe me.

Th: What happened when you said that? What's coming up for you right now, as you're sitting here with me?

Comment: We begin with the client in State 1, articulating her hopes for the future. However, as Rosalind expresses her intention to be there for her husband, anxiety starts to break through, heralding the upsetting emotions that are not too far behind.

The Processing of Emotional Suffering: State 2

Ct: Yeah, it's just that there's been a lot of pain in our marriage and ... It's hard to think that because a lot of times ... I just like ... we have a picture of our wedding, on our bedroom wall, and in it, we're kissing and—[drop down from the general to the specific, more right-brain mediated, tears, State 2 is here]

Th: Make room for yourself, it's okay ... it's really okay ... [support, dyadic affect regulation]

Ct: (blows out her cheeks trying to control pain, starts crying) ... and you can see the innocence there and the pure essence of love and thinking you have your life ahead of you and then ...

Th: Take your time ... take your time [dyadic affect regulation]

Ct: ... and my just going into it being completely open and honest and from the beginning having trouble and you think it's going to go one way, and it doesn't and ... things being brought into the marriage that you didn't know, just the deception and just not knowing ... And there was a time where I thought something was my problem the whole time, but in reality Neil was struggling with the pornography and stuff and my just being blind to that and the whole time blaming myself for me being not desirable enough or stuff like that...

Th: So there's pain coming from a very, very deep place. [empathy]

Ct: Yeah, and every time I feel like I've dealt with it, but it's still there.

Th: Is it okay that it's coming up? [asking for permission, collaborative relationship]

Ct: Yeah, because I think it needs to, because I don't think I'll get past it if it doesn't ... so yeah— [patient's transformance drive engaged]

Th: There is something about your telling me about that picture and the purity, and the innocence and the love in it ... Something about that touches this deep, deep place inside of you ... So much pain. [State 2 work: re-engaging vivid picture to facilitate deepening of affect]

Ct: It's ... it's hard for me to be vulnerable at times because of those experiences that I've had.

Th: You're doing a beautiful job with me. [affirmation]

Ct: Thank you ... Yeah, it is. I just want to be ... I want to be free of it. [transformance]

Th: It's a lot to carry. [empathy]

Ct: I didn't think it would still be here— (deep pain, starts crying again) [State 2 affects: grief]

Th: It's okay, it's okay ... Let it come. [facilitate deepening of affect]

Ct: Yeah, I mean I just feel there's a lot of joy in my life and then you find that person that you want to be with, and I didn't think I'd be here at twenty-five years old and already feeling such pain and having gone through a lot of really dark stuff. I guess I just have to grieve that in a way that that's what it is and then try to pick back up and keep going.

Th: So you're grieving for that young, innocent, in love ... [facilitate processing of affects associated with suffering, here, grief]

Ct: Yeah, I kind of want to slap that girl and be like ... "well, it's reality, you know." [deepening emotional experience brings forth characteristic dynamics, in this case, self-attack for vulnerability]

Th: Whoa! That felt so painful when you said, "I kind of want to slap that girl." I think that girl was already slapped—by life ... I want to see if we can somehow be with truth of what happened, and how wrenching for you it was. And see if we can help her, and not slap her. [therapist offers compassionate alternative to the self-punishment; track closely to see whether she can receive it, and make use of it]

Ct: (nods, with dismay at realization of her meanness toward herself) Yeah, that's true. Help her ...

Th: Really help her ...

Ct: (head nod, looks very emotional)

Th: ... Is there more? If it comes up, just make room for it, it's okay.

Ct: (another wave, sobs)

Th: Yeah ... it's okay ... it's okay ... just let it come ... (as patient is sobbing) just let it come ... [dyadic affect regulation]

Ct: I just didn't think this stuff was still so real ...

Th: What are these tears about?

Ct: I'm just feeling the pain of what it was like for me. I just ... I remember where I was and ... In our first apartment and I was just sitting there alone, out in our family room and he was in the bedroom, and we had just had a fight over sex and me not feeling desirable and him just not wanting it or whatever, and my just feeling completely like "what have I done wrong, you know, what's going on, I don't understand." And I was just very alone in that moment, very alone ... And I didn't want to talk to anybody about it because I was so shameful—Yeah, and I didn't know the other stuff that was going on with him at that time and … It was just a very lonely place, at that moment. **[a moment of integration marks the completion of the processing of that wave of grief]**

Comment: A wave of deep grief comes to the fore marking State 2. Its deepening stirs up the client's self-punitiveness. The therapist urges compassion toward self instead, which the client readily accepts, which allows left and right brain to come together to create meaningful narrative and greater prefrontal cortex mediation. The next round of State 2 work involves intra-relational attachment-based parts work (Lamagna & Gleiser, 2007) to deepen the healing of the self-to-self relationship.

The Processing of Emotional Suffering: State 2 Continued

Th: So what do you feel towards that "you," there and then, in that moment? It was a younger you … this happened a couple of years ago … you were in the family room … what do you feel towards her?

Ct: Compassion. I wish I could just hug her and say "It's okay." **[action tendency of care toward self in response to the experience of pain]**

Th: Can you let yourself do that? Just let yourself do that. How do you hug her? **[getting right brain involved to make it more real, wire it in, make it specific]**

Ct: I just give her a big hug and just let her cry and just say "It's okay, it's not you; there's just crap in the world that's going to happen …"

Th: It's okay … it's not you. **[selective mirroring, amplification]**

Ct: Yeah. "It's not you. And you had no control over it, you couldn't control that. So just be free of it." And also I just keep envisioning just taking my hand— **[continues with spontaneous visualization of more reparative actions—the process now has a mind of its own]** just, you know, just saying "You can do it." **[secure self-to-self attachment]**

Th: So what's it like for her, this younger version of yourself, to be met with such love and compassion? **[having explored the expressive side of caregiving, we now explore the receptive aspects]**

Ct: It's freeing. It's huge, it takes a weight off because there's understanding and also knowledge that … it's out of my control. (*deep exhale*) **[transformation]**

Comment. The State 2 intra-relational work transforms the self-attack results into self-to-self attachment, compassion, and new understanding. The image of unburdening, i.e., "it takes the weight off," along with the post-affective breakthrough affects of "freeing," and "huge," mark the emergent transformation.

Metaprocessing Transformational Experience: State 3

Th: Yeah ... Stay with that, physically with that feeling inside. Just notice what it feels like. And if you don't mind sharing it ... [invitation to collaboration]

Ct: Yeah, it feels very light and ... [transformational affects] Yeah, it feels like that huge weight I just had on myself was just totally removed ... [unburdening]

Th: Let yourself be with that, just be with that. [encouragement to experientially explore transformation]

Ct: (big proud smile) I think I feel stronger and more empowered. [transformational affects: mastery affects]

Th: That's a nice smile. [mirroring positive affect]

Ct: Yeah, I guess, it's really weird ... not weird, just, I mean ... [transformational affects: tremulous affects] I don't know, I feel more empowered (points to her chest) Just a sense of lightness. [transformational affects]

Th: What do you feel here? (therapist points to her own chest) [somatic mirroring, somatic localization of affect]

Ct: It's just like, not like a hole but ... just kind of—(gestures the vanishing of the weight she used to feel)

Th: Right, that's where the weight was, now the weight is lifted ...

Ct: ... It's gone! [transformation: unburdening] And I just feel like I can just ... that it was okay for me then to feel that pain but it but ... it's hard to explain. (giggles)

Th: Take your time ... take your time ... there's a ton going on. [dyadic affect regulation]

Ct: Yeah ... I mean, it's weird because, in a way, it's like me comforting me, you know, and me helping me seeing that I can do it. [new narrative emerges, new self-to-self relationship]

Th: And that it's not your fault. [therapist participates in the construction of the narrative]

Ct: Yeah, and it's not my fault, it's not under my control that ... [continues to integrate and weave new narrative]

Th: So just stay with that and just feel what is emerging, what's coming up as you are with yourself, with compassion and love. [encouragement to explore the new experience]

Ct: Yeah, I'm just feeling free of it. [transformational affects]

Th: And what does free feel like? What does it feel like in your chest, what does it feel like in your eyes? [metaprocessing: elaboration of somatic correlates of transformational experience]

Ct: It just feels like I'm weightless, I guess; it feels like I can go out and save the world and like that I'm free of it [transformational affects: mastery affects] ... Yeah!

Th: That's very touching. It's exciting too. [affective self-disclosure]

Ct: It is. It's exciting that I can do this … because I feel like a huge part of me is always looking for affirmation but, if I can do it for myself … **[continues to integrate new self-confidence into her emergent new narrative]**

Comment: Metaprocessing the client's transformational experience gives rise to a new autobiographical narrative, marked by empowerment and self-compassion. It is a perfect platform for re-processing the self-punitiveness that we witnessed earlier in the session, this time from the vantage point of new capacities and the emergent valuable worthy self. Given that neuroplasticity requires both novelty and repetition (Doidge, 2007; Siegel, 2010a), we will use this opportunity to do another round of experiential work to reprocess the old maladaptive patterns to further transform them and thus rewire and support the emerging new adaptive, positive patterns.

In the work that follows, going back to the old maladaptive self-punitive pattern evokes a fresh wave of grief, this time for herself, i.e., the metatherapeutic process of mourning-the-self. Its metaprocessing leads to the emergence of core state, and the tremendous integrative transformational opportunities of State 4 work. We see a spiraling process where integration leads to further mourning-for-the-self, which in turn leads to deepened self-compassion and then wave upon wave of integration, new meaning, new truth, and a transcendent new experience of self-love.

Another Round of Processing Leads to Further Transformation: State 3 Continued

Th: I want to go back to something that happened and look at it in light of where we are now. Your first impulse or when you said, "I kind of want to slap that girl." **[i.e., to slap herself, back to target]**

Ct: I can't believe I said that … **[disbelief is marker of changing relation to self]**

Th: Now that makes you sad.

Ct: (*painful compassionate affect*) Yeah, it does … She didn't know. It wasn't her fault. **[beginning of mourning-for-the-self and the rise of self-compassion]**

Th: Just stay with that sadness for a moment … The part that strikes me is that when I offered "Don't slap her, let's be with her," it's like, you responded with "Yes!" like you've been waiting to do this all this time. **[validate transformance capacity]**

Ct: (*rise of emotional pain*) Yeah, the thought of it … yeah. **[positive sign how unbearable self-punitiveness is becoming]**

Th: What do you feel being able to give compassion to her? **[deepening new self-to-self relationship]**

Ct: It's huge because … it really is huge … Because I don't give myself that at all. I don't give myself the chance to just be okay with … with … um … myself, I guess, and know that I can't control everything and it's not … it's not me … I don't know how to explain it but … **[new narrative]**

Th: You are doing such a brilliant job, just give yourself a little bit of time to sort of catch up with what you're learning, the words will come. **[validation of the tremulous aspect]**

Ct: (*nods, crying*) Just need to love myself.

Th: It's you letting yourself do what you need to do in the tears and in the compassion … Just let it come. Something very profound is happening. **[affirmation of transformation]**

Ct: I am enough. **[core state: undoing of belief of being inadequate, emergence of belief in the self and its worthiness]**

Th: You are enough. **[mirroring, affirmation]**

Ct: … I see myself as beautiful. **[core state: self-affirmation]**

Th: I see you as beautiful, but I want to hear from you: inside, what happens as you see yourself as beautiful? **[encouraging exploration and transformational experience]**

Ct: That I guess I could, you could say, I see myself in God's eyes and see who he's meant for me to be. **[core state]** … And I'm finally grasping that. **[core state]**

Comment: The preceding is an amazing statement: "I see myself as beautiful. I see myself in God's eyes and see who he's meant for me to be. And I'm finally grasping that." Phenomena have a mind of their own and are there for the observing, for anyone who is interested in them. We return to the therapy session, and we continue metaprocessing, elaborating core state, and the client's core sense of a worthy self.

Repeated Rounds of Metaprocessing and the Upward Spiral of Positive Affect: State 4

Ct: I've done so much in my life, and I don't think I've ever really taken a moment to think like "Wow, you did that!" And so like, with that, so in doing that stuff … I know I kind of like, it's kind of like I took the beauty and went … (*makes motion with her hand*)

Th: Just stay, just let it come, wherever it's taking you. **[dyadic affect regulation, affirming confidence]** You're seeing yourself … just breathe … and just notice what comes up, as you look at yourself and see yourself. **[ongoing metaprocessing: focusing on transformational experience]**

Ct: I can see such a strong woman, when I gave birth to my daughter, and I did it without any drugs and I was in such a calm place, so in tune with my body and with myself. Neil was there holding my hand and helping me, but I was so in tune with me. And in that place, I felt such a calmness and peace and confidence that I could do it and … just like looking at that person and she was just beautiful. I think the thing is you can't control what happens to yourself in that moment. [core state: self-affirmation]

Th: *Par excellence. (we both laugh)*

Ct: Yeah. And so just letting go and letting what was happening happen because it needed to, that was … it was huge, and I felt so amazing after it and just letting go and letting what happens—(*makes birth giving motions with her arms*) [core state: letting go] (*laughs*) I keep going like this, (*makes birth giving motions with her arms*)

Th: Well, you're giving birth, you're giving birth … [co-construction of meaning: re-birth of the self]

Ct: Yeah.

Th: Stay with it, you're giving birth, stay with it, just go with that motion … (*she makes the same motion again*) [encouragement from guide]

Ct: Yeah, just, freeing, just letting myself be, just letting myself be. Just letting myself be and not telling myself things that need to be, but just being … supporting myself … being. [core state—core self]

Th: What do you notice inside? I see the light in your eyes, I see this amazing smile. What's inside? [invitation to ground transformation in the body]

Ct: Inside is just like … like a seed that's growing into a beautiful tree and it's just out there, its roots in the dirt and it's just growing, you know, and nobody's telling it it needs to grow. [organic growth]

Th: Yes, nobody's barking, nobody's slapping. [contrasting the new with the old]

Ct: Yes, and it's just doing it. [transformation language: effortlessness]

Th: It's just doing it.

Ct: And it's just waving in the wind because, you know, it's just going and being and that's how I'm feeling about myself right now … It's very freeing. It's freeing to know that I can love myself and I can give myself a chance. [transformation language: freedom; love and affirmation]

Th: So what's it like to have gone through this process with my witnessing it and being with you in it?

Ct: It's huge.

Th: What's that like?

Ct: It's very … I feel like a warrior woman, yeah … [transformational language of strength] I just, I feel like all different pieces have been coming together for this moment to help me grow and to experience that growth right at this moment, you know, it's just like a flower is blooming, I guess. I'm into all of these plant analogies. (*laughs*) [transformation language: organic growth]

Th: Well I think you're completely right on, it's something organic.

Ct: This is really great. Thank you.

Th: How will this affect you with Neil?

Ct: It's huge because I can show more compassion towards him if I can show compassion towards myself and more love and loving myself and being confident in myself and being able to be confident in him, hopefully being able to show that to him, show that about myself, yeah … (*head nod*). I need a nap!

Th: I think you've earned a solid night's sleep! (*shared amusement*)

Th: So we'll bring this to a close but just before we do, tell me what you're taking away from this and coming back to the couples work.

Ct: … It's huge … I feel like we both have our raw hearts here, and in that moment that we both shared of connecting in the pain that we have and me connecting with Neil's pain and telling him that I'm here for him, like "I've got your back."

Th: "I'll fight for you."

Ct: "I'll fight for you," and now in this moment, in a way I guess I am telling myself that I will fight for myself as well. Like I can fight for myself.

Th: I bow before you! This is awesome.

Closing Reflections

We have come full circle. The session began in a positive, yet brittle, place, with the restoration of Rosalind's compassion for her husband, and her fierce advocacy on his behalf: "I'll fight for you." However, raw vulnerable painful feelings that had not been fully processed and old characterological patterns of self-punitiveness broke through. The co-creation of a positive embodied affect-facilitating bond allowed us to work experientially, helping Rosalind to bear and experience the disowned emotions underlying those patterns. Fully processing those emotions led her to experience liberation and unburdening, as well as self-compassion. Here we see how AEDP's metaprocessing methodology expands transformation. The client and I go on to experientially explore her transformational experiences and the emergent positive affects of innate healing that accompany them as assiduously as we previously processed her suffering and the negative affects that accompanied it.

AEDP's affirmative stance, transformational phenomenology and metaprocessing methodology constitute its particular way of putting positive neuroplasticity into action. Rewiring thus occurs through: *privileging transformation phenomena and maintaining a steady transformation focus; co-constructing relational safety and an embodied, attachment-based affect-facilitating bond;*

applying *dyadic mindfulness* to internal experience; keeping one's finger on the pulse of transformational experience through moment-to-moment tracking guided by transformational phenomenology; experientially *processing emotional experience* to transform suffering into resilience and access deep transformational affect states; *metaprocessing transformational experience* and the resulting transformational affects to bring in "fuel for life," i.e., energy and vitality into the system; and *promoting maximal integration and consolidation of therapeutic results* by metaprocessing core state phenomena, to allow new meaning and new truth to come forth, leading to the natural emergence of a new narrative of self. In this way, AEDP's metatherapeutic method accesses and experientially works with "facts of the sort dear to mystics" (James, 1890), and is deeply similar to many contemplative practices (Bushell et al., 2009) in not being finite. We come full circle.

Notes

1 By positive we do not mean necessarily happy, but rather experiences that have the subjective felt sense for the client of being "right," and "true," the way being able to right a crooked picture on the wall *feels right* once it is properly aligned.

2 My thanks to Krystina Kyser for pointing out the "compass" function of the phenomenology of the transformational process.

3 Both the adaptive action tendencies released by successful emotion processing (State 2) and the transformational affects that come to the fore with the metaprocessing of transformational experience (State 2) are positive affective phenomena, positive in the sense of feeling good and right.

4 It is here that gaze-up phenomena are most frequently encountered.

22

From Trauma to Transformation

Accelerating Resilience, Recovery, and Integration Through Embodied Transformational Therapy

Joseph Loizzo

I. Tapping Our Power to Change: An Introduction to Embodied Transformational Therapy

Today's confluence of breakthrough research and diverse methods of mind/body health and well-being has coalesced in a new multi-disciplinary consensus and broader spectrum of accepted therapeutic approaches. Centered around a revolutionary new science of human nature and a radically optimistic framework of plasticity, learning and change, this watershed has prompted a dialogue about mental health and well-being that not only crosses the lines between distinct schools of psychotherapy, but also the lines between Eastern and Western, ancient and modern, scientific and spiritual approaches to mind/body healing. Nowhere is the promise of this new watershed more apparent than in the surprising convergence of comparative neuropsychology, trauma care and embodied contemplative science and practice that gave rise to the transformational method of Embodied Transformational Therapy.

What is Embodied Transformational Therapy (ETT)? ETT is an evolutionary depth-psychology and embodied transformational practice based on the premise that all humans, given the right maps and tools, and enough time, support and skilled mentoring, can gradually fully transform not just their historic trauma, but also the unconscious self-protective perception, affect, reactivity and neurogenomic processing that drive our default traumatic mode of being and living. The exceptional promise and effectiveness of ETT stems from the fact that its model and methods approach embodiment in a fundamentally different way than contemporary embodied approaches to healing. Instead of seeing and treating embodiment as most contemporary approaches do—at

DOI: 10.4324/9781003243588-25

the level of gross anatomy and physiology, often observed and engaged externally—it sees and treats it at the level of subtle and extremely subtle anatomy and physiology, observed and engaged both internally and externally through coordinated, trained interoception and self-regulation.

Baseline, Transformation and Completion: The Alchemical Framework of ETT

The evolutionary psychology of ETT models human mind/body health across three broad conditions: i) the baseline condition, which includes the whole network of varying degrees and kinds of individual and collective mind/body suffering, stemming from chronic stress and trauma and rooted in default self-protective mind/brain processing; ii) the healing journey, which describes a three phase arc of progress in embodied transformation of stress and trauma into personal and social well-being through corrective learning, practice and integration and iii) the final condition, which describes the culmination of that journey as we approach the ideal of a fully conscious, fully integrated embodiment of individual, interpersonal and communal freedom and well-being.

ETT's model of the baseline condition of human life links an embodied depth-psychology with an evolutionary neuropsychology to describe how the human mind and nervous system get fragmented by default self-protective instincts and networks in ways that cause or aggravate human suffering. Specifically, its baseline model of our default, self-protective mind, brain, body and life helps explain how the fragmenting stress-reactive consciousness and neural processing we are born with expose our minds, brains and bodies to corrosive chronic stress and trauma, while blocking access to our full capacities for healing, learning, integration and well-being (Loizzo, 2009). It also serves to map the default structure and function of the embodied mind and nervous system—at gross, subtle and extremely subtle levels—as a basis for the work of conscious self-discovery, self-regulation and self-transformation of mind, brain, body and life in the course of ETT (Loizzo, 2014).

The healing journey of ETT maps the arc of transforming trauma and our traumatic mode of being into well-being across three broad phases. The three sequential phases are: Bonding—co-creating a confidential, congenial mentoring relationship; Revision—deconstructing and reconstructing traumatic narratives and worst-case perceptions of self and world; and Realization—transmuting our traumatic, fragmented body/mind, nervous system and world into an integrated, creative embodiment of lucid awareness and prosocial well-being. The three phases are mapped as parts of one continuous process of embodied self-world transformation in which the mentoring bond serves as a crucible and catalyst for change; congenial imagery and narrative transform traumatic perception from the top down; and embodied transformational affects, flow states and lucid intuitions transmute traumatic interoception and neural processing from the bottom up (Loizzo, 2018).

The final condition mapped as the destination of the healing journey of ETT and the consummation of all positive human development is modeled as the full realization and complete integration of four dimensions of embodied prosocial well-being. These four dimensions are: i) an intuitive sensibility of sheer joy and awe; ii) an intuitive objectivity of formless openness to reality as is; iii) a playful personality of sublimated flow and iv) the artful expression of unconditional care and love. The seeds for the fruition of these four dimensions of well-being are natural capacities innate in every human mind and nervous system at the baseline condition. In the course of the healing journey, they are brought to awareness in the encounter between therapist and client during the bonding phase, gradually accessed and nurtured in the revision phase, and brought to maturity in the course of the realization phase.

The Interdisciplinary, Inter-Traditional Sources and Development of ETT

ETT reflects a confluence of sources and methods that could not have come together at any prior point in history. Its most proximate source is C.G. Jung's pioneering work integrating psychoanalysis with the transformational psychology and practice of Western alchemy and Tibetan Buddhism. When in high school I borrowed *The Practice of Psychotherapy* from my father's office shelf, I was struck by the power of Jung's essay on the alchemical psychology of the transference (Jung, 1954). Yet I was equally struck by how fossilized and enigmatic his alchemical sources were. I never dreamed then that I would soon be studying in college with a former Tibetan Buddhist monk steeped in alchemy's Indian sister tradition, the Optimal Integral Process (Tib. bLa-med rNal-byor kyi rGyud, Skt. Anuttara-Yoga-Tantra), which combines ritual arts and yogic practices to access and transform the core depths of embodied mind (Cozort, 2005; Yeshe, 2014). While deeply resonant with Western alchemy and also studied at a distance by Jung, this 15-century-old transformational science and practice is the most extensively documented, widely disseminated and robustly preserved psychology of its kind in human history (Loizzo, 2012). Thanks to that fateful encounter with Thurman as a freshman, I have spent the last 50 years studying and practicing in this tradition under the guidance of some of its greatest living masters: H.H. the Dalai Lama, two of his personal tutors—the late Yongzin Ling Rimpoche and Tsanshab Serkhong Rimpoche—and my closest teacher, the late Ngawang Gelek Demo Rimpoche.

While Jung believed this powerful Eastern psychology would not be accessible to the Western mind, my encounter with Thurman and his teachers taught me otherwise. Yet unlike Thurman, I was not only interested in studying the Buddhist Tantras as a scholar-practitioner. I believed this living tradition could powerfully deepen and accelerate not just my own personal healing but that of the many who seek integration through psychotherapy. Fortunately, as I completed medical school and entered psychiatry training at Harvard, I joined a community of pioneering clinicians and researchers who helped me see how a transformational approach integrating the Buddhist Tantras might look today, including Leston Havens, Daniel Brown, Bessel van der Kolk and Herbert Benson.

After psychiatric training, when I returned to New York to pursue graduate studies at Columbia, I was fortunate enough to be part of a circle of scholars who had gathered around Thurman to help clearly explain and translate for the first time the profound transformational psychology of the Buddhist Tantras, including Christian Wedemeyer, David Gray, Thomas Yarnall and Vesna Wallace. Meanwhile, my work in the psychiatry department put me in dialogue with researchers who were revolutionizing our understanding of the neuropsychology of stress, trauma and transformation, including Eric Kandel, Bruce McEwan, Stephen Porges and Steven Cole. My dear friend and colleague Pilar Jennings helped me see how Jung's approach to the self and the unconscious informed the recent contributions of self-psychology and intersubjective psychoanalysis. Finally, in this phase of my journey I've been fortunate to work in dialogue with two Tibetan doctors at the confluence of Western and Buddhist psychology, Drs Nida Chenagtsang and Lobsang Rapgay, who have helped validate the cross-cultural understanding and integration behind ETT.

II. The Embodied Neuropsychology of Stress and Trauma: The Baseline Human Condition

While mainstream psychology and psychotherapy in the West have centered the disease model of modern biomedicine over both general psychology and public mental health, decades of research have shown that the most common forms of mental suffering—anxiety, depression, addiction, personality disorders, PTSD—are more closely linked to the pervasive impact of chronic stress and trauma than to the genetically-based brain disorders long postulated by Western psychiatry (Shulkin et al., 1998). ETT assumes this new consensus on the functional origins of mind/body suffering, aligning it more closely with the developmental models of relational, systemic and existential approaches to psychotherapy, as well as with the evolutionary-developmental models of Buddhist psychology. This functional approach is more consistent with the new science of neural plasticity, highlighting the developmental and behavioral sources of mind/brain impairments and fostering a new optimism about our human potential for healing, learning and transformation reflected in the rise of positive psychology and transformational therapies like ETT (Kandel, 1998; Davidson & Begley, 2013).

While the basic framework of Buddhist psychology—the Buddha's first teaching of four noble truths—is traditionally seen as medical model in that it offers a diagnosis, etiology, prognosis and treatment of what ails us, it is as far from the modern allopathic medical model as a healing framework can be. This is clear when we survey its four key principles. In brief, the first truth takes an existential approach to suffering in its many forms as an inexorable part of the common condition of all human/nonhuman life; the second truth explores the evolutionary-developmental root causes of that condition; the third truth offers a radically positive approach to psychology affirming our boundless potential for self-healing; and the fourth truth prescribes a contemplative learning approach to healing ourselves and others in eight steps that cultivate three healing disciplines of wisdom, meditation and ethics. While informed by the self-healing of classical Buddhist psychology, ETT extends that approach in the revised form assumed by the transformational depth-psychology of the Optimal Integral Process (OIP).

The threefold model of ETT—spanning the baseline, healing and final conditions—specifically draws on the OIP model, which maps the process of transformation alchemically into three phases: basis, path and fruit. The basis combines the first three truths of the Buddha's fourfold healing framework: an understanding that the default mode of the embodied mind and nervous system embeds suffering into the very structure and function of mind, brain and body; because it is shaped by an intergenerational continuum of evolutionary causality and developmental conditioning which blocks conscious access to the boundless reservoir of transformational healing, growth and change innate in all living beings. In contrast, the second element of the OIP framework—the path—relates to the classical fourth truth, integrating the cultivation of the three disciplines of wisdom, meditation and ethics as practiced within the embodied transformational methods of the OIP. Finally, the third element of the OIP framework—the fruit—corresponds to the developmental result of the transformational path, not explicitly spelled out in the fourfold framework, that is: the integrated embodiment of a mind liberated by wisdom, a personality transformed by meditative sublimation and a way of being and living in the world that manifests the consummation of human moral and social development (Wedemeyer, 2007).

The Two-Pronged Approach of ETT: De-Pathologizing Suffering and Affirming Potential

Like the basic state of OIP, the baseline condition assumed in ETT describes the range of individual, interpersonal and systemic mind/body ills in a de-pathologizing and de-stigmatizing way, as varied expressions of a deeper common human suffering, affecting people of all constitutions from all walks of life to varying degrees and in diverse forms. Despite recognizing many factors—evolutionary, developmental, social and environmental—contributing to the unique ways people suffer, ETT sees the root cause driving them all as that default survival mode of worst-case perception, reactive emotion and self-protective reflexes which exposes our minds, brains and bodies to the toxic effects of cumulative stress and trauma, anchoring the compulsive worldviews, narratives and habits that lead many individuals and groups to harm themselves and others, whether intentionally or not. More than just a conscious software of learned biases and traits, this default mode depends on an unconscious operating system of conditioned reactions and innate reflexes shaped through development, which persistently activates and reinforces evolutionary survival networks and the neurophysiology of stress and trauma across the whole brain and body.

Another way to flesh out the grip of the default survival mode on the baseline human condition is to consider the striking finding of a five-to-tenfold evolutionary negativity bias to attend, retain and organize mind/body processing around potentially threatening input and experience over neutral or positive input and experience (Vaish et al., 2008). This dramatic survival bias inexorably structures human cognitive, affective, behavioral and sociocultural development around self-protective instincts and conditionings like the stress-response and traumatic memories. And it also explains why the self-protective survival mode drives the cycle of compulsive chronic stress-reactivity and re-enactment of trauma, shifting the whole bell curve of human well-being tragically into the negative zone of preventable illness, avoidable suffering, accelerated aging and premature death.

While acknowledging how pervasive and deep-rooted suffering is in the human condition, ETT recognizes another whole spectrum of innate capacities—for healing, learning, thriving and transformation—also present in each and every one of us at baseline. Though every bit as universal and innate, our access to these capacities for well-being is generally constrained by the self-protective death grip the survival mode has on the default structure and function of the embodied mind and nervous system. So besides its de-pathologizing functional take on human suffering, ETT also assumes at the outset a radically optimistic stance that recognizes and engages the fundamental natural capacities for healing and transformation waiting to be accessed at the core of every human mind and nervous system.

This two-pronged approach—de-pathologizing suffering and affirming our core capacity for healing—means that ETT starts out with a radical optimism and change orientation that gives us two legs up on what ails us before treatment even begins. This proactive stance on our baseline condition also sets the stage for the healing journey of transformation ahead, by laying the groundwork for the two-pronged methodology of ETT—catalyzing change from the start by working to override the self-protective default mode of stress and to empower instead the transformational mode of safe connection and well-being.

The Hybrid Learning Methodology and Developmental Pedagogy of ETT

In practice, the therapeutic optimism of ETT depends in no small part on its adapting the hybrid methodology and developmental pedagogy of the Nalanda tradition of contemplative learning preserved in Tibet. As in that tradition, individual mentoring in ETT is seen as only one part of a four-dimensional approach to deepening and accelerating individual/communal healing and transformation. The other three parts are educational classes in contemplative methods of stress-reduction and self-healing; the client's commitment to a personal practice of study, reflection and meditation to actively reduce stress and access their full healing potential and the opportunity to experience/belong to a community of people dedicated to a life path of individual and collective transformation.

While the ETT therapist actively works to help clients to understand and counter-stress and to learn practical ways they can access their full potential for transformation and well-being, individual mentoring is focused on holding and responding to the client's moment-to-moment experience of suffering and healing, not on teaching ideas or skills. Even when introducing ideas or skills is responsive to the client's immediate experience, the ETT therapist must take care to introduce them in ways that are sensitive to their client's incli-nations, challenges and capacities, given where they currently are in their process of healing and development. For instance, if a client is in the phase of building readiness and trust in the relationship and process, the therapist must take care to disclose only those ideas and skills that are attuned to the client's present needs, and not to disclose any ideas or skills that relate to more advanced phases of the path. And of course, the effectiveness of that disclo-sure will entirely depend on whether it touches or moves the client on their own very personal journey of understanding and transformation.

Beyond the select ideas and skills the therapist introduces in individual therapy, most of the psychoeducation and skills-learning that deepens and accelerates healing in ETT takes place outside of therapy sessions. As in other modern contemplative therapies like MBCT, DBT and CFT, the first place that happens is in psychoeducational classes. To offer an educational context resonant with ETT, I've developed two contemplative learning pro-grams adapting simplified versions of the same OIP curriculum that informs this therapy. Compassion-Based Resilience Training (CBRT) is an eight to ten-week modular, evidence-based introduction to the whole spectrum of contemplative insights and skills assumed by ETT. As discussed by Fiona Brandon in her chapter in Part Two of this volume, CBRT teaches the basic science and practice of self-healing through mindfulness training, and the basic science and practice of social healing through compassion training, as well as the basic science and practice of embodied healing through embod-ied contemplative practices like imagery and breath-work. Another psych-oeducational format I use that teaches the same contemplative curriculum in the language and context of work-related stress and work-life thriving is Boundless Leadership, a six-month modular, evidence-based program I devel-oped with my colleague Elazar Aslan.

Contemplative learning programs like these not only help clients gain insights and practices we know are powerful forces for healing and change, but also guide them to develop their own personal practice of learning and medita-tion. This step is critical since such a practice empowers them to develop the strength to be the prime agents in their own healing journey of transforma-tion. For the sake of accessibility and inclusiveness, it's vital to recognize that a personal practice need not be a formal meditation practice. It could involve the sustained study of different maps and tools of transformation, sustained reflection through practices like journaling, participating in religious rituals, pursuing an art form or spending time in nature. Or it may involve physical trainings like yoga, exercise or sports which reduce stress and generate flow states and traits. Whatever form it takes, the dimension of personal practice is absolutely indispensable to the deepening and acceleration of healing possible though ETT.

Finally, the fourth dimension of the ETT method is community. Here again, the form and content of the community matters less than its most active ingredient: the human experience of authentic belonging. This experience could come in the form of engaging in process-oriented psychotherapy groups, contemplative therapies or psychoeducational programs like the ones described above. It might come through membership in healing communities bound by a shared spiritual or contemplative practice tradition. It might come through relying on spiritual self-help communities like 12-step recovery. Or it might come from joining a transformational community devoted to helping people heal racial, gender or other systemic traumas and fostering liberative psychosocial/institutional/cultural change. This communal dimension of ETT is every bit as indispensable as the personal practice dimension, because we human beings do not suffer or heal alone, as solitary individuals or in isolated dyads, but suffer or thrive in nested groups—families, lineages, institutions, communities, specific cultures and multi-cultural societies. Given the extended social dimension of our human nature and ways of life, healing or change that does not also include healing and change in that communal dimension can never be complete.

Living, Breathing Quantum Complexity: ETT's Unprecedented Neuroecopsychology[1]

The final key to ETT's distinctive approach to our baseline condition is that it sees and treats the human psyche as embodied in a more complex, dynamic way than previous scientific psychologies or psychotherapies. While most modern psychologies recognize that the psyche is embedded in the evolutionary matrix of neurobiology and the interpersonal matrix of development, they have tended to assume that it is passively shaped by neural processing and caregiver interactions rather than actively co-creating them. Modern psychologies have also assumed that the psyche is not equally embedded in and actively co-creating the broader natural, social and cultural dimensions of its complex living environment. ETT on the other hand sees the psyche as embedded and causally active across the whole multi-dimensional complexity of its inner and outer environments. Specifically, it sees the psyche as the learning interface of an open, self-organizing, self-regulating and self-transcending system, making it an integral, even driving force shaping the development of its own living body and of its living social and natural environments (Varela et al., 1992). This distinctive view of the psyche at baseline integrates two groundbreaking models of the nature of life and mind, namely: the theory of living beings as complex open systems; and a psychobiological corollary of quantum physics. The simplest way to appreciate the radical nature of this depth psychology is to consider how it models the two main dimensions of psychic life—the mind/body dimension and the internal/external, subject/object dimension.

While clinicians, neuroscientists and philosophers today overwhelmingly assume a materialist model which reduces mind to an emergent property of brain function, ETT assumes a radical model of mind and brain/body as interdependent and inseparable complex systems in constant and mutual two-way interaction. According to that model, mind and brain/body cooperate at three distinct levels: 1) the neocortical level of waking consciousness and gross cognitive/sensorimotor processing; 2) the limbic level of imaginative/dream consciousness and subliminal affective processing and 3) the core brain level of intuitive/sleep/orgasmic consciousness and interoceptive visceral processing. At the gross and subliminal levels, mind and brain, organism and environment, all cooperate as distinct yet mutually interdependent and interactive systems that together support the self-organization, self-regulation and self-transcendence of each individual embodied mind. Yet at the extremely subtle level which is the primal source of these two more differentiated levels, mind and nervous system, organism and environment, all operate as one undifferentiated non-binary process in which intuitive visceral learning and neurogenomic information processing, internal conscious processing and the external information processing of nature and other lives are four inseparable and indistinguishable wave-forms of one and the same conscious bioenergy field (Loizzo, 2016).

In other words, ETT understands both mind and body and their internal and external environments in a distinctive framework you can think of as a psychobiological version of quantum mechanics. Just as modern physics views matter at its most elemental level as capable of manifesting both wave-like and particulate forms of an extremely subtle field of inseparable mass-energy-information, so in the case of living individuals and environments, ETT sees life at its most elemental level as capable of manifesting three wave-like forms of conscious information processing and three particulate forms of neurogenomic information processing, all continuously and inseparably emerging out of an extremely subtle field of conscious mass-energy-information. While this model portrays embodied mind in a radical way that challenges our felt sense of our own and others' minds and bodies as fundamentally and essentially separate, it offers a more scientifically cogent view of psyche and life that honors our embeddedness in nature and our deep natural capacity for change as more basic to who we are than the relatively distinct mind/body patterns we tend to identify with. In this way, EET's transformative power starts before the first therapist-client encounter, because it sees and treats the embodied mind not as a solid mass of genetic coding, hard-wired circuits and trait-based conditioned programming, but as a spacious, open field of conscious life energy and information humming with boundless untapped potential for self-transcendence through learning and adaptation.

In addition to modeling the individual's full potential for embodied psychic change, ETT also applies its unique framework of living quantum complexity to model the full potential of couples, families, organizations and societies for embodied interpersonal and sociocultural change. Once we see individual humans as spacious, open fields of conscious life energy and information—as primed for self-transcendence—it's easier to see human relationships and communities as also naturally primed for change, however dense and static they seem right now. And of course, as a final corollary to this transformational view, this same framework of quantum complexity also applies to the natural world, helping us more deeply understand and sense our embeddedness and essential inseparability with all life and our planet, priming us to own our full potential to more fully appreciate and steward the environment we share.

There is one final wrinkle we need to address in the baseline condition. If we accept ETT's highly positive view of our nature and potential for change, how do we understand why embodied learning and deep transformation are so difficult for most human individuals and groups to access most of the time? This seeming contradiction brings us back to where we began—understanding the powerful death-grip our default survival mode and self-protective instincts have on our full natural capacity for conscious self-regulation, embodied learning and self-transcendent change. This default constriction of our psyche and soma is inevitable given the self-protective legacies of evolution and early childhood, and is only reinforced by the survival-driven mindset shared by many if not most human cultures. Yet we also know that this constriction is not inexorable. Given an environment of social co-regulation, genuine empathy, belonging and care, we humans can and do readily shift out of survival mode into a thriving mode that unlocks our boundless generative capacities for conscious self-regulation, embodied learning and self-transcendence (Porges, 2011). So the first challenge of any psychotherapy, including

ETT, is to foster that co-regulating environment that allows people to relax and release their default defensive mode enough to begin tapping into the capacities they need to consciously heal, learn and change (Cozolino, 2006).

III. The Healing Journey: ETT's Three Phase Arc of Embodied Self-Transformation

Although the healing journey of ETT unfolds organically through its three phases, the multi-dimensional complexity of the mind/body process is such that the actual path any one client takes towards healing will necessarily involve a blurring, mixing and overlapping of phases. This is especially true since healing, like early development, is a spotty, discontinuous process, in which advances alternate with regressions, and leaps forward necessitate a process of repetition and reiteration in order for learning and change to consolidate. In addition, each client's psyche and soma will inevitably weave a different path through the healing terrain of ETT, depending on their distinct lived experience, temperament, learning style and inclination. With these caveats in mind, let's turn to consider the general three-phase model.

III.A Phase One—Bonding: The Crucible and Catalyst of Therapeutic Relationship

Bonding, the first phase in ETT's healing journey, follows three basic premises about human nature. First, it follows from the premise that the capacity for healing, learning and change are fundamental to the psyche as a complex system open to constant exchange with its inner and outer environments, and that accessing that capacity will offer the most direct, unhindered and effective path of healing. Second, it follows from the premise that accessing the psyche's full capacity for healing, learning and change critically depends on the extent to which it is operating in its self-protective default survival mode or in its generative self-transcendent thriving mode. Third, it follows from the premise that the rate-limiting variable that determines which mode the psyche is in, and how primed it is for change, is how consistently and robustly the cues it is receiving from its internal and external environment are cues of safety and connection rather than of danger and disconnection.

Given this background, it only makes sense that the bonding phase of ETT aims at insuring that both parties to the therapy are as ready, willing and able as humanly possible to co-create a confidential, congenial mentoring relationship. Practically, this relationship can be defined as a mutual rapport which supports a robust and consistent interchange of cues of safety and connection, sustained by an equally robust capacity to acknowledge, repair and restore that interchange when it is interrupted by unintended or extraneous cues of danger and disconnection. Cues of safety and connection include such positive social emotional signs as facial expressions, body language, vocal tone and verbal expressions indicating empathy, concern, care, respect and encouragement (Porges, 2011; Ekman, 2007). This mode of stable social cooperation and communication allows for an optimal intersubjective experience in which a deep-felt sense of safety, trust and confidence supports and complements an equally profound sense of bravery, curiosity and congeniality.

Of course, the co-creation of the mentoring bond does not imply that therapist and client are equally responsible for developing or sustaining it, or that the roles they play in the process are identical or symmetrical. What it does mean is that both parties bring specific social emotional capacities to their encounter that work in complementary ways to co-create and sustain a bond of confidentiality and congeniality which supports them both to access, communicate and cooperate in thriving mode. Typically, throughout this initial phase, most of the work of sending cues of safety and connection will come from the therapist, based on their more deeply and fully developed capacities for self-awareness, self-regulation and self-transcendence. The essential work on the client's side is to adopt those cues with receptivity, curiosity and confidence to prime and enhance their temporarily more limited capacities for self-awareness and self-regulation, in order to access and engage their thriving mode.

The complementary work of co-creating a mentoring bond reflects the reality revealed by psychotherapy research—that the lion's share of the therapeutic outcome depends on the extent to which both parties bring social emotional strengths that support the relational process at the core of the work. In Lambert's meta-analysis of outcome date, for instance, 40% of positive outcomes is related to personal qualities or resources the client brings into the relationship (such as self-awareness, self-other compassion, insight), while 30% is related to personal qualities the therapist brings (such as empathy, affirmation, attunement, genuineness) (Lambert, 1992).

Beyond those key factors, the client's capacity to respond to cues of safety with enhanced self-regulation (often dismissed as the placebo effect) and their expectancy (confidence in the process that boosts motivation and expectation of results) together account for an additional 15% of the outcome. Although specific theory and technique accounted for only 15% of positive outcomes in Lambert's study, other analyses suggest that the capacity to draw on them to offer a clear therapeutic framework and articulate consensual goals may account for a significant share of the common factors therapists bring, expanding their overall impact beyond that fraction (Hofmann & Barlow, 2014). Finally, to the extent that training in and internalizing theory and method may help therapists develop key qualities, the role of theory and method in practice and over time may be greater than Lambert's work would suggest.

Preliminary Capacities for Forming a Confidential, Congenial Mentoring Bond

Viewing this first phase in light of the map of the path developed in the OIP, the capacity of therapist and client to co-create a working mentoring bond is seen as presupposing a prior journey in which both parties develop key preliminary abilities. In the most general terms, the preliminary abilities clients must be working towards fall into three categories: renunciation, the complex ability to face compulsive habits that cause suffering, break free of them and cultivate healing alternatives that foster well-being; compassion, the complex ability to meet the suffering of others with empathic presence, empathic concern, the urge to help and to act with wisdom and skill to relieve it; and wisdom, the ability to stay open to the ever-changing, infinitely complex relativity of all life and all things in a way that awakens deep humility and awe, continuous learning and self-transcendence. These three basic capacities in turn support the client's ability to envision their own transformation, recognize their need for skilled guidance on the path, and commit to co-creating and working within the crucible of a confidential, congenial mentoring bond (Berzin, 2010).

Of course, the therapist needs to bring these same fundamental capacities to co-creating the bond, only hopefully far more deeply developed and fully embodied. In addition, they must have the wisdom to recognize the client's innate potential for transformation, the compassion to accept their developmental level, learning style, personal aspirations and current obstacles, as well as the expressive mastery to adapt the presentation of the path at successive stages to the client's evolving needs and capacities. Additionally, the therapist must be adept at receiving and sustaining the client's idealizing transference, and accepting and working though negative transference, while gradually mirroring and pointing out the client's innate potential and actual strengths, fostering their internalizing the ideals projected onto the therapist and the transforming of self-image, self-concept and lived experience accordingly. Finally, the therapist must have substantially completed their own transformation from compulsion and trauma to freedom and well-being, so that they can embody them not just at the level of cognition, perception and affect but also at the level of visceral interoception and neural processing (Loizzo, 2012).

III.B Phase Two—Revision: Deconstructing and Reconstructing the Traumatic Self-World

Revision, the second phase of the healing journey of ETT involves the painstaking teamwork of uncovering traumatic narratives, memories and perceptions of self and world, analyzing them deeply and repeatedly enough that they can be deconstructed and unlearned, and holding the space for transformational affects, insights and corrective experiences to give birth to a radically affirming new vision and narrative of self and world (Dahl et al., 2015). Beyond this very general structure, ETT's distinctive approach to the revision phase combines elements of the OIP with contemporary systems of transformational practice like Jungian analysis, self-psychology, intersubjective analysis, EMDR and Richard Schwartz's internal family systems (IFS) approach. In what follows, I will survey the distinctive methodology of ETT's revision phase under five headings: i) transparency, ii) congeniality, iii) juxtaposition, iv) repetition and v) reconnection.

Transparency: The First Feature of the Revision Phase

The first distinctive feature of ETT's method of restructuring habits of thinking, imagining, perceiving and emoting is the fundamental importance of transparency through all aspects of the revision process. The term transparency refers to an insight-oriented way of working with symbolic constructions—conscious or unconscious, historical or therapeutic—which recognizes, critiques and sees through the unconscious objectification/reification of any and all constructions, no matter how gross or subtle. This profound and exquisitely careful way of working with symbolic content is absolutely vital to the success of the corrective operation of the revision stage, in the same way that maintaining an antiseptic operating field is vital to the success of a surgical procedure. By painstakingly purging both uncovered constructs and therapeutic constructions of even the slightest taints of objectification/reification, ETT enables the transparent—i.e., fully conscious—exploration, excision and reconstruction of traumatic experience without seeding the psychic space with reified content that harbors aspects of prior compulsive self-states and worldviews and the traumatic precepts and affects that anchor them.

What this means in practice is that no word, narrative, image, metaphor or experience, including those suggested by the therapeutic framework itself, can be safely shared within the therapy without being purged by an explicit de-reifying reminder that it does not name, identify, refer or relate to any self, part or object that is unitary, autonomous, unchanging, objective or non-relative. In addition, to counter the risk of reifying even these negative reminders, transparency also involves taking care not to name or refer to any self, personality, identity, part or nature, without an explicit reminder that it is entirely fluid, relational, evolving, transitory and contextual, arising within the open psychosomatic-psychosocial field of boundless possibility that is the primal common source of all actual experience. In short, transparency means keeping the therapeutic meaning-making space as free and clear as possible, by continually evacuating it of any and all reified content that arises, leaving it as much as possible in its open mode of continual, self-transcendent transformation and creativity—the "groundless ground" of personal freedom and prosocial well-being.

Congeniality: The Second Feature of the Revision Phase

The second feature of the revision phase is congeniality. Congeniality refers to the way both the content and process of therapeutic revision reflect the intimate mirroring bond that is the living, breathing crucible and catalyst for the healing journey of transformation. Content-wise, this means that the language and imagery that hold and guide the work of deconstruction and reconstruction reflect the dyadic process of the idealizing transference, revolving around the idea and image of integrated freedom and prosocial well-being projected by the client onto the therapist, as well as the potential for embodied integration the therapist sees in/mirrors for the client. In this way, both parties to the therapy co-create and share a vision of self, other and world that is congenial in that it is born of and embodies the creative synthesis of two sensibilities, a synthetic "we" with a mind of its own, as in Jessica Benjamin's notion of an intersubjective "third" (Benjamin, 2017). Given that the content of the revision phase reflects the congeniality of the mentoring bond, all the related ideas and images that emerge in the process—images of a transformed outer and inner environment and of the transformation process itself—will also reflect the congenial bond that is their source.

Process-wise, congeniality refers to the way in which the client's journey of deconstructing the traumatic self-world and consciously creating a new life of real freedom and well-being is held as mirroring the therapist's own prior journey of deconstruction and conscious creation. This process-oriented congeniality structures the path of transformation in a non-shaming, de-pathologizing way, as a common human journey prompted and guided by the mentoring bond, and maps that journey as a three-stage process of fully embodied transformation. That map takes the client through a dissolution process in which we die to the old self and world, a transition process in which we reemerge from that "death" to conceive and develop a fully conscious creative spirit and energy, and a manifestation process in which we embody and integrate a whole new way of being and living.

The final aspect of congeniality is the embodied dimension of mutual genuineness, through which both parties are connecting in an intersubjective state of shared immediacy or authenticity in the present moment. This aspect of congeniality reflects the deepest level of co-regulation, where both parties cooperate to create an intersubjective field of embodied safety and trust that allows them both to sustain a moment-to-moment connection with their own and one another's affective, visceral and sensorimotor experience, and/or to repair that connection when it is temporarily disrupted. You can think of this embodied congeniality as the soft underbelly of symbolic transparency, since it presupposes that neither party is so caught up in reified conceptual or perceptual constructs that they are cut off from real time interoceptive access to their immediate embodied experience.

Juxtaposition: The Third Feature of the Revision Phase

The third feature of ETT's revision phase is juxtaposition. Juxtaposition refers to the way both deconstructive and reconstructive formulations that advance the revision must be framed to be effective—that is, in a specific form and content that is precisely targeted to counter and correct the cognitive and affective components of the client's traumatic self-state and worldview. In other words, the therapeutic constructions that will best advance the work of revision are those whose form and content most directly expose, counter and correct the specific habits of worst-case perception and affective reaction conditioned by any particular person's traumatic experience. The logic of this feature of the revision phase follows from the neuroplastic mechanism by which memories and reactions learned through conditioning are modified or extinguished—that is, by the juxtaposition of corrective experiences which directly contradict or disprove prior learning, destabilize the neural connections encoding it, and given enough repetition, eventually reconsolidate or erase what had been learned (Ecker & Bridges, 2020).

Of course, given the complexity of traumatic experience and learning, the need for fully embodied de-conditioning also requires that the corrective constructions of the revision phase suggest a deeper, embodied sense that ensures the juxtaposition and unlearning will eventually be completely realized. To the extent that traumatic experience involves fragmentation of self-world constructs, for instance, juxtaposition typically involves a range of different self-states or parts as well as range of corrective images of the other and the outer world. And since embodied learning also involves a whole range of sensorimotor experience, juxtaposition typically involves connecting words and images with synesthetic experiences of sound, scent, taste, touch, physical movement and/or interoceptive visceral sensations.

Finally, to be complete, the therapeutic constructions of the revision phase must juxtapose precisely with traumatic conditioning not just in content but also in process. This requirement overlaps with the process-oriented dimension of congeniality, which insures that the process of a client's transformation is mapped in a way that mirrors the process of the mentor's journey and that of all those who successfully travel it. Just as traumatic constructs of self and world act as the seeds for traumatic narratives that relate the unfolding of that self and world from the origin point of birth, through the transitions of development and maturation, up to the culmination of death, so too therapeutic self-world constructions must be set within the unfolding of therapeutic narratives of liberation, transformation and triumph. In general, what this means is that therapeutic self-world constructs must be set within narratives that portray the origin and development of a life of genuine freedom, starting with the death-like dissolution of reified traumatic life, transitioning through the emergence of a fully conscious native spirit of liberated creativity, and culminating in the full embodiment of a triumphant new self and life of fully integrated well-being.

Repetition: The Fourth Feature of the Revision Phase

The next-to-last feature of the revision phase in ETT is repetition. As with juxtaposition, this feature of the work of revision reflects the mechanistic requirements of neuroplastic change, as the final common pathway of embodied learning (Ecker & Bridges, 2020). Once the cognitive and affective imprints of traumatic memories have been destabilized by juxtaposition with a therapeutic construction/corrective experience, they will need to be repeatedly challenged by the de-reifying insight/experience prompted by repeated juxtapositions in order to be increasingly reconsolidated and erased. While that process typically begins with a flash of initial insight, whether within or between sessions, my clinical experience aligns with the research findings that such insight needs to be revisited repeatedly in order to generate lasting change. In my experience, this process takes not hours or days but months and years, and typically involves a gradual process of incremental, deepening unlearning, presumably yielding a succession of reconsolidations that only gradually moves towards full erasure.

In terms of the complementary work of reconstruction that completes this phase, the emergence of an authentic positive vision of transformation that fosters the development of a new self and world of prosocial well-being also requires repetition in order to prompt the gradual process of neuroplastic learning and embodiment. As with deconstruction, this new learning also takes place through a long sequence of repeated therapeutic constructions, refinements, insights and realizations, only gradually leading to internalization and fully embodied integration. This gradual process of embodied learning and integration accounts for the final feature of the revision phase—reconnection.

Reconnection: The Fifth Feature of the Revision Phase

The final feature of the revision phase is reconnection. As we shift our self-construct and narrative away from traumatic memories and mind/body states, the revision process begins to undo traumatic dissociation and reconnect us with the full range of our embodied experience including our full capacity for emotional, visceral and bodily states of well-being. Key to this process of reconnection are two complementary modes of work. First comes the reconnection of traumatic self-states and memories with vital points within the body where traumatic affects, autonomic reactivity and aversive sensorimotor stimuli can be accessed, held and released. Second comes the reconnection of therapeutic insight and symbolic consciousness with the transformational affects, autonomic balance and pleasant sensorimotor stimuli that emerge out of the release of trauma and renewed access to mind/body states of well-being. Both of these aspects of reconnection effectively transpose or embed the critical and creative constructs of the juxtaposed therapeutic material into the interoceptive space of lived, felt somatic experience.

III.C Phase Three—Realization: Fully Embodying a Whole Self and World of Well-Being

While the revision phase helps transform traumatic constructs and narratives into transparent vision and expression through the top-down art of insight-oriented congenial dialogue, the realization phase refers to the deeper work of transmuting our traumatically fragmented body/mind, nervous system and being in the world into an integrated embodiment of lucid intuition and prosocial well-being, through the bottom-up arts of sublimation and embodied co-regulation. The healing power of this phase is supported by the emerging new science that confirms the most optimistic assessments of our human potential for consciously accessing our normally unconscious deep visceral affects, autonomic mind/body regulation, neural structure and function, even cellular gene regulation, and of transforming them from their default self-protective mode into an optimal mode of integrated, embodied prosocial well-being (Davidson & Begley, 2013; Fredrickson et al., 2013). While this new science affirms our human potential for radical transformation of our visceral affect, autonomic regulation, neural wiring and epigenetics, it only maps the most general dimensions of the realization process itself. Beyond this very general structure, ETT's distinctive approach to the realization phase combines elements of the OIP with contemporary systems of transformational practice like Reichian, Bioenergetic and Gestalt analysis, Accelerated Experiential Dynamic Psychotherapy (AEDP), Somatic Experiencing (SE), Sensorimotor Psychotherapy (SMP) and Polyvagal Therapy (PVT). In what follows, I survey the distinctive methodology of ETT's realization phase under five headings: i) de-materialization, ii) sublimation, iii) lucid intuition, iv) dreamlike embodiment and v) integration.

De-Materialization: The First Feature of the Realization Phase

The first feature of the realization phase is de-materialization, which refers to the work of seeing through our reified traumatic constructs of the body as a gross physical object in the world and developing an immediate felt sense of the body as a subtle, fluid and complex process of interoceptive sensation, visceral affect, sensorimotor energy and experienced neurochemistry. In other words, de-materialization picks up where the work of reconnection in the revision phase left off. As we begin to de-reify traumatic self-states and narratives and reconnect constructive awareness with the full range of embodied affects, energies and physiological states in each moment, we begin to develop a whole new felt sense of what it means to inhabit a human body. That sense is of the body not as the three-dimensional solid we see in the mirror, nor as the bodily self-image we construct by comparing our appearance with others, nor the sense of bounded physicality we feel through touch, nor the object of all the words and gestures others express in response to our embodied presence. It is the de-objectified sense of the body we experience from the inside out; the de-materialized sense of our internal environment as a fluid, living, breathing field of intimate interiority and intersubjectivity; the de-identified sense of the inner world as a microcosm of all life and nature—a whole invisible universe of ever-shifting voices, images, moods, sensations, shapes, colors, tones, scents, tastes, textures, intentions and movements.

In the most basic sense, the work of de-materializing the body is to unlock and explore the infinite scope, depth and complexity of embodied experience. Of course, essential to that inner journey of discovery is a profound sense of safe connection, open-mindedness and radical acceptance, a sense that most of us need to borrow from trustworthy guides with full confidence in our capacity to explore the depth and breadth of our embodied experience, to befriend our inner landscape and to clear away obstacles and cultivate the boundless potential of our human nature. As with most voyages into the unknown, this one depends on the guidance of someone who has already rigorously explored and developed their own inner terrain, as well as a set of maps and tools that empower us to traverse obstacles and direct our progress.

Many traditions of transformational practice offer some sort of map of the nervous system which constitutes the interface between mind and the de-materialized affect-energy body, maps such as the model of the alchemical vessel and fountain, the hermetic map of the caduceus, the Kabbalistic map of the sefirot or the yogic map of the subtle body assumed in the OIP (Jung, 1954; Yates, 1991; White, 1996). ETT sees these maps as guides to train interoceptive exploration, experiential access and conscious self-regulation of central nervous system networks and processes that support basic mind/body functions, from cardiovascular function, respiration and metabolism to cognition, perception, emotion and sensation. The OIP subtle body map, for instance, can effectively guide therapists and clients to extend interoceptive awareness to visceral regions where the autonomic activation of trauma can be readily sensed through autonomic afferents, and where the use of bottom-up practices like breath exercises, self-massage or gentle movement can help down-regulate bodily stress-reactivity and support the work of relaxing, releasing and transforming embodied trauma (Loizzo, 2018).

Of course, these maps are not the actual terrain of the subtle affect-energy body, much less the extremely subtle mind-energy field that sustains our full capacity for transformation and self-transcendence. They simply help both therapists and clients navigate their interoceptive experience in a systematic and replicable way that allows for shared exploration and intimate learning, gradually priming the development of embodied self-awareness and self-regulation of the central nervous system. In my research and clinical experience, this journey involves observing the interplay between paying close top-down attention to the range of visceral sensation and observing the effects of bottom-up exercises such as deep breathing, breath slowing, breath holding, forced breathing, self-massage, posture shifts and gentle movement. The journey usually begins with investigating the felt sense of embodied traumatic stress reactivity—whether around the head and neck, throat and shoulders, chest, abdomen, pelvis or limbs. Soon enough, given the mix of top-down embracing awareness with bottom-up autonomic calming, this inward journey leads to embodied experiences of relief and release, which reconnect conscious awareness with the transformational affect-energy states and neural networks of well-being.

This gradual shift in the quality of interoceptive awareness from facing and embracing embodied trauma to experiencing release and well-being is modeled in an intriguing way by the subtle body map. This map, familiar to many from Hatha yoga, depicts the central nervous system as a series of six main neural networks emanating from a central channel that follows the midline neural axis from the forehead to the sacrum and is intertwined along the way with two smaller side channels, which represent the two branches of the autonomic nervous system (Loizzo, 2014). The calming and balancing of the two polar side channels by concerted top-down and bottom-up methods helps relax and release the constriction which their extreme reactivity imposes on access to the central neural networks that sustain autonomic balance, blissful reward affect, energy and chemistry, as well as focused, centered, flow states of consciousness. This access to the central channel—that is, to the modulating influence of integrative structures like the medial prefrontal cortex, anterior cingulate and myelinated vagus on hypothalamic regulation of the brain's reward and activating systems—permits cultivating self-regulation of affect, energy, neurochemistry and awareness such that we can gradually access and integrate the primal mind-energy field of blissful openness that supports our full potential for transformation and self-transcendence (Loizzo, 2016).

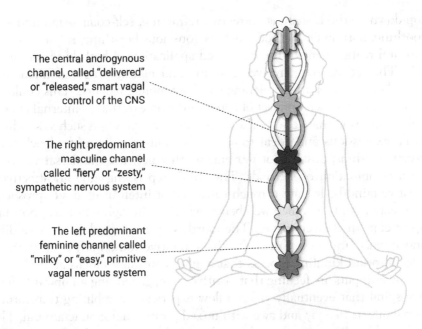

The central androgynous channel, called "delivered" or "released," smart vagal control of the CNS

The right predominant masculine channel called "fiery" or "zesty," sympathetic nervous system

The left predominant feminine channel called "milky" or "easy," primitive vagal nervous system

Figure 22.1 Subtle Body Map of the Autonomic Nervous System (Lotus and Pixel, Used with Permission)

Sublimation: The Second Feature of the Realization Phase

Sublimation, the capacity to consciously transform traumatic visceral affect, neural energy and chemistry into the positive affect, energy and chemistry of prosocial well-being is the second key feature of ETT's realization phase. While the term—derived from alchemy via psychoanalysis—is often regarded with skepticism or invoked in ways that make it seem mysterious or vague, sublimation in fact refers to the full development and operation of an innate human capacity for conscious self-regulation of affect and its associated neural energy and chemistry. As such, in ETT it is recognized not only as the rate-limiting factor in social emotional development but also as the foundation of all embodied learning, self-regulation and self-transcendence. What has led many from Freud on to see sublimation as rarefied or inaccessible is the fact that it spans the entire arc of a complex mind/body process which links at least five distinct steps of self-regulation together into one complete pathway of radical transformation.

The simplest way to bring this complex ability down to earth is to break it down into its component steps. The first step is conscious recognition and down-regulation of affective-autonomic stress reactivity. This could involve top-down methods such as corrective reframing, self-compassion and self-soothing, bottom-up methods such as conscious breathing, self-massage or postural realignment or the concerted application of both kinds of methods. The second step involves entering and maintaining a non-reactive, mind/body state of affect tolerance and autonomic balance. This could be based on a top-down mindset of equanimity; on external or internal cues of safe connection that activate the myelinated ventral vagus such as soothing facial expressions and vocal tones; on bottom-up calming feedback from breath rhythms, postures or movements that activate the dorsal vagus or on a combination of methods. The third step is engaging an affectively positive mind/body state through sustained or intensified cues of prosocial connection and embodied well-being, whether through top-down, bottom-up or combined mechanisms. The fourth step is up-regulating, expanding and intensifying an existing affectively positive mind/body state through a feedforward kindling process that applies continuous focus and effort to whatever inputs are feeding that positive state, generating an upward affective spiral that eventually yields a flow experience combining transformational affects like joy and awe with mixed positive autonomic arousal. The fifth and final step involves channeling and harnessing the flow accessed by the upward affective spiral towards disidentifying with/releasing embodied traumatic affect, energy and chemistry and identifying with/ cultivating the prosocial affect, energy and chemistry of well-being and its embodied expression and action instead.

Lucid Intuition: The Third Feature of the Realization Phase

The third feature of the ETT realization phase is lucid intuition. As the phrase suggests, lucid intuition refers to the fully conscious self-regulation of embodied modes of interoception and neuroception that normally remain unconscious yet powerfully shape our affective, energetic, sensorimotor and neural processing. The preverbal biases and assessments formed by implicit and procedural learning in the course of development constitute a whole network of largely unconscious perceptual habit that anchors our traumatic experience of embodied life, restricting access to full experience of embodied prosocial well-being. Lucid intuition is the result of a painstaking process of gradually exposing and correcting unconscious affective biases and perceptual distortions conditioned by stress and trauma so that we can recover and consciously access the full natural capacity of our interoceptive and neuroceptive faculties. Given the need to access the embodied experience of prosocial well-being in order to expose, correct and release traumatic conditioning, lucid intuition assumes a well-developed capacity for sublimation to provide a platform of transformational affect-energy states of well-being.

What grows out of this work is the capacity to link constructed, symbolic modes of perception with more immediate, embodied modes of interoception and neuroception in such a way that we can access and embody our full capacity for radical openness and self-transcendence at all levels of the mind/body process. While intuition has traditionally been understood in one of two polar ways—either skeptically as an unreliable subjective impression, or romantically as an infallible embodied wisdom—ETT sees it as an embodied mode of perception, that is, as an embodied intelligence like emotional intelligence which is no more and no less reliable in general than symbolically constructed modes of perception like thinking, imagination or recognition. On the other hand, it sees lucid intuition as far more reliable than either unexamined, untrained intuition or unexamined, untested symbolic knowledge. Like knowledge or emotion subjected to thorough analysis, lucid intuition is more reliable because it reflects a consciously cross-checked and trained mode of embodied perception which has been thoroughly examined, tested and refined by critical reflection, experiential testing and intersubjective validation.

Of course, given the multi-dimensional complexity of human intelligence and learning, ETT does not approach lucid intuition as monolithic or its cultivation as a one-track process. Based on its quantum complexity model of the mind/body process, derived from the OIP, ETT differentiates distinct levels and types of lucid intuition depending on whether they operate at the gross, subtle or subtlest level of mind/body processing (Thurman, 2010). At the level of waking consciousness and gross cognitive/sensorimotor processing, it recognizes five modes of lucid intuition that operate in relation to each of five gross mind/body systems—physical, hedonic, motivational, conceptual and perceptual. At the subtle level of dream/imaginative consciousness and subliminal emotional processing, it recognizes three modes of lucid intuition that operate in relation to attachment, aversion and isolation-oriented conditioned biases and unconscious instincts. And at the level of the subtlest deep sleep/orgasmic consciousness and interoceptive visceral processing, it recognizes a primordial source mode of lucid intuition that operates in relation to the non-binary, bias-and-instinct-free realm of self-transcendent openness, peak positive affect-energy and neurogenomic fluidity.

The general form of all these lucid intuitions is an embodied felt sense of the de-reifying insights of radical open-mindedness, transparency and

de-materialization that increasingly clear the learning space for ETT's bonding, revision and realization phases. For ETT, the lucid intuition that helps
render the physical body transparent is the reflective intuition, which is built
on a felt sense of the intimate spacious interiority of the living body. The
lucid intuition that helps render hedonic pain-pleasure-numbness sensation
transparent is the empathic intuition, since it de-personalizes hedonic sensation with an unbiased felt sense of the hedonic vulnerability and sensitivity
shared by all embodied beings. The lucid intuition that helps render the motivational system transparent is the success intuition, which helps ensure successful goal-execution with the felt sense of confidence born of artful social
teamwork. The lucid intuition that helps render conceptuality transparent is
the discerning intuition, which elevates conceptuality to the level of a science or fine art by appreciating the exquisite, infinite distinctiveness of each
unique individual person, place or thing that can be conceived. The lucid
intuition that helps render the perceptual system transparent is the transcendence intuition, which deepens perceptiveness to the level of visionary
insight or transcendent wisdom by seeing through any mediating perceptual
habit or bias that may limit continued openness to the infinite complexity and
ungraspable relationality of anything and everything that can be perceived.

The three forms of lucid intuition that operate at the subtle level reflect the
learned capacity to disidentify with normally unconscious conditioned and
instinctive patterns of embodied affective reactivity/impulsivity so we can
access visceral interoception and neuroception from a space of fully conscious
unbiased awareness and prosocial affective well-being. For ETT, the first of
these three modes is the pacifying intuition, which allows one to down-regulate and disidentify with anxious attachment patterns, fearful autonomic
arousal and attachment instincts, and to access instead the felt sense of
embodied self-confidence, trust and prosocial openness. The second mode,
the caring intuition, allows one to down-regulate and disidentify with avoidant attachment patterns, aggressive autonomic arousal and self-protective
instincts, and to access instead the felt sense of affective tolerance, visceral
acceptance and prosocial connectedness. The third mode, the engaging intuition, allows one to down-regulate and disidentify with disorganized attachment patterns, dissociative freeze activation and primal protective instincts,
and to access instead the felt sense of safely embodied presence, grounded
openness and prosocial engagement.

The lucid intuition that operates at the subtlest level—translucence intuition—reflects the learned capacity to consciously access and fully embody
the non-binary, bias-and-instinct-free source mode of the mind/body process,

which supports the psyche's capacity for primal self-transcendent openness, prosocial affect-energy and neurogenomic fluidity. In addition to bringing awareness and self-regulation to the primal source of all states and forms of consciousness—the original face or native ground of our being—it also brings them to the bioelectrochemical field that supports the embodied mind's boundless potential for self-transcendence through learning and transformation. In short, the translucence intuition reflects the psyche's full self-awareness and self-regulation of its normally unconscious essential nature—as a spacious field of potential primed for learning and self-transcendence, indivisible from the mass-energy-information field of neuroplasticity and genomic fluidity. Essentially, this subtlest lucid intuition reflects the final intuitive realization that renders the mind/body process fully transparent, de-materialized and de-objectified. What begins as an altered state of immersion in spacious sleeplike/orgasmic dissolution and absorption eventually becomes a stable trait that allows the mind to realize its primal nature—as a translucent openness to any and all energy and information in the internal and external environment.

Dreamlike Embodiment: The Fourth Feature of the Realization Phase

The gradual dawning of lucid intuition opens the door to the fourth feature of the ETT realization phase—dreamlike embodiment. As the journey into our interiority de-materializes the traumatic felt sense of embodiment, allowing for growing awareness and self-regulation of the affective energy and lucid intuition of well-being, it forever transforms our normally unconscious relationship with living in a human body. Given widening access to the full range and depth of embodied experience, the capacity for shifting affect and energy through sublimation, and a consequent shift in the center of gravity towards a deeper, more fluid sense of embodied well-being, comes a whole new take on embodiment. In stark contrast to the default reified sense of the body as given, based on the normally unconscious instinct-driven process of early childhood conditioning, this new lived experience of being in a human body is characterized by self-awareness, flexibility and conscious sculpting of the felt sense of embodied personhood. This new relationship with embodiment is further enhanced by the emergence of lucid intuitions which help de-materialize reified perceptions and sensations of having a body and effectively render transparent not just the default childhood body-sense but the whole spectrum of embodied experience. It allows us to acquire a taste for the "unbearable lightness" or dreamy fluidity of our most intimate felt sense of embodied being, as if we were really inhabiting not a solid physical body with feet on the ground but a living, breathing person-shaped waveform floating or swimming though groundless fields of positively charged, information-rich bioenergy.

The combined effect of the various shifts in embodiment that arise in the course of the ETT path gradually leads to a profound sense of disorientation regarding the new, transparent experience of mind/body states. Clients who go through a de-reification of familiar constructs of self and world in the revision phase and go on to experience a de-materialization of familiar mind/body states in the realization phase typically report feeling "strange," "odd," "uneasy" or "uncomfortable" in the context of a markedly positive sense of relief and well-being. This positive disorientation is quite unlike the derealization and depersonalization that arise out of dissociative defenses against stress and trauma. Instead, this disorientation grows out of the contrast between default traumatic mind/body states and states that feel unfamiliar not just because they are novel but also because they are grounded in well-being affects and energies rather than in the stress-reactive affects and energies of trauma. The equivalent of the destabilization of traumatic memories through juxtaposition in the revision phase, this disorientation in the realization phase reflects a transition in which the unconscious stress affects and visceral energies of trauma are exposed, destabilized and de-conditioned by the conscious therapeutic experience of positive affects and energies of embodied safety and well-being.

Of course, given the repeated deconditioning of traumatic embodiment and exposure to the prosocial affects and energies of embodied well-being, the felt sense of the body in the realization phase eventually moves through disorientation to become stable and familiar as a new normal. Yet the fact that this new positive form of embodiment has emerged in the full light of consciousness rather than through unconscious development means that the new normal feels radically different from the default sense of the body as a solid physical object in the world. In particular, it takes on a sense of the essential lightness of being—a sense that the body is not a fixed solid but a shifting, insubstantial appearance reflected like a dream or illusion in the de-materialized interior space of embodied mind. This new sense of the body as dreamlike and illusory is further enhanced by the emergence of lucid intuitions which de-materialize the whole spectrum of the lived experience of the mind/body process at all levels and in all states. Of course, this broad shift towards a more lucid and fluid way of being embodied is not happening in a vacuum or in isolation; it emerges as a natural internalization and experiential validation by the client of the therapist's felt sense of embodied life, available to the client as a lived possibility within the intersubjective field of the mentoring bond.

This healing sense of the body as like a dream body or illusion is what ETT calls dreamlike embodiment. And given that it emerges out of the conscious interior space cleared by de-materialization, sublimation and lucid intuition; dreamlike embodiment is to conditioned embodiment what philosophy, art or science are to unexamined life. Given the new normal of heightened conscious awareness of the body as a whole spectrum of living breathing experience, what naturally emerges is a new sense of embodiment not only as a broad range of optional ways of being, or embodied self-states, but also as a creative freedom and responsibility to choose among the options and sculpt out of them a particular tone and style of embodiment in any given place and time. This new sense allows for a more inclusive embrace of all previously fragmented self-states, and a gradual healing integration of these parts into a field of awareness that allows a fluid, transparent teamwork among the long estranged and alienated selves. Thanks to this new creative sense of dreamlike embodiment, one naturally evolves a more artful relationship with embodied personhood. Like an actor, one comes to relate to personhood less as unitary or given than as the unfolding of an intentional creative process, which allows for a wide range and aesthetic fine-tuning of embodiment as an instrument for the social expression and communication of experience and character.

Integration: The Fifth Feature of the Realization Phase

Integration, the fifth and last feature of the ETT realization phase, refers to the work of artfully inhabiting a transparent, de-materialized sense of the mind/body process through gradually weaving lucid intuition together with dreamlike embodiment into a consciously chosen, fully integrated way of being. As in the course of normal development, this work involves a continuous repetition of mind/body state changes, oscillating between experiences of dissolution or de-differentiation on the one hand, and reemergence or differentiation on the other. Repeating these transitions over time deepens the experiential shifts prompted by de-reifying, deconstructive insight/dematerializing reflection, followed by the emergence of newfound mind/body states of integrated well-being. Such experiential oscillations recapitulate the natural transitions that shape development throughout the lifecycle, such as the wake–sleep cycle, hormonal cycles, seasonal cycles, the state changes of sexual intimacy and the existential changes of death/near-death and birth/reemergence.

The path of integration is based on alternately bringing lucid intuition to help de-materialize and dissolve traumatic mind/body states through fearless insight, and then using that intuition to consciously guide the emergence of a chosen dreamlike embodiment through weaving positive energies, affects and modes of expression into a lucid, fully embodied integrity of prosocial well-being. The integration process involves not just healing dissociated self-states or parts with their traumatic affects and autonomic reactivities, but actively harnessing the expanded self-awareness and access to well-being to consciously envision and craft a new spectrum of optimal ways of being and living in the world.

In this sense, ETT maps and traverses the whole journey of psychic health, from facing and healing trauma to the highest levels of positive mind/body health and embodied prosocial well-being. And since this healing journey involves increasing access to and integration of the radically open, self-transcendent potential we humans share with all life and nature, an individual's integration of fully lucid, fully embodied well-being is not just a personal shift, but inexorably catalyzes reciprocal shifts in others, in society and in the larger world. We have all had temporary glimpses of this kind of self-transcendent shift, as when the experience of falling deeply in love shifts our whole sense of being in the world away from a dense, solid sense of separateness and isolation towards a more buoyant and fluid sense of fully belonging and being deeply connected through a field of boundless possibility. The difference is, instead of that powerful shift emerging involuntarily based on our psychobiological instincts and conditionings, and decaying inevitably over time, it emerges as the result of conscious access to our primal mind/body capacities for prosocial well-being, not simply as a transient state but as a consciously learned, continuously practiced and finally fully integrated stable trait.

III.D The Final Condition: Reaping the Harvest of Lucid Positive Human Development

The final condition described in ETT's map of human development reflects the culmination not just of the healing journey but of the lifelong process of deepening and integrating the changes made in the course of that journey. It offers a generic model of the final realization and full integration of the human potential dormant in all of us at baseline, which can be gradually accessed and cultivated through ETT and in the course of life after therapy. In that sense, the final condition represents a general model of the highest reaches of positive human development, as seen from the vantage of ETT.

The model depicts optimal well-being as full final freedom from self-protective habits and instincts that obstruct open processing either along the mind/body axis, along the subject/object axis or both. In keeping with ETT's view of the baseline condition of human life, this freedom reflects the learned capacity of waking consciousness to interoceptively access and intentionally live from the extremely subtle field of conscious mass-energy-information which holds our full potential for learning and change, and hence acts as the prime source for the development of psychosomatic and psychosocial well-being. Specifically, the final condition is mapped as the full realization and complete integration of four dimensions of embodied prosocial well-being. These four dimensions are: i) an intuitive sensibility of sheer joy and awe; ii) an intuitive objectivity of formless openness to reality as it is; iii) a playful personality of sublimated flow and iv) the artful expression of unconditional care and love.

Understanding the Four Dimensions of Fully Embodied Prosocial Well-Being

As I mentioned above, the seeds for the fruition of these four dimensions of well-being are natural capacities innate in every human mind and nervous system at baseline. In the course of the healing journey, they are brought to awareness in the encounter between the two parties during the bonding phase, gradually accessed and nurtured in the revision phase, and brought to maturity in the course of the realization phase and the continued growth that follows. Now that we've surveyed the main features of each of those phases, it may help to trace the four dimensions of the final condition back to their seeds and the path of their cultivation through the healing journey.

While the four dimensions of embodied well-being are listed above in the order of their final emergence out of the conscious energy-information field which is their primary source, it's vital to note that that is not the order in which they are generally accessed and cultivated within the healing journey. Typically, these four domains are accessed in the reverse order from their emergence in the final condition, that is: access to unconditional care and love comes first; the play of sublimation and flow second; access to the intuitive objectivity of formless openness next and the acquired taste for the intuitive sensibility of peak affects like awe and joy last. The reason for this is simple enough. Progress along the path to well-being tends to follow an arc from the most accessible to waking consciousness to the least, that is—from the gross level of waking consciousness and sensorimotor processing towards the very subtlest level of orgasmic consciousness and interoceptive visceral processing. In other words, this normal progression reflects the incremental nature of the therapeutic work of bringing self-awareness and self-regulation to increasingly subtle and primal levels of consciousness and neurobiology.

Bringing mindful awareness to waking-state experience and processing in most cases is more readily accessible, while accessing the deeper, more primal dimensions of well-being—sublimation, lucid intuition, embodied joy—involve deeper and subtler levels of embodied self-awareness and self-regulation. Of course, this is not to suggest that the progression in any one individual or group is so linear or predictable. In practice, as I shared above, the process of access and cultivation often takes a circuitous, non-linear path, based on individual differences in forms of suffering, learning style, inclination and so on. Nonetheless, in my personal and clinical experience this organic logic does apply to the overall progress of most individuals, most of the time.

The same organic logic also sheds light on the seeds of well-being lying dormant at the baseline condition and helps clarify the underpinnings of the therapeutic logic of ETT. Specifically, the "seeds" of the four dimensions of prosocial well-being can be traced to the four levels of consciousness and their respective forms of neurophysiological processing, and so can be mapped onto the structure and function of the nervous system. (Note that this mapping refines the three main levels of the ETT mind/body model into four by distinguishing deep sleep from orgasm and dividing core brain processing into upper and lower levels.) In particular, the seed of unconditional care and love maps onto waking neocortical processing in the brain model and forebrain-crown circuits sensed in the head on the embodied model; the seed of sublimation maps onto dreamlike limbic system processing in the brain model and the expressive circuit sensed at the throat in the embodied model; the seed of intuitive objectivity maps onto the deep sleep hypothalamic-midbrain processing in the brain model and the perceptual circuit sensed at the heart in the embodied model; and the intuitive sensibility of joy and awe maps onto brainstem somatosensory processing in the brain model and the hedonic sensitivity/motivational circuits sensed at the navel and sacrum in the embodied model.

The depth-psychological structure of the healing journey of ETT and its four-dimensional mapping of fully embodied prosocial well-being show the radical transformational aim of this approach. The full scope of optimal well-being accessible through ETT reflects a complete transformation of all four levels of consciousness and neural processing from their traumatic survival mode into a fully integrated mode of embodied prosocial

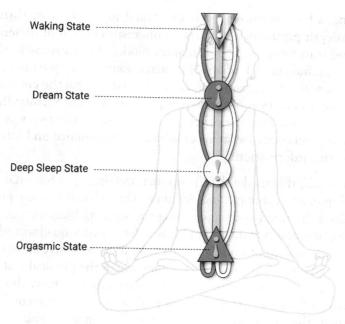

Waking State

Dream State

Deep Sleep State

Orgasmic State

Figure 22.2 Subtle Body Map of States of Consciousness (Lotus and Pixel, Used with Permission)

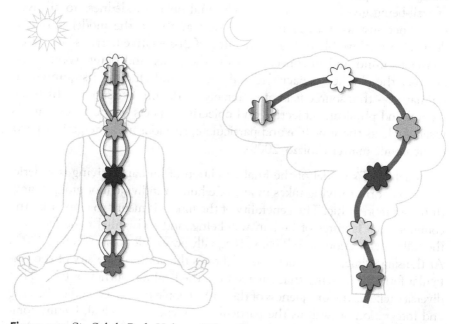

Figure 22.3 Six Subtle Body Hubs and Their Corresponding Brain Mapping (Lotus and Pixel, Used with Permission)

well-being, which promotes both individual and collective thriving. In terms of depth psychology, the way to understand the four dimensions of well-being is in terms of ETT's complex model of the psyche as the open mind-energy matrix out of which emerge four main systems of mutual interaction and interdependence. On one hand, the psyche emerges out of the two-way interaction of the psychophysical systems of embodied mind and conscious body; on the other, it emerges out of the two-way interaction of the psychosocial systems of subjective experience and intersubjective/objective information.

In other words, this model depicts optimal well-being as full final freedom from self-protective habits and instincts that obstruct open processing either along the mind/body axis, along the subject/object axis or both. In that sense, unconditional care and love refers to that quadrant where the physical embodiment of well-being gives rise to its objective expression; the play of sublimation refers to that quadrant where the physical embodiment of well-being gives rise to the subjective experience of flow; the intuitive objectivity of formless openness refers to that quadrant of mental embodiment where the optimistic openness of well-being gives rise to evolving knowledge of objective reality; and the intuitive sensibility of joy and awe refers to that quadrant of mental embodiment where the affective positivity of well-being gives rise to an unconditional open-mindedness to all lived experience just as it is. A more holistic way to see the model is that it depicts optimal well-being as the healing of dissociative barriers—between conscious mind and unconscious body, the inner and outer world—that obstruct the psyche's capacity to fully access and channel its quintessential nature—that source field of extremely subtle mind-energy in which the mental and physical, subjective and objective aspects of the psyche are as inseparable as the wavelike and particulate, spacious and energetic aspects of subatomic matter (Loizzo, 2009).

Although ETT's model of the final condition of human thriving is generic, the actual form thriving takes in any one human individual or group is anything but monolithic. The generality of the model is meant to emphasize the common core features of human well-being, and to highlight the fact that the fullest realization of well-being is equally accessible to all (Brown, 2009). At the same time, the model also celebrates the endless diversity of the particular forms of thriving that emerge from the healing journey of ETT. That diversity reflects the uniqueness of the paths people take to embodied healing and integration, as well as the particular way each individual, family, community and society chooses to realize and express human flourishing. As a pointer to that diversity, the model also assumes a typology of different forms and styles of well-being that, albeit still generic, indicates the particularity of the final condition. The generic types of embodied prosocial well-being it describes include people who lead with the physical expression of care; with empathic sensitivity; with analytic or aesthetic expressiveness; with altruistic engagement and action and with philosophical-psychospiritual depth. Further differentiating these types, each is seen as expressed sometimes in a style of gentleness, sometimes in a style of fierce intensity, and sometimes in a style that combines gentle and fierce qualities. Of course, even this 15-fold typology does not exhaust the distinctiveness of each individual and group's complete fruition of prosocial well-being.

Given this brief unpacking of the final condition, we have completed our survey of the theory and practice framework of ETT. Before we turn to a case study that fleshes out the arc of this method, I offer Table 22.1 as an overview of the framework.

Table 22.1 The Alchemical Framework of Embodied Transformational Therapy (by Joseph Loizzo)

Basic Mental State	Neural/Subtle Body Basis	Phases of the Therapeutic Path	Fruits/Dimensions of Well-Being
Waking State	Neocortex/ Sensed in the Forehead-Crown Circuits	Bonding Phase 1 Renunciation 2 Compassion 3 Transcendent Insight	Artful Expression of Unconditional Care and Love
Dream State	Limbic System/ Sensed at the Throat Circuit	Revision Phase 1 Transparency 2 Congeniality 3 Juxtaposition 4 Repetition 5 Reconnection	Playful Personality of Sublimation and Flow
Deep Sleep State	Hypothalamus-Midbrain/ Sensed at the Heart Circuit	Realization Phase I 1 De-Materialization 2 Sublimation 3 Lucid Intuition	Intuitive Objectivity of Formless Openness
Orgasmic State	Pons-Medulla/Sensed at the Navel-Sacrum Circuits	Realization Phase II 4 Dreamy Embodiment 5 Integration	Intuitive Sensibility of Sheer Joy and Awe

IV Clinical Application: A Case Study of Embodied Transformational Therapy

Sharon, a cis-gendered heterosexual white female, was in her mid-40s when she came to see me struggling with chronic feelings of guilt, shame and anxiety, compounded by self-blaming rumination and self-destructive behavior. Although she'd been plagued by these feelings and habits since she was in middle school, she had managed, based on her sharp intellect, emotional intelligence and strong self-discipline to complete a PhD, secure an academic leadership position and form a successful second marriage. Now that she'd created the outer life she wanted, she sought out therapy since her success failed to bring the inner confidence and peace she expected it would. A highly articulate yet self-effacing woman with shoulder-length auburn curls and a dignified creative flair, Sharon's dark eyes revealed an undertone of insecurity and sadness that belied her obvious humor and playful affect.

As Sharon shared her origin story, speaking with animation on my office couch, I began to sense what she might need from a therapist to form a confidential, congenial mentoring bond. What she shared was the story of an emotional orphan. Born with a highly analytical verbal mind, a richly active imagination and an intensely engaging emotional style, her inner life had a range and complexity neither of her parents could understand, much less accept or meet. Her dad recognized her analytical mind, but as an emotionally repressed midwestern man, was highly critical of Sharon's imagination and emotional intensity. Her alcoholic mom, whose childhood physical handicap left her narcissistically wounded and emotionally abusive, felt threatened by Sharon's rich inner life and resented the intellectual affinity she shared with her dad. The family dynamic was aggravated by her younger sister, whose temperament closely resembled their mom's, leading to a symbiotic bond between the sister and mom that left my client the odd woman out. Since she only partially identified with her dad and was envied and disavowed by her mom and sister, she found herself in the most vulnerable position in the family, caught in the crossfire between her dad's internalized patriarchal oppression and her mom's and sister's internalized misogyny.

What Sharon needed—to be seen, loved and encouraged as a gifted young woman with a rich, complex inner life—was something neither of her parents could offer, but most therapists could. The one wrinkle I saw was the need she naturally felt to identify with a woman who could mirror her gender-nonconforming constellation of qualities and offer a complex feminist role model to help her celebrate and integrate her full potential in the face of her family conditioning and the dominant culture of patriarchy. Fortunately, Sharon had sensed this need ever since a family move forced the loss of a best child-hood friend, her psychic twin, precipitating a grief reaction. Not having the validation of her friend meant she was stuck with her repressive and attacking family, reliving the early trauma of feeling unseen, abandoned and judged by her parents and sister. The re-traumatization was compounded by the way her family pathologized her grief—sending her to a psychiatrist who labelled her "depressive" and prescribed medication. All this happened at such a critical time in her development that it got woven into a traumatic narrative that she was defective, unlovable and did not belong either in the company of women or in the world of men.

Fortunately for Sharon, she had the emotional and intellectual resources to imagine a path to well-being and wholeness, by becoming a teacher who could be there as a mentor for other young people like herself and pro-tect them from the developmental trauma she suffered. This path is what allowed her to continue to excel at school despite her inner turmoil, and eventually to go on to college and graduate study focused on feminism, where she met several strong feminist mentors. Unfortunately, her present work environment was more reminiscent of her family of origin than the academic family she made for herself as an adult. While she was beloved by her students and fellow faculty, the combination of having a highly narcis-sistic, emotionally abusive boss and feeling unmet by her caring but obses-sive husband recapitulated the perfect storm of her childhood in a way that precipitated a mid-life crisis.

From our first meeting, it was clear to me that Sharon had all the necessary prerequisites to form an effective mentoring bond except one—the positive expectation that she could disidentify with her trauma and radically trans-form herself and her life. While I sensed she may eventually need a feminine role model, I trusted the inner wisdom that led her to seek help from an emotionally focused male therapist/feminist ally at this critical point in her life. So we began our work together already squarely in the revision phase, by exposing and de-reifying her identification with the traumatic, pathologizing self-construct and narrative she internalized from her family and initial treat-ment experience. The reconstructive work of that first phase was made easier by the fact that Sharon's own intellectual journey had already led her through deconstructive feminist criticism to a keen understanding of the way her combination of intellect, imagination and emotion exposed her to crossfire for defying both sides of the binary logic of patriarchal gender identities and roles. The work that remained was rendering transparent the way her role as the family's identified patient was simply covering up for the original trauma of being exposed to a double dose of the family's internalized patriarchy.

This opened the door to our co-creating a congenial ideal self-narrative to juxtapose against her trauma, correcting Sharon's shame-based sense that she was defective or flawed with the healing insight that she was the witness, truth-teller and altruist who chose to expose and transform the systemic oppression her family was enmeshed in. Since we began our work together, she had found inspiration in the liberative wisdom of Buddhism and had begun a regular practice of mindfulness, self-compassion and breath work. So when it came time to flesh out a new vision and narrative for herself, given her vivid literary imagination and rich dream life, she found herself drawn to Tibetan visualization, especially to one of the fierce feminine wisdom archetypes that was central in the OIP (Gray, 2007). Visualization, the first stage of the OIP, involves daily repetition of a performance script in which one identifies with an ideal archetype associated with a congenial mentor and rehearses completely transforming one's perception, experience and action in the world in light of that identification. The archetype Sharon gravitated to offered the strong feminine role model she needed, and allowed her to channel her past and present, male- and female-identified human mentors to serve as flesh-and-blood models for her new way of being. Given its built-in linkage to the subtle body interoceptive map of the nervous system, this practice also afforded her specific guidance for how to reconnect with her full range of embodied experience, both through embedding internalized links to the mentor/archetype's image and voice at vital points within the body, and through supporting somatic trauma healing and transformation with bottom-up practices of self-massage and breath work (Yeshe, 2015).

The congenial vision and narrative of the fierce wisdom goddess helped to catalyze Sharon's work in the revision phase, offering both a shared map to juxtapose against her traumatic self-world image and a model for the emergence of a transformational vision and story of a whole new way of being. At the same time, it empowered her to let go of her traumatic self-doubt and anxious attachment style, so she could feel more confident in asserting herself with her difficult boss and with her emotionally constricted husband. This boost in confidence and secure embodiment prepared her to negotiate for a new leadership role at work, focused on creating a whole new curriculum with the experiential, inclusive and socially engaged mission to inspire and empower diverse students to be agents of change. And it also helped her confront her husband and insist he seek psychotherapy to better access and express his emotions.

The shifts Sharon was making in her experience and engagement with herself and her world gradually opened the door to the realization phase of her healing journey. Reconnecting with the full range of her embodied experience, from being able to bear and release embodied trauma to accessing embodied states of well-being, deepened and expanded her growing felt sense of her body as a rich and complex inner world. This greater ease and comfort with her own interoceptive experience allowed her to witness, bear and care for the somatic forms of traumatic reactivity triggered by social criticism and rejection—including sensations of heaviness, fatigue and fainting and a strong urge to withdraw and hide. Gradually she found herself able to relax and shift these sensations with deep abdominal breathing, which helped her maintain the clarity and confidence to navigate social criticism and rejection from her boss, sister or mother without falling into traumatic habits of shame-paralysis and self-blame. Instead, she began to access the capacity to shift the stress affect and energy of her trauma into affect-energy states of release, well-being and joyful flow.

Given her increasing capacity to shift and sublimate traumatic affects and energies, Sharon began to glimpse and access the lucid intuition she would need to transform two of the most stubborn embodied trauma patterns that had plagued her since childhood. The first of these was a recurrent nightmare that would often follow triggering experiences of social attack. That dream was a night terror in which she found herself forced to pack for a trip she wasn't expecting or prepared for, felt unable to get her things together in time to travel with her family, and then found herself judged and abandoned by her family. We agreed that this nightmare reflected the reenactment of the traumatic move her family made when Sharon was in middle school, but that insight did little to change the course or frequency of the dreams. Given her deepening self-awareness, self-regulation and intuition, at some point she began to notice she was becoming more lucid in processing her nightmare and even lucid in parts of some of her dreams. We worked together to prepare her to exploit this window by choosing to turn her dream body (either in the dream or retroactively on awakening) into her fierce wisdom goddess, say no to her family's agenda, and consciously separate from them to find her own place of embodied safety and congenial community. Although Sharon's ability to bring lucid intuition to revising her dreams was sporadic, the few instances in which it worked dramatically reduced the density and charge of her anxiety dreams, bringing a palpable promise of deeper change.

The second pattern Sharon had struggled with since her grief reaction to being abruptly separated from her childhood best friend was compulsive nail-biting. Also typically activated by experiences of social criticism or rejection, this self-destructive compulsion often left her nail beds exposed and exquisitely painful. Here too her deepening lucid intuition enabled her at times to observe and release the compulsive urge before it got mindlessly acted out, allowing her to harness the affect, energy and chemistry of relief into sensing her body as the dreamlike embodiment of the fierce wisdom goddess. I suggested Sharon work to cultivate these experiences of deeply embodied release and transformation by practicing self-massage to help her body access the embodied affect-energy of prosocial well-being.

V ETT: A Contemporary Inter-Traditional Method of Embodied Self-Transcendence

Sharon's healing journey is just one of the many I have been honored to be part of over the years I've been practicing ETT. Although she was exceptionally primed for this work, and actively integrated traditional wisdom and methods into her therapy, many of the clients I have followed over the years have needed more time forming a congenial bond or crafting healing visions and narratives of self-transcendence that reflect their own culture and sensibility. Unfortunately, the limits of this chapter preclude any further unpacking of the practical application and the range and scope of this therapeutic approach. While I have presented ETT as a structured evidence-based contemporary therapy, one of its great strengths is that it relies not just on the latest scientific breakthroughs and the first century of Western psychotherapy, but is also grounded in a 15-century living tradition of embodied self-transformation and self-transcendence developed in classical India and preserved in Tibet (Wedemeyer, 2007). The timeless tradition of OIP is not only the inspiration for this therapy's distinctive models of human nature and transformational change, but also the source of its multi-dimensional methodology, and many of its powerful mind/body methods of healing and change. As a living hybrid of this timeless tradition with recent Western psychotherapy, ETT is unique in being a rigorously inter-traditional approach to embodied healing. In addition to having such deep, hybrid roots, ETT is also unique in that its radical view of humanity's full natural potential for individual and collective self-transcendence offers a remarkably prescient and promising path for linking personal transformation with the familial, societal and civilizational transformation we all need at this pivotal time on planet Earth (Wallace, 2001).

Note

1   I define neuroecopsychology as the study of the human psyche understood in light of complexity theory, that is as a living system of conscious learning and adaptation, constantly interactive with and inseparable from neurogenomic information systems internally and sociocultural and natural information systems externally.

References

Ahmed, F. (2010). Epigenetics: Tales of adversity. *Nature, 468*(7327), S20. https://doi.org/10.1038/468S20a

Ainsworth, M. (1978). The Bowlby-Ainsworth attachment theory. *Behavioral and Brain Sciences, 1*(3), 436–438. https://doi.org/10.1017/S0140525X00075828

American Medical Association. (2021). *The AMA's Strategic Plan to Embed Racial Justice and Advance Health Equity*. https://www.ama-assn.org/about/leadership/ama-s-strategic-plan-embed-racial-justice-and-advance-health-equity

Amihai, I., & Kozhevnikov, M. (2014). Arousal vs. relaxation: A comparison of the neurophysiological and cognitive correlates of Vajrayana and Theravada meditative practices. *PloS One, 9*(7), e102990. https://doi.org/10.1371/journal.pone.0102990

Arpaia, J., & Rapgay, L. (2003). *Tibetan Wisdom for Modern Life: Spirituality, Relationships, Performance, and Health*. Motilal Banarsidass.

Austin, J. H. (2014). *Zen-Brain Horizons: Toward a Living Zen*. MIT Press.

Baer, R. A. (2003). Mindfulness training as a clinical intervention: A conceptual and empirical review. *Clinical Psychology: Science and Practice, 10*(2), 125–143. https://doi.apa.org/doi/10.1093/clipsy.bpg015

Baker, H. S., & Baker, M. N. (1987). Heinz Kohut's self psychology: An overview. *The American Journal of Psychiatry, 144*(1), 1–9. https://doi.org/10.1176/ajp.144.1.1

Banai, E., Mikulincer, M., & Shaver, P. R. (2005). "Selfobject" needs in Kohut's self psychology: Links with attachment, self-cohesion, affect regulation, and adjustment. *Psychoanalytic Psychology, 22*(2), 224–260. https://doi.org/10.1037/0736-9735.22.2.224

Bankard, J. (2015). Training emotion cultivates morality: How loving-kindness meditation hones compassion and increases prosocial behavior. *Journal of Religion and Health, 54*(6), 2324–2343. https://10.1007/s10943-014-9999-8

Banyan, C. D., & Klein, G. E. (2001). *Hypnosis and Hypnotherapy: Basic to Advanced Techniques for the Professional*. Abbot Press.

Baradon, T. (Ed.). (2009). *Relational Trauma in Infancy: Psychoanalytic, Attachment and Neuropsychological Contributions to Parent-Infant Psychotherapy*. Routledge.

Batchelor, S. (1998). *Buddhism Without Beliefs: A Contemporary Guide to Awakening*. Riverhead Books.

Baum, S., Guze, V., Hall, D., Madden, A., Panvini, R., Rhoads, E., Schneider, J., Silberstein, J., & Tuccillo, E. (2011). *Modern Bioenergetics: An Integrative Approach to Psychotherapy*. New York Society for Bioenergetic Analysis. http://bioenergetics -nyc.org/wp-content/themes/nysba/pdfs/NYSBA-Monograph-July2015.pdf

Bays, J. C. (2011). *How to Train a Wild Elephant: And Other Adventures in Mindfulness*. Shambhala Publications.

Beary, J. F., & Benson, H. (1974). A simple psychophysiologic technique which elicits the hypometabolic changes of the relaxation response. *Psychosomatic Medicine*, 36(2), 115–120. https://doi.org/10.1097/00006842-197403000-00003

Beaumont, E., Galpin, A., & Jenkins, P. (2012). 'Being kinder to myself': A prospective comparative study, exploring post-trauma therapy outcome measures, for two groups of clients, receiving either cognitive behaviour therapy or cognitive behaviour therapy and compassionate mind training. *Counselling Psychology Review*, 27(1), 31–43.

Beblo, T., Fernando, S., Klocke, S., Griepenstroh, J., Aschenbrenner, S., & Driessen, M. (2012). Increased suppression of negative and positive emotions in major depression. *Journal of Affective Disorders*, 141(2–3), 474–479. https://doi.org/10 .1016/j.jad.2012.03.019

Beck, A. T. (1976). *Cognitive Therapy and the Emotional Disorders* (p. 356). International Universities Press.

Benjamin, J. (2017). *Beyond Doer and Done to: Recognition Theory, Intersubjectivity and the Third*. Routledge.

Benson, H., Lehmann, J. W., Malhotra, M. S., Goldman, R. F., Hopkins, J., & Epstein, M. D. (1982). Body temperature changes during the practice of g Tum-mo yoga. *Nature*, 295(5846), 234–236. https://doi.org/10.1038/295234a0

Benson, H., Malhotra, M. S., Goldman, R. F., Jacobs, G. D., & Hopkins, P. J. (1990). Three case reports of the metabolic and electroencephalographic changes during advanced Buddhist meditation techniques. *Behavioral Medicine (Washington, D.C.)*, 16(2), 90–95. https://doi.org/10.1080/08964289.1990.9934596

Berzin, A. (2010). *Introduction to the Kalachakra Initiation*. Snow Lion Publications.

Bion, W. R. (1970). *Attention and Interpretation: A Scientific Approach to Insight in Psycho-Analysis and Groups*. Tavistock Publications.

Bion, W. R. (2013). Notes on memory and desire. In J. Aguayo & B. Malin (Eds.), *Wilfred Bion: Los Angeles Seminars and Supervision* (pp. 133–149). Routledge. (Original work published 1967).

Birnbaum, R. (2003). *The Healing Buddha* (Rev. ed.). Shambhala Publications.

Bishop, S. R., Lau, M., Shapiro, S., Carlson, L., Anderson, N. D., Carmody, J., Segal, Z. V., Abbey, S., Speca, M., Velting, D., & Devins, G. (2004). Mindfulness: A proposed operational definition. *Clinical Psychology: Science and Practice, 11*(3), 230–241. https://doi.org/10.1093/clipsy.bph077

Bowlby, J. (1988). *A Secure Base: Parent-Child Attachment and Healthy Human Development*. Basic Books.

Brach, T. (2004). *Radical Acceptance: Embracing Your Life with the Heart of a Buddha*. Bantam Books.

Brach, T. (2016). *True Refuge: Finding Peace and Freedom in Your Own Awakened Heart*. Bantam Books.

Braehler, C. (2020). *Fierce Self-Compassion: Empowering Yourself in the Face of Harm & Injustice*. [Audio course]. https://www.selfcompassioninclinicalpractice.com/p/fierce-self-compassion-empowering-yourself-against-harm-injustice

Braehler, C. (in press). Self-compassion in trauma treatment. In A. Finlay-Jones & K. Neff (Eds.), *Handbook of Self-Compassion*. Springer.

Braehler, C., & Neff, K. (2020). Self-compassion. In PTSD. In M. Tull, & N. Kimbrel (Eds.), *Emotion in Posttraumatic Stress Disorder: Etiology, Assessment, Neurobiology, and Treatment* (pp. 567–596). Academic Press.

Braehler, C., Gumley, A., Harper, J., Wallace, S., Norrie, J., & Gilbert, P. (2013a). Exploring change processes in compassion focused therapy in psychosis: Results of a feasibility randomized controlled trial. *The British Journal of Clinical Psychology, 52*(2), 199–214. https://doi.org/10.1111/bjc.12009

Braehler, C., Harper, J., & Gilbert, P. (2013b). Compassion focused group therapy for recovery after psychosis. In C. Steel (Ed.), *CBT for Schizophrenia: Evidence Based Interventions and Future Directions* (pp. 236–266). Wiley-Blackwell.

Braun, T. D., Park, C. L., & Gorin, A. (2016). Self-compassion, body image, and disordered eating: A review of the literature. *Body Image, 17*, 117–131. https://doi.org/10.1016/j.bodyim.2016.03.003

Breines, J. G., & Chen, S. (2012). Self-compassion increases self-improvement motivation. *Personality and Social Psychology Bulletin, 38*(9), 1133–1143. https://doi.org/10.1177/0146167212445599

Brewer, J. A., & Garrison, K. A. (2014). The posterior cingulate cortex as a plausible mechanistic target of meditation: Findings from neuroimaging. *Annals of the New York Academy of Sciences, 1307*, 19–27. https://doi.org/10.1111/nyas.12246

Brewer, J. A., Worhunsky, P. D., Gray, J. R., Tang, Y.-Y., Weber, J., & Kober, H. (2011). Meditation experience is associated with differences in default mode network activity and connectivity. *Proceedings of the National Academy of Sciences of the United States of America, 108*(50), 20254–20259. https://doi.org/10.1073/pnas.1112029108

Bromberg, P. M. (1996). Standing in the spaces: The multiplicity of self and the psychoanalytic relationship. *Contemporary Psychoanalysis, 32*(4), 509–535. https://doi.org/10.1080/00107530.1996.10746334

Brooks, V. R. (1981). *Minority Stress and Lesbian Women.* Lexington Books.

Brotherson, S. (2005). *Understanding Brain Development in Young Children.* NDSU Extension Service.

Broussard, D. M. (2013). *The Cerebellum: Learning Movement, Language, and Social Skills.* Wiley-Blackwell Press.

Brown, D. (2009). Mastery of the mind East and West: Excellence in being and doing and everyday happiness. *Annals of the New York Academy of Sciences, 1172,* 231–251. https://doi.org/10.1196/annals.1393.018

Bushell, W. C., Olivo, E. L., & Theise, N. D. (Eds.). (2009). *Longevity, Regeneration, and Optimal Health: Integrating Eastern and Western Perspectives.* Annals of the New York Academy of Sciences.

Buss, D. M. (2000). The evolution of happiness. *American Psychologist, 55*(1), 15–23. https://doi.apa.org/doi/10.1037/0003-066X.55.1.15

Caplan, M. (2012). *The Soft Overcomes the Hard: Walking the Spiritual Path with Excruciating Humility.* https://www.huffpost.com/entry/the-soft-overcomes-the-hard_b_1457587

Caplan, M., Portillo, P., & Seely, L. (2013). Yoga psychotherapy: The integration of Western psychological theory and ancient yogic wisdom. *Journal of Transpersonal Psychology, 45*(2), 139–158.

Carey, N. (2013). *The Epigenetics Revolution: How Modern Biology Is Rewriting Our Understanding of Genetics, Disease, and Inheritance.* Columbia University Press.

Cass, V. C. (1984). Homosexual identity formation: Testing a theoretical model. *The Journal of Sex Research, 20*(2), 143–167. https://doi.org/10.1080/00224498409551214.

Chah, A. (2004). *A Still Forest Pool: The Insight Meditation of Achaan Chah* (J. Kornfield & P. Breiter, Eds.). Quest Books.

Chambers, R., Lo, B. C. Y., & Allen, N. B. (2008). The impact of intensive mindfulness training on attentional control, cognitive style, and affect. *Cognitive Therapy and Research, 32*(3), 303–322. https://doi.org/10.1007/s10608-007-9119-0.

Chavez-Dueñas, N. Y., Adames, H. Y., Perez-Chavez, J. G., & Salas, S. P. (2019). Healing ethno-racial trauma in Latinx immigrant communities: Cultivating hope, resistance, and action. *The American Psychologist, 74*(1), 49–62. https://doi.org/10.1037/amp0000289

Chenagtsang, N. (2016). *Mirror of Light: A Commentary on Yuthog's Ati Yoga* (B. Joffe, Trans.; Vol. 1). Sky Press.

Chenagtsang, N. (2018). *Karmamudra: The Yoga of Bliss: Sexuality in Tibetan Medicine* (B. Joffe, Ed.). Sky Press.

Chödrön, P. (1991). *Wisdom of No Escape: And the Path of Loving-Kindness.* Shambhala.

Chödrön, P. (2000). *When Things Fall Apart: Heart Advice for Difficult Times.* Shambhala Publications.

Clarke, K., & Yellow Bird, M. (2021). *Decolonizing Pathways to Integrative Healing in Social Work.* Routledge.

Cohen, S., Evans, G. W., Stokols, D., & Krantz, D. S. (1986). *Behavior, Health, and Environmental Stress.* Plenum Press. https://doi.org/10.1007/978-1-4757-9380-2

Comas-Díaz, L. (1981). Effects of cognitive and behavioral group treatment in the depressive symptomatology of Puerto Rican women. *Journal of Consulting and Clinical Psychology, 49,* 627–632.

Comas-Díaz, L. (1987). Feminist therapy with Hispanic/Latina women: Myth or reality? *Women and Therapy, 6*(4), 39–61.

Comas-Díaz, L. (Ed.). (1994). *Women of Color: Integrating Ethnic and Gender Identities in Psychotherapy.* Guilford Press.

Comas-Díaz, L. (2012). *Multicultural Care: A Clinician's Guide to Cultural Competence.* American Psychological Association.

Comas-Díaz, L., & Greene, B. (2013). *Psychological Health of Women of Color: Intersections, Challenges, and Opportunities.* Praeger.

Comas-Díaz, L., & Griffith, E. E. H. B. (Eds.). (1988). *Clinical Guidelines in Cross Cultural Mental Health.* Wiley.

Comas-Díaz, L., Hall, G. N., & Neville, H. A. (2019). Racial trauma: Theory, research, and healing: Introduction to the special issue. *American Psychologist, 74*(1), 1–5.

Comas-Díaz, L., Lykes, M. B., & Alarcón, R. D. (1998). Ethnic conflict and the psychology of liberation in Guatemala, Peru and Puerto Rico. *American Psychologist, 53,* 778–792. https://doi.org/10.1037/0003-066X.53.7.778

Corsini, R. J., & Wedding, D. (2000). *Current Psychotherapies* (6th ed.). F. E. Peacock Publishers, Inc.

Cozolino, L. (2006). *The Neuroscience of Human Relationships: Attachment and the Developing Brain.* W. W. Norton & Company.

Cozort, D. (2005). *Highest Yoga Tantra: An Introduction to the Esoteric Buddhism of Tibet.* Snow Lion Publications.

Craig, A. D. (2005). Forebrain emotional asymmetry: A neuroanatomical basis? *Trends in Cognitive Sciences, 9*(12), 566–571. https://doi.org/10.1016/j.tics.2005.10.005

Dahl, C. J., Lutz, A., & Davidson, R. J. (2015). Reconstructing and deconstructing the self: Cognitive mechanisms in meditation practice. *Trends in Cognitive Sciences, 19*(9), 515–523. https://doi.org/10.1016/j.tics.2015.07.001

Dahm, K. A., Meyer, E. C., Neff, K. D., Kimbrel, N. A., Gulliver, S. B., & Morissette, S. B. (2015). Mindfulness, self-compassion, posttraumatic stress disorder symptoms, and functional disability in U.S. Iraq and Afghanistan war veterans. *Journal of Traumatic Stress, 28*(5), 460–464. https://doi.org/10.1002/jts.22045

Dalai Lama. (2009). *The Union of Bliss and Emptiness: Teachings on the Practice of Guru Yoga* (T. Jinpa, Trans.). Snow Lion Publications.

Dalai Lama, & Berzin, A. (1997). *The Ganden/Kagyü Tradition of Mahamudra.* Snow Lion Publications.

Dalai Lama, Tsong-ka-pa, & Hopkins, J. (1987). *Tantra in Tibet.* Snow Lion.

Dale, S. K., Weber, K. M., Cohen, M. H., Kelso, G. A., Cruise, R. C., & Brody, L. R. (2014). Resilience moderates the association between childhood sexual abuse and depressive symptoms among women with and at-risk for HIV. *AIDS and Behavior, 19*(8), 1379–1387. https://doi.org/10.1007/s10461-014-0855-3.

Damasio, A. R. (2003). *Looking for Spinoza: Joy, Sorrow and the Feeling Brain.* Harcourt.

Darwin, C. (1965). *The Expression of Emotion in Man and Animals.* University of Chicago Press. (Original work published 1872).

Davidson, R., & Begley, S. (2013). *The Emotional Life of Your Brain: How Its Unique Patterns Affect the Way You Think, Feel, and Live—And How You Can Change Them.* Plume Books.

Davis, D. M., & Hayes, J. A. (2011). What are the benefits of mindfulness: A practice review of psychotherapy-related research. *Psychotherapy, 48*(2), 198–208. https://doi.apa.org/doi/10.1037/a0022062

De Mello, A. (1984). *The Song of the Bird.* Image Books.

DelMonte, M. M. (1995). Meditation and the unconscious. *Journal of Contemporary Psychotherapy, 25*(3), 223–242.

Depue, R. A., & Morrone-Strupinsky, J. V. (2005). A neurobehavioral model of affiliative bonding: Implications for conceptualizing a human trait of affiliation. *The Behavioral and Brain Sciences*, 28(3), 313–350; discussion 350–395. https://doi.org/10.1017/S0140525X05000063

Desbordes, G., Gard, T., Hoge, E. A., Hölzel, B. K., Kerr, C., Lazar, S. W., Olendzki, A., & Vago, D. R. (2014). Moving beyond mindfulness: Defining equanimity as an outcome measure in meditation and contemplative. *Research. Mindfulness*, 6(2), 356–372. https://doi.org/10.1007/s12671-013-0269-8

Desbordes, G., Negi, L. T., Pace, T. W. W., Wallace, B. A., Raison, C. L., & Schwartz, E. L. (2012). Effects of mindful-attention and compassion meditation training on amygdala response to emotional stimuli in an ordinary, non-meditative state. *Frontiers in Human Neuroscience*, 6, Article 292. https://doi.org/10.3389/fnhum.2012.00292

Dhonden, Y. (2000). *Healing from the Source: The Science and Lore of Tibetan Medicine* (B. A. Wallace, Ed. & Trans.). Snow Lion.

Diedrich, A., Grant, M., Hofmann, S. G., Hiller, W., & Berking, M. (2014). Self-compassion as an emotion regulation strategy in major depressive disorder. *Behaviour Research and Therapy*, 58, 43–51. https://doi.org/10.1016/j.brat.2014.05.006

Diedrich, A., Hofmann, S. G., Cuijpers, P., & Berking, M. (2016). Self-compassion enhances the efficacy of explicit cognitive reappraisal as an emotion regulation strategy in individuals with major depressive disorder. *Behaviour Research and Therapy*, 82, 1–10. https://doi.org/10.1016/j.brat.2016.04.003

Dobson, O., Price, E. L., & DiTommaso, E. (2022). Recollected caregiver sensitivity and adult attachment interact to predict mental health and coping. *Personality and Individual Differences*, 187, Article 111398. https://doi.org/10.1016/j.paid.2021.111398

Dobzhansky, T. (1982). *Genetics and the Origin of Species*. Columbia University Press. (Original work published 1937).

Dōgen. (1994). Bendōwa. In G. Nishijima & C. Cross (Eds. & Trans.), *Master Dōgen's Shōbōgenzō, Book 1* (pp. 1–24). Wind Bell Publications. (Original work 1231).

Dōgen. (1997). Zanmai O Zanmai. In G. Nishijima & C. Cross (Eds. & Trans.), *Master Dōgen's Shōbōgenzō, Book 3* (pp. 281–284). Wind Bell Publications. (Original work 1244).

Dōgen. (2002). Fukanzazengi: (Universal Promotion of the Principles of Zazen). In N. Waddell & M. Abe (Trans.), *The Heart of Dōgen's Shōbōgenzō* . State University Press of New York Press. (Original work 1227).

Doidge, N. (2007). *The Brain That Changes Itself: Stories of Personal Triumph from the Frontiers of Brain Science*. Penguin Books.

Doidge, N. (2016). *The Brain's Way of Healing: Remarkable Discoveries and Recoveries from the Frontiers of Neuroplasticity*. Penguin Books.

Dominelli, L. (2002). *Anti-Oppressive Social Work Theory and Practice* (J. Campling, Ed.). Palgrave Macmillan. https://doi.org/10.1007/978-1-4039-1400-2.

Dudley, K. J., Li, X., Kobor, M. S., Kippin, T. E., & Bredy, T. W. (2011). Epigenetic mechanisms mediating vulnerability and resilience to psychiatric disorders. *Neuroscience and Biobehavioral Reviews*, 35(7), 1544–1551. https://doi.org/10.1016/j.neubiorev.2010.12.016

Duschinsky, R. (2020). *Cornerstones of Attachment Research*. Oxford University Press.

Dusek, J. A., Hibberd, P. L., Buczynski, B., Chang, B.-H., Dusek, K. C., Johnston, J. M., Wohlhueter, A. L., Benson, H., & Zusman, R. M. (2008). Stress management versus lifestyle modification on systolic hypertension and medication elimination: A randomized trial. *Journal of Alternative and Complementary Medicine (New York, N.Y.)*, 14(2), 129–138. https://doi.org/10.1089/acm.2007.0623

Easwaran, E. (2007). *The Dhammapada* (2nd ed.). Nilgiri Press.

Eberhardt, J. (2019). *Biased: Uncovering the Hidden Prejudice That Shapes What We See, Think, and Do*. Viking Books.

Eberhardt, J. L. (n.d.). *Academic Publications*. Jennifer L. Eberhardt. https://web.stanford.edu/~eberhard/publications.html

Eberhardt, J. L. (2019). *Biased: Uncovering the Hidden Prejudice That Shapes What We See, Think, and Do*. Viking.

Ecker, B., & Bridges, S. K. (2020). How the science of memory reconsolidation advances the effectiveness and unification of psychotherapy. *Clinical Social Work*, 48, 287–300. https://doi.org/10.1007/s10615-020-00754-z

Edmondson, A. (1999). Psychological safety and learning behavior in work teams. *Administrative Science Quarterly*, 44(2), 350–383. https://doi.org/10.2307/2666999.

Edmondson, A. C. (2019). *The Fearless Organization: Creating Psychological Safety in the Workplace for Learning, Innovation, and Growth*. Wiley.

Ehret, A. M., Joormann, J., & Berking, M. (2015). Examining risk and resilience factors for depression: The role of self-criticism and self-compassion. *Cognition and Emotion*, 29(8), 1496–1504. https://doi.org/10.1080/02699931.2014.992394

Ekman, P. (2007). *Emotions Revealed: Faces and Feelings to Improve Communication and Emotional Life* (2nd ed.). Henry Holt and Company.

Ellis, A. (1962). *Reason and Emotion in Psychotherapy*. Lyle Stuart.

Emerson, H. (2019, August 14). *Addressing the Roots of Racial Trauma: An Interview with Psychologist Lillian Comas-Díaz*. Mad in America: Science, Psychiatry and Social Justice. https://www.madinamerica.com/2019/08/racism-impacts-everyone-interview-psychologist-lillian-comas-diaz/

Emery, A. K. D. (2020). *The Protective Influence of Self-Compassion Against Internalized Racism Among African Americans* [Doctoral dissertation]. University of Nebraska-Lincoln.

Engen, H. G., & Singer, T. (2015). Compassion-based emotion regulation up-regulates experienced positive affect and associated neural networks. *Social Cognitive and Affective Neuroscience, 10*(9), 1291–1301. https://doi.org/10.1093/scan/nsv008

Entringer, S., Epel, E. S., Lin, J., Buss, C., Shahbaba, B., Blackburn, E. H., Simhan, H. N., & Wadhwa, P. D. (2013). Maternal psychosocial stress during pregnancy is associated with newborn leukocyte telomere length. *American Journal of Obstetrics and Gynecology, 208*(2), 134.e1–134.e7. https://doi.org/10.1016/j.ajog.2012.11.033

Epstein, M. (1995). *Thoughts Without a Thinker: Psychotherapy from a Buddhist Perspective*. Basic Books.

Epstein, M. (2001). *Going on Being: Buddhism and the Way of Change*. Broadway Books.

Erdynast, A., & Rapgay, L. (2009). Developmental levels of conceptions of compassion in the ethical decision-making of Western Buddhist practitioners. *Journal of Adult Development, 16*(1), 1–12. https://doi.org/10.1007/s10804-008-9041-z

Erskine, R. G., Clark, B., Evans, K. R., Goldberg, C., Hyams, H., James, S., & O'Reilly-Knapp, M. (1994). The dynamics of shame: A roundtable discussion. *Transactional Analysis Journal, 24*(2), 80–85. https://doi.org/10.1177/036215379402400203

Fairfax, H. (2008). The use of mindfulness in obsessive compulsive disorder: Suggestions for its application and integration in existing treatment. *Clinical Psychology & Psychotherapy, 15*(1), 53–59. https://doi.org/10.1002/cpp.557

Fanon, F. (1963). *The Wretched of the Earth* (C. Farrington, Trans.). Grove Press. (Original work published 1961).

Fanon, F. (1965). *A Dying Colonialism* (H. Chevalier, Trans.). Grove Press. (Original work published 1959).

Fanon, F. (1967). *Black Skin, White Masks* (C. L. Markmann, Trans.). Grove Press. (Original work published 1952).

Fanon, F. (1969). *Toward the African Revolution* (H. Chevalier, Trans.). (Original work published 1964). Grove Press.

Farb, N. A. S., Segal, Z. V., & Anderson, A. K. (2013). Mindfulness meditation training alters cortical representations of interoceptive attention. *Social Cognitive and Affective Neuroscience, 8*(1), 15–26. https://doi.org/10.1093/scan/nss066

Fassinger, R. E., Shullman, S. L., & Stevenson, M. R. (2010). Toward an affirmative lesbian, gay, bisexual, and transgender leadership paradigm. *American Psychologist*, 65(3), 201–215. https://doi.org/10.1037/a0018597.

Feinstein, B. A. (2020). The rejection sensitivity model as a framework for understanding sexual minority mental health. *Archives of Sexual Behavior*, 49(7), 2247–2258. https://doi.org/10.1007/s10508-019-1428-3

Felitti, V. J., Anda, R. F., Nordenberg, D., Williamson, D. F., Spitz, A. M., Edwards, V., Koss, M. P., & Marks, J. S. (1998). Relationship of childhood abuse and household dysfunction to many of the leading causes of death in adults: The Adverse Childhood Experiences (ACE) Study. *American Journal of Preventive Medicine*, 14(4), 245–258. https://doi.org/10.1016/s0749-3797(98)00017-8

Ferngren, G. B. (2002). *Science and Religion: A Historical Introduction*. Johns Hopkins University Press.

Field, T. (2014). *Touch* (2nd ed.). Bradford Books.

Figley, C. R. (1995). Compassion fatigue: Toward a new understanding of the costs of caring. In B. H. Stamm (Ed.), *Secondary Traumatic Stress: Self-Care Issues for Clinicians, Researchers, and Educators* (pp. 3–28). Sidran Press.

Fosha, D. (2000a). Meta-therapeutic processes and the affects of transformation: Affirmation and the healing affects. *Journal of Psychotherapy Integration*, 10(1), 71–97. https://doi.org/10.1023/A:1009422511959

Fosha, D. (2000b). *The Transforming Power of Affect: A Model for Accelerated Change*. Basic Books.

Fosha, D. (2003). Dyadic regulation and experiential work with emotion and relatedness in trauma and disordered attachment. In M. F. Solomon & D. J. Siegel (Eds.), *Healing Trauma: Attachment, Mind, Body, And Brain*. W. W. Norton and Company.

Fosha, D. (2005). Emotion, true self, true other, core state: Toward a clinical theory of affective change process. *Psychoanalytic Review*, 92(4), 513–552. https://doi.org/10.1521/prev.2005.92.4.513

Fosha, D. (2008). Transformance, recognition of self by self, and effective action. In K. J. Schneider (Ed.), *Existential-Integrative Psychotherapy: Guideposts to the Core of Practice* (pp. 290–320). Routledge.

Fosha, D. (2009a). Emotion and recognition at work: Energy, vitality, pleasure, truth, desire & the emergent phenomenology of transformational experience. In D. Fosha, D. J. Siegel, & M. F. Solomon (Eds.), *The Healing Power of Emotion: Affective Neuroscience, Development, Clinical Practice* (pp. 172–203). W.W. Norton and Company.

Fosha, D. (2009b). Healing attachment trauma with attachment (...and then some! In M. Kerman (Ed.), *Clinical Pearls of Wisdom: 21 Leading Therapists Offer Their Key Insights* (pp. 43–56). W. W. Norton and Company.

Fosha, D. (2009c). Positive affects and the transformation of suffering into flourishing. *Annals of the New York Academy of Sciences, 1172*, 252–262. https://doi.org/10.1111/j.1749-6632.2009.04501.x

Fosha, D. (2013a). A heaven in a wild flower: Self, dissociation, and treatment in the context of the neurobiological core self. *Psychoanalytic Inquiry, 33*(5), 496–523. https://psycnet.apa.org/doi/10.1080/07351690.2013.815067

Fosha, D. (2013b). Turbocharging the affects of healing and redressing the evolutionary tilt. In D. J. Siegel & M. F. Solomon (Eds.), *Healing Moments in Psychotherapy* (pp. 129–168). W. W. Norton and Company.

Fosha, D., & Yeung, D. (2006). Accelerated experiential-dynamic psychotherapy: The seamless integration of emotional transformation and dyadic relatedness at work. In G. Stricker & J. Gold (Eds.), *A Casebook of Integrative Psychotherapy* (pp. 165–184). American Psychological Association.

Fox, K. C. R., Zakarauskas, P., Dixon, M., Ellamil, M., Thompson, E., & Christoff, K. (2012). Meditation experience predicts introspective accuracy. *PloS One, 7*(9), e45370. https://doi.org/10.1371/journal.pone.0045370

Frank, J., & Frank, J. (1993). *Persuasion and Healing: A Comparative Study of Psychotherapy* (3rd ed.). Johns Hopkins University Press.

Fredrickson, B. L. (2009). *Positivity: Groundbreaking Research Reveals How to Embrace the Hidden Strength of Positive Emotions, Overcome Negativity, and Thrive*. Random House.

Fredrickson, B. L., Grewen, K. M., Coffey, K. A., Algoe, S. B., Firestine, A. M., Arevalo, J. M. G., Ma, J., & Cole, S. W. (2013). A functional genomic perspective on human well-being. *Proceedings of the National Academy of Sciences of the United States of America, 110*(33), 13684–13689. https://doi.org/10.1073/pnas.1305419110

French, B. H., Lewis, J. A., Mosley, D. V., Adames, H. Y., Chavez-Dueñas, N. Y., Chen, G. A., & Neville, H. A. (2020). Toward a psychological framework of radical healing in communities of color. *The Counseling Psychologist, 48*(1), 14–46. https://doi.org/10.1177/0011000019843506

Freud, S. (1958). Recommendations to Physicians Practising Psycho-analysis. In J. Strachey (Ed. & Trans.), *The Standard Edition of the Complete Psychological Works of Sigmund Freud (Vol. XII)* (pp. 111–120). The Hogarth Press. (Original work published 1912).

Freud, S. (1962). *Civilization and Its Discontents* (J. Strachey, Trans.). W. W. Norton & Company. (Original work published 1930).

Freud, S. (1964). Analysis terminable and interminable. In J. Strachey (Ed.), & J. Strachey (Trans.), *The Standard Edition of the Complete Psychological Works of Sigmund Freud (Vol. XXIII)* (pp. 209–253). The Hogarth Press. (Original work published 1937).

Frijda, N. H. (1986). *The Emotions*. Cambridge University Press.

Gale, C., Gilbert, P., Read, N., & Goss, K. (2014). An evaluation of the impact of introducing compassion focused therapy to a standard treatment programme for people with eating disorders. *Clinical Psychology & Psychotherapy, 21*(1), 1–12. https://doi.org/10.1002/cpp.1806

Gardner, H. (2006). *Multiple Intelligences: New Horizons in Theory and Practice* (Rev. ed.). Basic Books.

Garland, E. L., Fredrickson, B., Kring, A. M., Johnson, D. P., Meyer, P. S., & Penn, D. L. (2010). Upward spirals of positive emotions counter downward spirals of negativity: Insights from the broaden-and-build theory and affective neuroscience on the treatment of emotion dysfunctions and deficits in psychopathology. *Clinical Psychology Review, 30*(7), 849–864. https://doi.org/10.1016/j.cpr.2010.03.002

Germer, C. K. (2009). *The Mindful Path to Self-Compassion: Freeing Yourself from Destructive Thoughts and Emotions*. Guilford Press.

Germer, C. K., & Neff, K. D. (2016). *Mindful Self-Compassion (MSC) Training Program* [Unpublished manual].

Germer, C. K., Siegel, R. D., & Fulton, P. R. (Eds.). (2013). *Mindfulness and Psychotherapy* (2nd ed.). Guilford Press.

Gilbert, P. (2009). Introducing compassion-focused therapy. *Advances in Psychiatric Treatment, 15*(3), 199–208. https://doi.org/10.1192/apt.bp.107.005264

Gilbert, P. (2010). *The Compassionate Mind: A New Approach to Life's Challenges*. New Harbinger Publications.

Gilbert, P. (Ed.). (2017). *Compassion: Concepts, Research and Applications*. Routledge.

Gilbert, P., & Andrews, B. (1998). *Shame: Interpersonal Behavior, Psychopathology, and Culture*. Oxford University Press.

Gilbert, P., & Choden. (2014). *Mindful Compassion: How the Science of Compassion Can Help You Understand Your Emotions, Live in the Present, and Connect Deeply with Others*. New Harbinger Publications.

Gilbert, P., & Procter, S. (2006). Compassionate mind training for people with high shame and self-criticism: Overview and pilot study of a group therapy approach. *Clinical Psychology & Psychotherapy, 13*(6), 353–379. https://doi.org/10.1002/cpp.507

Gilbert, P., McEwan, K., Catarino, F., & Baião, R. (2014a). Fears of negative emotions in relation to fears of happiness, compassion, alexithymia and psychopathology in a depressed population: A preliminary study. *Journal of Depression and Anxiety, S2*(01), Article 01. https://doi.org/10.4172/2167-1044.S2-004

Gilbert, P., McEwan, K., Catarino, F., & Baião, R. (2014b). Fears of compassion in a depressed population implication for psychotherapy. *Journal of Depression and Anxiety.* https://doi.org/10.4172/2167-1044.S2-003

Gilbert, P., McEwan, K., Catarino, F., Baião, R., & Palmeira, L. (2014c). Fears of happiness and compassion in relationship with depression, alexithymia, and attachment security in a depressed sample. *The British Journal of Clinical Psychology, 53*(2), 228–244. https://doi.org/10.1111/bjc.12037

Gilbert, P., McEwan, K., Gibbons, L., Chotai, S., Duarte, J., & Matos, M. (2012). Fears of compassion and happiness in relation to alexithymia, mindfulness, and self-criticism. *Psychology and Psychotherapy: Theory, Research and Practice, 85*(4), 374–390. https://doi.org/10.1111/j.2044-8341.2011.02046.x

Gilbert, P., McEwan, K., Matos, M., & Rivis, A. (2011). Fears of compassion: Development of three self-report measures. *Psychology and Psychotherapy: Theory, Research and Practice, 84*(3), 239–255.

Glasser, W. (1965). *Reality Therapy: A New Approach to Psychiatry.* Harper & Row.

Goldstein, J. (2016). *Mindfulness: A Practical Guide to Awakening.* Sounds True.

Gray, D. B. (2007). *The Cakrasamvara Tantra (The Discourse of Śri Heruka): A Study and Annotated Translation.* American Institute of Buddhist Studies.

Gray, M., Coates, J., & Yellow Bird, M. (Eds.). (2008). *Indigenous Social Work Around the World: Towards Culturally Relevant Education and Practice.* Ashgate Publishing.

Gray, M., Coates, J., Yellow Bird, M., & Hetherington, T. (Eds.). (2013). *Decolonizing Social Work.* Ashgate Publishing.

Gross, R. M. (1998). *Soaring and Settling: Buddhist Perspectives on Contemporary Social and Religious Issues.* Continuum.

Gunaratana, B. H. (2011). *Mindfulness in Plain English.* Wisdom Publications.

Hamilton, J. P., Furman, D. J., Chang, C., Thomason, M. E., Dennis, E., & Gotlib, I. H. (2011). Default-mode and task-positive network activity in major depressive disorder: Implications for adaptive and maladaptive rumination. *Biological Psychiatry, 70*(4), 327–333. https://doi.org/10.1016/j.biopsych.2011.02.003

Hanh, T. N. (2014). *No Mud, No Lotus: The Art of Transforming Suffering.* Parallax Press.

Hanson, R. (2009). *Buddha's Brain: The Practical Neuroscience of Happiness, Love, and Wisdom.* New Harbinger Press.

Hanson, R. (2013). *Hardwiring Happiness: The New Brain Science of Contentment, Calm, and Confidence.* Harmony Books.

Hayes, S. C., Villatte, M., Levin, M., & Hildebrandt, M. (2011). Open, aware, and active: Contextual approaches as an emerging trend in the behavioral and cognitive therapies. *Annual Review of Clinical Psychology, 7*, 141–168. https://doi.org/10.1146/annurev-clinpsy-032210-104449

Hazan, C., & Shaver, P. (1987). Romantic love conceptualized as an attachment process. *Journal of Personality and Social Psychology, 52*(3), 511–524. https://10.1037//0022-3514.52.3.511

Hebb, D. O. (2002). *The Organization of Behavior: A Neuropsychological Theory.* The Psychology Press. (Original work published 1949).

Heller, H. C., Elsner, R., & Rao, N. (1987). Voluntary hypometabolism in an Indian Yogi. *Journal of Thermal Biology, 12*(2), 171–173. https://doi.org/10.1016/0306-4565(87)90060-X

Helms, J. E. (1992). *A Race Is a Nice Thing to Have: A Guide to Being a White Person or Understanding the White Persons in Your Life.* Content Communications.

Henry, W. P., Schacht, T. E., & Strupp, H. H. (1990). Patient and therapist introject, interpersonal process, and differential psychotherapy outcome. *Journal of Consulting and Clinical Psychology, 58*(6), 768–774. https://doi.apa.org/doi/10.1037/0022-006X.58.6.768

Hofmann, S. G., & Barlow, D. H. (2014). Evidence-based psychological interventions and the common factors approach: The beginnings of a rapprochement? *Psychotherapy, 51*(4), 510–513. https://doi.org/10.1037/a0037045.

Holmes, J. (2014). *John Bowlby and Attachment Theory* (2nd ed.). Routledge. https://doi.org/10.4324/9781315879772

Hölzel, B. K., Carmody, J., Evans, K. C., Hoge, E. A., Dusek, J. A., Morgan, L., Pitman, R. K., & Lazar, S. W. (2010). Stress reduction correlates with structural changes in the amygdala. *Social Cognitive and Affective Neuroscience, 5*(1), 11–17. https://doi.org/10.1093/scan/nsp034

Hölzel, B. K., Lazar, S. W., Gard, T., Schuman-Olivier, Z., Vago, D. R., & Ott, U. (2011). How does mindfulness meditation work? Proposing mechanisms of action from a conceptual and neural perspective. *Perspectives on Psychological Science: A Journal of the Association for Psychological Science, 6*(6), 537–559. https://doi.org/10.1177/1745691611419671

Hopkins, J. (Ed.). (1980). *Compassion in Tibetan Buddhism / Tsong-ka-pa. With Kensur Lekden's Meditations of a Tantric Abbot* (J. Hopkins, Trans.). Ryder.

Hopkins, J. (2007). *Nāgārjuna's Precious Garland: Buddhist Advice for Living and Liberation.* Snow Lion Press.

Iwakabe, S., & Conceicao, N. (2016). Metatherapeutic processing as a change-based therapeutic immediacy task: Building a initial process model using a modified task-analytic research strategy. *Journal of Psychotherapy Integration, 26*(3), 230–247. https://doi.apa.org/doi/10.1037/int0000016

Iyengar, B. K. S. (2005). *Light on Life: The Yoga Journey to Wholeness, Inner Peace, and Ultimate Freedom*. Rodale.

James, W. (1890). The hidden self. *Scribner's, 7*(3), 361–373.

James, W. (1950). *The Principles of Psychology: Vol. Vols. 1 & 2*. Dover Publications. (Original work published 1890)

Jinpa, T. (2005). *Mind Training: The Great Collection*. Wisdom Publications.

Johnson, S. (2008). *Hold Me Tight: Seven Conversations for a Lifetime of Love*. Little, Brown Spark.

Johnson, S., & Brubacher, L. (2016). Deepening attachment emotion in emotionally focused couple therapy (EFT). In G. R. Weeks, S. T. Fife, & C. M. Peterson (Eds.), *Techniques for the Couple Therapist: Essential Interventions from the Experts* (pp. 155–160). Routledge. https://doi.org/10.4324/9781315747330-32

Josipovic, Z. (2014). Neural correlates of nondual awareness in meditation. *Annals of the New York Academy of Sciences, 1307*, 9–18. https://doi.org/10.1111/nyas.12261

Josipovic, Z., Dinstein, I., Weber, J., & Heeger, D. J. (2011). Influence of meditation on anti-correlated networks in the brain. *Frontiers in Human Neuroscience, 5*, 183. https://doi.org/10.3389/fnhum.2011.00183

Jung, C. G. (1954). *The Practice of Psychotherapy: Essays on the Psychology of the Transference and Other Subjects* (R. F. C. Hull, Trans.). Pantheon Books.

Jung, C. G. (1981). Archetypes of the collective unconscious. In G. Adler & R. F. C. Hull (Eds. & Trans.), *The Archetypes and The Collective Unconscious (Collected Works of C.G. Jung Vol. 9 Part 1)* (2nd ed.). Princeton University Press. (Original work published 1934)

Jung, C. G. (1983). *Mysterium Coniunctionis* (R. F. C. Hull, Trans.). Pantheon.

Kabat-Zinn, J. (1982). An outpatient program in behavioral medicine for chronic pain patients based on the practice of mindfulness meditation: Theoretical considerations and preliminary results. *General Hospital Psychiatry, 4*(1), 33–47. https://doi.org/10.1016/0163-8343(82)90026-3

Kabat-Zinn, J. (2003). Mindfulness-based interventions in context: Past, present, and future. *Clinical Psychology: Science and Practice, 10*(2), 144–156. https://doi.apa.org/doi/10.1093/clipsy.bpg016

Kabat-Zinn, J. (2013). *Full Catastrophe Living: Using the Wisdom of Your Body and Mind* (Rev. ed.). Bantam Books.

Kabat-Zinn, J., Lipworth, L., Burney, R., & Sellers, W. (1987). Four-year follow-up of a meditation-based program for the self-regulation of chronic pain: Treatment outcomes and compliance. *The Clinical Journal of Pain, 2*(3), 159–173.

Kabat-Zinn, J., Massion, A. O., Kristeller, J., Peterson, L. G., Fletcher, K. E., Pbert, L., Lenderking, W. R., & Santorelli, S. F. (1992). Effectiveness of a meditation-based stress reduction program in the treatment of anxiety disorders. *The American Journal of Psychiatry, 149*(7), 936–943. https://doi.org/10.1176/ajp.149.7.936

Kaliman, P., Alvarez-López, M. J., Cosín-Tomás, M., Rosenkranz, M. A., Lutz, A., & Davidson, R. J. (2014). Rapid changes in histone deacetylases and inflammatory gene expression in expert meditators. *Psychoneuroendocrinology, 40*, 96–107. https://doi.org/10.1016/j.psyneuen.2013.11.004

Kalyani, B. G., Venkatasubramanian, G., Arasappa, R., Rao, N. P., Kalmady, S. V., Behere, R. V., Rao, H., Vasudev, M. K., & Gangadhar, B. N. (2011). Neurohemodynamic correlates of "OM" chanting: A pilot functional magnetic resonance imaging study. *International Journal of Yoga, 4*(1), 3–6. https://doi.org/10.4103/0973-6131.78171

Kandel, E. R. (1998). A new intellectual framework for psychiatry. *The American Journal of Psychiatry, 155*(4), 457–469. https://doi.org/10.1176/ajp.155.4.457

Kandel, E. R. (1999). Biology and the future of psychoanalysis: A new intellectual framework for psychiatry revisited. *The American Journal of Psychiatry, 156*(4), 505–524. https://doi.org/10.1176/ajp.156.4.505

Karen, R. (1994). *Becoming Attached: Unfolding the Mystery of the Infant–Mother Bond and Its Impact on Later Life.* Warner Books.

Karen, R. (1998). *Becoming Attached: First Relationships and How They Shape Our Capacity to Love.* Oxford University Press.

Kelly, A. C., & Tasca, G. A. (2016). Within-persons predictors of change during eating disorders treatment: An examination of self-compassion, self-criticism, shame, and eating disorder symptoms. *The International Journal of Eating Disorders, 49*(7), 716–722. https://doi.org/10.1002/eat.22527

Kelly, A. C., Carter, J. C., Zuroff, D. C., & Borairi, S. (2013). Self-compassion and fear of self-compassion interact to predict response to eating disorders treatment: A preliminary investigation. *Psychotherapy Research: Journal of the Society for Psychotherapy Research, 23*(3), 252–264. https://doi.org/10.1080/10503307.2012.717310

Kernberg, O. F. (1990). New perspectives in psychoanalytic affect theory. In R. Plutchik & H. Kellerman (Eds.), *Emotion: Theory, Research, and Experience, Volume 5: Emotion, Psychopathology, and Psychotherapy* (pp. 115–131). Academic Press. https://doi.org/10.1016/B978-0-12-558705-1.50011-7

Kernberg, O. F. (2006). Psychoanalytic affect theory in the light of contemporary neurobiological findings. *International Congress Series, 1286*, 106–117. https://doi.org/10.1016/j.ics.2005.10.011

Khoury, B., Lecomte, T., Fortin, G., Masse, M., Therien, P., Bouchard, V., Chapleau, M.-A., Paquin, K., & Hofmann, S. G. (2013). Mindfulness-based therapy: A comprehensive meta-analysis. *Clinical Psychology Review, 33*(6), 763–771. https://doi.org/10.1016/j.cpr.2013.05.005

Kim, S., Thibodeau, R., & Jorgensen, R. S. (2011). Shame, guilt, and depressive symptoms: A meta-analytic review. *Psychological Bulletin, 137*(1), 68–96. https://doi.org/10.1037/a0021466

The King Center. (n.d.). *The King Philosophy - Nonviolence365®*. Retrieved June 17, 2022, from https://thekingcenter.org/about-tkc/the-king-philosophy/

Klein, M. (1975). *Envy and Gratitude and Other Works 1946–1963*. The Free Press.

Klimecki, O. M., Leiberg, S., Lamm, C., & Singer, T. (2013). Functional neural plasticity and associated changes in positive affect after compassion training. *Cerebral Cortex, 23*(7), 1552–1561. https://doi.org/10.1093/cercor/bhs142

Klimecki, O. M., Leiberg, S., Ricard, M., & Singer, T. (2013). Differential pattern of functional brain plasticity after compassion and empathy training. *Social Cognitive and Affective Neuroscience, 23*(7), 1552–1561. https://doi.org/10.1093/scan/nst060

Knafo, D. (2002). Revisiting Ernst Kris's concept of Regression in the service of the ego in art. *Psychoanalytic Psychology, 19*(1), 24–49. https://doi.org/10.1037/0736-9735.19.1.24

Kohut, H. (1971). *The Analysis of the Self: A Systematic Approach to the Psychoanalytic Treatment of Narcissistic Personality Disorders*. University of Chicago Press.

Kohut, H. (1977). *The Restoration of the Self*. University Of Chicago Press.

Kohut, H. (1984). *How Does Analysis Cure?* (A. Goldberg & P. E. Stepansky, Eds.). University of Chicago Press.

Kohut, H., & Wolf, E. S. (1978). The disorders of the self and their treatment: An outline. *The International Journal of Psychoanalysis, 59*(4), 413–425.

Kok, B. E., Coffey, K. A., Cohn, M. A., Catalino, L. I., Vacharkulksemsuk, T., Algoe, S. B., Brantley, M., & Fredrickson, B. L. (2013). How positive emotions build physical health: Perceived positive social connections account for the upward spiral between positive emotions and vagal tone. *Psychological Science, 24*(7), 1123–1132. https://doi.org/10.1177/0956797612470827

Kosslyn, S. M., DiGirolamo, G. J., Thompson, W. L., & Alpert, N. M. (1998). Mental rotation of objects versus hands: Neural mechanisms revealed by positron emission tomography. *Psychophysiology, 35*(2), 151–161.

Kosslyn, S. M., Thompson, W. L., Costantini-Ferrando, M. F., Alpert, N. M., & Spiegel, D. (2000). Hypnotic visual illusion alters color processing in the brain.

The American Journal of Psychiatry, 157(8), 1279–1284. https://doi.org/10.1176/appi
.ajp.157.8.1279

Kosslyn, S. M., Thompson, W. L., & Ganis, G. (2006). *The Case for Mental Imagery*.
Oxford University Press.

Kozhevnikov, M., Elliott, J., Shephard, J., & Gramann, K. (2013). Neurocognitive
and somatic components of temperature increases during g-tummo meditation:
Legend and reality. *PloS One, 8*(3), e58244. https://doi.org/10.1371/journal.pone
.0058244

Kozhevnikov, M., Louchakova, O., Josipovic, Z., & Motes, M. A. (2009). The
enhancement of visuospatial processing efficiency through Buddhist Deity
meditation. *Psychological Science, 20*(5), 645–653. https://doi.org/10.1111/j.1467
-9280.2009.02345.x

Krieger, T., Altenstein, D., Baettig, I., Doerig, N., & Holtforth, M. G. (2013). Self-
compassion in depression: Associations with depressive symptoms, rumination,
and avoidance in depressed outpatients. *Behavior Therapy, 44*(3), 501–513. https://
doi.org/10.1016/j.beth.2013.04.004

Kristeller, J. L., & Hallett, C. B. (1999). An exploratory study of a meditation-based
intervention for binge eating disorder. *Journal of Health Psychology, 4*(3), 357–363.
https://doi.org/10.1177/135910539900400305

Kristeller, J., & Rapgay, L. (2013). Buddhism: A blend of religion, spirituality,
and psychology. In *APA Handbook of Psychology, Religion, and Spirituality
(vol 1): Context, Theory, and Research* (pp. 635–652). American Psychological
Association. https://doi.org/10.1037/14045-035

Kuyken, W., Byford, S., Taylor, R. S., Watkins, E., Holden, E., White, K., Barrett,
B., Byng, R., Evans, A., Mullan, E., & Teasdale, J. D. (2008). Mindfulness-based
cognitive therapy to prevent relapse in recurrent depression. *Journal of Consulting
and Clinical Psychology, 76*(6), 966–978. https://doi.org/10.1037/a0013786

Laithwaite, H., O'Hanlon, M., Collins, P., Doyle, P., Abraham, L., Porter, S., & Gumley,
A. (2009). Recovery After Psychosis (RAP): A compassion focused programme
for individuals residing in high security settings. *Behavioural and Cognitive
Psychotherapy, 37*(5), 511–526. https://doi.org/10.1017/S1352465809990233

Lamagna, J., & Gleiser, K. A. (2007). Building a secure internal attachment: An
intra-relational approach to ego strengthening and emotional processing with
chronically traumatized clients. *Journal of Trauma and Dissociation, 8*(1), 25–52.
https://doi.org/10.1300/J229v08n01_03

Lambert, M. J. (1992). Psychotherapy outcome research: Implications for integrative
and eclectical therapists. In J. C. Norcross & M. R. Goldfried (Eds.), *Handbook of
Psychotherapy Integration* (pp. 94–129). Basic Books.

Lambert, M. J., & Barley, D. E. (2001). Research summary on the therapeutic relationship and psychotherapy outcome. *Psychotherapy: Theory, Research, Practice, Training, 38*(4), 357–361. https://doi.apa.org/doi/10.1037/0033-3204.38.4.357

Lamrimpa, G. (1999). *Transcending Time: An Explanation of the Kalachakra Six-Session Guruyoga* (P. B. Fitze, Ed.; B. A. Wallace, Trans.). Wisdom Publications.

Lati, R., & Hopkins, J. (1985). *Death, Intermediate State and Rebirth in Tibetan Buddhism.* Snow Lion Publications.

Lati, Rinpoche. (1981). *Mind in Tibetan Buddhism: Oral Commentary on Ge-shay Jam-bel-sam-pel's Presentation of Awareness and Knowledge, Composite of All the Important Points, Opener of the Eye of New Intelligence* (E. Napper, Ed. & Trans.; Rev. ed.). Snow Lion.

Lazar, S. W., Bush, G., Gollub, R. L., Fricchione, G. L., Khalsa, G., & Benson, H. (2000). Functional brain mapping of the relaxation response and meditation. *NeuroReport, 11*(7), 1581–1585.

Lazar, S. W., Kerr, C. E., Wasserman, R. H., Gray, J. R., Greve, D. N., Treadway, M. T., McGarvey, M., Quinn, B. T., Dusek, J. A., Benson, H., Rauch, S. L., Moore, C. I., & Fischl, B. (2005). Meditation experience is associated with increased cortical thickness. *NeuroReport, 16*(17), 1893–1897. https://doi.org/10.1097/01.wnr.0000186598.66243.19

Leary, M. R., Tate, E. B., Adams, C. E., Allen, A. B., & Hancock, J. (2007). Self-compassion and reactions to unpleasant self-relevant events: The implications of treating oneself kindly. *Journal of Personality and Social Psychology, 92*(5), 887–904. https://doi.org/10.1037/0022-3514.92.5.887

LeBlanc, A. J., Frost, D. M., & Bowen, K. (2018). Legal marriage, unequal recognition, and mental health among same-sex couples. *Journal of Marriage and Family, 80*(2), 397–408. https://doi.org/10.1111/jomf.12460

Lee, D. A. (2005). The perfect nurturer: A model to develop a compassionate mind within the context of cognitive therapy. In *Compassion: Conceptualisations, Research and Use in Psychotherapy* (pp. 326–351). Routledge. https://doi.org/10.1080/09638230500513175

Leiberg, S., Klimecki, O., & Singer, T. (2011). Short-term compassion training increases prosocial behavior in a newly developed prosocial game. *PloS One, 6*(3), e17798. https://doi.org/10.1371/journal.pone.0017798

Lieberman, A. F., Padrón, E., Van Horn, P., & Harris, W. W. (2005). Angels in the nursery: The intergenerational transmission of benevolent parental influences. *Infant Mental Health Journal, 26*(6), 504–520. https://doi.org/10.1002/imhj.20071

Lieberman, M. D. (2013). *Social: Why Our Brains Are Wired to Connect.* Crown.

Linden, W., Stossel, C., & Maurice, J. (1996). Psychosocial interventions for patients with coronary artery disease: A meta-analysis. *Archives of Internal Medicine, 156*(7), 745–752.

Linehan, M. M. (1993a). *Cognitive-Behavioral Treatment of Borderline Personality Disorder.* Guilford Press.

Linehan, M. M. (1993b). *Skills Training Manual for Treating Borderline Personality Disorder.* Guilford Press.

Linehan, M. M., Armstrong, H. E., Suarez, A., Allmon, D., & Heard, H. L. (1991). Cognitive-behavioral treatment of chronically parasuicidal borderline patients. *Archives of General Psychiatry, 48*(12), 1060–1064. https://doi.org/10.1001/archpsyc.1991.01810360024003

Lipton, B., & Fosha, D. (2011). Attachment as a transformative process in AEDP: Operationalizing the intersection of attachment theory and affective neuroscience. *Journal of Psychotherapy Integration, 21*(3), 253–279. https://doi.apa.org/doi/10.1037/a0025421

Llinás, R. R. (2001). *I of the Vortex: From Neurons to Self.* MIT Press.

Loizzo, J. (2000). Meditation and psychotherapy: Stress, allostasis and enriched learning. In P. Muskin (Ed.), *Complementary and Alternative Medicine and Psychiatry.* American Psychiatric Association Press.

Loizzo, J. (2009). Optimizing learning and quality of life throughout the lifespan: A global framework for research and application. *Annals of the New York Academy of Sciences, 1172,* 186–198. https://doi.org/10.1196/annals.1393.006

Loizzo, J. (2012). *Sustainable Happiness: The Mind Science of Well-Being, Altruism, and Inspiration.* Routledge.

Loizzo, J. (2014a). Personal agency across generations: Translating the evolutionary psychology of karma. In C. K. Wedemeyer, J. D. Dunne, & T. Yarnall (Eds.), *In Vimalakirti's House: A Festschrift in Honor of Robert A. F. Thurman on the Occasion of his 70th Birthday.* American Institute of Buddhist Studies.

Loizzo, J. (2014b). Meditation research, past, present, and future: Perspectives from the Nalanda contemplative science tradition. *Annals of the New York Academy of Sciences, 1307*(1), 43–54. https://doi.org/10.1111/nyas.12273

Loizzo, J. (2017). Contemplative psychotherapy: The art and science of sustainable happiness. In *Advances in Contemplative Psychotherapy: Accelerating Healing and Transformation* (1st ed., pp. 1–13). Routledge.

Loizzo, J. (2018). Vajrayāna buddhism. In P. Bilimoria (Ed.), *History of Indian Philosophy* (pp. 360–370). Routledge.

Loizzo, J. (2021). *Compassion-Based Resilience Training Student Manual.* Nalanda Institute for Contemplative Science.

Loizzo, J., Charlson, M., & Peterson, J. (2009). A program in contemplative self-healing: Stress, allostasis, and learning in the Indo-Tibetan tradition. *Annals of the New York Academy of Sciences, 1172*, 123–147. https://doi.org/10.1111/j.1749-6632.2009.04398.x

Loizzo, J. J. (2015). Buddhist perspectives on psychiatric ethics. In J. Z. Sadler, K. W. M. Fulford, & C. van Staden (Eds.), *The Oxford Handbook of Psychiatric Ethics* (Vol. 1). Oxford University Press.

Loizzo, J. J. (2016). The subtle body: An interoceptive map of central nervous system function and meditative mind-brain-body integration. *Annals of the New York Academy of Sciences, 1373*(1), 78–95. https://doi.org/10.1111/nyas.13065

Loizzo, J. J. (2018). Can embodied contemplative practices accelerate resilience training and trauma recovery? *Frontiers in Human Neuroscience, 12*, 134. https://doi.org/10.3389/fnhum.2018.00134

Loizzo, J. J., Peterson, J. C., Charlson, M. E., Wolf, E. J., Altemus, M., Briggs, W. M., Vahdat, L. T., & Caputo, T. A. (2010). The effect of a contemplative self-healing program on quality of life in women with breast and gynecologic cancers. *Alternative Therapies in Health and Medicine, 16*(3), 30–37.

Longe, O., Maratos, F. A., Gilbert, P., Evans, G., Volker, F., Rockliff, H., & Rippon, G. (2010). Having a word with yourself: Neural correlates of self-criticism and self-reassurance. *NeuroImage, 49*(2), 1849–1856. https://doi.org/10.1016/j.neuroimage.2009.09.019

Lopez, S. J., Pedrotti, J. T., & Snyder, C. R. (2014). *Positive Psychology: The Scientific and Practical Explorations of Human Strengths* (3rd ed.). SAGE.

Lü, W., Wang, Z., & Liu, Y. (2013). A pilot study on changes of cardiac vagal tone in individuals with low trait positive affect: The effect of positive psychotherapy. *International Journal of Psychophysiology: Official Journal of the International Organization of Psychophysiology, 88*(2), 213–217. https://doi.org/10.1016/j.ijpsycho.2013.04.012

Lucre, K. M., & Corten, N. (2013). An exploration of group compassion-focused therapy for personality disorder. *Psychology and Psychotherapy: Theory, Research and Practice, 86*(4), 387–400. https://doi.org/10.1111/j.2044-8341.2012.02068.x

Luders, E. K., Toga, A. W., Lepore, N., & Gaser, C. (2009). The underlying anatomical correlates of long-term meditation: Larger hippocampal and frontal volumes of gray matter. *Neuroimage, 45*(3), 672–678. https://doi.org/10.1016/j.neuroimage.2008.12.061

Lutz, A., Brefczynski-Lewis, J., Johnstone, T., & Davidson, R. J. (2008). Regulation of the neural circuitry of emotion by compassion meditation: Effects of meditative expertise. *PloS One, 3*(3), e1897. https://doi.org/10.1371/journal.pone.0001897

Lutz, A., Dunne, J. D., & Davidson, R. J. (2007). Meditation and the neuroscience of consciousness: An introduction. In P. D. Zelazo, M. Moscovitch, & E. Thompson (Eds.), *The Cambridge Handbook of Consciousness* (pp. 499–551). Cambridge University Press. https://doi.org/10.1017/CBO9780511816789.020

Lutz, A., Greischar, L. L., Rawlings, N. B., Ricard, M., & Davidson, R. J. (2004). Long-term meditators self-induce high amplitude gamma synchrony during mental practice. *Proceedings of the National Academy of Sciences of the United States of America, 101*(46), 16369–16373. https://doi.org/10.1073/pnas.0407401101

Lyons-Ruth, K. (2006). The interface between attachment and intersubjectivity: Perspective from the longitudinal study of disorganized attachment. *Psychoanalytic Inquiry, 26*(4), 595–616. https://doi.org/10.1080/07351690701310656

MacBeth, A., & Gumley, A. (2012). Exploring compassion: A meta-analysis of the association between self-compassion and psychopathology. *Clinical Psychology Review, 32*(6), 545–552. https://doi.org/10.1016/j.cpr.2012.06.003

Main, M. (1999). Epilogue. Attachment theory: Eighteen points with suggestions for future studies. In J. Cassidy & P. R. Shaver (Eds.), *Handbook of Attachment: Theory, Research and Clinical Applications* (pp. 845–888). Guilford Press.

Majied, K. (2010). The impact of sexual orientation and gender expression bias on African American students. *The Journal of Negro Education, 79*(2), 151–165.

Majied, K. (2013). Sexuality and contemporary issues in Black parenting. *Journal of Human Behavior in the Social Environment, 23*(2), 267–277. https://doi.org/10.1080/10911359.2013.747405

Majied, K. (2020). On being Lailah's daughter: Blessons from umieversity on actualizing enlightenment. In P.A. Yetunde & C. A. Giles (Eds.), *Black & Buddhist: What Buddhism Can Teach Us About Race, Resilience, Transformation & Freedom*. Shambhala.

Majied, K. (in press). *Joyfully Just: Liberating Meditaton Practices*. Sounds True.

Majied, K. F. (2003). *The Impact of Racism and Homophobia on Depression* [Doctoral dissertation, State University of New York at Albany]. ProQuest Dissertations Publishing.

Majied, K. F. (2010). The impact of sexual orientation and gender expression bias on African American students. *The Journal of Negro Education, 79*(2), 151–165.

Majied, K. F. (2015). Racism and homophobia in Cuba: A historical and contemporary overview. *Journal of Human Behavior in the Social Environment, 25*(1), 26–34. https://doi.org/10.1080/10911359.2014.953428

Majied, K., & Moss-Knight, T. (2012). Social work research considerations with sexual minorities in the African Diaspora. *Journal of Social Work Values and Ethics, 9*(2), 56–67.

Manuel, E. (2015). *The Way of Tenderness: Awakening Through Race, Sexuality, and Gender*. Wisdom Publications.

Marchetti, I., Koster, E. H. W., Sonuga-Barke, E. J., & De Raedt, R. (2012). The default mode network and recurrent depression: A neurobiological model of cognitive risk factors. *Neuropsychology Review, 22*(3), 229–251. https://doi.org/10.1007/s11065-012-9199-9

Marin, N. (Ed.). (2020). *Black Imagination: Black Voices on Black Futures*. McSweeney's Publishing.

Marlatt, G. A., & Gordon, D. M. (Eds.). (1985). *Relapse Prevention: Maintenance Strategies in the Treatment of Addictive Behaviors*. Guilford Press.

Mascaro, J. S., Rilling, J. K., Tenzin Negi, L., & Raison, C. L. (2013). Compassion meditation enhances empathic accuracy and related neural activity. *Social Cognitive and Affective Neuroscience, 8*(1), 48–55. https://doi.org/10.1093/scan/nss095

Mason, L. I., Alexander, C. N., Travis, F. T., Marsh, G., Orme-Johnson, D. W., Gackenbach, J., Mason, D. C., Rainforth, M., & Walton, K. G. (1997). Electrophysiological correlates of higher states of consciousness during sleep in long-term practitioners of the Transcendental Meditation program. *Sleep, 20*(2), 102–110. https://doi.org/10.1093/sleep/20.2.102

Matos, M., Pinto-Gouveia, J., & Costa, V. (2013). Understanding the importance of attachment in shame traumatic memory relation to depression: The impact of emotion regulation processes. *Clinical Psychology & Psychotherapy, 20*(2), 149–165. https://doi.org/10.1002/cpp.786

Matos, M., Pinto-Gouveia, J., & Gilbert, P. (2013). The effect of shame and shame memories on paranoid ideation and social anxiety. *Clinical Psychology & Psychotherapy, 20*(4), 334–349.

McEwen, B., & Lasley, E. (2002). *The End of Stress as We Know It*. Joseph Henry Press.

McPherran, M. L. (1999). *The Religion of Socrates*. Penn State University Press.

McWilliams, N. (2004). *Psychodynamic Psychotherapy: A Practitioner's Guide*. Guilford Press.

Meichenbaum, D. (1977). *Cognitive Behavior Modification: An Integrative Approach*. Plenum Press.

Mellet, E., Petit, L., Mazoyer, B., Denis, M., & Tzourio, N. (1998). Reopening the mental imagery debate: Lessons from functional anatomy. *NeuroImage, 8*(2), 129–139. https://doi.org/10.1006/nimg.1998.0355

Menakem, R. ((2017). *My Grandmother's Hands: Racialized Trauma and the Pathway to Mending Our Hearts and Bodies*. Central Recovery Press.

Meyer, I. H. (1995). Minority stress and mental health in gay men. *Journal of Health and Social Behavior, 36*(1), 38–56.

Meyer, I. H. (2003). Prejudice, social stress, and mental health in lesbian, gay, and bisexual populations: Conceptual issues and research evidence. *Psychological Bulletin, 129*(5), 674–697. https://doi.org/10.1037/0033-2909.129.5.674

Meyer, I. H. (2019). Rejection sensitivity and minority stress: A challenge for clinicians and interventionists. *Archives of Sexual Behavior, 49*(7), 2287–2289. https://doi.org/10.1007/s10508-019-01597-7

Mid Staffordshire NHS Foundation Trust Public Inquiry. (2013). Nursing. In *Report of the Mid Staffordshire NHS Foundation Trust Public Enquiry* (Vol. 3, pp. 1497–1544). The Stationery Office.

Mikulincer, M., Shaver, P. R., & Pereg, D. (2003). Attachment theory and affect regulation: The dynamics, development, and cognitive consequences of attachment-related strategies. *Motivation and Emotion, 27*(2), 77–102. https://doi.org/10.1023/A:1024515519160

Miller, J. J., Fletcher, K. F., & Kabat-Zinn, J. (1995). Three-year follow-up and clinical implications of a mindfulness-based stress reduction intervention in the treatment of anxiety disorders. *General Hospital Psychiatry, 17*(3), 192–200. https://doi.org/10.1016/0163-8343(95)00025-M

Moacanin, R. (1986). *Jung's Psychology and Tibetan Buddhism: Western and Eastern Paths to the Heart.* Wisdom Publications.

Molino, A. (Ed.). (1999). *The Couch and the Tree: Dialogues in Psychoanalysis and Buddhism.* North Point Press.

Muller-Ortega, P. E. (1997). *The Triadic Heart of Siva: Kaula Tantricism of Abhinavagupta In The Non-Dual Shaivism of Kashmir.* Shri Satguru Publications.

Mullin, G. C. (Ed.). (2005). *The Six Yogas of Naropa: Tsongkhapa's Commentary Entitled A Book of Three Inspirations: A Treatise on the Stages of Training in the Profound Path of Naro's Six Dharmas* (G. C. Mullin, Trans.). Snow Lion Publications.

Neale, M. (2011). *McMindfulness and Frozen Yoga: Rediscovering the Essential Teachings of Ethics and Wisdom.* https://bit.ly/3aGSNmH

Neale, M. (2012). *What Buddhist Psychotherapy Really Is.* https://bit.ly/3NEv0Cu

Neff, K. (2015). *Self-Compassion: The Proven Power of Being Kind to Yourself.* William Morrow.

Neff, K. D. (2003). The development and validation of a scale to measure self-compassion. *Self and Identity, 2*(3), 223–250. https://doi.org/10.1080/15298860309027

Neff, K. D., & Germer, C. K. (2013). A pilot study and randomized controlled trial of the mindful self-compassion program. *Journal of Clinical Psychology, 69*(1), 28–44. https://doi.org/10.1002/jclp.21923

Neff, K. D., Kirkpatrick, K. L., & Rude, S. S. (2007). Self-compassion and adaptive psychological functioning. *Journal of Research in Personality, 41*(1), 139–154.

Nemirovsky, C. (2021). Relational and intersubjective psychoanalysis. In J. Filc (Trans.), *Winnicott and Kohut on Intersubjectivity and Complex Disorders: New Perspectives for Psychoanalysis, Psychotherapy and Psychiatry* (pp. 103–110). Routledge.

Norcross, J. (Ed.). (2011). *Psychotherapy Relationships That Work: Evidence-Based Responsiveness.* Oxford University Press.

Ogden, T. H. (2004). An introduction to the reading of Bion. *The International Journal of Psycho-Analysis, 85*(Pt 2), 285–300. https://doi.org/10.1516/002075704773889751

Oliver, M. (2004). The summer day. In *New and Selected Poems* (Vol. 1, p. 94). Beacon Press.

Orange, D. M., Atwood, G. E., & Stolorow, R. D. (1997). *Working Intersubjectively: Contextualism in Psychoanalytic Practice.* The Analytic Press.

Palmo, T. (2002). *Reflections on a Mountain Lake: Teachings on Practical Buddhism.* Snow Lion Publications.

Pando-Mars, K. (2016). Tailoring AEDP Interventions to attachment style. *Transformance: The AEDP Journal, 6*(2). https://aedpinstitute.org/transformance-journal/transformance-volume-6-issue-2/

Pearlin, L. I. (1989). The sociological study of stress. *Journal of Health and Social Behavior, 30*(3), 241–256.

Pederson, O. (2009). *The First Universities: Studium Generale and the Origins of University Education in Europe.* Cambridge University Press.

Pepping, C. A., O'Donovan, A., & Davis, P. J. (2013). The positive effects of mindfulness on self-esteem. *The Journal of Positive Psychology, 8*(5), 376–386. https://doi.org/10.1080/17439760.2013.807353.

Peterson, C. (2006). *A Primer in Positive Psychology.* Oxford University Press.

Petty, S. (2016). *Seeing, Reckoning & Acting: A Practice Toward Deep Equity.* Change Elemental. https://changeelemental.org/resources/seeing-reckoning-acting-a-practice-toward-deep-equity/

Petty, S. (2017). Waking up to all of ourselves: Inner work, social justice, & systems change. *Social Justice, Inner Work & Contemplative Practice, [Special Issue]. ICEA Journal, 1*(1), 1–14. http://www.contemplativemind.org/files/ICEA_vol1_2017.pdf

Petty, S., & Leach, M. (2020). *Systems Change & Deep Equity: Pathways Toward Sustainable Impact, Beyond "Eureka!," Unawareness & Unwitting Harm*. Change Elemental.   https://changeelemental.org/resources/systems-change-and-deep -equity-monograph/

Pinto-Gouveia, J., & Matos, M. (2011). Can shame memories become a key to identity? The centrality of shame memories predicts psychopathology. *Applied Cognitive Psychology, 25*(2), 281–290. https://doi.org/10.1002/acp.1689

Pinto-Gouveia, J., Duarte, C., Matos, M., & Fráguas, S. (2014). The protective role of self-compassion in relation to psychopathology symptoms and quality of life in chronic and in cancer patients. *Clinical Psychology & Psychotherapy, 21*(4), 311–323. https://doi.org/10.1002/cpp.1838

Porges, S. W. (2007). The polyvagal perspective. *Biological Psychology, 74*(2), 116–143. https://doi.org/10.1016/j.biopsycho.2006.06.009

Porges, S. W. (2009). Reciprocal influences between body and brain in the perception of affect: A polyvagal perspective. In D. Fosha, D. J. Siegel, & M. F. Solomon (Eds.), *The Healing Power of Emotion: Affective Neuroscience, Development & Clinical Practice*. W. W. Norton & Company.

Porges, S. W. (2011). *The Polyvagal Theory: Neurophysiological Foundations of Emotions, Attachment, Communication and Self-Regulation*. W. W. Norton & Company.

Porges, S. W., & Furman, S. A. (2011). The early development of the autonomic nervous system provides a neural platform for social behavior: A polyvagal perspective. *Infant and Child Development, 20*(1), 106–118. https://doi.org/10.1002 /icd.688

Porter, C. L., Yang, C., Jorgensen, N. A., & Evans-Stout, C. (2022). Development of mother-infant co-regulation: The role of infant vagal tone and temperament at 6, 9, and 12 months of age. *Infant Behavior & Development, 67*, Article 101708. https://doi.org/10.1016/j.infbeh.2022.101708

Powell, J. A. (2015). *Racing to Justice: Transforming Our Conceptions of Self and Other to Build an Inclusive Society*. Indiana University Press.

Pribram, K. H. (2013). *The Form Within: My Point of View*. Prospecta Press.

Rakel, D. P., Hoeft, T. J., Barrett, B. P., Chewning, B. A., Craig, B. M., & Niu, M. (2009). Practitioner empathy and the duration of the common cold. *Family Medicine, 41*(7), 494–501.

Rapgay, L. (2005). *The Tibetan Book of Healing*. Lotus Press.

Rapgay, L., & Bystrisky, A. (2009). Classical mindfulness: An introduction to its theory and practice for clinical application. *Annals of the New York Academy of Sciences, 1172*(1), 148–162. https://doi.org/10.1111/j.1749-6632.2009. 04405.x

Rappe, S. (2007). *Reading Neoplatonism: Non-discursive Thinking in the Texts of Plotinus, Proclus, and Damascius*. Cambridge University Press.

Rayburn, C. A., & Comas-Díaz, L. (Eds.). (2008). *WomanSoul: The Inner Life of Women's Spirituality*. Praeger.

Ricard, M., & Thuan, T. X. (2004). *The Quantum and the Lotus: A Journey to the Frontiers Where Science and Buddhism Meet*. Broadway Books.

Riggle, E. D. B., Mohr, J. J., Rostosky, S. S., Fingerhut, A. W., & Balsam, K. F. (2014). A multifactor lesbian, gay, and bisexual positive identity measure (LGB-PIM). *Psychology of Sexual Orientation and Gender Diversity, 1*(4), 398. https://doi.org/10.1037/sgd0000057

Rockliff, H., Gilbert, P., McEwan, K., Lightman, S., & Glover, D. (2008). A pilot exploration of heart rate variability and salivary cortisol responses to compassion-focused imagery. *Clinical Neuropsychiatry: Journal of Treatment Evaluation, 5*(3), 132–139.

Ross, C. E., & Mirowsky, J. (1989). Explaining the social patterns of depression: Control and problem solving—Or support and talking? *Journal of Health and Social Behavior, 30*(2), 206–219. https://psycnet.apa.org/doi/10.2307/2137014

Rossman, M. L. (2000). *Guided Imagery for Self-Healing*. New World Library.

Rubin, J. B. (1996). *Psychotherapy and Buddhism: Toward an Integration*. Springer Science+Business.

Russell, E., & Fosha, D. (2008). Transformational affects and core state in AEDP: The emergence and consolidation of joy, hope, gratitude and confidence in the (solid goodness of the) self. *Journal of Psychotherapy Integration, 18*(2), 167–190. https://doi.apa.org/doi/10.1037/1053-0479.18.2.167

Russell, E. M. (2015). *Restoring Resilience: Discovering Your Clients' Capacity for Healing*. W. W. Norton & Company.

Ryff, C. D. (2014). Psychological well-being revisited: Advances in the science and practice of eudaimonia. *Psychotherapy & Psychosomatics, 83*, 10–28. https://doi.org/10.1159/000353263

Salzberg, S. (2002). *Loving Kindness: The Revolutionary Art of Happiness*. Shambhala Publishing.

Salzberg, S. (2010). *Real Happiness: The Power of Meditation*. Workman Publishing.

Salzberg, S. (2013). *Real Happiness at Work: Meditations for Accomplishment, Achievement, and Peace*. Workman Publishing.

Sanderson, A. (1985). Purity and power among the Brāhmans of Kashmir. In M. Carrithers, S. Collins, & S. Lukes (Eds.), *The Category of the Person: Anthropology, Philosophy, History* (pp. 190–215). Cambridge University Press.

Sattler, F. A., Nater, U. M., & Mewes, R. (2021). Gay men's stress response to a general and a specific social stressor. *Journal of Neural Transmission, 128*(9), 1325–1333. https://doi.org/10.1007/s00702-021-02380-6

Sbarra, D. A., Smith, H. L., & Mehl, M. R. (2012). When leaving your ex, love yourself: Observational ratings of self-compassion predict the course of emotional recovery following marital separation. *Psychological Science, 23*(3), 261–269. https://doi.org/10.1177/0956797611429466

Schanche, E., Stiles, T. C., McCullough, L., Svartberg, M., & Nielsen, G. H. (2011). The relationship between activating affects, inhibitory affects, and self-compassion in patients with Cluster C personality disorders. *Psychotherapy (Chicago, Ill.), 48*(3), 293–303. https://doi.org/10.1037/a0022012

Schore, A. N. (2001). Effects of a secure attachment relationship on right brain development, affect regulation, and infant mental health. *Infant Mental Health Journal, 22,* 7–66. https://doi.org/10.1002/1097-0355(200101/04)22:1<7::AID-IMHJ2>3.0.CO;2-N

Schore, A. N. (2009). Right brain affect regulation: An essential mechanism of development, trauma, dissociation, and psychotherapy. In D. Fosha, D. J. Siegel, & M. F. Solomon (Eds.), *The Healing Power of Emotion: Affective Neuroscience, Development & Clinical Practice* (pp. 112–144). W. W. Norton & Company.

Schore, A. N. (2010). Relational trauma and the developing right brain: The neurobiology of broken attachment bonds. In T. Baradon (Ed.), *Relational Trauma in Infancy: Psychoanalytic, Attachment and Neuropsychological Contributions to Parent–Infant Psychotherapy* (pp. 19–47). Routledge.

Schore, A. N. (2012). *The Science and Art of Psychotherapy.* W. W. Norton & Company.

Schroeder, V. M., & Kelley, M. L. (2010). Family environment and parent-child relationships as related to executive functioning in children. *Early Child Development and Care, 180*(10), 1285–1298. https://psycnet.apa.org/doi/10.1080/03004430902981512

Schulkin, J., Gold, P. W., & McEwen, B. S. (1998). Induction of corticotropin-releasing hormone gene expression by glucocorticoids: Implication for understanding the states of fear and anxiety and allostatic load. *Psychoneuroendocrinology, 23*(3), 219–243. https://doi.org/10.1016/s0306-4530(97)00099-1.

Schwartz, R. C. (1995). *Internal Family Systems Therapy.* Guilford Press.

Segal, J. (2004). *Melanie Klein* (2nd ed.). Sage Publications.

Segal, Z. V., Williams, J. M. G., & Teasdale, J. D. (2013). *Mindfulness-Based Cognitive Therapy for Depression* (2nd ed.). Guilford Press.

Seppälä, E. M., Simon-Thomas, E., Brown, S. L., Worline, M. C., Cameron, C. D., & Doty, J. R. (2017). *The Oxford Handbook of Compassion Science.* Oxford University Press. https://10.1093/oxfordhb/9780190464684.001.0001

Shamar Rinpoche. (2014). *The Path to Awakening: How Buddhism's Seven Points of Mind Training Can Lead You to a Life of Enlightenment and Happiness* (L. Braitstein, Ed. & Trans.). Delphinium Books.

Shannahoff-Khalsa, D. (1991). Lateralized rhythms of the central and autonomic nervous systems. *International Journal of Psychophysiology, 11*(3), 225–251. https://doi.org/10.1016/0167-8760(91)90017-r

Shannahoff-Khalsa, D. (2008). Psychophysiological states: The ultradian dynamics of mind–Body interactions. *International Review of Neurobiology, 80,* 1–220.

Shannahoff-Khalsa, D. S. (2007). Selective unilateral autonomic activation: Implications for psychiatry. *CNS Spectrums, 12*(8), 625–634. https://doi.org/10.1017/s1092852900021428

Shantideva. (1997). *A Guide to the Bodhisattava Way of Life (Bodhicaryāvatāra)* (V. A. Wallace & B. A. Wallace, Trans.). Snow Lion Publications.

Shāntideva. (2006). *The Way of the Bodhisattava: A Translation of the Bodhicharyāvatāra* (Padmakara Translation Group, Trans.; Rev. ed.). Shambhala.

Shaw, M. (2022). *Passionate Enlightenment: Women in Tantric Buddhism* (Princeton Classics ed.). Princeton University Press.

Sheinbaum, T., Kwapil, T. R., Ballespí, S., Mitjavila, M., Chun, C. A., Silvia, P. J., & Barrantes-Vidal, N. (2015). Attachment style predicts affect, cognitive appraisals, and social functioning in daily life. *Frontiers in Psychology, 6*(296). https://doi.org/10.3389/fpsyg.2015.00296

Sheldrake, R. (2009). *Morphic Resonance: The Nature of Formative Causation.* Park Street Press.

Siegel, D. J. (2007). *The Mindful Brain: Reflection and Attunement in the Cultivation of Well-Being.* W. W. Norton & Company.

Siegel, D. J. (2009). Mindful awareness, mindsight, and neural integration. *The Humanistic Psychologist, 37*(2), 137–158. https://doi.org/10.1080/08873260902892220

Siegel, D. J. (2010a). *The Mindful Therapist: A Clinician's Guide to Mindsight and Neural Integration.* W. W. Norton & Company.

Siegel, D. J. (2010b). *Mindsight: The New Science of Personal Transformation.* Bantam Books.

Siegel, D. J. (2012). *Pocket Guide to Interpersonal Neurobiology: An Integrative Handbook of the Mind.* W.W. Norton & Co.

Siegel, D. J. (2015). *How Relationships and the Brain Interact to Shape Who We* (2nd ed.). Guilford Press.

Siegel, D. J. (2017). *Mind: A Journey to the Heart of Being Human.* W. W. Norton and Company.

Siegel, D. J. (2020). *The Developing Mind: How Relationships and the Brain Interact to Shape Who We Are* (3rd ed.). Guilford Press.

Siegel, D. J., & Bryson, T. P. (2011). *The Whole-Brain Child: 12 Revolutionary Strategies to Nurture Your Child's Developing Mind.* Delacorte Press.

Singer, T., & Bolz, M. (2013). *Compassion: Bridging Practice and Science.* Max Planck Institute for Human Cognitive and Brain Sciences. http://www.compassion -training.org/?lang=en&page=download

Singer, T., & Klimecki, O. M. (2014). Empathy and compassion. *Current Biology, 24*(18), R875–R878. https://doi.org/10.1016/j.cub.2014.06.054

Spalding, K. L., Bergmann, O., Alkass, K., Bernard, S., Salehpour, M., Huttner, H. B., Boström, E., Westerlund, I., Vial, C., Buchholz, B. A., Possnert, G., Mash, D. C., Druid, H., & Frisén, J. (2013). Dynamics of hippocampal neurogenesis in adult humans. *Cell, 153*(6), 1219–1227. https://doi.org/10.1016/j.cell.2013. 05.002

Spillius, E. B. (Ed.). (1988). *Melanie Klein Today: Developments in Theory and Practice (Volume 1: Mainly Theory).* Psychology Press.

Stern, D. N. (1985). *The Interpersonal World of the Infant: A View from Psychoanalysis and Developmental Psychology.* Basic Books.

Strong, S. D. (2021). Contemplative psychotherapy: Clinician mindfulness, Buddhist psychology, and the therapeutic common factors. *Journal of Psychotherapy Integration, 31*(2), 146–162. https://doi.org/10.1037/int0000191

Sulloway, F. J. (1992). *Freud, Biologist of the Mind: Beyond the Psychoanalytic Legend.* Harvard University Press.

Tan, K. K. H., Treharne, G. J., Ellis, S. J., Schmidt, J. M., & Veale, J. F. (2020). Gender minority stress: A critical review. *Journal of Homosexuality, 67*(10), 1471–1489. https://doi.org/10.1080/00918369.2019.1591789

Tang, Y.-Y., Hölzel, B. K., & Posner, M. I. (2015). The neuroscience of mindfulness meditation. *Nature Reviews. Neuroscience, 16*(4), 213–225. https://doi.org/10.1038 /nrn3916

Tatum, B. (1994). Teaching White students about racism: The search for White allies and the restoration of hope. *The Teachers College Record, 95*(4), 462–476.

Tatum, B. D. (1992). Talking about race, learning about racism: The application of racial identity development theory in the classroom. *Harvard Educational Review, 62*(1), 1–25. https://doi.org/10.17763/haer.62.1.146k5v980r703023

Tatum, B. D. (1997). *"Why Are All the Black Kids Sitting Together in the Cafeteria?": And Other Conversations About the Development of Racial Identity.* Basic Books.

Tatum, B. D. (2000). *Assimilation Blues: Black Families in White Communities, Who Succeeds and Why*. Basic Books.

Tatum, B. D. (2004). Family life and school experience: Factors in the racial identity development of Black youth in White communities. *Journal of Social Issues, 60*(1), 117–135. https://doi.org/10.1111/j.0022-4537.2004.00102.x

Tatum, B. D. (2007). *Can We Talk About Race?: And Other Conversations in an Era of School Resegregation*. Beacon Press.

Tatum, B. D. (2010). The complexity of identity: "Who am I?" In M. Adams, W. J. Blumenfeld, H. W. Hackman, H. W. Hackman, & X. Zúñiga (Eds.), *Readings for Diversity and Social Justice: An Anthology on Racism, Sexism, Anti-Semitism, Heterosexism, Classism and Ableism* (pp. 9–14). Routledge.

Tatum, B. D. (2017, Summer/Fall). "Why are all the Black kids still sitting together in the cafeteria?" and other conversations about race in the 21st century. *Liberal Education, 46–55*.

Teasdale, J. D., Segal, Z., & Williams, J. M. (1995). How does cognitive therapy prevent depressive relapse and why should attentional control (mindfulness) training help? *Behaviour Research and Therapy, 33*(1), 25–39. https://doi.org/10.1016/0005-7967(94)e0011-7

Teasdale, J. D., Segal, Z. V., Williams, J. M., Ridgeway, V. A., Soulsby, J. M., & Lau, M. A. (2000). Prevention of relapse/recurrence in major depression by mindfulness-based cognitive therapy. *Journal of Consulting and Clinical Psychology, 68*(4), 615–623. https://doi.org/10.1037//0022-006x.68.4.615

Testa, R. J., Habarth, J., Peta, J., Balsam, K., & Bockting, W. (2015). Development of the gender minority stress and resilience measure. *Psychology of Sexual Orientation and Gender Diversity, 2*(1), 65–77. https://doi.org/10.1037/sgd0000081.

Thera, N. (1972). *The Power of Mindfulness*. Unity Press.

Thera, N. (1994). *The Four Sublime States: Contemplations on Love, Compassion, Sympathetic Joy and Equanimity*. Access to Insight (BCBS Edition). http://www.accesstoinsight.org/lib/authors/nyanaponika/wheel006.html

Thomson, A. (2008). *Bodies of Thought: Science, Religion, and the Soul in the Early Enlightenment*. Oxford University Press.

Thurman, R. (2005). *The Jewel Tree of Tibet: The Enlightenment Engine of Tibetan Buddhism*. Free Press.

Thurman, R. A. F. (1991). *The Central Philosophy of Tibet: A Study and Translation of Jey Tsong Khapa's Essence of True Eloquence*. Princeton University Press.

Thurman, R. A. F. (1996). *Essential Tibetan Buddhism*. HarperOne.

Thurman, R. A. F. (2010). *Brilliant Illumination of the Lamp of the Five Stages (Rim Lnga Rab Tu Gsal Ba'i Sgron Me): Practical Instructions in the King of Tantras, the*

Glorious Esoteric Community by Tsong Khapa Losang Drakpa (T. F. Yarnall, Ed.). American Institute of Buddhist Studies.

Travis, L. A., Bliwise, N. G., Binder, J. L., & Horne-Moyer, H. L. (2001). Changes in clients' attachment styles over the course of time-limited dynamic psychotherapy. *Psychotherapy: Theory, Research, Practice, Training, 38*(2), 149–159. https://doi.apa .org/doi/10.1037/0033-3204.38.2.149

Treisman, K. (2016). *Working with Relational and Developmental Trauma in Children and Adolescents.* https://doi.org/10.4324/9781315672762

Trevarthen, C. (2009). The functions of emotion in infancy: The regulation and communication of rhythm, sympathy, and meaning in human development. In D. Fosha, D. J. Siegel, & M. F. Solomon (Eds.), *The Healing Power of Emotion: Affective Neuroscience, Development, and Clinical Practice* (pp. 55–85). Norton.

Trevarthen, C., & Aitken, K. J. (2001). Infant intersubjectivity: Research, theory, and clinical applications. *Journal of Child Psychology and Psychiatry, and Allied Disciplines, 42*(1), 3–48.

Tronick, E. Z. (1998). Dyadically expanded states of consciousness and the process of therapeutic change. *Infant Mental Health Journal, 19*(3), 290–299. https://doi.org /10.1002/(SICI)1097-0355(199823)19:3<290::AID-IMHJ4>3.0.CO;2-Q

Ulanov, A. (2004). *Spiritual Aspects of Clinical Work.* Daimon Verlag.

Ulanov, A., & Ulanov, B. (1999). *The Healing Imagination: The Meeting of Psyche and Soul.* Daimon Verlag.

Vago, D. R. (2014). Mapping modalities of self-awareness in mindfulness practice: A potential mechanism for clarifying habits of mind. *Annals of the New York Academy of Sciences, 1307,* 28–42. https://doi.org/10.1111/nyas.12270

Vago, D. R., & Silbersweig, D. A. (2012). Self-awareness, self-regulation, and self-transcendence (S-ART): A framework for understanding the neurobiological mechanisms of mindfulness. *Frontiers in Human Neuroscience, 6,* 296. https://doi .org/10.3389/fnhum.2012.00296

Vaish, A., Grossman, T., & Woodward, A. (2008). Not all emotions are created equal: The negativity bias in social-emotional development. *Psychological Bulletin, 134*(3), 383–403. https://doi.org/10.1037/0033-2909.134.3.383

van der Kolk, B. A. (2002). The assessment and treatment of complex PTSD. In *Treating Trauma Survivors with PTSD.* American Psychiatric Press.

van der Kolk, B. A. (2014). *The Body Keeps the Score: Brain, Mind, and Body in the Healing of Trauma.* Penguin Books.

van der Velden, A. M., Kuyken, W., Wattar, U., Crane, C., Pallesen, K. J., Dahlgaard, J., Fjorback, L. O., & Piet, J. (2015). A systematic review of mechanisms of change in mindfulness-based cognitive therapy in the treatment of recurrent major depressive disorder. *Clinical Psychology Review, 37*, 26–39. https://doi.org/10.1016/j.cpr.2015.02.001

Van Gordon, W., Sapthiang, S., & Shonin, E. (2022). Contemplative psychology: History, key assumptions, and future directions. *Perspectives on Psychological Science, 17*(1), 99–107. https://doi.org/10.1177/1745691620984479

Varela, F. J. (Ed.). (2002). *Sleeping, Dreaming and Dying: An Exploration of Consciousness with the Dalai Lama* (B. A. Wallace & T. Jinpa, Trans.). Wisdom.

Varela, F. J., Thompson, E. T., & Rosch, E. (1992). *The Embodied Mind: Cognitive Science and Human Experience.* MIT Press.

Vestergaard-Poulsen, P., van Beek, M., Skewes, J., Bjarkam, C. R., Stubberup, M., Bertelsen, J., & Roepstorff, A. (2009). Long-term meditation is associated with increased gray matter density in the brain stem. *NeuroReport, 20*(2), 170–174. https://doi.org/10.1097/WNR.0b013e328320012a

Vettese, L. C., Dyer, C. E., Li, W. L., & Wekerle, C. (2011). Does self-compassion mitigate the association between childhood maltreatment and later emotion regulation difficulties? A preliminary investigation. *International Journal of Mental Health and Addiction, 9*(5), 480–491. https://doi.org/10.1007/s11469-011-9340-7.

Voigt, R., Camp, N. P., Prabhakaran, V., Hamilton, W. L., Hetey, R. C., Griffiths, C. M., Jurgens, D., Jurafsky, D., & Eberhardt, J. L. (2017). Language from police body camera footage shows racial disparities in officer respect. *Proceedings of the National Academy of Sciences, 114*, 6521–6526. https://doi.org/10.1073/pnas.1702413114

Wallace, B. A. (2005). *Genuine Happiness: Meditation as the Path to Fulfillment.* Wiley.

Wallace, B. A. (2007). *Contemplative Science: Where Buddhism and Neuroscience Converge.* Columbia University Press.

Wallace, B. A. (2011). *Contemplative Science: Where Buddhism and Neuroscience Converge.* Columbia University Press.

Wallace, B. A., & Shapiro, S. L. (2006). Mental balance and well-being: Building bridges between Buddhism and Western psychology. *The American Psychologist, 61*(7), 690–701. https://doi.org/10.1037/0003-066X.61.7.690

Wallace, B. A., & Wilhelm, S. (1993). *Tibetan Buddhism from the Ground Up: A Practical Approach for Modern Life.* Wisdom.

Wallace, V. A. (2001). *The Inner Kālacakratanta: A Buddhist Tantric View of the Individual.* Oxford University Press.

Waziyatawin, & Yellow Bird, M. (Eds.). (2012). *For Indigenous Minds Only: A Decolonization Handbook.* School of American Research/SAR Press.

Wedemeyer, C. K. (2007). *Āryadeva's Lamp That Integrates the Practices (Caryāmelāpakapradīpa) the Gradual Path of Vajrayāna Buddhism According to the Esoteric Noble Tradition.* American Institute of Buddhist Studies.

Weick, A., Kreider, J., & Chamberlain, R. (2009). Key dimensions of the strengths perspective in case management, clinical practice, and community practice. In D. Saleebey (Ed.), *The Strengths Perspective in Social Work Practice* (5th ed., pp. 108–120). Pearson.

Welwood, J. (2000). Between heaven and earth: Principles of inner work. In *Toward a Psychology of Awakening: Buddhism, Psychotherapy, and the Path of Personal and Spiritual Transformation* (pp. 11–21). Shambhala Publications.

Weng, H. Y., Fox, A. S., Shackman, A. J., Stodola, D. E., Caldwell, J. Z. K., Olson, M. C., Rogers, G. M., & Davidson, R. J. (2013). Compassion training alters altruism and neural responses to suffering. *Psychological Science, 24*(7), 1171–1180. https://doi.org/10.1177/0956797612469537

Wheeler, G. (1997). Self and shame: A Gestalt approach. *Gestalt Review, 1*(3), 221–244. https://doi.org/10.2307/44394019

White, D. G. (1996). *The Alchemical Body: Siddha Traditions in Medieval India.* University of Chicago Press.

White, M., & Epston, D. (1990). *Narrative Means to Therapeutic Ends.* W. W. Norton & Company.

Williams, A. K., Owens, R., & Syedullah, J. (2016). *Radical Dharma: Talking Race, Love, and Liberation.* North Atlantic Books.

Willis, J. (2008). *Dreaming Me: Black, Baptist, and Buddhist: One Woman's Spiritual Journey.* Wisdom Publications.

Winnicott, D. W. (1958). *Collected Papers: Through Paediatrics to Psycho-Analysis.* Basic Books.

Winnicott, D. W. (1965). *The Maturational Processes and the Facilitating Environment: Studies in the Theory of Emotional Development.* Hogarth Press.

Winnicott, D. W. (1975). *The Child, the Family, and the Outside World.* Penguin.

Wong, C. C. Y., Knee, C. R., Neighbors, C., & Zvolensky, M. J. (2019). Hacking stigma by loving yourself: A mediated-moderation model of self-compassion and stigma. *Mindfulness, 10*(3), 415–433. https://doi.org/10.1007/s12671-018-0984-2

Wood, A. M., Froh, J. J., & Geraghty, A. W. A. (2010). Gratitude and well-being: A review and theoretical integration. *Clinical Psychology Review, 30*(7), 890–905. https://doi.org/10.1016/j.cpr.2010.03.005

Yarnall, T. F. (2013). *Great Treatise on the Stages of Mantra (Sngags Rim Chen Mo): Chapters XI–XII (The Creation Stage) by Tsong Khapa Losang Drakpa.* American Institute of Buddhist Studies.

Yates, F. A. (1991). *Giordano Bruno and the Hermetic Tradition*. University of Chicago Press.

Yellow Bird, M. (2013). Neurodecolonization: Applying mindfulness research to decolonizing social work. In M. Gray, J. Coates, M. Yellow Bird, & T. Hetherington (Eds.), *Decolonizing Social Work*. Ashgate Publishing.

Yellow Bird, M. (n.d.). *Neurodecolonization*. Neurodecolonization and Indigenous Mindfulness. https://www.indigenousmindfulness.com/about

Yellow Bird, M., Gehl, M., Hatton-Bowers, H., Hicks, L. M., & Reno-Smith, D. (2020). *Defunding Mindfulness: While We Sit on Our Cushions, Systemic Racism Runs Rampant*. Zero to Three. https://www.zerotothree.org/resource/perspectives-defunding-mindfulness-while-we-sit-on-our-cushions-systemic-racism-runs-rampant/

Yeshe, L. T. (2014). *Introduction to Tantra: The Transformation of Desire* (J. Landaw, Ed.; Rev. ed.). Wisdom Publications.

Yeshe, L. T. (2015). *The Bliss of Inner Fire: Heart Practice of the Six Yogas of Naropa*. Wisdom Publications.

Yeung, D., & Fosha, D. (2015). Accelerated experiential dynamic psychotherapy. In E. S. Neukrug (Ed.), *The SAGE Encyclopedia of Theory in Counseling and Psychotherapy*. SAGE Reference.

Young-Eisendrath, P. (2019). *Love between Equals: Relationship as a Spiritual Path*. Shambhala.

Zessin, U., Dickhäuser, O., & Garbade, S. (2015). The relationship between self-compassion and well-being: A meta-analysis. *Applied Psychology. Health and Well-Being, 7*(3), 340–364. https://doi.org/10.1111/aphw.12051

Zetzel, E. R., & Meissner, W. W. (1974). *Basic Concepts of Psychoanalytic Psychiatry*. Basic Books.

Zimbardo, P. (2008). *The Lucifer Effect: Understanding How Good People Turn Evil*. Random House.

Zopa, L. (2001). *Ultimate Healing: The Power of Compassion* (A. Cameron, Ed.). Wisdom Publications.

Index

Page numbers in **bold** denote tables, those in *italic* denote figures.

9781032153063